Coercion, Cooperation, and Ethics in International Relations

Coercion, Cooperation, and Ethics in International Relations

Richard Ned Lebow

Routledge
Taylor & Francis Group
New York   London

Routledge is an imprint of the
Taylor & Francis Group, an informa business

Routledge
Taylor & Francis Group
270 Madison Avenue
New York, NY 10016

Routledge
Taylor & Francis Group
2 Park Square
Milton Park, Abingdon
Oxon OX14 4RN

© 2007 by Taylor & Francis Group, LLC
Routledge is an imprint of Taylor & Francis Group, an Informa business

Printed in the United States of America on acid-free paper
10 9 8 7 6 5 4 3 2 1

International Standard Book Number-10: 0-415-95525-4 (Softcover) 0-415-95524-6 (Hardcover)
International Standard Book Number-13: 978-0-415-95525-6 (Softcover) 978-0-415-95524-9 (Hardcover)

Library of Congress Cataloging-in-Publication Data

Lebow, Richard Ned.
Coercion, cooperation, and ethics in international relations / Richard Ned Lebow.
p. cm.
ISBN 0-415-95524-6 (hardback) -- ISBN 0-415-95525-4 (pbk.)
1. International relations--Moral and ethical aspects. 2. Deterrence (Strategy) 3. Deterrence (Strategy)--Moral and ethical aspects. 4. International cooperation. I. Title.

JZ1306.L43 2006
172'.4--dc22   2006016526

**Visit the Taylor & Francis Web site at
http://www.taylorandfrancis.com**

**and the Routledge Web site at
http://www.routledge-ny.com**

to Naomi and Jacob

Contents

Preface

I am grateful to Robert Tempio, formerly of Routledge, for convincing me to publish a collection culled from four decades of my articles and chapters. It turned out to be a useful intellectual exercise for me to think about the categories in terms of how they could be grouped and the ways in which my research agenda has evolved since my first publications in the late 1960s. I tend to spend my time looking forward, to my next projects, not backward, to those that have already appeared in print. In the course of this project I discovered that looking backward can help you look forward by encouraging a broader understanding of one's research trajectory. Knowing more about what motivates one's research, how this has changed or remained constant over time, and the ways in which seemingly disparate strands of research are related, invigorates and enlightens present and contemplated projects.

I have particularly diverse interests, and choosing which of them to represent was difficult. My early work was more in comparative politics than international relations, and I chose to include two selections. One of them, on divided nations and partitioned countries, written in the early 1970s, is interesting not only for its arguments, but for illustrating the extent to which most of these conflicts are still with us and are among the most intractable of all international problems. The following six chapters on deterrence and compellence represent the core of my research in the 1970s and 1980s, and were very much a response to the Cold War. Their lessons transcend that conflict, and all the more so as American policymakers never seem to have learned them. I include two chapters on cooperation, the flip-side of conflict management, so to speak. They critique the role of deterrence in conflict resolution—confirmed tautologically by American deterrence theorists and policymakers—and offer a different perspective on the problem. I include three selections that draw on Greek philosophy, literature, and history, and use them to reflect upon our discipline, the nature of power and influence, and the extent to which knowledge can reduce tragedy in international relations. I conclude with an essay that lays out what I believe to be a useful goal and direction for international relations theory.

I considered including another section on counterfactuals, as I have done considerable work on them over the years. This collection is already large enough, and I am going to publish a separate volume on counterfactuals that includes past and current research of an historical and experimental nature.

Works written even two years ago cry out for revision, and all the more so for articles and chapters written decades back. Revision was not an attractive option as it would derail current projects, some of which build on documents and insights that have since become available. My early work on the Cold War advanced what were radical propositions at the time (e.g., that the Cuban missile crisis was due to Khrushchev's miscalculation, not Kennedy's alleged failure to practice deterrence firmly; that deterrence is at least as likely to provoke rather than prevent confrontations; that China and the Soviet Union also thought they were acting defensively, not offensively, as perceived in the West). Subsequent evidence from Soviet and Chinese archives, memoirs by former Soviet and Chinese policymakers, and interviews with them confirm these propositions.

Two of my chapters are coauthored with Janice Gross Stein, and I am grateful to her for permission to reprint them. Working with Janice was a pleasure, and this and other articles and books we wrote together led to a far better product than I could have produced by myself.

Some of my articles and chapters were published before we became more conscious of the need for gender-neutral language. I have left them unchanged, but readers will note that sometime in the 1980s I stop referring to "he" and "him" unless the people in question are men.

In addition to Rob Tempio, I am grateful to Charlotte Roh and Lynn Goeller at Routledge for their support and assistance. I would also like to acknowledge the financial support I received from various foundations and other sources to research and write these chapters and articles included in this volume. Thanks go to the Canadian Institute for International Peace and Security, the Carnegie Corporation, the Council for Advanced Research at the Naval War College, the Institute of War and Peace Studies of Columbia University, the Inter-University Consortium for World Order Studies, the MacArthur Foundation, the Research Foundation of the City University of New York, the U.S. Institute of Peace and the Rockefeller Foundation and their Bellagio Center, and the Dickey Center of Dartmouth College.

Acknowledgments

The author and publisher would like to thank the following copyright holders for granting permission to reproduce material in this work:

"Conclusions," *Divided Nations in a Divided World,* coauthored with Gregory Henderson, in Gregory Henderson, Richard Ned Lebow, and John G. Stoessinger, *Divided Nations in a Divided World* (New York: David McKay, 1974), pp. 433–456.

"Colonial Policies and Their Payoffs," in Richard Ned Lebow, *White Britain and Black Ireland: The Influence of Stereotypes on Colonial Policy* (Philadelphia: Institute for the Study of Human Issues, 1976), pp. 89–114.

"Cognitive Closure and Crisis Politics," in Richard Ned Lebow, *Between Peace and War: The Nature of International Crisis* (Baltimore: Johns Hopkins University, 1981), pp. 101–47.

"Beyond Deterrence," coauthored with Janice Stein, *Journal of Social Issues* 43, no. 4 (1987), 5–71.

"Nuclear Deterrence in Retrospect," coauthored with Janice Stein, in *We All Lost the Cold War* (Princeton: Princeton University Press, 1994), ch. 14.

"Reason Divorced from Reality: Thomas Schelling and Strategic Bargaining," to appear in *International Politics.* An earlier version appeared in *International Journal* 51 (Summer 1996), pp. 555–76, under the title, "Thomas Schelling and Strategic Bargaining."

"Beyond Parsimony: Rethinking Theories of Coercive Bargaining," *European Journal of International Relations* 4, No. 1 (1998), pp. 31–66.

"Transitions and Transformations: Building International Cooperation," *Security Studies* 6 (Spring 1997), pp. 154–79.

"Thucydides the Constructivist," *American Political Science Review* 95 (September 2001), pp. 547–60.

"Reason, Emotion and Cooperation," *International Politics*, 42, no. 3 (2005), pp. 283–313.

"Power, Persuasion and Justice," *Millennium* 33, no. 3 (Spring 2005), pp. 551–82.

"Tragedy, Politics and Political Science," *International Relations* 19 (Spring 2005), pp. 329–36.

"Robert McNamara: Max Weber's Worst Nightmare," *International Relations* 20, no. 2 (June 2006), pp. 211–24.

Introduction

My interest in foreign policy and international relations dates back to my childhood in Queens, New York. World War II was underway in my neighborhood well before Pearl Harbor as so many of its residents and my childhood friends were refugees from the Nazis, fascists, or communists—or two of the three in the case of an Estonian family on an adjacent block. American entry into the war brought blackouts, oil skin curtains, rationing, scrap drives, and a Saturday morning parade of fathers proudly shouldering farm implements up 65th Avenue to the communal "victory garden," where they fought fascist weeds and nurtured allied vegetables.

One of my friends, from Italy, had been torpedoed while crossing the Atlantic. My babysitter Bert and his sister Inge, forced to go to school in Switzerland by the Nazis, had smuggled gold coins across the border inside cut out school books until they and their family fled across the river in the darkness of night. The German Catholic family across the street had two sons in the U.S. air force, both of whose bombers were shot down, but they were fortunately liberated by advancing allies forces on the eve of VE Day. World War II was a local event and engaged my attention.

It also aroused my emotions as news reaching the block from Europe in the early postwar years was generally bad. Neighbors learned of the loss of families and friends in death camps. New kids arrived, some with nervous ticks or scarred faces, and others with an uncontrollable urge to seek cover under their school desks in response to any loud noise. I do not remember when it happened, but a desire developed and strengthened to understand what had caused this awful suffering and what might be done to make the world a happier place for another generation of kids.

School provided none of the answers. Discipline was strict, the curriculum boring, and the pace of learning agonizingly slow. We sat in front of sloping wooden desks with holes for no longer used inkwells. Each desk was attached to the chair in front, and desks and chairs were arranged in parallel rows. Teachers had the unfortunate habit of having us read aloud, one pupil at a time, working their way down one row and up the next. In the early grades, I amused myself by drawing or looking at the maze of water and electrical pipes on the ceiling. I would start at one place, picked at random, and try to trace the shortest and then the most elaborate route to other locations on the pipes. The school was on Yellowstone Boulevard and large windows provided a vista of urban sprawl and fast disappearing farms. On the horizon was a small, odd-shaped structure that resembled a Mayan or Aztec step pyramid. When really bored, I would conjure up images of Aztec priests using stone knives to cut out the hearts of screaming teachers, held in place by my most robust classmates. By third grade, I brought independent reading to school. In a variant of Bert and Inge's ploy, I covered the books with the same oil cloth used for school books, or placed them inside open text books that I was supposed to be reading. Occasionally I was caught and sent to the principal's office and then to the library as punishment. Wonderful Mrs. Austin, the librarian, knew exactly what was going on, and welcomed me with new and interesting books, among them, I remember, Life's *Picture History of World War II*, with an engaging text by John Dos Passos. I read a lot of history and anything I could get my hands on concerning the Nazis and World War II.

High school was almost as tedious, and it was no longer possible to get sent to the library. I played "hooky" a lot, spent hours in the New York Public Library, the Marshall Chess Club, and Ebbet's Field. My knowledge of modern history became more extensive and I made my initial forays into literature and social science. Karl Mannheim's *Ideology and Utopia* was over my head, but I found Eric Fromm's *Escape from Freedom* and Hans Morgenthau's *Politics Among Nations* easier going. I did not get that much out of these readings at the time because I did not know how to evaluate arguments or integrate them and their authors into broader intellectual frameworks. So mostly, I assimilated information that became a resource I could draw on at later stages of my career.

My real education began at the University of Chicago in the late 1950s. Chicago required its most distinguished faculty to teach introductory courses, and I had the benefit of Saul Bellow, Reuel Denney, and Daniel Boorstin in my first year of study. I later took or audited courses and seminars with Richard McKeown in philosophy, Edward Shils, and Morris Janowitz in sociology, Hannah Arendt of the Committee on Social Thought and Herman Finer, Hans Morgenthau, David Easton, and Leo Strauss in political science. I became a research assistant for Finer and then for Morgenthau, which was certainly more stimulating than earlier jobs in the library stacks, medical records room, and the morgue. Chicago taught me how to read a text carefully, to make an argument, and perhaps most importantly, to listen with respect and an open mind to the arguments of others. Many of my professors were European émigrés, and it was only when I went to graduate school at Yale that I discovered—and not from my mentors Hajo Holton and Karl Deutsch—that in English, "Plaaato" is pronounced "Plato" and "Tukidides" as "Thucydides."

Its relative proximity to Smith aside, the most enjoyable aspect of Yale was the student body. My cohort, and here I include students a year ahead or behind, included Janice Stein, Oran Young, Nick Onuf, Pat Morgan, Roy Lickleider, Nan

Henry (now Keohane), Bob Putnam, Ed Tufte, Joel Aberbach, Dick Merelman, Don Rothschild, and Jim Scott. I learned at least as much from them as I did from my professors. In 1964, Tom Schelling came to Yale to deliver a series of lectures that Yale University Press would later publish as *Arms and Influence*. Several of us attended the talks and were impressed by Schelling's brilliance, but equally struck by his political naiveté. In one of the post-lecture Q & A's, Janice Stein voiced her doubts about Schelling's belief that a massive bombing campaign against North Vietnam would likely compel Hanoi to halt the rebellion in the South. She pointed out that North Vietnam had little industrial infrastructure or other high value targets to destroy. Perhaps a bombing campaign would not so much compel Hanoi to give into America's demands as it would strengthen the resolve of the North Vietnamese people to support their regime in its resistance to foreign intervention. All Schelling could say in reply was that the United States had the capability to drop more bombs on Vietnam than it had on Germany and Japan in World War II.

My most interesting seminars at Yale were with Karl Deutsch, Harold Lasswell, and historian, Hajo Holborn. The first two were prominent leaders of the behavioral revolution and were as optimistic about the ability of social scientists to understand political relationships as they were pessimistic about the wisdom of governments to use such knowledge wisely.

Deutsch was a brilliant lecturer, and novel ideas flowed from his fertile mind in a veritable cascade. My seminar paper for his class applied the concepts of mobilization and assimilation from his *Nationalism and Social Communication* to the Afro-American community in the South to understand the likely appeal of the nascent Black nationalist movement. After two weeks of conducting surveys and intensive interviews, an FBI agent arrived at the fraternity house where I was staying on the University of Alabama campus in Tuscaloosa to drive me to Atlanta and put me on a flight north. There was a plot afoot to do me harm, he explained, but would not provide any evidence that might have made this credible. I was deeply suspicious but ultimately convinced to go to Atlanta. Two days later, three civil rights workers—Cheney, Schwerner, and Goodman—were murdered in Mississippi. I was shocked and angered, but grateful to be back in New Haven.

Yale would ultimately prove to be as inhospitable as Tuscaloosa. As I was interested in international relations from an interdisciplinary perspective, I had made the mistake of applying to the committee on international relations rather than to the department of political science. I did not know at the time that the committee had been set up as a kind of Jurassic Park for dinosaurs the department wanted to marginalize as they pushed ahead with the behavioral revolution. I got off on the wrong foot with the director, a China scholar, ardent supporter of Chiang Kai-chek, and sometime advocate of a preemptive nuclear strike against Red China. Relations deteriorated further, I surmise, as result of my outspoken opposition to the Kennedy's administration's growing involvement in Vietnam. I had developed an early sensitivity to this issue in Paris, where I had spent the summer of 1963.

I lived at the Cité Universitaire and had become friendly with a group of Vietnamese students who had a lot to say about recent developments in their country.

In 1965, Deutsch was on leave and the professor in question graded the international relations components of my comprehensive examination. He failed me on this test and my retake and expelled me from the program. Professors Deutsch and Holborn subsequently spoke to Yale President Kingman Brewster, who agreed to continue my registration and fellowship for a term so I would not be drafted and sent off to Vietnam. They advised me to finish my education elsewhere, and Deutsch called his friend John Stoessinger to arrange for my admission into the recently established Ph.D. program at the City University of New York. I became their first graduate in 1968 and stayed on to teach at City College and the Graduate Center. At the Graduate Center, I had the good fortune to study with John Herz, Ivo Duchacek, John Stoessinger, Melvin Richter, and Isaiah Berlin.

My college and graduate school years coincided with the civil rights movement, several of the most acute crises of the Cold War, America's tragic involvement in Indochina and the Chinese cultural revolution. I was deeply interested in all of these developments, and a part-time activist in the civil rights and anti-war movements. I was struck by the different ways supporters and opponents of the war ordered their narratives, and the diametrically opposed ways they generally responded to the same information. This phenomenon stood in sharp contrast to the expectations of the rationalist models of decision making then increasingly in vogue. So did the decline in public support for the war as the 1960s wore on. Changes in belief systems were dramatic, not incremental as Bayesian logic would predict, and often in response to events, like the Tet Offensive, that could readily be assimilated to either the pro- or anti-war narratives. For these reasons, I was drawn to psychological approaches to decision making and devoured the small but stimulating literature on the subject.

Colonialism and its aftermath

My dissertation drew on this literature to address the problem of racism and prejudice. Most psychological studies at the time were rooted in Freudian conceptions that treated prejudice as a pathology. The famous authoritarian personality study and its "F scale" is a case in point. Freud had attempted to generalize from individuals to society on the basis of the distribution of certain personality types and the degree of libidinal repression. Harold Lasswell extended this line of inquiry in *World Politics and Personal Insecurity*, published in 1935.[1] Eric Fromm's *Escape from Freedom* represented another variant, and attempted a synthesis of Freud and Marx.[2]

I was very impressed by these studies but disturbed by their empirical implications. To the extent that prejudice was an expression of deep-seated psychological causes, there was little hope that it could be eradicated by education or greater exposure to people who were its targets. The psychological literature nevertheless recognized, and even stressed, the extent to which manifestations of prejudice rose and fell as a function of demographic, economic, and political changes. This obvious tension between psychological and social causes encouraged me to wonder if there were other, situational causes of prejudice that might more readily be ameliorated by education of changing conditions. Leon Festinger's work on cognitive dissonance seemed to point in this direction.[3] He had made the case for situationally induced anxiety and distortions in information processing, as when smokers were presented with information that it was harmful to their health. I theorized that slavery and colonialism created strong dissonance by virtue of the contradictions they posed to the proclaimed, and more to the point, assimilated values of the society. Dissonance should be particularly pronounced in liberal societies, and before the modern era, in societies that colonized or enslaved people of the same religion of ethnic group.

Guided by these propositions, I selected the Anglo-Irish colonial relationship as a case study in which to evaluate these propositions. Unlike most other colonized people, the Irish were white, Christian, and European; they had even Christianized their colonizer, which was a nice reversal on the usual course of events. Yet, the stereotype of the Irish shared many features with that of Blacks in the United States: they were depicted as childlike, hospitable, full of rhythm, frequently inebriated, and gratuitously violent, especially when drunk. I traced the origins of the stereotype back to the Anglo-Norman need to justify their twelfth century conquest of Ireland and rude treatment of its inhabitants. It subsequently helped to reduce dissonance produced by the contradiction between the repressive and destructive policies of colonialism and the Christian beliefs of the colonizers. To square the two, it was necessary to remove the Irish from the realm in which these principles applied. This could be done by portraying them as sub-human and unfeeling, or childlike and in need of a firm hand. By the nineteenth century, the largely unchanged stereotype continued to justify British rule in Ireland. The English convinced themselves that they were providing the only possible rational government for a priest-ridden, ignorant people incapable of governing themselves. When protest and nationalist movements arose, British preconceptions kept the majority of politicians and public opinion from realizing the true nature of the protest and the extent of its popular support. The stereotype became a perceptual prison, British officials were unable to respond appropriately to the demands of Repeaters, Young Irelanders, and Fenians. As a consequence, the set of stereotypes that justified British colonialism also contributed to its failure and demise.

The last chapter of *White Britain and Black Ireland*, reprinted here as reading number one, extends my argument to colonialism more generally. I argue that the most enduring colonial systems are paradoxically those in which the metropolitan power makes the least effort to educate the populace or integrate them into the wider political community. Paradoxically, the least stable are the most liberal, where efforts are made to win the loyalty of the colonial population, or at least its elite, by holding out the prospect of their integration in the national community. Legitimacy is difficult to establish, and requires not only the expenditure of considerable resources, but responsiveness to the needs of the population in question. Empathy is unlikely to develop when stereotypes impede understanding, as they do in almost all colonial situations. The strategy of integration in these circumstances raises expectations that cannot be fulfilled and only further alienates the colonial population. As in Ireland, agitation for autonomy, independence, and even rebellion, is likely to develop. Liberal powers find it difficult to resort to the kind of repression necessary to squelch such movements effectively. Britain and France, the quintessential liberal colonial powers, both behaved in ways that encouraged independence movements and made them difficult to suppress. Portugal and Spain, by contrast, did little to educate indigenous peoples or to build local infrastructure, and held on to their empires until they liberalized at home.

I conducted most of the research for my dissertation and book that grew out of it in libraries and archives in Britain and Ireland. I visited Northern Ireland, where, in the course of the late 1960s, a Catholic civil rights movement developed. I befriended some of these activists and learned first-hand about the situation in Belfast and Derry, and the ways in which protest has an important international dimension. Local discrimination aside, one of the catalysts of the North Irish civil disobedience campaign was the American civil rights movement. In its first large protest, a sit-in at the segregated housing estate in Caledon, in the Dungannon Rural District, ended with the protestors singing "We Shall Overcome."

My interest in Ireland became increasingly contemporary, and I made several research trips to Belfast and other locations in Northern Ireland. With Gregory Henderson and John Stoessinger, I edited a book on divided nations and partitioned countries published in 1974.[4] I wrote the case study on Ireland and coauthored the conclusion with Gregory Henderson. The book examines generic problems of division and those specific to divided nations (e.g., the two Germanys, Chinas, Vietnams, and Koreas) and partitioned countries (former colonies divided into two or more countries at the time of independence because of communal divisions). In the intervening years, Germany and Vietnam have unified, and some progress toward peace has been made in Northern Ireland, and perhaps in Cyprus as well. North and South Korea and China and Taiwan continue to be volatile relationships, as do Israel-Palestine and India-Pakistan. The collapse of the Soviet empire, and Yugoslavia and Czechoslovakia in its wake, spawned additional partitioned countries. Azerbaijan and Armenia fought a costly war over disputed territory, and the breakup of Yugoslavia was accompanied by equally nasty and still unresolved conflicts. Partitioned countries may be the most intractable of all international conflicts, and our study of their dynamics remains relevant to understanding the present day world. I accordingly include our conclusions as reading number two.

On my visits to Northern Ireland I collected data on sectarian assassination, a phenomenon that developed in 1970–1971. I managed to speak to some of the "lads" responsible for this violence and learned something about the organization of the Protestant paramilitary groups responsible for them. There was a striking contrast between the Irish Republic Army (IRA)—soon to splinter into "official" and "provisional" factions—and their Protestant counterparts. The Provisional IRA, responsible for most of the violence on the Catholic side, was organized in cells, but these cells were part of a larger organization with a hierarchy and history. The Ulster Defence Association (UDA) and Ulster Volunteer Force (UVF) squads were more local and ad hoc, and their leaders were men, who by the force of their charisma, could impose their wills on their colleagues. New recruits were often driven to the edge of Catholic ghettos and forced to pull the trigger once the leader had chosen a target. Acts of murder of this kind put recruits on the wrong side of the law and psychologically in thrall to the leader.

The two sides also attacked largely different targets. The IRA went after the British army and the symbols of the Protestant power structure: police, banks, hotels. The IRA was an elusive target, so the UDA and the UVF had to make do with attacks on young men from Catholic working class ghettos, the kind of person likely to join the IRA. Violence on both sides waxed and waned as a function of capabilities, but even more the political situation. The real enemies of paramilitary groups were middle class politicians in their own communities, and violence would escalate whenever there was any hint of a possible accommodation. It aimed, and usually succeeded, in polarizing public opinion and making accommodation more difficult, if not impossible.[5] This pattern would be repeated in the Middle East and Indian subcontinent.

Deterrence

I received my tenure in 1971, and with it, the freedom to invest in what would turn out to be an eight-year study of international crisis. Crisis management was a "hot topic" in international relations, and driven by the seeming lesson of Berlin and Cuba that better techniques could reduce the likelihood of superpower war. I was sympathetic to this goal, but more interested in the broader role of crisis in conflict, and the difference, if any, in crises between nuclear versus conventionally armed states.

I compiled a list of 26 war-threatening crises between 1898 and 1967, and coded them along a number of dimension, including the number of states involved, the duration and outcome of the crisis and the arsenals of their protagonists. In the course of my research, I subdivided crises into four analytical categories. In *Justification of Hostility* crises (e.g., Second *Lusitania*, German-Polish crisis of 1939, the Gulf of Tonkin), the initiator is intent on war, and the goal of the crisis is to mobilize domestic and international support by making the other side appear responsible for war. Four of five Justification of Hostility crises in my sample resulted in war. *Spinoff* crises grow out of existing wars (or those expected to begin shortly), and arise from the initiator's perceived need to improve its strategic position in that conflict at the expense of a third party. Examples include the Spanish-American crisis of 1898, the First *Lusitania* crisis of 1915, and the Russo-Finnish crisis of 1939. Five of eight crises ended in war. *Accident* crises, of which I had only representative—the Dogger Bank Affair of 1905—are unintended and the result of bad judgment or unauthorized actions by subordinates. Participants are keen to find a solution, as Britain and Russia did in this instance, but only when Russia backed down at the last minute. *Brinksmanship* crises, by far my largest category, are triggered by a deliberate challenge of an adversary's commitment in the hope or expectation that a successful challenge will help cope with pressing strategic or domestic problems. Thirteen of my cases were Brinksmanship, among them the Fashoda crisis of 1898, the First Moroccan crisis of 1905, the Sino-Indian and Cuban missile crises of 1962. In ten of these confrontations the initiator miscalculated, and had to back down or go to war.

I began my research committed to all of the conventional assumptions about deterrence. I expected to find that commitments that were challenged were incredible because the defender had inadequate capability to defend them or seemed to lack resolve to do so. To my surprise, I found no positive relationship between challenges and the apparent credibility of commitments. To probe this anomaly, I designed a more rigorous test of credibility that relied on contemporary third party assessments of the four conditions deterrence theorists expected commitments to meet. Commitments had to be well-defined, communicated to adversaries, defensible and efforts had to be made to communicate resolve to defend them if they were challenged. These evaluations confirmed my earlier assessment. The next step was a comparative study of the decision-making processes of initiators of Brinksmanship crises who were forced to back down or accept war. I found a pattern of motivated bias in every case. Key policy makers were more sensitive to their own political needs than they were to those of the leaders and states they challenged. They largely ignored, denied or explained away information they received suggesting that the challenged states were likely to defend their commitments. To the extent that they needed to mount a successful challenge to cope with domestic and strategic problems, they convinced themselves they would succeed. Once committed to challenges, they engaged in bolstering and other forms of postdecisional rationalization, and became even more insensitive to information and warnings that suggested their challenge was likely to end in disaster. A number of Brinksmanship crises led to war because leaders recognized their miscalculations too belatedly to search for a peaceful outcome.

The third reading in this volume is a chapter drawn from *Between Peace and War: The Nature of International Crisis*.[6] It provides succinct overviews of cognitive and motivational approaches to decision making and documents the ways in which prior expectations, motivated bias and commitment led to denial and sluggish steering in Germany in the July 1914 crisis and were a major cause of World War I. At the critical moment of the crisis, Kaiser Wilhelm suffered a dissociative reaction and was incommunicado at his palace in Potsdam for almost 24 hours. *Between Peace and War* discusses two other cases in detail where motivated bias contributed to war: the U.S. decision to cross the 38th parallel in Korea in 1950, and the Indian challenge of China in 1962. I document three other dissociative reactions: Stalin in 1941, Nehru in 1962, and Nasser in 1967.

Janice Stein and I would later explore the role of motivated bias in intelligence failure and more recent international crises. In *Psychology and Deterrence*, which we coauthored with Robert Jervis, we published case studies of Egyptian and Israeli decision making in 1973 and Argentina and Britain in 1981.[7] Patrick Morgan and Jack Snyder also contributed interesting chapters to the volume. Stein and I coauthored a more extensive critique of deterrence in the form of three articles for a special issue of the *Journal of Social Issues* that also contains commentaries on our work by psychologists, historians and political scientists.[8] We go beyond deterrence in this piece to look at the alternative strategy of reassurance. Whereas deterrence and compellence seek to bring about desired outcomes by raising the costs of non-compliance, reassurance attempts to do so by increasing the rewards of compliance. Our article examines the conditions under which these strategies are likely to succeed and fail, and how they can be combined in a more sophisticated approach to conflict management. It is reprinted here as reading number four.

During the 1980s I wrote a book or the problems of nuclear crisis management, in which I explored the possible interactions between a tightly coupled warning and response system and the kinds of human errors associated with stress.[9] With the advent to power of Mikhail Gorbachev in the Soviet Union and his policy of *glasnost* (openness), it became possible for the first time to gain access to Soviet archives and private collections of documents in the possession of Soviet officials and former officials. Janice and I exploited *glasnost* to explore the role of deterrence and compellence during the Cold War. One of us was invited to several of the conferences run on the Cuban missile crisis by the John F. Kennedy School of Government, and we both conducted extensive interviews with former American, Soviet, Israeli, and Egyptian officials who had played important roles in that crisis and in the superpower crisis arising from the October 1973 Middle East war.

Ten years earlier, I had published an article challenging the conventional wisdom in the West about the origins of the Cuban missile crisis.[10] President Kennedy had what can only be called a neurotic obsession about his resolve, and interpreted the secret Soviet missile deployment in Cuba in the summer and fall of 1962 as the result of his failure to stand firm in Laos, Berlin, and the June 1961 Vienna summit that preceded the latter crisis.[11] Kennedy shared his concern for his resolve with his advisors and Eli Abel, a capable journalist who wrote a best-selling book on the missile crisis.[12] Graham Allison, author of what became for many years the standard scholarly work on the crisis, lent further credence to this interpretation. "Even up to the day of discovery," he insisted, "a man in Moscow, listening to the array of messages emanating from Washington, could have had grounds for reasonable doubt about the U.S. government's reaction."[13] This conclusion was speculation, as there was precious little evidence about Soviet decision making available at the time. The principal source was two volumes of memoirs by Nikita Khrushchev, badly translated into English.[14] In the second of these books, Khrushchev speaks of his respect for Kennedy and his fortitude in defending his country's foreign policy.[15] Kennedy also appeared to have satisfied the four conditions of deterrence, having carefully defined his commitment, communicated to Moscow by public and private channels, beefed up American forces in the Caribbean, where the United States had an overwhelming military advantage, and sought by a variety of means to convey resolve. None of the American students of the crisis considered the possibility that Khrushchev had miscalculated. I speculated about the combination of motives that might have driven Khrushchev to deploy missiles in Cuba and convince himself that he could get away with it. If so, the American president and analysts of the crisis, working within the framework of deterrence, had confirmed it falsely and tautologically. The need to demonstrate resolve tightened its hold on the American psyche.

Interviews, Soviet documents, and transcripts from conferences make it apparent that Khrushchev sent missiles to Cuba to deter an expected American invasion, offset America's first strike strategic capability and gain revenge for Kennedy's deployment of Jupiter missiles in Turkey.[16] We believe that Khrushchev also hoped the missiles would push Kennedy toward an accommodation, which he desperately wanted to free resources for his economic programs.[17] Khrushchev never doubted Kennedy's resolve. Fidel Castro pleaded within him to send the missiles openly to Cuba, the way Kennedy had to Turkey. Khrushchev refused on the grounds that the president would send the American navy to intercept or sink the ships transporting the missiles and their warheads. We found compelling evidence in support of my earlier speculation that it was Khrushchev, not Kennedy, who miscalculated. He was warned by high officials and advisors, among them Andrei Gromyko, Anastas I. Mikoyan, and Oleg Troyanovsky, that the missiles in Cuba would be discovered before they became operational and provoke a serious crisis with the United States. Khrushchev brushed their warnings aside, never ordered or undertook an independent evaluation of the risks, took refuge in the assurances of people unqualified to offer them, and forced reluctant members of the Politburo to sign the document authorizing the deployment.[18]

Our research on the Cuban missile and 1973 Middle East crises also unearthed new information about the dynamics of these confrontations. It revealed that mutual clarification of interests and reassurance were at least as important as compellence in bringing about a peaceful resolution of the missile crisis. The 1973 crisis, by contrast, was resolved because of a cease-fire that removed the principal ground of contention. When Israel was recovering from the surprise, coordinated Syrian-Egyptian attack and on the offensive against Egyptian armies, Kissinger flew to Moscow to seek a cease-fire, and continued on to Jerusalem to urge the Israelis to agree to halt the fighting The Israeli army fought on, repulsed the Syrians, crossed the Canal, and all but surrounded the two Egyptian armies on the Suez front. The Soviets were now anxious to save their clients, and the Politburo authorized Brezhnev to pursue a joint political-military initiative with the United States to enforce the cease-fire.[19]

Brezhnev was convinced that Kissinger had taken advantage of him, and had secretly urged Israel to step up their offensive while Moscow was putting pressure on Egypt and Syria to accept a cease-fire. Kissinger had done nothing of the kind, and the Americans were actually putting pressure on Israel to halt its offensive along the Canal while the Politburo was meeting. Brezhnev added an authorized sentence to the message he sent to the American president in which he suggested that the Soviet Union would consider acting alone if the United States did not join it in putting an end to the fighting. In fact, the fighting had all but stopped, but nobody in Moscow knew this because Soviet battlefield intelligence was almost 72 hours behind time. The Americans, who had timely intelligence, put the worst possible interpretation on Brezhnev's letter. For different reasons, Secretary of State Henry Kissinger, Secretary of Defense James Schlesinger, CIA Director William Colby, and Chairman of the Joint-Chiefs of Staff Admiral Thomas Moorer agreed to respond with a nuclear alert. They ordered that American strategic forces be brought up to "DefCon 3," where they had not been since the Cuban missile crisis. They did so on their own authority when Alexander L. Haig, with Nixon in the residential wing of the White House, informed them that the president was too drunk to come to the telephone. The American nuclear alert, intended by Kissinger to deter Soviet military intervention, completely baffled the Politburo. The crisis petered out when Moscow finally learned that the fighting had stopped.[20]

Compellence

Compellence is the sister strategy of deterrence. It uses threats of punishment to bring about, rather than prevent some action. Thomas Schelling and Robert Jervis both contend that it is more difficult to achieve because the action it requires is visible, unlike restraint, and more likely to lead to loss of face. They and other scholars deduced a host of further propositions about coercive strategies and the bargaining advantages conferred by reputation, the military balance, interests and roles (challenger vs. defender). These propositions are rational and logically consistent but rest on a set of generally unarticulated behavioral and political assumptions. By the late 1980s, they were at the core of a burgeoning literature on coercive bargaining that encompassed case studies, game theoretic treatments and formal models. They were also ingrained in the American national security community, where they had important consequences for policy.

In reading six, "Beyond Parsimony: Rethinking Theories of Coercive Bargaining," originally published in the *European Journal of International Relations*, I identify the most important political and behavioral assumptions of this literature. I interrogate them using empirical evidence from the origins, dynamics and outcome of the Cuban missile crisis. While only one case, the missile crisis helped to spawn so much of this literature, and is widely used to illustrate the propositions I critique. I argue that the political assumptions misconstrue the process of risk assessment, exaggerate the ability of leaders to estimate the risks inherent in their threats or to form reasonable estimates of adversarial evaluations of their resolve. These problems may help explain why deterrence and compellence often fail when practiced by rational and attentive actors against equally rational and attentive targets. Some of the political and behavioral assumptions of deterrence are unique to these strategies, but most are shared with other rational theories of bargaining. My critique accordingly has important implications for these theories, and they are spelled out in the conclusion.

Theories and strategies take on a life of their own. This is certainly true of deterrence, which became something of a self-fulfilling prophecy for American scholars and policymakers. This mind set continued well into the 1990s, after the Cold War was over. It has been relatively immune to evidence that Soviet leaders never questioned American resolve, unless it was to worry that successive administrations were trigger happy and prone to threaten or use force in situations were diplomacy was more appropriate. The most graphic evidence I encountered of the hold this mind set had on otherwise intelligent people was an encounter with Jim Fearon at a talk I gave at the University of Chicago. I thanked him for a recent article in which he wrote that if the work Janice Stein and I had done on deterrence was valid, it was among the most important findings of postwar international relations research. I missed the intended irony, he explained. He rejected our arguments out of hand. On what grounds, I asked. "If what you claim about deterrence is true," he replied, "it would make a mockery of a vast literature that builds on the assumptions that you dismiss."

I noted earlier that I attended Thomas Schelling's lectures at Yale that were published in 1966 as *Arms and Influence*. The book was enormously influential, and together with his earlier work, *The Strategy of Conflict*, gave a powerful boost to theoretical work on coercive bargaining.[21] Much of it was game theoretical, and later, the subject of formal models. Following Schelling, this literature was deductive, assumed incomplete information and bargaining in the form of sequential moves. It became increasingly divorced from empirical reality; game theoretic approaches searched for equilibria in increasingly complex games, while formal modelers sought proofs based on the internal logic of their arguments.

Those studies that sought to root their assumptions in empirical reality were often historically uninformed. A prominent example is Bruce Bueno de Mesquita's, *The War Trap*, based on the premise that leaders go to war because they expect to win, as, he insists, they do in practice.[22] Benjamin Valentino and I found that in the 30 wars fought since 1945 involving a minimum of 1,000 casualties, only 7 of the initiators achieved their wartime goals [see Table 1]. If we relax our criterion for success, and make it simply the defeat of the other sides' armed forces, the number of successful initiators rises only to 10.

The real war trap is directly antithetical to the one posited by Bueno de Mesquita. What we need to explain is far more paradoxical: the propensity of leaders to go to war in conditions where they are likely to lose. And the explanation is not incomplete information; in many, if not most, of the cases, information was available beforehand indicating that war was likely to lead to disaster. Examples include India's challenge of China in 1962, the U.S. intervention in Vietnam in the mid-1960s, and China's invasion of Vietnam in 1979. In other cases, where the

Table I.1

War	Dates	Military Victory	Achieves War Aims
India - Pakistan (First Kashmir) Side A: India Side B: Pakistan	1947–1949	No	No
War of Israeli Independence (Israel vs. Palestine/Arab coalition) Side A: COALITION: Egypt (A1), Iraq (A2), Jordan (A3), Syria (A4) Side B: Israel	1948–1949	No	No
China-Tibet I Side A: China Side B: Tibet	1950	Yes	Yes
Korean Side A: COALITION: China (A1), North Korea (A2) Side B: USA	1949–1953	No	No
Russo-Hungarian Side A: Hungary Side B: Russia (Soviet Union)	1956	Yes	Yes
Sinai/Suez Side A: Egypt Side B: COALITION: Israel (B1), France (B2), UK (B3)	1956	Yes	Yes
Vietnam Side A: North Vietnam Side B: USA	1959–1975	No	No
Indo-Chinese Side A: China Side B: India	1962	Yes	Yes
Second Kashmir Side A: India Side B: Pakistan	1965	No	No
Six Day War Side A: COALITION: Egypt (A1), Iraq (A2), Syria (A3) Side B: Israel	1967	No	No
US vs. Cambodia	1971	No	No
Israeli-Egyptian (War of Attrition) Side A: Egypt Side B: Israel	1969–1970	No	No

(Continued)

Table I.1   (Continued)

War	Dates	Military Victory	Achieves War Aims
Football (El Salvador vs. Honduras) Side A: El Salvador Side B: Honduras	1969	Yes	Yes
India - Pakistan (Bangladesh) Side A: India Side B: Pakistan	1971	Yes	Yes
Yom Kippur Side A: COALITION: Egypt (A1), Syria (A2) Side B: Israel	1973	No	No
Cyprus Side A: Greece Side B: Turkey	1974	Yes	Yes
Vietnamese-Cambodian Side A: Cambodia Side B: Vietnam	1977–79	Yes	No
Ethiopia-Somalia (Ogaden) Side A: COALITION: Cuba (A1), Ethiopia (A2) Side B: Somalia	1977–78	No	No
Ugandan-Tanzanian Side A: Tanzania Side B: Uganda	1978–79	No	No
First Sino-Vietnamese Side A: China Side B: Vietnam	1979	No	No
Iran-Iraq Side A: Iran Side B: Iraq	1980–88	No	No
Falklands/Malvinas War (UK vs. Argentina) Side A: Argentina Side B: UK	1982	No	No
Israel-Syria (Lebanon) Side A: Israel Side B: Syria	1982	No	No
Second Sino-Vietnamese Side A: China Side B: Vietnam	1987	No	No

the Castro regime in Cuba which, he believed, the United States was intent on overthrowing.[24] The Taiwan Straits crisis of 1954–55 is another example. It was provoked by Chinese shelling of the offshore islands of Qemoy and Matsu, then occupied by Taiwanese forces. Mao Zedong and the Chinese Politburo ordered the shelling, we now know, to deter what they believed was an imminent and major military move against the Chinese mainland by Taiwan and the United States. In a mirror image of American postcrisis assessment, the Chinese considered their action a success when the expected attack failed to materialize.[25]

I next undertook a critique of Thomas Schelling, the most celebrated exponent of rationalist models of coercive bargaining. His writings illustrate the theoretical and policy dangers of ignoring politics, culture and morality in search of deductive, rational understandings. The examples Schelling uses to illustrate his arguments demonstrate the difficulties inherent in the search for a universal, abstract approach to bargaining. They indicate that tactics, signals, noise, and reference points only take on meaning in context, and that context is a function of the history, culture and the prior experience of actors with each other. People cannot communicate without a common language, and Schelling errs in assuming that everyone speaks the language of twentieth century Western microeconomics. The ultimate irony may be the extent to which Schelling's works on bargaining are unwitting prisoners of a particular language and context. The assumptions he makes about the nature and modalities of coercive bargaining reflect a parochial, American view of the world. They lead him to misrepresent the dynamics of the bargaining encounters he uses to justify his approach. He recognizes that the coercive bargaining equation has two sides to it: the ability to inflict punishment, and the ability to absorb pain. In analyzing Vietnam, he focuses only on the U.S. ability to inflict punishment through a campaign of aerial bombardment. He ignores—as did the Johnson administration—the Vietnamese ability to absorb pain, which in the end proved to be decisive. It explains why the United States won every battle but still lost the war.

The most striking omission in Schelling's analysis is ethics. His only reference to morality in *Arms and Influence* concerns the French in Algeria, and is intended to highlight the differences between that conflict and American intervention in Vietnam. The Algerian rebels waged a war of terror against their French and Algerian opponents. The French Army opposed them with force and sought to eliminate their military capability. When this strategy failed, he notes, the French turned to terror, with no more effect. Algeria showed that relying on coercive terror in return may prove not only degrading, but incompatible with the purpose it is intended to serve. Schelling is naively confident that this would not happen in Vietnam because the United States had found a way to coerce the North Vietnamese government without using force against its population.[26] Hans Morgenthau insisted that both the ends and the means of foreign policy had to be consistent with the prevailing moral code—for both ethical and practical reasons. Schelling's brand of realism—and American policy in Indochina—dispenses with all morality on the grounds that it had no place in a dangerous world populated by cutthroat adversaries and frightened allies. In doing so, it does away with what Americans publicly proclaim was the key distinguishing feature between themeselves and their communist adversaries.

In 1994, I sent my Schelling critique to *International Security*, who returned it with a note from the editor explaining that it was "too negative" to send out for review! I published it in *International Studies*, the leading Canadian journal of international relations.[27] In 1993, the National Academy of Sciences gave Schelling an award for "behavioral research relevant to the prevention of nuclear war." In 2005 he was corecipient of the Nobel Prize in economics, in part for his work on coercive bargaining and strategy. In the circumstances, I thought it appropriate to revisit Schelling and revise and update my critique. It was published by *International Politics* in June 2006, and reprinted here as reading number seven.

Arms and Influence was written with the Vietnam conflict very much in mind, but Schelling had only an indirect influence on American policy in that conflict. Robert McNamara, by contrast, was one of the principal architects of American intervention in Vietnam in his capacity as secretary of defense in the Johnson administration. For many years, he was silent on the subject of the war, and only began to speak out in the 1990s. McNamara's talks and books on the subject are intended to rehabilitate his reputation, although they are presented as objective efforts to explore the causes of the war and the failure of the United States and Vietnam to reach an accommodation. McNamara received more publicity in the Errol Morris film—*The Fog of War*—winner of the 2004 Oscar for the best documentary. In this film, McNamara assumes the pose of a wise old sage reflecting on the evils of the twentieth century.

Max Weber recognized that politicians continually face ethical dilemmas, and must sometimes use "morally dubious" means to achieve appropriate ends. He knew too that leaders must trust in their own judgments, as there is no objective way of judging among competing sets of values. He nevertheless expected good leaders to have values, and to follow an "ethic of responsibility," which entailed efforts to evaluate ends and means in terms of those values.[28] Weber gave Nietzsche's dichotomy a modern twist by reframing it as a conflict between charisma and bureaucracy. He associated charisma with human creativity, which found its fullest expression in the man of culture (*Kulturmensch*). Bureaucracy stifles this creativity by organizing life around dehumanizing routines and empowering the expert but soulless technician (*Fachmensch*). As reason shaped the structure and ends (*Zweckrationalität*) of all kinds of human activities, including religion, art, and the academy, it led to a corresponding disenchantment with nature and the mysteries of life, and with it, a loss of wholeness and decline in communal identification.[29]

In "Robert McNamara: Max Weber's Worst Nightmare," published in *International Relations*, and here reprinted as reading number eight, I portray McNamara as the quintessential *Fachmensch*.[30] As a target planner in World War II, an executive, and later president, of Ford Motor Company, secretary of defense, and president of the World Bank, he was driven by the belief that most problems are amenable to technical solutions, and that clear, logical thinking and good data can discover those solutions and make their implementation more effective and efficient. The technocratic approach to problems has led to remarkable progress, especially in the material domain, but it has not come without costs. In Robert McNamara's case, it is responsible for his accomplishments and his failings, and presents us with a micro case in which to assess the consequences of policies formulated in an ethical vacuum.

The Schelling and McNamara selections have great contemporary relevance in light of the Iraq War. This indicates that little has changed in the theory and practice of coercive bargaining. The former has become immeasurably more sophisticated, but it is still based on the same questionable assumption that politics and culture can be ignored because the logic and language of bargaining are universal. Yet almost every study of international crisis reveals how signals are missed or misinterpreted, as are "moves," so central to all formulations of bargaining. Formal bargaining theories may do a good job of capturing behavior in highly formalized settings—like auctions at Christie's—where actors have been socialized to a set of procedures that makes communication transparent and effective. But few bargaining encounters in international relations have these characteristics. The problem of influence is more difficult still because it depends on knowledge of others' preferences. In the absence of such knowledge, there is no way of knowing if threats or rewards are likely to influence their cost calculus, and if they do so, in what direction. There are no technical fixes for these problems. They are context-dependent, require knowledge about other actors, their cultures and their preferences. The goal of a parsimonious bargaining theory based on realist principles is a conceit. The most such theories can do is to offer a first cut into a problem, that is to help actors structure their situation and to provide a framework they can fill in with relevant local knowledge.

The policy problem runs along a parallel track. Here too, there is no substitute for local knowledge, and for the same reasons. Policy based on grand schemes, whether those of academic realists like John Mearsheimer or the neoconservative ideologues in the Bush administration, are premised on the universal applicability of foundational principles, from which policy options are then deduced. In practice, such initiatives will almost inevitably fail because they do not take local conditions into account, or the host of other considerations, domestic and international, that shape outcomes. More fundamentally, the Iraq disaster is a reflection of crude and simplistic view of the world (in contrast to the more sophisticated wisdom of classical realism) that greatly overvalues military and economic capability—and especially, their alleged power to coerce, while ignoring the power of resistance based on appeals to principles, honor and self-esteem.

Cooperation

This section of book reprints two articles that address the theory and substance of cooperation. "Reason, Emotion and Cooperation," first published in *Interna-*

tional Politics, is a different kind of attack on rational models of cooperation.[31] In contrast to my critique of the strategic bargaining literature, I do not object to the use of rational models *per se*, as decisions to cooperate, unlike decisions to go to war, often reflect rational deliberation. My critique concerns in the first instance the mechanisms employed by these approaches to explain cooperation.

The realist, liberal institutionalist, social capital, "tit-for-tat," and "thin" constructivist explanations for cooperation rely on the explanatory mechanisms imported from micro-economics: coordination, transparency, and arrangements or strategies that reduce the shadow of the future by making cooperation more beneficial and defection more costly. They assume, rather than explain, the presence of an underlying propensity to cooperate that allow these mechanisms and strategies to work. In tit-for-tat, for example, cooperation requires a pre-existing disposition to cooperate. When this is not present, as in the simulations Axelrod ran with American policy makers during the Cold War, defection is the norm. All these approaches to cooperation rest on questionable ontological assumptions; their unit of analysis, the autonomous, egoistic actor is a fiction of the Enlightenment. Most actors, states included, have social identities that lead them to frame their interests at least in part in collective terms. This is what explains their propensity to cooperate with another group of actors, and their willingness to do so in instances that may not appear to be in their interest.

Rational models of decision making—and some psychological approaches—ignore affect or consider it detrimental to good judgment. Sophocles, Thucydides, and Aristotle, by contrast, recognized that cooperation and the communities it sustains depend on friendship (*philia*).[32] Friendship expands citizens' horizons, enables them to develop empathy, collective identities, and conceptions of self-interest that include the well-being of others. For Plato, the most important purpose of dialogue is not the substantive consensus it can foster, but the good will and friendship it creates among interlocutors. Friendship promotes trust and a propensity to listen and take seriously to what others have to say and cooperate with them toward common ends. Cooperation, in turn, creates and sustains common identities that make interests converge and facilitates further cooperation in the kind of community Democritus called a *homonoia*.[33]

Good judgment is also a product of reason and emotion. As Aristotle observes, we emulate people we admire, and use our reason to reflect upon their actions and ours to understand why, and under what conditions, certain courses of action succeed or fail.[34] We need good character traits to make good judgments, and these also come through experience and emulation of mentors.[35] The findings of modern neuroscience lend considerable credence to the Aristotelian perspective. They indicate that affect plays an important positive role in decision making at every stage of the process. It helps us select what information is worthy of attention and how it should be evaluated and acted upon.[36] To understand both cooperation and good judgment, we must study the complex interaction between reason and emotion, and identity and good judgment.

"Transitions and Transformations: Building International Cooperation," published in *Security Studies* in 1997, posits two stages of accommodation between adversarial states. The initial stage is characterized by a significant reduction in the perceived probability of war. Examples include Egyptian-Israeli relations after the 1979 peace treaty, and Sino-American relations in the aftermath of President Nixon's visit to the People's Republic of China in April 1971. Some conflicts move to a second stage of accommodation, characterized by "normal" political, economic and social relations. Examples include Anglo-French relations in the decade after their 1904 *Entente Cordiale*. Stage one involves negotiations, some of them secret, between national leaders or their most trusted advisors, assisted perhaps by the good offices of third parties. There is also an important internal dynamic, as leaders on both sides must have sufficient latitude to implement any accord they reach. This usually requires efforts to neutralize or co-opt domestic opponents. Stage two accommodation involves cooperation at the highest levels of government, but also negotiations and the implementation of agreements by middle levels of bureaucracies. It requires a dense network of trade and investment, cultural, and educational exchanges as well as visits by ordinary citizens. As relations normalize, the locus of contacts shifts from governments to businesses, non-profit organizations, professional associations, and even individuals.

My article theorizes about the causes of stage one accommodation. It does so on the basis of three historical case studies: Anglo-French relations between the Fashoda crisis of 1898 and the *Entente* of 1904, Egyptian-Israeli relations between the 1973 October War and the Peace Treaty of 1979, and the end of the Cold War from the selection of Mikhail Gorbachev as general secretary in 1986 to the unification of Germany in 1991. I find two principal and reinforcing incentives for accommodation in all my cases, and a third enabling condition in two of them. The first and primary incentive is a commitment by a leader to a program of far-reaching domestic reforms that are seen to require accommodation with a foreign adversary. This is essential to free resources or to bring about the domestic conditions necessary to pursue reforms. French Prime Minister Théophile Delcassé sought an understanding with Britain to reorient French foreign policy in light of the threat posed by Germany. He also wanted an accommodation to facilitate major domestic reforms that would strengthen the Third Republic by reducing the power of the army and the church. President Anwar Sadat of Egypt wanted to restructure the Egyptian economy, removing many state controls and reorienting it toward the West in the hope of attracting investment and trade. To do this, he had to extract Egypt from the Arab-Israeli conflict and its dependence on the Soviet Union. Foreign and domestic concerns were both critical for Gorbachev, who wanted to reduce defense spending and jump start the Soviet economy and needed to end the Cold War to undercut the power of the Soviet military-industrial complex and their claims on scarce resources.

The second incentive concerns the escalating costs of conflict. In each case, the leaders in question had concluded that conflict with their adversary was expensive, risky and unwinnable. For the French, the Fashoda crisis of 1898 brought the country to the brink of war with Britain at the same time it was in the acute *faux Henri* phase of the Dreyfus Affair. French humiliation at Fashoda exposed the absurdity of challenging Britain. Arabs convinced themselves that they had lost every war with Israel because they were unprepared, uncoordinated, and lacked the military initiative. The Egyptian-Syrian surprise attack on Israel in October 1973 benefited from all these advantages, and in addition, the latest Soviet weapons and new tactics to counter Israel's' advantage in armor. Despite initial successes on both fronts, the war was a military disaster for both Syria and Egypt. Sadat recognized that his only opportunity to gain back the Sinai was through diplomacy and the good offices of the United States. Gorbachev and his principal advisors regarded the Cold War as the legacy of Stalinism that had taken on a life of its own. They recognized that every attempt to gain a unilateral advantage was offset by a counter-move that left them at least as disadvantaged as before. Graphic evidence was provided by the deployment in the 1980s of a new generation of nuclear-tipped missiles in Europe. NATO had countered with the deployment of Pershing-2 rockets and cruise missiles, the former threatening to Soviet command and control.

Overtures to wind down conflicts can be very costly if spurned by the adversary. They make leaders look weak in the eyes of adversaries, encouraging further challenges, and provide ammunition to domestic opponents, who may exploit a foreign setback to challenge their authority. The third, enabling condition is the belief that adversaries will respond positively to peace feelers. In the Anglo-French and Egyptian-Israeli cases, as in the Sino-American relations, there were extensive secret talks that led to the outlines of a deal before any public announcements were made. The Soviet-American accommodation is different in the sense that Gorbachev began a public peace offensive at the height of turbulent relations with the United States, led by a seemingly uncompromising president who referred to the Soviet Union as the "evil empire." There is good reason to believe that Gorbachev convinced himself that he would succeed because he knew he had to if he was going to pursue *glasnost* and *perestroika* successfully. In a subsequent publication—the concluding chapter Janice Stein and I wrote for *Ending the Cold War*—we argue that Gorbachev's behavior can only be described as motivated bias.[37]

I close this section with two caveats. Three cases can generate propositions but not substantiate them. I remain hopeful that someone will evaluate this explanation for accommodation across a broader sample of cases. My second cautionary note concerns the important role of miscalculation, which may be as important in making peace as it is making war. The Anglo-French *Entente Cordiale* worked well for both countries. Delcassé gained British support for French penetration of Morocco, backing in the two Moroccan crises provoked by Germany and joint military planning that enabled the early and critical intervention of the British Expeditionary Force in the opening stage of the First World War. His parliamentary coalition, *La Défense Républicaine*, successfully carried through its reforms and ensured the democratic consolidation of the Third Republic. Sadat and Gorbachev were not so fortunate. Sadat reoriented Egypt's foreign policy, but this did little to improve the economy, as it remained mired in corruption and handicapped by heavy-handed state interference. In October 1981, Sadat was assassinated by Muslim extremists infuriated by his peace treaty with Israel. Gorbachev successfully ended the Cold War, but his economic reforms were insufficient to improve the economy and were resisted, if not sabotaged, by hardliners. His reforms hastened the collapse of communism in Eastern Europe, the reunification of Germany under the auspices of NATO, and the breakup of the Soviet Union. One must wonder if either leader would have chosen accommodation if they had had a better understanding of where that path was likely to lead.

Ancient Greeks

In my last year of high school I treated myself to an inexpensive Modern Library edition of Greek tragedies. I read the plays with interest, but without real understanding in the absence of context, maturity, and expert guidance. What I did appreciate was the spare and abstract nature of the plot line and dialogue, which struck me as somewhat similar to the minimalist prints of Utamaro and Hiroshige, artists who had recently engaged my interest. In university, I had a more serious exposure to the Greeks. I read selections from Plato and Thucydides in "Introduction to Western Civilization," and more thoroughly in philosophy and international relations courses. I wrote a course paper on the contradiction I detected between Thucydides' authorial claim about the causes of war and those indicated by his narrative account. In Book 1.23.6, he writes that "the growth of the power of Athens, and the alarm which this inspired in Sparta, made war inevitable."[38] The narrative of Book I suggests that the war was due to Athenian hubris, Spartan concern for their standing, and reinforcing miscalculations by great and small powers alike.

I revisited this question in the 1980s, when I co-taught a course on hegemony in the ancient and modern worlds with Cornell colleague and historian Barry Strauss[39] It allowed me to reread Thucydides and discuss the text with an authority on fifth century Greece. Barry and I subsequently organized a conference and edited a book on the subject of hegemony.[40] The conference, at the Princeton villa in Cadenabbia, Italy, provided useful feedback on my paper, but still left me with a nagging mystery: how to account for the discrepancy between the argument and narrative of Book One.

In the following decade, I worked on other problems. I wrote a book on nuclear crisis management that examined the ways in which stress and its behavioral consequences in an acute crisis could defeat the procedures designed to prevent the accidental or unauthorized launch of nuclear weapons.[41] With Hans Bethe, Richard Garwin, Kurt Gottfried, Franklyn Long, and Carl Sagan, I coauthored the first book to attack the scientific and political premises of Ronald Reagan's Strategic Defense Initiative, better known as "Star Wars." I wrote a book on bargaining, stimulated by a class I taught on the subject, and my experience in running bargaining simulations for the U.S. government, the NATO Defence College and various other groups.[42] In the early 1990s, Janice Stein and I completed our research for *We All Lost the Cold War*. I then turned my attention to the end of that conflict and coauthored a book on the subject with Richard Herrmann.[43]

Ending the Cold War brought together scholars from differing intellectual perspectives to design a collaborative strategy for determining how and why the Cold War ended. We agreed to focus on five turning points: Gorbachev's accession to power, the Soviet decision to withdraw from Afghanistan and reduce other Soviet commitments in the Third World, the breakthrough in arms control signaled but the Intermediate Range Nuclear Forces Treaty (INF) of December 1987, the liberation of Eastern Europe, and the reunification of Germany. Our authors investigated each of these turning points from the perspectives of four competing explanations: material forces, ideas, domestic politics, and leaders. Rather than pitting them against each other, the goal was to find ways in which these explanations were synergistic as much as competing. Contributors were also asked to use counterfactuals to discover what and how much they needed to undo to prevent the positive outcomes these turning points represent. For evidence, we relied on extensive interviews, collaboration with the Cold War History Project to obtain relevant documents from Soviet, American, and Eastern European archives, and four oral history conferences that brought together leading policymakers from the Soviet Union, the United States, and Western Europe.

The most fascinating of these conferences was a two-day meeting in Moscow with the most prominent Soviet officials who had opposed the foreign policy of Mikhail Gorbachev. Participants included former Head of the KGB Vladimir Kryuchkov, former Minister of Defense Dimitri Yazov, former Vice President Gennady Yanayev, and First Deputy Chairman of the Soviet Defense Council Oleg Baklanov, all members of the "gang of eight" that attempted the unsuccessful coup against Gorbachev in August 1991. In discussing the coup, it became evident that none of its planners had ever talked about what they would do once in power beyond revoking the All Union Treaty that would have allowed Soviet Republics to keep draftees on their own territory, threatening the survival of the Red Army, and with it the Soviet Union. Nor had they ever considered what to do if Republics refused to recognize the coup, which is what happened. Kryuchkov, we discovered, was still rankled by Yazov's refusal to order Soviet troops to fire on the crowd that had gathered in front of the "White House" to protest the coup and protect Russian President Boris Yeltsin, who was mobilizing support against it. Yazov explained that he had made certain that the forces he ordered into the streets were not armed; he was convinced that their presence would intimidate any opposition. When this failed, he was unwilling to order Soviet troops to fire on Muscovites. The unofficial high point of the meeting came when a cell phone sounded in the attaché case of Baklanov's driver cum body guard. He looked around uncomfortably, then hunched over the case to shroud its contents as he opened it to answer the phone. At least half of our small group caught a good glimpse of the phone, wads of $100 dollar bills with rubber bands around them, and a large pearl-handled revolver.

In the 1990s, I wrote several articles and book chapters about counterfactuals. I intend to include several of them in a volume I am preparing on counterfactuals and politics. Toward the end of the decade, I returned to the problem of Thucydides. In *Tragic Vision of Politics: Ethics, Interests and Orders*, I sought to resurrect the wisdom of classical realism through the texts of Thucydides, Carl von Clausewitz, and Hans J. Morgenthau. I advance the counter-intuitive argument that interest and ethics are reconcilable at the deepest level of understanding; that interests cannot be formulated intelligently outside of a language of justice. I use this formulation to critique post-Cold War American foreign policy.

Thucydides, Clausewitz, and Morgenthau share a tragic understanding of life and politics. I argue that Greek tragedy provides the basis for an alternative and more productive ontology for the social sciences. The dominant ontology assumes that the egoistic, autonomous actor without any history is a proper starting point for analysis. The Greeks recognized that people are rarely clustered at the poles of any social continuum (e.g., self- versus social identity, interest vs. honor, family vs. civic obligations), and that when they are, the consequences are invariably destructive. At most times in most societies, human commitments and behavior is arrayed somewhere along the continuum between the extremes that tragedy problematizes. Most people and their societies make uneasy, often illogical, uncomfortable and usually unstable compromises in favor of unwavering commitments to any set of values or responsibilities. Like tragedy, we must start from the premise that these polarities define the extremes of the human condition and are not good starting points for understanding behavior. We must represent, not suppress, the diversity and inherent instability of human identities, interests and motives, and their complex interactions with the discourses, social practices, and institutions they generate and sustain.

Tragic Vision of Politics is unambiguously a work of social science, but relies on ancient and modern literature for some its most important insights. It opens with a short story, "Nixon in Hell," which I wrote to introduce its principal normative argument: that leaders of government and institutions should be held accountable to the same ethical standards of behavior as private individuals. Like tragedy, and art more generally, the story serves its purpose by arousing the emotions as well as engaging the minds of readers. The Greeks understood that cooperation and conflict alike result from the interplay of emotions and reason, and I use their understanding and my story to critique existing theories of cooperation, develop the outlines of an alternative approach and make the case for the instrumental value of ethical behavior.

My two chapters on Thucydides address the origins of the Peloponnesian War and his broader political project: warning future generations of the destructive consequences of reason's failure of to restrain appetite and spirit. The chapter on the origins of the war finally resolves to my satisfaction the apparent contradiction between Thucydides' authorial statement and the narrative of Book I. The follow-on chapter reads his history as a layered, sophistic text, where tensions and contradictions within and between levels draw readers to deeper levels of understanding. Reading number eleven, an article published in the *American Political Science Review*, is an abbreviated presentation of the argument of this chapter. I marshal textual, linguistic, and contextual evidence to critique traditional realist readings of Thucydides—and especially of the Melian Dialogue—and argue that he is as much the father of constructivism as he is of realism. The most superficial level of Thucydides' history examines the destructive consequences of domestic and foreign policies framed outside of a language of justice. His deeper political-philosophical aim is to explore the relationship between convention (*nomos*) and nature (*phusis*) and its implications for civilization. Thucydides suggests that *nomos* helps to construct identities and channels and restrains the behavior of individuals and societies. Speech and reason (*logos*) make *nomos* possible because all conventions depend on shared meanings. The positive feedback loop between *logoi* (words) and *erga* (deeds) was responsible for Greek civilization, while their unraveling was responsible for the international and civil strife of the Peloponnesian War. International security and civil order depend upon recovering the meaning of words and the conventions they enable.[44]

Modern realist conceptions of power emphasize its material basis and divorce the analysis and application of power from ethical considerations. Ancient Greeks, by contrast, were equally sensitive to the social bases of power, how its exercise might strengthen or weaken the personal or communal bonds on which influence ultimately rests. Greek playwrights and philosophers distinguish between power exercised through persuasion (*peithō*), which strengthens these bonds, and power that weakens them because it relies on coercion, bribery, and deceit (*dolos*). Binary Greek concepts for persuasion, power, and hegemony provide the basis for a critique of realist conceptions of power and post-Cold War American foreign policy. "Power and Ethics," originally published in *Millennium*, and reproduced here as reading number twelve, draws on a range of Greek sources, but especially Sophocles' play *Philoctetes*, to explore the complicated relationships among material capabilities, power and influence.[45]

The third reading in this section, "Tragedy, Politics and Political Science," was originally published in *International Relations* as part of an extended debate on the role of tragedy in international relations. The three other participants—Mervyn Frost, James Mayall, and Nicholas Rengger—present a range of views on the utility of tragedy as analytical category, the underlying causes of tragedy in international relations and the extent to which knowledge of tragedy might minimize its likelihood and consequences. I argue that the concept of tragedy is particularly relevant to a world of competing ethical and intellectual perspectives. Hubristic efforts to impose one's authority and values on others by force in such a world are almost certain to meet resistance and lead to outcomes diametrically opposed to those sought. The Anglo-American invasion of Iraq is a quintessential example, and best understood as tragedy in the classic Greek sense of the term.

My interest in the Greeks continues, and I am currently at work on a theory of international relations based on the Greek understanding of the human psyche. It is richer than its modern counterparts and generates important insights into preference formation and the causes of political order and instability at the individual, state and international levels. It also facilitates generalizations about the ways in which order or its decline at any level affects order at adjacent levels.[46] I will return to this question in the conclusion.

Notes

1   Harold Lasswell, *World Politics and Personal Insecurity* (New York: McGraw-Hill, 1935).
2   Eric Fromm, *Escape from Freedom* (New York: Holt, Rinehart & Winston, 1941).
3   Leon Festinger, *A Theory of Cognitive dissonance* (Evanston, Il: Row, Peterson, 1957).
4   Gregory Henderson, Richard Ned Lebow and John G. Stoessinger, *Divided Nations in a Divided World* (New York: David McKay, 1974).
5   Richard Ned Lebow, "The Origins of Sectarian Assassination: The Case of Belfast," *Journal of International Affairs* 32 (Spring 1978), pp. 43–61.
6   Richard Ned Lebow, *Between Peace and War: The Nature of International Crisis* (Baltimore: Johns Hopkins University Press, 1981).
7   Robert Jervis, Richard Ned Lebow, and Janice Gross Stein, *Psychology and Deterrence* (Baltimore: The Johns Hopkins University Press, 1985). Richard Ned Lebow and Janice Gross Stein, *When Does Deterrence Succeed and How Do We Know?*, with Janice Gross Stein (Ottawa: Canadian Institute for International Peace and Security, 1990); "Preventing War in the Middle East: When Do Deterrence and Reassurance Work," in Steven Spiegel, ed., *Conflict Management in the Middle East* (Boulder, CO: Westview Press, 1991); "Deterrence: The Elusive Dependent Variable," *World Politics* 42 (April 1990), pp. 336–69; "Rational Deterrence Theory: I Think Therefore I Deter," *World Politics* 41 (January 1989), 208–24.
8   Richard Ned Lebow and Janice Gross Stein, "Beyond Deterrence," *Journal of Social Issues* 43, No. 4 (1987), pp. 5–71; "Beyond Deterrence: Building Better Theory," pp. 155–69, and "Conventional and Nuclear Deterrence: Are the Lessons Transferable?," pp. 171–91.
9   Richard Ned Lebow, *Nuclear Crisis Management: A Dangerous Illusion* (Ithaca, NY: Cornell University Press, January 1987).
10   Richard Ned Lebow, "The Cuban Missile Crisis: Reading the Lessons Correctly," *Political Science Quarterly* 98 (Autumn 1983), 431–58.
11   The charge that Khrushchev took Kennedy's measure at Vienna and found him wanting, originated with James Reston, *New York Times Magazine*, November 15, 1964, p. 126.
12   Elie Abel, *The Missiles of October* (Philadelphia: Lippincott, 1962).
13   Graham T. Allison, *Essence of Decision: Explaining the Cuban Missile Crisis* (Boston: Little, Brown, 1971), pp. 235–37.

14 Nikita S. Khrushchev, *Khrushchev Remembers*, trans. Strobe Talbott (Boston: Little, Brown, 1970), and *Khrushchev Remembers: The Last Testament*, trans. and ed. Strobe Talbott (New York: Bantam, 1976).

15 *Khrushchev Remembers: The Last Testament*, pp. 566–67; Lebow and Stein, *We All Lost the Cold War* (Princeton, NJ: Princeton University Press, 1994), pp. 70–72, for the testimony of other Soviet officials.

16 Richard Ned Lebow and Janice Gross Stein, *We All Lost the Cold War*, ch. 2; Raymond L. Garthoff, *Reflections on the Cuban Missile Crisis*, rev. ed. (Washington, D.C.: Brookings, 1989), pp. 6–42.

17 Lebow and Stein, *We All Lost the Cold War*, ch. 3.

18 Ibid.

19 Ibid., chs. 8 and 9.

20 Ibid, pp. 251–58.

21 Thomas Schelling, *The Strategy of Conflict* (Cambridge: Harvard University Press, 1960).

22 Bruce Bueno de Mesquita, *The War Trap* (New Haven, CT: Yale University Press, 1981).

23 Richard Ned Lebow and Janice Gross Stein, "Deterrence: The Elusive Dependent Variable," *World Politics* 42 (April 1990), 336–69. Paul Huth and Bruce Russett, "What Makes Deterrence Work? Cases from 1900 to 1980," *World Politics* 36 (July 1984), pp. 496–526, and "Deterrence Failure and Crisis Escalation," *International Studies Quarterly* 32 (March 1988), pp. 29–46.

24 Lebow and Stein, *We All Lost the Cold War*, ch. 2.

25 Lebow and Stein, "Deterrence: The Elusive Dependent Variable."

26 Schelling, *Arms and Influence*, p. 174.

27 Richard Ned Lebow, "Thomas Schelling and Strategic Bargaining," *International Studies* 51 (Summer 1996), pp. 555–76.

28 Max Weber, "Politics as a Vocation," trans. and ed. H. H. Gerth and C. Wright Mills (New York: Galaxy, 1958), pp. 75, 121–23, 125–26.

29 Max Weber, "The Profession and Vocation of Politics," in *Political Writings*, ed. Peter Lassmann and Ronald Speirs (Cambridge: Cambridge University Press, 1994), pp. 309–69.

30 Richard Ned Lebow, "Robert S. McNamara: Max Weber's Nightmare," *International Relations*, 20(2) (June 2006), pp. 211-24.

31 Richard Ned Lebow, "Reason, Emotion and Cooperation," *International Politics*, 42(3) (2005), pp. 283–313.

32 Aristotle, *Nicomachean Ethics*, 1155a14, 1159b25, 1161a23, 1161b12, and Politics, 1280b39. Thucydides, II.43.1 has Pericles describe *philia* as the foundation of alliances as well as cities.

33 Hermann Diels and Walther Kranz, *Die Fragmente der Vorsokratiker*, 7th ed. (Berlin: Weidmannsche Verlagsbuchhandlung, 1956), frg. 68B255.

34 Aristotle, *Nicomachean Ethics*, 1.7.1099a4-5, 1.13.1103a2, distinguishes practical from theoretical reason; 6.1.1139a29-30, 1139a29-30 defines *phronesis* and how it helps non-rational desires to achieve their proper virtue.

35 Ibid, Books VIII and IX.

36 Gerald Clore, including "Cognitive Phenomenology: Feelings and the Construction of Judgment," in Leonard Martin and Abraham Tesser, eds., *The Construction of*

Social Judgments (Hillsdale, NJ: Erlbaum, 1992), pp. 133–63, and Gerald Clore et al, "Affective Feelings as Feedback: Some Cognitive Consequences," in Leonard Martin and Gerald Clore, eds., *Theories of Mood and* Cognition (Mahway, NJ: Erlbaum, 2002), pp. 27–62; Antonio Damasio, *Descartes' Error: Emotion, Reason, and the Human* Brain (New York: Putnam, 1996); Jeffrey Gray, *The Psychology of Fear and Stress*, 2nd ed. (Cambridge: Cambridge University Press, 1987). For a good review of the literature, see Rose McDermott, "The Feeling of Rationality: The Meaning of Neuroscientific Advances for Political Science" *Perspectives in Politics*, 2 (December 2004), pp. 691–706.

37 Richard Ned Lebow and Janice Gross Stein, "Understanding the End of the Cold War as a Non-Linear Confluence," in Herrmann and Lebow, *Ending the Cold War*, pp. 189–218.

38 Thucydides, I.23. Translation from the Richard Crawley translation in Robert B. Strassler, ed., *The Landmark Thucydides: A Comprehensive Guide to the Peloponnesian War* (New York: Free Press, 1996), I.23.

39 Richard Ned Lebow and Barry R. Strauss, eds., *Hegemonic Rivalry: From Thucydides to the Nuclear Age* (Boulder, CO: Westview Press, 1991).

40 Richard Ned Lebow and Barry R. Strauss, *Hegemonic Rivalry: From Thucydides to the Nuclear Age* (Boulder, CO: Westview Press, 1991).

41 Richard Ned Lebow, *Nuclear Crisis Management: A Dangerous Illusion* (Ithaca, NY: Cornell University Press, January 1987).

42 Richard Ned Lebow, *The Art of Bargaining* (Baltimore: Johns Hopkins University Press, 1996).

43 Richard K. Herrmann and Richard Ned Lebow, eds., *Ending the Cold War* (New York: Palgrave-Macmillan, 2004).

44 Richard Ned Lebow, "Thucydides the Constructivist," *American Political Science Review* 95 (September 2001), pp. 547–60.

45 Richard Ned Lebow, "Power and Ethics," *Millennium 33*(3) (Spring 2005), pp. 551–82.

46 Richard Ned Lebow, *Recognition, Honor andd Standing: A Paradigm of Politics and International Relations* (Cambridge: Cambridge University Press, forthcoming).

Part I
Colonialism and its aftermath

1 Colonial policies and their payoffs

In the nineteenth century all colonial powers, like Britain in Ireland, were presented with two alternative sets of goals. The traditional conception of empire envisaged colonies as territories to be exploited. A newer conception, not fully articulated until after the French Revolution, was that colonies provided additional land and people whose integration into the political unit would strengthen the nation. The former conception relied upon superior military power to keep the people quiescent; the latter, upon responsiveness to make them loyal.

Unlike many political questions of the nineteenth century, this one did not lend itself to a compromise that would partially fulfill both conceptions. The alternative goals were by their very nature mutually exclusive. If colonial powers desired to maintain their empires, they were compelled to make a choice between the two. An examination of the strategies required to implement the goals will help to illustrate the increasing dilemma faced by metropolitan powers.

A strategy of coercion is dictated by a goal of exploitation. To the extent that the colony is exploited at the expense of the inhabitants the colonizer must rely upon his superior power to preserve control. Such a strategy requires a minimal material commitment, can lead to an immediate "payoff," but is less likely to result in a stable political connection.

The colonizer's authority depends on his ability to enforce obedience by the subject population. The colonized must be made to realize that rebellion is doomed to failure or entails intolerable cost to the insurgents. The payoff of such a strategy is both material and psychological. The metropolitan power can exact tribute or forced labor, exploit the material wealth and economic resources of the colony and utilize its geographic position for military advantage vis-à-vis other powers. A coercion strategy is also rewarding in the sense that domination gained through force and control exercised through terror enable individuals, classes or societies to give expression to inner frustrations and anxieties.[1]

The drawbacks of basing authority on coercion are manifold. The colonizer's authority is likely to be accepted only as long as his power and his will to use it remain unquestioned. Should the metropolitan country suffer a relative decline in power by reason of internal disruption or foreign conflict, or should the colonized territory redress the military imbalance by securing the support of a third power, the danger of rebellion will increase. The Irish, for example, remained poised for rebellion throughout the centuries before the Union. Actual insurgency occurred, however, only when military factors favored the chances of rebellion. In 1640, when Britain was internally divided by civil war, in 1690, when it was threatened by Louis XIV, and again in 1798, when it was locked in a deadly struggle with Napoleon, the Irish capitalized upon Britain's weakness and the opportunity for foreign support and rose in rebellion.

The colonizer's authority is equally likely to be challenged should he grow "soft," his military spirit dampened by the spoils of success, by the rigor of frequent battle or by changes in the ethics of his society. This was, no doubt, an important calculation of the leaders of the Irish insurrection in 1920–1921.

Colonies ruled by such methods can present the specter of constant rebellion. If the power of the colonizer is called into question for any of the reasons discussed, the cost of preserving domination may become so high as to offset the profit extracted from the colony. In the case of Ireland this probably occurred some time in the middle of the nineteenth century. While maintenance can develop into a costly burden, withdrawal may be perceived as an even more disastrous outcome because of the precedent it could set for other, similar situations—the domino theory—or because it would leave behind a hostile population likely to pose a threat to the former colonizer. Both of these considerations were paramount in the minds of those Englishmen who opposed repeal of the Union.

The rather Machiavellian moral to be learned from this dilemma is that rule based on coercion must never be allowed to be questioned to the extent that a serious threat to domination develops. There are two means which can be employed to prevent such a situation from arising.

The most commonly adopted course is aimed at preserving the colonizer's credibility by terror and violence. This has been the standard technique resorted to by most conquerors. Genghis Khan, for example, was so effective in terrorizing the Russian princes and people during his brief campaigns in Russia that when the hordes retired behind the Asian steppes they considered it unnecessary to leave behind a force of occupation. In the hundred years that followed Russian strength vis-à-vis the Tartars steadily increased but the yearly tribute to Astrakhan was nevertheless dutifully delivered for fear of the consequences should it be withheld.

In the modern world the use of terror and violence as a deterrent has lost much of its efficacy. The maintenance of the colonizer's credibility in the eyes of the native population is in itself no longer effective in preventing rebellion. When struggles take on ideological significance the level of endurance of all the participants is raised. Action is inspired that is frequently suicidal in cost. When people rebel in the name of religious freedom, human liberty or national independence, the extent of their opponent's destructive capacity is no longer the most relevant consideration because the insurgents no longer perceive death as the worst of all possible outcomes. The Russian boyars would have dismissed as absurd the suggestion that they begin a futile rebellion for the sake of national honor. But the Irishmen who calmly faced death in the springtime of their lives in the Easter Rebellion of 1916 did so willingly. The insurgency began with a conscious recognition on their part that it was doomed to failure. The cry of "Give me liberty or give me death"—or the more contemporary "Better dead than red"—reflects the transcendent importance ideological principles occupy in the modern individual's value hierarchy.

If the politically relevant population of the colony can no longer be effectively controlled by the destructive capability of the colonizer, the only recourse likely to be effective in preserving domination is a policy designed to prevent the development of an elite capable of leading a revolution. Perhaps the ultimate application of this logic is to be found in Hitler's projected plans for eastern Europe.

The Nazis intended to exterminate a large percentage of the native population, including all those who had received an education. German settlers were to repopulate the land, while the remaining inhabitants were to be reduced to hewers of wood and drawers of water, mere slaves who would carry out necessary but menial agricultural and mechanical labor. Deprived of organizational and military skills, illiterate and uneducated, the population would have been transformed into beasts of burden, human only in their physical form and potential. Such a population—assuming it had no contact with the outside world—would have posed little threat to the German ascendancy.

At the opposite end of the political spectrum from the strategy of coercion is the strategy designed to integrate the colonial population into the national political community. The aim of this strategy is to secure the loyalty of the colonial subjects by legitimizing the colonial connection in their eyes.

A political system develops legitimacy when it is consistently able to meet the needs and fulfill the expectations of the population over which it wields authority. The more often its ability in this regard is demonstrated over time, the more the people come to associate their individual success with the success and survival of the system. As support for the system grows, its authority to make decisions affecting the lives and fortunes of the population is less frequently questioned. Compliance gradually becomes a habit.

A political system derives great advantages from having secured the loyalty of the population. Among other things, it obtains a certain degree of latitude for its actions by reason of the reservoir of support it has built up. This support, a credit that can be drawn upon during times of crisis, enables the system to survive reverses which otherwise might have proved fatal.

Legitimacy, however, is more difficult to achieve than rule based on coercion, and it entails a higher expenditure of resources. A heavy load is placed on the decision-making apparatus of the metropolitan power. Its institutions must develop means to judge the needs of the population and must be capable of bringing the resources of the state to bear where they are required. This in itself requires a considerable expenditure of time, money and effort. In addition, these resources must be expended over a long period of time before any payoff becomes apparent. Scholars who have studied the integration process have found that the advantages the colonized community derives from amalgamation must outweigh the burdens.

It is only after the colony's politically relevant population perceives that it is likely to attain a higher degree of wealth, status, honor and security by virtue of integration, and in fact realizes these goals, that it is likely to assume the responsibilities of the relationship.[2]

Perhaps the most difficult commitment is of a psychological nature. The colonizer cannot preserve his exclusiveness and sense of superiority over the colonized if meaningful social contact and communication are to be established. Without such communication it is impossible to develop the mutual understanding, trust and predictability of behavior that are so essential to responsiveness. No level of administrative capability and material expenditure will compensate for the lack. Unless a high degree of empathy develops, the metropolitan society will most likely be extremely reluctant to consent to the high cost of a strategy of integration and to grant the opportunities for upward mobility so essential to that strategy's success.

Herein lies the danger of the strategy of integration. If for any reason the metropolitan power proves unresponsive to the needs of the colonized or fails to create the mobility that the population has been led to expect, the integration will be unsuccessful. The colonial power will have created expectations that have not been fulfilled and probably will alienate the community it sought to integrate. In such a case, as in Ireland, rebellion or at least agitation for autonomy is likely to develop.

Ironically, the probability for the success of a rebellion is likely to be considerably greater than if the metropolitan power had never attempted integration. Unlike a coercive strategy, which aims to prevent a native elite from developing, a strategy designed to achieve integration encourages mobility and political participation. An unsuccessful attempt at integration, by providing some mobility and some political participation, will create an elite without at the same time securing the loyalties of that elite to the larger political unit. The very cadres necessary to organize and carry out rebellion will be formed. The strategy of integration can therefore be viewed as a gamble with high rewards and equally high risks. If it is successful, the payoff is highly rewarding; if it is unsuccessful, the result is likely to be disaster.

The British policy: a curious amalgam

British policy toward Ireland in the centuries before the Union is accurately characterized as a strategy of coercion. Ireland was a colony whose land and people were ruthlessly exploited to serve British interests. British dominion, exercised by a minority of soldiers, settlers, and administrators ruling over an alien and restless people, rested on the threat and actual application of force and terror. Settlers were encouraged to farm land expropriated from the indigenous inhabitants and were given arbitrary and absolute power over the lives and fortunes of the natives.

Although the British relied principally upon their preponderant military power to guarantee their authority in Ireland, after 1640 they employed the additional tactic of policies designed to prevent a native elite from developing. The Penal Laws, legislated after Cromwell's suppression of the Irish insurgents, forbade Irish Catholics to serve in the army, to enter politics, to own land, to practice a profession, to import or export, to send their children to a Catholic school in Ireland or abroad for an education. Such repressive measures, coupled with a further expropriation of Irish lands (and even a policy of extermination), were consciously designed to reduce the wealth, power and organizational capabilities of the Irish people. Like eastern Europe, Ireland was to be reduced to a productive, untroublesome asset. The interests of the native inhabitants were entirely sacrificed to the interests of the metropolitan power.

In the first 50 years after the Union British policy toward Ireland became a curious amalgam of the two basic strategies that satisfied the conditions of neither but deepened the pitfalls of both. The avowed goal of successive British governments was the integration of the Irish people into the British nation. To some extent policies designed to achieve this goal were implemented. Discriminatory restrictions against Irish Catholics and the Catholic religion were largely removed. The Penal Laws had been struck down in the decades before the Union, and Catholic emancipation was granted several decades afterwards. The Catholic church was allowed to operate without legal interference and was even given some state support. The government allocated more funds for Irish education—both parochial and secular—and actively promoted job mobility within the civil service. The outlay for the development of roads and other transportation facilities, public health, and social services also increased many-fold in the first 50 years of Union.

As a result, there was an increase in literacy and education, an increase in wealth (though not between 1830 and 1850), and a corresponding increase in the store of specialized technical and administrative skills among the Irish people. Although the Ireland of 1850 was still a predominantly agrarian country, the middle class, which had begun to emerge at the beginning of the century, had increased its size and solidified its power. An Irish intelligentsia had emerged that fully participated in the avant-garde political and artistic trends of the European intellectual elite.

There was the other side to the coin. Throughout this period the British continued to exploit Ireland. At the beginning of the century, British industrialists had rigged the commercial clauses of the Union in such a way that they were easily able to destroy infant Irish industry and guarantee a large market in Ireland for finished British goods. British industrialists also exploited the chronic unemployment of Ireland by paying substandard wages to Irish workers imported from that island. The Protestant church continued to receive a substantial part of Irish revenues, even though it did little to contribute to the well-being or spiritual welfare of the majority of the Irish people. The Irish administration, although it became progressively more responsive to Irish interests after 1830, still included many individuals who viewed their jobs as mere sinecures or as rewards for past service. The British parliament continued to legislate differently for Ireland and England and refused to grant the Irish those basic civil liberties all Englishmen believed to be their natural inheritance. Above all, the Irish landed interests, through a notorious abuse of their arbitrary power, mercilessly exploited the Irish peasantry and contributed more than anyone else to the economic malaise of the countryside.

Exploitation and responsiveness were mutually exclusive. Therefore the reforms designed to meet the demands of the Irish people were unsuccessful in promoting reconciliation because they did not redress the core grievances arising from continuing exploitation and oppression. The Irish, for example, were given parliamentary representation, yet it proved ineffectual in guaranteeing the civil liberties of the Irish people. Irishmen were employed by the British administration in Ireland, but policy was still formulated by bureaucrats who were largely unresponsive to Irish needs. The Catholic church was made legal in Ireland and even subsidized by the state, but the established church continued to draw heavily on the Irish revenues. Reform, rather than statisfying Irish demands made the hopelessness of their position even more apparent and thus fanned the flames of their discontent.

The political, religious, and economic reforms, coupled with the increasing British commitment of resources in Ireland, created conditions in which a middle class and native intelligentsia could develop. However, change and reform were not sufficiently far-reaching to fulfill the expectations of these classes for wealth, prestige, honor, and equality. Aware of the possibilities for change, furious with the inequalities still remaining, and possessing technical and administrative skills and increasing capital, these classes mobilized the masses to support their demands and became the spearhead of the national movement. The Repeal movement, which had asked only for equality, was eclipsed by national movements like Young Ireland, the Fenians, and Sinn Fein that demanded independence. In the end, it was the nationalist movement which secured the loyalty of the Irish people and successfully challenged British rule.

A paradigm of colonial history

The conclusions reached by Rupert Emerson in his impressive study *From Empire to Nation* suggest that the same contradictory dualism which characterized the Anglo-Irish relationship was a general feature of European colonial policy.[3] Emerson offers a paradigm of colonial history to explain the developmental sequence of colonial peoples from subject status to independence.

Emerson divides the colonial period in Asia and Africa into three stages, each representative of a distinct attitude manifested by the native population toward Western rule. According to him, the first period was characterized by a xenophobic rejection of colonial rule. The indigenous inhabitants, led by their traditional leaders, rose in rebellion against the alien invader. The colonial power's values, political forms, and physical presence were violently rejected by the society. The Boxer Rebellion, the Indian mutiny, and the uprising of the Mahdi in the Sudan were all representative of this phase of interaction between the colonizer and the colonized. Such attempts to expel the foreigners and return to the traditional way of life were unsuccessful. The power of the traditional elite was frequently broken by the uprising, and often they retained a negligible influence only by reason of the grace accorded to them by the occupying nation. In such cases they proved useful as an administrative link between the colonial authorities and the native population. Over successive generations, this arrangement frequently proved fruitful to both parties, and the colonial power was able to retain the loyalties of this class until independence.

The second period was characterized by a swing from xenophobic rejection to emulation. The change developed gradually, and only after radical alterations in the indigenous patterns of life had been effected by European occupation. A modern market economy developed alongside the precolonial subsistence economy. Urban centers, the loci of the European community, grew in size and importance and attracted natives from the hinterland. The cities were the centers of operation for overseas companies and the expanding colonial administration and were increasingly populated by a rising class of native entrepreneurs. As colonial governments and metropolitan commercial enterprises extended their operations, they found it necessary to introduce modern health services, to establish schools and to train elements of the native population in the skills and techniques of industrial society. This was partly a function of need and partly a response, Emerson argues, to growing pressures at home to improve the lot of the natives. Missionaries and charitable organizations tended the bodies and minds of natives as well as their souls.

Thus urbanization and the spread of literacy, the growth of secular education and the diffusion of technical and administrative skills among the native population were byproducts of European colonial rule. These changes gave rise to a Europeanized element in the colony, concentrated in the urban centers and coexisting with the majority of the native population that remained rooted in its traditional ways. A new class of native had emerged. Fluent in the language of the colonizer, skilled in the techniques of the West, and schooled in the ideas and values of European civilization, members of these new elite demanded the power, wealth, and status accorded Europeans with similar qualifications. These *evolués*, as the French called them—often educated at Oxford, the Sorbonne, or The Hague—rejected their old cultures and openly embraced the new. They considered themselves not so much Ibo, Arab, or Malay as English, French, or Dutch.

Some members of this first generation of culturally uprooted individuals were able to achieve high mobility in their adopted societies. This was especially evident in the French colonies, where assimilation was the avowed policy of the government. Two examples are Félix Houphouet-Boigny of the Ivory Coast, who became a cabinet minister, and Léopold Senghor, a noted poet (in the French language) who was honored by membership in the prestigious French Academy. Such persons, however, represented a minority of the emerging native elite; most others like them were refused positions for which they believed their training and experience qualified them. Although competent and hardworking and honest in their adoption of European customs, they remained "natives" to the colonialists, who refused to bestow upon them the status freely granted less qualified members of the European community. In short, they remained frustrated in their attempt to achieve the benefits of the new order.

These frustrated Europeanized elements of the colony, Emerson argues, were not blind to the anomaly between word and deed. Colonial governments sought justification in the name of secular enlightenment and frequently articulated their "mission" as the diffusion of the benefits of Western civilization. To the colonial population this appeared to be sheer hypocrisy, as they saw themselves being denied these very benefits.

Bitterness in the face of such discrimination—justified by colonialists on the basis of racial or ethnic differences—was sharpened by the all-too-obvious contrast between this treatment and the ideas of equality and human dignity the elite had imbibed from their European education. The Declaration of the Rights of Man was a far cry from the realities of life in the colony. They also could not help but perceive the manner in which their fellow natives were treated as compared to the growing concern and solicitude shown the masses in Europe. As Europeans were achieving the rights of political participation and were being given the opportunity of deciding their own destinies, the colonial population was being denied these same rights. Two distinct political and administrative codes had developed, one for the European at home or in the colonies and another for the native. Governments quick to respond to the needs of their European citizens were blithely unresponsive to the demands of their colonial subjects. The result was that the Europeanized elements of the native population grew to believe that as long as colonial domination continued they and their fellows would remain in a subordinate status.

The reaction to this impasse led to the third and final stage of colonialism. The disillusioned *evolués* rejected assimilation into Western society in favor of assertion of their native culture. Emerson and others argue that colonial nationalism was an attempt by these elite to create a new environment, a new society in which they could achieve the power, wealth, and status denied them by both the traditional and the Western societies. At the same time, they were motivated by a concern to obtain justice, good government, and economic well-being for the mass of the colonial population. Colonial nationalism was a synthesis of the two cultures: European rule was rejected, but not the attributes of Western power; the complacence and rigid hierarchy of traditional society were deprecated, but not its cultural achievements, its language and some of its other traditions. National-ist leaders embraced the methods of the West in order to turn them against the colonial powers.

The native intelligentsia drew increasing support from other classes of society to whom nationalism also offered an attractive vehicle through which to satisfy their ambitions. Native professional men and entrepreneurs, civil servants and trade unionists—all drawn from the urbanized and culturally uprooted seg-ment of society—swelled the ranks of the national movement. The money and organizational cadres necessary to mobilize the masses were drawn from these social groups. Frustrated by the contrast between their poverty and the wealth of the Europeans, and indignant over their lack of status in their own country, the masses were easily aroused by a movement that promised to raise their standard of living and confer upon them a new dignity.

If Emerson is correct, then the European colonial powers appear to have fol-lowed in Africa and Asia the same curious amalgam of the two strategies of colo-nialism that Britain pursued with regard to Ireland. On the one hand, the colony was exploited in order to provide raw materials, cheap labor, military conscripts, and wider markets for Western capital and goods. To insure the success of these ventures, the native population was denied any share of real political power in the colony and deprived of much of its wealth. On the other hand, the policies of the colonial administrations gave rise to a small but articulate class of native entre-preneurs and intellectuals, skilled in the techniques of the West, familiar with the ideals of European society, and demanding their share of the wealth, power, and prestige.

In this connection it must be noted that the rise of such a class was not a nec-essary function of colonial rule. Certainly some natives had to be taught to read and had to be exposed to the techniques of Western society, but those Western powers that professed democratic values at home encouraged such development far beyond the mere requirements of administration in the colony. Education and enlightenment became goals in themselves. Students were sent to the great European universities, where they drank in the currents of egalitarian and radical thought. They returned home with an even greater awareness of the differences between their societies and European ones and with greater expectations as to their mobility, which, we have seen, remained unfulfilled. This proved to be a tre-mendous impetus to the development of national movements, for it increased the size of the cadres that would organize the movements. At the same time, educa-tion and innovation within the colonies swelled the number of those who looked to these men for leadership. The proof that education fostered nationalism can be seen in the fact that those great colonial powers, such as Spain and Portugal, which made no pretext of bringing secular enlightenment to their colonies were the last to face the challenge of organized independence movements.

It was not difficult for colonial powers to admit a few *evolués* into their ranks. This required no radical restructuring of colonial society. When, however, greater numbers of natives began to demand similar privileges and opportunities, the colonial regimes were presented with a serious challenge. Like Britain in Ireland they were forced to make a choice between two alternative and mutually exclusive strategies. Like Britain in Ireland they appeared unable to do so and thus contributed to—if not caused—the rise of an alienated elite that challenged the basis of colonial authority.

The stereotype revisited

It is apparent from this analysis that the same irrational strategy pursued in Ireland was pursued in other colonial relationships as well. Could it be that the same perceptive myopia was the cause in these other cases?

In Ireland we have seen how a stereotyped image of the native was invented to justify colonial occupation. The stereotype functioned as a tension-reduction mechanism and, eventually, as a perceptual prison that blinded the British government to the reality of political and economic conditions in Ireland. As a result the British government initiated policies which were irrational in the sense that they fulfilled neither the goal of integration nor that of exploitation. What evidence is there of the existence of a similar perceptual blindness in other colonial situations?

Sensitive observers have provided us with ample evidence of stereotyped images of natives in almost all colonial situations. Descriptions of these stereotypes and commentary about their effects abound in both fictional and nonfictional studies of colonialism.

The original colonial novel, built on the theme of the Dutch experience in Indonesia, was probably *Max Havelaar*, first published in 1860.[4] The stereotypic qualities attributed to the Indonesian native hardly differed from those which characterized Paddy. With reference to the French colonial empire, the novels of Albert Memmi serve to illuminate the many striking parallels between the stereotypes of Irish and Algerians.[5] Similarly, ample evidence can be found in the English-speaking world. The theme of colonial stereotypes is at the core of George Orwell's *Burmese Days*, E. M. Forster's *Passage to India*, and several of the novels of Graham Greene.[6] Forster provided a particularly insightful analysis of how such images served to solidify the colonial community and set the colonizer apart from the native. Forster and Orwell also stressed a perceptual gap created by the images, making meaningful communication between the worlds of colonizer and colonized all but impossible.

The stereotype of the Black American is another example. Its content and effects have been treated in novels like those of Mark Twain, Richard Wright, and James Baldwin, and in serious academic investigations, the most impressive of which remains Gunnar Myrdal's *An American Dilemma*.[7]

The most fascinating aspect of the content of the stereotypes found in such works is that, while they describe such widely differing environments and peoples as those of Ireland and Indonesia, Algeria, Black America, Burma, and Nigeria, the characteristics that colonizers attributed to the natives are remarkably uniform. With almost monotonous regularity colonial natives have been described as indolent and complacent, cowardly but brazenly rash, violent, uncivilized, and incapable of hard work. On the more complimentary side, they have been characterized as hospitable, good-natured, possessing a natural talent for song and dance, and, frequently, as curious but incapable of a prolonged span of attention. In short, the image of simple creatures in need of paternal domination emerged very clearly. Each image, of course, varied slightly from the other, to include obvious differences in native mores, but the panoply of characteristics remained basically the same and effectively differentiated the natives from the white man.

Some observers have even suggested the function that the image of such characteristics fulfilled. Albert Memmi, in *The Colonizer and the Colonized*, commented on the utility of the belief that all natives are lazy. "It seems to receive unanimous approval," he wrote, "of colonizers from Liberia to Laos, via the Maghreb."

It is easy to see to what extent this description is useful. It occupies an important place in the dialectics exalting the colonizer and humbling the colonized. Furthermore, it is economically fruitful. Nothing could better justify the colonizer's privileged position than his industry, and nothing could better justify the colonized's destitution than his indolence. The mythical portrait of the colonized therefore includes an unbelievable laziness, and that of the colonizer, a virtuous taste for action. At the same time, the colonizer suggests that employing the colonized is not very profitable, thereby authorizing his unreasonable wages.[8]

The same might be and has, in fact, been said with reference to a series of other beliefs which functioned, as in the case of Ireland, to reduce tension and justify colonial policy. Jean Paul Sartre said in this connection:

How can an elite of usurpers, aware of their mediocrity, establish their privileges? By one means only: debasing the colonized to exalt themselves, denying the title of humanity to the natives, and defining them as simply absences of qualities—animals, not humans. This does not prove hard to do, for the system deprives them of everything. Colonialist practice has engraved the colonialist idea into things themselves; it is the movement of things that designates colonizer and colonized alike. This oppression justifies itself through oppression: the oppressors produce and maintain by force the evils that render the oppressed, in their eyes, more and more like what they would have to be like to deserve their fate.[9]

Thus, Sartre concludes, colonial stereotypes become self-fulfilling and self-justifying images.

It is only natural to progress one step beyond this stage and examine the effect such images had upon policy. If the stereotypes were functional in reducing tension in other colonies besides Ireland, and if they dominated perception and became self-fulfilling—which evidence seems to suggest—then it is equally likely that as in the case of Ireland they became perceptual prisons through which colonial policy was evaluated and formulated. The existence of stereotyped images which distorted reality into harmony with the psychological needs of the colonizing society would explain not only the failure of colonial powers to perceive the necessity of choice between the two alternative strategies we have discussed, but also their inability to react rationally to the challenge of nationalist movements.

If the stereotype operated as a perceptual prison, then, as in Ireland, the characteristics attributed to the native population suggested the assumptions within which colonial policy was formulated. The most important of these assumptions were the following beliefs: (1) that the natives were incapable of self-government; (2) a corollary, that the native inhabitants were in need of the strong parental authority of the colonial power; (3) that colonial rule, therefore, was in the best interests of the native; and (4) another corollary, that the natives knew this.

The colonialists, of course, believed that the natives recognized the natural authority of the white man and were accordingly loyal to the colonial regime. These assumptions created the parameters for colonial policy. They limited the number and range of policy alternatives which were thought to be applicable to colonial administration. Policies outside the parameters set by the assumptions would be rejected, because accepting them would challenge the validity of the assumptions.

Rigid adherence to either the strategy of coercion or the strategy of integration involved policies beyond these parameters. On the one hand, the natives could not be ruled entirely by force and coercion and be denied all opportunities to partake of the wealth of the colony because this would clearly invalidate the colonialist's claim to have the best interests of the native in mind. On the other hand, promoting integration of the natives into the national community was equally unthinkable because they were perceived as being incapable of self-government and unable to cope with the privileges and responsibilities granted to the domestic population. The image of the native, therefore, dictated a colonial strategy halfway between the two basic alternatives.

Colonial powers professing to adhere to democratic values accordingly encouraged native education, introduced certain social services, and provided some job mobility for talented colonials. At the same time, their assumptions led them to deny the native any real exercise of political power or opportunity to achieve economic and social equality with the people of the colonizer's own nation. The colonial administration developed little empathy with the natives, could not perceive them as equals, and was unable to accept their demands for equality as reasonable. Thus the native elite whose development was stimulated by colonial policies was also alienated by them. Increasingly it turned to nationalism as the solution to its dilemma.

The assumptions formulated in terms of the stereotyped image also provide an explanation for the irrational response of the colonial powers to native nationalism or protest. Once the colonial power was confronted with a rising protest movement, it had two practical alternatives to pursue: to accept the challenge and crush the movement, or to meet the demands of the native politicians in the hope of minimizing the appeal of nationalism and perhaps postponing or preventing the day when the leaders would demand total independence. But most colonial powers were unable to choose between these alternatives. Most of them could not perceive native political movements as a real threat because they remained convinced not only that independence was impossible, but that the vast majority of native inhabitants were content with their administration and were only being misled by agitators. The protest movements were accordingly explained away, as in Ireland, in terms of the ambitions of self-seeking, vicious agitators, or deluded madmen. At the same time, the colonial powers could not bring themselves to take action which would really have repressed such protest. Certainly leaders were jailed, meetings broken up and civil liberties partially suspended. The leaders were, however, usually released after short sentences; their supporters were repressed but not exterminated; censorship was imposed, but the nationalist presses were not smashed; and civil liberties were only temporarily suspended. In Ireland, for example, Daniel O'Connell was found guilty of treason by a rigged jury, but the decision was reversed by the House of Lords. The Young Ireland revolutionaries, captured alter the rebellion of 1848, were not hanged but only temporarily deported, and the Irish press, which more than ever was agitating for independence, continued to indict the policies of the British government.

The histories of independence movements in India, Nigeria, Kenya, Algeria, and Indonesia are not dissimilar. The values of the colonial administrators and the pressures exerted by public opinion at home generally prevented the reprisals and garrison-slate tactics that characterized the policies of colonial powers like Portugal and Spain. Some pretense of democratic government had to be preserved if the colonizers were still to claim justification of their policies in terms of the model of colonial government they themselves had propagated.[10]

The colonialist response, therefore, usually consisted of a combination of mild repression and minor reform. Colonial administrators continued to believe that the protests of the natives were not really motivated by political concerns. They assumed that the masses neither understood nor wanted independence and the political machinery it entailed, and that their political aspirations were merely the result of passions inflamed by agitators seeking power.

Lord Lloyd, high commissioner of Egypt in the 1920s, whose attitude may be taken to be representative of the views of most colonial administrators, concluded:

> Good administration is their [the natives'] only desire and concern—and it is because we have allowed administration to be obscured by political issues that we have brought such heavy troubles upon the shoulders of all

concerned. In these countries the real problem has been administrative, and we have chosen to regard it as political.[11]

The proper focus of colonial rule, therefore, was to provide peace and quiet from above so that the common people could pursue their goals. Accordingly, greater attention was paid to administrative than to political matters (although some minor concessions were granted in the economic and political spheres).

The result was to demonstrate to the people of the colony that history was on the side of the nationalists. Though their demands were still unmet, the political agitators were allowed to continue operating. Their defiance of the colonial government with relative impunity from reprisal, and their partial success in gaining concessions, strengthened their hand and increased their power among the natives of the colony. In the end the colonial government was presented with a real confrontation. Colonial powers were given the choice of granting independence, as happened in India, Nigeria and French Equatorial Africa, or of throwing overboard all pretext of democracy and attempting to rule the colonies as occupied countries, as happened in Indochina, Algeria, and Ireland. By the time the confrontation developed, however, the power of the national movements had increased and the means necessary to preserve colonial rule had become so contradictory to the values of a democratic society that there was fierce resistance at home to the use of those means. These factors, coupled with the fact that the international balance of power favored the independence movements, sealed the fate of widespread colonial empire.

In sum, the successful maintenance of colonial rule depended on rigid adherence to either of the two basic strategies. Halfway measures and compromise proved fatal to dominion. A choice had to be made. If the metropolitan power ruled the colonies as territories to be exploited at the expense of their inhabitants, it could not shrink from adopting coercive measures—inhumane as they may have appeared—if colonial authority was to be preserved. If, on the other hand, authority was to be maintained by securing the loyalty of the native population, the metropolitan power could not exploit the colony at the expense of its inhabitants. The colonizer had to develop empathy and accept the sacrifices required to legitimate the political connection.

Britain and France—the two primary examples of a democratic colonial power—were unable to commit themselves to either strategy. The majority of the political elites in both nations were unwilling to relinquish the advantages they believed metropolitan powers should derive from governing colonies and were unable to see independence as a practical alternative. At the same time, however, they viewed with increasing repugnance authority that rested entirely upon coercion. They were very reluctant to endorse the means required to preserve political power in the colonies. The problem can equally well be stated in reverse. As a result of the changing political climate of the nineteenth century, Britain and France were compelled to legitimate their authority in the eyes of the colonial population but were unable or unwilling to make the sacrifices required by such a course of action.

As the century unfolded, the dilemma grew more oppressive. In certain respects it reflected a basic paradox of the age. The nineteenth century was an era in which liberalism made great gains. The liberal ideology carried with it a commitment to government conducted in the interests of the majority of the people. Great emphasis was placed on the morality of political behavior. As liberalism outgrew its early doctrinaire tenets and incorporated ideas put forward by those concerned with social justice, an increasing emphasis was placed on improving the condition of the lower classes and extending spiritual and material welfare and the right of political participation to more and more people.

The nineteenth century was also an age in which political struggles were increasingly viewed in an ideological context. When the nation-state replaced the dynastic political unit and mass participation became a relevant factor, both the means and ends of political action underwent a significant change. Political differences and rivalries between nations tended to be defined in an ideological context in order to obtain from the population the sacrifices required to pursue foreign-policy goals. This was true of colonial rivalries as well as those in other areas. Colonization could be justified by the need to preclude takeover by a foreign power with a hostile ideology. And formerly unacceptable means and sacrifices were justified by the overriding importance of the ultimate goal.

Although colonial government was subject to increasing moral criticism, the nineteenth century will be remembered as the great age of Western colonial expansion. Colonies were perceived as vitally important sources of political and economic power in the struggle for the mastery of Europe. From 1870 to the end of the century, European penetration into colonial territories increased, as did the total territory effectively controlled by the metropolitan powers.

Many Europeans, especially those of a liberal persuasion, were forced to choose between their principles and what was regarded by them as political necessity. The majority of the liberals, seduced by arguments in favor of imperial expansion, envisaged colonial empire as a prerequisite to national power and even national survival. Somehow, principles and necessity had to be reconciled.

There was an additional dilemma at work as well. Because political rivalries had been structured in an ideological context, those persons who believed that their nation represented freedom and justice, as opposed to the tyranny of the rival, could not easily espouse political behavior—even if they thought it necessary—that contradicted the very goals for which the struggle was supposedly being waged. Englishmen who condemned French barbarities and undemocratic practices in Algeria could hardly admit that they pursued a similar policy in Ireland and India. The reverse held true, of course, for the French.

Thus the dilemma created by the conflict between the emerging value consensus of European democratic society and the means of political behavior in the colonies increased in intensity during the century. There can be little doubt that it produced a great psychological problem for the actors involved. Tension was generated that somehow had to be reduced. The means employed, this study has argued, was a perceptual sleight of hand, a stereotyped image of reality, which enabled those suffering from the dilemma to rationalize into harmony the contradiction between moral belief and political necessity. This solution had a profound effect on later policy. For while it proved useful in reducing tension, it did so at the expense of a realistic perception of colonial affairs. In the end its influence on policy proved disastrous and contributed to the collapse of colonial empire.

Notes

1   See Joseph Schumpeter, *Imperialism and Social Classes*, trans. Heinz Norden (New York, A. M. Kelley, 1951).
2   Karl Deutsch et al., *Political Community and the North Atlantic Area* (Princeton, NJ, 1957), 21.
3   Rupert Emerson, *From Empire to Nation* (Cambridge, MA, 1960).
4   Edward Douwes Dekker, Max Havelaar, or *The Coffee Sales of the Netherlands Trading Company*, trans. W. Siebenhaar (New York, 1927).
5   See Albert Memmi, *Portrait d'un juif l'impasse* (Paris, 1962), and *La statue de sel* (Paris, 1966).
6   George Orwell, *Burmese Days* (London, 1935); E. M. Forster, *A Passage to India* (New York, 1924). For Graham Greene's treatment of stereotypes see especially *The Heart of the Matter* (London, 1948).
7   See Richard Wright, *Native Son* (New York, 1940); James Baldwin, *Go Tell It on the Mountain* (New York, 1953), and *Notes of a Native Son* (Boston, 1962); Gunnar Myrdal et al., *An American Dilemma: The Negro Problem and Modern Democracy* (New York, 1962).
8   Albert Memmi, *The Colonizer and the Colonized* (New York, 1965), 79.
9   Quoted in Memmi, *The Colonizer and the Colonized*, xxvi.
10 Ibid., passim.
11 Quoted in Emerson, *From Empire to Nation*, 38.

2 Divided nations and partitioned countries

Gregory Henderson and Richard Ned Lebow

The ideal nation-state is a political unit synonymous with a nationality. Such polities abound in textbooks but are rare in the real world. Most nations contain more than one nationality, and nationalities themselves are frequently divided among two or more states. A list of countries, for example, that comprise 90% of all the members of one ethnic group and contain a minority population of 5% or less would be very short indeed. Japan alone among the great powers would appear on the list, and certainly no more than a handful of newly independent countries would qualify. Division, therefore, is a basic and universal problem; and since nations have multiplied in the last generation, so also has division. Divisions and divisiveness have profound political ramifications. The desire for unification or autonomy motivates the participants in a majority of current international conflicts and has led directly to most of the wars fought since 1945.

Unfortunately for the scholar, the phenomenon of division is as varied as it is ubiquitous. This variety poses serious problems of classification and probably precludes a truly comprehensive treatment of division. Accordingly, the editors have found it necessary to impose careful limits on this study and have confined it to instances of division in which there was a period of prior political unity. In some cases, Germany and China, for example, this unity was the result of organic historical development. In others, as with the Indian subcontinent, it was imposed by force from the outside. Nevertheless, such unity, and the economic, administrative, and political structures associated with it, forms a convenient starting point for the study of division. The subsequent dissolution of these bonds is the common analytic thread binding the cases together. Group divisions solely within countries, such as the conflict between the Ibo and Hausa in Nigeria, have been excluded from study, as have the strivings for unity of ethnic groups like the Basques and Kurds, divided among several countries but possessing no history of prior structural unity.

Even within the universe of cases to be examined, considerable variation occurs with respect to both the origins of division and the patterns of political relationships that have prevailed in the postpartition period. Two distinct categories of division emerge, however. These are divided nations and partitioned countries.

Divided nations are countries with marked ethnic homogeneity, a common historical tradition and experience of successful political unity, that have been subsequently divided into two separate political units. The division is artificial in the sense that it was imposed from the outside, usually by great powers at the close of a war, or, in the case of China, has endured only by reason of great-power involvement. Germany, Korea, China, and Vietnam belong to this category of division, as do Cambodia and Laos where de facto division has emerged more recently. The division of the Mongols, once united in a single empire, belongs somewhat more exceptionally to this category, having been imposed by the great powers long ago and over a longer period of time.

Partitioned countries are divisions resulting from internal causes; by reason of ethnic, linguistic, or religious conflict between or among groups formerly residing within one political unit. These divisions are most frequently associated with the breakup of colonial empires. Thus, Austria-Hungary divided into all or part of eight states, the British Raj into five, French Indochina into four, and the Palestine Mandate into two.[1] Cyprus (de facto divided) also belongs to this category, as do other cases—Holland and Belgium, for example—not represented in this study. The editors have resisted imposing subcategorization on the basis of the kind of conflict that promoted partition because division is never the result of a single axis of cleavage. Religious cleavages in Ireland, for example, also reflect perceived ethnic differences, as they do in India and Pakistan. Linguistic differences usually have ethnic or historical overtones, and ethnic differences, as in the case of Palestine, are often reinforced by linguistic and religious diversity.

Divided nations

The case studies suggest that the two categories of division are further differentiated from each other by the political problems that achieve prominence in the postpartition period. In particular, two different kinds of issues appear to lie at the roots of postpartition conflict in each category. With respect to divided nations these are the problems of identity and successor status.

Identity

Nations generally define their identities in terms of the common traditions, history, and culture of their people. This uniqueness forms the psychological cement which binds a nation together and distinguishes it from its neighbors. Nevertheless, divided nations have found it impossible to structure their identities solely on this basis because, at the time of partition, each dyad of divided nations was to a considerable degree ethnically, linguistically, and culturally identical. Accordingly, no such claim to "national" uniqueness was possible. Even in cases where some cultural differences existed, as in Vietnam, they were perceived to be an insufficient foundation upon which to build a new national identity. Moreover, while the political elites in some divided nations have encouraged cultural divergence—the People's Republic of China, for example, has introduced a reformed script and North Korea has abandoned the use of Chinese characters—both leaders and peoples have been reluctant to renounce the notion of a common nationality, with the exception of East Germany which now claims national uniqueness on the basis of its socialist system. Willy Brandt best articulated this sentiment at the signing of the recent German agreement when he declared, in contradiction to the East German claim, that East Germany and West Germany might be separate states but their peoples constituted only one nation. The one-nation concept has been repeatedly affirmed by leaders of most other divided nations as well.

The fact that each divided nation, with the exception of the two Chinas and the two Germanies, are roughly equal in size and population, has also effectively precluded any credible claim to be the sole de facto representative of the entire nation. Leaders of divided nations have, therefore, turned to ideology as the main instrument both for structuring separate identities and justifying the separate existence of their polity. The cold war and the neat division of all divided nations into communist and noncommunist states has greatly facilitated this development. It has encouraged each side of a division to espouse its social, economic, and political truths and to lay-claim to being the nucleus of a future unified nationhood. Given the sharp internal political effects of ideological confrontation, it is not surprising that despite the waning of the cold war, the intensity of ideological conflict between most divided nations endures. It is still uncertain as to how efficacious ideological differentiation will ultimately prove in structuring separate identities; initially its success seems considerable. But the level of hostility generated by such confrontation has clearly been costly to all parties concerned. It has precluded meaningful economic cooperation and necessitated exceptionally high per capita expenditures on military establishments.

Successor status

The universe immutably rules that two objects cannot occupy the same space at the same time. This physical law appears to have its political corollary. Divided nations are splinter states of a nation with prior juridical status. Most divided nations have at some point in their history claimed to be the sole legitimate successor of the former nation-state. They have asserted legal identity with the previous national entity and have refused to recognize the de jure existence of their opposite numbers.[2] Both Koreas and both Chinas adhere to this position, as does North Vietnam; until recently, so did West Germany. East Germany and South Vietnam do not. The conflict over representation is, of course, no arid legal squabble but a reflection of the goal held by each divided state claiming sole-representation status for ultimate unification through the destruction of its opponent state. The claim to sole-representation status and the corresponding effort to deter third parties from recognizing the other side is designed to buttress one's own identity and legitimacy while weakening that of the other side. The Hallstein Doctrine of West Germany carried this claim to its logical extreme by stipulating the severance of relations with any country that recognized East Germany. The economic might of West Germany gave her sufficient leverage to implement this policy and resulted in the isolation of East Germany from the noncommunist world for 25 years. Both Chinas and both Koreas have their own version of this doctrine.

The last few years have witnessed some easing of the diplomatic conflict between the two Germanies and, to a less-definite extent, the two Koreas, and progress has been made toward resolving the successor conflict by mutual acceptance of a "two state, one nation" solution. Given the stability and economic revival of East Germany and the corresponding desire of numerous underdeveloped countries to establish relations with it, West Germany found the Hallstein Doctrine beginning to work against its own best interests. Accordingly, it has finally been abandoned and West Germany has recognized the juridical existence of East Germany in return for other concessions. The two Koreas may be moving toward this position; the two Germanies have already entered the UN, and the two Koreas might conceivably do so. Both Chinas, of course, still adhere to their version of the Hallstein Doctrine and Taiwan refers to the mainland government as the "rebel group" while the People's Republic of China derides the Taiwan regime as the "remnant clique." Given the recent successes of the People's Republic, there is little reason to expect any similar compromise.

Prognosis

The phenomenon of divided nations has endured long enough for us to hazard generalizations about the patterns of interstate relations that have emerged in the postpartition period and even to suggest some likely future outcomes. Three possible "solutions" emerge: a solution being defined as either reunification or mutual acceptance of the status quo and, with it, normalization of relations. The first solution, that of unification imposed through the military conquest of one divided nation by another, was tried by North Korea, the People's Republic of China, and North Vietnam but was defeated in all three instances by American military intervention. An attempt by South Korea, the United States, and their allies to unify Korea by force was similarly defeated by the intervention of the People's Republic. With the possible exception of the three states of Indochina, where cease-fires are fragile, military solutions are not likely to be attempted by any other divided states in the foreseeable future.

Unification may also result from the political victory of one side over the other. According to this scenario, the internal political and economic weakness of one of the divided states leads to the collapse of its regime accompanied by strong popular sentiment in favor of unification. Unification is then accomplished without significant military resistance. Most divided states have harbored this goal and have pursued policies (e.g., propaganda, nonrecognition, sabotage) designed to facilitate it. Despite this, only in China and Indochina is such an outcome at all likely. In the case of Vietnam, the continuing inability of the South Vietnamese government to legitimize itself, and the corresponding existence of large numbers of well-organized cadres favoring unification on the terms of the North, have nourished North Vietnamese hopes of such a victory. The same is true in Cambodia and Laos. It is, of course, too early to predict the outcome of these struggles.

In the case of China, the possibility of political victory is a function of the unique structural attributes of that division. In all the other cases, with the partial exception of Germany, the disparity in size, population, and economic resources between divided states is not exceptionally great. With respect to the two Chinas, this disparity is tremendous and has ultimately given the People's Republic a decisive advantage. The emergence of the People's Republic as a great power prompted the United States, formerly the major backer of the government on Taiwan, to reconsider its China policy. The subsequent American initiatives toward détente with the People's Republic accelerated the steady erosion of Taiwan's international position. More nations now recognize the People's Republic than do Taiwan, and the People's Republic now occupies China's seat in the United Nations and affiliated international organizations. The next few years are likely to see the further isolation of Taiwan. Nixon's trip to the People's Republic, his promise to withdraw all American personnel from Taiwan, and more recently, Japanese diplomatic and economic initiatives toward the People's Republic, have all constituted profound psychological blows to the Nationalist regime. The passing of Chiang Kai-shek is likely to weaken the regime further while perhaps encouraging, for the first time, some dialogue with the mainland. It is by no means improbable that some kind of federation or even unification, largely on terms dictated by the People's Republic, will occur later in the century.

The third possible solution may be termed peaceful coexistence and has presently the best chance of emerging in the German and Korean cases. Each of the states resulting from these divisions, with the possible exception of East Germany, entertained hopes of promoting the internal collapse of its opponent and of imposing unification on its own terms. Both Koreas also made unsuccessful bids for the military conquest of the other side. These policies failing, a stalemate has emerged: each state is economically resurgent and relatively stable politically, and each receives continuing support from its respective superpower ally. Neither Korea nor Germany can realistically expect to destroy its rival; indeed, each has begun to perceive strong internal incentives for reducing hostility. The decline of the cold war and the changing pattern of superpower relations that has accompanied it, has also provided external incentives for rapprochement. Rapprochement has proceeded the furthest in Germany where the recent agreement between the two states marks a historic break with the turbulent past and may well lead to close economic cooperation and wide cultural contacts as it has led to full normalization of relations.

Within coexistence or between it and reunification lies a possible in-between zone which no nation has yet entered (with the very partial exception of the Nordic states or Luxembourg and Belgium which are not aiming at unification). This zone—not static state—would be inhabited by a number of possible federative modalities in which the chiefs of state and, perhaps, some upper bodies remain separate but consultative and under them, ministries, operating bodies, or ad hoc committees (including canals, railways, postal service, electricity, etc.) are run jointly, perhaps in or from neutral territory such as the demilitarized zones of Korea or Vietnam. Presumably, joint operation would gradually expand so that communicating coexistence would have some gradual means of developing into reunification. Kim Il-sung in Korea has proposed federation before reunification and splinters of the idea are in the agreement on Vietnam. Totally alien to the old *Staatswissenschaft* theory, the various possible convergence capsules adumbrated above have the virtue of avoiding the quantum jump from two states to one, with all its difficulty and risk.

Finally, whether describable as a "solution" or not, it remains quite possible that divided nations may continue for extended periods in the state of division and hostility which has generally characterized them until today.

A paradigm of division

Case studies suggest that relations between divided nations change as a function of (1) the degree of stability and legitimacy of each divided state; (2) relations between each divided state and its respective superpower; and (3) relations between the superpowers themselves. Stated in the form of an hypothesis: As divided nations develop internal strength and hostility between their respective superpower backers decreases, they are likely to possess greater freedom of action and seek improved relations with each other. This process can be described in terms of stages, each marked by changes in the aforementioned variables and each indicative of improved relations between the divided states. Before describing these stages, several caveats are in order. All divided nations begin life in Stage I (intense mutual hostility) but do not necessarily pass through the other stages in the course of their existence. The dilemma of division may in fact be resolved, as was discussed earlier, by military conquest or political victory in the course of Stage I. Stage II (declining hostility) actually represents a quantum leap in the relations between divided states and is only reached as the result of a peculiar and fortuitous combination of circumstances which so far, apply only to Germany and Korea. Stage IV (unification) marks another quantum leap and, as yet, no divided nations have reached this stage.

Stage I initial division

Defining characteristic: intense hostility between units. This hostility is marked by:

1 mutual nonrecognition
2 sole claim to successor status by at least one of the units

3 intense ideological conflict
4 attempts to fortify and close the border by at least one unit
5 attempts to subvert the opponent regime through both propaganda and fifth column activity
6 possible militarization of the conflict

Reasons

External: Superpower occupation or leverage coupled with intense superpower conflict leads to the establishment or support of mutually antagonistic political elites each harboring the expectation of supplanting the other.

Internal: New regimes—especially when perceived to be puppet governments—have difficulties in establishing legitimacy and encourage interunit hostility for internal political purposes. Such hostility is usually aggravated by the existence of large numbers of refugees who seek military confrontation as their means of return home.

Stage II middle-term division

Defining characteristic: declining hostility between units. This is marked by:

1 tacit or formal acceptance of coexistence and a corresponding dilution of claims to sole-successor status
2 decline in the intensity of ideological confrontation
3 decline in the salience of the border permitting a wider exchange of persons and ideas
4 decline in both overt and covert attempts to subvert the opponent regime
5 decline in mutual perceptions of the likelihood of military confrontation

Symbolic acts often associated with Stage II include:

1 exchange of visits between leaders
2 public statements renouncing military solutions to division and/or in favor of unification by common consent
3 agreements with respect to border questions, visitation, and repatriation of families
4 public recognition of the partition line as an "inviolable" boundary
5 common entrance into international organizations

Reasons

External: Recognition of a political-military stalemate between units and the counterproductive nature of hostility with respect to relations with important third parties. Decline in tensions between rival superpowers allowing greater latitude for the expression of internal pressures toward détente. In some instances (e.g., East Germany), there is actually strong superpower pressure to improve interunit relations.

Internal: Mutual success in achieving legitimacy reduces each unit's need to employ hostility as an internal political prop. Economic success has the same effect and further reduces dependence on superpowers. The successful absorption of refugees also functions to permit greater flexibility toward the other unit. Positive incentives toward détente emerge with equal salience. Chief among these are economic advantages: interunit trade and the economic benefits resulting from decreased expenditure on costly military establishments. On the political side, the populations of both units still perceive the division of families and cities as artificial and agreements mitigating these human costs of division are likely to have profound internal political payoffs for elites.

Stage III rapprochement

None of the divided nations has yet entered Stage III but the experience of the two Irelands in the 1950s and early 1960s suggests the pattern of relations that is likely to prevail. Rapprochement is marked by:

1 close economic cooperation with respect to tourism, trade, and development leading to the creation of limited but joint administrative apparatus which can expand gradually
2 political cooperation with respect to common external questions (foreign aid, cultural programs, relations with neighbor states) and later, with respect to security vis-à-vis both internal and external threats
3 a further decline in the salience of the border and a corresponding increase in the mobility of persons and ideas
4 the creation of intergovernmental linkages at all levels from traffic control to security, and with it, the establishment of formal consultative machinery

Reasons

Greater internal stability coupled with a continuing decline in cold war tensions further diminishes the external and internal restraints on interunit cooperation. The passing of the generation of leaders in both units whose political career was associated with the division and initial period of intense hostility also functions to remove restraints on cooperation. With respect to positive incentives, the successful experience of prior limited cooperation is likely to be instrumental in generating popular demands for more extensive cooperation while making political elites more receptive to such cooperation. However, there are likely to be limits to this "spillover" effect that will probably halt the process of cooperation short of actual unification. These restraints, a function of the political, economic, and administrative divergence that has occurred during the span of the division, will prove very difficult to overcome. They are:

1 The existence of two independent sets of leaders and of political and administrative institutions, each with considerable reluctance to merge by reason of parochial power considerations. The fear of redundancy is especially important here.
2 The divergence of administrative procedures and values encouraging bureaucratic resistance to merger.
3 Economic disparities between states and between groups and classes present in both units are likely to motivate resistance to unification within the more affluent state and among groups and classes in either unit who occupy a favored position likely to diminish with unification.
4 Prior ideological and foreign commitments that tie the hands of leaders on both sides.
5 The opposition of communist and noncommunist systems qua systems.
6 Fear of penetration resulting in loss of legitimacy and even domestic control. This is a real fear in totalitarian regimes like East Germany which suspect that greater contact with a nontotalitarian government will lead to greater internal demands for liberalization. Perhaps this explains why East Germany has recently chosen to emphasize its national uniqueness—a measure designed to reduce the impact of post-treaty penetration from West Germany.

Stage IV unification (no data)

Internal divergence and contradictory foreign commitments may remain an effective barrier to unity despite the intensity of feeling in favor of it in both units. The external restraints on unification may prove the most difficult to overcome. In the case of Germany, for example, both units are well integrated into conflicting alliance systems. East Germany is a member of the Warsaw Pact and COMECON. West Germany belongs to NATO and her economy is integrated with that of other Western European members of the EEC. Barring the demise of U.S.-USSR rivalry and the ensuing economic integration of Europe, German unification is not likely to prove acceptable to the superpowers.

Even assuming that this stage of cooperation will be reached, it is more likely to result in a kind of loose federation than in actual unification. This might involve free mobility of persons, extensive economic cooperation and some symbolic representations of unity such as a common flag, national anthem, athletic teams and cultural organizations. Perhaps, both units might agree to a single president in whom sovereignty reposes but whose actual authority is limited to ceremonial functions.

Partitioned countries

As legend has it, King Solomon was once confronted by two women quarreling over possession of a child. Each woman claimed to be the rightful mother and asked Solomon to award the child to her. The wise king proposed a compromise. He would cut the child in two and give half to each woman. One of the women, appalled at the thought of harming the child, pleaded with Solomon to give her rival custody of the child instead. Her concern for the child's welfare convinced the king that she was the true mother and he awarded the child to her. Ethnic groups have made similar conflicting claims with respect to territory, and like Solomon, colonial powers and the United Nations have been asked to arbitrate the disputes. Like Solomon, they have frequently offered to divide the claim between the contesting parties. Alas, none of the claimants has ever been so horrified by the thought of division as to suggest that the entire territory be awarded to its opponent. As a consequence, colonial powers and the United Nations have actually wielded the knife and divided disputed territories in two. As one might expect, such division has rarely resolved the conflict.

Partition was nevertheless intended to resolve conflict by separating hostile ethnic communities and allowing each to satisfy its demands for nationhood in separate political units. Case studies suggest that this political surgery has not proved very successful; postpartition relations between most divided groups are still marked by intense hostility; in several instances this hostility has led to war. The cases further suggest that the operation's failure was due in large part to the patients' anatomies, which made it impossible to separate the conflicting communities effectively. As a result, substantial minorities were included in one or both successor states and hostility between these minorities and the dominant communities helped promote interstate conflict. In addition, conflicting groups have rarely agreed as to where the boundary between them ought to be drawn—if indeed, they have accepted partition to begin with. This has led to bitter territorial disputes which continue to poison relations in the postpartition period.

Minority problems

In every country that was ultimately partitioned, the conflicting ethnic groups were to some extent geographically intermingled. Usually this resulted from past patterns of migration, but in two cases, those of Ireland and Israel, continued intermingling represented deliberate attempts by ethnic groups to improve their security position and heighten their territorial claims. Such intermingling made it impossible to draw partition lines that neatly separated the antagonistic communities; in Cyprus, where the distribution of Greeks and Turks resembles a patchwork quilt, it has precluded the attempt at partition altogether. Each successor state was therefore left with a minority population which, in the cases of Northern Ireland and Israel, amounted to a very significant proportion of the total population.

Following partition, population transfers rectified this situation somewhat, the most notable being that between India and Pakistan which uprooted millions. Population transfer took place on a smaller scale in the Middle East, where 750,000 Arabs fled Israel and an equivalent number of Jews emigrated from Arab states to Israel, and in Ireland, where 50,000 Catholics were expelled from the North and a smaller number of Southern Protestants chose to emigrate to Britain. Major population transfers have not yet occurred between Pakistan and Bangladesh but are likely in the future, with Bengalis in Pakistan choosing repatriation and Biharis in Bangladesh opting for Pakistan.

While population transfers reduced the size of minorities in partitioned countries, they did so at the cost of tremendous human suffering and left refugees with bitter memories who have helped to keep these conflicts alive. Nowhere is this more apparent than in the Middle East where the Arab states' refusal to absorb Palestinian refugees and Israel's equal refusal to permit their return has led to their internment in refugee camps. These camps have functioned as spawning grounds of frustration and anger which have twice helped to plunge the Middle East into war. Until the refugee problem is resolved, there is little likelihood that the Arab-Israeli conflict will abate.

Significant minorities still exist in most partitioned countries. In India, the Muslim population of Kashmir wishes unification with Pakistan and has been a constant source of friction between the two states. In the Middle East, the existence of a substantial Arab minority in Israel—and, since 1967, of an even greater number of Arabs in Jerusalem, the West Bank, and the Gaza Strip—has forced Israel to implement security measures that contribute to Arab-Israeli hostility. The inhumane treatment of Jewish minorities in Arab states—especially in Iraq—has angered Israelis; public opinion polls reveal that Jewish immigrants from Arab states have the most uncompromising attitudes toward Israel's neighbors. The most dramatic example of the impact of minority problems on interstate relations is, of course, Ireland. After almost 50 years of partition, the two Irelands had finally embarked on a path of cooperation that was rapidly leading to full normalization of relations. The violent Protestant reaction to Northern Catholic demands for civil rights and the civil strife that ensued destroyed this détente, however, and once again put the two states on a collision course.

Territorial dispute

With the exception of Pakistan and Bangladesh, which have no contiguous territory, no partitioned country was able to agree on a mutually acceptable border. In every instance, fighting broke out and the de facto border became the cease-fire line between the conflicting groups. Inevitably, one or both sides were dissatisfied with this line and laid claim to additional territory on the basis of historical association and/or ethnic consanguinity. In the case of Palestine, the Arab side even denies the right of Israel to exist as a nation and lays claim to the total territory of Palestine.

Disputed territories remain key sources of conflict in almost every case of partition. In Ireland, conflicting claims to countries Fermanagh and Tyrone poisoned North-South relations for decades, and many Irish Catholics still deny the right of Northern Ireland to exist at all. In the interwar years, irredenta plagued Eastern European politics with the splinter states of the Austro-Hungarian Empire making territorial claims on one another. Indeed, only the dominant Soviet presence in the area has brought the abeyance of such claims; should Soviet influence recede, there is every reason to suspect that Teschen, Transylvania, and Temesvar would once again become contested.

The two most violent territorial disputes are associated with the partitions of India and Palestine. In 1948 the Arab states waged an unsuccessful war to deprive Israel of her existence. In 1956 and 1967 Arabs fought to restore at least the partition line proposed by the United Nations in 1947. Arab states are now pledged to liberate the territories conquered by Israel in 1967. Israel, on the other hand, has never found her frontiers consonant with her security interests and is unlikely to relinquish much of the territory she has conquered since 1967, let alone since 1947. This dispute has already led to three wars and still dominates the politics of the region. The same is true of the Indian subcontinent where two wars have arisen from conflicting claims over Kashmir and other territory.

Prognosis

Unfortunately, our authors do not express much hope of resolving outstanding issues between partitioned countries in the near future. Judging from history, this pessimism appears justified. Minority groups have usually succeeded in obtaining full equality and toleration only in periods when the majority group enjoyed economic prosperity and political security. Neither condition is likely to be met in most partitioned countries given the current intensity of interstate conflict. Thus, with the possible exception of Northern Ireland, where British intervention is promoting Catholic rights, internal communal conflict and interstate hostility are likely to continue to aggravate one another.

Nor are the passions associated with irredenta likely to abate significantly. Once again, only in Ireland, where the salience of the border has declined over fifty years and where joint membership in the EEC may further blur territorial division, is hope of resolution real. Territorial disputes are defused only slowly and short of dramatic resolution by war, those associated with partition are likely to be part of the international scene for some time to come. The damaging aspects of such conflicts are readily apparent. Hostility generated by such disputes demands proportionately high per capita expenditures on military establishments which in turn diminish the funds available for development. Moreover, expressions of hostility and plans for war have a way of becoming self-fulfilling and have led to a series of military confrontations in both the Middle East and the Indian subcontinent which have had a disastrous impact on the economies of several states involved and, in the case of both the Arabs and Pakistanis, have destroyed the viability of successive regimes. Defeat in war and ensuing political and economic discontent have brought political elites to focus popular discontent on foreign enemies, thus reinforcing the intensity of the original conflict. No evidence suggests that this upward spiral of hostility is about to be reversed.

General conclusion

Recognition of the important differences between the two categories of division should not discourage a discussion of aspects of division that are common to both categories nor should it curb the search for criteria by which the dangers of division can be assessed. This unity is clearly not to be sought in the causes of division, for these are exceedingly diverse. Rather, it is to be sought in the psychological arena. The starting point of this inquiry is the realization that the cement holding social systems together is psychological. Divisions of whatever sort are thus vital though varied portions of the psychological map on which all nations and societies are inscribed.

To declare the underlying units of divisions a psychological one is clearly only a beginning. Obviously, since societies are involved, the province of study is social psychology, and since tension and hostilization within groups are modal to the problem, group dynamics ought to provide the best framework for comparative study. When this study has progressed sufficiently, some degree of measurement and prediction should become possible. For behind the diversity of division and the despair to which it gives rise lie half-seen rules and measurements of tension and cohesion, criteria of hostility and hostilization, and perhaps cool paths toward cures to be hewn eventually from the dishevelment of political history and the emotions, often the hysteria, of communal strife.

The first general conclusion to which the studies in this volume lead is that the unity of nations—probably of most if not all nations—is quite fragile, far more fragile than the nations are willing to admit. Group dynamics suggests, and our cases tend to confirm, that the cohesion of a group is inversely related to its size. Group allegiance is largely a function of repeated satisfaction gained from participation in group decisions and, if the group has common values and objectives, from sharing in the positive payoffs of group activity. The larger the group, the more difficult it becomes to satisfy disparate individual needs; increasingly sophisticated and responsive organizational structures must be developed to perform this function. On the whole, therefore, greater unities always stand in danger of being reduced to lesser, more intimate, and more interactive parts.

In speaking of greater unities easily reduced to component parts, empires like those of Rome, Spain, and Austria-Hungary, composed of many highly distinctive entities which could generate their own independence movements, come first to mind. India, Pakistan, Indochina are as easily frangible. However, the most striking examples of the frangibility of nations comes not from these obvious cases but from the division of far more homogeneous states, notably Korea and Germany. Neither of these states had internal reasons for division and both had been happily united for some time—in Korea's case, since the seventh century AD. In both instances, division was artificial, and in Korea's case, division at the 38th parallel established a new high in arbitrariness. Yet, four new states have come from these divisions and have proved viable and indeed successful in the face of all expectations and predictions to the contrary. All four have proved more creative and energetic than the great majority of undivided nations. They are among the most rapidly developing of all the world's polities and have demonstrated beyond question that ethnic, linguistic, or religious differentiation is quite unnecessary for a successful division. Like a worm cut into two parts, each of which can crawl away and grow, peoples as homogeneous as any in the world can be divided and survive as separate units. Under certain conditions of force, of lack of recourse, and of hostility, it is probable that no nation in the world could not be with some success divided. The recent signs of détente between the two Germanies and the two Koreas notwithstanding, all four states have achieved sharp identities of their own. So could, potentially, most states of the present world if they were to be divided. Certainly, there is every indication that the two Chinas and the two Vietnams either have achieved or can achieve equally striking and satisfactory new identities. So, undoubtedly, could Cambodia and Laos if two wholly separate and complete governments were to become fully operational in each part.

The latter instances point to another general conclusion also strongly affirmed by students of group dynamics: that the establishment of new and separate identities involves the institution of separate organizational structures and the success of the new identities in no small degree depends on the separateness and the fullness with which these organizations operate. In simplest operational terms, Austria was saved from division because central government for the entire country was never wholly abandoned. Against every intention except the Russians', Korea's unity was lost when separate administrations became fully operational and when the territories in which these administrations functioned were sealed off from one another. There are an infinite number of other, more subtle illustrations. In Ireland, for example, the institutions of the Catholic and Protestant churches, segregated educational institutions, and the special anniversaries and parades of each community are important components and gauges of disunity. In India, where Moslem and Hindu communities were always to some extent separate, the politicization of these identities was aggravated by the formation of the Congress party and the competition to control the legislatures of the Indian states. A completely separate identity and accompanying hostility was the clear outgrowth of the establishment of separate governments. Where no separate governments exist, as with India's remaining 40 million Muslims, identities, though distinct, are far less sharp and hostility less intense. The analysis of division is thus in a very important degree an organizational study; the level of division hostilities is importantly a function of organization.

A further conclusion is that the growth of new identities depends very much on the fullness and the intensity with which the new units and their organizations—especially their separate governments—operate. This conclusion relates to the doctrine of interaction in group formation. The formal division of a country greatly increases social and political activity. An era of crisis is born. Refugees stream across the new border, rarely in modest numbers as in Ireland, Cyprus, and Mongolia, but more often in large numbers as in Germany, Korea, Vietnam, China, Laos, and Cambodia. In some cases, heavy migration takes place in both directions, as with India, Pakistan, Palestine, and Rwanda-Urundi. The influx of refugees creates an intense demand for services separated from those of the other side and conducted in an atmosphere hostile to the other side.

The severing of integrated economies further intensifies demands for separate administrative entities. In a developed economy such as that of Germany, the diminution of major exchange through rail, road, and other means aggravated the general economic collapse of 1945 and created extensive demands on separate administrations. In Korea, the same was true when vital north-south rail, road, and shipping communications ended abruptly and, somewhat later, when the entire South was plunged into darkness with the cutting of power from the North. In economies always more separate, such as those of the two Chinas, or in the underdeveloped economies of Cambodia and Laos, or in Ireland, where communications have never really been severed, the effects have been less as have the economic demands on separate governments to create separate facilities. Developed states in this sense appear to suffer more from severance, underdeveloped states less. A medium-developed economy, e.g., Korea, perhaps suffers the most because its capacity to create viable separate economies is less than in Germany. The effort to do so is correspondingly more difficult and more damaging relative to the economy as a whole.

Economic rupture is, in short, one criterion by which to measure the relative effects and strains of division. Its impact on divisiveness cannot be measured in terms of dollar or trade damage alone but must also be reckoned in terms of the relative demands on the separate administrations whose reactive efforts deepen both the actuality and psychology of divisiveness. The political demands for separate administrations are usually quite profound and, especially in the early stages of division, outbid the rational demands of united economies. Hence, such nations as the two Koreas, the two Chinas, and the two Germanies proceeded with comparatively small outcry to duplicate facilities once obtained from the severed partner. Even in desperate poverty, Rwanda and Urundi largely ignore the clear advantages of economic cooperation. Ultimately, economic needs may prove an important channel for reunification or détente, especially in the case of medium-developed states like Korea where the expense of continuing duplication threatens greater political dependence on foreign nations.

Political activity is therefore primary in its effects on division. In all cases it appears to rise enormously in the wake of division and to function as the most basic instrument in the creation of separate institutions and of emotions which kindle the psychology of division.

Both the forms and the results of the political activity of division are impressive. Government—separate government and, usually, explicitly hostile government—in each divided part became the major objective of conflicting groups, and political parties became the vehicle by which this was accomplished. Division is, therefore, one of the chief catalysts of political mobilization and party development. In Ireland the struggle between Catholic nationalists and Protestants loyal to Britain produced major party movements on both sides, and the nationalists so effectively mobilized an impoverished and largely illiterate rural population that even in Ireland's diaspora its people have, in different national settings, maintained their reputation for political organization. The lengthy prelude to the division of Palestine was a tremendous catalyst to the rise of parties and political activity not only in Israel but in all neighboring Arab states as well. India is an even more arresting example. The formation of the Congress party spurred the rise of Muslim political movements which mobilized the cause of Muslim separatism. These movements became the progenitors of Pakistan and continue today to be bulwarks of its cause. In an ironically similar sequence, lack of cohesion between political movements in East Pakistan and West Pakistan mobilized separatist opinion and heralded the Pakistan-Bangladesh cleavage. Political-party formation and mobilization is far less developed in Cambodia and Laos, but even here division has stimulated substantially more political activity than existed before and may well become the crucial stimulus for the development of more effective political entities with broader participation than was possible before division took place.

Party activity is perhaps the most striking form of the group-reinforcement process so basic to the building of viable national divisions. It is, of course, far from the only one and is usually the culmination of much other group activity encouraging divisiveness. Churches, for example, have played such a role in European and to some extent in Muslim culture. Their special rites, processions, and traditions have provided moral rationalizations for uncompromising and confrontatory stands. In the divisions of Ireland, Cyprus, Palestine, and India-Pakistan, one sees what may hopefully be among the last acts of this long tragedy.

The confrontatory role of churches is also apparent in descending order of importance in Vietnam, Korea, and China where religion has functioned to validate morally and ideologically the extremity of opposition to communist states by anticommunist political elites and refugees. The role of religion and church institutions as rallying points of persecuted or refugee minorities is ancient and familiar to early Christian, Jewish, Buddhist, and Muslim history. Its confrontatory role in more recent divisions, while not wholly new, has mounting significance because of both the relative ideological poverty of anticommunist nations in cold war divisions and the sheer numbers of refugees associated with such divisions. Germany has been the exception here because the refugees in West Germany are not a religious minority in any meaningful sense. This fact combined with the understanding leadership within the German church has made religion and Protestant Christianity a bridge and not a fortress of confrontatory conviction between the two Germanies.

Political party and religious activity are only the most signal and overt of refugee activities encouraging polarization. Refugees have need of, and tend to join, organizations of many kinds. Having direct experience of conditions on the other side of the division, they are liable to establish themselves as guardians of confrontation and to enter defense and control bodies. Leadership in army, police, and intelligence bodies in Taiwan, South Korea, and South Vietnam tended to be exerted by refugees. Refugees have also played marked leadership roles in the divisions of Palestine, Germany, Pakistan, and even Laos. In time of particular threat, refugees have often formed their own youth and other defense groups as in the immediate post-World War II period in South Korea and in the Middle East where Palestinian guerrillas have been a major source of continuing hostility between Israel and the Arab states. Nevertheless, the polarization induced by refugees tends to be limited largely to the refugee generation. Unless refugees, as in the Palestine situation, are kept in camps and are unintegrated into a new national society, the original spirit of antagonism is rarely inherited by their socially integrated children.

Once formed, the more intense the confrontative activity of the organizations on either side of a division, the deeper the division will run. Just as strikes and confrontation crystallize class division, conflicting contact between divided states acts as a catalyst to group division. Here, the violence of the initial break usually plays a key role. Usually the break is violent—but not always. In Rwanda-Urundi unity was putative only and a break never came. In Mongolia the break occurred in pieces and partly through migration over a long period of time. In Ireland the break occurred long enough ago to have been personally witnessed by only a thinning minority of the population and tends to merge with the violence of a long-previous and long-remembered history. In Laos and Cambodia the break is both violent and recent, but it has been less definite. At the present time, no settled borders and no fully established regimes exist in either Laos or Cambodia; thus, there are less-definite entities for emotions to cohere around. A condition not entirely dissimilar pertains in Cyprus, though the entities are more definite there and, being infinitely smaller, are far better known and psychologically grasped. In all other cases covered, the break has occurred in the last generation and has been more or less violent. It has involved the active and continued maintenance of armed forces (as, of course, it does in Cyprus, Laos, and Cambodia). In the case of Pakistan-Bangladesh alone, this condition is greatly palliated by the noncontiguity of the borders. For China, the sea provides less of a palliative.

The character of the border is another variable. The most divisive borders are unstable, illegitimate, and subject to warfare—as with the fighting lines dividing Laos, Cambodia, and, to a lesser extent, Cyprus, India-Pakistan, and Palestine.

More legitimate but hermetically sealed borders which allow no friendly intercourse—as in Korea, Vietnam, and China—come next. They invoke hostility by troop concentrations, military action, or incidents while the stability of the relatively legitimized line encourages a definite psychological perception of the national entity which then forms part of the psychology of division. Borders allowing limited and controlled communication (Germany) or near-normal communication (Ireland, Mongolia, and, off-and-on, Rwanda-Urundi) probably contribute more to the tempering than to the escalation of hostility. A movement toward communicating borders is, obviously, highly desirable.

War is the ultimate expression of hostility arising from division. The threat of division to world peace is both manifold and profound. Indeed, all wars and most important military actions since 1945 have been associated with one or another of the divisions covered in this volume. The savagery of fighting between the two parts of divided countries may well exceed that between wholly foreign countries—a sad reminder that brothers make the worst enemies. During the Korean War, South Koreans told vivid stories of the cruelty of the North Korean invaders, far greater than that of the Red Chinese troops, and North Koreans frequently had more to fear from South Koreans than from American or other allied troops. In these tragedies, as in Vietnam, in the inter-Muslim slaughters of Bangladesh, and in Ireland and Cambodia, is ample evidence of the awesome dynamics of division.

Only the future politics of Korea and Indochina will show whether war between the divisions of fairly homogeneous states has any more redeeming side. It is possible that the horror of what war involves may have cathartic influences on the emotional vortices and ideological differences of national divisions. Some contact, even if usually hostile, may in some circumstances be better than none. The sight of destroyed villages and torn bodies of the same hue and birth may arouse more human feeling and pity than the flow of hostile propaganda across political boundaries. The escalation of military budgets, the wastage of scarce national resources in armies few wish to use may even arouse sobering national reactions. In Korea these reactions seem already to have begun. It is too soon to say whether war may have an ultimately ambivalent influence on the hostilities of divided countries; it is possible. For the present, however, it must still be judged the ultimate escalator of divisiveness.

Many other factors affect, or may affect, the psychological and the realistic complexes that maintain divisions. Among them are ethnic, linguistic, and religious homogeneity; population distribution; stability and legitimacy of government; distribution of natural resources; degree of development; level of education; length of historical experience; the influence of neighboring states and the great powers: ideology and propaganda. A rough and exploratory attempt to measure the impact of these factors on hostilization in relation to the cases covered in this volume has been made in the Appendix.

The relative importance of each of these factors for divisions is hard to assay. Population distribution has fairly clear importance, especially when correlated with the character of the borders involved. Dense settlement—as in Korea, Pakistan-India, and Cyprus—is an obvious intensifier of the forces discussed above. Low population density—e.g., in Mongolia and to some extent in Cambodia and Laos—tends to make hostilization forces less intense.

Ethnic and linguistic differences undoubtedly increase the possibility that a division will or may occur; they provide powerful ground for the rallying of separate groups as was prominent in the split of Pakistan and Bangladesh. Contrary to what might have been thought before World War II, however, these differences may not greatly increase the vortex of divisiveness in states that have already been divided. Of the wars or military actions now in progress in divided countries (Vietnam, Laos, Cambodia) or in war-torn Korea, ethnic and linguistic differences are either absent or play no significant part. The last generation has proved that a divided homogeneous nation can be uncompromisingly and savagely hostile as an unhomogeneous one—if not more so.

Resource distribution and degree of development are factors that can also contribute to the emotions of deprivation. Yet, in a manner running against the grain of the Marxian thesis, it is extraordinary, on the whole, how little economic and developmental factors inject themselves into the psychological and emotional complex of national division. They are overwhelmingly rational factors, and divided nations have generally shown astonishing ingenuity in adapting themselves to imposed economic adversities. Indeed, the deprivation of a resource, a service, or a productive unit by the division of a nation appears to have an effect comparable to a similar loss caused by war. The nation is challenged to make up the loss and, in the process, often develops rapidly.

Something similar might be said for the legitimacy and even stability of government. For when a nation is lacking in these, it tends to be challenged to make up for them. Its competitiveness with its divided partner in this respect seems to be a more important contributor than economic factors to the psychology of division. Such an inference can be drawn from the strivings of both East Germany and North Korea to achieve international recognition. Recognition by foreign powers and the buttress to legitimacy it entails has been, for the two Koreas, the two Germanies, and the two Vietnams, so bitter a field of competition in the last years as to undermine increasingly their respective versions of the Hallstein Doctrine and open the prospect of widespread recognition of both parts of these divided nations.

Length of historical experience is hard to appraise, but it does appear to play a modest role in affecting the divisiveness of sundered countries. Ireland seems to be the division in which this factor has played the greatest role. Appeals to history and the creation of a myth around which people can rally and from which they are loath to retreat has been central to the Irish problem, and more than any other factor it has helped to maintain enmity after 50 years of partition. On the whole, recent experience sadly shows that countries with long histories of unity are as easily sundered as a country whose unity is brief, though they do not cleave themselves voluntarily. Whether appeals to long history will be effective as a stimulus to reunification, the example of Korea is likely soon to show. Such appeals have been rhetorically important in starting talks between the two Koreas. Were there ever to be a hope for Mongolian unity, appeals to history would certainly have to play a key role in rallying Mongols to achieve it.

The influence of great powers and of neighboring states on the achievement and maintenance of division within nations is too large a subject for adequate treatment within this conclusion, which seeks, instead, to stress the internal dynamics of division. Nevertheless, it is clear that such outside influence is great. It is decisive in divided nations; these countries can be united only with great-power consent. The influence of great powers and neighboring states on the partitioned countries is also critical. Great Britain's role in Ireland has constituted the historical reason for Ireland's disunity, and many would say that it continues so to constitute it today. The role of Greece and Turkey in Cyprus has similarly constituted the grounds for division in that island, while the role of the United Nations in peacekeeping in Cyprus continues to be vital. Rwanda-Urundi's unity was connived against by the occupying colonial power while the force favoring it has been the United Nations. Great Britain authored the plan for the partition of Palestine, and the involvement of the United States and the Soviet Union in this question through the years is deep and well known as is, of course, that of the surrounding Arab states. The interest of outside powers in the India-Pakistan division is considerable but less decisive than the former role of Great Britain as colonial overlord of the subcontinent. While Pakistan and Bangladesh might have ultimately separated in any case, the armed force of India was decisive in the actual wrenching of Bangladesh from Pakistan. In short, the role of great or neighboring powers has been decisive in all cases of division except for India-Pakistan—and even in that instance the role of Great Britain was important.

It is in the domain of ideology that the internal and external strains affecting division converge. On the one hand, ideology usually has been transmitted to divided countries by colonial powers, occupying superpowers, or interested third parties anxious to foment subversion. On the other hand, division created internal needs for ideological identification. Confrontation, crisis, strife, and the groups and institutions that division breed produced a need for organizational cement and belief in action which only ideology could provide. The communist portions of divided states such as mainland China and North Korea developed into more ideological polities than the Soviet Union itself. Ideology, in turn, bred propaganda, and divided states became propaganda states. And propaganda, having hostility as a major object, bred further hostilization.

As a result, divided countries became increasingly and rather swiftly mobilized. Beginning in early nineteenth-century Ireland, one can see this process sweeping toward its crescendo in the nearly total mobilization of the masses achieved by the People's Republic of China and by the Democratic People's Republic of Korea. A particularly interesting example of the result of mass participation is cited by Craig Baxter in "India and Pakistan," in Henderson, Gregory, Richard

Ned Lebow and John G. Stoessinger, *Divided Nations in a Divides World* (New York: David McKay, 1974, pp. 267–98) the case of India when Gandhi invoked a mass movement for avowedly peaceful political purposes. Problems that had been communal suddenly became national. Sentiments once localized had to be appeased in oratory and elections at the national level. The flexibility needed to avert the Muslim-Hindu crisis was overwhelmed and leadership saw its force dulled or found itself prostituted for mass ends. What was prologue to division in India became the handwriting on the wall in other cases of division.

"If it is into the waters of passion that you plunge your oar you will be borne away" ends the first sentence of a famous Japanese novel. In dividing, nations have plunged themselves and their peoples into an increasingly ideologized and politicized world. Confrontation has induced in them a quicker pace of political mobilization than has overtaken most nations. The milieu of divided countries has been one of polarization and of propaganda, sometimes of the creation of national myth and destiny. The result has not encouraged the forces of compromise and rationality needed to reduce the tensions created—let alone provide solutions to division.

It may be that we stand on the borders of a new era. The Brandt initiatives in Germany have shown a way toward compromise and rationality. Korea may be following or may find its own way. In Vietnam a war ends haltingly, hopefully enduringly. In no recent case has a state once divided reunited, nor is any state approaching unification now. For some, such as Laos and Cambodia, division may harden sooner than it recedes or yield only to traumatic armed conflict. Like Goethe's sorcerer's apprentice, the world may not be freed of the spirits it has summoned.

The path, if it is to be taken, is clear. It is the path of communication. Once organizations created out of hostilization begin to speak to each other, propaganda will recede, ideology will soften slightly, and the organizations in which separateness has inhered will change. If this communication can develop into an expanding number of joint functions and tasks for organizations on both sides of divisions, group-reinforcement processes will begin to foster unity rather than disunity. If this stage can be succeeded by attempts at reductions in armed forces, emotional tensions will ebb and prospects for rapprochement or unity will brighten. Meanwhile, the habits and institutions of disunity will be hard to overcome, and the important stories of division told here will continue to hold sober lessons on how societies behave.

Notes

1   In this sense, the countries of Indochina can be said to be doubly divided. Each is a successor state of the former French colony and each in turn is divided between rival communist and noncommunist governments.
2   See the excellent discussion of the legal aspects of this problem in John Herz's chapter on Germany.

References

Deutsch, M. (1983). The prevention of World War III: A psychological perspective. *Political Psychology, 4,* 3–31.

French, J. R. P., Jr., & Raven, B. H. (1959). The bases of social power. In D. Cartwright (Ed.), *Studies in social power* (pp. 150–167). Ann Arbor, MI: Institute of Social Research.

Jervis, R. (1976). *Perception and misperception in international politics.* Princeton, NJ: Princeton University Press.

Milburn, T. (1961). The concept of deterrence: Some logical and psychological considerations. *Journal of Social Issues, 17*(3), 3–11.

Osgood, C. E. (1959). Suggestions for winning the real war with Communism. *Journal of Conflict Resolution,* 3, 295–325.

Pruitt, D. G., & Rubin, J. Z. (1986). *Social conflict: Escalation, stalemate, and settlement.* New York: Random House.

Russell, R. W. (Ed.) (1961). Psychology and policy in a nuclear age. *Journal of Social Issues, 17*(3).

Tetlock, P. E. (1983). Policymakers' images of international conflict. *Journal of Social Issues, 39*(1), 67–86.

White, R. K (1984). *Fearful warriors.* New York: Free Press.

Part II
Deterrence

3 Cognitive closure and crisis politics

The Austrians should move, the sooner the better, and the Russians—although friends of Serbia—will not intervene.

Theobald von Bethmann-Hollweg, July 5, 1914

If war does not break out, if the czar is unwilling, or alarmed, if France counsels peace, we shall have the prospect of splitting the Entente.

Theobald von Bethmann-Hollweg, July 6, 1914

We have not willed war, it has been forced upon us.

Theobald von Bethmann-Hollweg, August 4, 1914

Traditional social science theory depicted decision making as an essentially rational process. This paradigm assumed that policy makers processed information in a relatively straightforward and honest manner in order to discover the best policy alternative. To do this, they identified the alternatives, estimated the probability of success of each, and assessed their impact upon the values they sought to maximize. Policy makers were thought of as receptive to new information. As they learned more about a particular problem they were expected to make more complex and sophisticated judgments about the implications of the various policy alternatives they considered. The rational actor paradigm also assumed that policy makers confronted trade-offs squarely, that they accepted the need to make choices between the benefits and costs of competing alternatives in order to select the best policy.

Considerable research points to the conclusion that decision making in practice differs notably from the rational process we have just described.[1] This finding has prompted efforts to develop alternative paradigms of decision making, several of which have already been formulated in considerable detail. Each of these several paradigms claims to represent a more accurate description of the decision-making process than that of the rational actor model. The variety of models and approaches to decision making that have been developed in recent years has added immeasurably to our understanding of the decision-making process. The models have made us aware of the complexity of this process and the multiplicity of personal, political, institutional, and cultural considerations that can shape decisions. For this very reason no one perspective provides a satisfactory explanation of decision making. Each offers its own particular insights and is more or less useful depending upon the analytical concerns of the investigator and the nature of the decision involved.

For our purposes the psychological perspective on decision making appears to be the most relevant by virtue of the insights it offers into the causes and effects of misperception. Use of the psychological approach is complicated by the fact that there is as yet no integrated statement of psychological principles and processes that could be considered to represent a paradigm of decision making.[2] There are instead several different schools of thought, each of which attempts to explain nonrational processes in terms of different causation. The state of psychological theory therefore mirrors that of decision-making theory as a whole. As it is often necessary to employ more than one decision-making perspective to understand the genesis of a policy, so one must exploit more than one psychological theory or approach in order to explain the nonrational processes that are involved. In the pages that follow I will accordingly describe two psychological approaches, one cognitive the other motivational, that will be used in analyzing my case material.

Cognitive consistency, and misperception

The cognitive approach emphasizes the ways in which human cognitive limitations distort decision making by gross simplifications in problem representation and information processing. Some psychologists have suggested that human beings may be incapable of carrying out the procedures associated with rational decision making.[3] Whether or not this is actually the case, there is growing evidence that people process and interpret information according to a set of mental rules that bear little relationship to those of formal logic. Robert Abelson refers to these as yet poorly understood procedures as "psychologic."[4]

One principle of psychologic that has received considerable empirical verification is the principle of "cognitive consistency." Numerous experiments point to the conclusion that people try to keep their beliefs, feelings, actions, and cognitions mutually consistent. Thus, we tend to believe that people we like act in ways we approve of, have values similar to ours, and oppose people and institutions we dislike. People we dislike, we expect to act in ways repugnant to us, have values totally dissimilar from ours, and to support people and institutions we disapprove of.[5] Psychologists have theorized that cognitive consistency is an economic way or organizing cognition because it facilitates the interpretation, retention, and recall of information.[6] While this may or may not be true, our apparent need for cognitive order also has some adverse implications for decision making because it suggests the existence of systematic bias in favor of information consistent with information that we have already assimilated.

At the present time, considerable work is being done to analyze the various ramifications of cognitive consistency for decision making. To date, the most comprehensive effort is that of Robert Jervis whose work is especially relevant for our purposes, because he has made the foreign policy process the specific focus of his study.[7]

Jervis contends that it is impossible to explain crucial foreign policy decisions without reference to policy makers' beliefs about the world and the motives of other actors in it. These beliefs, organized as "images," shape the way in which policy makers respond to external stimuli. He suggests that the primary source of images is sterotyped interpretations of dramatic historical events, especially wars and revolutions. These upheavals have a particularly strong impact upon the thinking of younger people whose opinions about the world are still highly impressionable. Images formed by adolescents and young adults can still shape their approach to international problems years later when they may occupy important positions of authority. Jervis believes that this may explain why "generals are prepared to fight the last war and diplomats prepared to avoid it."[8]

Lessons learned from history are reinforced or modified by what policy makers learn from first-hand experience. Jervis finds that events that are personally experienced can be a "powerful determinant" of images. This too may be a source of perceptual distortion because personal experiences may be unrepresentative or misleading. As with historical lessons, events experienced early in adult life have a disproportional impact upon perceptual predispositions.[9]

The major part of Jervis' study is devoted to analyzing the ways in which images, once formed, affect foreign policy behavior. From the outset he makes an important distinction between what he calls "rational" and "irrational" consistency. The principle of consistency, he argues, helps us to make sense of new information as it draws upon our accumulated experience, formulated as a set of expectations and beliefs. It also provides continuity to our behavior. But the pursuit of consistency becomes irrational when it closes our minds to new information or different points of view. Even irrational consistency can be useful in the short run because it helps to make a decision when the time comes to act. However, persistent denial of new information diminishes our ability to learn from the environment. Policy makers must strike a balance between persistence and continuity on the one hand and openness and flexibility on the other. Jervis marshals considerable evidence to indicate that they more often err in the direction of being too wedded to established beliefs and defend images long after they have lost their utility.[10]

Irrational consistency can leave its mark on every stage of the decision-making process. Most importantly, it affects the policy maker's receptivity to information relevant to a decision. Once an expectation or belief has taken hold, new information is assimilated to it. This means that policy makers are more responsive to information that supports their existing beliefs than they are to information that challenges them. When confronted with critical information, they tend to misunderstand it, twist its meaning to make it consistent, explain it away, deny it, or simply ignore it.

To the extent that policy makers are confident in their expectations, they are also likely to make a decision before sufficient information has been collected or evaluated. Jervis refers to this phenomenon as "premature cognitive closure" and sees it as a major cause of institutional inertia. As all but the most unambiguous evidence will be interpreted to confirm the wisdom of established policy and the images of reality upon which it is based, policy makers will proceed a long way down a blind alley before realizing that something is wrong.[11]

When policy makers finally recognize the need to reformulate an image, they are likely to adopt the first one that provides a decent fit. This "perceptual satisficing" means that images change incrementally, that a large number of exceptions, special cases, and other superficial alterations will be made in preference to rethinking the validity of the assumptions on which the image is based. It also means that tentative beliefs or expectations, often made on the basis of very incomplete information, come to exercise a profound influence on policy because once they are even provisionally established incoming information is assimilated to them. This, in turn, lends credence to their perceived validity.[12]

The tautological nature of information processing is further facilitated by the "masking effect" of preexisting beliefs. As information compatible with an established belief will be interpreted in terms of it, the development of alternative beliefs that the information might also support is inhibited. Thus, the belief that the other side is bluffing, as Jervis points out, is likely to mask the perception that it means what it says because the behaviors that follow from these two intentions resemble each other so closely.[13]

The second way in which irrational consistency influences decision making is by desensitizing policy makers to the need to make value "trade-offs." Instead of recognizing that a favored option may advance one or even several valued objectives, but does so at the expense of some other valued objective, policy makers are more likely to perceive the option as simultaneously supporting all of their objectives. As they come to favor an option, policy makers may even alter some of their earlier expectations or establish new ones all in the direction of strengthening the case for the favored policy.

The failure to recognize trade-offs leads to "belief system overkill." Advocates of a policy advance multiple, independent, and mutually reinforcing arguments in its favor. They become convinced that it is not just better than other alternatives but superior in every way. Opponents, on the other hand, tend to attack it as ill considered in all its ramifications. In this regard, Jervis cites Dean Acheson's description of Arthur Vandenberg's characteristic stand: "He declared the end unattainable, the means harebrained, and the cost staggering." Cognitions ordered in this way facilitate choice as they make it appear that all considerations point toward the same conclusion. Nothing therefore has to be sacrificed. But, as Jervis points out, "the real world is not as benign as these perceptions, values are indeed sacrificed and important choices are made, only they are made inadvertently."[14]

The final way irrational consistency is manifested is in the form of postdecisional rationalization, a phenomenon described by Leon Festinger in his theory of cognitive dissonance.[15] Festinger argues that people seek strong justification for their behavior and rearrange their beliefs in order to lend support to their actions. Following a decision they spread apart the alternatives, upgrading the attractiveness of the one they have chosen and downgrading that of the alternative they have rejected. By doing so they convince themselves that there were overwhelming reasons for deciding or acting as they did. Festinger insists that people only spread apart the alternatives *after* they have made a decision. The decision must also result in some kind of commitment and the person making it must feel that it was a free decision, i.e., that he had the choice to decide otherwise.[16]

Subsequent research indicates that decisional conflict is positively correlated with the appeal of the rejected alternatives, their dissimilarity from the chosen alternatives and the perceived importance of the choice. In other words, the more difficult the decision, the greater the need to engage in postdecisional rationalization. According to Jervis, foreign policy decisions are often characterized by these criteria, and statesmen respond by upgrading their expectations about their chosen policy. By making their decision appear even more correct in retrospect they increase the amount of negative feedback required to reverse it. Postdecisional rationalization therefore makes policy makers less responsive to the import of critical information.[17]

Decisional conflicts and defensive avoidance

Whereas Jervis stresses the ways in which cognitive processes distort decision making, another school of psychology emphasizes the importance of motivation as a source of perceptual distortion. They see human beings as having a strong need to maintain images of the self or the environment conducive to their emotional well-being. This need interferes with their ability to act rationally. Harold Lieff observes:

> An important aspect of emotional thinking, including anxious and fearful thinking, is its selectivity. Under the influence of anxiety, a person is apt to select certain items in his environment and ignore others, all in the direction of either falsely proving that he was justified in considering the situation frightening and in responding accordingly, or conversely, of seeking reasons for false reassurances that his anxiety is misplaced and unnecessary. If he falsely justifies his fear, his anxieties will be augmented by the selective response, setting up a vicious circle of anxiety—distorted perception—increased anxiety. If, on the other hand, he falsely reassures himself by selective thinking, appropriate anxieties may be reduced, and he may then fail to take the necessary precautions.[18]

The work of Irving Janis and Leon Mann represents one of the most thought-provoking attempts to construct a motivational model of decision making. They start from the assumption that decision makers are emotional beings, not rational calculators, that they are beset by doubts and uncertainties, struggle with incongruous longings, antipathies, and loyalties, and are reluctant to make irrevocable choices. Important decisions therefore generate conflict, defined as simultaneous opposing tendencies to accept and reject a given course of action. This conflict and the psychological stress it generates become acute when a decision maker realizes that there is risk of serious loss associated with any course of action open to him.* More often than not, he will respond to such situations by procrastinating, rationalizing, or denying his responsibility for the decision making.[19]

Janis and Mann present their "conflict model" of decision making in terms of the sequence of questions policy makers must ask when confronted with new information about policies to which they are committed. Their answers to these questions determine which of five possible patterns of coping they will adopt (see Figure 3.1).

The first of the questions pertains to the risks to the policy maker of not changing his policy or taking some kind of protective action. If he assesses the risks as low, there is no stress and he can ignore the information. Janis and Mann refer to this state as "unconflicted inertia." Sometimes this is a sensible appraisal as when policy makers ignore warnings of doom from critics motivated by paranoia or partisan advantage. It is dysfunctional when it is a means of avoiding the stress associated with confronting a difficult decision head on."

If the perceived risks are thought to be serious, the policy maker must attempt to identify other courses of action open to him. If his search reveals a feasible alternative, Janis and Mann expect that it will be adopted without conflict. "Unconflicted change," as this pattern of coping is called, may once again reflect a realistic response to threatening information although it can also be a means of avoiding stress. Unconflicted change is dysfunctional when it mediates a pattern of "incrementalism." This happens when the original policy is only marginally changed in response to threatening information and then changed slightly again when more trouble is encountered. Such a crude satisficing strategy tends to ignore the range of alternative policies, some of which may be more appropriate to the situation. Janis and Mann suggest that this is most likely to occur when a policy maker is deeply committed to his prior course of action and fears that significant deviation from it will subject him to disapproval or other penalties.[21]

If the policy maker perceives that serious risks are inherent in his current policy, but upon first assessment is unable to identify an acceptable alternative, he experiences psychological stress. He becomes emotionally aroused and preoccupied with finding a less risky but nevertheless feasible policy alternative. If, after further investigation, he concludes that it is unrealistic to hope for a better strategy, he will terminate his search for one despite his continuing dissatisfac-

---

* Psychological stress is used by Janis and Mann to designate "unpleasant emotional states evoked by threatening environmental events or stimuli." Common unpleasant emotional states include anxiety, guilt and shame.

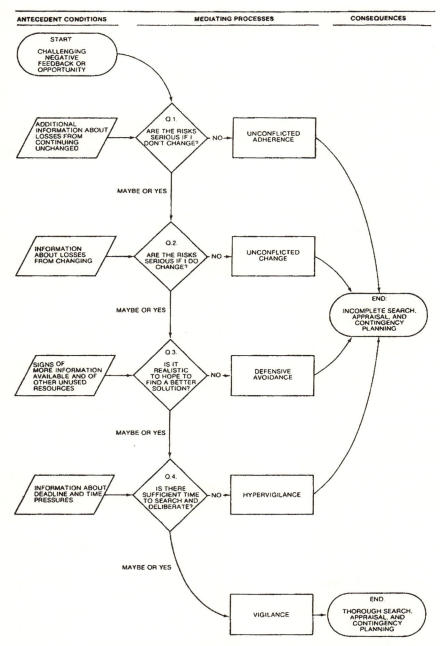

Figure 3.1 A Conflict-Theory Model of Decision Making Applicable to All Consequential Decisions. Source: Irving L. Janis and Leon Mann, Decision Making: A Psychological Analysis of Conflict, Choice, and Commitment (New York: The Free Press, 1977), p. 70. Reprinted by permission of the publisher.

tion with the available options. This results in a pattern of "defensive avoidance," characterized by efforts to avoid fear-arousing warnings.[22]

Janis and Mann identify three forms of defensive avoidance: procrastination, shifting responsibility for the decision, and bolstering. The first two are self-explanatory. Bolstering is an umbrella term that describes a number of psychological tactics designed to allow policy makers to entertain expectations of a successful outcome. Bolstering occurs when the policy maker has lost hope of finding an altogether satisfactory policy option and is unable to postpone a decision or foist the responsibility for it onto someone else. Instead, he commits himself to the least objectionable alternative and proceeds to exaggerate its positive consequences or minimize its negative ones. He may also deny the existence of his aversive feelings, emphasize the remoteness of the consequence, or attempt to minimize his personal responsibility for the decision once it is made. The policy maker continues to think about the problem but wards off anxiety by practicing selective attention and other forms of distorted information processing.[23]

Bolstering can serve a useful purpose. It helps a policy maker forced to settle for a less than satisfactory course of action to overcome residual conflict and move more confidently toward commitment. But bolstering has detrimental consequences when it occurs before the policy maker has made a careful search of the alternatives. It lulls him into believing that he has made a good decision when in fact he has avoided making a vigilant appraisal of the possible alternatives in order to escape from the conflict this would engender.[24]

If the policy maker finds an alternative that holds out the prospect of avoiding serious loss he must then inquire if he has sufficient time to implement it. If his answer to this question is no, his response will be one of "hypervigilance." This pattern of coping is also likely to be adopted if the time pressures are such that the policy maker does not even believe it possible to initiate a search for an acceptable alternative. Hypervigilance is characterized by indiscriminate openness to all information and a corresponding failure to determine whether or not that information is relevant, reliable, or supportive. Decisions made by persons in a hypervigilant state are likely to be unduly influenced by the will and opinions of others. In its most extreme form, panic, decisions are formulated in terms of the most simple-minded rules, e.g., "Do what others around you are doing." This is why a fire in a theater may prompt the audience to rush irrationally toward only one of several accessible exits.[25]

The patterns described above—unconflicted inertia, unconflicted change, defensive avoidance, and hypervigilance—are all means of coping with psychological stress. But they are hardly likely to lead to good decisions as each pattern is characterized by some kind of cognitive distortion. "High quality" decision making occurs when a policy maker is able to answer "yes," or at least "maybe," to all four questions. "Vigilance," the pattern of coping that leads to good decisions, is therefore associated with the following conditions: the policy maker realizes that his current policy will encounter serious difficulties; he sees no obvious satisfactory alternative but believes that a good alternative can probably be found and implemented in the time available to him.[26]

The preceding argument makes it apparent that Janis and Mann believe that stress can facilitate good decision making but only under circumstances so specific that they are not likely to recur very often. In less than ideal circumstances stress can be so acute as to compel the policy maker to adopt a decision-making strategy to protect him from it. Any of these patterns of coping will impair the quality of the decision.

Cognitive processes and decision-making pathologies

The studies we have just described represent two of the most provocative and comprehensive attempts to apply psychological insights to the study of political behavior. Unfortunately for those concerned with developing a psychological paradigm, the principal arguments of these two works are derived from sufficiently different premises to preclude their reformulation into an integrated model of decision making. For Jervis, the starting point is the human need to develop simple rules for processing information in order to make sense of an extraordinarily complex and uncertain environment. Janis and Mann take as their fundamental assumption the human desire to avoid fear, shame, and guilt. Jervis describes cognitive consistency as the most important organizing principle of cognition. Janis and Mann contend that aversion of psychological stress is the most important drive affecting cognition. Whereas Jervis concludes that expectations condition our interpretation of events and our receptivity to information, Janis and Mann argue for the importance of preferences. For Jervis, we see what we *expect* to see, for Janis and Mann, what we *want* to see.[27]

Despite the differences between these scholars they are in fundamental agreement about the important implications of cognitive, distortion for decision making. Each in his own way emphasizes the tendency of policy makers to fail to see trade-off relationships, engage in postdecisional rationalization, and remain insensitive to information that challenges the viability of their commitments. In essence, they are advancing competing explanations for some of the same observable behavior, behavior they both describe as detrimental to good decision making.

The several kinds of cognitive distortions Jervis and Janis and Mann refer to result in specific kinds of deviations from rational decision making. These deviations might usefully be described as decision-making "pathologies." To the extent that they are present they diminish the probability that effective policy will be formulated or implemented. For the purpose of analyzing crisis performance the most important of these pathologies appear to be: (1) the overvaluation of past performance as against present reality, (2) overconfidence in policies to which decision makers are committed, and (3) insensitivity to information critical of these policies. These pathologies warrant some elaboration.

Overvaluation of past success

Policy makers, according to Jervis, learn from history and their own personal experience. Their understanding of why events turned out the way they did constitutes the framework in terms of which they analyze current problems. It facilitates their ability to cope with these problems and provides continuity to their behavior.

Lessons from the past can discourage productive thinking to the extent that they represent superficial learning and are applied too reflexively. Jervis makes the case that this is a common occurrence because people rarely seek out or grasp the underlying causes of an outcome but instead assume that it was a result of the most salient aspects of the situation. This phenomenon gives rise to the tendency to apply a solution that worked in the past to a present problem because the two situations bear a superficial resemblance. Jervis observes: "People pay more attention to *what* has happened than to *why* it has happened. Thus learning is superficial, overgeneralized, and based on *post hoc ergo propter hoc* reasoning. As a result, the lessons learned will be applied to a wide variety of situations without a careful effort to determine whether the cases are similar on crucial dimensions."[28]

Examples of this kind of learning abound in the political and historical literature. A good case in point is the lesson drawn by the British military establishment and most military writers from the allied disaster at Gallipoli in World War I. Because Gallipoli failed, they became obdurate in their opinion that an amphibious assault against a defended shore was impractical and even suicidal. It took the Unites States Marine Corps., which undertook a detailed study of *why* Gallipoli failed (e.g., faulty doctrine, ineffective techniques, poor leadership, and utter lack of coordination) to demonstrate the efficacy of amphibious warfare.[29]

Success may discourage productive learning even more than failure as there is much less incentive or political need to carry out any kind of postmortem following a resounding success. If this is true, the greatest danger of superficial learning is that a policy, successful in one context, will be used again in a different and inappropriate context. The chance of this happening is enhanced by the strong organizational bias in favor of executing programs already in the repertory.[30] The Bay of Pigs invasion is a case in point. The CIA, ordered to overthrow Castro with no overt American participation, resurrected the plan they had used successfully in 1954 to topple the Arbenz government in Guatemala. Although the two situations had only a superficial similarity, this plan was implemented with only minor modifications, with results that are well known.[31] Some critics of American foreign policy have suggested that a similar process occurred with the containment policy. Due to its apparent success in Europe it was applied to Asia with consequences that now appear disastrous.[32]

Overconfidence

Jervis theorizes that irrational consistency encourages overconfidence at every stage of the decision-making process. Before a decision is made policy makers attempt to avoid value trade-offs by spreading the alternatives. In doing so they tend not only to make the favored alternative more attractive but also to judge it more likely to succeed. As policy decisions often hinge on estimates of their probability of success it is not surprising that Jervis finds that people who differ about the value of an objective are likely to disagree about the possibility of attaining it and the costs that this will entail. Those who favor the policy will almost invariably estimate the chances of success as high and the associated costs as lower than do their opponents.[33]

After a decision is made, postdecisional rationalization enters the picture. It too is a means of minimizing internal conflict by providing increased support for a person's actions. For by revising upwards the expected favorable consequences of a policy and its probability of success, policy makers further enhance their confidence in the policy. By this point their confidence may far exceed whatever promise of success would be indicated by a more objective analysis of the situation.[34]

Janis and Mann also describe overconfidence as a common decision-making pathology but attribute it to different causes and specify a different set of conditions for its appearance. For them it is a form of bolstering, the variety of psychological tactics that policy makers employ to maintain their expectations of an outcome with high gains and minimal losses. Policy makers will display overconfidence and other forms of defensive avoidance to the degree that they (1) confront high decisional conflict resulting from two clashing kinds of threat and, (2) believe that they will not find a better alternative for coping with this threat than their present defective policy. Janis and Mann write: "Whenever we have no hope of finding a better solution than the least objectionable one, we can always take advantage of the difficulties of predicting what might happen. We can bolster our decision by tampering with the probabilities in order to restore our emotional equanimity. If we use our imagination we can always picture a beautiful outcome by toning down the losses and highlighting the gains."[35]

Insensitivity to warnings

An important corollary of cognitive consistency theory is that people resist cues that challenge their expectations. They may misinterpret them to make them supportive, rationalize them away, or ignore them. Jervis finds that resistance to critical information increases in proportion to a policy maker's confidence in his course of action, the extent of his commitment to it, and the ambiguity of information he receives about it. Under these conditions even the most negative feedback may have little impact upon the policy maker.[36]

For Janis and Mann, insensitivity to warnings is a hallmark of defensive avoidance. When this becomes the dominant pattern of coping "the person tries to keep himself from being exposed to communications that might reveal the shortcomings of the course of action he has chosen." When actually confronted with disturbing information he will alter its implications through a process of wishful thinking. This often takes the form of rationalizations which argue against the prospect of serious loss if the current policy is unchanged. Janis and Mann find that extraordinary circumstances with irrefutable negative feedback may be required to overcome such defenses.[37]

Selective attention, denial, or almost any other psychological tactic used by policy makers to cope with critical information can be institutionalized. Merely by making their expectations or preferences known, policy makers encourage their subordinates to report or emphasize information supportive of those expectations and preferences. Policy makers can also purposely rig their intelligence networks and bureaucracies to achieve the same effect. Points of view thus confirmed can over time exercise an even stronger hold over those who are committed to them.[38] Some effort has been made to explain both the origins and duration of the Cold War in terms of such a process.[39] The danger here is that perceptual rigidity will impair personal and organizational performance. It encourages a dangerous degree of overconfidence which reduces the probability that policy makers will respond to information critical of their policies. Karl Deutsch warns: "If there are strong tendencies toward eventual failure inherent in all organizations, and particularly governments—as many pessimistic theories of politics allege—then such difficulties can perhaps be traced to their propensities to prefer self-referent symbols to new information from the outside world.[40]

Defensive avoidance and unconscious conflict

One further decision-making pathology must be considered. The paralysis or erratic steering that can result when defenses, erected to cope with anxiety, break down.

The human mind is particularly adept at developing defenses against information or impulses that threaten the attainment of important goals or the personality structure itself. Some of the more common defenses include repression, rationalization, denial, displacement, and acting out.[41] These defenses are not always effective. Fresh evidence of an unambiguous and unavoidable kind may break through a person's defenses and confront him with the reality he fears. This can encourage adaptive behavior. But it can also prompt him to adopt even more extreme defense mechanisms to cope with the anxiety this evidence generates. This latter response is likely to the extent that there are important causes of decisional conflict at the unconscious level.[42] Even these defenses may prove transitory and ineffective. As a general rule, the more intense and prolonged the defense the greater the probability of breakdown when it finally collapses. In the words of a famous pugilist: "The bigger they are the harder they fall."

Psychiatrists find that there is a very common (but not universal) pattern associated with the breakdown of defense and coping mechanisms:

FEAR
REPRESSION
CHRONIC ANXIETY
DECREASE IN DEFENSE AND COPING MECHANISMS
SYNDROMES OF ANXIETY REACTIONS[43]

In this formulation fear is a response to an *external* threat whereas anxiety relates to *internal* conflict. As Ernst Kris notes, external stress is reacted to in proportion to the internal tension or anxiety already existing. When internal tension or anxiety is great fear leads to repression. Repression produces chronic anxiety, all or part of which is usually outside of conscious awareness. In conditions of great psychological stress, defense mechanisms may not be effective in repressing anxiety.[44] An "anxiety reaction" may follow.[45]

A person suffering from an anxiety reaction almost always displays apprehension, helplessness, and a pervasive sense of nervous tension. Other clinical manifestations include headaches, indigestion, anorexia, palpitations, genitourinary problems, insomnia, irritability, and inability to concentrate. When confronted with the need to act, such a person is likely to be indecisive. He may cast about frantically seeking the advice of others or may oscillate between opposing courses of action, unable to accept responsibility for a decision. He is also likely to mistrust his own judgment and be easily influenced by the views of others. His ability to perform tasks effectively when they relate to the source of anxiety will be low. Commenting on his experience with anxiety reactions, one psychiatrist observes:

> The smallest obstacle may be insurmountable: the next day is the harbinger of death; the next visitor, the bearer of bad news; the next event, the beginning of catastrophe. Overly concerned with what others think of him the patient is constantly trying to make a favorable impression but is never satisfied with his performance. Uncertain of himself, he may belittle and degrade others in a misguided effort to raise his own self-esteem, all the while castigating himself for his failures. Although the patient with an anxiety reaction may exhibit considerable drive, it usually has a compulsive quality and is accompanied by misgivings regarding his competence to perform the task.[46]

Free-floating anxiety may alternatively be manifested in what Eugen Kahn refers to as a "stun reaction," characterized by withdrawal, passivity, and even psychomotor retardation.[47] The person in question attempts to escape anxiety by refusing to contemplate or confront the problem associated with it. The stun reaction is usually of limited duration and may be preliminary to an anxiety reaction which commences upon emergence from withdrawal.

Free-floating anxiety invariably leads to the adoption of more extreme defense mechanisms to cope with the tension associated with it. Two of the most common mechanisms are projection and marked denial. Both are usually ineffectual and transitory in nature.

In projection the individual attributes his own feelings and impulses to another person because he is unable to accept responsibility for them or tolerate the anxiety they produce. Projection also provides an explanation for failure and protects a person from having to acknowledge a painful and humiliating defeat. Projection invariably contains elements of persecution, jealousy, and sometimes compensatory delusions of grandeur. Frequent resort to projection to preserve an unstable personality structure is a classical manifestation of paranoia.[48]

Marked denial, as the term implies, consists of ignoring a threatening experience or its memory when it can no longer be relegated to the subconscious. Like projection, this defense can only be maintained at considerable cost to a person's ability to act effectively. In its extreme form, marked denial is a manifestation of a "dissociative reaction," a state where a person's thoughts, feelings, or actions are not associated or integrated with important information from his environment as they normally or logically would be. A dissociative reaction in effect consists of a jamming of one's circuits. Clinical symptoms include trance states (characterized by unresponsiveness to the environment, immobility, and apparent absorption with something deep within the self), estrangements and paramnesia (detachment and disengagement from persons, places, situations, and concepts), fugue (flight, entered into abruptly, often with amnesia and lack of care for one's person or surroundings), frenzied behavior (episodes of violent, outlandish, or bizarre behavior) and dissociative delerium (including hallucinations, wild emotional outpourings, and release of primary process material).[49]

A dissociative reaction is an extreme means of defending the ego against material that is too threatening to cope with on a conscious or unconscious level. It is most often manifested during periods of extreme stress. According to Louis Jolyon West: "Maturational shortcomings, emotional conflicts, and stressful life situations are thus superimposed upon each other to create a trap or impasse that cannot be resolved by the patient because of the overwhelming anxiety inherent in the available possible solutions."[50] The resolution brought about by a dissociative reaction is crippling but usually produces a beneficial change in the psychological economy of the individual.

Defense mechanisms can miscarry by leading to self-damaging behavior. Anxiety reactions, projection, and dissociative reactions hinder the willingness and effectiveness of persons to perform tasks related to the source of anxiety. These persons become indecisive or paralyzed or, if still capable of action, are likely to respond in ways that bear little relationship to the realities of the situation.

The implications of the preceding discussion for crisis management are obvious. Defense mechanisms are most likely to break down when the policy maker is inescapably confronted with the reality he has hitherto repressed. Such a situation is most likely to develop during the most acute stage of international crisis when the decision for peace or war hangs in the balance. A breakdown in the policy maker's defenses at this time may result in erratic behavior or his actual paralysis. Either condition is likely to "freeze" policy and contribute to the outbreak of war to the extent that it leaves the protagonists on a collision course.

The July crisis: a case study

Cognitive deficiencies were an important cause of war in the several brinkmanship crises included in our study that resulted in war. They were responsible for overconfidence. insensitivity to threatening information, and in at least one case contributed to the paralysis of national leadership during the most critical moment of the confrontation. The overall effect of these decision-making pathologies was to encourage policy makers to challenge important commitments of their adversaries with the erroneous expectation that their adversaries would back down. Once committed to such challenges, they remained insensitive to warnings that their adversaries were not going to give way and that their challenges, if pursued, were almost certain to lead to war.

Fully adequate documentation of this contention would require lengthy case studies of all of the brinkmanship crises that led to war. This is clearly out of the question. This chapter will examine German policy in the July crisis which, in the author's opinion, is a particularly telling example of the causal relationship between cognitive impairment, miscalculation, and war.

The story of the July crisis has been told many times. The purpose in doing so has usually been to assign guilt or responsibility for the war to one or more of the powers. A more useful question is how it happened. Most historians agree that none of the nations involved in the crisis aspired to provoke a general continental war, although the Germans were certainly more willing than others to face up to that possibility. European leaders nevertheless proved incapable of averting this catastrophe. The reasons for their failure are numerous and can ultimately be traced to lack of foresight in all the European capitals. However, this problem was most pronounced in Berlin and the miscalculations of German leaders were more instrumental in bringing about war than were the faulty judgments of any other set of policy makers. The poor performance of German policy makers can best be understood in terms of the cognitive closure of the German political system.

German policy in the July crisis was based on a series of erroneous assumptions as to the probable Russian, French, and British reactions to the destruction of Serbia by Austria-Hungary. Berlin was confident of its ability to localize an Austro-Serbian war despite all the indications to the contrary and actually urged Vienna to ignore all proposals for moderation. German leaders did not realize the extent of their miscalculation until very late in the crisis. At this point they still might have averted war had they revised their strategy and urged caution upon Vienna. Instead, they vacillated. They considered diametrically opposed courses of action and then passively accepted the coming of war as something they were powerless to avoid. By not revising her crisis scenario, Germany remained on a collision course with Russia, France, and Britain. She did nothing to prevent the war that was within her power to avoid.

The German foreign office had for some years viewed Austria-Hungary as the second "sick man" of Europe and had urged Vienna to pursue an aggressive policy in the Balkans in order to recover her self-confidence and international position. In keeping with this policy German political and military leaders encouraged the Austrians to seize upon the assassination of Franz Ferdinand as a convenient pretext to destroy Serbia.[51] Bethmann-Hollweg, the imperial chancellor and Jagow, the secretary of state for foreign affairs, explained the German position in a circular dispatch to the German ministers in St. Petersburg, Paris, and London: "If the Austro-Hungarian government is not going to abdicate forever as a great power, she has no choice but to enforce acceptance by the Serbian government of her demands by strong pressures and if necessary, by resort to military measures. The choice of methods must be left to her.[52]

Germany herself had no interest in Serbia. Aside from strengthening Austria, her objective was to separate Russia from France, a goal that motivated Bethmann-Hollweg throughout the course of the crisis. The chancellor even hinted to his colleagues that he meant to enforce this break at the risk of war.[53]

German leaders did not shy away from the prospect of an Austro-Serbian war because they were convinced that such a conflict could be "localized." Russia and France were thought unprepared for and disinclined to world war. The Germans also expected that Britain and France would if need be restrain Russia from any precipitous action. The Kaiser even entertained the hope that the upsurge of monarchial solidarity occasioned by the assassination might deter his cousin the czar from drawing his sword in defense of regicides. But even if the unexpected occurred and Russia and France intervened, the Germans still depended on British neutrality.[54] Count Szögyény, the Austrian ambassador in Berlin, could thus report to Vienna that emperor and chancellor alike were "absolute" in their insistence on the need for war with Serbia because Russia and France "were not yet ready" for such a conflict and would not intervene. Nor, he reported, did Berlin believe that Britain would "intervene in war which breaks out over a Balkan state, *even if it should lead to a conflict with Russia, possibly even France....*Not only have Anglo-German relations so improved that Germany feels that she need no longer fear a directly hostile attitude by Britain, but above all, Britain at this moment is anything but anxious for war, and has no wish whatsoever to pull the chestnuts out of the fire for Serbia, or in the last instance, for Russia."[55]

The German strategy was remarkably shortsighted. Even if the very questionable assumptions upon which this strategy was based had proven correct it still would have been self-defeating. The destruction of Serbia would only have aggravated Russo-German hostility, making Russia even more dependent on France and Britain and setting the stage for a renewed and more intense clash between the two blocs. This outcome aside, in practice, all of the assumptions of the German scenario proved to be ill-founded: the Austrian declaration of war on Serbia triggered a series of actions which embroiled Germany in a war with Russia, France, Belgium, and Britain. Moreover, German leaders received ample evidence that their scenario would lead to a Continental war *before* the Russian mobilization on July 30–31, the act which made that war almost unavoidable. Our inquiry must therefore seek to explain why German leaders based their foreign policy on such erroneous expectations and why they continued to adhere to them after they were proven invalid.

Some insight into the first question may be gained by examining the Bosnian annexation crisis and the effect that their success in that crisis appeared to have exercised over German decision makers in 1914. Five years earlier, in 1909, Aehrenthal, the Austrian foreign minister, had provoked a confrontation with Serbia and Russia by unilaterally announcing his intention to annex Bosnia-Herzogovina. nominally a province of the Ottoman Empire. Neither Serbia nor Russia was at first willing to accept this high-handed *fait accompli*. Both countries demanded compensation, and Serbia even mobilized her army to demonstrate resolve. But in the end, Russia was forced to acquiesce in the Austrian initiative and to exert pressure on Serbia to do likewise.[56]

The Russian capitulation was prompted by her military unpreparedness and diplomatic isolation. Neither the Russian army nor civil administration had fully recovered from the disastrous 1905 war with Japan and the revolution that followed in its wake. Russia's ally France also made it clear that she would not be dragged into a European war over a Balkan quarrel. On the other hand, Bülow, the German chancellor, stood firmly behind his ally, Austria. At the height of the crisis, he sent a curt ultimatum to St. Petersburg, demanding that Russia use her influence with Serbia to compel her acceptance of the Austrian action. Weakened by war, deserted by France, and faced with the combined might of Germany and Austria-Hungary, Russia reluctantly chose diplomatic humiliation in preference to certain defeat in war.

The Bosnian crisis appears to have exercised a profound influence upon German policy in 1914. To begin with, Bethmann-Hollweg's scenario was almost a carbon copy of Bülow's policy in 1909. At that time, Austria had initiated a *démarche* with Serbia, while Germany threatened Russia with war to keep her from intervening. Gottlieb von Jagow, appointed foreign secretary in January 1913, confirms that this similarity was more than mere coincidence: "Every policy had its consequences, even the policy of Bülow, although it had no steady line and scant farsightedness and consisted more of see-sawing and juggling. We were thrown back on Austria not only by the treaty of alliance but also by the way the European Powers were grouped—to no small degree the consequence of Bülow's policy. In 1914 we had no intention of aping Bülow's performance in 1909. But how could we leave Austria in the lurch?"[57]

The Bosnian crisis was the crucible in which German policy in 1914 took form. The chancellor in particular put great store in the possibility of repeating the success of 1909. Bülow's own comments to this effect—if they are to be believed—are quite revealing. Before leaving office in 1909 he alleges that he warned Bethmann-Hollweg not to try to repeat his policy but that the new chancellor was unconvinced and resented the advice.[58]

As we noted earlier, past success may blind decision makers to present reality. This appears to have happened in Berlin. German leaders replayed the Bosnian crisis and hoped to achieve an equally favorable outcome. But 1909 and 1914 bore only a superficial similarity and the conditions that had facilitated Bülow's coup in 1909 were no longer operative. Even before the crisis began there was every indication that Russia would not submit a second time to diplomatic humiliation. German leaders remained oblivious to this political reality.

The Austrian ultimatum in 1914 in effect demanded that Serbia relinquish her sovereignty. As Serbia was something of a Russian client, her acquiescence to Austrian demands would have dealt a serious blow to Russian influence in the Balkans. In Russian eyes this was tantamount to renouncing the czarist empire's status as a great power. The stakes were therefore greater in 1914 than they had been in 1909. So was Russia's ability to defend her interests. She had largely recovered from the dual disaster of defeat abroad and revolution at home, and her rearmament program was well advanced although not scheduled for completion until 1916. This time around Russia could also rely upon her major ally for support. In 1909 France had urged restraint. In 1914 the French agreed that Russia should oppose Austrian efforts to subjugate Serbia, and the French Minister in St. Petersburg exaggerated the extent of his government's support. Finally, it must be remembered that Russia's impotence in the Bosnian crisis had been a difficult emotional blow for its leaders. It led to a determination, shared by Slavophils and pro-Westerners alike, never to suffer such a humiliation again.[59]

The Russian refusal to countenance Serbia's destruction was a consideration, Bülow later admitted, "That should have been apparent to any normal German diplomat."[60] But German leaders, including the chancellor, failed to grasp the essential differences between 1909 and 1914 and held steadfast to their view that Russia would back down.[61] On July 18, two days before the dispatch of the Austrian ultimatum, Jagow outlined to the German minister in London Berlin's reasons for optimism:

> We must do our best to localize the conflict between Austria and Serbia. Whether this can be achieved depends in the first place on Russia and in the second place on the moderating influence exercised by her brethren of the Entente. The more resolute Austria shows herself and the more energetically we support her, the sooner will Russia stop her outcry. To be sure, they will make a great to-do in St. Petersburg, but when all is said and done, Russia is at present not ready for war.... In a few years, Russia will be ready to fight. Then she will crush us by the number of her soldiers. By then she will have built her Baltic Fleet and her strategic railways. Our group will in the meantime grow weaker and weaker. In Russia they probably know this, and for this reason Russia definitely wants peace for a few years longer.[62]

Jervis observes that misperceptions often endure because of the "masking effect" of preexisting beliefs. Information highly compatible with an established belief will be interpreted in terms of that belief. This will inhibit the development of alternative explanations for the information. The example Jervis offers, mistaking a serious threat for a bluff, is particularly germane to our analysis. He suggests that "the belief that the other side is bluffing is likely to mask the perception that it will actually fight because the behaviors that follow from these two intentions closely resemble each other."[63] This may help explain why up to the very eve of Russian mobilization, the Kaiser, Bethmann-Hollweg, and Jagow remained optimistic about the possibility of Russian neutrality. All the Russian protests, including first hints and then threats of mobilization, were exactly what would be expected from the Russian leaders if they were in fact bluffing. Their warnings accordingly fell on deaf ears. Albertini, reviewing the evidence to this effect, concludes: "However much the German Government might affirm that if war had to come, it was better for it to come at once than later, it may well be doubted whether they would so lightheartedly have embarked on the adventure if they had been convinced of immediate Russian intervention. They took the plunge reckoning on the acquiescence of all of the three Entente Powers and at worst on the neutrality of England. An extraordinary illusion![64]

One of the more important reasons why German leaders cherished their illusion until the very denouement of the crisis was that they were encouraged to do so by their diplomats. The German diplomatic corps performed badly during the crisis; with one exception, its members failed to criticize policy even when they knew it to fly in the face of reality, and limited their role to carrying out the instructions given them by Berlin. The explanation for this institutional malaise can be traced back to Bismarck's efforts to make the foreign office totally responsive to his directives. His often repeated maxim was: "At my command, and without knowing why, my diplomats must fall into rank like soldiers." Many foreign office officials were terrified of Bismarck and even those who were not, generally hastened to carry out his instructions to the letter. One veteran diplomat observed that "wax would be a hard metal compared to our pliancy toward the chancellor's will." Bismarck also made certain that German ministers abroad occupied an institutionally inferior position and were on the whole subordinate to counselors in the Wilhelmstrasse. These counselors, jealous of their own prerogatives, did their best to prevent ambassadors from developing independent positions of authority. They rarely consulted them about policy and sometimes did not even inform them about the rationale behind the initiative they were expected to help implement. German ambassadors frequently had to plead ignorance when questioned about policy by their host governments.[65]

Following Bismarck, ambassadorial morale declined precipitously as his less skillful successors encroached even further upon the limited prerogatives of the diplomats. Embittered envoys began to refer to the Wilhelmstrasse as the *Giftbude* (poisonous den). Much of the blame for this state of affairs can be laid at the foot of Friedrich von Holstein, senior counselor of the political division and the most influential official in the foreign office between Bismarck's resignation in 1890 and his own retirement in 1906. Holstein was easily offended, relentlessly vindictive, and probably paranoid. He was obsessed by the possibility of Bismarck's return to power and, with the backing of the Kaiser, purged the foreign office of anyone who had been closely associated with the former chancellor. In their place he recruited younger men who owed their loyalty to him and whose reports from abroad faithfully reflected his own view of the world. The toadyism demanded by Holstein from his subordinates was reinforced by the brutal manner in which he treated diplomats who offered professional judgments at variance with his. The fate of Prince Lichnowsky, minister in Vienna until 1904, was known to everyone. His career has been sidetracked as a result of his independent and outspoken reporting. Lichnowsky commented about Holstein:

> He quite lost touch with realities and lived in a world of illusions. He even went so far as to give his protégés instructions as to what should be the tenor of their reports. If one of our representatives abroad reported things this fantast and misanthrope did not wish to read, he henceforth had to reckon with Holstein as his enemy and expect a reprimand or a removal to some less desirable post. As a rule Holstein protected only mediocrities or diplomats who were content to be a putty in his hands. Officials of ability or character he dreaded. It thus very often came about that men who were nonentities attained the most important posts.[66]

While Lichnowsky was something of a maverick and felt considerable antagonism toward Holstein, his description of the foreign office, as an obsequious and narrow-minded institution, was confirmed by other observers. It was an accepted truth within the European diplomatic community that for young German diplomats to succeed they had to report to Berlin only what it wanted to hear. Sergei Sazonov, Russian foreign minister in 1914, noted in his memoirs that German diplomatic representatives were notorious for currying favor with the prevailing mood in Berlin, "well-knowing that the only one among them who boldly spoke the truth and opposed the plans of the Wilhelmstrasse was derided as a 'good old Lichnowsky.'"[67] Ambitious men, keeping the precedent of Lichnowsky in mind, studiously avoided expressing unpopular opinions.

Berlin was to pay dearly for its failure to encourage its representatives abroad to express their mind. During the course of the July crisis Lichnowsky was the only German diplomat to raise objections to the German strategy, to undertake any personal initiatives, or even to seek clarification of his instructions. Schoen in Paris, Tschirschky in Vienna, and Pourtalès in St. Petersburg reported only on specific developments within the countries to which they were assigned and offered only opinions supportive of Germany's efforts to localize an Austro-Serbian war.

The case of Count Friedrich von Pourtalès is illustrative of how German ambassadors twisted words and distorted facts in order to present a rosy picture to the Wilhelmstrasse. Pourtalès, a wealthy aristocrat of Swiss origin, was a protegé of Holstein and had risen to the rank of minister without the requisite seniority, because of the intercession of his mentor. Pourtalès was a man of peace and it is ironic that his failure to speak up may have contributed to the outbreak of war. But the unrealistic German notion that Russia would stand aside and permit the destruction of Serbia endured in part because Pourtalès, who certainly knew better, was reluctant to say so to Berlin.

Pourtalès, minister in St. Petersburg since 1907, recognized that Sazonov was often accused of vacillation by the nationalists, who in turn were egged on by Maurice Paléologue, the new French ambassador. Pourtalès stated in his memoirs that it was his impression at the time that Sazonov was powerless against this group.[68] This was probably an exaggeration of the truth. But the growing nationalist clamor meant that Russian leaders who on the whole had no desire for war could nevertheless not permit the destruction of Serbia without alienating opinion upon which they depended for support. Sazonov made no secret of Russia's determination to defend Serbia's independence and warned German diplomats to this effect prior to the onset of the crisis.[69] However, Pourtalès made no attempt to convey the Russian position to Berlin. There is not a single cable or report among the German documents warning of the influence of the Slavophils or of Sazonov's determination to protect Serbia.

Rather, Pourtalès repeatedly speaks of Sazonov's "policy of bluff"—a phrase picked up and frequently repeated by his cousin Bethmann-Hollweg.[70]

In July 1914, Pourtalès minimized the impact of the assassination upon Russian political leaders and St. Petersburg society in general. He did not even send his first account of the Russian reaction to the event until July 13, more than two weeks after the event. On July 24, he reported that "public opinion here has until now shown remarkable indifference towards the Austro-Serbian conflict." He subsequently made no attempt to alter this impression despite the increasingly angry tone of the Russian press and foreign office spokesmen. By far his most egregious omission concerned the Russian reaction to localization of the conflict, that pious illusion upon which the entire German strategy in the crisis was based.[71]

On July 24, three days before Russia's partial mobilization, Pourtalès was asked by Berlin to broach the possibility of localization to Sazonov. According to Pourtalès' own memorandum of their meeting, the Russian foreign minister was enraged by the suggestion and "vented his feelings in boundless accusations against Austria-Hungary, declaring with the utmost resolution that Russia could not possibly admit that the Austro-Serbian differences should be settled between the two parties alone." Sazonov accused Vienna of looking for a pretext to "swallow" Serbia in which case, he insisted "Russia will go to war with Austria."[72] Observers allege that Pourtalès was agitated and distraught when he emerged from his hour-long interview with Sazonov.[73] This seems likely, as later in the day the ambassador confided to his diary that war with Russia seemed unavoidable unless Austria backed down.[74]

None of these forebodings were reported to Berlin. Pourtalès attempted instead to assuage the anxieties of Germany's leaders. He reported Sazonov's warning but dismissed it as an overreaction due to his "extremely agitated state of mind." He advised the foreign office that localization of the conflict was still a realistic objective because "Russia will not take up arms except in the case that Austria were to want to make territorial acquisitions at Serbia's expense. Even the wish for a Europeanization of the question seems to indicate that an immediate intervention is not to be anticipated." In his obvious attempt to send reassuring reports to Berlin Pourtalès continued to minimize the possibility of Russian intervention and suppressed as long as possible any information that might have indicated that Germany was on a collision course with Russia. Albertini concludes that the ambassador's reports represented a deliberate falsification of the mood in St. Petersburg and could only have encouraged Jagow, Bethmann-Hollweg, and the Kaiser in their illusions.[75]

In all fairness to Pourtalès, he certainly cannot be held solely responsible for the erroneous German expectation of Russian acquiescence to the destruction of Serbia. He did, after all, report Sazonov's tirades against Austria-Hungary as well as the foreign minister's threats to intervene if Austria attacked Serbia. That German leaders chose to ignore these warnings and put credence in the reassuring opinions of their ambassador was their own doing and indicative of the extent to which they practiced selective attention. Their ability to do this was certainly facilitated by the sheer quantity of cables and reports they received which forced them to choose which among them were most deserving of their attention. The large number of messages and their equally diverse origin also meant that much of the information policy makers received was contradictory. All of this abetted the temptation to take seriously only those reports that tended to confirm their own preconceived notions of how other nations were likely to act. German leaders succumbed to this temptation, as their faith in Pourtalès' dispatches illustrates. Selective attention had the effect of negating the efforts by Russia, France, and Britain to warn Germany of the probable outcome of her continuing support of Austrian designs against Serbia. August Bach comments: "Parallel with optimistic estimates of the situation in Berlin went a profound underestimation of the extent to which the other side would be prepared to intervene.... This was a dangerous mistake, but up to July 27 it was so predominant that the Berlin statesmen during those days, even in the most serious communications from London and St. Petersburg, only looked for the few clues which seemed to point to a way of escape."[76]

Nowhere was German delusion greater than with respect to the expectation of British neutrality, a cornerstone of German policy throughout the crisis. And in this instance Berlin's behavior cannot be attributed to misleading dispatches from its ambassador, for Lichnowsky, the German minister in London, stressed the likelihood of British intervention in a Franco-German war. His admonitions were ignored.[77] German leaders preferred to believe the more comforting analyses of Admiral Tirpitz, Wilhem von Stumm, a British specialist in the foreign office, and other well connected but even less well qualified observers.[78]

The cardinal principle of British diplomacy throughout the centuries had been to preserve a balance of power on the Continent in order to prevent any expansionist power from achieving Continental hegemony. The aggressive policies of Wilhelminian Germany had led British leaders to suspect Germany of harboring such ambitions and this encouraged Britain to seek rapprochement with France and Russia as a counterweight to German power.[79] A German victory over both France and Russia would leave the Teutonic powers supreme in Europe and constitute a grave threat to the economic well-being and phsyical security of the British Empire. Although Britain had made no firm commitment to defend France, her policies in the two Moroccan crises made it apparent that no British government was likely to ignore its vital interests and stand aside while Germany conquered France.[80]

To this must be added Britain's treaty commitment to defend Belgian neutrality. The strategic importance of Belgium to Britain made it unlikely that she would look for a way of evading her responsibility. The ports of the low countries, especially those of Belgium, were the best possible bases for an invasion of Britain, and for this reason generations of British leaders had considered it vital to keep control of them in friendly hands. When Belgium achieved its independence, Britain had insisted upon her neutrality and in return had pledged with the other major powers, including Germany, to guarantee her independence and territorial integrity. It is difficult to find plausible reasons for believing that the German war plan, which called for the invasion of France via Belgium, would not trigger British intervention.

Prior to July 1914, Lichnowsky had frequently apprised his government of this situation.[81] During the course of the crisis his warnings became more strident and specific. On July 22, he told Berlin of Grey's hope that Germany would urge Austria to make only moderate demands on Serbia. This prompted the Kaiser to exclaim: "Am I to do that? Wouldn't think of it!...These fellows [the Serbs] have been intriguing and murdering and they must be taken down a peg."[82] Lichnowsky was instructed to inform Grey that Germany did not know what Berchtold was going to demand (which was untrue) and "regarded the question as an internal affair of Austria-Hungary, in which we have no standing to intervene."[83]

As Lichnowsky had surmised, the Austrian ultimatum had an "utterly devastating effect" in London. On July 25, he warned Berlin that Britain could not possibly remain indifferent to a war between Germany and France and implored his superiors to accept the British offer of mediation.[84] The following day, after speaking with Arthur Nicolson, permanent undersecretary of state for foreign affairs, and William Tyrrell, private secretary to Edward Grey, Lichnowsky fired off two more cables urging moderation.[85] In them he declared: "Berlin's hope for localization was completely impossible and must be left out of practical politics."[86] On the 27th, the British cabinet, by now deeply suspicious of Germany's motives, ordered the fleet, already at sea on maneuvers, not to disperse. Lichnowsky reported this news and his belief that Grey and the foreign office now perceived the Serbian question to be a trial of strength between the Triple Alliance and Triple Entente. "England," he warned, "will range herself on the side of France and Russia, in order to show that she does not mean to tolerate a moral or still less a military defeat of her group. If, under these circumstances, it should come to war, we shall have England against us."[87] Lichnowsky courageously urged his government to "spare the German people a struggle in which they have nothing to win and everything to lose."[88]

The conviction that Britain would nevertheless stand aside was so deeply rooted that Lichnowsky's warnings were ignored and he was dismissed as "unduly pessimistic."[89] German leaders remained convinced of British neutrality until the night of July 29. On the 21st, for example, when Sazonov advised Pourtalès that London would disapprove of any Austrian attempt to crush Serbia, the Kaiser wrote in the margin of the dispatch: "He's wrong." As for the Russian foreign minister's warning that Germany and Austria must "reckon with Europe," he commented: "No! Russia yes!"[90] The Kaiser's complacency was encouraged by Bethmann-Hollweg who assured him on the 23rd, the day Austria delivered her ultimatum, that "it was impossible that England would enter the fray."[91] Three days later, following Britain's announcement that her fleet was to remain on a war footing, Jagow told Jules Cambon, who had stated his belief that Britain would intervene immediately in a Franco-German war: "You have your information, we have ours which is quite to the contrary. We are sure of English neutrality."[92]

Because of their unflagging confidence in the possibility of localizing an Austro-Serbian conflict, Bethmann-Hollweg and Jagow made no more than a pretense of supporting the four British offers of joint mediation conveyed to them between July 24 and 28. By giving the appearance of accepting the British proposals the chancellor hoped to convince Britain of Germany's peaceful intentions when in fact he was urging Austria to declare war on Serbia.[93] On July 28 Bethmann-Hollweg cabled Tschirschky, the German minister in Vienna: "You must most carefully avoid giving any impression that we want to hold Austria back. We are concerned only to find a *modus* to enable the realization of Austria-Hungary's aim without at the same time unleashing a world war, and should this after all prove unavoidable, to improve as far as possible the condition under which it is to be waged."[94]

As this dispatch makes clear, the chancellor was willing to accept the risk of war because he believed that Germany could fight it under favorable conditions. One of these conditions was British neutrality, and the following evening Bethmann-Hollweg made a clumsy attempt to secure a pledge to this effect from the British government. Late in the night of July 29, he summoned Sir Edward Goschen, the British ambassador, to his study and assured him that Germany "would not seek any territorial advantage in Europe at the expense of France" if

Britain remained neutral. The chancellor refused to extend his promise to include France's overseas colonies and when queried about Belgium replied only that her territorial integrity would be respected *after* the war "provided Belgium does not take sides against us."[95] Bethmann-Hollweg thus telegraphed Germany's intention of invading France via Belgium! Goschen, grasping the significance of the conversation, was too appalled to raise immediate objections and quickly excused himself in order to cable the incredible proposition to his government.[96]

No sooner had Goschen left Bethmann-Hollweg's study than the chancellor was handed a telegram from Lichnowsky the contents of which temporarily shattered the dearest assumptions of German policy. Grey had repeated his offer of mediation but added that Britain could not remain neutral if France became embroiled in a military conflict with Germany. The relevant portion of the cable read: "...as long as the conflict was confined to Austria and Russia, they [Britain] could stand aside. But if we and France were to become involved, the position would at once be different and the British Government might possibly find itself impelled to take rapid decisions. In this case it would not do to stand aside and wait for a long time, *if war breaks out it will be the greatest catastrophe that the world has ever seen*."[97]

Grey's cable confronted Germany with the apparent choice between forcing caution on Vienna or of accepting a European war with Britain ranged among her adversaries. To this must be added the fact already known to Berlin that Italy, nominally an ally, would remain neutral in such a war. Germany thus faced the prospect of a war fought under the most disadvantageous political conditions. It was incumbent upon German leaders to recognize the extent of their miscalculation and reverse their policy by attempting to restrain Austria.

Despite Vienna's commitment to settle the score once and for all, Germany might still have averted war by putting the Austrians on notice that Germany would not support them if they invaded Serbia. After all, the Austro-Hungarian consensus for war developed only in response to German prodding for decisive action. With Germany subsequently demanding restraint this consensus might have been expected to break up with Tisza and the Hungarians, and possibly the old emperor as well, insisting on a diplomatic resolution to the crisis. It seems likely that Austrian passivity would have forestalled Russian mobilization and might have given European statesmen sufficient time to work out the kind of settlement that was being mooted by Grey.

The above argument is predicated upon a German initiative, an about-face by Berlin that was probably unrealistic to expect. In this connection it must be remembered that Austria was Germany's only important ally. Berlin's encouragement of Viennese truculence had from the very beginning been based on the German belief that Austria's continuing utility as an ally, and perhaps her survival as a great power as well, depended upon her ability to act decisively and forcefully toward Serbia. For Berlin to reverse itself and attempt to restrain Austria would have meant renouncing her primary objective in the crisis and could have been expected to accelerate all the tendencies toward timidity and indecision within Austria that so disturbed the Germans. It would also have done nothing to encourage pro-German feeling among the Austrians. At the very least it would have seriously strained the alliance. German leaders faced a serious dilemma: they had to make a choice between a risky Continental war and what promised to be an equally disastrous peace. Perhaps their unwillingness to shed the illusion of British neutrality is best understood as the result of their inability to face this decision squarely. For only by retaining their belief in British neutrality could German leaders deny the trade-off among important values that this choice necessitated.

Despite the expected consequences of restraining Austria it was a tragedy for Europe that German leaders did not make more than a half-hearted effort to do this. Some historians contend that Germany's failure to reach out for the olive branch reflected a clear and conscious decision to accept war. German policy makers were far from averse to the idea of war, but their behavior during the final stages of the crisis in no way appears to be that of men cooly executing a Byzantine scenario designed to provoke war. The vacillation, uncertainty, and confusion that characterized the performance of at least Germany's political leaders seems rather to indicate considerable emotional turmoil and psychological stress. This in turn was probably the result of the cognitive closure of the German political system, a luxury for which the country was now about to pay a frightful price. Recognition of error might normally have been rectified by compensatory behavior. But in the case of Germany her leader's expectations that an Austro-Serbian war could be localized was so deeply ingrained and information to the contrary so studiously ignored for so long that the German policy makers went into shock when inescapably confronted with the extent of their illusions. Momentarily, German political leaders were incapable of any kind of decisive action and their opportunity to avert catastrophe slipped by.

The chancellor's actions during the 24-hour period beginning on the night of July 29–30 typify the erratic course of German policy at the height of the crisis. Grey's warning on the night of the 29th that Britain could hardly remain neutral in a Franco-German war appears to have had a shattering effect on Bethmann-Hollweg.[98] His response after at least superficially recovering his composure, was to attempt to reverse his policy. He drafted an urgent appeal to Vienna for restraint, dispatched to Tschirschky at 2:55 a.m. on the 30th. The chancellor enclosed almost the entire text of Lichnowsky's cable adding:

> if Austria rejects all mediation, we are faced with a conflagration in which England will fight against us, Italy and Roumania in all probability will not be with us and we should be two against four great powers. As a result of English hostility the brunt of the fighting would fall on Germany.... In these circumstances we must urgently and emphatically suggest to the Vienna cabinet acceptance of mediation on these honorable terms. The responsibility for

the consequence which would arise in case of refusal would be exceedingly grave for Austria and ourselves.[99]

Five minutes later Bethmann-Hollweg sent a second telegram, this time directly to the Ballplatz, urging resumption of direct negotiations between Austria and Russia. The chancellor warned Berchtold in blunt language: "We are prepared to fulfill our duty as allies but we must refuse to allow Vienna to frivolously drag us into a world conflagration without regard to our advice." He also cabled Lichnowsky, advising him to inform Grey that Austria had been "urgently advised" to accept mediation.[100]

The chancellor's approach to Vienna, the product of his panic on the night of July 29–30, was unquestionably sincere. But it was unlikely to force Vienna to reverse its policy toward Serbia. Until now Berlin had done nothing but urge aggressive action upon somewhat reluctant Austrian statesmen. Bethmann-Hollweg, Jagow, and Moltke had pushed Vienna for an immediate declaration of war, rejection of all offers of mediation, and speedy commencement of hostilities against Serbia. In response to this pressure the wavering Austrian cabinet had repressed its collective anxieties, screwed up its courage, and rejected the conciliatory Serbian reply to their ultimatum. On July 28 they declared war on Serbia and the following day the Austrian army began a bombardment of Belgrade. Having finally crossed their psychological Rubicon the Austrian leaders obviously felt a tremendous sense of psychological release and were hardly about to turn back willingly. Berchtold, the Austrian foreign minister, refused to even consider the idea and told the German ambassador so in no uncertain terms.[101]

Berchtold's angry rejoinder indicates that Austrian leaders were unprepared to reconsider their decision to go to war. There is considerable experimental evidence to the effect that reluctance to reopen a decision is proportionate to the difficulty of making it in the first place.[102] There can be no doubt as to the traumatic and politically difficult nature of the Austrian decision to go to war.[103] At the very least, therefore, German efforts to make Vienna change its policy were certain to meet resistance and hostility. Even if pursued with vigor they might not have succeeded in bringing about a reversal of Austrian policy.

Upon learning of Berchtold's negative reply, Bethmann-Hollweg, even without the knowledge of the latest in social science research, must have realized that a far more dramatic *démarche* was required if Austria was to be restrained. Perhaps he should have telephoned Berchtold and personally explained the gravity of the situation to him. Failing that he ought at least to have made a stronger representation by telegram. Austria should have been told that Germany had miscalculated, that war against Britain, France, and Russia was madness and that Berlin was accordingly compelled to withdraw ail promises of support unless Austria immediately agreed to halt her army in Belgrade, open direct negotiations with Russia, and if that failed to submit to mediation by the great powers. This the chancellor could not bring himself to do.

By the morning of the 30th Bethmann-Hollweg's resolve to find a way out of the crisis had weakened considerably. Although he had as yet received no reply to his cable of the night before he made no further attempt to contact Vienna by either telephone or cable. He also began to take seriously Moltke's demand for immediate mobilization, thought necessary by the general staff in light of reports of Russian military preparations.[104] The chancellor even agreed to consider Moltke's proposal for an ultimatum to Russia. But that evening, having still received no answer from Vienna, he decided to make a renewed plea for moderation. This cable, known as telegram 200 to historians, was dispatched at 9 p.m. and merely urged Austria to accept mediation.[105] Such a timorous message was even less likely than the cables of the night before to force reconsideration of war by Vienna.

Two and one-half hours later even this meager effort to preserve the peace was aborted. At 11:20 p.m., Zimmermann, undersecretary of state for foreign affairs, cabled Tschirschky *en clair*: "Please do not for the time being carry out Instruction No. 200."[106] In the interval between the two cables Moltke, having learned of the chancellor's plea for moderation from Zimmermann, had intervened and convinced Bethmann-Hollweg that because of Russian preparations for war Austrian acceptance of mediation would be disastrous to Germany's military position. This was utter nonsense because Berlin did not learn about Russia's general mobilization until 11:40 the following morning. But, Bethmann-Hollweg, unsure of himself and close to physical exhaustion, meekly acceded to Moltke's demand and later even agreed to urge military action on Vienna. He cabled Tschirschky: "I have suspended the execution of Instruction No. 200 because General Staff tells me that military preparations of our neighbors, especially in the east, compel speedy decisions if we do not wish to expose ourselves to surprises. General Staff urgently desires to be informed especially and with the least possible delay of decisions taken in Vienna, especially those of a military nature. Please act quickly so that we receive answer tomorrow."[107]

The chancellor's failure to pursue his *démarche* with Austria and his subsequent capitulation to the military were undoubtedly the result of complex causes about which we can only speculate. On one level his behavior appears to be a classic manifestation of hypervigilance. According to Janis, hyper-vigilance is evoked as a coping pattern when a person realizes that his current course of action threatens serious loss, that a satisfactory alternative may exist but that there is insufficient time in which to make a search for it. Hypervigilant persons make snap judgments, suffer from a mounting feeling of helplessness and are unduly influenced by the behavior of others around them. The situation Bethmann-Hollweg confronted on the night of July 29 met all the criteria for hypervigilance: Grey's cable had revealed the serious risks inherent in German policy; other alternatives, (e.g., restraining Austria) appeared to hold out some prospect of avoiding disaster, but there was insufficient time to think them through and implement a new policy in any coherent manner. The chancellor responded to this situation by becoming hypervigilant and his performance suffered from all the shortcomings associated with high emotional arousal.

To this point our analysis has been entirely situational and has ignored the personality of the policy maker involved. Despite the importance of the situation it is obvious that people respond differently to the same stimuli. Not everyone, for example, panics in response to a fire in a theatre even when those around him are losing their heads. In the case of Bethmann-Hollweg, there are reasons for believing that his emotional state enhanced the probability that he would resort to a hypervigilant pattern of coping.

The chancellor's character contained contradictory elements of motivation and fatalism. Even in the best of circumstances, his behavior was marked by a habitual hesitancy. He usually had to struggle to overcome or suspend his doubts about the feasibility and value of a proposed course of action. Once he did so he became resolute and animated in the execution of the policy as was certainly true of his implementation of the German strategy for the July crisis. In this particular instance at least his resolution may have been unconsciously motivated by his need to overcome the doubts he had about the wisdom of the policy which he and Germany had embarked upon. That he had such doubts is a matter of record and will be discussed elsewhere in this study. Let it suffice to say here that the chancellor was one of the few European leaders who perceived that a Continental war would unleash frightening forces that might destroy the very fabric of European society.

There are additional grounds for supposing that Bethmann-Hollweg went along with the challenge of the Entente for reasons which had nothing to do with its wisdom. For years the military had openly criticized him as a weakling. The generals, and some politicians as well, voiced their fear that he was leading Germany to a "Fashoda," a diplomatic capitulation that carried with it all the pejorative connotations that "Munich" does today and was invoked by hardliners to oppose any policy that incorporated an element of compromise. Fritz Stern suggests that Bethmann-Hollweg's resolution in the July crisis derived at least in part from "a feeling that his policy of so-called conciliatoriness had yielded nothing, strengthened by the weariness of the civilian who had for so long been attacked by his tougher colleagues." In support of this contention Stern observes that "It is a curious fact that in his [Bethmann-Hollweg's] postwar memoirs he defended his July course by arguing that the opposite course—accomodation of Russia—would have amounted to 'self-castration' [*Selbstentmannung*]—an unconscious allusion perhaps to frequent charges of civilian effeminacy."[108]

To the extent that the chancellor had struggled to suppress both his intellectual doubts about and emotional disinclination toward the course of action to which he was now committed, he became anxiety-ridden about its outcome. For the same reason, he was unresponsive to warnings that called the success of the policy into question. When, following the receipt of Grey's warning on the night of the 29th, he realized that his policy was doomed to fail, he panicked and began to search frantically for a means of escape. But, as is often the case with hypervigilant behavior, his solutions were not well conceived or skillfully implemented. In this connection, it might have been relevant that the chancellor was only very recently bereaved. His unsettled emotional state—his colleagues described him as extremely melancholy—may have contributed to his failure to cope effectively with the challenge posed by the crisis.

If Bethmann-Hollweg vacillated between confidence and pessimistic fatalism, the Kaiser was moody and sometimes outspokenly bellicose. In the opinion of those who knew him best, the Kaiser's aggressiveness was a facade designed to compensate for his own feelings of inadequacy. Bülow expressed the view that:

> William II did not want war. He feared it. His bellicose marginal notes prove nothing. His exaggerations were mainly meant to ring in the ears of privy councillors at the foreign office, just as his more menacing jingo speeches were intended to give the foreigner the impression that here was another Frederick the Great or Napoleon.... William II did not want war, if only because he did not trust his nerves not to give way under the strain of any really critical situation. The moment there was danger His Majesty would become uncomfortably conscious that he could never lead any army in the field.... He was well aware that he was neurasthenic, without real capacity as a general, and still less able, in spite of his naval hobby, to have led a squadron or even captained a ship.[109]

His rhetoric aside, the Kaiser often exercised a restraining influence on German military and political leaders. Admiral Tirpitz observed that "When the Emperor did not consider the peace to be threatened he liked to give full play to his reminiscences of famous ancestors." But, "in moments which he realized to be critical he proceeded with extraordinary caution."[110] The Kaiser's underlying caution was apparent in the Moroccan crises of 1906 and 1911; when confronted with the possibility of war with Britain, the Kaiser had prudently backed down. In July 1914 the Kaiser had declared a similar desire for peace when he fully grasped the gravity of the situation, but he proved unequal to the task of reorienting Germany's foreign policy.

From July 5 through 27 the Kaiser, convinced of the feasibility of localizing the conflict, gave his unconditional support to Austria. During these weeks Wilhelm was in his most blustering mood. He derided Berchtold as a "donkey" for showing too much caution and rejected all suggestions of great power mediation as unwarranted British meddling in the internal affairs of Austria-Hungary.[111] On July 27, in apparent response to Lichnowsky's warnings from London—although the foreign office had edited out many of his most trenchant observations in the copies of his cables they sent to the palace—Wilhelm began to moderate his position and expressed himself in favor of peace.[112] In contrast to his earlier pugnacious swaggering, his marginalia now reflected concern for finding a way out of the crisis.

The Kaiser's change of mood was quite apparent to Jagow and Bethmann-Hollweg. The two men conspired to withhold from the Kaiser Serbia's reply to Austria's ultimatum until they thought it too late for him to intervene and perhaps squash the momentarily expected Austrian declaration of war. When Wilhelm finally read the Serbian note early on the morning of the 28th he hailed it as "a brilliant achievement in a time limit of only forty-eight hours!" "It is more than one could have expected! A great moral success for Vienna; but with it all reason for war is gone and Giesl [the Austrian Ambassador to Serbia] ought to have quietly stayed on in Belgrade! After that I should never have ordered mobilization."[113]

Considering his prior pledges of unwavering support to Vienna, the Kaiser could not now bring himself to ask Austria to reverse her policy. Instead, he sought some compromise that would enable her to humiliate Serbia yet forestall Russian, French, and ultimately British intervention. The solution he hit upon was the ill-fated but nevertheless ingenious idea of a "Halt in Belgrade." Austria, the Kaiser hastened to inform Jagow, should occupy Belgrade as "security" for the enforcement of the Austrian demands already accepted by Serbia. This would appease Austrian national sentiment and the honor of her army.[114] Coupled with a statement by Austria that she neither planned to crush Serbia nor annex any territory, the Kaiser's formula might have been the first step on the path toward some kind of diplomatic settlement if Bethmann-Hollweg and Jagow had responded energetically and insisted upon Austrian acquiescence while pressing the other powers for support.[115] But on the 28th, the chancellor and the foreign minister were still convinced of their ability to localize the conflict. Bethmann-Hollweg was anxious to encourage, not forestall, an Austrian declaration of war and postponed sending the Kaiser's formula to Vienna until 10:15 that evening. He also modified the proposal to ensure that even if Austria deigned to accept it Russia almost certainly would not.[116]

Throughout the day of the 29th, the Kaiser had high hopes that his idea of a halt in Belgrade would preserve the peace of Europe. Nothing could have been further from the truth. Wilhelm was unaware of the true content of Bethman-Hollweg's cable to Vienna, or of Pourtalès' cable reporting Russia's partial mobilization and finally of Grey's stern warning received the night before. Albertini concludes: "No monarch believing himself to hold the threads of the situation could possibly have been more ill-informed, more devoid of any grasp of the situation, and this was so because Wilhelm did not maintain contact with his subordinates and had no knowledge of what they were doing."[117] The Kaiser's ignorance was due in part to deliberate efforts by Jagow, Moltke, and Bethmann-Hollweg to deceive their sovereign by distorting and withholding information—the three above-mentioned cables being cases in point. But it is also true that as the crisis became more acute Wilhelm voluntarily moved to the periphery of German decision making by taking up residence in Potsdam, 25 miles away from the nerve center of German foreign policy in the Wilhelmstrasse.

The Kaiser's isolation on July 30 can be considered even more irresponsible in light of the threatening news he received during the course of the day. Upon waking, he was handed a cable from the czar informing him of Russia's partial mobilization.[118] A few minutes later he read an alarmist report from the German naval attaché in London warning that "the British fleet will launch an instant and immediate attack on us at sea if it comes to war between us and France."[119]

At 1 p.m. he finally learned of Lichnowsky's cable of the night before conveying Grey's threat to intervene in a Franco-German war. Finally, at 7 p.m., the Kaiser received word that Sazonov had declared that Russia's partial mobilization could not be revoked.[120] Wilhelm was devastated by the turn of events.[121] His isolation, otherwise incomprehensible, is best interpreted as a desperate but unsatisfactory effort to cope with the psychological stress associated with the deepening crisis and growing prospect of war.

The Kaiser actually appears to have suffered an acute anxiety reaction on July 30. He was withdrawn and irritable, and displayed a sense of helplessness. He also exaggerated the gravity of the political situation and his own inability to do anything about it. His incredible misinterpretation that morning of the czar's cable is illustrative of his impaired cognitive functioning. The message merely repeated the already known fact that Russia had implemented military preparations against Austria-Hungary, adding that these measures had commenced five days previously. Wilhelm misread the cable and concluded that Russia had begun mobilizing against *Germany* five days earlier. The Kaiser instantly reverted to a mood of profound despair and aggressiveness. He dropped his interest in mediation and talked instead of mobilization in order to prevent Russia from gaining the upper hand. "I cannot commit myself to mediation any more," he wrote on the telegram, "since the Czar, who appealed for it, has at the same time been secretly mobilizing behind my back. It is only a maneuver to keep us dangling and increase the lead he has already gained over us. My task is at an end."[122] Bethmann-Hollweg's accompanying note received a similar annotation.[123]

Wilhelm's paranoid response was perhaps indicative of his need to resort to more extreme defense mechanisms to cope with the free-floating anxiety triggered by the breakdown of his former defenses. No longer able to deny the probability of Russian, French, and British intervention, yet unable to admit just how grievously he had miscalculated, Wilhelm chose instead to escape from his own aggressiveness and its consequences by portraying Germany and himself as helpless victims of the aggressive designs of other powers. Paranoid delusions of persecution are typically triggered by environmental or interpersonal stress, although they tend to occur only in persons who have formerly maintained an unstable psychological balance by resorting to denial or other defense mechanisms.[124] The Kaiser was such a person. He had long suffered from a psychophysiological disorder referred to by Freud and others as neurasthenia.[125] This neurosis is a manifestation of inability to cope with emotional conflicts and feelings of inferiority. In Wilheim's case, his feelings of inadequacy might be traced to the burden of living up to the accomplishments of his illustrious forebears. His well known physical defect, a shriveled left arm, certainly did nothing to alleviate whatever feelings of inferiority he felt. Unable to accept responsibility for his failure to localize the Austro-Serbian conflict, a failure which might be seen as confirmation of his own feared inadequacy, the Kaiser resorted to paranoid projection to cope with a reality that was in every sense too threatening for him to face honestly.

Projection was obvious in the minutes hastily scribbled by the Kaiser on the dispatches he received during the course of July 30. His response to Grey's warning is a striking case in point:

> England shows her hand at the moment when she thinks we are cornered and, in a manner of speaking, done for. The low-down shopkeeping knaves have been trying to take us in with banquets and speeches. The grossest deception is the King's message to me by Henry: 'We shall remain neutral and try to keep out of this as long as possible.' Grey makes the king out a liar and these words to Lichnowsky are utterances of the bad conscience he has for deceiving us. What is more, it is a threat combined with bluff, meant to detach us from Austria, stop our mobilizing and make us take the blame for war. He knows quite well that if he says a single, sharp, deterrent word to Paris or St. Petersburg and admonishes them to remain neutral, both will at once keep quiet. But he takes good care not to say the word and threatens us instead! Contemptible scoundrel! England *alone* bears the responsibility for peace or war, not we now! That must be made publicly clear.[126]

The full extent of the Kaiser's paranoia was revealed that evening in his lengthy minute on Pourtalès' cable reporting that Russia's partial mobilization (directed against Austria) could not be revoked.[127] War now seemed unavoidable and a catastrophe for which the Kaiser bore a fair share of responsibility. Since his accession to the throne he had repeatedly attempted to humiliate France and Russia and had antagonized Britain by senselessly challenging her naval superiority. His aggressive words even more than his policies had encouraged Germany's neighbors to shelve their own quarrels and band together to protect themselves. During the course of the crisis itself, the Kaiser had given a free hand to Austria and spurned all British offers of mediation. Unable to admit the bankruptcy of his policy, the Kaiser sought release in a traumatic projective discharge. This paroxysm of fury, worth quoting at length for what it reveals about the workings of an unsettled mind, was directed against Britain whom Wilhelm now accused of having worked painstakingly over the years to bring about Germany's destruction:

> Irresponsibility and weakness are to plunge the world into the most terrible war, aimed in the last resort at ruining Germany. For no doubt remains in my mind: England, Russia, and France—basing themselves on our *casus foederis* in relation to Austria—are in league to wage a war of annihilation against us, taking the Austro-Serbian conflict as a pretext. . . . In other words, we are either basely to betray our ally and leave him a prey to Russia—thereby breaking up the Triple Alliance—or, for our loyalty to the alliance, be fallen upon by the combined Triple *Entente* and punished.
>
> That is the real naked situation in a nutshell, slowly and surely prepared by Edward VII, carried forward and systematically developed in disavowed

conversations held by England with Paris and St. Petersburg; finally brought to a conclusion and put into operation by George V. The stupidity and clumsiness of our ally has been turned into a noose for our necks. So the famous 'encirclement of Germany' has at last become a complete actuality.

Edward VII in the grave is still stronger than I who am alive! And to think there have been people who believed England could be won over or pacified by this or that petty measure!!! Ceaselessly, relentlessly, she has pursued her aim by notes, proposals of [naval] holidays, scares, Haldane, etc. And we have fallen into the snare and have even introduced the keel-for-keel rate of naval construction in the pathetic hope of pacifying England thereby!!!… Now we have the English so-called thanks for it! … Now this whole trickery must be ruthlessly exposed and the mask of Christian pacifism roughly and publicly torn from the face [of Britain] and the pharisaical peace sham put in the pillory!! And our consuls in Turkey and India, agents, etc., must fire the whole Mohammedan world to fierce revolt against this hateful, lying, unprincipled nation of shopkeepers; for if we are to bleed to death, England will at least lose India.[128]

Despite Bülow's disclaimer that the Kaiser's marginalia were meant to ring in the ears of privy councillors, his diatribes of July 30 could not but influence Bethmann-Hollweg, unsure as the chancellor was as to the proper course of policy to pursue.[129] Moltke and the chancellor were both aware of Wilhelm's latest change of mood and Moltke, who had previously lain low when the emperor favored mediation, now pushed hard for military action.[130] It is probable that Bethmann-Hollweg's failure to follow up on his demand that Vienna moderate her policy and his later capitulation to Moltke were at least in part a response to his sovereign's dramatic about-face.[131] In this connection it should be remembered that an important behavioral attribute of hypervigilant persons is their unusual responsiveness to the directions or will of others. The Kaiser's psychological self-indulgence may thus have exercised an even greater influence upon his chancellor than it normally would have. If so, it had a tragic impact upon the course of German policy.

By the morning of the 31st, the Kaiser had temporarily recovered his composure and unaware of the decisions made in Berlin the previous evening expressed renewed interest in peace![132] After a leisurely lunch, Wilhelm departed from Potsdam for Berlin, concerned about taking security measures against Russia. Upon arriving, he should have been shocked by the state of affairs he discovered. His chief of staff and chancellor were near panic and discussing the need for the most desperate measures. Rumors of Russian mobilization brought back to Germany by agents of the general staff had enabled Moltke to convince Bethmann-Hollweg to agree to proclamation of *Kriegsgefahrzustand* (measures preparatory to mobilization) and the dispatch of an ultimatum to Russia. The ultimatum, they realized, was certain to be rejected and would have to be followed by a declaration of war.[133] Confronted with a consensus among his advisors for military action,

Wilhelm lacked the will to oppose their premature and disastrous recommendations. His assent set in motion the chain of events that led to war.[134]

Kriegsgefahrzustand was proclaimed and an ultimatum sent to Russia giving her 12 hours to agree to halt all military preparations against Germany and Austria-Hungary. On the following day, August 1, France and Germany mobilized and Germany declared war on Russia. On August 2, Germany invaded Luxembourg and demanded the right to cross Belgian territory, a request the Belgian government naturally denied. On August 3, Germany invaded Belgium and declared war on France. On August 4, Britain, having received no reply to her ultimatum, declared war on Germany.

It is indicative of the air of unreality that prevailed in Berlin that right up to and even after the British declaration of war the chancellor and Kaiser continued to entertain hopes of British neutrality.[135] On the 31st, for example, Bethmann-Hollweg dispatched a cable to Lichnowsky imploring him to induce the English press to treat Germany's actions sympathetically.[136] On August 1, the Kaiser took heart in response to a cable from Lichnowsky raising the possibility of French neutrality if Germany refrained from attacking her.[137] Although it was totally unrealistic to expect France to stand aside while Germany attacked Russia and almost inconceivable that Moltke would agree to shift his offensive to the Eastern front, a contingency for which the general staff was totally unprepared, the Kaiser was overjoyed. He sent for champagne![138]

What began as a diplomatic offensive passed beyond the bounds of politics because German political leaders did not possess either the courage or good sense to alter their policy in midcrisis. Inescapably confronted with the fact that an Austro-Serbian war could not be localized the chancellor and the Kaiser were overcome by anxiety. Neither man was fully willing to admit the probable outcome of continued support of Austrian bellicosity nor prepared to accept the responsibility for radical reorientation of German policy. Their actions from the fateful night of July 29–30 to the outbreak of war betrayed irresolution, bewilderment, and loss of self-confidence. The Kaiser oscillated between moods of profound optimism and despair. His hypervigilant chancellor vacillated between the very extremes of available policy options. At first appalled by the thought of a European war, he sought to restrain Austria. Later, influenced by Moltke, he again urged military action upon Vienna. Both Kaiser and chancellor ultimately lapsed into passive acceptance of the inevitability of war although they continued to clutch at the hope of British neutrality the way a drowning man grasps a life preserver. Their last minute diplomatic efforts were not designed to prevent war but rather to cast the blame for it on Russia. This in turn helped to make their expectation of war self-fulfilling.

The case study suggests that the cognitive distortions of German political leaders were a root cause of the failure of German policy. They led in the first place to the adoption of an unrealistic strategy based as it was on erroneous perceptions of how the other powers would respond to an Austrian attempt to subjugate Serbia. They were also responsible for the failure of German leaders to realize the extent of their miscalculations as the crisis unfolded. Evidence to this effect was either suppressed or ignored until the very dénouement of the crisis. Finally, when their cherished illusions were shattered, German leaders suffered a dramatic loss of self-confidence which resulted in erratic and irresponsible behavior.

The near paralysis of the German political leadership amounted to an abdication of control over the course of policy during the most fateful hours of the crisis. This breakdown in political decision making meant not only that German policy was on a predestined course but that the military, pushing for mobilization, met only half-hearted resistance from political leaders and effectively made the decisions that plunged Europe into a catastrophic war which hardly anyone desired and probably could have been avoided.

The German experience points to the conclusion that the most crucial consideration affecting the outcome of brinkmanship crises is the ability of governments to *learn* from the results of their past behavior and to *modify* their subsequent policies in response. Acute international crises place a special premium on this ability because crisis strategies are based on a set of prior expectations about the likely behavior of other actors the validity of which only becomes apparent during the course of the crisis itself. If these expectations prove erroneous, policy must be adjusted accordingly. Moreover, this must be done with dispatch because crisis decision making is often subject to severe time constraints. Policy must reflect a rapid and ongoing learning process for it to maximize the probability of success. As learning and steering capacity diminish, policy comes to resemble a stone rolling downhill; it can neither be recalled nor can its path be altered. If the assumptions underlying such policy are incorrect, as was the case with Germany in 1914, the crisis may well result in war despite contrary desires on the part of policy makers.

Notes

1 For example, Herbert A. Simon, *Administrative Behavior* (New York: Free Press, 1946); Charles E. Lindbloom, "The Science of 'Muddling Through,'" *Public Administration* 19 (Spring 1959): 74–88; Richard Cyert and James March, *A Behavioral Theory of the Firm* (Englewood Cliffs, NJ: Prentice–Hall, 1963); Graham T. Allison, *Essence of Decision: Explaining the Cuban Missile Crisis* (Boston: Little, Brown, 1971); John D. Steinbruner, *The Cybernetic Theory of Decision* (Princeton, NJ: Princeton University Press, 1974).

2 Donald R. Kinder and Janet A. Weiss, "In Lieu of Rationality: Psychological Perspectives on Foreign Policy Decision Making," *Journal of Conflict Resolution, 22* (December 1978): 707–35, offer a thoughtful analysis of the prospects for a psychological paradigm of decision making. Following a review of the relevant literature the authors identify four common themes they believe will be central to any paradigm. These are (1) the striving for cognitive consistency and its conservative impact upon perception and information processing, (2) systematic biases in causal analysis, (3) distorting effects of emotional stress, and (4) the cognitive construction of order and predictability within a disorderly and uncertain environment.

3 In addition, see G. A. Miller, "The Magical Number Seven Plus or Minus Two: Some Limits on Our Capability for Processing Information," *Psychological Review, 63* (March 1956): 81–94; K. R. Hammond, C. J. Hursch, and F. J. Todd, "Analyzing the Components of Clinical Judgements," *Psychological Review, 71* (November 1964): 438–56; L. R. Goldberg, "Simple Models or Simple Processes? Some Research on Clinical Judgements," *American Psychologist, 23* (July 1968): 483–96; N. Wiggins and E. S. Kohen, "Man vs. Model of Man Revisited: The Forecasting of Graduate School Success," *Journal of Personality and Social Psychology, 19* (July 1971): 100–6. The experimental literature is reviewed by Robert P. Abelson, "Social Psychology's Rational Man," in S. I. Benn and G. W. Mortimore, eds., *Rationality and the Social Sciences: Contributions to the Philosophy and Methodology of the Social Sciences* (Boston: Routledge & Kegan Paul, 1976), pp. 59–89; Melvin Manis, "Cognitive Social Psychology and Attitude Change," *American Behavioral Scientist, 21* (May–June 1978): 675–90.

4 Robert P. Abelson and Milton Rosenberg, "Symbolic Psycho–Logic," *Behavioral Science, 3* (January 1958): 1–13; Robert P. Abelson, "Psychological Implication," in Robert P. Abelson et al., *Theories of Cognitive Consistency: A Sourcebook* (Chicago: Rand McNally, 1968), pp. 112–39, and "Social Psychology's Rational Man," pp. 59–89

5 Abelson and Rosenberg, in "Symbolic Psycho–Logic," p. 5, define a consistent structure as one in which "All relations among 'good elements' [i.e., those that are positively valued] are positive (or null), all relations among 'bad elements' [i.e., those that are negatively valued] are positive (or null), and all relations among good and bad elements are negative (or null)." The literature on cognitive consistency is considerable. For discussion of this literature, see, Robert Zajonc, "Cognitive Theories in Social Psychology," in Gardner Lindzey and Elliot Aaronson, eds., *The Handbook of Social Psychology*, 2nd ed. (Reading, MA.: Addison–Wesley, 1968), vol. 1, pp. 345–53; Abelson et al., *Theories of Cognitive Consistency: A Sourcebook;* Stevan Sherman and Robert Wolosin, "Cognitive Biases in a Recognition Task" *Journal of Personality, 41* (September 1973): 395–411; Jesse Delia and Walter Crockett, "Social Schemas, Cognitive Complexity, and the Learning of Social Structures," *Journal of Personality, 41* (September 1973): 412–29.

6 The various explanations for cognitive consistency are discussed by Norman Feather, "A Structural Balance Approach to the Analysis of Communication Effects," in Leonard Berkowitz, ed., *Advances in Experimental Social Psychology* (New York: Academic Press, 1967), vol. 3, pp. 99–165.

7 Robert Jervis, "Hypotheses on Misperception," *World Politics* 20 (April 1968): 454–79, and *Perception and Misperception in International Politics* (Princeton, NJ: Princeton University Press, 1976). For other analyses by political scientists of the implications of cognitive processes for decision making, see Robert Axelrod, *Framework for a General Theory of Cognition and Choice* (Berkeley, CA: Institute of International Studies, 1972), and Robert Axelrod, ed., *Structure of Decision: The Cognitive Maps of Political Elites* (Princeton, NJ: Princeton University Press, 1976); Steinbruner, *The Cybernetic Theory of Decision.*

8 Jervis, *Perception and Misperception in International Politics*, pp. 117–24,187,262–70. Jervis' argument is reminiscent of V. O. Key's thesis that dramatic historical events like the civil war and the great depression significantly influenced the forma-

tion of party identification which then endured long after the event and the party's response to it. "A Theory of Critical Elections," *Journal of Politics, 17* (February 1955): 3–18.

9 Ibid., pp. 239–48.

10 Ibid., pp. 17–42, et passim.

11 Ibid., pp. 187–91.

12 Ibid., pp. 191–95.

13 Ibid., pp. 193–95.

14 Ibid., pp. 128–43.

15 Leon Festinger, *A Theory of Cognitive Dissonance* (Stanford, CA: Stanford University Press, 1957), and Leon Festinger, ed., *Conflict, Decision, and Dissonance* (Stanford, CA: Stanford University Press, 1964); also Jack W. Brehm and Arthur Cohen, *Explorations in Cognitive Dissonance* (New York: Wiley, 1962); Alliot Aronson, "The Theory of Cognitive Dissonance," in Berkowitz, *Advances in Experimental Social Psychology*, vol. 4, pp. 15–17; Robert A. Wicklund and Jack W. Brehm, *Perspectives on Cognitive Dissonance* (Hillsdale, N.J.: Erlbaum, 1976). For a discussion of the literature, see, Jervis, *Perception and Misperception in International Politics*, pp. 382–406; Irving L. Janis and Leon Mann, *Decision Making: A Psychological Analysis of Conflict, Choice, and Commitment* (New York: Free Press, 1977), pp. 309–38, 437–40.

16 Janis and Mann, in *Decision Making*, pp. 81–105, disagree with Festinger on this point. They describe the spreading of alternatives as a form of bolstering, which they see motivated by the need to ward off the stress of decisional conflict and only secondarily by a need to maintain cognitive consistency. Accordingly, they argue for the existence of predecisional bolstering, especially in instances where the conflicted policymaker believes that he already possesses all the relevant information that he will receive.

17 Jervis, *Perception and Misperception in International Politics*, pp. 382–406.

18 Harold Lieff, "Anxiety Reactions," in Alfred Freedman and Harold Kaplan, eds., *Comprehensive Textbook of Psychiatry* (Baltimore: Williams & Wilkins, 1967), pp. 859–60.

19 Janis and Mann, *Decision making*, p. 15.

20 Ibid., pp. 55–56.

21 Ibid., pp. 56–57, 73.

22 Ibid., pp. 57–58, 74, 107–33.

23 Ibid., pp. 74–95.

24 Ibid., pp. 76–79.

25 Ibid., pp. 59–60, 205.

26 Ibid., pp. 62–63.

27 Not only do the authors advance different explanations for cognitive failures, they also minimize the importance of the psychological principles upon which the opposing explanation is based. Jervis, pp. 356–81, devotes a chapter to analyzing the influence of desires and fears upon perceptions and concludes that "the conventional wisdom that wishful thinking pervades political decision making is not supported by the evidence from either experimental or natural settings." For their part, Janis and Mann, p. 85, insist that cognitive consistency may be "a weak need" in many individuals. The effort by these analysts to discredit the principles underlying a different approach is certainly consistent with the principle of cognitive consistency.

28 Jervis, *Perception and Misperception in International Politics*, pp. 227–28.
29 Sir Roger Keyes, *Amphibious Warfare and Combined Operations* (New York: Macmillan, 1943), p. 53; William D. Puleston, *The Dardanelles Expedition* (Annapolis, MD: United Stales Naval Institute, 1927), pp. 1–56. No less of a figure than R. H. Liddell Hart, in *The Defence of Britain* (London: Faber & Faber, 1939), p. 130, concluded that Gallipoli had demonstrated the near impossibility of modern amphibious warfare. He thought that such operations were even more difficult since the advent of airpower. The same argument was made by Alexander Kiralfy, "Sea Power in the Eastern War," *Brassey's Naval Annual, 1942* (London: Brassey's, 1942), pp. 150–60; For a discussion of the development of amphibious warfare in the United States, see, Jeter A. Isely and Philip A. Crowl, *The United States Marines and Amphibious War: Its Theory and Its Practice in the Pacific* (Princeton, NJ: Princeton University Press, 1951), pp. 3–44.
30 See Allison, *Essence of Decision*, pp. 67–100, for a discussion of organizational theory. This particular aspect of the theory is discussed in greater detail by Harold Wilensky, *Organizational Intelligence: Knowledge and Policy in Government and Industry* (New York: Basic Books, 1967), pp. 75–94.
31 Arthur M. Schlesinger, Jr., *A Thousand Days* (Boston: Houghton, Mifflin, 1965), pp. 255–58, 289, 293, 297; Theodore C. Sorensen, *Kennedy* (New York: Harper & Row, 1965), pp. 294–309; Peter C. Wyden, *The Bay of Pigs: The Untold Story* (New York: Simon & Shuster, 1979), pp. 323–24.
32 See, Hans J. Morgenthau, "The Unfinished Business of United States Foreign Policy," *Wisconsin Idea*, Fall 1953 and, "Vietnam: Another Korea?" *Commentary*, May 1962, in Hans J. Morgenthau, *Politics in the Twentieth Century*, vol. 2: *The Impasse of American Foreign Policy* (Chicago: University of Chicago Press, 1962), pp. 8–16, 365–75; John Lukacs, *A New History of the Cold War*, 3d rev. ed. (Garden City, NY: Doubleday, 1966), pp. 69–71, 161, 167; Robert E. Osgood, *Alliances and American Foreign Policy* (Baltimore: Johns Hopkins University Press, 1968), pp. 75–77; Stanley Hoffman, *Gulliver's Troubles, or the Setting of American Foreign Policy* (New York: McGraw-Hill, 1968), pp. 140,153–54; James A. Nathan and James K. Oliver, *United States Foreign Policy and World Order* (Boston: Little, Brown, 1976); John Lewis Gaddis, *Russia, the Soviet Union, and the United States: An Interpretive History* (New York: Wiley, 1978), pp. 187–89, 193–200, 207–13; Leslie H. Gelb with Richard K. Betts, *The Irony of Vietnam: The System Worked* (Washington, D.C.: Brookings Institution, 1979), pp. 78–79, 181–82.
33 Jervis, *Perception and Misperception in International Politics*, pp. 128–30.
34 Ibid., pp. 382–93.
35 Janis and Mann, *Decision Making*, pp. 79–80, 91–95.
36 Jervis, *Perception and Misperception in International Politics*, pp. 187–202.
37 Janis and Mann, *Decision Making*, pp. 74–79.
38 Richard W. Cottam, in *Foreign Policy Motivation: A General Theory and a Case Study* (Pittsburgh: University of Pittsburgh Press, 1977), pp. 10–11, argues that the role structure of foreign policy bureaucracy is likely to mirror the needs of policy as they were perceived when those roles were structured. But once the structure is created a bureaucratic interest develops in perpetuating the world view upon which that structure is based. "Even extraordinarily competent bureaucrats ... will tend to bring congruence to role and perceptions. Indeed, a central ingredient of bureaucratic inertia is the rigidification of perceptual assumptions."

39   See D. F. Fleming, in *The Cold War and its Origins, 1917–1960*, 2 vols. (Garden City, NY: Doubleday, 1961), Walter La Febre, in *America, Russia, and the Cold War, 1945–1966* (New York: Wiley, 1968), and Nathan and Oliver, in *United States Foreign Policy*, all of whom stress the importance of initial American images of the Soviet Union in shaping subsequent policy. For an interesting theoretical analysis of this problem, see, Glenn H. Snyder, " 'Prisoner's Dilemma' and 'Chicken' Models in International Politics," *International Studies Quarterly, 15* (March 1971): 66–103; Jervis, in *Perception and Misperception in International Politics*, pp. 58–111, also stresses the self-fulfilling nature of foreign policy judgements as to the intentions of other nations.

40   Karl W. Deutsch, *The Nerves of Government* (New York: Free Press, 1963), p. 215.

41   The classic description of defense mechanisms is Anna Freud, *The Ego and the Mechanisms of Defense* 1936, (New York: International Universities Press, 1953).

42   Sigmund Freud distinguished between "preconscious" and "unconscious" emotional impulses. The former refer to motivations that a person is unaware of at the time he acts but is capable of recognizing when given appropriate cues by others. Preconscious impulses are more likely to be counteracted by corrective information than are unconscious ones. The latter derive from fundamental sexual and aggressive drives and are kept from consciousness by repression and other defense mechanisms. Janis and Mann, in *Decision Making*, pp. 95–100, argue that preconscious emotional impulses, triggered by fatigue, alcohol, or crowd excitement, prompt impulsive and irrational choices later regretted by the policy maker.

43   Sigmund Freud, *The Problem of Anxiety* (New York: Norton, 1936); Norman A. Cameron, "Paranoid Reactions," Harold Lieff, "Anxiety Reactions," John C. Nemiah, "Conversion Reactions," and Louis J. West, "Dissociative Reactions," in Freedman and Kaplan, *Comprehensive Textbook of Psychiatry*, pp. 665–76, 875–85.

44   Gross stress can itself produce an insoluble conflict of vital goals or needs. For some of the literature on this subject, see, Abraham Kardiner and H. Spiegel, *War, Stress, and Neurotic Illness* (New York: Harper & Row, 1941); Robert J. Weiss and Henry E. Payson, "Gross Stress Reaction," and Norman Q. Brill, "Gross Stress Reaction: Traumatic War Neuroses," in Freedman and Kaplan, *Comprehensive Textbook of Psychiatry*, pp. 1027–31, 1031–35; Charles D. Spielberger and Irving G. Sarason, eds., *Stress and Anxiety*, 2 vols. (New York: Wiley, 1975).

45   The American Psychiatric Association's *Diagnostic and Statistical Manual, Mental Disorders* (Washington: American Psychiatric Association, 1952), p. 32, defines anxiety reaction as follows: "In this kind of reaction the anxiety is diffuse and not restricted to definite situations or objects, as in the case of phobic reactions. It is not controlled by any specific psychological defense mechanism as in other psycho-neurotic reactions. This reaction is characterized by anxious expectation and frequently associated with somatic symptomatology. The condition is to be differentiated from normal apprehensiveness or fear."

46   Lieff, "Anxiety Reactions," p. 865.

47   Eugen Kahn, "The Stun," *American Journal of Psychiatry* 118 (February 1962): 702–4.

48   Sigmund Freud, "The Neuro-Psychoses of Defense," (1894) and "Further Remarks on the Neuro-Psychoses of Defense," in, *The Standard Edition of the Complete Psychological Works of Sigmund Freud* (London: Hogarth, 1962), vol. 3, pp. 43–68,

159–85; Norman A. Cameron, "Paranoid Conditions and Paranoia," in Silvano Arieti and Eugene B. Brody, eds., *American Handbook of Psychiatry: Adult Clinical Psychiatry*, 2d ed. (New York: Basic Books, 1974), pp. 675–93; Daniel S. Jaffe, "The Mechanisms of Projection: Its Dual Role in Object Relations," *International Journal of Psycho-Analysis, 49* (1968), part 4, pp. 662–77; D. Swanson, P. Bohnert, and J. Smith, *The Paranoid* (Boston: Little, Brown, 1970).

49   The American Psychiatric Association's *Diagnostic and Statistical Manual, Mental Disorders*, p. 32, defines dissociative reaction as follows: "This reaction represents a type of gross personality distortion, the basis of which is a neurotic disturbance, although the diffuse dissociation seen in some cases may occasionally appear psychotic. The personality disorganization may result in running or 'freezing.' The repressed impulse giving rise to the anxiety may be discharged by, or deflected into, various symptomatic expressions, such as depersonalization, dissociated personality, stupor, fugue, amnesia, dream state, somnambulism, etc."

50   Louis J. West, in Freedman and Kaplan, *Comprehensive Textbook of Psychiatry*, p. 889.

51   Chapter 2 of Richard Ned Lebow, *Between Peace and War: The Nature of International Crisis* (Baltimore: Johns Hopkins University Press, 1981) offers an analysis of German policy in the early stages of the crisis.

52   Bethmann-Hollweg and Jagow to the ambassadors in Petersburg, Paris, and London, July 21, 1914. *the deutschen Dokumente zum Kriegsausbruch* 1914, ed. Max von Montgelas and Walter Schücking, 3 vols. (Berlin: Deutsche Verlagsgesellschaft für Politik und Geschichte, 1922), (hereafter cited as D.D.), vol. 1, no. 100.

53   On July 16, for example, the chancellor cabled Siegfried von Rodern, minister for Alsace-Lorraine: "We have grounds to assume and cannot but wish, that France, at the moment burdened with all sorts of cares, will do everything to restrain Russia from intervention....If we succeeded in not only keeping France quiet herself but in getting her to enjoin peace on St. Petersburg, this will have a repercussion on the Franco-Russian alliance highly favorable to ourselves." D. D. 1, no. 58; Konrad H. Jarausch, in "The Illusion of Limited War: Chancellor Bethmann-Hollweg's Calculated Risk, July 1914," *Journal of Central European History* 2 (March 1969): 48–76, and Fritz Stern, in "Bethmann Hollweg and the War: The Limits of Responsibility," in Leonard Kreiger and Fritz Stern, eds., *The Responsibility of Power: Historical Essays in Honor of Hajo Holborn* (Garden City, NY: Doubleday, 1969), pp. 271–307, attempt to reconstruct the chancellor's attitudes and objectives during the crisis on the basis of the diary entries of Kurt Riezler, his long-standing political confidant and secretary. Jarausch argues that Bethmann-Hollweg risked a general war in the hope and expectation of breaking up the Entente and bringing about a new alignment more favorable to Germany. Fritz Stern, in fundamental agreement with Jarausch, states that "The Riezler diary sustains the view that Bethmann in early July had resolved on a forward course; by means of forceful diplomacy and a local Austrian war against Serbia he intended to detach England or Russia from the Entente or—if that failed— to risk a general war over an opportune issue at a still opportune moment." More general interpretations of Bethmann-Hollweg's policy are to be found in Karl Dietrich Erdmann, "Zur Beurteilung Bethmann Hollwegs," *Geschichte in Wissenschaft und Unterricht* 15 (September 1964): 525–40, and Andreas Hillgruber, "Riezler's Theorie des kalkulierten Risikos und Bethmann Hollwegs politische Konzeption

in der Julikrise 1914,"*Historische Zeitschrift, 202* (April 1966): 333–351. The latter analyzes the chancellor's crisis policy in terms of Riezler's prewar writings.

54　On July 17, Biederman, Saxon chargé d'affaires in Berlin, reported to Dresden: "If, contrary to expectations, Austria were obliged to take measures against Serbia, people here reckon on a localization of the conflict, because England is altogether peaceably minded and neither France nor Russia appears to feel any inclination for war." Cited by August Bach, *Deutsche Gesandschaftsberichte zum Kriegsausbruch 1914* (Berlin: Deutsche Verlagsgesellschaft für Politik und Geschichte, 1937), p. 20. On July 20, Koster, Baden chargé d'affaires, wrote to Dusch, Baden minister for foreign affairs: "In circles here, even at the foreign ministry, the opinion prevails that Russia is bluffing and that, if only for reasons of domestic policy, she will think well before provoking a European war, the outcome of which is doubtful. Moreover, it must not be overlooked that the personal sympathies of the czar for Serbia as the native country of the men who murdered the Austrian heir apparent and his wife, are extremely slight. Ibid., pp. 66–67. On July 27, Sir Edward Goschen cabled Sir Arthur Nicolson: "I found Jagow ill and tired but nevertheless optimistic—his optimism being based, as he told me, on the idea that Russia was not in a position to make war." *British Documents on the Origins of the War*, 1898–1914, ed. G. P. Gooch and Harold Temperley, 11 vols. (London: His Majesty's Stationery Office, 1926–28) (hereafter referred to as B. D.), vol. 11, no. 677.

55　Szögyeny to Berchtold, July 12, 1914. *Österreich-Ungarns Aussenpolitik*, vol. 7, no. 10, 215.

56　For a general discussion of the Bosnian Annexation crisis, see Luigi Albertini, *The Origins of the War of 1914*, trans, and ed. Isabella M. Massey, 3 vols. (Oxford: Oxford University Press, 1952), vol. l, pp. 190–300, and A. J. P. Taylor, *The Struggle for the Mastery of Europe*, 1848–1918 (New York: Oxford University Press, 1971). The best single study of the crisis remains Bernadotte Schmidt, *The Annexation of Bosnia*, 1908–1909 (Cambridge: Cambridge University Press, 1937).

57　Cited in F.W.C. Thimme, *Front wider Bülow: Staatsmänner, Diplomaten und Forscher zu einer Denkwürdigkeiten* (Munich: Bruckmann, 1931), p. 217.

58　Bernard von Bülow, *Memoirs*, trans. F. A. Voigt, 4 vols., (Boston: Little, Brown, 1931), vol. 3, pp. 12–18, 126.

59　See, Albertini, *Origins of the War*, vol. 2, pp. 181–216, 290–328, 528–631.

60　Bülow, *Memoirs*, vol. 3, pp. 157–58.

61　In the years before 1914 German leaders vacillated in their approach toward Russia. The traditional view held that Russia and Germany were natural allies because they had no serious conflict of interest, and successive foreign ministers had toyed with the idea of dropping Austria in favor of Russia. By 1914, Russia, although still viewed as a potential colossus, had lost much of its appeal because of its increasingly pan-Slav foreign policy. The prevailing view in Berlin was that Russia must be forced into a showdown while she was still militarily unprepared for war. German leaders expected that Russia would back down when challenged because of her relative un preparedness. Jagow wrote Lichnowsky to this effect in June 1914. Bülow recorded in his memoirs that it was a universally shared assumption among policy makers in Berlin at that time. Harry F. Young, *Prince Lichnowsky and the Great War* (Athens, Ga.: University of Georgia Press, 1977), p. 110; Kurt Riezler, *Tagebücher, Aufsätze, Dokumente*, ed. Karl Dietrich Erdmann (Göttingen: Vandenhoeck and Ruprecht, 1972), pp. 188–89; Bülow, *Memoirs*, vol. 3 pp. 159.

62 Jagow to Lichnowsky, July 18, 1914, D. D. 1, no. 72. The belief that St. Petersburg would not go to war because her military preparations were as yet incomplete reveals another way in which German leaders were seduced by irrational consistency. The German military reasoned that Russia would not risk war until she had a reasonable chance of victory, and the very earliest they expected this to occur was 1916 when her railway net and military reforms would be completed. They accordingly relied upon the progress of these measures as their strategic indicators of Russian intentions. By looking only at Russian military capability the Germans ignored the possibility that compelling political reasons might lead Russian leaders to contemplate war before their long-term strategic preparations were completed. This is of course what happened.

The use of incorrect or oversimplified strategic and tactical indicators is probably a major cause of intelligence failure. *The Agranat Report*, the official Israeli inquiry into the intelligence failure of 1973, attributes the failure to predict the Arab attack in part to military intelligence's reliance on an erroneous strategic conception for predicting a general attack. This indicator was based on exactly the same "military logic" that misled the German General Staff.

63 Jervis, *Perception and Misperception in International Politics*, pp. 193–95.

64 Albertini, *Origins of the War*, vol. 2, p. 161.

65 Prince Karl Max Lichnowsky, *Heading for the Abyss: Reminiscences by Prince Lichnowsky*, trans. Sefton Delmer, (London: Constable, 1928), pp. vi–xx; Young, *Prince Lichnowsky*, pp. 46–47; Lamar Cecil, *The German Diplomatic Service, 1871–1914* (Princeton, NJ: Princeton University Press, 1976), pp. 227, 242–48; and Gerhard Ritter, *The Sword and the Scepter: The Problem of Militarism in Germany* (translation of 2d rev. ed., *Staatskunst und Kriegshandwerk*), trans. Heinz Norden (Coral Gables, FL: University of Miami Press, 1970), vol. 2: *The European Powers and the Wilhelminian Empire*, vol. 2, pp. 128–29, all report on the attempt to control more closely the reports of the military attachés.

66 Lichnowsky, *Heading for the Abyss*, p. xx; Young, *Prince Lichnowsky*, pp. 18–22, 139, 171, 175; Cecil, *German Diplomatic Service*, pp. 244–45, 262–66, 291–300.

67 Cecil, in *German Diplomatic Service*, p. 287, observes that "Lichnowsky, whose independence of mind and arrogance were pronounced, refused to be intimidated by Holstein, who therefore resented his influence with the state secretary"; Sergei Sazonov, *Fateful Years, 1909–1916; the Reminiscences of Sergei Sazonov* (New York: Stokes, 1928), pp. 165–66.

68 Friedrich von Pourtalès, *Am Scheidewege zwischen Krieg und Frieden: Meine letzten Verhandlungen in Petersburg, Ende Juli 1914* (Berlin: Deutsche Verlagsgesellschaft für Politik und Geschichte, 1919), pp. 10–11.

69 Lichnowsky observes: "It cannot be said that Russian statesmen ever for a moment left us in doubt as to their attitude. They regarded the attack on Serbia as a *casus belli*, a 'question of life and death,' as M. Sazonov put it, and they were the better able to adopt this attitude as after their reconciliation with Japan, their treaty of 1907 with England concerning Asiatic questions had relieved them of all anxiety as to Russian policy in the Far East," *Heading for the Abyss*, p. 20; Albertini, in *Origins of the War*, vol. 2, pp. 181–96, discusses Russia's situation on the eve of the crisis and Sazonov's warning to Germany that Russia would not accept the subjugation of Serbia by Austria.

70 This is the conclusion of Albertini, in *Origins of the War*, vol. 2, p. 183.
71 Pourtalès to the Foreign Office, July 24, 1914, D. D. 1, no. 204. For other reports relevant to assessing Pourtalès' performance, see D. D. 1, nos. 53, 120, 130, 134, 160, 203, 217, 238, and 288.
72 Pourtalès to the Foreign Office, July 25, 1914, D. D. 1, no. 160.
73 Daily Summation of the Russian Foreign Ministry, July 24, 1914, in Otto Hötzsch, ed., *Die internationalen Beziehungen im Zeitalter des Imperialismus; Dokumente aus den Archiven der zarischen und derprovisorischen Regierung* (Berlin: Reimar Hobbing, 1932–36), ser. 1, vol. 5 no. 25.
74 Pourtalès, p. 19.
75 Pourtalès to the Foreign Office, July 25, 1914, D.D. 1, no. 204; Albertini, *Origins of the War*, vol. 2, pp. 183, 301–2.
76 August Bach, *Deutsche gesandschaftberichte zum Kriegsausbruch 1914* (Berlin: Quaderverlag, 1937), p. 20.
77 For reasons noted earlier, Lichnowsky was out of favor in Berlin and had been retired from his position as minister in Vienna. He was apparently brought out of retirement in 1912 to become minister in London because the preferred candidate for the job was thought to be too young. According to Lichnowsky, in *Heading for the Abyss*, p. 20, "Some elderly gentleman had therefore to be found, if possible with one foot in the grave, who would mark time in London until the young official in question had arrived at the necessary years of maturity." Even so, Lichnowsky was only offered the post after the first alternate selection refused it and the second died!
78 Tirpitz., author of the "risk theory," argued that England would hesitate to go to war against a serious naval rival. For his views and their influence on other German leaders, see. Volker R. Berghahn, *Der Tirpitz-Plan: Genesis und Verfall einer innenpolitischen Krisenstrategie unter Wilhehn II* (Düsseldorf: Droste Verlag. 1971). Stumm had served as councilor at the embassy in London and in 1914 was desk officer for Great Britain and director of the political division of the Foreign Office. Richard von Kühlmann, in *Erinnerungen* (Heidelberg: Lambert Schneider, 1948), pp. 404–5, relates that Grey thought Stumm incapable of seeing two sides to a question and that Sir William Tyrrell believed him to be mentally unstable and voiced his opposition to Stumm's possible appointment as minister in London. Stumm apparently bore a life-long grudge against Lichnowsky for edging him out in competition for that post. This may account for the vehemence with which he opposed and disparaged Lichnowsky's opinions. Young, in *Prince Lichnowsky*, pp. 64–66, 81–82, 112–13, argues that Stumm's animosity toward Lichnowsky led him to minimize the likelihood of British intervention and to rebuke Lichnowsky for his anxiety on this account. This in turn distorted Berlin's conduct of foreign affairs as great store was put in Stumm's knowledge of English affairs. Bülow, in his *Memoirs*, vol. 3, pp. 149–50, charges that along with Bethmann-Hollweg and Jagow, Stumm bore a primary responsibility for the war. The chancellor and foreign secretary also took comfort in reports from Albert Ballin and Prince Haldane. Ballin, president of the Hamburg-Amerika shipping line, dined with Churchill, Haldane, and Grey in London on July 24 and afterwards reported to his government that Churchill had confided to him that the British wished to avoid any war. Ballin apparently came away with the impression that "a moderately skilled German diplomatist could very well have conic to an understanding with England and France, which could have assured peace and prevented Russia

from beginning war." Bernard Huldermann, *Albert Ballin*, trans. W. J. Eggers, 4th ed. (London: Cassell, 1922), pp. 301–2. Ballin's report was followed by a cable from Prince Heinrich relaying a conversation he had had with King George on July 26 in which "Georgie" allegedly assured him that "we shall try to keep out of this and shall remain neutral." Prince Heinrich to Wilhelm. July 28, 1914, D. D. 1, No. 207.

79 British perceptions of Germany in the decade prior to 1914 are discussed in chapter 9.

80 Some historians of the July crisis, among them Sidney Fay, have suggested that German leaders may also have been misled by Britain's failure to state categorically from the outset that she would intervene in a war between Germany and France. The author is unconvinced by this argument. Given Britain's commitment to Belgium, her enduring interest in the balance of power on the Continent, her prior support of France in two crises with Germany and the obvious political reasons that constrained her from speaking out,. it should have been apparent to all but the most unsophisticated observer of British politics that no inferences about British intentions could be drawn from her reluctance to commit herself publicly to the defense of France. It seems more likely that Britain's refusal to make such a commitment provided the Germans with a rationalization for their belief in British neutrality, a belief to which they were already deeply committed. Some evidence for this assertion can be adduced from the fact that when British leaders did speak out the Kaiser and his circle were reluctant to believe them. They continued to entertain hopes of British neutrality as late as August 1 despite numerous British statements by then that this was hardly likely. We can speculate that German leaders had a need to see reality as consonant with their needs. But whatever the reason for Germany's miscalculation, it ought to be recognized as a German problem for which there is no plausible external explanation. The efforts by Fay and others to devise such explanations presage the attempts by later analysts to find good reasons for Khrushchev to have believed that he could get away with putting Soviet missiles in Cuba. All these explanations are based on the very dubious assumption that policy making in Berlin and Moscow was an essentially rational process.

81 In 1916. Lichnowsky declared: "There could be no possible doubt as to what England's attitude would be and it was therefore quite incomprehensible to me how the German Chancellor, in spite of Sir Edward Grey's repeated warnings and my own written and oral reports, could be so taken by surprise by the British declaration of war." Lichnowsky, *Heading for the Abyss*, p. 31: Young. *Prince Lichnowksy*, pp. 92–127.

82 Wilhelm's marginalia on Lichnowsky to Jagow, July 22, 1914, D. D. 1, nos. 118–21.

83 Jagow to Lichnowsky, July 23, 1914, D. D. 1, no. 124.

84 Lichnowsky to the Foreign Office, July 25, 1914. D. C. 1, nos. 163, 179.

85 Lichnowsky to the Foreign Office, July 26, 1914. D. D. 1, nos. 218. 236.

86 Ibid., no. 236.

87 Lichnowsky to the Foreign Office, 27, 1914. D. D. 1, no 265. This cable was not shown to Wilhelm.

88 Ibid., No. 236.

89 Bethmann-Hollweg to Lichnowsky, June 16, 1914. *The grosse Politik der europäischen Kabinette, 1871–1914* (Berlin, 1922–27), vol. 39, pp. 628–29; Peter Hatton, "Britain and Germany 1914: The July Crisis and War Aims," *Past and Present* no. 36 (Febru-

ary 1967), pp. 138–60; Konrad H. Jarausch, *The Enigmatic Chancellor; Bethmann Hollweg and the Hubris of Imperial Germany* (New Haven, CT: Yale University Press, 1973), pp. 142–43, 167–70.

90 Pourtalès to Bethmann-Hollweg, July 21, 1914, D. D. 1, no. 120.

91 Bethmann-Hollweg to Wilhelm II, 23, 1914, German foreign office, *Weltkrieg*, vol. 3, quoted in Jarausch, "The Illusion of Limited War: Chancellor Bethmann-Hollweg's Calculated Risk, July 1914," p. 62.

92 Raymond Récouly. *Les Heures tragiques d'Avant-Guèrre* (Paris: Renaissance du Livre, 1932). p. 23.

93 On July 23, Grey proposed that Germany urge moderation on Austria while Britain exerted pressure on Russia to moderate Serbia. The Kaiser rejected "these condescending orders" out of hand. Lichnowsky to Jagow, July 23, 1914, D. D. 1. no. 121; On July 25, Grey suggested that Berlin put pressure on Austria to accept the Serbian reply to her ultimatum. Bethmann-Hollweg passed on the British note to Austria without commenting on it, the diplomatic equivalent to rejection. Lichnowsky to Jagow, July 25, 1914, D. D. 1, no. 179; On July 27, Grey appealed once again to Berlin to use its influence in Vienna while London appealed to St. Petersburg for moderation. This time the chancellor did not even pass along the request to Berchtold. Lichnowsky to the Foreign Office, July 27, 1914, D. D. 1, no. 258; Finally, on July 28, Lichnowsky transmitted a fourth offer, this time from King George V and Grey, proposing a conference of European ambassadors. Lichnowsky noted that Nicolson and Tyrrell saw such a conference as "the only possibility of avoiding general war." Lichnowsky to the Foreign Office, July 28, 1914, D. D. 1, nos. 201, 218, and 238. Jagow and Bethmann-Hollweg were unresponsive to this suggestion as well.

94 Bethmann-Hollweg to Tschirschky, July 28, 1914, D. D. 2, no. 323.

95 Bethmann-Hollweg's notes of his interview with Goschen, July 29, 1914, D. D. 2, no. 373.

96 Goschen to Grey, July 30, 1914. B. D. 11, no. 293. Grey thought the offer "infamous" and concluded that Germany was ready to go to war in the hope of humiliating the Entente diplomatically. Grey to Goschen, July 30, 1914, B. D. 11, no. 303.

97 Lichnowsky to the Foreign Office, 29, 1914, D. D. 2, no. 368. The underlined sentence is in English in the original text.

98 In some ways the German reaction to British intervention is enigmatic. The Schlieffen Plan, as the Chancellor knew, called for a short war with France. If the campaign in fact lasted only six weeks, as everybody but Moltke expected, British intervention was not envisaged as a serious military threat. The Germans seriously underestimated Britain's ability to put an effective expeditionary force on the Continent and did not believe that her naval power would have any decisive significance in a short war. But German military planners hedged their bets because, unlike Hitler, they gave up the additional mobility they would have gained by invading Holland in the expectation of receiving goods through her neutral ports.

99 Bethmann-Hollweg to Tschirschky, July 30, 1914, D. D. 2, no. 395.

100 Bethmann-Hollweg to Berchtold, July 30, 1914, D. D. 2, no. 396; Bethmann-Hollweg to Lichnowsky, July 30, 1914, U. D. 2, no. 393.

101 Tschirschky to the Foreign Office, July 30, 1914, D. D. 2, no. 388; Bethmann-Hollweg had already received a hint as to Berchtold's state of mind in an earlier cable from Tschirschky reporting that Berchtold was reluctant even to consider the idea of

a halt in Belgrade and had put off giving him any reply. Tschirschky to the Foreign Office, July 29, 1914, D. D. 2, no. 338.

102 Jervis, *Perception and Misperception in International Politics,* pp. 383–406; Janis and Mann, *Decision Making,* pp. 309–38.

103 This decision is analyzed in chapter 2.

104 See Ritter, *The Sword and the Sceptor,* vol. 2, pp. 227–76, for the role of the German and Austrian general staffs in the crisis.

105 The message, drafted by Bethmann-Hollweg himself, had outlined the efforts to preserve the peace being undertaken by Britain and noted that if Vienna rejected mediation it would be taken as proof that she desired war, putting Germany in turn "in an untenable position position in the eyes of our own people." The chancellor concluded: "We can therefore only recommend most urgently that Austria should accept Grey's proposal....Your Excellency [Tschirschky] should express this view in the strongest terms to Count Berchtold and, if necessary, to Count Tisza." The inclusion of Tisza was significant because he was known to be the most influential Austro-Hungarian leader with serious doubts about the wisdom of war against Serbia. Bethmann-Hollweg to Tschirschky, July 30, 1914, D. D. 2, no. 441.

106 Zimmermann to Tschirschky, July 30, 1914, D. D. 2, no. 450.

107 Bethmann-Hollweg to Tschirschky, July 30 and 31, 1914, D. D. 2, nos. 451, 479.

108 Walter Goerlitz, ed., *Der Kaiser... Aufzeichnungen, des Chefs des Marinekabinetts Admiral Georg Alexander V. Müller über die Ära Wilhelms II* (Göttingen: Munsterschmidtverlag. 1965), pp. 77, 140; Theobald von Bethmann Hollweg, *Betrachtungen zum Weltkriege,* 2 vols. (Berlin: Reimar Hobbing, 1919–22), vol. l, pp. 142–43; Stern, "Bethmann Hollweg and the War: The Limits of Responsibility." p. 286–88.

109 Bülow, *Memoirs,* vol. 3, p. 149.

110 Tirpitz. *Politische Dokumente, 2* vols. (Berlin: Cotta, 1924–26), vol. 1, p. 242.

111 On July 23, for example, the Kaiser, in response to Grey's hope that Austria would not submit crushing demands to Serbia, commented in the margin of Lichnowsky's cable: "Grey makes the mistake of putting Serbia on a level with Austria and other great powers! That is monstrous. Serbia is a band of robbers that must be arrested for its crimes! I will not meddle with anything the Emperor alone is competent to deal with. I have been expecting this telegram and it does not surprise me! Real British reasoning and condescending way of giving orders which, I insist, must be turned down." Lichnowsky to Jagow, July 23, 1914. D. D. 1, no. 121.

112 It was only "in accordance with His Majesty's orders" that Bethmann-Hollweg forwarded Grey's plea for mediation to Vienna. Bethmann-Hollweg to Tschirschky, July 27, 1914, D. D. 1, no. 258; Herman Kantorowicz, *Gutachten zur Kriegsschuldfrage 1914,* ed. Imanuel Geiss (Frankfurt: Europäische Verlagsanstalt, 1967), p. 93.

113 The Kaiser's marginalia on the Serbian reply to the Austrian ultimatum. July 28, 1914, D. D. 2, no. 271.

114 Wilhelm to Jagow, July 28, 1914, D. D. 2, no. 293.

115 Grey himself proposed an almost identical compromise to Lichnowsky on the 29th thereby suggesting the British support would have been forthcoming for the Kaiser's formula. Lichnowsky to the Foreign Office, July 29, 1914.

116 Bethmann-Hollweg to Tschirschky, July 28, 1914, D. D. 2, no. 323. While the Kaiser thought it sufficient for Austria to occupy Belgrade, Bethmann-Hollweg proposed that she occupy additional territory. More importantly, whereas Wilhelm thought the

remaining points could "well be cleared up by negotiations," the chancellor changed the proposal to insist on "integral fulfillment of Austrian demands."

117 Albertini, *Origins of the War,* vol. 3, pp. 36–37.

118 Pourtalès to the Foreign Office, July 29, 1914; Nicholas to Wilhelm, 30 July 30, 1914; and Bethmann-Hollweg to Wilhelm, July 30, 1914, D. D. 2, nos. 343, 390, and 399.

119 Lichnowsky to the Foreign Office, 29, 1914, and Bethmann-Hollweg to Wilhelm, July 30, 1914, D. D. 2, nos. 368, 399.

120 Bethmann Hollweg to Wilhelm, 30 July 1914, and Pourtalès to the Foreign Office, July 30, 1914, D. D. 2, nos. 399, 407, and 401.

121 Goerlitz, *Regierte der Kaiser? Kriegstagebücher,* p. 37, shows in effect that the Kaiser preserved at least his outward calm upon reading the morning's cable from London, but exploded when confronted with Lichnowsky's report.

122 Minute on Nicholas to Wilhelm, July 30, 1914, D. D. 2, no. 390.

123 "His [the czar's] first telegram expressly said that he would probably be compelled to take measures which would lead to a European war. He thereby takes the blame on his own shoulders. In reality the measures were already in full swing and he has simply been lying to me... the wish that T should not let myself be deterred from my role as mediator by his mobilization measures are childish and meant only to set a trap for us! I regard my mediatory action as mistaken since without straightforwardly awaiting its effects, the czar, without a hint to me, has already been mobilizing behind my back." Minute on Bethmann-Hollweg to Wilhelm, July 30, 1914, D. D. 2, no. 399.

124 Norman A. Cameron, "Paranoid Reactions," in Freedman and Kaplan, *Comprehensive Textbook of Psychiatry,* pp. 665–75, and "Paranoid Conditions and Paranioa," in Arieti and Brody, *American Handbook of Psychiatry,* pp. 508–40; J. S. Tyhurst, "Paranoid Patterns." in A. H. Leighton, J. A. Clausen, and R. N. Wilson, eds., *Explorations in Social Psychiatry* (New York: Basic Books, 1957), pp. 31–42.

125 This syndrome is characterized by feelings of fatigue, worry, and inadequacy, by lack of zest and interest, and often by headaches, undue sensitivity to light and noise, and functional disturbances of digestion and circulation.

126 Wilheim's minute on Lichnowsky to the Foreign Office, July 29, 1914, D. D. 2, no. 368.

127 Pourtalès to the Foreign Office, July 30, 1914, D. D. 2, no. 401.

128 Minutes on above.

129 Jonathan Steinberg, in *Yesterday's Deterrent: Tirpitz and the Birth of the German Battle Fleet* (New York: Macmillan, 1965), p. 26, observes correctly if a bit floridly that the Kaiser "evidently generated a peculiar excitement in those around him and his lightning changes in disposition were like the flickering brilliance of a powerful electric storm."

130 That Bethmann-Hollweg had received Wilhelm's comments on the czar's telegram that morning is evidenced by his acknowledgement of the Kaiser's suggestions in a letter sent off at 11:15 a.m. Bethmann-Hollweg to Wilhelm, July 30, 1914, D. D. 2, no. 408.

131 Albertini, in *Origins of the War,* vol. 3, pp. 4–14, makes this argument.

132 This was apparent in conciliatory telegrams dispatched to King George and Czar Nicholas even though Wilhelm had already learned of the Russian mobilization. The cable to King George made reference to the Russian mobilization and asked Britain

to urge restraint on Russia. Wilhelm to George V, Wilhelm to Nicholas II, July 31, 1914, D. D. 2, nos. 477 and 480.

133 This subject is discussed in chapter 7 of *Between Peace and War.*.

134 Germany learned of the Russian general mobilization at 11:40 a.m. on July 31. Pourtalès to the Foreign Office, July 31, 1914, D. D. 2, no. 473.

135 When, at the start of the war, the cruisers *Goeben* and *Breslau* evaded a superior British naval force, the German admiralty and chancellor concluded not that the British navy had blundered but rather that Britain was unwilling to strike any "heavy blows" against Germany. Egmont Zechlin, "Cabinet versus Economic Warfare in Germany: Policy and Strategy during the Early Months of the First World War," in H. W. Koch, ed., *The Origins of the First World War* (London: Macmillan, 1972), p. 187, cited in Jervis, *Perception and Misperception in International Politics,* p. 323.

136 Bethmann-Hollweg to Lichnowsky, July 31, 1914, D. D. 3, no. 513.

137 Lichnowsky to the Foreign Office, 1 August 1914, D. D. 3, no. 570. For the best analysis of this episode see, Harry F. Young, "The Misunderstanding of August 1, 1914," *Journal of Modern History, 48* (December 1976): 644–65.

138 In support of the interpretation of the Kaiser's behavior advanced in this chapter it should be pointed out that his response to the July crisis was merely one manifestation of a behavioral pattern that he displayed throughout his life. The German general staff, for example, had for years played up to the Kaiser's well known need to indulge himself psychologically by arranging for the army he commanded at maneuvers to emerge victorious every year. This continued until Moltke made the Kaiser's noninterference in these exercises a condition of his accession to the position of chief of staff. Wilhelm's inability to face unpleasant realities surfaced most prominently after the retreat from the Marne. His appearances at army headquarters were less frequent as was his interference in the conduct of the war. Muttering, it was alleged, "I never wanted this," he retreated into a dream world of more comforting illusions. Alistair Horne writes: "When at his Western operational H. Q. at Charleville-Mézières, his day was leisurely, consisting of chatting with, and decorating, heroes from the front, and taking frequent walks around nearby Sedan, where he liked to ruminate over the simpler glories of the past. In the evenings, at dinner, members of his staff were detailed to feed him with the 'trench anecdotes' he so delighted in. Highly colored, these anecdotes had to glorify feats of Teutonic heroism and demonstrate the ridiculousness of the enemy. To the more proximate realities of war, the Kaiser closed his mind, and even the favorite, Falkenhayn. was not safe from reproof when he attempted to dissipate those rosy Hohenzollern illusions that had been the despair of poor Moltke." *The Price of Glory: Verdun 1916* (Harmondsworth: Penguin Books, 1964), pp. 45–46.

4 Beyond deterrence

Richard Ned Lebow and Janice Gross Stein

Deterrence is an attempt to influence another actor's assessment of its own interests. It seeks to prevent an undesired behavior by convincing the party who may
be contemplating such an action that its cost will exceed any possible gain. Deterrence presupposes that decisions are made in response to some kind of rational
cost–benefit calculus, that this calculus can be successfully manipulated from
the outside, and that the best way to do so is to increase the cost side of the ledger. This chapter challenges all three assumptions. It argues that deterrence is a
flawed strategy of conflict management, applicable only to a limited number of
cases, and spells out many of the reasons why this is so. Our critique of deterrence
has three interlocking components: political, psychological, and practical. Each
exposes a different set of problems of deterrence in theory and practice.

The political component examines the motivations behind foreign policy
challenges. Deterrence is unabashedly a theory of "opportunity." It asserts that
adversaries seek opportunities to make gains, and that when they find these opportunities they pounce. It accordingly prescribes a credible capacity to inflict unacceptable costs as the best means to prevent challenges. Empirical investigations
of cases of conflict point to an alternative explanation for a resort to force, which
we term a theory of "need." The evidence indicates that strategic vulnerabilities
and domestic political needs often constitute incentives to use force. When leaders become desperate, they may resort to force even when the military balance
is unfavorable and there are no grounds to doubt adversarial resolve. Deterrence
may be an inappropriate and even dangerous strategy in these circumstances. For
if leaders are driven less by the prospect of gain than they are by the fear of loss,
deterrent policies can provoke the very behavior they are designed to forestall by
intensifying the pressures on the challenger to act.

The psychological component is also related to the motivation of deterrence
challenges. To the extent that policy makers believe in the necessity of challenging the commitments of their adversaries, they become predisposed to see their
objectives as attainable. When they do so, pronounced and identifiable motivated
errors can occur. Leaders can distort their assessments of threat and be insensitive to warnings that the policies to which they are committed are likely to end in
disaster. Policy makers can convince themselves, despite evidence to the contrary,
that they can challenge an important adversarial commitment without provoking
war. Because they know the extent to which they are powerless to back down,

they expect their adversaries to accommodate them. Policy makers may also seek comfort in the illusion that their country will emerge victorious at little cost if the crisis gets out of hand and leads to war. Deterrence can thus be defeated by wishful thinking.

The practical component describes some of the most important obstacles to the successful implementation of deterrence. These derive from the distorting effects of cognitive biases and heuristics, political and cultural barriers to empathy, and the differing cognitive contexts that deterrer and would-be challengers are apt to use to frame and interpret signals. Problems of this kind are not unique to deterrence; they are embedded in the very structure of international relations. They nevertheless constitute particularly severe impediments to deterrence because of the deterrer's need to understand the world as it appears to the leaders of a would-be challenger in order to manipulate effectively their cost-benefit calculus. Failure to do so correctly can result in deterrent policies that succeed in making the proscribed behavior more attractive to a challenger.

All three components of our critique challenge core assumptions of deterrence. They also explain why deterrence is a risky and unreliable strategy. The problems associated with each component can independently confound deterrence. In practice they are often linked; political and practical factors interact with psychological processes to multiply the obstacles to success.

The drawbacks to deterrence that we identify do not lead us to conclude that it should be discarded. Part II of our essay, which analyzes deterrence successes, indicates that it still has an important role to play in the management of international conflict. We do argue, however, that scholars and statesmen must recognize the limits and inherent unpredictability of deterrence, and that they must make greater use of other strategies of conflict management Part III describes some of these strategies and their relationship to deterrence.

Data and method

Most of the evidence on which we base our analysis comes from historical case studies that we have published in *Psychology and Deterrence* (Jervis, Lebow, & Stein, 1985) or in *Between Peace and War* (Lebow, 1981). Both books analyzed deterrence encounters from the perspective of both sides: they examined the calculations, expectations, and actions of the challenger as well as those of the would-be deterrer. Because the interaction between adversaries is central to the understanding of deterrence successes and failures, case studies that look at the expectations and behavior of both are far more useful than analyses of the deliberations and policies of only one of the parties.

Most of the cases in those two volumes are *immediate* deterrence failures. This is in large part a function of the extraordinarily difficult problem of inferring success through counterfactual argument. The success of deterrence generally results in no action and can remain largely invisible to outsiders.

To identify a universe of cases of successful deterrence, analysts must first establish what would-be challengers intended to do and, far more problematic, what they would have done had the defender not threatened retaliation. Both tasks are most easily accomplished in cases of immediate deterrence when defenders anticipate a challenge, and threaten to punish or to deny a would-be challenger its objectives in an attempt to deter (Morgan, 1977). The more complete and reliable the historical evidence of the calculations of the challenger as well as the defender, the easier it is to define the relevant universe of cases.

Even then, restricting the analysis to cases of immediate deterrence biases the results in important ways. Because leaders have already begun to consider a use of force, these cases constitute the most demanding and rigorous test of deterrence. Undoubtedly, the bias that is built into the selection of cases inflates the rate of deterrence failure.

The alternative is identification of cases of *general* deterrence. General deterrence refers to the existing power relationships between adversaries and works by preventing a would-be challenger from even considering a use of force because of the obviously adverse consequences of military action. When it works, it leaves no evidentiary trail and, consequently, provides no clear criterion for case selection. As we shall argue, the success of general deterrence can be inferred only through counterfactual argument rather than evidence and is often subject to intense controversy. For these reasons, analysts of deterrence generally restrict their selection to cases of immediate deterrence and it is this evidence that we examine. Nevertheless, restricting our analysis to deterrence failures imposes costs. Explanations of the causes of failure can only be tentative, since some of the factors that appear to account for failure may also be at work when deterrence succeeds. Hypotheses derived from a controlled comparison of cases of deterrence failure will ultimately have to be validated against identified instances of deterrence success (Huth & Russett, 1984).

What is a deterrence failure? The goal of deterrence is to dissuade another actor from carrying out a proscribed behavior. In the context of international relations, the most important objective of deterrence is prevention of a use of force. To do this, the theory stipulates that the deterrer must carefully define the unacceptable behavior, communicate a commitment to punish transgressors (or deny them their objectives), possess the means to do so, and demonstrate the resolve to carry through its threat.[1] When these conditions are met and the proscribed behavior still occurs, we can speak of a deterrence failure (Brodie, 1959; Kaplan, 1958; Kaufmann, 1954; Kissinger, 1960, pp. 40–41; Milburn, 1959; Quester, 1966; Schelling, 1966, p. 374).

Researchers can and do disagree among themselves about the extent to which any or all of these conditions were met in a specific instance. These disagreements usually concern the credibility of the threat, something deterrence theorists consider to be the quintessential condition of the strategy's success. Unfortunately, it is also the most difficult to assess. This difficulty in assessment hinders a determination of whether a deterrence failure was due to the inadequacy of the strategy or merely to the failure of leaders to implement it adequately. Deterrence supporters invariably argue the latter when we make the case for the former (Lebow, 1987a; Orme, 1987).

The ongoing debate about the efficacy of deterrence is fueled by the inherent subjectivity of all interpretations of historical events. To reduce the impact of subjectivity and bias, we use a sample large enough to minimize the significance of disagreements about individual cases. Our arguments are therefore based on 10 examples of deterrence failure.[2] These cases are interesting not only because they document a pattern of deterrence failure, but also because they illustrate diverse reasons why failures occur. Evidence from conflicts where leaders used other kinds of strategies of conflict management will also be introduced where it is relevant.

Before proceeding, we must note the further difficulty of presenting arguments based on the evidence from case studies. In contrast to experimental or survey research, it is impossible to summarize data of this kind in a succinct manner. Nor would such a summary establish the validity of the findings even if we could demonstrate that the nature of the data base and the data analysis conformed to accepted research practice. As we have already observed, the reader must be convinced of the correctness of our interpretation of individual cases. Consequently, it is important to make explicit the basis for our interpretation of the evidence. For this reason we have chosen to incorporate as much case material as space permits. Readers interested in the data are referred to *Psychology and Deterrence* (Jervis et al., 1985), *Between Peace and War* (Lebow, 1981), and several journal articles (Lebow, 1983, 1984, 1987a, b; Stein, 1985c, 1987) for a fuller exposition of the cases.

Part I: a critique of deterrence

Political failings

Any strategy of conflict management should begin with a theory of the nature and causes of aggression. At the very least, such a theory should describe the mediating conditions and etiology of the malady that it seeks to control or prevent. Theories of deterrence fail to do even this. They finesse entirely the fundamental issue of the nature or causes of aggression by assuming both the existence of marked hostility between adversaries and a desire on the part of leaders of one to commit acts of aggression against the other. Deterrence further assumes that these leaders are under no political or strategic compunction to act aggressively, but that they will do so if they see an opportunity in the form of a vulnerable commitment of their adversary. It accordingly prescribes defensible, credible commitments as the most important means of discouraging aggression.

Case studies of international conflict contradict this depiction of international relations in important ways. They indicate that the existence of a vulnerable commitment is neither a necessary nor a sufficient condition for a challenge. At different times in history, "vulnerable" commitments have not been challenged while commitments that most observers would consider credible have been challenged. The evidence suggests, then, that deterrence theory has failed to identify correctly both the immediate and the underlying causes of aggression.

Deterrence theory assumes—and this is quintessentially American—that utility can be equated with narrow calculations of cost and gain, that is, in terms of the political, material, and physical well-being of leaders and their states. This disregards a host of other values—emotional, intangible, unquantifiable things—that history reveals to be at least as important for most peoples, Americans included. Why, for example, did the Confederacy challenge the North, which was clearly superior in military power and potential? Why did Southerners continue their struggle at tremendous human and economic cost long after leaders and soldiers alike recognized it to be a lost cause? Any number of other examples can be cited where people wittingly began or continued a struggle against great or even impossible odds. From Masada to the Irish Easter Rising, from Thermopylae to the resistance of the beleaguered Finns in 1940, history records countless stories of peoples who waged costly struggles with little or no expectation of success. Honor, anger, and national self-respect proved more compelling motives for action than pragmatic calculations of material loss and gain would have been reasons for acquiescence or passivity.

Deterrence also mistakes the symptoms of aggression for its causes. Specifically, it ignores the political and strategic vulnerabilities that can interact with cognitive and motivational processes to compel leaders to choose force.

In a previous study, Ned Lebow (1981) analyzed a class of acute international crisis, *brinksmanship,* whose defining characteristic was the challenger's expectation that its adversary would back away from its commitment in preference to war. He found that, much more often than not, brinksmanship challenges were initiated without good evidence that the adversary lacked either the capability or the resolve to defend its commitment; on the contrary, in most instances the evidence available at the time pointed to the opposite conclusion. The commitments in question appeared to meet the four necessary conditions of deterrence: they were clearly defined, repeatedly publicized, defensible, and the defending states gave every indication of their resolve to use force to defend their commitments. Not surprisingly, most of these challenges resulted in setbacks for the initiators, who were themselves compelled either to retreat or to go to war.

Faulty judgment by challengers could most often be attributed to their perceived need to carry out a challenge in response to pressing foreign and domestic threats. The policy makers involved believed these threats could be overcome only by a successful challenge of an adversary's commitment. Brinksmanship was conceived of as a necessary and forceful response to danger, as a means of protecting national strategic or domestic political interests before time ran out. Whether or not their assessment of international and domestic constraints was correct is a separate question for research. What is relevant is that leaders perceived acute domestic pressure, international danger, or both.

The extent to which policy makers contemplating challenges of their adversaries are inner directed and inwardly focused is also a central theme of Janice Gross Stein's (1985a, b) two contributions to *Psychology and Deterrence*. In her analysis of the five occasions between 1969 and 1973 when Egyptian leaders seriously contemplated the use of force against Israel, Stein argues that decision making in all of these instances departed significantly from the postulates of deterrence theory. All five decisions revealed a consistent and almost exclusive concentration by Egyptian leaders on their own purposes, political needs, and constraints. These leaders spoke in almost apocalyptic terms of Egypt's need to liberate the Sinai before détente between the superpowers progressed to the stage where Egyptian military action became impossible. They alluded again and again to the escalating domestic crisis that could be arrested only if the humiliation of 1967 were erased by a successful military campaign. By contrast, Israel's interests, and the imperatives for action that could be expected to flow from these interests, were not at all salient for Egyptian leaders. They thought only of the growing domestic and international constraints, and of the intolerable costs of inaction.

In 1969, the Egyptian failure to consider the relative interests of both sides resulted in a serious error. Egyptian leaders did not miscalculate Israel's credibility, but rather the scope of Israel's military response. They attached a very low probability to the possibility that Israel would carry the war of attrition onto Egyptian territory in order to maintain its position in the Sinai, a miscalculation of major proportions given the magnitude of the punishment Israel in fact inflicted upon Egypt.

Egypt's inability to understand that Israel's leaders believed defense of the Sinai was important, not only for the strategic depth and warning time it provided but also as an indicator of resolve, was merely one cause of its miscalculation in 1969. Egyptian leaders overestimated their own capacity to determine the course of a war of attrition and underestimated that of Israel. They also developed a strategy to fight the war, to culminate in a crossing of the canal, that was predicated on a fatal inconsistency: the belief that Egypt could inflict numerous casualties on Israel in the course of a war of attrition, but that Israel would refrain from escalating that conflict in order to reduce its casualties.

These faulty assessments and strategic contradictions are best explained as a motivated response to the strategic dilemma faced by Egyptian planners in 1969. Egypt could neither accept the status quo nor sustain the kind of military effort that would have been necessary to recapture the Sinai. Instead, Egypt embarked upon a poorly conceived limited military action. The wishful thinking and biased estimates were a form of bolstering; this was the way Egyptian leaders convinced themselves that their strategy would succeed. Israel's deterrent failed, not because of any lack of capability or resolve, but because Egypt's calculations were so flawed that they defeated deterrence.

Egyptian decision making in 1969 provides an example of what is probably the most frequent cause of serious miscalculation in international crisis: the inability of leaders to find a satisfactory way to reconcile two competing kinds of threats. The psychological stress that arises from this decisional dilemma is usually resolved by the adoption of defensive avoidance as a coping strategy. Leaders commit themselves to a course of action and deny information that indicates that their policy might not succeed (Janis & Mann, 1977, pp. 57–58). In the Egyptian case, the decisional dilemma that prompted defensive avoidance was the result of incompatibility between domestic imperatives and foreign realities. The domestic threat—i.e., political and economic losses—was the overriding consideration for Egyptian policy makers. Their estimates of their vulnerability motivated miscalculation and culminated in the failure of deterrence.

The Egyptian decision to use force in 1973 is even more damaging to the logic of deterrence than their motivated miscalculation in 1969. Egyptian leaders chose to use force in 1973 not because they miscalculated Israel's resolve or response, but because they felt so intolerably vulnerable and constrained. If Egyptian leaders had miscalculated, proponents of deterrence might argue that human error accounted for its failure. Economists advance similar kinds of arguments: the strategy is not flawed, only the people who use it. Egypt's leaders decided to challenge deterrence not because they erred, but because they considered the domestic and foreign costs of inaction unbearably high. They correctly anticipated a major military response by Israel, and they expected to suffer significant casualties and losses. Nevertheless, they planned a limited military action to disrupt the status quo and hoped for an internationally imposed ceasefire before their limited gains could be reversed. In 1973, Egyptian leaders considered their military capabilities inferior to those of Israel, but chose to use force because they anticipated grave domestic and strategic consequences from continuing inaction.

The same domestic considerations that compelled Egyptian leaders to challenge Israel also provided the incentives for Egyptian military planners to devise a strategy that compensated for their military weakness. Human ingenuity and careful organization succeeded in exploiting the flexibility of multipurpose conventional weaponry to circumvent many of the constraints of military inferiority. Egyptian officers strove to achieve defensive superiority iii what they planned to keep a limited battle zone (Stein, 1985a).

The Japanese decision to attack the United States in December 1941 seems analogous to the Egyptian decision of 1973. Like the Egyptians, the Japanese fully recognized the military superiority of their adversary, particularly the greater naval power and vastly superior economic base of the United States. The Japanese nevertheless felt compelled to attack the United States in the hope that a limited victory would facilitate a favorable settlement of their festering and costly conflict with China.

As the Egyptians were to do more than 30 years later, the Japanese military devised an ingenious and daring strategy to compensate for their adversary's advantages; they relied on air power and surprise to neutralize U.S. naval power in the Pacific. They too deluded themselves that their foe would accept the political consequences of a disastrous initial defeat instead of fighting to regain the initiative. The Japanese strategy was an act of desperation. Japan's leaders opted for war only after they were persuaded that the military balance between themselves and their adversaries would never again be as favorable as it was in 1941; time was working against them. They were also convinced that they could not attain their objectives by diplomacy (Borg & Okamoto, 1973; Butow, 1961; Hosoya, 1968; Ienaga, 1978; Ike, 1967; Russett, 1967).

The Japanese case highlights the importance of an uncongenial strategic environment as an incentive for a challenge. Leaders who anticipate an unfavorable decline in the relative balance of power may see no alternative to military action. President Anwar el-Sadat, for example, estimated that the longer he postponed war, the stronger Israel would become. This assumption helped create a mood of desperation in Cairo, so much so that Sadat repeatedly purged the Egyptian military command until he found generals who were confident that they could design around Israel's air and armored capability.

The Egyptian and Japanese cases indicate that a defender's capability and resolve are only some of the factors that challengers consider when they contemplate war. They are also influenced by domestic political pressures that push them toward action and by their judgments about future trends in the military balance. A pessimistic estimate of the probability of achieving important goals by peaceful means can also create frustration and constitute an incentive to act. This was very much so in Egypt in 1973 and in Japan in 1941. Both these cases illustrate how frustration, pessimism, and a sense of weakness in response to an unfavorable domestic and strategic environment can outweigh considerations of military inferiority.

How deterrence can backfire

When challengers are vulnerable or feel themselves vulnerable, a deterrer's effort to make important commitments more defensible and credible will have uncertain and unpredictable effects. At best, deterrence will be benign; it will simply have no effect. But it can also be malignant by intensifying precisely those pressures that are pushing leaders toward a choice of force. Japan and Europe in 1914 illustrate this dynamic.

The United States and other Western powers first froze Japanese assets and then imposed an oil embargo upon Japan in July–August 1941 in the hope of moderating Tokyo's policies. These actions became the catalysts for Japan's decision to go to war. Its leaders feared the embargo would deprive them of the capability to continue their conflict with China and, more seriously, would ultimately make them vulnerable to their adversaries. American strategy accordingly created a mood of desperation in Tokyo, an essential precondition of the attack on Pearl Harbor that followed.

Snyder (1985) examines the vulnerability that can arise in uncongenial strategic environments and explores the impact of security dilemmas on the outbreak of war in 1914. The distinguishing characteristic of a security dilemma is that behavior perceived by adversaries as threatening and aggressive is actually a defensive response to an inhospitable strategic environment. A "perceptual security dilemma" develops, Snyder argues, when strategic and psychological factors interact, and when strategic assessments are exaggerated or distorted by perceptual biases. In effect, leaders overrate the advantages of the offensive, the magnitude of power shifts, and the hostility of their adversaries.

In 1914, the major continental powers confronted elements of a security dilemma. As French fortifications improved in the 1880s, German security required the vulnerability of Russian forces in Poland; without this vulnerability, the German general staff feared that Russia and France could mobilize to full strength and then attack jointly. Russian security, however, excluded precisely such a weakness: Russia could not tolerate a decisive German advantage in a short war and so planned to increase its standing forces 40% by 1917. With French financial assistance, Russia also constructed new railways to transport these forces more rapidly to its western borders. Defensive preparations by Russia constituted an offensive threat to Germany and, conversely, a defensive strategy by Germany seemed to require offensives directed against France and Russia. Offense and defense thus became virtually indistinguishable.

Although the strategic environment was inhospitable and dangerous, Germany's military leaders greatly exaggerated the dangers and, as Snyder (1985, p. 170) demonstrates, reasoned inside out. They overrated the hostility of their adversaries and consequently assumed the inevitability of a two-front war. Once they did, the attractiveness of a preventive war-fighting strategy became overwhelming; German military leaders saw preventive war as the only alternative to their vulnerability. Indeed, the general staff gave no serious consideration after 1890 to the possibility of a defensive strategy against Russia and France. From then until 1914, the German military did not overestimate their offensive capabilities and then chose force, as deterrence theory would predict; on the contrary, they exaggerated the hostility of their adversaries in ways that psychological theories expect and then argued that an offensive capability was the least unsatisfactory option. Because of this choice, Germany's neighbors confronted a real security dilemma.

In this kind of strategic environment, military deterrence of Germany was a wholly inappropriate strategy of conflict avoidance. An attempt by either Russia or France to deter by threat of retaliation or through a show of force could only fuel the fear of an adversary that was already alarmed and, in so doing, further destabilize an already unstable environment. The Russian mobilization designed to deter, for example, could not help but alarm German military leaders committed to an offensive preemptive strategy. In 1914, when Germany's leaders chose to use force, they did so not because they saw an opportunity for gain but because they feared the strategic consequences of inaction. In an environment where already unfavorable strategic assessments were overlain by exaggerated fear and a sense of vulnerability, deterrence could only provoke the use of force that it was designed to prevent.

Psychological problems

The psychological component of our critique is also related to the motivation behind deterrence challenges. Once committed to a challenge, policy makers become predisposed to see their objective as attainable. Motivated error can result in flawed assessments and unrealistic expectations; leaders may believe an adversary will back down when challenged or, alternatively, that it will fight precisely the kind of war the challenger expects. Once committed to a challenge, policy makers may also become insensitive to warnings that their chosen course of action is likely to result in disaster. In these circumstances, deterrence, no matter how well it is practiced, can be defeated by a challenger's wishful thinking.

Flawed assessments

Like the Egyptian choice to initiate a war of attrition in 1969, the Japanese decision to attack Pearl Harbor exemplifies a strategic decision based on wishful thinking and flawed assessments. The Japanese military chose a limited war strategy because they estimated that it was the only kind of war they could hope to win against the United States, given its superior economic and military power. They persuaded themselves that a successful counterforce strike against U.S. naval units in the Pacific would convince Washington to withdraw from the Western Pacific and give Japan freedom of action in the region. The American reaction was, of course, nothing of the kind. Public opinion in the United States, enraged by the "sneak attack," became intent on waging war *a l'outrance* against Japan. President Franklin Delano Roosevelt and Chairman of the Joint Chiefs of Staff George C. Marshall had a difficult time throughout the war in concentrating America's principal military effort against Germany, which they rightly considered the more serious threat, because public opinion demanded the punishment of Japan.

The origins of World War I also illustrate how wishful thinking can defeat deterrence. German policy in the July crisis was based on a series of erroneous assumptions about the probable Russian, French, and British reaction to an attack by Austria–Hungary on Serbia. Berlin was confident of its ability to localize an Austro–Serbian war despite all the indications to the contrary and, throughout the crisis, urged Vienna to ignore pleas from the other great powers for moderation.

Germany's strategy was remarkably shortsighted. All of the assumptions on which German policy were based proved ill-founded; Austria's declaration of war on Serbia triggered a series of responses that embroiled Germany in a war with Russia, France, Belgium, and Britain. Moreover, even if the unrealistic assumptions on which German strategy was based had proven correct, it still would have been self-defeating. Serbia's defeat would have aggravated Russo–German hostility, increased Russia's dependence on France and Britain, and created the preconditions for another, far more intense clash between the two blocs.

Germany's strategy can best be understood as a response to the contradictions between its leaders' perception of their political needs and of the constraints of their external environment. The former dictated support of Austria, Germany's principal ally, in order to maintain the all-important alliance. The latter demanded caution because Germany's civilian leaders hoped to avoid responsibility for a European war that its generals were uncertain of their ability to win. These contradictions were reconciled in a strategy premised on the illusion that Austria, with German support, could wage a limited war in the Balkans without provoking the intervention of the other great powers. German leaders were only disabused of their illusion when it was too late to stop a sequence of military preparations that they had helped to initiate (Lebow, 1981, pp. 26–29, 119–124; 1984).

Insensitivity to warnings

Motivated errors can play a major role in blocking receptivity to signals. Once leaders have committed themselves to a challenge, efforts by defenders to make their commitments credible will at best have a marginal impact on their adversaries' behavior. Even the most elaborate efforts to demonstrate prowess and resolve may prove insufficient for discouraging a challenger who is convinced that a use of force is necessary to preserve vital strategic and political interests.

Janis and Mann (1977), in their analysis of decision making, suggest that policy makers who embrace a course of action, but recognize that their initiative entails serious risk, will experience psychological stress. They will become emotionally upset and preoccupied with finding a less risky alternative. If, after further investigation, they conclude that it is unrealistic to hope for a better strategy, they will terminate their search despite their continuing dissatisfaction with available options. The result is a pattern of "defensive avoidance," characterized by efforts to avoid, dismiss, and deny warnings that increase anxiety and fear.

Janis and Mann (1977, pp. 57–58, 107–133) identify three forms of defensive avoidance: procrastination, shifting responsibility for the decision to others, and bolstering. The first two are self-explanatory. Bolstering refers to a set of psychological tactics that policy makers use to create expectations of a successful outcome. Bolstering occurs when policy makers have lost hope of finding an altogether satisfactory policy option, and are unable to postpone a decision or shift responsibility to others. Instead, they commit themselves to the least objectionable alternative, and proceed to exaggerate its positive consequences or to minimize its costs. They may also deny the existence of aversive feelings, emphasize the remoteness of the consequence, or attempt to minimize personal responsibility for the decision once it is made. Policy makers continue to think about the problem, but ward off anxiety by practicing selective attention and other forms of distorted information processing.

Bolstering can serve a useful purpose. It helps a policy maker who is forced to settle for a less than satisfactory course of action to overcome residual conflict, and move more confidently toward decision and action. But bolstering has detrimental consequences when it occurs before leaders have made a careful search of the alternatives. It lulls them into believing they have made a good decision, when in fact they have avoided making a vigilant appraisal of the possible alternatives in order to escape from the conflict that would ensue.

Janis and Mann (1977) consider insensitivity to warnings a hallmark of defensive avoidance. When this becomes the dominant pattern of coping, "the person tries to keep himself from being exposed to communications that might reveal the shortcomings of the course of action he has chosen" (pp. 74–79). When actually confronted with disturbing information, leaders will alter its implications through a process of wishful thinking; they rationalize and deny the prospect of serious loss. Extraordinary circumstances with irrefutable negative feedback may be required to overcome such defenses.

Selective attention, denial, or almost any other psychological tactic used by policy makers to cope with critical information can be institutionalized. Merely by making their expectations or preferences known, policy makers encourage their subordinates to report or emphasize information supportive of those expectations and preferences. Policy makers can also structure their intelligence networks and bureaucracies to achieve the same effect. Perspectives thus confirmed and reconfirmed over time become more and more resistant to discrepant information and more difficult to refute.

In an earlier study, Lebow (1981, pp. 101–228) described in some detail how this process occurred in Germany in 1914, in the United States in 1950 with regard to the possibility of Chinese entry into the Korean War, and in India in 1962 during its border dispute with China. In all three instances, policy makers, responding to perceived domestic and strategic imperatives, became committed to risky military policies. They resorted to defensive avoidance to insulate themselves from the resulting stress. They subsequently allowed or encouraged their respective political–military bureaucracies to submit reports supportive of the policies to which the leadership was committed. Institutionalized in this way, defensive avoidance succeeded in blinding the policy makers to repeated warnings of impending disaster.

Motivated bias is a response to personal needs or external pressures. Evidence drawn from these cases suggests that at least one mediating condition of motivated bias is a choice by policy makers of a course of action that they recognize could result in substantial loss. Once challengers become committed to such an action, even the most strenuous efforts by a deterrer to define a commitment and give it credibility may have little impact. Motivated bias, in the form of faulty assessment of an adversary's resolve, overconfidence, and insensitivity to warnings can defeat even well-articulated and well-executed deterrence.

Problems in applying deterrence

Deterrence is beset by a host of practical problems. Among the most important is the difficulty of communicating capability and resolve to would-be challengers. Theories of deterrence assume that everyone understands, so to speak, the meaning of barking guard dogs, barbed wire, and "No Trespassing" signs. This is not so. Signals only acquire meaning in the context in which they are interpreted. When sender and recipient use quite different contexts to frame, communicate, or interpret signals, the opportunities for miscalculation and misjudgment multiply. Although this problem is endemic to international relations and is not limited to deterrence, it nevertheless can seriously limit the prospects of its success (Jervis, 1979, pp. 305–310; Lebow, 1985a).

A second problem, and one more specific to deterrence, concerns the difficulty of reconstructing the cost–benefit calculus of another actor. Deterrence requires the party intent on forestalling a challenge to manipulate the cost–benefit calculus of a would-be challenger. If credible threats of punishment always increased the cost side of the ledger—something deterrence theory takes for granted—then it would be unnecessary for deterrers to understand the value hierarchy and outcome preferences of target states. This convenient assumption is not borne out in practice. As we have seen, leaders may be driven not primarily by "opportunity" but rather by "vulnerability." When they are, increasing the costs of military action may have no effect on their unwillingness to tolerate the high costs of inaction.

Deterrence threats in these circumstances can also provoke the very behavior they are designed to prevent. This happens when, contrary to the deterrer's expectations, they intensify the pressures on the challenger to act. Unfortunately, the kinds of considerations that determine how a threat will influence an adversary's cost–benefit calculus are often invisible from the outside.

One of the authors (Ned) had a demonstration of this in his own life while working on the conclusions to *Psychology and Deterrence*. His son Eli, then aged five, had hit his almost two-year-old brother, David, several times during the course of the day. The reason for Eli's hostility seemed apparent: David had been ill with the flu and had received a lot of attention from his parents. Ned, upon arriving home from the office, decided to practice deterrence. He carefully defined his commitment ("Eli, if you hit your brother again, I'll take away your LEGO"—there was nothing Eli valued so much at the time as his LEGO) and communicated it as clearly as possible ("Eli, are you listening to me...?"). He also unquestionably possessed the means and the will to implement his threat (Eli knew that his father was lusting after an opportunity to have the LEGO all to himself to build a rocket).

Five minutes later Eli hit his brother again in full sight of his parents. Ned stormed off to carry out his threat. He later pondered the incident and wondered if his action had not encouraged Eli to hit David. He sensed that Eli was feeling hostile toward David but, being a sensitive child, probably felt guilty at the same time. Eli was therefore feeling cross-pressured until his father resolved his emotional dilemma by threatening him. Now Eli could express his hostility but then expiate his guilt through punishment. Perhaps this was why Eli accepted his punishment so calmly.

There are many international analogues to this familial deterrence failure. They are analogues in the sense that the process is the same: deterrers provoke the kind of behavior they have sought to prevent because of the unexpected effect of their intervention on the cost–benefit calculus of a challenger. They differ, of course, in that the calculations involved are conscious and political, not unconscious and psychological. Perhaps the best contemporary example is the Cuban missile crisis. Here, too, a deterrent action appears to have helped provoke a serious challenge because of the unexpected way in which it affected the challenger's perceptions of its interests.

Cuba: a case study   Several hypotheses have been advanced to explain why the Soviet Union placed missiles in Cuba in September and October of 1962. By far the most widely accepted is the Soviet need to redress the strategic balance (Abel, 1966, p. 28; Allison, 1971, pp. 52–56; Hilsman, 1967, pp. 200–202; Horelick & Rush, 1966, p. 141; Tatu, 1968, p. 231). According to this interpretation, the Russian decision to put missiles in Cuba was triggered by the sudden realization that the United States was capable of launching an effective first strike against the Soviet Union. At that time the Soviet Union possessed a very small fleet of long-range bombers, a sizable number of medium-range ballistic missiles (MRBMs) and intermediate-range ballistic missiles (IRBMs), and a small number of intercontinental ballistic missiles (ICBMs). All of these weapons were based in the Soviet Union and were of limited use in any retaliatory strike against the United States. The bombers were slow and easy to detect; they could not be expected to penetrate American air defenses. The medium- and intermediate-range ballistic missiles were excellent weapons, but they were incapable of reaching the continental United States, and the first-generation ICBMs, for which the Soviets had great hopes, proved too unreliable and vulnerable to serve as a practical weapon. Only a few of them were actually deployed.

American estimates of the size and effectiveness of the Soviet missile force had been highly speculative after May 1960, when U-2 overflights of the Soviet Union were discontinued. This situation was rectified in the late summer of 1961 by the introduction of satellite reconnaissance, which gave American intelligence a more accurate assessment of the number of Soviet missiles. At that time a far-reaching political decision was made to tell Moscow that Washington knew of its vulnerability.

The risk inherent in such a course of action was not fully appreciated by President John F. Kennedy, who feared only that the Soviets would now speed up their ICBM program. The president and his advisors were more sensitive to the need to moderate Premier Nikita Khrushchev's bellicosity, alarmingly manifest in his several Berlin ultimata, and thought this could be accomplished by communicating their awareness of American strategic superiority. The message was first conveyed by Roswell Gilpatric, deputy secretary of defense, in a speech delivered in November 1961 and was subsequently reinforced through other channels.

For Soviet leaders, the political implications of this message must have been staggering. Almost overnight the Kremlin was confronted with the realization that its nuclear arsenal was not an effective deterrent. In the words of Roger Hilsman,

> It was not so much the fact that the Americans had military superiority—that was not news to the Soviets. What was bound to frighten them most was that the Americans knew that they had military superiority. For the Soviets quickly realized that to have reached this conclusion, the Americans must have made an intelligence breakthrough and found a way to pinpoint the location of the Soviet missiles that had been deployed as well as to calculate their total numbers. A "soft" ICBM system with somewhat cumbersome launching techniques...is an effective weapon for both a first strike...and a second, retaliatory strike so long as the location of the launching pads can be kept secret. However, if the enemy has a map with all the pads plotted, the system will retain some of its utility as a first-strike weapon, but almost none at all as a second-strike weapon. The whole Soviet ICBM system was suddenly obsolescent. (1967, p. 164)

The Soviets were in a quandary. The missile gap could be closed by a crash program to develop more effective second-generation ICBMs and perhaps a submersible delivery system. Such an effort was extremely costly and likely to meet strong opposition within the Soviet hierarchy. More importantly, a crash program did nothing to solve the short-term but paralyzing Soviet strategic inferiority that could be exploited by American leaders. The deployment of missiles in Cuba can be interpreted as a bold attempt to resolve this dilemma. The American warning had the paradoxical impact of provoking the action it was designed to deter.

An alternative explanation of the failure of deterrence in Cuba has been proposed. Proponents of deterrence tend to argue that the strategy failed because Khrushchev considered Kennedy weak, doubted his resolve, and therefore discounted his warning. In support of their argument, they cite the president's youth, his performance at the summit meeting in Vienna, and his decision not to supply air cover for the irregular forces that invaded the Bay of Pigs. In short, they suggest that it was the ineptness of the strategist rather than the difficulties inherent in the strategy that explain the failure of deterrence (Abel, 1966; Horelick, 1964; Lebow, 1983, 1987a).

The evidence for this interpretation is far from persuasive. Khrushchev subsequently spoke of the tough exchanges he had had with Kennedy in Vienna. Moreover, as one of President Kennedy's closest advisers observed, the political damage to the president that ensued from the Bay of Pigs could suggest to an adversary that he would be especially sensitive to a challenge and, if anything, likely to respond more vigorously (Sorensen, 1965, p. 675). It appears, rather, that Kennedy projected his sense of vulnerability onto the estimates of his adversary. Kennedy worried that Khrushchev doubted his resolve and construed the Soviet decision to introduce missiles into Cuba as supporting evidence (Schlesinger, 1965, p. 391). The president's interpretation was widely accepted at the time, in large part because it was consistent with the prevailing emphasis on deterrence and resolve.

The Soviet decision to challenge deterrence is better explained by the interaction of organizational concerns, bureaucratic rivalries, and internal politics with a perception of strategic inferiority to generate a decision to challenge deterrence. The primary motive for putting missiles into Cuba may have been Soviet perceptions of their strategic vulnerability, but other considerations also probably played a role. The initiative may have been perceived as a solution to a number of different problems confronted by influential groups within the Soviet hierarchy.

Because the deployment of missiles in Cuba would achieve strategic goals cheaply, it would free funds for the hard-pressed industrial sector. It also provided an opening for the army to strike a blow at its rival, the recently created Strategic Rocket Forces (SRF). The SRF had been put in charge of all intercontinental missiles, but the weapons slated for Cuba, MRBMs and IRBMs, were controlled by the army and would, at least temporarily, restore its primacy in the strategic sphere (Allison, 1971, pp. 237–244; Horelick & Rush, 1966, p. 141; Schlesinger, 1965, p. 18). The successful emplacement of missiles also promised to advance the domestic political interests of Khrushchev and his supporters, who must certainly have felt the need for a major success after the failure of their two Berlin offensives and of their domestic agricultural programs.

The initiative met not only domestic economic and political needs but promised substantial foreign benefits in addition to the strategic purposes it would serve. The foreign ministry probably saw the prospective missile bases in Cuba as a means of dramatizing Soviet support for Fidel Castro, and also of demonstrating resolve to Peking. If it succeeded, the initiative would also give Khrushchev additional "chips" to play in the ongoing conflict over Berlin.

For all of these reasons, Allison (1971, pp. 237–244) suggests, a powerful coalition emerged in favor of putting missiles into Cuba, a coalition that consisted of bureaucrats and political leaders who each saw the emplacement of missiles as advancing their particular needs. It may be that Kennedy's warning, which signaled to the Soviet leadership that the United States knew the Soviet Union would find itself in a position of pronounced strategic inferiority for the foreseeable future, served as the catalyst to bring all these special interests into play. Without this signal, it seems unlikely that these disparate purposes would have been sufficiently compelling to lead Soviet leaders to undertake such a risky venture. It may also be that Kennedy's warning would have been insufficient to provoke a challenge in the absence of these diverse motives. To the extent that either hypothesis is correct, the Soviet decision hinged on the presence of two different kinds of reinforcing incentives. The impact of the first, Kennedy's warning, was entirely misunderstood by the Americans who expected it to moderate Soviet behavior. The second, the institutional and internal political motives, were invisible to the Americans and probably would have remained so even if they had been more sensitive to the role that considerations of this kind can play.

The argument can be made that the Soviet Union is a special case, that the selection of this case biases the interpretation of the evidence. It is undeniable that secrecy is a defining characteristic of the Soviet political system, effectively hiding the policy-making process from view. This is also true in more open societies like the United States, however, where the specific role that bureaucratic, organizational, political, and personal factors play in a policy decision may only become apparent long after the fact. The general opaqueness of foreign policy decision making means that deterrence in some ways resembles a game of Russian roulette: its outcome depends on all-important factors hidden from the view of one of the central players.

If the policy-making process is difficult to fathom from the outside, the deterrer's difficulties are compounded when the challenger's policy making is seriously flawed. When the challenger's calculus is based on a set of unrealistic assumptions about the political–military environment or the likely response of the deterrer to a challenge, attempts by outsiders to model the challenger's policy making are almost certain to be far from the mark. After all, officials in the state attempting to deter are hardly likely to premise their analysis on what they know to be erroneous expectations about their own behavior. This "regress of expectations," built into the logic of deterrence, makes the strategy extremely risky in practice.

Deterrence failures: an overview

Deterrence purports to describe an *interactive* process between the defender of a commitment and a would-be challenger. The defending state is expected to define and publicize its commitment, and to do its best to make that commitment credible in the eyes of its adversary. Would-be challengers are expected to assess accurately the defender's capability and resolve. The repetitive cycle of test and challenge is expected to provide both sides with an increasingly sophisticated understanding of each other's interests, propensity for risk taking, threshold of provocation, and style of foreign policy behavior.

Our analysis of case studies of adversarial relationships indicates that the expectations that deterrence has about deterrer and challenger bear little relation to reality. Challengers frequently focus on their own needs and do not consider, or distort if they do, the needs, interests, and capabilities of their adversaries. Moreover, at times they are motivated not by opportunity, as deterrence theory expects, but rather by vulnerability and perceived weakness. Deterrers, in turn, may interpret the motives or objectives of a challenger in a manner consistent with their expectations, with little regard to the competing expectations of the challenger. Both sides may also prove insensitive to each other's signals. Under these conditions, deterrence is likely to fail. Even recurrent deterrence episodes may not facilitate greater mutual understanding. On the contrary, experience may actually hinder learning to the extent that it encourages tautological confirmation of misleading or inappropriate lessons.

Part II: when does deterrence deter?

This section of the chapter examines a different set of cases: deterrence successes and instances where deterrence might have succeeded had it been tried. First, we seek to identify cases of successful deterrence to establish a valid set of cases for analysis; at present there is no consensus on when—much less why—deterrence has succeeded. Analysis of deterrence successes is important both to generate hypotheses about the conditions of successful deterrence and to validate propositions derived exclusively from the study of deterrence failures.

Deterrence successes

Deterrence failures are identifiable because they leave readily observable traces both at the time and after the fact. At the time they result in crises or wars, and after the fact they usually generate substantial documentation such as reports from commissions of inquiry and memoirs of participants. Deterrence successes, by contrast, can remain entirely invisible to outsiders. Who is to know if and when leaders were dissuaded from using force by the threats of their adversary? Decisions of this kind are likely to leave few public traces at the time and even after the fact; leaders are understandably reluctant to publicize their impotence and frustration in the face of superior force. For this reason, almost all of our evidence about deterrence successes is circumstantial and highly speculative.

The scholarly literature in international relations nevertheless contains numerous references to putative deterrence successes. These range from the sweeping assertion, common to conservative treatments of Western security, that the American nuclear umbrella has for over 40 years prevented a Soviet invasion of Western Europe to more discrete claims about the efficacy of deterrence in specific encounters or crises.

To evaluate these claims, we need a working definition of a deterrence "success." Unfortunately, defining a deterrence success can be as difficult as identifying one. The strictest definition, and one accepted by many proponents of deterrence, is a situation in which a state's leaders want to resort to force, prepare to do so, but ultimately decide to refrain because of the military capability and demonstrated resolve of their adversary (Brodie, 1959; George & Smoke, 1974, pp. 5, 516–517; Huth & Russett, 1984; Kaplan, 1958). Most of the claims for deterrence successes made by scholars appear to conform to this definition; they identify incidents characterized by visible military preparations, coupled with threats of the use of force, which triggered counterpreparations on the part of the would-be deterrer, followed by moderation on the part of the challenger. The critical inference here is that the challenger's moderation is a response to the deterrer's resolve and not the result of other constraints or considerations.

Deterrence encounters

There is no consensus among scholars of international relations on which cases conform to these criteria of deterrence success. Nevertheless, a claim of success is often made in a number of specific historical situations. These include the Berlin crises of 1948, 1959, and 1961; the Taiwan Straits in 1954 and 1958–1959; Cuba in 1962; and Jordan–Syria in 1970. Even a cursory examination of these cases reveals, however, that most of them fail to satisfy the criteria for a deterrence success.

To judge any of the Berlin crises a deterrence success, it must be shown that the American commitment to defend Berlin dissuaded the Soviet Union from using force to conquer that city. Soviet leaders could have done so directly by ordering their forces into the city, or indirectly by interdiction of the air and road corridors leading to the city from the West. In 1948–1949, the Soviet Union denied all road and rail access to the city from the West, but it did not attempt to close the air corridors. A hastily organized airlift supplied food and fuel to West Berliners and maintained Western authority in the city. Between 1958 and 1961, Soviet leaders again applied pressure on West Berlin indirectly through East German interference with access routes to the city. For a second time—the events of 1958–1961 are best considered part of a single drawn-out crisis—the West held firm and the crisis subsided.

On both occasions the Soviet Union stopped short of using the kind of force that would have been necessary to eject the Western powers from Berlin. In 1948–1949, Moscow refrained from interfering with the airlift once Britain and the United States indicated that they would not tolerate interdiction of the flights. In the second Berlin crisis, both East Germany and the Soviet Union made a number of serious threats, but were even more restrained in their behavior.

In 1948–1949, and to a lesser extent, in 1958–1961, American leaders viewed the Berlin blockade as additional evidence of Moscow's intention to extend its control throughout all of Eastern Europe (George & Smoke, 1974, pp. 431–437; Shlaim, 1983, pp. 43–109). Given this assumption, these leaders as well as many analysts subsequently attributed Soviet caution in both confrontations to Moscow's fear of war with the United States. There is reason, however, to question this interpretation of Moscow's goals and the related claim of success for deterrence.

For 1948–1949, by far the more serious of the crises, several respected chroniclers of the confrontation believe Moscow was motivated largely by a defensive set of concerns (Davison, 1958; George & Smoke, 1974, pp. 107–136; Shlaim, 1983). Stalin, they argue, was intent on aborting the birth of an independent and unified West Germany whose economy and security would be tightly linked to the West. He saw the creation of a such a state as a serious threat to Soviet security; reparations would cease; Soviet influence would diminish, based as it was on the instrumentalities of four-power occupation; and most important, a revitalized and possibly rearmed Germany would threaten Soviet control of the rump eastern zone. These analysts see the blockade not as a prelude to the occupation of Berlin but as an attempt to pressure the Western powers to abandon their plans for an independent West Germany. Marshall Sokolovsky, the Soviet military governor of Germany, made this objective quite clear at the outset of the blockade (Clay, 1950, p. 367). If this now widely accepted interpretation of Soviet behavior is correct, the choice of a blockade as a strategy cannot be explained as the result of successful deterrence. As George and Smoke (1974) point out, "Far from being a second-best strategy...the blockade may have been viewed by Stalin as a *preferred* option for pursuing his complex objectives" (p. 135).

A more persuasive claim might be made, George and Smoke suggest, that deterrence prevented the Soviet Union from escalating the conflict when the airlift began to defeat the blockade. But here again, the question of motive is all-important. It is not at all apparent that the conquest of Berlin, with or without Western resistance, would have strengthened Stalin's capacity to maintain a weak and divided Germany; it certainly would not have prevented the unification of western zones of occupation. More likely, occupation of all of Berlin would have deprived him of his most important source of leverage with the Western allies: his ability to threaten their tenuous and vulnerable presence in the city. If this reconstruction of Stalin's calculations is correct, then his restraint cannot be attributed to the deterrent strategy of the West.

Interpretation of Soviet motives in the subsequent Berlin confrontations is also open to question. Like Stalin before him, Khrushchev and his East German ally, Walter Ulbricht, exploited their ability to threaten the Western position in Berlin in the hope of extracting political concessions. They sought formal recognition of East Germany to legitimize that state and, with it, the Soviet position in Eastern Europe (George & Smoke, 1974, pp. 431–437). Again, occupation of Berlin would not have accomplished their purposes, which required the compliance, not the opposition, of the United States. The use of force would have been counterproductive; it would have defeated Soviet objectives. If this interpretation is correct, Soviet restraint cannot be attributed to Western deterrence.

The Taiwan Straits crises of 1954–1955 and 1958 offer another illustration of the difficulty that analysts confront in trying to assess the extent to which deterrence was responsible for a challenger's moderation. To do so, we need valid evidence of the challenger's motives, which is almost always unavailable at the time and can remain so long afterward. In both Taiwan Straits crises, the People's Republic of China (PRC) shelled offshore islands occupied by Nationalist Chinese forces but did not attempt to invade those islands. In 1955, and again in 1958, the PRC stopped its shelling when the United States demonstrated that it could still resupply the islands by sea.

Some analysts subsequently claimed that this show of resolve by the United States succeeded in deterring China and in compelling it to cease its artillery fire. They believe the shelling was offensive in intent and a planned prelude to an invasion. George and Smoke (1974) argue, "If, as seems likely, Peking did intend to wrest Quemoy and Matsu, the most important of the offshore islands in the Taiwan Strait, from the Nationalists, then one can regard American actions during the crisis as achieving a partial deterrence success" (p. 266). In their opinion, however, it was also a partial deterrence failure because the American commitment "did not deter Peking from employing lesser options at its disposal to create controlled pressures with which to test and, if possible, to erode the U.S. commitment" (p. 266; see also Kalicki, 1975, pp. 122–123). They view the 1958 crisis in a similar light; once again, Peking was deterred from the high-risk strategy of an invasion but not from the lower risk initiative of an artillery assault (George & Smoke, 1974, pp. 363–376).

Others consider that the motives of PRC leaders were largely defensive and that they intended no provocation beyond the artillery barrage. Writing about the 1958 crisis, Melvin Gurtov and Byong-Moo Hwang advance the thesis that "Mao's first concern was to deflect a dangerous and growing threat to China's security at a time of rapid domestic change and military weakness. He tried to do this with a limited, low-risk preemptive move against the offshore islands in order to bring the Americans to their senses about their ally on Taiwan" (Gurtov & Hwang, 1980, pp. 63–97; see also Tsou, 1959; Whiting, 1978, pp. 240–241). They cite as evidence: the logistics of the PRC operation at the time, which Pentagon experts discounted as a prelude to an attack on the offshore islands; Chinese public statements, which maintained throughout the crisis that the bombardment was "punitive" and "retaliatory," not the first step to the liberation of Taiwan; and Khrushchev's recollections of his conversations with Mao Zedong. According to Khrushchev (1970), Mao insisted that "we don't want Chiang to be too far away from us. We want to keep him within our reach. Having him [on Quemoy and Matsu] means we can get at him with our shore batteries as well as our air force. If we'd occupied the islands, we would have lost the ability to cause him discomfort any time we want" (p. 263).

Circumstantial evidence and recent historical opinion tends to support the defensive interpretation of Chinese behavior in these crises. However, in the absence of the relevant Chinese documents, it is impossible to establish with certainty which, if either, of these interpretations is correct. George and Smoke (1974, p. 527), to their credit, recognize the highly speculative nature of their conclusions. Other deterrence scholars, however, treat Chinese motives as offensive and then use their analysis, without qualification, to classify the outcome of these crises as deterrence successes. They admit no uncertainty in their reconstruction of Chinese calculations and then use that reconstruction to conclude that deterrence had succeeded.

A review of the literature suggests that the policy an analyst promotes is often a function of this crucial evaluation of an adversary's intentions. During the Cold War, those who saw the Soviet Union and the PRC as aggressive, determined to exploit any opportunity to expand, also adopted deterrence as their preferred strategy of conflict management (George & Smoke, 1974, pp. 587–592; Herz, 1964; Luard, 1967). They interpreted moderation by either set of leaders as evidence of the success of deterrence, did not consider that restraint could have resulted from other causes, and concluded that deterrence was the only appropriate response to such adversaries. The merits of deterrence were thus confirmed tautologically over time in a series of Cold War confrontations like crises over Berlin and Taiwan. Its efficacy established through counterfactual argument and tautological reasoning, deterrence gradually began to dominate American foreign policy in theory and practice.

The Cuban missile crisis nicely illustrates this process of reasoning which culminates in questionable if not mistaken claims of success for deterrence. American leaders at the time considered the Soviet emplacement of missiles to be further evidence of the offensive purposes of the Soviet leadership. Critics of this interpretation, as we have seen, suggest an alternative, defensive explanation of Khrushchev's decision. The dispute over Soviet motives and goals raises serious questions about a claim of successful deterrence.

Even if Soviet intentions were not in dispute, classification of this case as a deterrence success is dubious. It simply fails to meet the criteria of success (George & Smoke, 1974, p. 447). President Kennedy defined the proscribed action—no offensive weapons were to be deployed on the island—and communicated his commitment to the Russians through different channels on several occasions. Khrushchev challenged Kennedy's commitment and put missiles into Cuba, an act that triggered a Soviet–American crisis when it was discovered. The onset of crisis between the two superpowers over Cuba is more properly characterized as a deterrence failure, and this is how we treated it in Part I. The outcome of the crisis is a different matter. Through a partial blockade of Cuba and the threat of an air strike, Kennedy convinced Khrushchev to agree to remove the Soviet missiles. The outcome must be judged a success for coercive diplomacy.

The American attempt to prevent an attack by Syria against Jordan in September 1970 is also treated by many analysts as a success for deterrence. Closer inspection reveals, however, that like the Cuban missile crisis, the onset of the crisis testified to the failure of deterrence while its outcome was similarly a success for compellence. On September 17, 1970, after four aircraft were hijacked by the Popular Front for the Liberation of Palestine and forced to land, with their hostages, in Jordan, fighting broke out between the Jordanian army and Palestinian guerrilla forces. President Nixon immediately and explicitly warned the leaders of Iraq and Syria not to intervene, and directly threatened military retaliation (Stein, 1987). At the same time, a third aircraft carrier was dispatched to the Sixth Fleet and an amphibious task force was ordered to stay in position, 36 hours off the coast of Lebanon (Kissinger, 1979, p. 614). Nevertheless, three days later, Syrian tanks crossed the border into Jordan and, that afternoon, two additional armored brigades joined the attacking forces. A beleaguered King Hussein urgently requested assistance as it became painfully clear that the extension of American deterrence had failed.

The United States quickly shifted to a strategy of coercive diplomacy: it augmented its forces in the Mediterranean; it appealed to the Soviet Union to impress on Syria the importance of the withdrawal of its armored forces from Jordan; and it began to coordinate its military response with Israel, which moved its forces ostentatiously into position on Syria's flank. After an emboldened King Hussein attacked advancing Syrian armor, Damascus began to withdraw its forces behind its border. Because the outcome of the crisis was satisfactory to American policy makers, proponents of deterrence did what they had done in their interpretation of Cuba: They glossed over the failure of deterrence in their retrospective analysis of their management of the conflict.

Deterrence in relationships

Proponents of deterrence are sensitive to the need to view conflicts diachronically. They argue that an examination of patterns of conflict over time can demonstrate the efficacy of deterrence as a strategy of conflict management. In this connection, they point to several protracted conflicts where, they claim, deterrence has prevented war. Assertions of this kind are routinely made about the Soviet–American and Sino–Soviet conflicts. Some scholars argue that deterrence has also been temporarily successful at various times in preventing war between the Arab states and Israel. All of these relationships have been characterized by acute hostility. The first two have been punctuated by periodic crises and, in the case of the Sino–Soviet conflict, by limited military engagements, but have not spilled over into general war. The absence of serious crises in recent years in Soviet–American relations has been construed as additional evidence in support of deterrence.

In analyzing the role of deterrence in these conflicts, it is important to differentiate between deterrence as a strategy of conflict management and deterrence as an expression of existing power relationships. The latter, which Morgan (1977) refers to as *general* deterrence, is quite independent of efforts by a state to define and publicize a commitment, and to threaten war in its defense. The former, the subject of our study, refers to a conscious effort by leaders to manipulate the risk of war in order to influence the behavior of an adversary. Such threats are, of course, based on underlying power relationships but they are not synonymous with them. For deterrence to be judged a successful *strategy,* war must be averted through the deliberate efforts of me deterrer to dissuade a challenger from resorting to force.

The first of our cases, Soviet–American relations, is commonly cited as a deterrence success. Typical of such claims is the assertion in a recent and highly respected book by Seweryn Bialer (1986) that "nuclear deterrence has prevented a direct Soviet–American military confrontation" (p. 362). Citing Soviet–American relations as an example of a deterrence success presupposes that Moscow would have invaded Western Europe in the absence of an American commitment to retaliate, if need be, with nuclear strikes against the Soviet Union and its Eastern European allies.

There is, however, little even in the way of circumstantial evidence to support this presupposition. Most military analysts question whether Soviet leaders at any time intended to invade Europe or to attack the United States. The Soviet Union, they maintain, had neither the incentive to attack nor, for many years, did it make any serious effort to acquire the kinds of conventional and strategic forces that would have been necessary to fight such a war (Evangelista. 1983–1984; Wolfe, 1970). Drastically reduced in size in the years following the surrender of Germany, Joseph Stalin's postwar army did not have the capability to conduct an offensive in Western Europe. American leaders, belatedly aware of the postwar Soviet demobilization, exaggerated the potency and size of the Soviet army throughout the 1950s in order to build European support for NATO and its budgetary requirements (Evangelista, 1983–1984).

The Soviet Union also lacked the economic capabilities to engage the United States in a major conflict in Europe. The Soviet economy had been badly damaged by the war, and desperately needed time and resources to recover, whereas the United States emerged with its economy invigorated and with uncontested command of the world's seas. The evidence suggests that Stalin's principal objective in Western Europe was economic, and his abiding interest in reparations from the Western occupation zones required the goodwill, not the hostility, of the United States, the United Kingdom, and France (Davison, 1958; Gaddis, 1972, pp. 234–241; Shlaim, 1983; Ulam, 1968, pp. 400–401).

If Stalin was deterred from invading Western Europe it was the result of Soviet weaknesses rather than western strengths. Self-deterrence continued to function through the 1960s, perhaps well into the 1970s. The Warsaw Pact was organized only in 1957 and, even then, no attempt was made to equip its forces with the latest weapons or to integrate its disparate national forces into a unified command until the latter part of the 1960s. Analysts of the East–West military balance disagree, as they always have among themselves, about the Warsaw Pact's ability to invade Western Europe. They concur, however, that it was at least 20 years after the end of World War II before the Soviet Union made a serious attempt to equip and deploy the kinds of forces that would be necessary to undertake this kind of military action (Holloway, 1984; Lewis, 1982; MccGwire, 1987; Tiedtke, 1978; Wolfe, 1970).

Sino–Soviet relations are even more difficult to interpret. The Chinese lay claim to 1,540 square kilometers of Soviet territory, which they insist was illegally occupied by czarist Russia. On several occasions there have been border clashes on islands in the Amur River occupied by the Soviet Union and claimed by China. Peking was apparently responsible for the most serious of these incidents, the clash in March 1969. Some scholars argue that the resort to force by China was an expression of an internal struggle for influence; others hold that it was a considered response to a series of prior Soviet provocations (Brown, 1976; Nelsen, 1972). Moscow had been openly supporting rebellion in Xinjiang and Inner Mongolia, building up its forces along China's periphery, and encroaching on islands in the Ussuri River to which it laid claim. These scholars suggest that it was the Chinese who were attempting to deter; through a limited use of force they hoped to deter further Soviet encroachments on Chinese territory and to impel Soviet leaders to reassess their border policy (Gurtov & Hwang, 1980).

If Chinese leaders were attempting to deter and to contain the Soviet Union, they did not succeed. On the contrary, following the clash in 1969, the Soviet Union dramatically stepped up its military buildup in the Far East. By the time of Mao's death in 1976, there were 43 Soviet divisions in place, supported by modern combat aircraft, prepositioned munitions, and an expanding communications and transportation network. Moscow had also redeployed one-quarter of its SS-4 and SS-5 missiles from the Western military districts to the Far East (Gelman, 1982; Lieberthal, 1978; Stuart, 1982). The Soviet buildup in turn failed to moderate Chinese foreign policy. Instead, it encouraged Peking to accelerate its military modernization, conventional and nuclear, and to seek political rapprochement with the United States. The Chinese also shifted the bulk of their army from the south, where it had faced American forces in Indochina, to the north, opposite Soviet forces. China's actions further heightened Moscow's concern for its security in the Far East.

Deterrence in the context of Sino–Soviet relations can hardly be judged a success. It seems to have triggered an escalatory spiral of mutual hostility and military preparations, and to have been an important cause of China's subsequent incursion into Vietnam. Ironically, China provoked a border incident with the Soviet Union at a time when it was domestically divided and militarily weak. Since this demonstration of force, despite some inflammatory rhetoric, Peking has been militarily restrained along the Soviet border. Some Chinese scholars attribute that caution to China's new strength; in their opinion Chinese leaders no longer perceived the need to demonstrate resolve to its internal and external adversaries (Gurtov & Hwang, 1980, pp. 242–259). If this proposition is correct, then the Soviet buildup has not only been unnecessary but contrary to Soviet interests; it has provoked rather than deterred Chinese military and political countermeasures.

The Syrian–Israel example raises a problem of a different kind. Again, analysts looking at the relationship over time argue that fear of the military consequences of war with Israel has deterred President Hafiz al-Assad from launching an offensive to regain all or part of the Golan Heights. Given the continuing military asymmetry in favor of Israel, they expect it to continue to do so. Whether or not deterrence will continue to succeed, however, is problematic precisely because of the growing political and psychological pressures in Syria that have defeated deterrence elsewhere.

Syria has engaged in an extensive military buildup since 1982, a buildup that has imposed heavy costs on an already severely troubled economy. Some military analysts suggest that the strengthening of Syria's armed forces has created a temporary "window of military opportunity," which will stay open only a few years (Lebow & Levite, 1987). Under these conditions, Syrian military leaders are likely to argue forcefully that time is working against them. External inducements to a use of force are compounded by intense domestic rivalry and competition, and by the failing health of Syria's leader, Hafiz al-Assad; it is principally Assad's leadership that has assured the predominance of Alawite generals in the Syrian army. Constrained at home and abroad, as was Sadat before him, Assad gives evidence of pushing his army into devising a scenario that plans around Israel's military superiority. Paradoxically, if this interpretation is correct, deterrence may not only fail to prevent a use of force but contribute to the outbreak of war, as it did between Egypt and Israel in 1969 and 1973. Again, Israel has relied almost exclusively on deterrence without an accompanying political strategy designed to address, at least in part, the factors that would motivate Syria to resort to force. In so doing, it has helped create the conditions that we associate with challenges.

In our judgment, the strongest argument for successful deterrence can be made in two cases rarely mentioned in the deterrence literature. These are Cuban–American and Nicaraguan–American relations. Successive American governments would have liked to overthrow Castro. The Kennedy administration mounted an operation to do so with Cuban exiles, but the president stopped short of committing the American planes and troops that would have been essential to the operation's success. President Ronald Reagan's administration has conducted a number of covert operations designed to overthrow the government of Nicaragua, and provides financial support and training for anti-Sandinista forces. But it too has been unwilling to launch an invasion.

American reluctance to invade Cuba and Nicaragua cannot be explained satisfactorily by Soviet support for either country. The Soviet Union can do little to defend either government should the United States invade. Nor can these regimes defend themselves successfully against a full-scale American attack. Unlike Grenada, however, they can put up stiff and continuing resistance to an American occupation. It is probably the prospect of an open-ended commitment to maintain American troops engaged in an ongoing struggle against guerrilla forces that deters Washington. Recognizing that such a conflict would be politically unacceptable in the United States, the Cuban and Nicaraguan governments have both attempted to deter military action by the United States by raising American estimates of the military cost of an invasion and occupation.

If deterrence has worked in these two cases, it has done so for reasons often ignored by deterrence theorists. Successful deterrence was not the result of a favorable military balance but rather of the ability of the deterrer to inflict unacceptable political costs on the would-be challenger. To be sure, those political costs were directly related to the deterrer's military capability but they were by no means synonymous. Deterrence was proportional in the sense that the deterrer had only a limited capability to inflict harm on the challenger. However, this limited capability was enough to deter, given American leaders' estimates of the political constraints they faced. Although the United States in both cases possessed undisputed military superiority and the capability to invade, it was unable to translate these assets into political leverage. This was so in large part because of American estimates of the asymmetry in political constraints, an asymmetry that they considered favorable to the deterrer. Both these cases underline the importance of political as opposed to military factors in shaping the outcome of deterrence.

Counterfactuals

Our case-by-case review makes it apparent that there are few unambiguous examples of post-1945 deterrence successes. Some of these cases can not simply be considered successes; in others, the claims are plausible but unsupported. If and when it becomes available, documentation may substantiate these claims, but until it does, claims of success can at best be tentative. The absence of good and reliable evidence has inevitably led advocates of deterrence to build their case primarily on counterfactuals, to allege that deterrence would have worked had it been attempted. Early studies of deterrence almost invariably cited Munich and the Korean War as prototypic cases where deterrence might have worked had leaders tried (George & Smoke, 1974, p. 142). That proponents of deterrence rely so heavily on counterfactuals to establish the usefulness of their strategy does not speak well for deterrence. The support for deterrence becomes weaker still when we examine some of these cases.

Munich has always been the most important counterfactual case for advocates of deterrence. Together with most historians of the 1930s, they have lamented the failure of Britain and France to try seriously deterring Germany. They assume that Adolf Hitler would have backed down had Britain and France remained unequivocal in their commitment to defend Czechoslovakia. German documents make it apparent, however, that, by 1938, Hitler wanted war. Indeed, he was disappointed that Prime Minister Neville Chamberlain was as accommodating as he was at Munich and made new demands at the last moment in the hope of forestalling an agreement. By 1938, resolve, commitment, and a serious attempt to deter by Britain and France would not have succeeded any better than appeasement in preventing war (Weinberg, 1970–1980).

Had Britain and France stood firm a few years earlier, the future of Europe might have been different. In 1936, when Hitler ordered the German army into the demilitarized Rhineland, his generals estimated that they could not overcome French military resistance. Together with disaffected senior diplomats, they might have conspired to remove Hitler from power had Britain and France opposed remilitarization with force. Indeed, as late as 1938, army and foreign office officials made preparations for a coup but lost confidence when the Western powers capitulated once again (Bullock, 1964, pp. 333–334, 566–567; Craig, 1964, pp. 486–487; Deutsch, 1978; Rothfels, 1962, pp. 57–63).

Britain and France did not try to deter in large part because of the widespread desire in both capitals to avoid war. At the time, it was not at all self-evident to British and French leaders that Hitler was motivated by opportunity, that he aspired to more than a return to the pre-Versailles political and territorial status quo. If Hitler's purposes had been so limited, then Anglo–French tolerance of his remilitarization of the Rhineland would have been a reasonable policy, while its alternative—French military intervention—could have triggered an unnecessary war.

Without a doubt, the tragedy of the 1930s was the failure of European statesmen to recognize that Hitler sought the opportunity to exploit the weaknesses of others; his ambitions were unlimited. It would not have been enough, however, for the leaders alone to have recognized the danger Hitler posed. For democratic states to deter adversaries credibly, they must have the strong and obvious support of their publics. British and French opinion were each deeply divided over domestic issues as a result of ongoing economic and social cleavages, but both were pre-eminently antiwar; neither would have supported an attempt at deterrence against Hitler's Germany in 1935, 1936, or 1937. Not until March 1939, in response to Hitler's occupation of Czechoslovakia, did the British public appreciate the threat posed by Nazi Germany and support military action. In France, a significant segment of opinion continued to believe well into the war that French socialists constituted a greater danger than did Nazi Germany. Without strong public support it would have been impractical to have attempted to deter Germany.

In the autumn of 1938, threats of war would not have had a great deal of credibility. Indeed, it is surprising that, when Britain and France finally extended deterrence to Poland in March 1939, Hitler attached as much credibility as he did to their threat to go to war. He expected Britain to fight a limited war and then, within months, to negotiate a separate peace. Given the past performance of the Chamberlain government and the residual antiwar sentiment in Britain, it is difficult to understand why Hitler found the threat at ail believable.

Ironically, analysts have consistently misused Munich as the paradigm of deterrence failure. By 1938, deterrence was irrelevant because Hitler was intent on war. When it was finally tried the following year, deterrence failed for precisely this reason. In 1936, when deterrence might have succeeded in stopping Hitler, it was impractical because neither the British nor French people were prepared to risk war to preserve the Versailles settlement. Those who criticize the Western powers for not vigorously opposing Hitler's first acts of aggression ignore the political constraints that operated within Britain and France, and that precluded deterrence as a strategy. Indeed, this argument reflects the tendency of deterrence theorists to treat war avoidance as a problem between unitary actors, and to ignore entirely the domestic political, psychological, and economic factors that can either reinforce or defeat deterrence, or even entirely preclude the attempt to deter.

A somewhat stronger case can be made for the role that deterrence might have played in preventing the Korean War. Nevertheless, analysis of this case must proceed with considerable caution because of the lack of good documentation on North Korean intentions and decision processes. Proponents of deterrence and Cold War historians routinely assert that North Korea was tempted to invade the South because American actions, prior to June 1950, gave it every reason to believe Washington would not commit its limited forces in the Pacific to the defense of South Korea. Critical of Secretary of State Dean Acheson's designation of Korea as outside the defense perimeter of the United States, they argue that a highly publicized American commitment to defend South Korea would have deterred North Korea's President Kim Il-sung and the Soviet Union. It is conceivable that a vigorously articulated deterrent threat may have had such an impact. But there is another, equally plausible possibility.

North Korean strategy was built around a lightning attack that would capture Seoul, within the day's march of the 38th parallel, and envelop the bulk of the South Korean army, stationed between Seoul and the border. Even if there had been an American commitment to defend South Korea, Kim Il-sung and his advisors might have discounted its credibility because the United States did not then have the forces in place to defend South Korea (George & Smoke, 1974, p. 538). Only a sizable American presence in Korea could have reinforced a deterrent threat, but President Truman, Acheson, and the Joint Chiefs of Staff all opposed the commitment of American forces, precisely because they feared being drawn into a land war on the Asia mainland.

In reviewing these cases, we do not seek to establish the validity of any particular interpretation. Indeed, in most cases, the available documentation does not yet permit a definitive account. We do propose, however, that there are other—and, in the case of Munich, more plausible—interpretations of these encounters than those proposed by advocates of deterrence. Moreover, even when the proposition that deterrence might have succeeded had it been tried is plausible, it is, of course, impossible to substantiate. Often the best that can be done is to advance a logically and politically consistent counterfactual argument for what might have happened if one of the actors had behaved differently.

Counterfactual argument is not restricted to those cases where deterrence might have worked had it been tried. On the contrary, all attempts to establish the success of deterrence are based on counterfactual argument; proponents of deterrence argue that war would have occurred had deterrence not been used. This too is a "what if" proposition; it is the mirror image of the argument put forward in cases where advocates of deterrence allege that it would have worked had it been tried. As we have seen, historical arguments designed to show why certain outcomes did not occur can easily lend themselves to tautological reasoning. If the reasoning is not tautological—and it need not necessarily be—nevertheless, when proponents of deterrence claim that deterrence succeeded or that it would have succeeded had it been used in time, their arguments are at best speculative. This is hardly a secure foundation on which to build a strategy of conflict management.

Deterrence in the long term

Evidence drawn from these cases of deterrence failures and putative successes suggests that deterrence is a risky and uncertain strategy. It indicates that the utility of deterrence is limited to a narrow range of conflicts: those in which adversarial leaders are motivated largely by the prospect of gain rather than by the fear of loss, have the freedom to exercise restraint, are not misled by grossly distorted assessments of the political–military situation, and are vulnerable to the kinds of threats that a would-be deterrer is capable of making credible. Deterrence must also be practiced early on, before an adversary commits itself to a challenge and becomes correspondingly insensitive to warnings that its action is likely to meet with retaliation. Unless these conditions are met, deterrence will at best be ineffective and at worst counterproductive.

These conditions apply only to deterrence in the short term—that is, to specific deterrence encounters. Proponents of deterrence generally concentrate their attention on these kinds of cases. However, our analysis of deterrence would be incomplete if we failed to examine its implications for the management of adversarial relationships in the longer term. Here we ask whether and why deterrence facilitates or retards the resolution of international conflict.

Deterrence theorists maintain that it can facilitate conflict resolution by convincing a challenger that its fundamental objectives cannot be met through a use of force. This realization may provoke a reorientation of policy and lay the groundwork for a subsequent accommodation. The relationship between Egypt and Israel in the last decade can be read this way. George and Smoke (1974, p. 5) note that deterrence may also give the parties to a dispute time to work out an accommodation and, in so doing, reduce tensions and the potential for overt conflict. However, deterrence can also retard conflict resolution by exacerbating the causes of the conflict or by creating new incentives to use force. Three different processes can contribute to this negative outcome.

As we have observed, deterrence can intensify the pressures on adversarial leaders to resort to force. It did so in the Cuban missile crisis and it may well have done so in the second crisis over the Taiwan Straits. In the wake of the 1954–1955 crisis, the United States reinforced deterrence in the Straits. President Eisenhower committed the United States to the defense of Taiwan and the offshore islands and, in 1957, authorized the deployment of nuclear-tipped surface-to-surface Matador missiles on Taiwan. To the president's annoyance, however, Chiang Kai-shek began a major military buildup on the islands and by 1958 had stationed 100,000 troops there, one-third of his total ground forces. It is probable that, to leaders in Peking, the increased military preparedness and troop deployments indicated that Washington was preparing to "unleash" Chiang. A series of provocative speeches by Secretary of State John Foster Dulles, suggesting that Chinese Nationalist forces might invade the mainland if significant domestic unrest provided the opportunity, fueled the Chinese perception of threat. Gurtov and Hwang (1980, pp. 63–98) suggest that it was this heightened perception of threat that led the Chinese leadership to demonstrate resolve through a renewed artillery assault on Quemoy and Matsu.

Deterrence can also intensify conflict by encouraging defenders to develop an exaggerated concern for their bargaining reputation. Deterrence does not attach great significance to the impact of the interests at stake in influencing an adversary's judgments of a commitment's credibility. It assumes—incorrectly, according to several empirical studies—that the most important component of credibility is the defender's record in honoring past commitments (George & Smoke, 1974, pp. 550–561; Jervis et al., 1985; Maxwell, 1968; Snyder & Diesing, 1977, pp. 183–184). Thomas Schelling, author of one of the most influential studies of deterrence, emphasized the interdependent nature of commitments; failure to defend one, he argued, will make willingness to defend any commitment questionable in the eyes of an adversary. "We tell the Soviets," Schelling (1966) wrote, "that we have to react here because, if we did not, they would not believe us when we said that we will react there" (p. 374).

Sensitivity to their bargaining reputation encourages leaders to make or to exaggerate the importance of commitments that lack substantive worth. Schelling (1966), for one, defended the value, indeed the necessity, of purely symbolic commitments. "Few parts of the world," he confessed, "Are intrinsically worth the risk of serious war by themselves, especially when taken slice by slice, but defending them or running risks to protect them may preserve one's commitments to action in other parts of the world and at later times" (p. 194). Along with other deterrence theorists, Schelling ignored the possibility of escalation inherent in the interconnection among commitments.

The U.S. commitment to the defense of Quemoy and Matsu is a striking example of this kind of deterrence logic and of its dangers. The Eisenhower administration recognized that neither island was of any value to the defense of Taiwan; they were useful only as possible stepping-stones for an invasion of the mainland, something Washington never contemplated. American leaders acknowledged, moreover, that the islands were militarily exposed, since they were only a few miles from the Chinese mainland and well within range of shore-based artillery. But Eisenhower feared the loss of the islands would undercut deterrence throughout Asia and accordingly he committed the United States to their defense. The paradoxical effect of the president's commitment was to encourage Chiang, now secure in the expectation that Washington was committed to the defense of the islands, to carry out the provocative buildup on Quemoy and Matsu that helped provoke a war-threatening confrontation. Had there been no American commitment, we can speculate that there would not have been a second crisis over the Taiwan Straits; its principal cause would have been absent.

Symbolic commitments are also entangling because they tend to become more important to policymakers than commitments made in defense of substantive interests. Their exaggerated importance is probably due in large part to the pernicious effect of postdecisional rationalization. Once the commitment is made, leaders, generally uncomfortable about risking war for abstract, symbolic reasons, seek to justify the commitment to themselves and to others. This need to rationalize motivates them to "discover" important substantive justifications for commitments—justifications irrelevant to their original calculations.

In the case of the Taiwan Straits, top-level administration officials, who previously had questioned the importance of the offshore islands, subsequently came to see them as the linchpin of security throughout Asia (Halperin & Tsou, 1967). George and Smoke (1974, pp. 386, 578) report that the most senior policy makers subscribed in all solemnity to an astonishing version of the "domino" theory. In a classified policy statement meant only for internal use, Eisenhower and Dulles both argued that loss of the islands would likely not only endanger the survival of the Nationalist regime on Taiwan, but also that of pro-American governments in Japan, Korea, the Philippines, Thailand, and Vietnam, and would also bring Cambodia, Laos, Burma, Malaya, and Indonesia under the control of communist forces.

The most far-reaching expression of this "logic" was Vietnam. American leaders committed forces to Vietnam in large part because they were persuaded that failure to defend their commitment in Southeast Asia would encourage Moscow to doubt U.S. resolve elsewhere in the world. In a major policy address in April 1965, President Lyndon Johnson (1965–1969) told the American people, "To leave Vietnam to its fate would shake...confidence...in the value of America's word" (p. 395). Secretary of State Dean Rusk (1971) warned that "the communist world would draw conclusions that would lead to our ruin and almost certainly to a catastrophic war" (p. 23).

Despite the adverse consequences of Vietnam, the American belief in the interdependence of commitments appears undiminished and continues to influence policy. In 1974–1975 it prompted President Ford's administration to provide covert aid to two of the contending factions in the Angolan civil war. When Congress compelled the administration to terminate this support, an irate Henry Kissinger (1977) predicted that this "would lead to further Soviet and Cuban pressures on the mistaken assumption that America has lost the will to counter adventurism or even to help others to do so" (p. 360). President Carter's administration employed similar arguments to justify its commitment to defend the Persian Gulf. More recently, members of the Reagan administration have argued vigorously that the Soviet Union would become even more emboldened throughout the Third World if the United States failed to help Central American governments combat left-wing military challenges.

Finally, deterrence can intensify conflict by encouraging leaders to interpret even ambiguous actions as challenges that require a response. This exaggerated sensitivity to challenge is very much a function of the heavy emphasis that deterrence places on a state's bargaining reputation. As Schelling (1966) has warned, "If you are invited to play a game of 'chicken' and you refuse, you have just lost" (p. 118). Invitations to play chicken in the international arena, however, are rarely direct and unambiguous. Challenges must be inferred from the context of events that, given the inherent complexity of international affairs, gives policy makers considerable leeway in determining their meaning. Challenges are particularly difficult to substantiate because they are generally defined in terms of the intent of an action rather than its effect. Leaders are much more likely to perceive a challenge when they believe damage to their state's interests and reputation is the principal goal of another's actions, not just its byproduct (Jones & Davis, 1965).

As the motivations of others are rarely transparent, not even in retrospect, the identification of a challenge entails a high degree of subjective attribution. Leaders are therefore likely to interpret events in accord with their preconceptions or political needs. The Reagan, administration's view of the issues at stake in Central America nicely illustrates this process. By emphasizing the alleged links between Cuba and left-wing movements in the region, the current administration defines the challenge as communist-inspired probes of America power and resolve. Ronald Reagan, Alexander Haig, George Shultz, and Caspar Weinberger have repeatedly asserted that if these revolutionary movements succeeded in gaining or maintaining power—as have the Sandinistas in Nicaragua—the Soviet Union and Cuba, encouraged by the failure of the United States to display resolve, would intensify their efforts at subversion throughout the hemisphere.

Critics of the administration dispute this interpretation and, indeed, question the existence of a challenge to the United States. They argue that revolutionary movements in Central America are indigenous and primarily a response to the region's economic backwardness and tradition of repressive governments. Consequently, the United States becomes a target of left-wing forces only insofar as it is the primary supporter of their local adversaries. Critics of the administration challenge the fundamental assumption that indigenous revolutionary movements constitute a test of American resolve.

The three processes that we have just described are important contributing causes of tension, misunderstanding, and fear between adversaries. They point to the greatest long-term danger of deterrence: its propensity to make the worst expectations about an adversary self-fulfilling. Threats and military preparations, the currency of deterrence, inevitably arouse the fear and suspicion of those they are directed against. As we have observed, at times they tend to provoke the very behavior that they are designed to prevent. Over time, military preparations, initially a consequence of tensions between states, can become an important cause. This kind of dynamic has operated between the United States and the Soviet Union, between Israel and the Arab states, and in the Sino–Soviet conflict. It was also a marked component of Sino–American relations in the 1950s and 1960s. In all these cases, the misunderstanding and tension caused by deterrence, overlain on the substantive issues that divided the protagonists, made these conflicts more acute, more difficult to manage, and less amenable to resolution.

The outlines of the policy dilemma are clear. Protagonists to a conflict need deterrence to prevent their adversaries from resorting to force, but the use of deterrence can simultaneously make the conflict more acute and more likely to erupt into war. Because deterrence can be ineffective, uncertain, and risky, it must be supplemented by other strategies of conflict management. These strategies, which we group together under the rubric of *reassurance,* at times might substitute for deterrence or, more likely, complement deterrence and reduce some of its obvious risks.

Part III: deterrence and reassurance

Strategies of reassurance begin from a different set of assumptions than does deterrence. They too presume ongoing hostility but, unlike deterrence, root the source of that hostility not primarily in adversaries' search for opportunity but rather in their sense of acute vulnerability. Reassurance dictates that defenders try to communicate to their adversaries their benign intentions. They do so to reduce the fear, misunderstanding, and insecurity that are often responsible for unintended escalation to war.[3]

The test of the effectiveness of strategies of reassurance is their contribution to the avoidance of war among adversarial leaders who are hostile and suspicious of one another. Even when leaders consider their conflict with their adversary to be incapable of resolution, they can nevertheless attempt to reassure their adversaries through a broad range of strategies in an effort to avoid accidental or miscalculated war. In so doing, they may simultaneously help alleviate the underlying causes of adversarial hostility.

To examine the utility of reassurance and the conditions that constrain its effectiveness, we look at several examples of reassurance strategies that vary in the scope of their objectives. Beginning with the most ambitious, leaders can attempt to shift the trajectory of the conflict and induce cooperation through reciprocal bargaining strategies. A variant of a reciprocal strategy, *tit for tat,* has recently received a great deal of attention. To compensate for some of the weaknesses of tit for tat, leaders can also try to break out of habitual conflict through less conventional methods of unilateral and irrevocable concessions. If they are pessimistic about or disinterested in these more ambitious strategies, leaders can try through more modest strategies to compensate for some of the obvious weaknesses of deterrence. They can attempt through self-restraint not to exacerbate the pressures and constraints that operate on an adversary who may choose force because of the costs of inaction. They can also try informally to develop "norms of competition" to regulate their conflict and reduce the likelihood of miscalculated war. In a closely related strategy, they can attempt to put in place informal or formal regimes designed specifically to build confidence, reduce uncertainty, and diminish the probability of miscalculated war.

These are only a few among many possible variants of strategies of reassurance. They are neither mutually exclusive nor logically exhaustive. Moreover, the evidence in support of these strategies is an uneven mix of quantitative and qualitative data, single case study, comparative case analysis, and laboratory experiment. Five strategies of reassurance have been chosen for analysis largely because there is some relevant evidence of their interaction with deterrence.

Finally, strategies of reassurance, like deterrence, are difficult to implement. They too must overcome strategic, political, and psychological obstacles. Cognitive barriers to signaling, for example, can just as readily obstruct reassurance as they can deterrence. Other obstacles are specific to reassurance, and derive from the political and psychological constraints that leaders face when they seek to reassure an adversary. We attempt to identify these obstacles and to assess their impact on the management of conflict.

Reassurance through reciprocity

Reciprocity has long been at the center of theoretical concerns among sociologists, psychologists, game theorists, and analysts of the international political economy. Its utility as a strategy of reassurance on security issues, however, has recently begun to receive serious attention (Axelrod, 1984; Keohane, 1986; Larson, 1986, 1987). When the issue is one of security, reciprocal behavior is most usefully conceived as a pattern of contingent, sequential, and diffuse exchange among interdependent adversaries (Larson, 1986). Different streams of evidence from experiments, computer simulations, analyses of international interaction, and historical cases converge to suggest that a strategy of reciprocity can be effective in inducing an adversary to cooperate. Reciprocal strategies do better than either consistent cooperation or consistent competitiveness.

In experimental studies, the player who cooperates consistently is frequently exploited by the other (Deutsch, Epstein Canavan, & Gumpert, 1967; Oskamp, 1971; Shure, Meeker, & Hansford, 1965). Indeed, in games of "chicken" where the payoffs for a fight are lower than those for being exploited, a strategy of consistent competition was more successful in eliciting cooperation from the other side than was consistent cooperation (Sermat, 1964, 1967). However, an unconditionally competitive strategy can result in a "lock-in" of competitive responses (Rapoport & Chammah, 1965; Sermat, 1964, 1967). This is especially so when both sides are about equal in strength and resolve.

Evidence from both experimental studies and analyses of international bargaining suggests that a graduated strategy that begins with competition and then moves to cooperation is more successful (Leng & Walker, 1982; Oskamp, 1971). An analysis of bargaining strategies during international crises suggests that an initial period of coercive bargaining is necessary to establish resolve; after this initial period, one or the other party is able to make concessions without appearing weak (Snyder & Diesing, 1977). However, an opening strategy of coercion risks a spiral of escalation that can be difficult to break.

Contingent strategies are more effective than any of the variants of noncontingent strategies in eliciting cooperation from an adversary (Oskamp, 1971; Patchen, 1987; Wilson, 1971). in a series of computer tournaments recently designed by Robert Axelrod (1984), a variant of a reciprocal strategy, tit for tat, proved most effective in inducing cooperation among egoistic players in an anarchic environment. Tit for tat succeeds because of its special attributes; it generally cooperates on the first move and thereafter replicates what the previous player has just done. It is therefore "nice," "forgiving," but "firm": nice, because it begins cooperatively in an effort to promote reciprocal concession; forgiving, because it does not retaliate immediately after a single defection; but firm, because thereafter it reciprocates defection with defection and thereby reduces the risk of exploitation for those who use the strategy. The stability of cooperation can be improved further if retaliation is marginally less than provocation. In large part because of this admixture of controlled firmness and conciliation, Axelrod suggests, tit for tat holds broad promise as a strategy of conflict management.

Huth's and Russett's (1988) analysis of the impact of bargaining strategies on the outcome of deterrence sustains the effectiveness of reciprocal strategies. In their study of 60 cases of extended deterrence, they emphasize the stabilizing effects of reciprocity, and propose that deterrence is more likely to succeed if defenders bargain with firm-but-fair reciprocal strategies and more likely to fail if they follow either noncontingent conciliatory or bullying strategies.

Contemporary historians have also looked at the impact of tit for tat in inducing cooperation among adversaries on specific, limited issues of international security. The informal moratorium on nuclear testing between 1958 and 1961, for example, was achieved through its use. In March 1958, the Soviet government announced that it was unilaterally halting all tests of nuclear weapons. Despite his previous insistence that he would not agree to a moratorium unless there were progress toward disarmament, President Eisenhower reluctantly reciprocated and neither power tested until 1961 (Divine, 1978). More recently, however, the Soviet Union, using the same kind of strategy on the same issue, failed to induce reciprocal cooperation on nuclear testing from the United States, even though it repeatedly extended its unilateral moratorium.

Several of the characteristics of tit for tat may limit its applicability as a strategy of reassurance on security issues. Paradoxically, its attractions can become liabilities when the strategy is used outside the laboratory in the international environment. Proponents of tit for tat extol its simplicity: unlike deterrence, it does not assume rationality, or altruism, trust, and communication, and it can be self-policing. As long as the participants value their future relationship, as long as the "shadow of the future" is long, players will learn to cooperate through trial and error (Axelrod, 1984, pp. 125–126, 173–174; Oye, 1985). Experimental studies show, however, that people learn to reciprocate by reasoning and making inferences about the other side's motives and future action (Oskamp, 1971, pp. 243, 256).

First, the preferences of the participants are likely to be critical to the outcome of the strategy. Axelrod experiments only with self-interested egoists rather than with participants who concentrate on relative gain. Experimental studies suggest that players do not optimize when they seek to obtain higher relative gains (Kuhlman & Marshello, 1975; Kuhlman & Wimberley, 1976; McClintock & McNeel, 1966a, b; Messick & McClintock, 1968; Messick & Thorngate, 1967). When experimenters separate players who emphasize relative gain, they find that competitors are likely to defect regardless of the strategy they encounter, even tit for tat.[4] Moreover, cooperators are frequently assimilated to competitors; when matched against competitors, they defect out of self-defense. Even more alarming, competitors do not recognize that their opponent responded in self-defense; on the contrary, they believe their adversary was motivated very much by the factors that governed their own behavior (Kelley & Stahelski, 1970; Kuhlman & Marshello, 1975).

Outside the laboratory, in international security disputes, adversaries are even more likely to be interested in maximizing relative differences. It is not their own gains, but their gains relative to those of their adversary that may be crucial in a conflict over security. Psychological experiments suggest that asymmetries of power make competitive play more likely (Marwell, Ratcliff, & Schmitt, 1969). There is evidence that such asymmetries can prevent the parties from even beginning a process of bargaining. President Gamar Abdel Nasser, for example, insisted that asymmetries in capabilities between Egypt and Israel after 1967 precluded negotiation and reciprocal concession. Under these conditions, tit for tat may not promote reciprocal cooperation.

Tit for tat also pays no attention to the cognitive schemata of the players, nor to the impact of standard heuristics and errors of attribution, estimation, and judgment—a deficiency that, as we have seen, gravely weakens theories of deterrence. A cooperative move is unlikely to be reciprocated if an adversary has long-standing and deeply held negative images that have been reinforced over time. In February 1971, for example, President Sadat (1977, pp. 302–303) offered to sign a peace agreement in return for a full withdrawal from all the territory that Israel had captured in 1967. The offer to Israel was unprecedented: no Arab leader had ever publicly indicated a willingness to sign an agreement with Israel. Not surprisingly, however, Israel's leaders systematically discounted the significance of the offer; they attributed the conciliatory gesture to the political weakness of the new president and to the success of Israel's deterrent strategy. Because the bad-faith image of Egypt was deeply entrenched, reconfirmed by more than two decades of active hostility, Israel's leaders not unexpectedly dismissed a conciliatory offer when one finally came. Under these circumstances, a single cooperative move was insufficiently reassuring to penetrate strongly negative images. Secretary of State John Foster Dulles also held such a bad-faith image of the Soviet Union. Consequently, he dismissed almost every conciliatory Soviet action as designed to deceive the United States and to create an illusory sense of complacency (Holsti, 1967; Larson, 1985, pp. 29–34; Stuart & Starr, 1982).

Studies of attribution find that people tend to explain the cooperative actions of others as due to situational factors and attribute their own cooperative behavior to their disposition (Nisbett & Ross, 1980; Ross, 1977). This was precisely the process of attribution that Israel's leaders used in 1971 when they explained Sadat's cooperative offer by his political weakness at home, by the growing economic crisis in Egypt, and by the dearth of strategic options available to Egyptian leaders. Here, the fundamental attribution error interacted with prevailing cognitive images to defeat the possibility of reciprocation.

Drawing on theories of social exchange, Deborah Larson (1986, p. 21) suggests that the way a target interprets the initiator's motives is crucial to the success of reciprocity. Particularly important is the attribution that an adversary made the concession freely and voluntarily, rather than accidentally or through compulsion (Blau, 1964; Enzle & Schopflocher, 1978; Gouldner, 1960; Greenberg & Frisch, 1972; Kelley & Thibaut, 1978). People are also more inclined to be receptive if they consider their opponent's motives to be benign. If they estimate that their opponent is engaged in deceit or has ulterior motives, they do not feel obliged to reciprocate (Nemeth, 1970; Schopler & Thompson, 1968). Whether leaders interpret an action as conciliatory or aggressive is often a function of their perception of the goals and strategy that motivate the action (Jervis, 1976, pp. 58–113).

Not only do cognitive schemata, heuristics, and biases affect the interpretation of the meaning of action, but motivational biases do so as well. Frequently, leaders give opposite labels to the same behavior when they initiate the action and when it is carried out by an adversary (Larson, 1985, pp. 37–38;). The United States, for example, labels Soviet arms sales to the Middle East as obstructionist and dangerous to the peace process, but describes its own substantial sales as an essential prerequisite of peacemaking. Affect and cognition interact to shape the inferences that American leaders make about their own as well as Soviet behavior. The action does not speak for itself.

Finally, experimental and simulated studies of tit for tat ignore the social, political, and strategic context in which the strategy is used. Experimental studies, for example, have identified asymmetries of power as crucial explanatory variables of the type of strategies players use (Marwell, et al. 1969). An opponent is also more likely to cooperate in response to a conciliatory action when the initiator of the action is equal or stronger in capabilities than the target (Chertkoff & Esser,

1976; Linskold & Aronoff, 1980). Differences in capability have not yet been systematically built into analyses of tit for tat. Nor have the strategic fears and needs that can compound strategic dilemmas and culminate in motivated error been given systematic attention; the success of tit for tat has not been explored in different kinds of strategic environments.

The social context in which tit for tat is used is also largely ignored in most of the experimental, simulated, and interaction studies. Leaders may differ, for example, in their perceptions of reciprocity and in the functional measures of equivalence that they use. These differences between the United States and the Soviet Union, for example, were starkly evident as the process of détente unraveled. Measures of equivalence in international security are defined by leaders' perceptions and expectations rather than by objective criteria, and are subject to cognitive and motivated bias.

The difficulty in establishing common criteria of reciprocity can be mitigated to some extent if leaders share social norms. As Axelrod (1986) observes, shared norms may increase the salience of collective interests and thus influence people's preference structures. In so doing, they decrease competitive play and make reciprocal bargaining more likely. Systematic evidence of the impact of shared norms, however, and of common criteria of legitimacy on reciprocal bargaining is still scarce (Gouldner, 1960). Moreover, as is evident from the analysis of shared norms of competition that follows, obstacles to their development among adversaries are considerable.

If tit for tat is to be useful as a strategy of conflict management among adversaries, the research agenda must be expanded beyond unitary, rational egoists to include both a range of preferences and the subjective meanings that leaders attach to the actions of their adversary. The learning model that underlies tit for tat is flawed and inadequate. Many of the cognitive and motivational errors that confound the interpretation of deterrent threats can also impede an accurate reading of a conciliatory action designed to promote reciprocity. The strategy also must be situated within its context. Differences in cultural, political, and strategic contexts can further complicate the prospects of a tit for tat strategy. Much like formal theories of deterrence, analysis of tit for tat remains largely contextual.

Variants of reciprocal strategies have been designed to compensate for some of the obvious weaknesses of tit for tat. First, outside the laboratory it is often difficult to start a cooperative sequence of action. An adversary may not always identify a cooperative action or indeed pay attention to a change embedded in recurrent behavior. We have already noted Israel's dismissal of Sadat's conciliatory offer in 1971. Second, even though tit for tat begins with a cooperative action, if the adversary defects both sides can easily be locked in to an escalating spiral of conflict. As Axelrod (1984) acknowledges, tit for tat can culminate in an "unending echo of alternating defections" (p. 176).

Experimental studies find that variants of reciprocal strategies like GRIT (Graduated and Reciprocated Initiatives in Tension-reduction), which incorporate conciliatory initiatives taken independently of the other's actions, are more effective than tit for tat in eliciting cooperation (Lindskold, 1978; Lindskold & Collins, 1978; Lindskold, Walters, & Koutsourais, 1983; Osgood, 1980; Pilisuk & Skolnick, 1968). Moreover, they were as effective among players who were judged generally competitive by their previous play as they were among those who were generally cooperative. A second variation that is also effective is a reciprocal strategy that is slow to retaliate and slow to return to cooperation; this variant of reciprocity allows for initial misperception (Bixenstine & Gaebelein, 1971; Pruitt & Kimmel, 1977). Similarly, the strategy of the "reformed sinner" elicits reciprocity; it begins with defection for a few moves to establish resolve before moving to contingent cooperation (Benton, Kelley, & Liebling, 1972; Harford & Solomon, 1967).

All these variants of a reciprocal strategy require attribution of the other's intentions and reasoning. In addition, because exchange in reciprocal strategies in international security disputes is sequential, they all require the willingness to accept the risk of an undesirable outcome. To reduce that risk and to improve the likelihood of reciprocal cooperation, adversaries may attempt to build in procedures for inspection, to decompose their concessions, to make their concessions reversible, or to rely on irrevocable commitments (Larson, 1988 ms. pp. 9, 16–17, 23–24). The advantages of verifiability and inspection are obvious, and have received a great deal of attention. Strategies of decomposition or fragmentation were widely used by Henry Kissinger as he negotiated disengagement agreements in a "step-by-step" process in the Middle East (Stein, 1983). Experimental studies show that the prisoner's dilemma disappears when players can choose sequentially in full knowledge of the other's move and can reverse their decision to cooperate (Deutsch, 1958; Wagner, 1983). We turn now to an examination of a strategy of irrevocable commitment designed to break out of a lock-in of conflictual exchange.

Reassurance through "irrevocable commitment"

When leaders recognize that misperception and stereotyping govern their adversary's judgments as well as their own, they can try, by making an irrevocable commitment, to reassure their adversary of their benign intentions (Schelling, 1960, pp. 131–137). In so doing, they attempt to change the trajectory of the conflict through "learning" and to make a cooperative reciprocal strategy possible. President Anwar el-Sadat of Egypt, for example, designed a strategy of irrevocable commitment to break through the prevailing images of Israel's leaders and public, and to break out of a locked-in pattern of conflictual bargaining. He deliberately chose to make a large, dramatic, and risky concession.

Dissatisfied with the progress of negotiations in the autumn of 1977 and alarmed at the prospect of reintroducing the Soviet Union into the bargaining process, Sadat searched for a dramatic move that would reduce the suspicion and distrust between Egypt and Israel. It was this suspicion, built up over decades, he argued, that constrained the attempt to negotiate the issues at stake and fueled the cycle of wars. He first considered asking the five permanent members of the United Nations' Security Council to meet in Jerusalem with the parties to the Arab–Israel conflict but was dissuaded by President Carter, who warned that such a strategy would fail (Carter, 1982, p. 307; Sadat, 1977, pp. 306–307). Secret negotiations between Egypt's deputy prime minister and Israel's foreign minister followed in Morocco, where each agreed to make a critical concession: Israel indicated its willingness to return the Sinai peninsula to Egyptian sovereignty and Egypt agreed to establish full peace and diplomatic relations with Israel; the broad outlines of an agreement were in place.

Shortly thereafter, in a speech to the People's Assembly in Cairo, Sadat offered to travel to Jerusalem to address Israel's parliament personally in an effort to persuade its members of the sincerity of Egyptian intentions. The reaction was outrage in the Arab world, incredulity among the Israeli public, and alarm among some of the senior military in Israel who considered the proposed visit a ruse to provide cover for a renewed attack. Within days, however, Sadat came to Jerusalem and spoke to the Knesset of the Egyptian terms for peace. Egyptian demands were unchanged, but Israel's leaders and public paid attention to the deed rather than to the words. In large part through this single dramatic act of reassurance, Sadat changed the trajectory of the conflict as both Egypt and Israel repudiated the use of force as their principal strategy of conflict management.

Why did reassurance succeed? Several factors were at play, some general and some specific to the historical context. First, the initiative was irreversible: once the president of Egypt traveled to Jerusalem, he could not undo the deed. Because it could not be reversed, the action was treated as a valid indicator of Egyptian intentions rather than as a signal that could be manipulated (Jervis, 1970). Israel's leadership and public recognized the irreversibility of the action and, consequently, gave it great weight.

Second, the substantial political cost to President Sadat of breaking the longstanding Arab taboo of not treating directly with Israel was also apparent to Israel's leaders. Dissension within the Egyptian government was pronounced; the Egyptian foreign minister resigned in protest. A tidal wave of criticism from the Arab world engulfed the Egyptian leader and Arab states moved in near-unison to sever diplomatic relations with Egypt. Experimental studies suggest that people determine the motives of a donor by how much the gift costs the giver: the greater the relative cost to the donor, the less likely ulterior motives (Komorita, 1973; Pruitt, 1981, pp. 124–125). These studies in attribution are consistent with evidence of the impact of the cognitive heuristic of "proportionality" (Lebow & Cohen, 1986; Stein, 1993). Israel's leaders reasoned that Egypt's president would not incur such heavy costs were he not sincere.

Third, Sadat's arrival in Jerusalem challenged the most important set of beliefs about Arab goals among Israel's leadership and public. A broad cross section of

Israelis had assumed that Arab leaders were unrelentingly hostile, so much so that they were unprepared to meet Israel's leaders face to face. Once these core beliefs were shaken, it became easier for Israelis, as cognitive psychologists predict, to revise associated assumptions and expectations.

Fourth, President Sadat spoke over the heads of Israel's leadership directly to Israel's public. With his flair for the dramatic, he created the psychological and political symbols that would mobilize the people to press their more cautious and restrained leaders. In so doing, he removed a constraint on Israel's leaders and created a political inducement to action. The strategy of reassurance had multiple audiences and multiple constituencies.

Fifth, the president of Egypt adopted a strategy of reassurance only after he judged that the conflict between Egypt and Israel had "ripened for resolution" (Stein, 1983; Zartman, 1985). In 1977, both sets of leaders shared a common aversion to war. Sadat's initiative took place after a war that both sides lost. The military outcome of the war in 1973 persuaded civilian and military leaders in Egypt of Israel's superior military capability under almost any set of conditions. Israel's leaders, in turn, became pessimistic for the first time about the capacity of deterrence, based on superior military capability, to prevent war. In 1977, the challenger, Egypt, was deterred because it was persuaded of the futility of the use of force, while the deterrer, Israel, had become skeptical of the efficacy of deterrence as an exclusive strategy of conflict management. Because they were pessimistic about the benefits of a further use of force, they were willing to consider seriously political alternatives that required major political concessions, even though they knew these concessions would be politically costly among their respective constituencies.

Under this very special set of conditions, reassurance through irrevocable commitment succeeded brilliantly. We must be very careful, however, in extrapolating from this single case. The two critical components that make an irrevocable commitment reassuring to an adversary are its obviously high cost to the leaders who issue the commitment and its irreversibility. It is often very difficult and very risky to design a commitment that is both high in cost and irreversible. Reliance on verbal declaration of good intentions to reduce an adversary's fears may not persuade. The aphorism, "words are cheap," is especially apt; promises made can be withdrawn. When, for example, King Edward VII went to Kiel in 1904 to try to reassure German leaders of the benign intentions of Britain's entente with France, he failed. German leaders inferred instead that the behavior of the British monarch was designed to blind Germany to the aggressive intentions of the entente and to create a false sense of security. This interpretation was consistent with German expectations; consequently, the British attempt at reassurance magnified the German estimate of the threat posed by the entente (Paléologue, 1932, pp. 48–49).

A suspicious adversary is likely to discount a reassuring verbal message because it can be reversed, often with little cost. A recent simulation of tacit bargaining in arms control finds that leaders are rarely certain enough about an opponent's response to make a large cooperative gesture, while the opponent is rarely trusting enough to respond enthusiastically to a small one (Downs & Rocke, 1987). In designing strategies of reassurance, therefore, leaders face a difficult trade-off: they are more likely to make offers that are reversible and less costly, but reversible low-cost offers are far less persuasive to an adversary as an indicator of intentions.

Like deterrence, outside the laboratory, reassurance through irrevocable commitment also requires a degree of freedom from domestic political and bureaucratic constraints. In Egypt after the October War, Sadat had great autonomy in decision making and, indeed, could withstand the resignation of his foreign minister. This kind of autonomy is far more difficult to achieve in highly institutionalized and open societies where interests are vested in existing strategies. The making of an irrevocable commitment to leaders long identified as antagonists can also be difficult to justify to the public. Public opinion may be a less powerful constraint, however, than are organized private and institutional interests that benefit from ongoing hostility. The favorable response of publics in Israel, and in the United States after President Nixon's visit to China, testifies to their flexibility.

Finally, an irrevocable commitment is more likely to reassure when both parties share a common aversion to war. To return again to the conflict between Egypt and Israel, Israel's leaders, after 1973, were far less optimistic that deterrence could prevent war and were pessimistic about the future benefits of a use of force. And, although we have no access to evidence that is directly relevant, the circumstantial evidence indicates that Egypt was deterred after 1973. Deterrence was based not on explicit threats issued by Israel's leaders nor on their conscious manipulation of risk, but rather on Egyptian estimates of Israel's continuing military superiority. In this case, general deterrence facilitated—indeed promoted—a high-cost, high-risk strategy of reassurance predicated on the assumption that an adversary could learn and change.

Reassurance through self-restraint

Leaders may be pessimistic about the possibility of changing their adversary's long-term intentions, but nevertheless recognize the political conditions that can compel an opponent to use force in the immediate future and attempt to prevent these pressures from becoming dangerously intense. This is no easy task. It may be very difficult to reduce the domestic political and economic pressures that are so often critical to a challenger's decision to use force. These kinds of factors are often not subject to manipulation, especially from the outside. However, even if defenders cannot directly affect the political environment of their opponent, at the least they can try to refrain from actions that would be likely to exacerbate the pressures on their adversary. Evidence of the impact of strategies of self-restraint, however, is both uneven and mixed.

In 1987, India and Pakistan found themselves caught up in a cycle of escalating troop movements. In the autumn of 1986, India announced plans for unusually large war games scheduled for February and March of 1987 at a newly completed training site in the Rajasthan desert near the border of the Pakistani province of Sind. Prune Minister Rajiv Gandhi described the operations as routine and assured Pakistan that India had no hostile intent. Given the unprecedented size of the Indian maneuvers, however, verbal reassurances were not enough to allay the fears of military leaders in Pakistan. Pakistani leaders also expressed concern that secessionists in Sind might ally with Indian forces. In response, Pakistan deployed military divisions just across the border from the Indian states of Punjab, Jammu, and Kashmir. These areas have been the site of fighting between India and Pakistan in the past.

Officials in both India and Pakistan admitted that neither wanted war. None of their disputes was sufficient, in and of themselves, to provoke war, and both recognized India's military superiority. Despite the mutually acknowledged difference in military capability, however, leaders in Pakistan and India both sent additional troops to the border area even as they expressed alarm that an accidental shot by either side could lead to full-scale fighting.

As both India and Pakistan became increasingly alarmed, both pledged to exercise self-restraint and agreed to high-level discussions designed to ease tension and allay mutual fear. The two delegations to the talks, led by Abdus Sattar, the foreign secretary of Pakistan, and Alfred Gonsalves, the acting foreign secretary in India, approved a partial withdrawal of approximately 80,000 of the 340,000 heavily armed soldiers who faced each other along the north-central border and agreed on further negotiations to arrange withdrawal of the remainder. The agreement further provided that, until the Indian army exercises ended, Pakistan continue to deploy its armor and troops in the Punjab. The two sides also undertook to exercise "the maximum restraint" and to avoid all provocative actions along the border. Neither side was confident that deterrence alone could prevent war and each recognized the need for self-restraint. The language each used to describe the agreement is revealing: Humayan Khan, the Pakistani ambassador to India, explained that "it was a question of mutual reassurances" since each side felt provoked by the other; and Gonsalves, India's chief negotiator, added that Pakistan had been reassured of India's intentions (Weisman, 1987).

A strategy of self-restraint can reduce some of the obvious risks of deterrence. Because it uses the language of reassurance rather than of threat, it can allay the fears of leaders caught in a process of escalation, as it did in India and Pakistan, and reduce the likelihood of miscalculation. However, it can be both demanding of and dangerous for those who use it. It is demanding because it requires leaders to monitor their adversary's political pressures, its strategic dilemmas, its leaders' estimates of the political and strategic costs of inaction, and their assessment of the alternatives. A strategy of self-restraint encourages leaders to consider their adversary's calculus within the broadest possible political and strategic context.

Like deterrence, it requires leaders to view the world through the eyes of their adversaries and, as we have seen, there are formidable cognitive and motivational impediments to reconstructing the calculus of another set of leaders. Perhaps because leaders pay attention to the vulnerabilities of their adversary as well as to its opportunities when they consider self-restraint, they may be able to overcome at least some of these impediments. At a minimum, they are more likely to do so than leaders who consider only deterrence.

A strategy of self-restraint is not only demanding, it can also be dangerous if it culminates in miscalculated escalation. When deterrers are attentive to the weaknesses of an opponent, to the possibility that they may provoke an adversary who is as yet uncommitted to a use of force, then they are more likely to exercise restraint. Would-be challengers, however, may misinterpret restraint and caution as weakness and lack of resolve. Britain's failure to deter Argentina in 1982 is a case in point.

Britain was extremely sensitive to what its leaders considered important domestic constraints on the Argentinian leadership. Attuned to the political weakness of their opponents, British leaders refrained from making overt threats or visible military preparations to defend the Falklands. Lord Carrington, British foreign minister at the time, later confessed, "[We] feared that it would lead to war by strengthening the hand of extremists in the *Junta*" (*Times*, 1982). The British government also responded with extraordinary timidity to a private Argentinian attempt to assert sovereignty over the South Georgia Islands, an obvious prelude to a challenge in the Falklands. HMS *Endurance,* an Antarctic survey ship sent to the islands in the aftermath of the incident, was then hastily withdrawn when three Argentinian warships appeared on the scene. Nicanor Costa Méndez, then Argentina's foreign minister, subsequently explained that the retreat of the *Endurance* after Carrington's earlier promise to Parliament that it would remain on station as long as necessary helped convince the junta that it had nothing to fear from Britain (Lebow, 1985b). The impact of the strategy of restraint was the obverse of what British leaders had intended: it strengthened the resolve of those committed to military action and allayed the anxieties of more moderate men like Costa Méndez who were now persuaded that a use of force would probably succeed.

Argentina's leaders went to war because of their belief that Britain would tolerate a use of force. The British dilemma—whether to try to prevent miscalculated escalation through self-restraint or to deter a premeditated challenge through threat and demonstration of resolve—is a recurrent problem in the choice of a strategy of conflict management. The policy problem is compounded by the fact that strategies designed to prevent the occurrence of one often exacerbate the likelihood of the other. More troublesome still, it may not be apparent before the fact which of the two routes to war is the more likely.

The Sino–Indian border conflict, which erupted into war in 1962, also illustrates the kinds of difficulties that leaders face when they try to design a mixed strategy to avoid both miscalculated escalation and a calculated challenge (Lebow,

1981, pp. 148–228). In 1961 Chinese soldiers surrounded Indian outposts that had been set up in contested areas of the Ladakh district. After they demonstrated their ability to cut off several of these outposts, the Chinese subsequently withdrew, leaving the Indian pickets unharmed. Hoping to deter further encroachments by India, Peking intended the limited action as a demonstration of resolve, which would nevertheless allow Indian leaders to back down without loss of face because violence had been avoided. Government officials in New Delhi, however, misinterpreted the Chinese reluctance to fire on the pickets as a sign of timidity. They reasoned that Chinese forces had failed to press their tactical advantage because Peking feared the consequences of a wider conflict with India. As a result, Indian leaders became more optimistic about the prospects of a successful challenge and bolder in their efforts to occupy as much of the disputed territory, east and west, as they could.

China's mixed strategy of a limited demonstration of resolve followed by restraint failed to prevent war. It failed because of serious miscalculations by India's leaders of China's intentions and its capabilities (Lebow, 1981, pp. 153–168). Prime Minister Jawaharlal Nehru and Foreign Minister Krishna Menon were persuaded that China would want to avoid the condemnation of the non-aligned bloc that would follow if it were to use force. Indian leaders also incorrectly saw themselves as militarily superior and interpreted the apparent Chinese reluctance to fire on the Indian pickets as evidence of fear of military defeat. This faulty assessment of the military balance can be traced to a series of self-serving and entirely unrealistic intelligence reports from a highly politicized military bureaucracy. The Chinese, who formulated their military assessment on the basis of a more thorough and careful analysis of the capabilities of the two sides, could not know how badly the Indian leadership was misinformed. Unaware of the nature and extent of India's miscalculations, they acted with restraint. In so doing, they reinforced precisely those expectations among Indian leaders most likely to promote rather than prevent a challenge.

Evidence of the use of restraint in the context of general deterrence is still fragmentary and episodic. Analysts have not yet examined the documentary record to identify the relevant universe of cases. The limited evidence that is available of the interactive use of restraint and demonstration of resolve suggests that each carries with it the risk of serious error. An exercise of restraint may avoid provocation of a beleaguered or frightened adversary, but it may also increase the likelihood of miscalculated escalation. The language of threat and demonstration of resolve, on the other hand, may reduce the probability that a challenger will underestimate a deterrer's response, but it may also provoke a vulnerable and fearful opponent.

Reassurance through "norms of competition"

Adversaries can also reassure one another of the limits of their intentions through the development of informal, even tacit, norms of competition in areas of disputed interest. Informal, shared norms among adversaries may delegitimate certain kinds of mutually unacceptable action and, consequently, reduce the need to manipulate the risk of war. They may also establish mutually acceptable boundaries of behavior and reduce some of the uncertainty that can lead to miscalculated war.

Some experimental studies examine the impact of shared norms on the propensity of players to cooperate. In one experiment, players were allowed pregame discussion and negotiation; they subsequently invoked social sanctions against "cheats" and "greed," and they continued to cooperate despite the experimenter's use of increasing payoffs for defection (Bonacich, 1972). Shared norms may also transform players' preference structures and consequently change the game matrix to permit cooperation (Axelrod, 1986). It has also been suggested that a concession that is readily interpreted as adherence to a shared norm is less likely to be interpreted as evidence of weakness and provoke a miscalculated challenge (Stern, Axelrod, Jervis, & Radnor, 1989).

Analyses of historical cases also deal with the impact of shared norms on crisis prevention and on war avoidance. The United States and the Soviet Union attempted to develop explicit understandings of the limits of competition when they signed the Basic Principles Agreement in 1972 and, a year later, a more specific agreement on consultation to deal with crises that threatened to escalate to nuclear war. These agreements were not a success, in part because the formal documents masked significant disagreements and differences in interpretation. If anything, the unrealistic expectations they aroused, the disputes over interpreting the agreements, the consequent allegations of cheating and defection, and the ensuing distrust and anger exacerbated the management of the conflict between the two nuclear adversaries (Stein, 1988]).

The United States and the Soviet Union were far more successful in establishing less formal and less explicit norms of competition in Cuba, and then in the Middle East (George, 1985). In both cases they did so because of a shared fear that their competition could escalate easily to a serious and dangerous confrontation. In 1962, President Kennedy declared that the United States would not invade Cuba, in return for an assurance that the Soviet Union would not again deploy offensive weapons on the island. There was some ambiguity, however, in subsequent years about the scope of the agreement and its duration. In August 1970, the Soviet Union inquired through diplomatic channels whether the agreement still remained in force. President Richard M. Nixon's administration reiterated its commitment to the shared norm and, shortly thereafter, invoked this understanding to object to the construction of a base in Cuba to service Soviet submarines.

Again in 1978, diplomatic discussions between Soviet and American officials focused on the replacement of older fighter-interceptor aircraft with newer ground-attack planes capable of carrying nuclear weapons. The Soviet Union reassured the United States of its intention to deploy only a limited number of aircraft and the matter was resolved.

The United States was less adept at handling the "discovery" of a brigade of Soviet combat forces in Cuba later that year. Although the brigade had been in Cuba since 1962. American intelligence focused attention on its presence in 1978. Although the shared norms did not appear to include ground forces, the Carter administration, under pressure from vocal critics in the Senate, nevertheless objected publicly that their presence violated the common understanding. The Soviet Union refused to withdraw the forces or to change their configuration, but reaffirmed the training mission of the forces that were present (Duffy, 1983).

Although the shared norm of competition was ambiguous, capable of multiple interpretation, and sensitive to domestic political processes, it nevertheless focused the attention of Soviet and American leaders on the boundaries of competition, and generally led to the mutual clarification of intentions and to a clearer definition of acceptable limits.

The usefulness of norms of competition in the Middle East provides a more dramatic illustration of their capability to regulate conflict. The United States and the Soviet Union have tacitly acknowledged that each may come to the assistance of its ally if it is threatened with a catastrophic military defeat by the ally of the other. To avoid such an intervention, the superpower must compel the regional ally who threatens to inflict such an overwhelming defeat to cease its military action (Dismukes & McConnell, 1979; George, 1985, p. 11). The Soviet Union invoked this tacit norm in 1967 and again in 1973, and although the United States attempted to deter Soviet intervention, it simultaneously moved to compel Israel to cease its military action and to reassure the Soviet Union immediately of its intention to do so. Deterrence and reassurance worked together and, indeed, it is difficult to disentangle the impact of one from the other on the effective management of that conflict (Stein, 1987).

In 1970, when Egypt's air defense capability had been destroyed, the Soviet Union also warned of its intention to intervene. This time, the Nixon administration responded only with a deterrent warning and made no attempt either to compel its ally to cease its air raids or to reassure the Soviet Union, not unexpectedly, deterrence failed as the Soviet Union introduced ground and air forces into Egypt. When the Soviet Union did so, however, the United States tacitly accepted the legitimacy of their presence and sought only to prevent their use in offensive activity. Implicitly, it acknowledged the legitimate Soviet interest in preventing a catastrophic military defeat of Egypt (George, 1985, p. 11; Stein, 1987).

Evidence of the preconditions and effectiveness of shared norms of competition is again episodic and unsatisfactory. Very little analysis has been done; there is as yet no systematic comparative analysis across cases of the success and failure of shared norms in managing conflict. George (1985) notes that these tacit and informal norms of competition in and of themselves do not provide a sufficiently stable basis for the management of conflict between the two superpowers; they lack both institutionalized arrangements and procedures for clarification of their ambiguities and extension to new situations. He suggests that shared norms of competition are likely to vary in utility according to the resources and strategies the superpowers can use, the domestic and international constraints they face, the leaders' capacity to formulate and differentiate their own interests as well as to evaluate the interests at stake for their adversary, the magnitude of each superpower's interest, and the symmetry of the distribution of interest. Tacit norms and patterns of restraint are more likely to emerge, for example, in areas of high-interest asymmetry than in areas of disputed or uncertain symmetry.

The preconditions for the development of effective norms of competition are rigorous, demanding, and unlikely to be met in many adversarial relationships. Indeed, the obstacles to success of shared norms are no less than those confronted by the strategy of deterrence. The cognitive and motivational limits to leaders' capacities to differentiate their own interests as well as to evaluate the interests at stake for their adversary are as severe as those that limit defenders' capacities to assess the interest of would-be challengers. Political pressures may encourage leaders to probe the limits of shared norms even as they incite would-be challengers to test the limits of commitment.

Given these obstacles, it is surprising that, in an area of disputed symmetry like the Middle East, the United States and the Soviet Union were able to agree tacitly on a shared norm to limit the most dangerous kind of conflict. When norms of competition are shared, the available evidence suggests that they do reduce some of the real risks of deterrence. Additional research is needed to identify those cases where shared norms of competition have succeeded and where they have failed. Only then can analysts assess the development and effectiveness of shared norms as a strategy of conflict management in the context of general deterrence.

Reassurance through limited security regimes

In an effort to reduce the likelihood of an unintended and unwanted war, adversaries have agreed, informally at times, on principles and put in place procedures to reduce the likelihood of accident or miscalculated war. Technically, these arrangements are referred to as *limited security regimes.*

The concept of "regime" was borrowed from international law and broadened to incorporate the range of shared norms, principles, rules, and procedures around which leaders' expectations converge (Krasner, 1982a). These principles and procedures may be formal or informal, tacit or explicit, but because some norms are shared, the behavior of leaders is constrained. A rich literature explores the creation and impact of regimes in the international political economy, but far less attention has been devoted to the analysis of the creation and impact of limited security regimes (Axelrod & Keohane, 1985; Keohane, 1984; Krachtowil & Ruggie, 1986; Lipson, 1984; Nye, 1986; Smith, 1987; Stein, 1985c; Young, 1986).

The creation of limited security regimes is most likely when leaders share a common aversion to war and to its consequences (A. Stein, 1982; Stein, 1985c). A shared fear of war is not restricted only to the nuclear powers; it occurs with

surprising frequency in the contemporary international system as military technology, conventional as well as nuclear, threatens ever greater destruction. The
evidence available suggests that limited security regimes among adversaries are
more likely to be created in the context of general deterrence, which enhances the
shared aversion to war (Nye, 1987; Stein, 1985c).

Also important is the configuration of interests among prospective members of
a regime. Limited security regimes can accommodate "egoists" more easily than
"competitors" as their principal participants. Leaders need not be interested in the
common good but can pursue their self-interest, irrespective of those of other participants. This capacity to accommodate egoists fits nicely with the evidence that
at times would-be challengers are inwardly focused, preoccupied with their own
needs and vulnerabilities. Regimes cannot, however, accommodate competitors
who seek to maximize the relative difference between their own gains and those
of their adversary (Messick & McClintock, 1968; Shubik, 1971).

The distribution of power also contributes in important ways to the creation of
international regimes. In the classical balance-of-power system, the weaker states
had little option but to accept the regime put in place by the great powers. In the
postwar world, the "hegemonic" position of the United States allowed it to create
regimes that facilitated cooperation among the advanced industrial states across a
wide variety of policy issues (Keohane, 1984; Keohane & Nye, 1977, pp. 38–60).
As a recent analysis of the nonproliferation regime demonstrates, however, the
presence of a hegemon is not a necessary prerequisite of the creation of a limited
security regime; on the contrary, collective action occurred in a period of hegemonic decline (Keohane, 1984, p. 46; Smith, 1987. pp. 268–269). New regimes
have often been created in the aftermath of an important change in the distribution of power, especially after a major war (Jervis, 1982, pp. 369–371).

Limited security regimes can be attractive to adversaries because they fulfill
important functions and provide valuable resources to their members that reduce
the risks of cooperation. Insofar as even limited security regimes provide reliable,
low-cost information about members' activities, they make action less opaque,
estimation less difficult, and reduce the likelihood of miscalculation. They reduce
uncertainty both about the behavior of adversaries and about the boundaries of
the conflict. In the limited security regime in place between Egypt and Israel
since 1974, for example, the United States has routinely circulated intelligence
information about the military dispositions of one to the other. They also link
issues together, lengthening the. "shadow of the future" and increasing the incentives to sacrifice immediate for future gain (Keohane, 1984, p. 88; Oye, 1985).[5]

Finally, adversaries may consider participation in a limited security regime if
it improves the accuracy of detection and reduces the likelihood of defection. A
regime may permit adversaries to monitor each other's actions with increased
confidence by providing more complete and reliable information, by increasing
surveillance capabilities for all parties, or by invoking the assistance of outsiders as monitors. It can give leaders more leeway than they otherwise would have

to meet a prospective defection by increasing available warning time (Stein, 1985c).

Evidence drawn from the Middle East illustrates the possibilities and benefits of limited, informal security regimes that, although they were negotiated under the most adverse conditions, nevertheless endured for a considerable period of time. It is not difficult to illustrate their utility in the management of conflict between Egypt and Israel in the last decade. Building upon a series of limited arrangements agreed upon in the context of general deterrence, Egypt and Israel, with the help of the United States, were ultimately able to agree on a set of principles and to put in place a complex series of procedures designed to reduce the probability of mis-calculated escalation. Limited arms control provisions, creation of buffer zones, sharing of intelligence information, the deployment of an international force, and the involvement of the United States as a third-party guarantor, presently work within the framework of a formally agreed-upon limited security regime to reduce uncertainty, clarify intentions, and minimize the risk of unintended war.

While it is not difficult to establish the relevance of a limited security regime in the favorable military and political conditions created by the war in 1973, the prospects of creating and maintaining a limited regime in the far harsher climate after the Suez war in 1956 are less obvious. In this sense, the experiment after 1956 can serve as a critical case. In the mid-1950s, Egypt and Israel were parties to a bitter conflict that had twice erupted into war and each suspected the other of the intention to expand. Analysts argue that these conditions preclude the creation of even a limited security regime (Jervis, 1982; Lipson, 1984). Yet some important preconditions were present.

After the war in 1956, general deterrence was reestablished. Israel, the deterrer, was then a status quo power with obvious military superiority and little interest in a use of force. Egypt, the challenger, was unprepared militarily and economically for further fighting. Politically, however, Egypt was unable and unwilling to consider any agreement whose function was more extensive than the avoidance of unwanted war; an adversarial relationship was still very much present. Nevertheless, both sides perceived war as costly and unattractive, at least for the moment, and they were both interested in procedures that could reduce the probability of an accidental conflict and simultaneously minimize the risk of a surprise attack. They were prepared to negotiate informally—indeed, indirectly and tacitly—a limited set of principles and procedures narrowly focused on the management of security in the Sinai peninsula.

The informal and limited regime had several components. Israel insisted publicly and Egypt acquiesced tacitly that there was to be no blockade of the Straits of Tiran at the southeastern tip of the peninsula. Egypt also agreed to the deployment of a United Nations' peacekeeping force (UNEF) just inside the eastern border of the Sinai, on Egyptian territory. This force was formally charged with patrolling, manning sensitive border positions, and preventing infiltration across the border.

The United Nations' force was not so much a fire brigade as a fire alarm. Its most important function was not explicit but tacit: it could not prevent an attack but it could provide valuable warning time of an impending attack in at least two ways. Both Egypt and Israel expected that the withdrawal of the force would require time-consuming multilateral discussions at United Nations headquarters in New York. This would provide valuable advance warning to the deterrer of an impending defection by the challenger. Moreover, because a demand for the withdrawal of UNEF would signal a clear change in purpose, the challenger's intentions became far less opaque and easier to read. Consequently, agreement by Egypt to the deployment of an international force reassured Israel.

Another important component of the informal regime was a tacit consensus on the deployment of Egyptian forces in the Sinai. Egypt deployed only two divisions, well back in the western half of the desert, reinforced by no more than 250 tanks; this configuration of force did not represent an immediate threat to Israel (Evron, 1975). Although the scope of the arms control arrangements was limited and tacit, they nevertheless functioned as a hedge against accidental war and again as an effective early warning system. By limiting contact between the crack units of Israel's and Egypt's armed forces, the likelihood of war arising out of a chance, accidental encounter was reduced; in this sense, the limited, informal, and tacit components of the regime worked effectively to avoid an outcome that neither side wanted.

Because a massive deployment of the Egyptian army in the Sinai would have to precede any ground action, violation of these tacit rules would alert Israel to an impending attack. Israel's confidence in its general deterrent capability was therefore considerable as long as these rules were observed. Consequently, its leaders felt less need to resort to the language of threat or to engage in the conscious manipulation of the risk of war.

The informal, limited regime also permitted expectations to stabilize and converge about the management of security in the Sinai peninsula. The management of conflict therefore became easier as the actions of both parties became more predictable. Contrary to much of regime theory, expectations stabilized after rather than before the limited regime was in place as both sides began to learn.

Although the limited security regime was tacitly negotiated, narrowly focused, and informal, it persisted for 11 years and reassured both Egypt and Israel through important changes in the distribution of political and military power. Indeed, at times it protected President Nasser from the pressures of his Arab constituency. The proposition that even limited reassurance in the context of general deterrence was of considerable value to both challenger and defender is sustained by the special conditions that attended the disruption of the regime.

The regime was not destroyed through a premeditated repudiation but rather as a result of serious miscalculation, first by President Nasser and then by the Secretary-General of the United Nations, U Thant. The president of Egypt, under considerable pressure from his Arab constituency, asked for a partial withdrawal of UNEF but the secretary-general insisted on a complete withdrawal of the force if changes in its status were made. In so doing, U Thant not only removed the smoke detector from an overheated environment, but also dismantled a system of crisis management that provided time for outsiders to search for political solutions. When the peacekeeping force was pulled out, both Egypt and Israel immediately recognized that a war that neither had sought directly was now unavoidable. The experiment in reassurance, however, was not in vain; some learning had taken place. Seven years and two wars later, Egypt, Israel, and the United States began the painstaking process of creating a better institutionalized, more explicit, more broadly focused security regime. This successor regime permitted considerable learning and a change in both Egypt's and Israel's definitions of their interests. Today, in the context of ongoing general deterrence, these revised definitions of interests set the parameters for the management of the conflict between Egypt and Israel.

Reassurance through the creation of limited security regimes has not been restricted only to Egypt and Israel. The United States and the Soviet Union agreed in 1967 to the demilitarization of outer space in an effort to limit the scope of their conflict. In 1970 they actively promoted the nonproliferation regime and, in 1972, negotiated a limited regime to reduce the likelihood of accident and miscalculated conflict at sea (Lynn-Jones, 1985). They have also regulated their conflict in central Europe through the Austrian State Treaty, the Berlin agreements, and the Final Act of the Conference on Security and Cooperation in Europe.

Most recently, the superpowers and their allies negotiated a limited security regime designed to build confidence in central Europe. Advance notification and inspection of large military maneuvers are expected to reduce uncertainty, reassure an alarmed adversary, clarify intentions, and diminish the likelihood of accidental war. All of these limited security regimes were created in the context of an ongoing adversarial relationship in which both sides continued to rely on general deterrence to prevent war. Within this context, both sets of leaders attended not to the aggressive intentions of the other but rather to their shared fears and common aversion to war.

Reassurance through the creation of limited and focused security regimes can be of considerable help in reducing fear, uncertainty, and misunderstanding between adversaries. At a minimum, adversaries gain access to more reliable and less expensive information about each other's activities, which can reduce uncertainty, the incidence of miscalculation, and an inappropriate manipulation of the risk of war. In a complex international environment that is often information poor and technologically driven, lower cost and more valid information can be a considerable advantage in more effective management of conflict.

There are serious obstacles to the creation of limited security regimes even when adversaries share a powerful common aversion to war. First, the cost of unreciprocated participation is inordinately high because security is prerequisite to all other values and even minor miscalculations can have large consequences (Jervis, 1982). The defection of an adversary from a regime is almost certain to have graver consequences when the issue is security than, for example, when it is economic. The magnitude of the consequences of error makes limited security regimes especially difficult and risky to build. Closely related to the absolute scope of potential loss in security disputes is the difficulty in estimating the probability of loss. As the earlier analysis of deterrence suggests, estimating the motives and intentions of adversaries is very difficult, as is interpreting an opponent's behavior. Precisely because the consequences of error are so great, leaders have an understandably pronounced fear of deception (Lipson, 1984).

Fear of a surprise attack can encourage leaders to try to build limited security regimes, but it can also make their attainment immeasurably more difficult. Leaders who otherwise might prefer to participate in a limited security regime may nevertheless refrain if they fear a devastating surprise attack. If the advantage to the side who strikes first is large, then leaders are not likely to weigh future benefits heavily in an uncertain and dangerous present. On security issues it is often difficult and dangerous to forego present advantage for future benefit (Oye, 1985). In short, the critical obstacles to the creation of security regimes lie in the unique dangers and consequences of error, dangers that are manifest in the extraordinary difficulties of detection and the grave consequences of defection (Stein, 1985c).

Nevertheless, analysis of the creation and maintenance of limited security regimes is valuable insofar as it highlights the frameworks that adversaries have created to improve the management of their conflict. The episodic evidence available suggests that creation of a limited security regime is likely when adversaries share a mutual aversion to war, when general deterrence is in place, and when neither party seeks to maximize relative gain on the specific issue. A careful reading of the very small number of studies of limited security regimes suggests that the relationship between deterrence and reassurance is interactive: general deterrence can be a critical precondition of limited security regimes among adversaries and reassurance can eliminate some of the discourse of threat that otherwise might inflame a frightened adversary. In this sense, general deterrence and reassurance can become reinforcing strategies of conflict management.

We still need to know a great deal more, however, about how limited security regimes are created and maintained. Current theories give inadequate weight to the cognitive and motivational factors that are crucial to the formation of regimes. Although the distribution of power and the configuration of interests are important variables, they do not adequately explain the creation of the non-proliferation regime or the limited security regimes in the Middle East (Smith, 1987; Stein, 1985c). What leaders know and what they learn is central; it is, after all, leaders' expectations and preferences that are treated as the critical intervening variables by analysts of international regimes. Nevertheless, there is no explicit theory of cognitive change, no explanation of how leaders' expectations stabilize, converge, and change.

There has been little systematic analysis, for example, of the impact of cognitive schemas, heuristics, and biases on leaders' expectations, nor is the analysis of the maintenance and demise of security regimes informed by an explicit theory of learning (Nye, 1987; Rosenau, 1986). How do leaders interpret and reinterpret shared norms? One of the significant benefits of international economic regimes is their autonomous impact, their "lag" effect, even after underlying political and economic conditions have changed. Even though interests change, the international institutions that were created remain in place and continue to regulate conflict in the international political economy (Krasner, 1982b). Can we expect the same beneficent impact from limited security regimes? Do leaders change their definition of their interests in part because of their participation in limited security regimes? Does sufficient learning occur to mitigate the intensity of some international conflicts (Nye, 1987)? If so, under what political and strategic conditions does this occur?

Nor do existing theories pay sufficient attention to motivational explanations of leaders's definitions of their interests. Although interests are essential variables in the explanation of regime creation, they generally are specified through microeconomic reasoning (Keohane, 1984). Insofar as leaders are motivated by the fear of war, however, models of rational choice may obscure the impact of fundamental psychological processes on leaders' preferences. Political and strategic needs, for example, may significantly affect the way leaders value the costs and benefits of a limited security regime.

Analyses of the creation, maintenance, and impact of limited security regimes have only just begun. The empirical studies are few (Jervis, 1982; Nye, 1987; Smith, 1987; Stein, 1985c) and the theory is still developing. Through controlled comparative analysis, historical cases can be identified for investigation and richer theoretical models developed. Explanations must assess the impact of domestic political processes as well as strategic conditions on leaders' needs and expectations and must model processes of learning and change. In short, the research agenda must explore when and how, in the context of general deterrence, adversaries' fears can best be exploited to put in place limited security regimes to reduce the likelihood of unwanted war.

Conclusions

This analysis of deterrence and reassurance has reviewed their theoretical assumptions, the fit of the theory with the available evidence, and the quality of the evidence that sustains arguments of their strengths and weaknesses. It has also explored their respective advantages and disadvantages as strategies of conflict management under different conditions. Theories of deterrence are generally unsatisfying: many of their fundamental assumptions are not sustained by the evidence nor do they generate conditional propositions about the utility of deterrence. Theories of reassurance draw widely from the behavioral sciences, but little attempt has been made either to integrate theoretical propositions or to test their validity in different kinds of international environments. Nor have their interactive effects been examined across a series of cases. Finally, scholars have yet to agree on the relevant universe of cases that can be used to test both sets of theories and their interaction. Consequently, the evidence available is fragmentary, often episodic, frequently open to multiple interpretation, and difficult to evaluate. It is, however, drawn increasingly from a wide range of experimental, simulated, and historical studies. It is within this context of flawed theory and uneven evidence that the following tentative propositions are put.

Evidence is beginning to cumulate from a range of historical studies about the factors that contribute to the failure of deterrence, but not enough is known about the conditions associated with its success, or with the success or failure of reassurance. Equally important, the interactive effects of these strategies under varying conditions need more attention. Pruitt and Rubin (1986) suggest that a combination of firmness and concern is most effective in managing social conflict. In the management of international conflict, the available evidence suggests that deterrence and reassurance are appropriate at different times in different sequences.

Deterrence is appropriate only when adversarial leaders are motivated largely by the prospect of gain rather than by the fear of loss, are free to exercise restraint, are not misled by grossly distorted assessments of the political–military situation, and are vulnerable to the kinds of threats a deterrer is capable of making credible. If challengers do not share these cognitive, motivational, and political attributes, a strategy of deterrence is likely to fail. The timing of deterrence is also important. The effectiveness of deterrence is enhanced if it is used early, before an adversary becomes committed to a use of force and becomes correspondingly insensitive to warnings and threats. If these conditions are not met, deterrence is likely to be at best ineffective and at worst provocative.

The evidence also suggests that when would-be challengers feel politically vulnerable or fear attack from abroad, deterrence as a strategy of conflict management may provoke the very response it is attempting to prevent. There is considerable support for this proposition from behavioral decision theory, which suggests that people will take much larger risks to avoid loss than to seek gain (Kahneman & Tversky, 1979). When leaders seek to avoid loss, deterrence is not only ineffective, it may be dangerous. Domestic political instability and/or strategic vulnerability may provoke motivated distortion of basic processes of inference, estimation, and judgment, which can defeat deterrence.

When would-be challengers are motivated largely by need and are seriously constrained at home and abroad, variants of reassurance can supplement deterrence. Reassurance promises to reduce the distrust and fear that can propel a challenger to use force. It can succeed, however, only with an adversary who is concerned primarily about its own security and does not seek to exploit. A great deal of evidence drawn from experimental, simulated, and historical studies suggests that a strategy of reciprocity that builds in unilateral cooperative actions may induce an adversary to cooperate and avoid a spiraling process of escalation. A wide range of studies demonstrates the need to use a mix of strategies to establish resolve and credibility as well as to persuade an adversary that an offer to cooperate is genuine. As in deterrence, however, the theoretical literature is insufficiently sensitive to the cognitive, motivational, political, and strategic factors that can limit the effectiveness of reciprocity. It is especially striking that the theoretical specification of reciprocal processes does not include learning or change, despite the importance of motive attributions, subjective preferences, and attitudes toward gain in affecting reciprocal cooperation.

Preliminary historical and comparative research suggests that more modestly conceived strategies may be effective in reducing some of the obvious risks of deterrence. In the context of general deterrence, self-restraint, the development of informal forms of competition, and limited security regimes can help reassure a vulnerable adversary and reduce the likelihood of unwanted war. To succeed, however, they must overcome some of the psychological, political, and strategic obstacles that confound deterrence.

Designing strategies of conflict management that combine components of deterrence and reassurance is no easy task. There are formidable obstacles to the success of these strategies, individually and collectively, and the risks of one are often the benefits of the other. No single strategy is likely to work across cases under different strategic, political, and psychological conditions. Nevertheless, sensitivity to the limiting conditions of each strategy, to their relative strengths and weaknesses, and to their interactive effects is essential to the management of international conflict short of war.

Acknowledgment

Research for this study was supported by grants from the Carnegie Corporation of New York to Richard Ned Lebow, and by a grant from the Canadian Institute of International Peace and Security to Richard Ned Lebow and Janice Gross Stein.

Notes

1 The definition of adequate communication and apparent resolve is difficult. For purposes of assessing the theory of deterrence, the appropriate test must be the judgment of disinterested third parties and not that of the would-be challenger. As we will show, the latter's receptivity to communications and its judgment about a commitment's credibility may be impaired by motivated biases.

2 These cases are Fashoda (1898), Korea (1903–1904), Agadir (1911), World War I (July 1914), the Chinese entry into the Korean War (1950), Cuba (1962), the Sino–Indian crisis of 1962, and the Arab–Israeli wars of 1967, 1969, and 1973.

3 In experimental studies, reassurance strategies are appropriate to games of prisoner's dilemma and chicken. For an examination of these payoff matrices and their application to international conflict, see Snyder and Diesing (1977).

4 Play in the prisoner's dilemma does not distinguish players with a relative gain orientation. The matrix does not permit the analyst to distinguish the motives behind a competitive move: the same choice, "D." maximizes both individual and relative gain (Larson, 1987, pp. 26–27).

5 This "functional" theory explains regime maintenance rather than the creation of regimes. Insofar as the functions that a limited security regime can perform are known to would-be members, however, they can become incentives to participate when adversaries share a common aversion to war.

References

Abel, E. (1966). *The missile crisis.* Philadelphia, PA: Lippincott.

Allison, G. (1971). *Essence of decision: Explaining the Cuban missile crisis.* Boston: Little, Brown.

Axelrod, R. (1984). *The evolution of cooperation.* New York: Basic Books.

Axelrod, R. (1986). An evolutionary approach to norms. *American Political Science Review, 80,* 1095–1111.

Axelrod, R., & Keohane, R. (1985). Achieving cooperation under anarchy. *World Politics, 38,* 226–254.

Benton, A. A., Kelley, H. H., & Liebling. B. (1972). Effects of extremity of offers and concession rate on the outcomes of bargaining. *Journal of Personality and Social Psychology, 24,* 73–83.

Bialer, S. (1986). *The Soviet paradox: External expansion, internal decline.* New York: Alfred Knopf.

Bixenstine, E., & Gaebelein, J. (1971). Strategies of 'real' opponents in eliciting cooperative choice in a prisoner's dilemma game. *Journal of Conflict Resolution, 15,* 157–166.

Blau, P. (1964). *Exchange and power in social life.* New York: John Wiley & Sons.

Bonachich, P. (1972). Norms and cohesion as adaptive responses to potential conflict: An experimental study. *Sociometry, 35,* 357–375.

Borg, D., & Okamoto, S. (Eds.) (1973). *Pearl Harbor as history: Japanese-American relations, 1931–1941.* New York: Columbia University Press.

Brodie, B. (1959). The anatomy of deterrence. *World Politics, 11,* 173–192.

Brown, R. G. (1976, Summer). Chinese politics and American policy: A new look at the triangle. *Foreign Policy, 23,* 3–23.

Bullock, A. (1964). *Hitler: A study in tyranny* (rev. ed.). New York: Harper & Row.

Butow, R. (1961). *Tojo and the coming of the war.* Stanford, CA: Stanford University Press.

Carter, J. (1982). *Keeping faith: Memoirs of a president.* New York: Bantam.

Chertkoff, J. M., & Esser, J. K. (1976). A review of experiments in explicit bargaining. *Journal of Experimental Social Psychology, 12,* 464–456.

Clay, L. D. (1950). *Decision in Germany.* Garden City, NY: Doubleday.

Craig, G. A. (1964). *The politics of the Prussian army, 1640–1945.* New York: Oxford.

Davison, W. P. (1958). *The Berlin blockade.* Princeton, NJ: Princeton University Press.

Deutsch, H. C. (1978). *Hitler and his generals: The hidden crisis, January–June 1938.* Minneapolis: University of Minnesota Press.

Deutsch, M. (1958). Trust and suspicion. *Journal of Conflict Resolution, 2,* 265–279.

Deutsch, M., Epstein, Y., Canavan, D., & Gumpert, P. (1967). Strategies of inducing cooperation: An experimental study. *Journal of Conflict Resolution, 11,* 345–360.

Dismukes, B., & McConnell, J. M. (Eds.) (1979). *Soviet naval diplomacy.* New York: Pergamon Press.

Divine, R. (1978). *Blowing on the wind: The nuclear test ban debate, 1954–1960.* New York: Oxford University Press.

Downs, G. W., & Rocke, D. M. (1987). Tacit bargaining and arms control. *World Politics, 39,* 297–325.

Duffy, G. (1983). Crisis prevention in Cuba. In A. George (Ed.), *Managing U.S.-Soviet rivalry: Problems in crisis prevention* (pp. 285–318). Boulder. CO: Westview Press.

Enzle, M., & Schopflocher, D. (1978). Instigation of attribution processes by attributional questions. *Personality and Social Psychology Bulletin, 4,* 595–599.

Evangelista, M. A. (1983–84, Winter). Stalin's postwar army reappraised. *International Security, 7,* 110–138.

Evron, Y. (1975). The demilitarization of the Sinai. In *Jerusalem Papers on Peace Problems.* Jerusalem: Leonard Davis Institute for International Relations.

Gaddis, J. L. (1972). *The United States and the origins of the Cold War, 1941–47.* New York: Columbia University Press.

Gelman, H. (1982). *The Soviet Far East buildup and Soviet risk-taking in China* (Rand Report R2943-AF). Santa Monica, CA: Rand.

George, A. (1985). *U.S.-Soviet global rivalry: Norms of competition.* Paper presented to the XIIIth World Congress of the International Political Science Association in Paris.

George, A. L., & Smoke, R. (1974). *Deterrence in American foreign policy: Theory and practice.* New York: Columbia University Press.

Gouldner, A. W. (1960). The norm of reciprocity: A preliminary statement. *American Sociological Review, 25,* 161–178.

Greenberg, M. S., & Frisch, D. M. (1972). Effect on intentionality on willingness to reciprocate a favor. *Journal of Experimental Social Psychology, 8,* 99–111.

Gurtov, M., & Hwang, B.-M. (1980). *China under threat: The politics of strategy and diplomacy.* Baltimore, MD: Johns Hopkins University Press.

Halperin, M. H., & Tsou, T. (1967). The 1958 Quemoy crisis. In M. H. Halperin (Ed.), *Sino-Soviet relations and arms control.* Cambridge, MA: MIT Press.

Harford, T., & Solomon, L. (1967). "Reformed sinner" and "Lapsed saint" strategies in the prisoner's dilemma game. *Journal of Conflict Resolution, 11,* 104–109.

Herz, J. (1964, Autumn). The relevancy and irrelevancy of appeasement. *Social Research, 31,* 296–320.

Hilsman, R. (1967). *To move a nation.* Garden City, NY: Doubleday.

Holloway, D. (1984). The Warsaw pact in transition. In D. Holloway & J. M. O. Sharp (Eds.), *The Warsaw pact: Alliance in transition* (pp. 19–38). Ithaca, NY: Cornell University Press.

Holsti, O. R. (1967). Cognitive dynamics and images of the enemy: Dulles and Russia. In D. J. Finlay, O. R. Holsti, & R. R. Fagen (Eds.), *Enemies in politics* (pp. 25–96). Chicago: Rand McNally.

Horelick, A. L. (1964). The Cuban missile crisis: An analysis of Soviet calculations and behavior. *World Politics, 16,* 380–382.

Horelick, A. L., & Rush, M. (1966). *Strategic power and Soviet foreign policy.* Chicago: University of Chicago Press.

Hosoya, C. (1968). Miscalculations in deterrence policy: Japanese-U.S. relations. 1938–1941. *Journal of Peace Research, 2,* 79–115.

Huth, P., & Russett. B. (1984). What makes deterrence work? Cases from 1900 to 1980. *World Politics, 36,* 496–526.

Huth, P., & Russett, B. (1988). Deterrence failure and escalation to war. *International Studies Quarterly, 32,* 29-45

Ienaga, S. (1978). *The Pacific war, 1931–1945*. New York: Pantheon.

Ike, N. (1967). *Japan's decision for war, records of 1941: Policy conferences*. Stanford, CA: Stanford University Press.

Janis, I. L., & Mann, L. (1977). *Decision making: A psychological analysis of conflict, choice and commitment*. New York: Free Press.

Jervis, R. (1970). *The logic of images in international relations*. Princeton, NJ: Princeton University Press.

Jervis, R. (1976). *Perception and misperception in international politics*. Princeton, NJ: Princeton University Press.

Jervis, R. (1979). Deterrence theory revisited *World Politics, 31,* 289–324.

Jervis, R. (1982). Security regimes. *International Organization, 36,* 357–378.

Jervis, R., Lebow, R. N., & Stein, J. G. (1985). *Psychology and deterrence*. Baltimore, MD: Johns Hopkins University Press.

Johnson, L. B. (1965–1969). Speech given at Johns Hopkins University, 7 April 1965. In *Public papers of the presidents of the United States: Lyndon B. Johnson, 1965*. Washington, D.C.: Government Printing Office.

Jones, E. E., & Davis, K. E. (1965). From acts to dispositions: The attribution process in person perception. In L. Berkowitz (Ed.), *Advances in experimental social psychology* (Vol. 2, pp. 219–266). New York: Academic Press.

Kahneman, D., & Tversky, A. (1979). Prospect theory: An analysis of decision under risk. *Econometrica, 47,* 263–291.

Kalicki, J. H. (1975). *The pattern of Sino-American crises*. New York: Cambridge University Press.

Kaplan, M. A. (1958, October). The calculus of deterrence. *World Politics, 11,* 20–44.

Kaufmann, W. W. (1954). *The requirements of deterrence*. Princeton, NJ: Center of International Studies.

Kelley, H. H., & Stahelski, A. J. (1970). Social interaction basis of cooperators and competitors' beliefs about others. *Journal of Personality and Social Psychology, 16,* 66–91.

Kelley, H. H., & Thibaut, J. W. (1978). *Interpersonal relations: A theory of interdependence*. New York: John Wiley & Sons.

Keohane, R. O. (1984). *After hegemony*. Princeton, NJ: Princeton University Press.

Keohane, R. O. (1986). Reciprocity in international relations. *International Organization, 40,* 1–28.

Keohane, R. O., & Nye, J. S. (1977). *Power and interdependence: World politics in transition*. Boston: Little, Brown.

Khrushchev, N. S. (1970). *Khrushchev remembers: The last testament,* (Strobe Talbott, Trans.). Boston: Little, Brown.

Kissinger, H. A. (1960). *The necessity of choice*. New York: Harper.

Kissinger, H. A. (1977). *American foreign policy* (3rd ed.). New York: Norton.

Kissinger, H. A. (1979). *The White House years*. Boston: Little, Brown.

Komorita, S. S. (1973). Concession-making and conflict resolution. *Journal of Conflict Resolution, 17,* 745–762.

Krachtowil, F., & Ruggie, J. G. (1986). International organization: A state of the art or an art of the state? *International Organization, 40,* 753–776.

Krasner, S. (Ed.) (1982a, Spring). International regimes [Special issue]. *International Organization.* 36(2).

Krasner, S. (1982b, Spring). Structural causes and regime consequences: Regimes as intervening variables. *International Organization, 36*(2), 185–205.

Kuhlman, M. D., & Marshello, A. F. J. (1975). Individual differences in game motivation as moderators of preprogrammed strategy effects in prisoner's dilemma. *Journal of Personality and Social Psychology, 32,* 922–931.

Kuhlman, D. M, & Wimberley, D. L. (1976). Expectations of choice behavior held by cooperators, competitors and individualists across four classes of experimental game. *Journal of Personality and Social Psychology, 34,* 69–81.

Larson, D. W. (1985). *Origins of containment: A psychological explanation.* Princeton, NJ: Princeton University Press.

Larson, D. W. (1986, August). *Game theory and the psychology of reciprocity.* Paper presented to the annual meeting of the American Political Science Association, Washington, DC.

Larson, D. W. (1987). The Austrian state treaty. *International Organization, 41*(1), 27–60.

Larson, D. W. (1998). Game theory and the psychology of reciprocity. In J. G. Stein (Ed.), International negotiation: A multidisciplinary perspective. *Negotiation Journal.* 4, 281–301

Lebow, R. N. (1981). *Between peace and war: The nature of international crisis.* Baltimore, MD: Johns Hopkins University Press.

Lebow, R. N. (1983). The Cuban missile crisis: Reading the lessons correctly. *Political Science Quarterly, 98,* 431–458.

Lebow, R. N. (1984, Summer). Windows of opportunity: Do states jump through them? *International Security, 9,* 147–186.

Lebow, R. N. (1985a). Conclusions. In R. Jervis, R. N. Lebow. & J. G. Stein (Eds.), *Psychology and deterrence* (pp. 204–211). Baltimore, MD: Johns Hopkins University Press.

Lebow, R. N. (1985b). Miscalculation in the South Atlantic: The origins of the Falklands war. In *Psychology and deterrence* (pp. 89–124). Baltimore, MD: The Johns Hopkins University Press.

Lebow, R. N. (1987a). Deterrence failure revisited: A reply to the critics. *International Security, 12,* 197–213.

Lebow, R. N. (1987b). The Kennedy administration and the Cuban missile crisis. Unpublished manuscript.

Lebow, R. N., & Cohen, D. F. (1986). *Afghanistan as inkblot: Assessing cognitive and motivational explanations of foreign policy.* Paper presented at the annual meeting of the International Society of Political Psychology, Amsterdam.

Lebow, R. N., & Levite, A. (1987). Can the next Arab-Israeli war be prevented? Unpublished manuscript.

Leng, R. J., & Walker, S. G. (1982). Comparing two studies of crisis bargaining: Confrontation, coercion, and reciprocity. *Journal of Conflict Resolution, 26,* 571–591.

Lewis, W. J. (1982). *The Warsaw Pact: Arms, doctrine, and strategy.* New York: McGraw-Hill.

Lieberthal, K. G. (1978). *Sino-Soviet conflict in the 1970s: Its evolution and implications for the strategic triangle* (Rand Report R2342-NA). Santa Monica, CA: Rand.

Lindskold, S. (1978). Trust development, the GRIT proposal, and effects of conciliatory acts on conflict and cooperation. *Psychological Bulletin, 85,* 772–793.

Lindskold, S., & Aronoff, J. R. (1980). Conciliatory strategies and relative power. *Journal of Experimental Social Psychology, 16,* 187–198.

Lindskold, S., & Collins, M. G. (1978). Inducing cooperation by groups and individuals. *Journal of Conflict Resolution, 22.* 679–690.

Lindskold, S., Walters, P. S., & Koutsourais, H. (1983). Cooperators, competitors, and response to GRIT. *Journal of Conflict Resolution, 27,* 521–532.

Lipson, C. (1984). International cooperation in economic and security affairs. *World Politics, 37*(1), 1–23.

Luard, E. (1967). Conciliation and deterrence. *World Politics, 19,* 167–189.

Lynn-Jones, S. (1985, Spring). A quiet success for arms control: Preventing incidents at sea. *International Security, 9,* 154–184.

Marwell, G., Ratcliff, K., & Schmitt, D. R. (1969). Minimizing differences in a maximizing difference game. *Journal of Personality and Social Psychology, 12,* 158–163.

Maxwell, S. (1968). *Rationality in deterrence.* Adelphi Paper No. 50. London: Institute for Strategic Studies.

McClintock, C. D., & McNeel, S. P. (1966a). Reward and score feedback as determinants of cooperative game behavior. *Journal of Personality and Social Psychology, 4,* 606–613.

McClintock, C. D., & McNeel, S. P. (1966b). Reward level and game playing behavior. *Journal of Conflict Resolution, 10,* 98–102.

MccGwire, M. (1987). *Military objectives in Soviet foreign policy.* Washington. DC: Brookings.

Messick, D. M., & McClintock, C. G. (1968). Motivational bases of choice in experimental games. *Journal of Experimental Social Psychology, 4,* 1–25.

Messick, D. M., & Thorngate, W. (1967). Relative gain maximization in experimental games. *Journal of Experimental Social Psychology, 3,* 85–101.

Milburn, T. W. (1959). What constitutes effective deterrence? *Journal of Conflict Resolution, 3,* 138–146.

Morgan, P. (1977). *Deterrence, a conceptual analysis.* Beverly Hills, CA: Sage.

Nelsen, H. (1972). The military forces in the cultural revolution. *China Quarterly. 51,* 444–474.

Nemeth, C. (1970). Bargaining and reciprocity. *Psychological Bulletin, 74,* 297–308.

Nisbett, R. E., & Ross, L. (1980). *Human inference: Strategies and shortcomings of social judgment.* Englewood Cliffs, NJ: Prentice-Hall.

Nye, J. S., Jr. (1987). *Nuclear learning and U.S.-Soviet security regimes. International Organization, 41.* 371–402.

Orme, J. (1987). Deterrence failures: A second look. *International Security, 12,* 3–40.

Osgood, C. (1980, May). The GRIT strategy. *Bulletin of Atomic Scientists,* pp. 58–60.

Oskamp, S. (1971). Effects of programmed strategies on cooperation in the prisoner's dilemma and other mixed-motive games. *Journal of Conflict Resolution, 15,* 225–259.

Oye, K. (1985). Explaining cooperation under anarchy: Hypotheses and strategies. *World Politics, 38(1),* 1–24.

Paléologue, M. (1932). *Un prélude à l'invasion de la Belgique: Le plan Schlieffen.* Paris: Plon et Nourrit.

Patchen, M. (1987). Strategies for eliciting cooperation from an adversary. *Journal of Conflict Resolution, 31,* 164–185.

Pilisuk, M., & Skolnick, P. (1968). Inducing trust: A test of the Osgood proposal. *Journal of Personality and Social Psychology, 8,* 122–133.

Pruitt, D. G. (1981). *Negotiation behavior.* New York: Academic Press.

Pruitt, D. G., & Kimmel, M. J. (1977). Twenty years of experimental gaming. *Annual Review of Psychology, 28,* 363–392.

Pruitt, D. G., & Rubin, J. Z. (1986). *Social conflict: Escalation, stalemate, and settlement.* New York: Random House.

Quester, G. (1966). *Deterrence before Hiroshima: The airpower background to modern strategy.* New York: John Wiley & Sons.

Rapoport, A., & Chammah, A. M. (1965). *Prisoner's dilemma.* Ann Arbor: University of Michigan Press.

Rosenau, J. (1986). Before cooperation: Hegemons, regimes, and habit-driven actors. *International Organization, 40,* 849–894.

Ross, L. (1977). The intuitive psychologist and his shortcomings: Distortions in the attribution process. In L. Berkowitz (Ed.), *Advances in experimental social psychology* (Vol. 10, pp. 174–241). New York: Academic Press.

Rothfels, H. (1962). *The German opposition to Hitler.* Chicago: Regnery.

Rusk, D. (1971). Memorandum, 1 July 1965. In *The Pentagon Papers: The Defense Department history of United States decision making on Vietnam* (Vol. 4). Boston: Beacon Press.

Russett, B. (1967). Pearl Harbor: Deterrence theory and decision theory. *Journal of Peace Research, 4*(2), 89–105.

Sadat, A. el-. (1977). *In search of identity: An autobiography.* New York: Harper & Row.

Schelling, T. (1960). *The strategy of conflict.* Cambridge, MA: Harvard University Press.

Schelling, T. (1966). *Arms and influence.* New Haven, CT: Yale University Press.

Schlesinger, A. M., Jr. (1965). *A thousand days: John F. Kennedy in the White House.* Boston: Houghton Mifflin.

Schopler J., & Thompson, V. D. (1968). Role of attribution processes in mediating amount of reciprocity for a favor. *Journal of Personality and Social Psychology, 2,* 243–250.

Sermat, V. (1964). Cooperative behavior in a mixed-motive game. *Journal of Social Psychology, 62,* 217–239.

Sermat, V. (1967). The effect of an initial cooperative or competitive treatment upon a subject's response to conditional cooperation. *Behavioral Science, 12,* 301–313.

Shlaim, A. (1983). *The United States and the Berlin blockade: 1948–1949.* Berkeley and Los Angeles: University of California Press.

Shubik, M. (1971). Game of status. *Behavioral Science, 16,* 117–129.

Shure, G. H., Meeker, R. J., & Hansford, E. A. (1965). The effectiveness of pacifist strategies in bargaining games. *Journal of Conflict Resolution, 9,* 106–116.

Smith, R. K. (1987). The non-proliferation regime and international relations. *International Organization, 41,* 253–281.

Snyder, G., & Diesing, P. (1977). *Conflict among nations.* Princeton, NJ: Princeton University Press.

Snyder, J. (1985). Perceptions of the security dilemma in 1914. In R. Jervis, R. N. Lebow, and J. G. Stein (Eds.), *Psychology and deterrence* (pp. 153–179). Baltimore, MD: Johns Hopkins University Press.

Sorensen, T. (1965). *Kennedy.* New York: Harper & Row.

Stein, A. (1982). Coordination and collaboration: Regimes in an anarchic world. *International Organization, 36*(2), 299–324.

Stein, J. G. (1983). The alchemy of peacemaking: The prerequisites and corequisites of progress in the Arab-Israeli conflict. *International Journal, 38*(4), 531–555.

Stein, J. G. (1983, Autumn). The alchemy of peacemaking: The prerequisites and corequisites of prog'ess in the Arab-Israeli conflict. *International Journal, 38*(4), 531–555.

Stein, J. G. (1985a). Calculation, miscalculation, and conventional deterrence I: The view from Cairo. In R. Jervis, R. N. Lebow, and J. G. Stein (Eds.), *Psychology and deterrence* (pp. 34–59). Baltimore, MD: Johns Hopkins University Press.

Stein, J. G. (1985b). Calculation, miscalculation, and conventional deterrence II: The view from Jerusalem. In R. Jervis, R. N. Lebow, and J. G. Stein (Eds.). *Psychology and deterrence* (pp. 60–88). Baltimore, MD: Johns Hopkins University Press.

Stein, J. G. (1985c). Detection and defection: Security 'regimes' and the management of international conflict. *International Journal, 40*(4), 599–627.

Stein, J. G. (1987). Extended deterrence in the Middle East: American strategy reconsidered. *World Politics, 39,* 326–352.

Stein, J. G. (1988). Managing the managers: Crisis prevention in the Middle East. In G. Winham (Ed.), *New Issues in Crisis Management.* Boulder, CO: Westview Press, 171-99.

Stein, J. G. (1993). Building politics into psychology: The misperception of threat. in N. J. Kressel, ed. *Political Psychology.* New York: Paragon House, 367-92.

Stern, P., Axelrod, R., Jervis, R., & Radnor, R.(1989). "Conclusions." In P. Stern, Axelrod, R., Jervis, R., & Radnor, R., eds *Deterrence* Washington, D.C.: National Research Council. 294-326.

Stuart, D. T. (1982, Fall). Prospects for Sino-European security cooperation. *Orbis, 26,* 721–747.

Stuart, D., & Starr, H. (1982). Inherent bad-faith reconsidered: Dulles, Kennedy, and Kissinger. *Political Psychology, 3,* 1–33.

Tatu, M. (1968). *Power in the Kremlin: From Khrushchev to Kosygin.* London: Collins.

Tiedtke, S. (1978). *Die Warschauer Vertragsorganisation: zum Verhältnis von Militär- und Entspan-nungspolitik in Osteuropa.* Munich: Oldenbourg.

Times. (1982, April 5). Lord Carrington in the House of Lords, April 4, 1982.

Tsou, T. (1959, Fall). Mao's limited war in the Taiwan Strait. *Orbis, 11,* 332–50.

Ulam, A. B. (1968). *Expansion and coexistence: The history of Soviet foreign policy, 1917–1967.* New York: Praeger.

Wagner, R. H. (1983). The theory of games and the problem of international cooperation. *American Political Science Review, 77,* 330–347.

Weinberg, G. (1970–1980). *The foreign policy of Hitler's Germany II.* Chicago: University of Chicago Press.

Weisman, S. R. (1987, February 5). India and Pakistan reach pact to ease tension over troops. *New York Times,* pp. 1, 3.

Whiting, A. S. (1978). *The Chinese calculus of deterrence: India and China.* Ann Arbor: University of Michigan Press.

Wilson, W. (1971). Reciprocation and other techniques for inducing cooperation in the prisoner's dilemma game. *Journal of Conflict Resolution, 15,* 196–198.

Wolfe, T. W. (1970). *Soviet power and Europe, 1945–1970.* Baltimore, MD: Johns Hopkins University Press.

Young, O. R. (1986). International regimes. Toward a new theory of institutions. *World Politics, 39*(1), 104–122.

Zartman, W. (1985). *Ripe for resolution.* Oxford: Oxford University Press.

5 Nuclear deterrence
in retrospect

Richard Ned Lebow and Janice Gross Stein

The role of nuclear weapons in Soviet-American relations has been hotly debated. Politicians, generals, and most academic strategists believe that America's nuclear arsenal restrained the Soviet Union throughout the Cold War. Critics maintain that nuclear weapons were a root cause of superpower conflict and a threat to peace. Controversy also surrounds the number and kinds of weapons necessary to deter, the political implications of the strategic balance, and the role of nuclear deterrence in hastening the collapse of the Soviet imperium.

These debates have had a distinctly theological quality. Partisans frequently defended their positions without recourse to relevant evidence. Some advocated strategic doctrines that were consistent with military postures that they supported. "War-fighting" doctrines were invoked by the air force to justify silo-busting weapons like the MX missile.[1] Mutual Assured Destruction (MAD) was espoused by arms controllers to oppose the deployment of particular weapons systems.

More careful analysts have been alert to the difficulty of making definitive judgments about deterrence in the absence of valid and reliable information about Soviet and Chinese objectives and calculations. McGeorge Bundy, in his masterful *Danger and Survival*, tells a cautionary tale of the impatience of leaders to acquire nuclear weapons, their largely futile attempts to exploit these weapons for political purposes and, finally, their efforts through arms control, to limit the dangers nuclear weapons pose to their owners as well as their targets. Bundy emphasizes the uncertainty of leaders about the dynamics of deterrence and their concerns about the risks of escalation in crisis.[2]

Richard K. Betts, in another exemplary study, illustrates how difficult it is to assess the efficacy of nuclear threats.[3] He found great disparity between the memories of American leaders and the historical record. Some of the nuclear threats American presidents claim were successful were never made.[4] Other threats were so oblique that it is difficult to classify them as threats. Betts was understandably reluctant to credit any nuclear threat with success in the absence of information about the internal deliberations of the target states. When these states behaved in ways that were consistent with their adversary's demands, it was often unclear if the threat was successful or irrelevant. Leaders could have complied because they had been deterred or compelled, they could have been influenced by considerations unrelated to the threat, or they could have intended originally to behave as they did.

Newly declassified documents and extensive interviews with Soviet and American officials permitted us to reconstruct the deliberations of leaders of both superpowers before, during, and after the two most serious nuclear crises of the last 30 years. This evidence sheds new light on some of the controversies at the center of the nuclear debate. Needless to say, definitive judgments must await the opening of archives and more complete information about the calculations of Soviet and American leaders in other crises, as well as those of other nuclear powers.

The four questions

Our analysis is organized around four questions. Each question addresses a major controversy about nuclear deterrence and its consequences. The first and most critical question is the contribution nuclear deterrence made to the prevention of World War III. The conventional wisdom regards deterrence as the principal pillar of the postwar peace between the superpowers. Critics charge that deterrence was beside the point or a threat to the peace. John Mueller, who makes the strongest argument for the irrelevance of nuclear weapons, maintains that the superpowers were restrained by their memories of World War II and their knowledge that even a conventional war would be many times more destructive.[5]

More outspoken critics of deterrence charge that it greatly exacerbated superpower tensions. The deployment of ever more sophisticated weapons of destruction convinced each superpower of the other's hostile intentions and sometimes provoked the kind of aggressive behavior deterrence was intended to prevent. The postwar peace endured despite deterrence.[6]

The second question, of interest to those who believe that deterrence worked, is why and how it works. Some advocates insist that it forestalled Soviet aggression; in its absence Moscow would have attacked Western Europe and possibly have sent forces to the Middle East.[7] More reserved supporters credit the reality of nuclear deterrence with moderating the foreign policies of both superpowers. They maintain that the destructiveness of nuclear weapons encouraged caution and restraint and provided a strong incentive for Moscow and Washington to make the concessions necessary to resolve their periodic crises.[8]

The third question concerns the military requirements of deterrence. In the 1960s, Defense Secretary Robert S. McNamara adopted MAD as the official American strategic doctrine. McNamara contended that the Soviet Union could be deterred by the American capability to destroy 50% of its population and industry in a retaliatory strike. He welcomed the effort by the Soviet Union to develop a similar capability in the expectation that secure retaliatory capabilities on both sides would foster stability.[9]

Many military officers and civilian strategists rejected MAD on the grounds that it was not credible to Moscow. To deter the Soviet Union, the United States needed to be able to prevail at any level of conflict. This required a much larger nuclear arsenal and highly accurate missiles necessary to dig out and destroy Soviet missiles in their silos and the underground bunkers where the political and military elite would take refuge in any conflict. "War-fighting" supplanted MAD as the official strategic doctrine during the presidency of Jimmy Carter. The Reagan administration spent vast sums of money to augment conventional forces and to buy the strategic weapons and command and control networks that Pentagon planners considered essential to war-fighting.[10]

An alternative approach to nuclear weapons, "finite deterrence," maintained that Soviet leaders were as cautious as their Western counterparts and just as frightened by the prospects of nuclear war. Nuclear deterrence was far more robust than proponents of either MAD or war-fighting acknowledged and required only limited capabilities—several-hundred nuclear weapons would probably suffice. The doctrine of finite deterrence never had visible support within the American government.[11]

Differences about the requirements of deterrence reflected deeper disagreements about the intentions of Soviet leaders. For war-fighters, the Soviet Union was an implacable foe. Its ruthless leaders would willingly sacrifice their people and industry in pursuit of world domination. They could only be restrained by superior capabilities and demonstrable resolve to use force in defense of vital interests. Partisans of MAD thought the Soviet Union aggressive but cautious. Soviet leaders sought to make gains but were even more anxious to preserve what they already had. The capability to destroy the Soviet Union as a modern industrial power was therefore sufficient to deter attack, but not necessarily to make its leaders behave in a restrained manner. Proponents of war-fighting and MAD stressed the overriding importance of resolve; Soviet leaders had to be convinced that the United States would retaliate if it or its allies were attacked and come to their assistance it they were challenged in other ways.

Finite deterrence was based on the premise that both superpowers had an overriding fear of nuclear war. Small and relatively unsophisticated nuclear arsenals were sufficient to reinforce this fear and the caution it engendered. Larger forces, especially those targeted against the other side's retaliatory capability, were counterproductive; they exacerbated the insecurity of its leaders, confirmed their belief in their adversary's hostility, and encouraged them to deploy similar weapons. Supporters of finite deterrence put much less emphasis on the need to demonstrate resolve. The possibility of retaliation, they believed, was enough to deter attack.

The fourth question concerns the broader political value of nuclear weapons. War fighters maintained that strategic superiority was politically useful and conferred bargaining leverage on a wide range of issues.[12] Most supporters of MAD contended that strategic advantages could only be translated into political influence in confrontations like the missile crisis, in which vital interests were at stake.[13] Other supporters of MAD, and all advocates of finite deterrence, denied that nuclear weapons could serve any purpose beyond deterrence.

Restraining, provocative, or irrelevant?

Students of deterrence distinguish between general and immediate deterrence. General deterrence relies on the existing power balance to prevent an adversary from seriously considering a military challenge because of its expected adverse consequences.[14] It is often a country's first line of defense against attack. Leaders resort to the strategy of immediate deterrence only after general deterrence has failed, or when they believe that a more explicit expression of their intent to defend their interests is necessary to buttress general deterrence. If immediate deterrence fails, leaders will find themselves in a crisis, as Kennedy did when American intelligence discovered Soviet missiles in Cuba, or at war, as Israel's leaders did in 1973. General and immediate deterrence represent a progression from a diffuse if real concern about an adversary's intentions to the expectation that a specific interest or commitment is about to be challenged.

Both forms of deterrence assume that adversaries are most likely to resort to force or threatening military deployments when they judge the military balance favorable and question the defender's resolve. General deterrence pays particular importance to the military dimension; it tries to discourage challenges by developing the capability to defend national commitments or inflict unacceptable punishment on an adversary. General deterrence is a long-term strategy. Five-year lead times and longer are common between a decision to develop a weapon and its deployment.

Immediate deterrence is a short-term strategy. Its purpose is to discourage an imminent attack or challenge of a specific commitment. The military component of immediate deterrence must rely on forces in being. To buttress their defensive capability and display resolve, leaders may deploy forces when they anticipate an attack or challenge, as Kennedy did in the aftermath of the summit in June 1961. In response to Khrushchev's ultimatum on Berlin, he sent additional ground and air forces to Germany and strengthened the American garrison in Berlin. These reinforcements were designed to communicate the administration's will to resist any encroachment against West Berlin or Western access routes to the city.

General deterrence

The origins of the missile crisis indicate that general deterrence, as practiced by both superpowers, was provocative rather than preventive. Soviet officials testified that the American strategic buildup, deployment of missiles in Turkey, and assertions of nuclear superiority, made them increasingly insecure. The president viewed all of these measures as prudent, defensive precautions. American actions had the unanticipated consequence of convincing Khrushchev of the need to protect the Soviet Union and Cuba from American military and political challenges.

Khrushchev was hardly the innocent victim of American paranoia. His nuclear threats and unfounded claims of nuclear superiority were the catalyst for Kennedy's decision to increase the scope and pace of the American strategic buildup. The new American programs and the Strategic Air Command's higher state of strategic readiness exacerbated Soviet perceptions of threat and contributed to Khrushchev's decision to send missiles to Cuba. In attempting to intimidate their adversaries, both leaders helped to bring about the kind of confrontation they were trying to avoid.

Kennedy later speculated, and Soviet officials have since confirmed, that his efforts to reinforce deterrence also encouraged Khrushchev to stiffen his position on Berlin.[15] The action and reaction that linked Berlin and Cuba were part of a larger cycle of insecurity and escalation that reached well back into the 1950s, if not to the beginning of the Cold War. The Soviet challenge to the Western position in Berlin in 1959–61 was motivated by Soviet concern about the viability of East Germany and secondarily by Soviet vulnerability to American nuclear-tipped missiles stationed in Western Europe. The American missiles had been deployed to assuage NATO fears about the conventional military balance on the central front, made more acute by the creation of the Warsaw Pact in 1955. The Warsaw Pact, many Western authorities now believe, represented an attempt by Moscow to consolidate its control over an increasingly restive Eastern Europe.[16]

Once the crisis erupted, general deterrence played an important moderating role. Kennedy and Khrushchev moved away from confrontation and toward compromise because they both feared war. Kennedy worried that escalation would set in motion a chain of events that could lead to nuclear war. Khrushchev's decision to withdraw the missiles indicated that he too was prepared to make sacrifices to avoid war. His capitulation in the face of American military pressure was a humiliating defeat for the Soviet Union and its leader. Soviet officials confirm that it was one factor in his removal from power a year later.[17] For many years, Americans portrayed the crisis as an unalloyed American triumph. Kennedy's concession on the Jupiters and his willingness on Saturday night to consider making that concession public indicate that, when the superpower leaders were "eyeball to eyeball," both sides blinked. One reason they did so was their fear of nuclear war and its consequences.

General deterrence also failed to prevent an Egyptian decision to use force in 1973. President Sadat and his military staff openly acknowledged Egyptian military inferiority. They had no doubt about Israel's resolve to defend itself if attacked. Sadat still chose to fight a limited war. He decided to attack Israel because of intense domestic political pressures to regain the Sinai. He had lost all hope in diplomacy after the failure of the Rogers missions, and although he recognized that the military balance was unfavorable, he expected it to get even worse in the future.

Israel's practice of general deterrence—it acquired a new generation of fighters and bombers—convinced Sadat to initiate military action sooner rather than later. Egyptian military planners devised a strategy intended to compensate for their military inferiority. Egyptian officers sought to capitalize on surprise, occupy the east bank of the Suez Canal, defend against Israeli counterattacks with a mobile missile screen, and press for an internationally imposed cease-fire before their limited gains could be reversed by a fully mobilized Israel. The parallels between 1962 and 1973 are striking. In both cases, attempts to reinforce general deterrence against vulnerable and hard-pressed opponents provoked rather than prevented unwanted challenges.

General deterrence had contradictory implications in the crisis that erupted between the United States and the Soviet Union at the end of the October War. Leaders of both superpowers were confident that the other feared war; general deterrence was robust. This confidence allowed the United States to alert its forces worldwide without fear of escalation. Brezhnev and some of his colleagues, on the other hand, worried about escalation if Soviet forces were deployed in positions in Egypt where they were likely to encounter advancing Israelis. The Politburo agreed that they did not want to be drawn into a military conflict that could escalate. Fear of war restrained the Soviet Union and contributed to the resolution of the crisis.

Immediate deterrence is intended to forestall a specific military deployment or use of force. For immediate deterrence to succeed, the defender's threats must convince adversaries that the likely costs of a challenge will more than offset any possible gains.[18] Immediate deterrence did not prevent the missile crisis. After Khrushchev had decided to send missiles to Cuba, Kennedy warned that he would not tolerate the introduction of Soviet missiles in Cuba. The president issued his threat in the belief that Khrushchev had no intention of establishing missile bases in Cuba. In the face of the president's warnings, Khrushchev proceeded with the secret deployment.

Students of the crisis disagree about why deterrence failed. Some contend that the strategy could not have worked, whereas others insist that Kennedy attempted deterrence too late.[19] Whatever the cause, the failure of deterrence exacerbated the most acute crisis of the Cold War. By making a public commitment to keep Soviet missiles out of Cuba, Kennedy dramatically increased the domestic political and foreign-policy costs of allowing the missiles to remain after they were discovered. A threat originally intended to deflect pressures on the administration to invade Cuba would have made that invasion very difficult to avoid if Soviet leaders had not agreed to withdraw their missiles.

Israel chose not to practice immediate deterrence in 1973. Its leaders were convinced that Egypt would only attack when it could neutralize Israel's air force. Confidence in general deterrence blinded Israel's leaders to the growing desperation of Sadat and his imperative to find a limited military strategy that would achieve his political objective. Israel's leaders worried instead that limited deterrent or defensive measures on their part might provoke Egypt to launch a miscalculated attack.

Even if Israel had practiced immediate deterrence, the evidence suggests that it would have made no difference. It is unlikely that public warnings and mobilization of the Israel Defense Forces would have deterred Egypt; Sadat had expected Israel to mobilize its reserves and reinforce the Bar-Lev Line in response to Egyptian military preparations. He was surprised and pleased that Israel did not take defensive measures and that Egyptian forces did not sustain the high casualties that he had anticipated and was prepared to accept.[20]

When the cease-fire negotiated jointly by Moscow and Washington failed to stop the fighting, Brezhnev threatened to consider unilateral intervention. The United States resorted to immediate deterrence to prevent a Soviet deployment. This was not the first time since the war began that Kissinger had attempted to deter Soviet military intervention. As early as October 12, he told Dobrynin that any attempt by the Soviet Union to intervene with force would "wreck the entire fabric of U.S.-Soviet relations."[21] Later that day, he warned the Soviet ambassador that any Soviet intervention, regardless of pretext, would be met by American force.[22] On the evening of October 24, when Brezhnev asked for joint intervention and threatened that he might act alone if necessary, the United States went to a DEFCON III alert.

Immediate deterrence was irrelevant since Brezhnev had no intention of sending Soviet forces to Egypt. Soviet leaders had difficulty understanding why President Nixon alerted American forces. Brezhnev and some of his colleagues were angered, dismayed, and humiliated. Immediate deterrence was at best irrelevant in resolving the crisis and, at worst, it damaged the long-term relationship between the superpowers.

Deterrence had diverse and contradictory consequences for superpower behavior. General and immediate deterrence were principal causes of the missile crisis, but general deterrence also facilitated its resolution. In 1973, general deterrence contributed to the outbreak of war between Egypt and Israel and provided an umbrella for competition between the United States and the Soviet Union in the Middle East. Immediate deterrence failed to prevent the superpower crisis that followed, but general deterrence constrained the Soviet leadership and helped to resolve the crisis. These differences can best be understood by distinguishing between the strategy and reality of nuclear deterrence.

The strategy of deterrence attempts to manipulate the risk of war for political ends. For much of the Cold War, Soviet and American policy makers doubted that their opposites were deterred by the prospect of nuclear war. They expended valuable resources trying to perfect the mix of strategic forces, nuclear doctrine, and targeting policy that would succeed in restraining their adversary. They also used military buildups, force deployments, and threats of war to try to coerce one another into making political concessions. In Berlin and Cuba, these attempts were unsuccessful but succeeded in greatly aggravating tensions.

The reality of deterrence derived from the inescapable fact that a superpower nuclear conflict would have been an unprecedented catastrophe for both sides. Superpower leaders understood this; by the late 1960s, if not earlier, they had come to believe that their countries could not survive a nuclear war. Fear of war, independent of the disparity in the strategic capabilities of the two sides, helped to keep both American and Soviet leaders from going over the brink and provided an important incentive for the mutual concessions that resolved the Cuban missile crisis. The moderation induced by the reality of deterrence helped to curtail the recklessness encouraged by the strategy of deterrence.

The contradictory consequences of deterrence are not fully captured by any of the competing interpretations. Proponents of deterrence have emphasized the positive contribution of the reality of deterrence but ignored the baneful consequences of the strategy. The critics of deterrence have identified some of the political and psychological mechanisms that made the strategy of deterrence provocative and dangerous. But many ignored the ways in which the reality of deterrence was an important source of restraint.

When and why does deterrence work?

Proponents of deterrence have advanced two contrasting reasons for its putative success. The conventional wisdom holds that deterrence restrained the Soviet Union by convincing its leaders that any military action against the United States or its allies would meet certain and effective opposition. Those who credit deterrence with preserving the peace assume that, in its absence, the Soviet Union would have been tempted to use force against its Western adversaries or their allies in the Middle East.

Throughout the years of Soviet-American rivalry, American leaders regarded their adversary as fundamentally aggressive and intent on expanding its influence by subversion, intimidation, or the use of force. Soviet leaders were frequently described as cold, rational calculators who were constantly probing for opportunities. They carefully weighed the costs and benefits and abstained from aggressive action only it its costs were expected to outweigh the gains. In this context, the peace always looked precarious to American leaders and the remarkable success in avoiding war needed an extraordinary explanation. The strategy of nuclear deterrence provided the explanation.

The strategy of deterrence seemed ideal for coping with a fundamentally aggressive and opportunity-driven adversary. It sought to prevent Soviet aggression by denying its leaders opportunities to exploit. The United States consequently developed impressive military capabilities—general deterrence—and publicly committed itself to the defense of specific interests—immediate deterrence—when it appeared that these interests might be challenged. The conventional wisdom, eloquently expressed in many of the scholarly writings on deterrence, assumed that Soviet aggression would wax and wane as a function of Soviet perceptions of American military capability and resolve. Soviet leaders would be most restrained when they regarded the military balance as unfavorable and American resolve as unquestionable.[23]

Our analyses of the crises in 1962 and 1973 do not support this assessment of deterrence. In 1962, the strategy of deterrence provoked a war-threatening crisis, and, in 1973, nuclear deterrence provided the umbrella under which each sought to make or protect gains at the expense of the other until they found themselves in a tense confrontation.

The alternative interpretation holds that fear of nuclear war made both super-powers more cautious than they otherwise would have been in their competition for global influence and thereby kept the peace. Although far more convincing than the argument that credits the strategy of nuclear deterrence with preserving the peace, this explanation also is not fully persuasive. The reality of nuclear deterrence had a restraining effect on both Kennedy and Khrushchev in 1962 and on Brezhnev in 1973. When superpower leaders believed that they were approaching the brink of war, fear of war pulled them back.[24]

It is difficult to judge how much of the fear of war can be attributed to nuclear weapons. At the time of the Korean War, the United States had only a limited nuclear arsenal, but Stalin may have exaggerated American ability to launch extensive nuclear strikes against the Soviet Union.[25] Robert McNamara subse-quently testified that President Kennedy worried primarily that the missile crisis would lead to a conventional war with the Soviet Union.[26] Other members of the Ex Comm disagree; they say it was the threat of nuclear war that was in the back of their minds and, probably, the president's.[27] McNamara also admits that he had little expectation that a conventional conflict could be contained. "I didn't know how we would stop the chain of military escalation once it began."[28]

Soviet leaders also worried about war in the missile crisis, but neither the writ-ten record nor the testimony of Soviet officials offers any evidence of the kind of war Khrushchev thought most likely. There is no evidence that Khrushchev or Kennedy speculated about war scenarios; they were desperately trying to resolve the crisis. They had no political or psychological incentive to investigate the con-sequences of failure—quite the reverse. Their fear of war remained strong but diffuse.

In 1973, the United States did not see war as a likely possibility, but Soviet leaders worried actively about war. They feared the consequences of a conven-tional Soviet-Israeli engagement somewhere between the canal and Cairo, or an accidental encounter at sea. However, there is no evidence that Soviet speculation progressed to more detailed consideration of how either could escalate to nuclear war. Again, the fear of war was strong but diffuse. Soviet leaders feared not only nuclear war but any kind of Soviet-American war. Their fear translated into self-deterrence; Brezhnev ruled out the commitment of Soviet forces on Egypt's behalf before the United States practiced deterrence.

The absence of superpower war is puzzling only if at least one of the superpow-ers was expansionist and aggressive. On the basis of the evidence now available, the image that each superpower held of the other as opportunity-driven aggressors can be discredited as crude stereotypes. Khrushchev and Brezhnev felt threatened by what they considered the predatory policies of their adversary, as did Ameri-can leaders by Soviet expansionist policies. For much of the Cold War, Soviet leaders were primarily concerned with preserving what they had, although like their American counterparts, they were not averse to making gains that appeared to entail little risk or cost. Serious confrontations between the superpowers arose only when one of them believed that its vital interests were threatened by the other.

With the benefit of hindsight, it is apparent that although both superpowers hoped to remake the world in their image, neither Moscow nor Washington was ever so dissatisfied with the status quo that it was tempted to go to war to force a change. It was not only the absence of opportunity that kept the peace, but also the absence of a strong motive for war. Without a compelling motive, leaders were unwilling to assume the burden and responsibility for war, even if they thought its outcome would be favorable. In the late 1950s and early 1960s, when the United States might have destroyed the Soviet Union in a first strike with relatively little damage to itself, American leaders never considered a preventive war. The Soviet Union never possessed such a strategic advantage, but there is no reason to suspect that Khrushchev or Brezhnev had any greater interest than Eisenhower and Kennedy in going to war. The reality of deterrence helped to restrain leaders on both sides, but their relative satisfaction with the status quo was an important cause of the long peace.

How much is enough?

There was never a consensus in Washington about what was necessary to deter the Soviet Union. Proponents of MAD maintained that Soviet leaders would be deterred by the prospect of their country's destruction. Robert McNamara's "whiz kids" at Defense calculated that MAD required the capability to destroy 50% of the Soviet Union's population and industry in a retaliatory strike.[29] McNamara recommended to Premier Aleksei Kosygin in 1967 that the Soviet Union acquire roughly the same kind of second-strike capability so that deterrence would become more stable. Many military officers and conservative civilian strategists rejected MAD on the grounds that it was not a credible strategy. No American president, they argued, could ever convince his Soviet counterpart that he would accept certain destruction of the United States to punish the Soviet Union for invading Western Europe. To deter Soviet aggression, the United States needed clear-cut, across-the-board strategic superiority to decapitate the Soviet political and military leadership, destroy their command, control, and communications network, penetrate hardened targets, and outright Soviet forces at every level.[30] Proponents of finite deterrence, the smallest of the three communities, argued that nuclear deterrence was robust and required only limited capabilities. Strategic thinkers in France and Israel have, of necessity, voiced this kind of argument.

The outcome of the missile crisis supports the argument of finite deterrence. The American advantage was overwhelming. The CIA estimated that the Soviet Union, which had only 100 missiles and a small fleet of obsolescent bombers, could attack the United States with at most 350 nuclear weapons. The United States had a strategic nuclear strike force of thirty-five-hundred weapons and far more accurate and reliable delivery systems. Because Soviet missiles were unreliable and Soviet bombers vulnerable to air defenses, it was possible that very few Soviet weapons would have reached their American targets. Had the missiles in Cuba been fully operational and armed with nuclear weapons, they would have augmented the Soviet arsenal by fewer than 60 warheads.[31]

Military superiority offered little comfort to the administration. It was not "usable superiority," McGeorge Bundy explained, because "if even one Soviet weapon landed on an American target, we would all be losers."[32] Robert McNamara insists that "The assumption that the strategic nuclear balance (or 'imbalance') mattered was absolutely wrong."[33] He recalled a CIA estimate that the Soviets might be able to deliver thirty warheads against the United States in a retaliatory attack. "Does anyone believe that a president or a secretary of defense would be willing to permit thirty warheads to fall on the United States? No way! And for that reason, neither we nor the Soviets would have acted any differently before or after the Cuban deployment."[34] In McNamara's judgment, no president would be willing "to consciously sacrifice an important part of our population or our land and place it in great jeopardy to a strike by Soviet strategic forces, whether it be one city, or two cities, or three cities." The Soviet Union had the capability to do this even before deploying any missiles in Cuba. "And therefore, we felt deterred from using our nuclear superiority and that was not changed by the introduction of nuclear weapons into Cuba."[35]

Proponents of war-fighting, MAD, and finite deterrence would all expect Khrushchev to be deterred by the one-sided American strategic advantage. Only proponents of finite deterrence would anticipate that Kennedy would be deterred by the small Soviet arsenal.

Ironically, Kennedy was not fully confident before or during the crisis that even overwhelming American strategic superiority would restrain the Soviet Union. Khrushchev, by contrast, was confident—before the crisis—that the small and inferior Soviet arsenal would deter Kennedy. He worried rather that the United States would exploit its strategic superiority for political purposes. His confidence in finite deterrence permitted him to deploy missiles in Cuba with the expectation that Kennedy would not go to war.

During the crisis, Khrushchev's confidence in deterrence wavered. He worried both that Kennedy would be unable to control the militants in the military and the CIA who did not share his sober recognition of the futility of war and that the crisis might spin out of control. These fears were partly responsible for the concessions that he made. Kennedy, too, worried that Khrushchev would be ousted by militants determined to go to war. Even when the United States had the overwhelming superiority that proponents of war-fighting recommend, Kennedy's confidence in deterrence was limited. He, too, then made the concessions necessary to resolve the crisis.

In making critical judgments about the robustness of deterrence during the crisis, Kennedy and Khrushchev paid little attention to the military balance. They concentrated instead on the political pressures that might push either side into using force. Their success in resolving the crisis increased their confidence that the other shared their horror of war.

Although deterrence was robust in 1962, not everybody drew the same positive lessons from the missile crisis as did Khrushchev and Kennedy. Influential members of the Soviet elite believed that the Kennedy administration had acted aggressively in Cuba because of its strategic advantage. Many Americans concluded that Khrushchev had retreated because of Soviet inferiority. The lesson of the missile crisis was clear: the United States needed to maintain its strategic advantage, or failing that, strategic parity. In Moscow, too, there was a renewed commitment to ending the strategic imbalance. The missile crisis did not trigger the Soviet strategic buildup of the 1960s—it had been authorized by Khrushchev before the missile crisis—but it mobilized additional support for that program and made it easier for Brezhnev to justify when resources grew scarce in the 1970s.[36]

The crisis in 1973, the most serious superpower confrontation since the missile crisis, occurred when the strategic balance was roughly equal and both sides had a secure second-strike capability. Proponents of finite deterrence would expect the reality of nuclear deterrence to be robust and the strategy of nuclear deterrence to fail unless the security of the homeland was threatened. Given the reality of nuclear deterrence when both sides had an assured capacity to retaliate, advocates of MAD would also expect the strategy of deterrence to fail unless vital interests were at stake. War-fighters would reason differently. Since neither side possessed "escalation dominance," the side that estimated a lower risk of war would have the advantage.

The predictions of the three schools with respect to the American alert cannot be tested directly, since deterrence was irrelevant. The Soviet Union had no intention of sending forces to Egypt before the United States alerted its forces. We can nevertheless assess the Soviet interpretation of the American attempt at deterrence and examine its fit with the expectations of the three schools. Soviet leaders dismissed the American nuclear alert as incredible. They could do so in a context in which nuclear weapons were regarded as so unusable that nuclear threats to defend anything but the homeland or vital interests were incredible. There is no evidence, moreover, that political leaders in Moscow made any attempt to assess the relative strategic balance. The Soviet interpretation is consistent with the expectations of finite deterrence and MAD and inconsistent with those of war-fighters.

Analysis of these two crises reveals that it was not the balance or even perceptions of the balance but rather the judgments leaders made about its meaning that were critical. The understanding lenders had of their adversary's intentions was much more important than their estimates of its relative capabilities. Deterrence was as robust in 1962 as proponents of finite deterrence expected, and at least as robust in 1973 as proponents of MAD anticipated. Yet, worst-case analyses remained the conventional wisdom for many years among militants in both the United States and the Soviet Union. Many on both sides continued to assume that the strategic balance was and would continue to be the critical determinant of superpower behavior.

War-fighters drew a direct relationship between the strategic balance and Soviet behavior. The Soviet Union would be most restrained when the United States had a strategic advantage and would behave more aggressively when the military balance tilted in their favor.[37] Proponents of finite deterrence denied that any relationship existed between the strategic balance and aggression, whereas adherents of MAD could be found on both sides of the debate. The proposition that the aggressiveness of Soviet leaders intensified or diminished in accordance with their perception of the strategic balance became the fundamental assumption of strategic analysis and force planning in the United States. Deterrence was considered primarily a military problem, and many American officials and strategists worked on the assumption that Washington could never have too powerful a military or too great a strategic advantage.[38]

The link between Soviet foreign policy and the military balance is an empirical question. To test this relationship, we examined Soviet-American relations from the beginning of the Cold War in 1947 to 1985, when Mikhail Gorbachev came to power. Drawing on formerly classified estimates of the strategic balance and public studies of the balance prepared by prominent strategic institutes, we developed a composite measure of the relative strategic potency of the two superpowers. Our analysis suggests that the nuclear balance went through three distinct phases. The first, 1948 to 1960, was a period of mounting American advantage. The second, 1961 to 1968, was characterized by a pronounced but declining American advantage. The third, 1968 to 1985, was an era of strategic parity."[39]

There is no positive correlation between shifts in Soviet assertiveness and shifts in the strategic balance. Soviet challenges are most pronounced in the late 1940s and early 1950s in central Europe and Korea and again in the late 1950s and early 1960s in Berlin and Cuba. A third, lesser period of assertiveness occurred from 1979 to 1982 in Africa and Afghanistan.[40] The first and second peaks occurred at a time when the United States had unquestioned nuclear superiority. The third peak coincides with the period of strategic parity, before the years of the putative American "window of vulnerability." During this period of alleged Soviet advantage, roughly 1982 to 1985, Soviet behavior was restrained. The relationship between the military balance and Soviet assertiveness is largely the reverse of that predicted by proponents of war-fighting. The United States had unquestioned supremacy from 1948 to 1952 and again from 1959 to 1962, the principal years of Soviet assertiveness. Soviet challenges were most pronounced when the Soviet Union was weak and the United States was strong.

This pattern challenges the proposition that aggression is motivated primarily by adversaries who seek continuously to exploit opportunities. When leaders became desperate, they behaved aggressively even though the military balance was unfavorable and they had no grounds to doubt their adversary's resolve. In the absence of compelling need, leaders often did not challenge even when opportunities for an assertive foreign policy were present.[41] A definitive answer to the question, "How much is enough?" must await detailed analyses of other nuclear crises with other leaders. Drawing on the analysis of leaders' thinking in these two cases and the broad pattern in their relationship during the Cold War, we can suggest a tentative answer: finite nuclear capabilities in the context of a shared fear of war. In this circumstance, a little deterrence goes a long way.

The political value of nuclear weapons

Just as there was no consensus during the Cold War on how much deterrence was enough, so there was no agreement on the political value of nuclear weapons. War-fighters contended that nuclear power was fungible; they insisted that strategic advantages could be successfully exploited for political purposes. Most proponents of MAD argued that nuclear threats were likely to be effective only in defense of a state's most vital interests. Proponents of finite deterrence took the most restrictive view of the political value of nuclear weapons. They argued that nuclear weapons could only deter attacks against one's own state and perhaps against one's closest allies.

War-fighters, who were dubious about the efficacy of deterrence and set the most demanding conditions, nevertheless expressed the greatest confidence in compellence. Advocates of finite deterrence, who maintained that nuclear deterrence was relatively easy to achieve, doubted that nuclear threats would succeed in compelling nuclear adversaries. Proponents of MAD thought deterrence was somewhat easier to achieve than compellence.

These seeming contradictions between the schools of war-fighting and finite deterrence can be reconciled by examining why each argued that deterrence and compellence would succeed or fail. For war-fighters, the critical factor was the military balance. When a state possessed a decisive strategic advantage, it could more convincingly demonstrate resolve and more readily deter and compel an adversary. Parity made deterrence possible but compellence extraordinarily difficult.

Advocates of finite deterrence reasoned that leaders had a pronounced fear of the consequences of nuclear war. This fear had a low threshold and was independent of the level of destruction leaders could inflict on their adversaries. The strategic balance was therefore irrelevant to deterrence, and strategic advantage did not make compellence any easier. So long as the target state had some nuclear retaliatory capability, nuclear threats for any purpose other than retaliation lacked credibility.

Proponents of MAD also denied the utility of strategic superiority. They placed the threshold of deterrence higher than did advocates of finite deterrence and argued that a state needed an unquestioned capability, after sustaining a first strike, to retaliate in sufficient force to destroy approximately 50% of its adversary's population and industry. Additional nuclear capabilities did not make deterrence any more secure. Some advocates of MAD believed that strategic advantages were critical for compellence but only in limited, well-specified circumstances. Like the advocates of finite deterrence, they argued that the unprecedented destructiveness of nuclear weapons made it very difficult to make credible nuclear threats against nuclear adversaries. Such threats would carry weight only when a state's most vital interests were unambiguously threatened.[42]

Proponents of war-fighting and MAD argued that the Cuban missile crisis was consistent with their expectations. They both maintained that Khrushchev sent missiles to Cuba because he doubted American resolve and withdrew them because he respected American military capability.[43] The crisis illustrated a general truth to war-fighters: strategic superiority confers important bargaining advantages in crisis. Advocates of MAD maintained that the missile crisis was a special case. Compellence succeeded not only because of the American military advantage, but because of the asymmetry of interests. The United States was defending a vital interest, the Soviet Union was not.[44]

Both arguments took as their starting point the apparently one-sided outcome of the crisis in favor of the United States. Khrushchev withdrew the Soviet missiles in return for a face-saving pledge from Kennedy not to invade Cuba. Proponents of war-fighting and MAD treated this pledge as largely symbolic because the administration had no intention of invading the island other than to remove the missiles. Both believed that the missiles would have significantly affected the military or political balance and therefore treated their withdrawal as a major concession.

These interpretations that congealed in the 1960s are contradicted by newly available evidence. Although the administration had ruled out an invasion of Cuba, Khrushchev considered Kennedy's pledge not to invade an extremely important concession. With other Soviet leaders, he was convinced that the United States was preparing to overthrow the Castro government and was only prevented from doing so by the missile deployment. In the eyes of the president and his secretary of defense, the missiles in Cuba had much less military value than many students of the crisis have alleged. Their withdrawal was important for domestic and foreign political reasons.

We now know that Kennedy made a second, important concession to Khrushchev: he agreed to remove the American Jupiter missiles from Turkey at a decent interval after the crisis. The decision to withdraw the missiles was not made before the crisis, as some administration officials contended, but was offered to Khrushchev as a concession. However, Kennedy insisted that the Kremlin keep it secret. The removal of the Jupiters had little military value but was of enormous symbolic importance to Khrushchev.

The outcome of the missile crisis is best explained by finite deterrence. The terms of the settlement did not reflect the strategic balance, but mutual fears of war. Despite pronounced Soviet strategic inferiority, the crisis ended in a compromise, not in a one-sided American victory. American leaders judged it too risky to rely on their strategic advantage to compel withdrawal of the Soviet missiles without making compensating concessions.

The advocates of finite deterrence, MAD, and war-fighting would all expect compellence to be very difficult in the strategic context of 1973. War-fighters would predict that neither the Soviet Union nor the United States could compel the other side to achieve political benefit since neither had a decisive strategic advantage. Under conditions of parity and a secure capability to retaliate, proponents of MAD and finite deterrence would predict that compellence would be very difficult unless vital interests were demonstrably at stake.

The failure of Soviet compellence in 1973 is consistent with the shared expectation of all three schools. Brezhnev did not succeed in compelling the United States to restrain Israel, even though it was very much in Washington's interest to stop the fighting. On the contrary, Brezhnev's attempt to compel backfired and escalated the crisis. Although Kissinger recognized Soviet interests, particularly the heavy cost of its humiliating failure to stop the fighting, he nevertheless interpreted Brezhnev's threat that he might consider unilateral action as a direct challenge to the reputation and resolve of the United States.

All three approaches expect, although for quite different reasons, strategic parity to confer no political advantage. To distinguish among the three schools, we need detailed evidence of the calculations of American leaders about the strategic balance. Yet, when Kissinger and his colleagues chose to respond to Brezhnev's threat that he might consider unilateral military action, they made no reference at all to the strategic balance.[45] When they chose not to comply with Brezhnev's threat, the strategic balance was not salient in their minds.

Our analysis of these two cases is most consistent with the arguments of finite deterrence. The overwhelming strategic advantage of the United States in the missile crisis was negated by the fear of war. When the strategic balance was roughly equal, the Soviet Union could not compel even when the United States recognized the strong Soviet interest in protecting an endangered ally and their own interest in saving the Egyptian Third Army. Our evidence suggests that nuclear weapons are unusable for any political purpose but the defense of vital interests.

Nuclear threats and nuclear weapons

The role of nuclear threats and nuclear weapons in Soviet-American relations during the Cold War runs counter to much of the conventional wisdom. Throughout the Cold War, superpower leaders expected their adversary to exploit any strategic advantage for political or military gain. Consequently, they devoted scarce resources to military spending to keep from being disadvantaged. For four decades Soviet and American leaders worried about the political and military consequences of strategic inferiority. These fears, coupled with the worst-case analysis each side used to estimate the other's strategic capabilities, fueled an increasingly expensive arms race. In the late 1940s, the Soviet Union made an intensive effort to develop its own nuclear arsenal in the aftermath of Hiroshima and Nagasaki. In the early 1950s, both sides developed thermonuclear weapons. Following the success of Sputnik in 1957, the United States accelerated its commitment to develop and deploy ICBMs. President Kennedy's decision to expand the scope of the American strategic buildup in the spring of 1961 triggered a reciprocal Soviet decision. The Reagan buildup of the 1980s was a response to Brezhnev's intensive spending of the previous decade and widespread concern that it had bought the Soviet Union a strategic advantage.

This pervasive fear of strategic inferiority was greatly exaggerated. We offer a set of general observations about the impact of nuclear threats and nuclear weapons that summarize our arguments based on the new evidence. These observations must remain tentative until additional evidence becomes available about other critical confrontations during the Cold War and about the role of nuclear weapons in Sino-American and Sino-Soviet relations.

1. Leaders who try to exploit real or imagined nuclear advantages for political gain are not likely to succeed. Khrushchev and Kennedy tried and failed to intimidate one another with claims of strategic superiority in the late 1950s and early 1960s. Khrushchev's threats and boasts strengthened Western resolve not to yield in Berlin and provoked Kennedy to order a major strategic buildup. Kennedy's threats against Cuba, his administration's assertion of strategic superiority, and the deployment of Jupiter missiles in Turkey—all intended to dissuade Khrushchev from challenging the West in Berlin—led directly to the Soviet decision to send missiles to Cuba. Both leaders were willing to assume the risks of a serious confrontation to avoid creating the impression of weakness or irresolution.

2. Credible nuclear threats are very difficult to make. The destructiveness of nuclear weapons makes nuclear threats more frightening but less credible. It is especially difficult to make nuclear threats credible when they are directed against nuclear adversaries who have the capability to retaliate in kind. Many Soviets worried about nuclear war during the missile crisis, but Khrushchev judged correctly that Kennedy would not initiate a nuclear war in response to the deployment of Soviet missiles. Khrushchev's principal concern was that the president would be pushed into attacking Cuba and that armed clashes between the invading Americans and the Soviet forces on the island committed to Cuba's defense would escalate into a wider and perhaps uncontrollable war.

In 1973, the American alert had even less influence on the Soviet leadership. It was inconceivable to Brezhnev and his colleagues that the United States would attack the Soviet Union with nuclear weapons. They did not believe that the interests at stake for either the United States or the Soviet Union justified war. The American nuclear threat was therefore incomprehensible and incredible.

3. Nuclear threats are fraught with risk. In both 1962 and 1973, American leaders were uninformed about the consequences and implications of strategic alerts. In 1973, they did not fully understand the technical meaning or the operational consequences of the DEFCON III alert and chose the alert in full confidence that it entailed no risks. During the missile crisis, when conventional and nuclear forces were moved to an even higher level of alert, it was very difficult to control alerted forces. Military routines and insubordination posed a serious threat to the resolution of the crisis.

Evidence from these two cases suggests that there are stark trade-offs between the political leverage that military preparations are expected to confer and the risks of inadvertent escalation they entail. American leaders had a poor understanding of these trade-offs: they significantly overvalued the political value of nuclear alerts and were relatively insensitive to their risks.[46]

4. Strategic buildups are more likely to provoke than to restrain adversaries because of their impact on the domestic balance of political power in the target state. Stalin, Khrushchev, and Brezhnev all believed that strategic advantage would restrain adversaries. Khrushchev believed that the West behaved cautiously in the 1950s because of a growing respect for the economic as well as the military power of the socialist camp. He was convinced that the visible demonstration of Soviet power, through nuclear threats and the deployment of missiles in Cuba, would strengthen the hands of the "sober realists" in Washington who favored accommodation with the Soviet Union. Khrushchev's actions had the reverse impact: they strengthened anti-Soviet militants by intensifying American fears of Soviet intentions and capabilities. Kennedy's warnings to Khrushchev not to deploy missiles in Cuba and his subsequent blockade were in large part a response to the growing domestic political pressures to act decisively against the Soviet Union and its Cuban ally.

Brezhnev's strategic buildup was a continuation of Khrushchev's program. American officials believed that the Soviet buildup continued after parity had been achieved. Soviet strategic spending appeared to confirm the predictions of militants in Washington that Moscow's goal was strategic superiority, even a first-strike capability. Brezhnev, on the other hand, expected Soviet nuclear capabilities to prevent the United States from engaging in "nuclear blackmail." Instead, it gave Republicans the ammunition to defeat President Carter and the SALT II agreement. The Soviet arms buildup and invasion of Afghanistan contributed to Ronald Reagan's landslide victory in 1980 and provided the justification for his administration's massive arms spending. American attempts to put pressure on the Soviet Union through arms buildups were equally counterproductive.

5. Nuclear deterrence is robust when leaders on both sides fear war and are aware of each other's fears. War-fighting, MAD, and finite deterrence all mistakenly equate stability with specific arms configurations. More important than the distribution of nuclear capabilities, or leaders' estimates of relative nuclear advantage, is their judgment of an adversary's intentions. The Cuban missile crisis was a critical turning point in Soviet-American relations because it convinced Kennedy and Khrushchev, and some of their most important advisors as well, that their adversary was as committed as they were to avoiding nuclear war. This mutually acknowledged fear of war made the other side's nuclear capabilities less threatening and paved the way for the first arms-control agreements.

By no means did all American and Soviet leaders share this interpretation. Large segments of the national security elites of both superpowers continued to regard their adversary as implacably hostile and willing to use nuclear weapons. Even when Brezhnev and Nixon acknowledged the other's fear of war, they used the umbrella of nuclear deterrence to compete vigorously for unilateral gain. Western militants did not begin to change their estimate of Soviet intentions until Gorbachev made clear his commitment to ending the arms race and the Cold War.

Deterrence in Hindsight

The Cold War began as a result of Soviet-American competition in Central Europe in the aftermath of Germany's defeat. Once recognized spheres of influence were established, confrontations between the superpowers in the heart of Europe diminished. Only Berlin continued to be a flash point until the superpowers reached an understanding about the two Germanies. The conventional and nuclear arms buildup that followed in the wake of the crises of the early Cold War was a reaction to the mutual insecurities they generated. By the 1970s, the growing arsenal and increasingly accurate weapons of mass destruction that each superpower aimed at the other had become the primary source of mutual insecurity and tension. Moscow and Washington no longer argued about the status quo in Europe but about the new weapons systems each deployed to threaten the other. Each thought that deterrence was far less robust than it was. Their search for deterrence reversed cause and effect and prolonged the Cold War.

The history of the Cold War provides compelling evidence of the pernicious effects of the open-ended quest for nuclear deterrence. But nuclear weapons also moderated superpower behavior, once leaders in Moscow and Washington recognized and acknowledged to the other that a nuclear war between them would almost certainly lead to their mutual destruction.

Since the late 1960s, when the Soviet Union developed an effective retaliatory capability, both superpowers had to live with nuclear vulnerability. There were always advocates of preemption, ballistic missile defense, or other illusory visions of security in a nuclear world. But nuclear vulnerability could not be eliminated. MAD was a reality from which there was no escape short of the most far-reaching arms control. Even after the dissolution of the Soviet Union and the proposed deep cuts in nuclear weapons, Russia and the United States will still possess enough nuclear weapons to destroy each other many times over.[47]

Nuclear vulnerability distinguished the Soviet-American conflict from conventional conflicts of the past or present. In conventional conflicts, leaders could believe that war might benefit their country. Leaders have often gone to war with this expectation, although more often than not they have been proven wrong. The consequences of war turned out very differently than expected by leaders in Iraq in 1980, Argentina in 1982, and Israel in 1982.

Fear of the consequences of nuclear war not only made it exceedingly improbable that either superpower would deliberately seek a military confrontation with the other; it made their leaders extremely reluctant to take any action that they considered would seriously raise the risk of war. Over the years they developed a much better appreciation of each other's interests. In the last years of the Soviet-American conflict, leaders on both sides acknowledged and refrained from any challenge of the other's vital interests.

The ultimate irony of nuclear deterrence may be the way in which the strategy of deterrence undercut much of the political stability the reality of deterrence should have created. The arms buildups, threatening military deployments, and the confrontational rhetoric that characterized the strategy of deterrence effectively obscured deep-seated, mutual fears of war. Fear of nuclear war made leaders inwardly cautious, but their public posturing convinced their adversaries that they were aggressive, risk-prone, and even irrational.

This kind of behavior was consistent with the strategy of deterrence. Leaders on both sides recognized that only a madman would use nuclear weapons against a nuclear adversary. To reinforce deterrence, they therefore tried, and to a disturbing degree, succeeded in convincing the other that they might be irrational enough or sufficiently out of control to implement their threats. Each consequently became less secure, more threatened, and less confident of the robust reality of deterrence. The strategy of deterrence was self-defeating; it provoked the kind of behavior it was designed to prevent.

The history of the Cold War suggests that nuclear deterrence should be viewed as a powerful but very dangerous medicine. Arsenic, formerly used to treat syphilis and schistosomiasis, and chemotherapy, routinely used to treat cancer, can kill or cure a patient. The outcome depends on the virulence of the disease, how early the disease is detected, the amount of drugs administered, and the resistance of the patient to both the disease and the cure. So it is with nuclear deterrence. Finite deterrence is stabilizing because it prompts mutual caution. Too much deterrence, or deterrence applied inappropriately to a frightened and vulnerable adversary, can fuel an arms race that makes both sides less rather than more secure and provoke the aggression that it is designed to prevent. As with any medicine, the key to successful deterrence is to administer correctly the proper dosage.

The superpowers "overdosed" on deterrence. It poisoned their relationship, but their leaders remained blind to its consequences. Instead, they interpreted the tension and crises that followed as evidence of the need for even more deterrence. Despite the changed political climate that makes it almost inconceivable that either Russia or the United States would initiate nuclear war, there are still influential people in Washington, and possibly in Moscow, who believe that new weapons are necessary to reinforce deterrence. Deeply embedded beliefs are extraordinarily resistant to change.

Postscript

Deterrence and the end of the cold war

> I like many others knew that the USSR needed radical change. Khrushchev tried it, Kosygin tried it. ...If I had not understood this, I would never have

accepted the position of General Secretary. At the end of 1986, we feared that the process of reform was slowing down and that the same fate could befall our reforms as befell Khrushchev's.

—**Mikhail S. Gorbachev**[1]

The final claim made for nuclear deterrence is that it helped to end the Cold War. As impeccable a liberal as *New York Times* columnist Tom Wicker reluctantly conceded that Star Wars and the massive military buildup in the Reagan administration had forced the Soviet Union to reorient its foreign and domestic policies.[2] The conventional wisdom has two components. American military capability and resolve allegedly convinced Soviet leaders that aggression anywhere would meet unyielding opposition. Forty years of arms competition also brought the Soviet economy to the edge of collapse. The Reagan buildup and Star Wars, the argument goes, were the straws that broke the Soviet camel's back. Moscow could not match the increased level of American defense spending and accordingly chose to end the Cold War.

We cannot examine these propositions about the impact of deterrence on the end of the Cold War with the same quality of evidence we used to assess the role of deterrence in superpower relations during the Cold War. Nevertheless, the absence of a large body of documents, interviews, and memoirs has not discouraged columnists and scholars from rendering judgments about the end of the Cold War. Nor will it prevent policy makers from using these interpretations as guides to action in the future. It is therefore essential that the conventional wisdom does not go unexamined. The limited evidence that is now available is not consistent with these two propositions about the role of deterrence in ending the Cold War. Within the confines of the available evidence, we sketch the outlines of a very different interpretation.

The end of the cold war

Soviet officials insist that Gorbachev's withdrawal of Soviet forces from Afghanistan, proposals for arms control, and domestic reforms took place despite the Reagan buildup. Mikhail Sergeevich Gorbachev came to power in March 1985 committed to liberalizing the domestic political process at home and improving relations with the West so that the Soviet Union could modernize its rigid economy. Within a month of assuming office, he announced his first unilateral initiative—a temporary freeze on the deployment of Soviet intermediate-range missiles in Europe—and in a series of subsequent proposals tried to signal his interest in arms control. President Reagan continued to speak of the Soviet Union as an "evil empire" and remained committed to his quest for a near-perfect ballistic-missile defense.

Gorbachev came to office imbued with a sense of the urgency of domestic reform and with a fundamentally different attitude toward the West. He was confident that the United States would not deliberately attack the Soviet Union and that the serious risk was an accidental or miscalculated .exchange.[3] In conversations with his military advisors, he rejected any plans that were premised on a war with the United States. "During the period of stagnation," he observed, "we had assumed that such a war was possible, but when I became general secretary, I refused to consider any such plans."[4] Since he saw no threat of attack from the United States, Gorbachev was not "afraid" of any military programs put forward by the Reagan administration and did not feel forced to match them. Rather, he saw arms spending as an unnecessary and wasteful expenditure of scarce resources. Deep arms reductions were not only important to the reform and development of the Soviet economy, hut also an imperative of the nuclear age.[5]

Rather than facilitating a change in Soviet foreign policy, Reagan's commitment to the Strategic Defense Initiative (SDI) complicated Gorbachev's task of persuading his own officials that arms control was in the Soviet interest. Conservatives, much of the military leadership, and captains of defense-related industries took SDI as further evidence of the hostile intentions of the United States and insisted on increased spending on offensive counter-measures. Gorbachev, Eduard Shevardnadze, Aleksandr Yakovlev, and many foreign-ministry officials did not feel threatened by Star Wars but were constrained and frustrated by the political impact of Reagan's policies at home.[6]

To break the impasse, Gorbachev used a two-pronged strategy. In successive summits he tried and finally convinced Reagan of his genuine interest in ending the arms race and restructuring East-West relations on a collaborative basis. When Reagan changed his estimate of Gorbachev, he also modified his assessment of the Soviet Union and became the leading dove of his administration. Gorbachev also worked hard to convince Western publics that he intended a radical departure from past Soviet policies. The withdrawal from Afghanistan, freeing of Soviet political prisoners, and liberalization of the Soviet political system evoked widespread sympathy and support in the West and generated strong public pressures on NATO governments to respond positively to his initiatives.

The first breakthrough—an agreement on intermediate nuclear forces (INF)—was the unintended result of the Reagan administration's need to placate American and European public opinion. American officials were deeply divided on the question of theater arms control and settled on the "double zero" proposal only because they thought that Moscow would reject the offer. The proposal required the Soviet Union, which had already deployed a new generation of nuclear delivery systems in Europe, to make deeper cuts in its arsenal than the United States, which had only just begun to field new weapons in Europe. Washington expected Gorbachev to reject the proposal and hoped thereby to make him appear responsible for the failure of arms control. They were astonished when he agreed in principle.[7] Soviet officials contend that Gorbachev accepted "double zero," not because of Soviet weakness, but in the expectation that it would trigger a reciprocal process of accommodation. President Gorbachev subsequently described the INF agreement as a watershed in Soviet-American relations. "Working on the treaty and the treaty itself," he said, "created trust and a network of personal links."[8] To Gorbachev, the absolute gain of accommodation was far more important than the relative distribution of military advantage in any particular arms-control agreement.[9]

Gorbachev's political persistence broke through Reagan's wall of mistrust. At their Reykjavik summit in October 1986, the two leaders talked seriously about eliminating all their ballistic missiles within ten years and significantly reducing their arsenals of nuclear weapons. No agreement was reached because Reagan was unwilling to limit SDI. The Reykjavik summit, as Gorbachev had hoped, nevertheless began a process of mutual reassurance and accommodation.[10] That process continued after an initially hesitant George Bush became a full-fledged partner. In hindsight, it is apparent that Gorbachev's initiatives began the process that brought the Cold War to an end.

Defense and the economy

The conventional wisdom assumes that the Soviet Union was forced to match American defense spending and to end the Cold War when it could no longer compete. There is no evidence that Soviet defense spending rose or fell in response to American defense spending. Revised estimates by the CIA indicate that Soviet defense expenditures remained more or less constant throughout the 1980s. Neither the Carter-Reagan buildup nor Star Wars had any impact on gross spending levels. Their only demonstrable impact was to shift in marginal ways the allocation of defense rubles. After SDI, more funds were earmarked to developing countermeasures to ballistic defense.[11]

If American defense spending bankrupted the Soviet economy and led Gorbachev to end the Cold War, a sharp decline in defense spending should have occurred under Gorbachev. Despite his rejection of military competition with the United States, CIA statistics show that Soviet defense spending remained relatively constant as a proportion of Soviet gross national product during the first four years of Gorbachev's tenure. The Soviet gross national product declined precipitously in the late 1980s and early 1990s; Gorbachev's domestic reforms had a profoundly negative impact on the Soviet economy. Soviet defense spending was reduced only in 1989 and did not shrink as rapidly as the overall economy. In the current decade, Soviet, and then Russian defense spending has consumed a higher percentage of disposable national income than it did in the Brezhnev years.[12]

From Stalin through Gorbachev, annual Soviet defense spending consumed about 25% of Soviet disposable income. This was an extraordinary burden on the economy. Not all Soviet leaders were blind to its likely consequences. In the early 1970s, some officials recognized that the economy would ultimately stagnate if the military continued to consume such a disproportionate share of resources.[13] Brezhnev, however, was even more heavily dependent than Khrushchev on the support of a coalition in which defense and heavy industry were well represented. In defense, as in other budgetary outlays, allocations reflected the relative political power of different sectors of the economy. Within the different sectors, spending and investment were controlled by bureaucracies with strong vested interests. As a result, not only military but also civilian speeding was frequently wasteful and inefficient. Logrolling among competing groups compounded the problem by increasing the aggregate level of spending.[14] Because Soviet defense spending under Brezhnev and Gorbachev was primarily a response to internal imperatives, it is not correlated with American defense spending. Nor is there any observable relationship between defense spending and changes in the political relationship between the superpowers, until the cuts in the American defense budget in 1991.

The proposition that American defense spending bankrupted the Soviet economy and forced an end to the Cold War is not sustained by the available evidence. The critical factor in the Soviet economic decline was the rigid "command economy" imposed by Stalin in the early 1930s. It offered little or no reward for individual or collective initiative, freed productive units from the competition normally imposed by the market, and centralized production and investment decisions in the hands of an unwieldy bureaucracy immune from market forces and consumer demands. The command economy predates the Cold War and was not a response to American deterrence.[15]

Why soviet foreign policy changed

To explain the dramatic reorientation of Soviet foreign policy, we need to look first at the domestic agendas of Soviet leaders. Khrushchev's and Gorbachev's efforts to transform East-West relations and Brezhnev's more limited attempt at detente were motivated in large part by their economic objectives.

Khrushchev sought an accommodation with the West to free manpower and resources for economic development. He hoped that success in reducing East-West tensions would enhance his domestic authority and make it more difficult for conservative forces to block his economic and political reforms. Gorbachev had a similar agenda and pursued a similar strategy. *Perestroika* required peaceful relations abroad to succeed at home. Accommodation with the West would permit a shift in resources from the military to productive investment; attract credits, investment, and technology from the West; and weaken the power of the conservatives opposed to Gorbachev and his reforms. Accommodation with the West was especially critical for Gorbachev because the Soviet economy had deteriorated sharply since the early 1970s and the brief detente between the United States and the Soviet Union. The impetus for domestic reform was structural; economic decline, or the threat of serious decline, motivated Gorbachev, like Khrushchev and Brezhnev, to implement domestic reforms and seek accommodation with the West.

The need to arrest economic decline and improve economic performance cannot by itself explain the scope of reforms or the kind of relationship Gorbachev tried to establish with the West. Only a few central Soviet leaders responded to economic imperatives by promoting a radical restructuring of the Soviet relationship with the West.[16] Almost all the fundamental components of Gorbachev's "new thinking" about security were politically contested.[17] Traditional thinkers powerfully placed within the defense ministry and the Soviet General Staff vigorously challenged the new concepts of security. Indeed, Gorbachev had to go outside the establishment to civilian and academic specialists on defense in the policy institutes in Moscow for new ideas about Soviet security.[18] Insofar as senior Soviet leaders and officials in the Gorbachev era disagreed fundamentally about the direction of Soviet foreign and defense policy, structural imperatives alone cannot adequately explain the change in Soviet thinking about security under Gorbachev.

Gorbachev differed significantly from Khrushchev and Brezhnev in his conception of security. Previous Soviet leaders had regarded the capitalist West as the enemy and had feared military aggression against the Soviet Union or its allies. Like their Western counterparts, they measured security in terms of military and economic power; Soviet military prowess and socialist solidarity were necessary to deter attack and restrain the capitalist powers. Khrushchev and Brezhnev wanted to improve relations with the West, but they remained committed to their ideological view of a world divided into two hostile camps. Unlike Stalin, they recognized that nuclear weapons had made war between the superpowers irrational and unlikely, but they believed in the fundamental antagonism between the incompatible systems of capitalism and socialism.

Gorbachev and his closest advisors rejected the traditional Soviet approach to security. In their view, it had helped to create and sustain the Cold War and had placed a heavy burden on the Soviet economy. *Perestroicki* were especially critical of the domestic consequences of postwar Soviet foreign policy; conflict with the West had been exploited by the Communist Party to justify its monopoly on power and suppression of dissent.[19]

Gorbachev's vision of Soviet security was cooperative rather than competitive. He and Eduard A. Shevardnadze repudiated the class basis of international relations that had dominated Soviet thinking about security since the Soviet state was created. They explicitly condemned as mistaken the thesis developed in the Khrushchev and Brezhnev years that peaceful coexistence was a specific form of the class struggle.[20] "New thinking" about security was based on five related propositions: the primacy of universal, "all-human" values over class conflict; the interdependence of ail nations; the impossibility of achieving victory in nuclear or large-scale conventional war; the need to seek security in political and economic rather than military terms; and the belief that neither Soviet nor Western security could be achieved unilaterally.[21] Gorbachev called for the development of "a new security model" based on "a policy of compromise" among former adversaries.[22]

National security was to be replaced by a "common, indivisible security, the same for all." The goal of the Soviet Union was to join a "common European house" that would foster security and prosperity through "a policy of cooperation based on mutual trust."[23]

Gorbachev, Shevardnadze, and other committed democrats believed in a complex, two-way relationship between domestic reform and foreign policy. Accommodation with the West would facilitate perestroika, but it was more than an instrument of reform and economic rejuvenation.[24] For the Soviet Union to join the family of nations, it had to become a democratic society with a demonstrable respect for the individual and collective rights of its citizens and allies. Granting independence to the countries of Eastern Europe was the international analogue to emptying the gulags, ending censorship in the media, and choosing members of the Supreme Soviet through free elections.

Gorbachev was able to pursue a more far-reaching and dramatic strategy of accommodation than his predecessors because of the evolution in the superpower relationship since the acute confrontations of the 1960s. He was much less fearful of Western intentions than Khrushchev and less concerned that the United States and its allies would exploit concessions as a sign of weakness. Khrushchev's fear of the West severely constrained his search for accommodation. He never considered, as did Gorbachev, that soft words and unilateral initiatives would evoke enough public sympathy and support so that Western governments would be pushed by their own domestic publics to reciprocate. Khrushchev did make some unilateral concessions; he reduced the size of the armed forces and proclaimed a short-lived moratorium on nuclear testing. When his actions were not reciprocated, the militant opposition at home forced him to revert to a confrontational policy. His inflammatory rhetoric in turn strengthened the forces in the West who opposed accommodation with the Soviet Union.

Gorbachev could not have succeeded in transforming East-West relations and ending the Cold War if the West had not become his willing partner. Unlike Khrushchev, whose quest for a German peace treaty frightened France and West Germany, Gorbachev met a receptive audience when he attempted to end the division of Europe. Disenchantment with the Cold War, opposition to the deployment of new weapons systems, and a widespread desire to end the division of Europe, given voice by well-organized peace movements, created a groundswell of support for exploring the possibilities of accommodation with the Soviet Union.

The impact of American policy

Throughout the Cold War, many leaders in the West argued that the internal structure and foreign-policy goals of the Soviet Union were ideologically determined and largely unaffected by the policies of other states. The West could only restrain Soviet aggression through a policy of strength. Many academic analysts rejected the argument that Soviet domestic and foreign policies were immutable.

They maintained that Western policies made a difference, but disagreed among themselves about the nature of the interaction between Soviet and American foreign and domestic policies.

Some scholars contended that the links were reciprocal. Soviet "orthodoxy," which favored heavy industry, restricted individual freedoms, and a strong military, was strengthened by an international environment that appeared to confirm the enemy image of the capitalist West. Conciliatory Western, policies could weaken the influence of Soviet militants and strengthen the hand of those officials who favored reform and accommodation with the West.[25] Other scholars subscribed only to the first of these propositions. Citing the Khrushchev experience, they agreed that a threatening international environment undermined reform and accommodation, but, drawing on the Brezhnev years, they denied the corollary that detente encouraged domestic liberalization.[26] The contrast between Gorbachev and Brezhnev led some specialists to argue that reform only came when the leadership confronted the prospect of domestic and foreign-policy disaster.[27]

The available evidence suggests a different proposition about the relationship between American and Soviet foreign policy. The critical factor was the agenda of Soviet leaders. American influence was limited when Soviet leaders were not seriously committed to internal reform. Confrontation then exacerbated Soviet-American tensions, but conciliation did not necessarily improve the relationship, nor did it encourage internal reforms. Jimmy Carter's efforts to transform Soviet-American relations had little effect because they came after Brezhnev had lost interest in domestic reform at home.

When the principal objective of Soviet leaders was economic reform and development, they were anxious to reach some kind of accommodation with the West. Gorbachev, like Khrushchev, was committed to domestic economic reform. Under these conditions, American policy, whether confrontational or conciliatory, had its greatest impact. Confrontation was most likely to provoke an aggressive response because it exacerbated the foreign-policy problems of Soviet leaders, undercut their domestic authority, and threatened their domestic economic goals. Conciliation was most likely to be reciprocated because Soviet leaders expected an improved relationship to enhance their authority at home, free scarce resources for development, and provide access to Western credits and technology.

If American policy did have an impact when Soviet leaders were committed to reform, then the strategy of deterrence likely prolonged the Cold War. The Cold War ended when Soviet leaders became committed to domestic reform and to a concept of common security that built on the reality of nuclear deterrence, and when Western leaders reassured and reciprocated. We cannot support these propositions with the kind of evidence we marshaled in support of our contention that the strategy of deterrence had complex but largely negative consequences for superpower relations during the Cold War. The same kind of detailed reconstruction of Soviet and American policy during the Gorbachev era will only be possible when documents, memoirs, and interviews of key participants become available. Until then, this alternative interpretation of the impact of the strategy of nuclear deterrence on the end of the Cold War may help to stimulate an important debate about the enduring lessons of the Cold War and its demise.

Notes

1 In keeping with the theological quality of the debate, followers of the "war-fighting" sect of deterrence had a sacred text: *Voyenaya mysl'*, the Soviet *Journal of Military Thought*. Many of the professional Soviet military discussions of the contingent uses of military power were misused to infer and attribute offensive military intentions to the Soviet Union.

2 McGeorge Bundy, *Danger and Survival: Choices About the Bomb in the First Fifty Years* (New York: Random House, 1988).

3 Richard K. Betts, *Nuclear Blackmail and Nuclear Balance* (Washington, D.C.: The Brookings Institution, 1987).

4 Harry Truman claimed to have compelled the Soviet Union to withdraw from Iran in 1946, but no documentary record of a nuclear threat can be found. See Betts, *Nuclear Blackmail and Nuclear Balance,* pp. 7–8; Richard W. Cottam, *Iran and the United States: A Cold War Case Study* (Pittsburgh: University of Pittsburgh Press, 1988).

5 John E. Mueller, *Retreat from Doomsday: The Obsolescence of Modern War* (New York: Basic Books, 1989). Kenneth N. Waltz, *Theory of International Politics* (Reading, MA.: Addison-Wesley, 1979), also disparaged the role of nuclear weapons and argued that bipolarity was responsible for the long peace. Waltz, "The Emerging Structure of International Politics," paper prepared for the August 1990 Annual Meeting of the American Political Science Association, subsequently acknowledged nuclear weapons as one of "the twin pillars" of the peace. See Richard Ned Lebow, "Explaining Stability and Change: A Critique of Realism," in Richard Ned Lebow and Thomas Risse-Kappen, eds., *International Relations Theory and the End of the Cold War,* forthcoming, for a critical examination of the realist position on the long peace.

6 Richard Ned Lebow, "Conventional vs. Nuclear Deterrence: Are the Lessons Transferable?" *Journal of Social Issues, 43*, 4 (1987), pp. 171–91.

7 McGeorge Bundy, "To Cap the Volcano," *Foreign Affairs,* 48, 1 (October 1969), pp. 1–20; Harvard Nuclear Study Group, *Living With Nuclear Weapons* (Cambridge, MA.: Harvard University Press, 1983); Klaus Knorr, "Controlling Nuclear War," *International Security* 9, 4 (Spring 1985), pp. 79–98; Michael Mandelbaum, *The Nuclear Question: The United States and Nuclear Weapons, 1946–76* (New York: Cambridge University Press, 1979); Robert W. Tucker, *The Nuclear Debate: Deterrence and the Lapse of Faith* (New York: Holmes & Meier, 1985).

8 For example, Raymond Aron, *The Great Debate: Theories of Nuclear Strategy,* trans. Ernst Pawel (Garden City, NY: Doubleday, 1965); Stanley Hoffmann, *The State of War: Essays on the Theory and Practice of International Politics* (New York: Praeger, 1965), p. 236; Betts, *Nuclear Blackmail*; Bundy, *Danger and Survival;* Robert Jervis, *The Meaning of the Nuclear Revolution: Statecraft and the Prospect of Armageddon* (Ithaca, NY: Cornell University Press, 1989).

9 For the evolution of McNamara's strategic thinking, see Desmond Ball, *Politics and Force Levels: The Strategic Missile Program of the Kennedy Administration* (Berke-

ley: University of California Press, 1980), especially pp. 171–93; Lawrence Freedman, *The Evolution of Nuclear Strategy* (New York: St. Martin's Press, 1983), pp. 331–71.

10 For war-fighting critics of MAD, see Daniel Graham, *Shall America Be Defended?: SALT II and Beyond* (New Rochelle, NY: Arlington House, 1979); Colin S. Gray, *Nuclear Strategy and National Style* (Lanham, MD: Hamilton Press, 1986); Colin S. Gray and Keith B. Payne, "Victory is Possible," *Foreign Policy, 39* (Summer 1980), pp. 14–27; Albert Wohlstetter, "Between an Unfree World and None," *Foreign Affairs, 63*(5) (Summer 1985), pp. 962–94; Fred Hoffman, "The SDI in U.S. Nuclear Strategy," *International Security, 10*(1) (Summer 1985), pp. 13–24.

11 Morton H. Halperin, *Nuclear Fallacy: Dispelling the Myth of Nuclear Strategy* (Cambridge: Ballinger, 1987); Adm. Noel Gayler, "The Way Out: A General Nuclear Settlement," in Gwyn Prins, ed., *The Nuclear Crisis Reader* (New York: Vintage Books, 1984), pp. 234–43.

12 Graham, *Shall America Be Defended?;* Gray, *Nuclear Strategy and National Style;* Wohlstetter, "Between an Unfree World and None."

13 Robert S. McNamara, "The Military Role of Nuclear Weapons: Perceptions and Misperceptions," *Foreign Affairs, 62* (Fall 1983), pp. 59–80, at p. 68; Jervis, *The Meaning of the Nuclear Revolution,* pp. 34–38; Alexander L. George, David K. Hall, and William E. Simons, *The Limits of Coercive Diplomacy: Laos, Cuba, Vietnam* (Boston: Little, Brown, 1971); Betts, *Nuclear Blackmail.*

14 This distinction was introduced by Patrick M. Morgan, *Deterrence: A Conceptual Analysis* (Beverly Hills, CA.: Sage, 1977).

15 Arthur Schlesinger, Jr., *A Thousand Days: John F. Kennedy in the White House* (Boston: Houghton, Mifflin, 1965), pp. 347–48. This point is also made by Alexander L. George and Richard Smoke, *Deterrence in American Foreign Policy: Theory and Practice* (New York: Columbia University Press, 1974), pp. 429, 579.

16 On the Warsaw Pact, see Robin Allison Remington, *The Changing Soviet Perception of the Warsaw Pact* (Cambridge, MA.: MIT Center for International Studies, 1967); Christopher D. Jones, *Soviet Influence in Eastern Europe: Political Autonomy and the Warsaw Pact* (New York: Praeger, 1981); David Holloway, "The Warsaw Pact in Transition," in David Holloway and Jane M. O. Sharp, eds., *The Warsaw Pact: Alliance in Transition?* (Ithaca, NY: Cornell University Press, 1984) pp. 19–38.

17 Interview, Leonid Zamyatin, Moscow, December 16, 1991; Sergei Khrushchev, *Khrushchev on Khrushchev: An Inside Account of the Man and His Era*, trans. William Taubman (Boston: Little, Brown, 1990), pp. 156–57; Oleg Troyanovsky, "The Caribbean Crisis: A View from the Kremlin," *International Affairs* (Moscow) 4–5 (April/May 1992), pp. 147–57, at p. 149.

18 See Richard Ned Lebow, *Between Peace and War: The Nature of International Crisis* (Baltimore: Johns Hopkins University Press, 1981), pp. 82–97, for a discussion of the four traditional prerequisites of deterrence. For discussion of the conditions essential to deterrence success, see Richard Ned Lebow and Janice Gross Stein, *When Does Deterrence Succeed and How Do We Know?* (Ottawa: Canadian Institute for International Peace and Security, 1990), pp. 59–69.

19 Chapter 3 of Lebow and Stein, *We All Lost the Cold War* reviews this debate.

20 Janice Gross Stein, "Calculation, Miscalculation, and Conventional Deterrence I: The View from Cairo," in Robert Jervis, Richard Ned Lebow, and Janice Gross Stein,

Psychology and Deterrence (Baltimore: Johns Hopkins University Press, 1985), pp. 31–59.

21   Henry Kissinger, *Years of Upheaval* (Boston: Little, Brown, 1982), p. 508.

22   Ibid., p. 510.

23   "United States Objectives and Programs for National Security," (NSC 68) (April 14, 1950), *Foreign Relations of the United States, 1950*, vol. I (Washington, D.C.: Government Printing Office, 1977), p. 264; Vernon Aspaturian, "Soviet Global Power and the Correlation of Forces," *Problems of Communism, 20* (May-June 1980), pp. 1–18; John J. Dziak, *Soviet Perceptions of Military Power: The Interaction of Theory and Practice* (New York: Crane, Russak, 1981); Edward N. Luttwak, "After Afghanistan What?" *Commentary, 69* (April 1980), pp. 1–18; Richard Pipes, "Why the Soviet Union Thinks It Could Fight and Win a Nuclear War," *Commentary, 64* (July 1977), pp. 21–34; Norman Podhoretz, "The Present Danger," *Commentary, 69* (April 1980), pp. 40–49.

24   There is also some evidence that the fear of war influenced Soviet behavior in Korea. Joseph Stalin authorized Kim Il Sung to attack South Korea in June 1950 in the expectation that the United States would not intervene. When Washington did intervene, Stalin, afraid that the North Korean attack would provoke a Soviet-American war, quickly signaled interest in a cease-fire. N. Khrushchev, *Khrushchev Remembers: The Glasnost Tapes*, trans, and ed. Jerrold L. Schecter with Vyacheslav L. Luchkov (Boston: Little, Brown, 1990), pp. 144–47.

25   Oleg Grinevsky contends that Stalin feared that even a few atomic bombs dropped on Moscow would have destroyed the communist experiment. Interview, Oleg Grinevsky, Stockholm, October 24, 1992.

26   David A. Welch, ed., *Proceedings of the Hawk's Cay Conference on the Cuban Missile Crisis, 5–8 March 1987* (Cambridge, MA: Harvard University, Center for Science and International Affairs, Working Paper 89–1, 1989), mimeograph, pp. 81–83, hereafter cited as *Hawks Cay Conference*.

27   Ibid., pp. 83ff.

28   Hawk's Cay Conference, author's record.

29   Ball, *Politics and Force Levels*, pp. 171–93; Freedman, *The Evolution of Nuclear Strategy*, pp. 331–71.

30   Sec Graham, *Shall America Be Defended?*; Gray, *Nuclear Strategy and National Style*; Gray and Payne, "Victory is Possible"; Wohlstetter, "Between an Unfree World and None."

31   Interview, Gen. Dimitri A. Volkogonov by Raymond L. Garthoff, Moscow, February 1, 1989; Anatoliy Gribkov, "Transcript of the Proceedings of the Havana Conference on the Cuban Missile Crisis, January 9–12 1992," mimeograph, in James G. Blight, Bruce J. Allyn, and David A. Welch, eds., *Cuba on the Brink: Castro, the Missile Crisis, and the Soviet Collapse* (New York: Pantheon Books, in press), pp. 18–21, hereafter cited as *Havana Conference*.

32   "Retrospective on the Cuban Missile Crisis," 22 January 1983, Atlanta, Ga. Participants: Dean Rusk, McGeorge Bundy, Edwin Martin, Donald Wilson, and Richard E. Neustadt (hereafter referred to as Retrospective), p. 6.

33   *Hawk's Cay Conference*, pp. 9–10.

34   Interview, Robert McNamara, Hawk's Cay, Florida, March 6, 1987.

35   Retrospective, p. 40.

36 Garthoff, *Reflections on the Cuban Missile Crisis*, 2d ed. rev. (Washington, D.C.: The Brookings Institution, 1989), pp. 158–86, on Soviet lessons from the crisis; Interviews, Leonid Zamyatin and Anatoliy F. Dobrynin, Moscow, December 16–17, 1991.

37 The assertion that the Soviet Union could only be constrained by superior military power became something close to dogma in the United States government. It received its most forceful expression in National Security Council Memorandum (NSC) 68, written on the eve of the Korean War in 1950. NSC 68 is generally recognized as the most influential American policy document of the Cold War. See John L. Gaddis, *Strategies of Containment: A Critical Appraisal of Postwar American National Security Policy* (New York: Oxford University Press, 1982), chap. 4; Paul Y. Hammond, "NSC-68: Prologue to Rearmament," in Warner R. Schilling, Paul Y. Hammond, and Glenn H. Snyder, eds., *Strategy, Politics, and Defense Budgets* (New York: Columbia University Press, 1962), pp. 267–338; "United States Objectives and Programs for National Security," pp. 234–92.

38 Soviet leaders, with a mirror image of their adversary, made the same assumption about American foreign policy. Khrushchev put missiles in Cuba in part to achieve psychological equality and constrain American foreign policy.

39 The accepted strategic wisdom, reflected in our analysis, holds that the United States had a decisive strategic advantage throughout the 1950s. It possessed an expanding capability to attack the Soviet Union with nuclear weapons without the prospect of direct retaliation. The Strategic Air Command had a large and growing fleet of strategic bombers based in the United States, Western Europe, and North Africa. This strike force was supplemented by carrier and land-based aircraft deployed along the Soviet periphery. The Soviet Union's bomber force was small, shorter range, and technologically primitive.

The relative military balance changed in the 1960s when both superpowers began to deploy ICBMs. In 1962, at the time of the Cuban missile crisis, the United States had some 3,500 warheads against approximately 300 for the Soviets. Only 20 of the Soviet warheads were on ICBMs. See Sagan, "SIOP-62: The Nuclear War Plan Briefing to President Kennedy," *International Security, 12*, I (Summer 1987), pp. 22–51; David A. Welch, ed., *Proceedings of the Cambridge Conference on the Cuban Missile Crisis, 11–12 October 1987* (Cambridge, MA.: Harvard University, Center for Science and International Affairs, April 1988), final version, mimeograph, pp. 52, 79, hereafter cited as *Cambridge Conference*. By the end of the 1960s, the Soviet Strategic Rocket Forces had deployed enough ICBMs to destroy about half of the population and industry of the United States. It had achieved the capability that McNamara considered essential for MAD.

Some time in the 1970s the Soviet Union achieved rough strategic parity. This balance prevailed until 1991, although some analysts have argued that one or the other possessed some margin of advantage. American missiles were more accurate throughout the 1970s. The United States was also the first to deploy multiple independently targeted reentry vehicles (MIRVs). It put three warheads on Minuteman missiles, and 14 on submarine-launched ballistic missiles (SLBMs). The Soviet Union began to deploy MIRVs in the late 1970s and, in the opinion of some analysts, gained a temporary strategic advantage because of the greater throw weight of their ICBMs. The SS-18 could carry 30 to 40 MIRVs, but in practice was deployed with a maximum of ten.

40 Soviet aggressiveness is a subjective phenomenon. To measure it, we polled a sample of international relations scholars and former government officials. They were carefully chosen to ensure representation of diverse political points of view. These experts were given a list of events that could be interpreted as Soviet challenges to the United States, its allies, or nonaligned states. They were asked to rank them in order of ascending gravity. The survey revealed a surprising concurrence among experts. A description of the survey and its results appears in Richard Ned Lebow and John Garofano, "Soviet Aggressiveness: Need or Opportunity?" mimeograph.

41 This kind of need-based explanation of aggression provides a convincing explanation of both Soviet and American foreign policy in the Cold War since the Khrushchev and Kennedy years. See Richard Ned Lebow, "Windows of Opportunity: Do States Jump Through Them?" *International Security, 9* (Summer 1984), pp. 147–86.

42 McNamara, "The Military Role of Nuclear Weapons"; Jervis, *The Meaning of the Nuclear Revolution;* George, Hall, and Simons, *The Limits of Coercive Diplomacy;* Betts, *Nuclear Blackmail.*

43 Albert and Roberta Wohlstetter, "Controlling the Risks in Cuba," *Adelphi Paper* no. 17 (London: International Institute for Strategic Studies, 1965), p. 16. See also, Herman Kahn, *On Escalation* (New York: Praeger, 1965), pp. 74–82; Thomas Schelling, *Arms and Influence* (New Haven, CN.: Yale University Press, 1966), pp. 80–83.

44 McNamara, "The Military Role of Nuclear Weapons"; Jervis, *The Meaning of the Nuclear Revolution,* pp. 34–38.

45 Years later, in an offhand comment, Kissinger claimed that he would not have felt secure enough to choose an alert if the Soviet Union had had a marked strategic advantage. Cited by Betts, *Nuclear Blackmail,* p. 125. This kind of indirect and fragmentary evidence fits best with the arguments of the war-fighters, largely because Kissinger thought very much as they did. It is of course debatable whether Kissinger would have acted differently had the United States been in a position of relative inferiority; the proposition has never been put to the test. Given Kissinger's heavy emphasis on reputation and resolve, it seems unlikely that he would have complied even if the Soviet Union had had a relative strategic advantage. Proponents of finite deterrence and MAD would argue that Soviet compellence was unlikely to succeed even if the Soviet Union had had a marked advantage because the interests at stake were not sufficiently important.

46 This theme is developed at length in Richard Ned Lebow, *Nuclear Crisis Management: A Dangerous Illusion* (Ithaca, NY: Cornell University Press, 1987).

47 By 2003, if the cuts proposed in the START II treaty are implemented, Russia will cut its missiles to 504 and its warheads to 3,000 and the United States will reduce its missiles to 500 and its warheads to 3,500.

Notes to Postscript

1 Interview, Mikhail S. Gorbachev, Toronto, 1 April 1993.

2 Tom Wicker, "Plenty of Credit," *New York Times,* December 5, 1989, p. A35, points to the irony that those who for years argued that a Communist-led Soviet Union could not be reformed, now claim credit for *perestroika* and the Soviet retreat from Eastern Europe.

3 Interview, Mikhail S. Gorbachev, Toronto, April 1, 1993.

4 Ibid.

5 Ibid. See also the comments by Soviet Foreign Minister Aleksandr Bessmertnykh and Anatoliy S. Chernyaev, advisor to President Gorbachev on foreign affairs, 1986–1991, "Retrospective on the End of the Cold War," Conference sponsored by the John Foster Dulles Program for the Study of Leadership in International Affairs, Woodrow Wilson School, Princeton University, 25–27 February 1993.

6 Interview, Mikhail S. Gorbachev, Toronto, April 1, 1993, and comments by Aleksandr Bessmertnykh, "Retrospective on the End of the Cold War."

7 Thomas Risse-Kappen, *The Zero Option: INF; West Germany, and Arms Control* (Boulder, Colo.: Westview, 1988); Richard Eichenberg, "Dual Track and Double Trouble: The Two-Level Politics of INF," Peter Evans, Harold Jacobsen, and Robert Putnam, eds., *Double-Edged Diplomacy: International Bargaining and Domestic Politics* (Berkeley: University of California Press, 1993; Fen Osler Hampson, Harald von Reikhoff, and John Roper, eds., *The Allies and Arms Control* (Baltimore: Johns Hopkins University Press, 1992); Don Oberdorfer, *The Turn: From the Cold War to a New Era, The United States and The Soviet Union, 1983–1990* (New York: Poseidon Press, 1991), pp. 169–74.

8 Interview, Mikhail S. Gorbachev, Toronto, April 1, 1993. See also the comments by Bessmertnykh, "Retrospective on the End of the Cold War."

9 Interviews, Fedor Burlatsky, Cambridge, October 12, 1987; Vadim Zagladin, Moscow, May 18, 1989; Oleg Grinevsky, Vienna and New York, October 11 and November 10,1991.

10 The arms proposal that Gorbachev tabled at Reykjavik was the Soviet analogue to Reagan's "double zero" proposal. Oleg Grinevsky, interview, Stockholm, April 25, 1992, reports that before the summit, Gorbachev asked his chief arms-control advisors, Viktor Karpov, Yuli Kvitinsky, and Oleg Grinevsky to prepare proposals for arms control. Defense Minister Dmitri Yazov and Chief of the General Staff Sergei Akhromeyev learned about the preparation of new proposals and strongly opposed the initiative because they were convinced that any likely arms-control agreement would be unfavorable to the Soviet Union. They went to see Gorbachev and asked if he was seriously interested in deep cuts in the arsenals of both superpowers. When he responded affirmatively, they advised him that any proposal prepared by professional arms controllers would be overly conservative and require elaborate negotiations of definitions and verification. Yazov and Akhromeyev told a gullible Gorbachev of their abhorrence of nuclear weapons—they made conventional wars difficult, if not impossible to fight—and offered to prepare proposals for Reykjavik that would represent a serious step toward nuclear disarmament. Gorbachev immediately transferred responsibility for preparation of arms-control proposals for the summit to Yazov and Akhromeyev. They prepared the proposal that Gorbachev presented at Reykjavik, convinced that President Reagan and his advisors would reject it out of hand. Yazov and Akhromeyev were astonished when Reagan expressed serious interest.

11 Franklyn D. Holzman, "Politics and Guesswork: CIA and DIA Estimates of Soviet Military Spending," *International Security, 14* (Fall 1989), pp. 101–31; Central Intelligence Agency and Defense Intelligence Agency, "Beyond Perestroika: The Soviet Economy in Crisis," paper prepared for the Technology and National Security Subcommittee of the Joint Economic Committee, U.S. Congress, May 14, 1991.

12 The Soviet government reported that overall output declined by 2% in 1990 and by 8% in the first quarter of 1991. Big cuts in defense spending began in 1989, and the annual decline has been on the order of about 6%. Because the economy is declining more rapidly than defense expenditure, defense as a percent of gross national product has increased. "Beyond Perestroika," pp. iv, 1, 11–12.

13 For criticism of the powerful role of the "defense lobby" under Brezhnev by younger officials and scholars, see Stephen F. Cohen and Katrina vanden Heuvel, *Voices of Glasnost: Interviews with Gorbachev's Reformers* (New York: Norton, 1989) and Georgi Arbatov, The System: *An Insider's Life in Soviet Politics* (New York: Random House, 1992).

14 For discussion of logrolling under Brezhnev, see Jack Snyder, *Myths of Empire* (Ithaca, NY: Cornell University Press, 1991) and Richard Anderson, *Competitive Politics and Soviet Foreign Policy: Authority-Building and Bargaining in the Brezhnev Politburo*, Ph.D. diss., University of California, Berkeley, 1989.

15 The command economy cannot be attributed to the Nazi threat because Stalin promulgated the first five-year plan in 1929 and collectivized agriculture in the early 1930s, before Hitler's rise to power.

16 Analysts of Soviet politics, writing in late 1989, argued that "new thinking" was limited to a few central Soviet leaders and advisors. A. Lynch, *Gorbachev's International Outlook: Intellectual Origins and Political Consequences*, Institute for East-West Security Studies, Occasional Paper no. 9 (Boulder, CO: Westview, 1989), p. 53.

17 For an explanation of "new thinking" and the political debate it provoked, see Janice Gross Stein, "Cognitive Psychology and Political Learning: Gorbachev as an Uncommitted Thinker and Motivated Learner," in Richard Ned Lebow and Thomas Risse-Kappen, eds., *International Relations Theory and the Transformation of the International System* (New York: Columbia University Press, 1995), pp. 223–58.

18 See Sarah E. Mendelson, "Internal Battles and External Wars: Politics, Learning, and the Soviet Withdrawal from Afghanistan," *World Politics, 45*(3) (April 1993), pp. 327–60; Jeff Checkel, "Ideas, Institutions, and the Gorbachev Foreign Policy Revolution," *World Politics, 45*(2) (January, 1993), pp. 271–300.

19 Interviews, Fedor Burlatsky, Cambridge, October 12, 1987; Vadim Zagladin, Moscow, May 18, 1989; Oleg Grinevsky, Vienna and New York, October 11 and November 10, 1991; Georgi Arbatov, Ithaca, N.Y., November 15, 1991; Anatoliy Dobrynin, Moscow, December 17, 1991.

20 See Mikhail Gorbachev, *Pravda*, October 21, 1986 and speech to the United Nations General Assembly, December 7, 1988, *Novosti*, no. 97, p. 13; and speech by Eduard A. Shevardnadze, in *Vestnik Ministerstva Inostrannykh Del USSR* 15, August 15, 1988, p. 33.

21 For Western discussion of "new thinking" in foreign policy, see David Holloway, "Gorbachev's New Thinking," *Foreign Affairs, 68* (Winter 1988–89), pp. 66–81; Robert Legvold, "The Revolution in Soviet Foreign Policy," *Foreign Affairs* 68, 1 (America and the World 1988/89), pp. 82–98; Stephen M. Meyer, "The Sources and Prospects of Gorbachev's New Political Thinking on Security," *International Security, 13*(2) (Fall 1988), pp. 124–63.

22 Mikhail Gorbachev, "Speech to the United Nations."

23 Mikhail Gorbachev, *Perestroika: New Thinking for Our Country and the World* (New York: Harper & Row, 1987), p. 187; Holloway, "Gorbachev's New Thinking."

24 By 1987, Gorbachev insisted that the unforgiving realities of the nuclear age demanded new concepts and new policies, independent of *perestroika* at home: "Some people say that the ambitious goals set forth by the policy of *perestroika* in our country have prompted the peace proposals we have lately made in the international arena. This is an oversimplification....True, we need normal international conditions for our internal progress. But we want a world free of war, without arms races, nuclear weapons, and violence; not only because this is an optimal condition for our internal development." Gorbachev, *Perestroika*, p. 11.

25 Stephen F. Cohen, "Soviet Domestic Politics and Foreign Policy," in Robbin F. Laird and Erik P. Hoffman, eds., *Soviet Foreign Policy in a Changing World* (New York: Aldine, 1986), pp. 66–83; Jerry F. Hough, "Soviet Succession: Issues and Personalities," *Problems of Communism, 31* (September-October 1982), p. 20–40; Raymond L. Garthoff, *Détente and Confrontation: American-Soviet Relations from Nixon to Reagan* (Washington, D.C.: The Brookings Institution, 1985); Jack Snyder, "International Leverage on Soviet Domestic Change," *World Politics, 42* (October 1989), pp. 1–30.

26 Aleksandr Yanov, *The Drama of the Soviet 1960s: A Lost Reform* (Berkeley, CA.: Institute of International Studies, 1984), pp. 97–98, 103–6; Timothy J. Colton, "The Changing Soviet Union and the World," in Laird and Hoffman, *Soviet Foreign Policy in a Changing World*, pp. 869–89.

27 This was also the original idea behind George Kennan's policy of containment; Richard Pipes, "Can the Soviet Union Reform?"; Laird and Hoffman, *Soviet Foreign Policy in a Changing World*, pp. 855–68; Harry Gelman, *The Brezhnev Politburo and the Decline of Detente* (Ithaca, NY: Cornell University Press, 1984). For a good critique, see Matthew Evangelista, "Sources of Moderation in Soviet Security Policy," in Philip E. Tetlock, Jo L. Husbands, Robert Jervis, Paul C. Stern, and Charles Tilly, eds., *Behavior, Society, and Nuclear War*, II (New York: Oxford University Press, 1991) 2 vols., pp. 254–354. Evangelista argues against a mechanistic formulation of the relationship between Soviet and American foreign policies.

Part III

Compellence

6 Beyond parsimony: rethinking theories of coercive bargaining

Theories of deterrence and compellence incorporate behavioral and political assumptions. In all but the most transparent environments, the behavioral assumptions place unrealistic informational and analytical requirements on policy makers. The political assumptions misconstrue the process of risk assessment, exaggerate the ability of leaders to estimate the risks inherent in their threats and shape adversarial estimates of their resolve. These problems explain why deterrence and compellence can tail when practiced by rational and attentive leaders against equally rational and attentive targets. Some of the political and behavioral assumptions of deterrence and compellence are unique, but others are shared with other rational theories of bargaining. My critique has implications for these theories, and they are spelled out in the conclusion. I illustrate my argument with examples from American and Soviet decision making in the Cuban missile crisis.

I begin by describing some of the controversies that worked their way through the several 'waves' of the deterrence literature (Brodie, 1946; Viner, 1946; Wolfers, 1962; Jervis, 1979). These controversies obscured the more important underlying consensus about core political and behavioral assumptions. I identify these assumptions, show how the behavioral assumptions derive from the political ones and why both are often unrealistic.

The gist of my argument concerns the overriding importance of the context in which bargaining occurs. Rational bargainers formulate goals by considering their interests in a specific context. Interests dictate bargaining goals, and readings of context lead to estimates of how well those goals can be achieved. A bargainer who considers its demands just, the balance of resources in its favor, and the other side desperate to reach a quick agreement, will expect to obtain more than it otherwise would. Readings of context depend on actors' frames of reference and the information available to them. Bargainers using different frames of reference, or "schemas" in the language of cognitive psychology, are likely to see different attributes of context as salient and make different estimates of the balance of bargaining power. This is most likely to happen in bargaining encounters where there is a high degree of conflict, the context in which deterrence and compellence are most frequently practiced.

Different readings of context can narrow or prevent a zone of agreement from emerging. Leaders who consider their country favored by the balance of interests, military power and resolve expect the other side to concede more. If both sides consider themselves so favored, they are unlikely to find common ground for agreement. They may also discount each other's threats because they are seen to be in support of unrealistic demands.

Credible threats must be appropriate and sufficient. To meet these criteria, leaders must know something about the target's preferences. But preferences are difficult to estimate in the absence of adequate information, and whatever information is available may be misinterpreted if filtered through inappropriate schemas. Threats based on faulty estimates of target preferences can unwittingly provoke the behavior they are designed to prevent if they convince their targets that compliance will be more costly than challenges (Rapoport, 1966; King, 1975; Jervis, 1979; Jervis et al., 1985; Lebow & Stein, 1987, 1994).

Different readings of context also confound attempts to communicate interests and resolve. Signals take on meaning in context, and when sender and recipient use different schemas to formulate and interpret signals they can easily be missed or misunderstood. Attempts to communicate concessions can actually be interpreted as signals of resolve and vice versa. Readings of context also shape assessments of risk and resolve and, contrary to the expectations of deterrence and compellence, those assessments can prove relatively impervious to outside attempts to influence them.

Case selection

A widely accepted strategy for casting doubt on a theory is to pick an easy case for the theory and show that its predictions do not hold. Cuba is an easy case for theories of deterrence and compellence because of the unrelenting environmental pressures on the superpowers to reach a settlement to avoid a catastrophic conventional or nuclear war. It is a hard case because the protagonists were from different political cultures, were locked into an acute and war-threatening conflict with a significant ideological component, there were no rules to structure their bargaining, and their leaders had little prior experience of each other. For all these reasons, effective communication was extraordinarily difficult. The missile crisis is not a fair test of parsimonious, rational theories of bargaining even though it has been widely used by scholars to demonstrate the putative explanatory power of such models (Brams, 1985; Langlois, 1989, 1991; Wagner, 1989). I treat the missile crisis as a "deviant-case" in Arend Lijphart's terminology (Lijphart, 1971; Eckstein, 1975). By demonstrating why a theory or model fails, the researcher hopes to identify the scope conditions of the theory or model and the variables or processes it must take into account to expand the domain in which it is applicable. I will argue that these variables and processes are sufficiently numerous and important as to confound the search for predictive theory.

Capabilities versus interests

Deterrence and compellence are strategies of coercive bargaining (Schelling, 1960, 1966; Art, 1980; Baldwin, 1985; Sagan, 1994; Herring, 1995). They use threats to persuade an actor to carry out, or refrain from carrying out, a specified behavior. Successful threats must hold out the prospect of enough loss to make compliance more attractive than noncompliance. Their implementation must also appear certain, or highly probable, in the absence of compliance. Implementation usually involves costs for threat makers too, and credibility is difficult to establish in proportion to the magnitude of those costs.

Recognizing the relationship between capability and resolve, first and second wave deterrence theorists emphasized the importance of the military balance (Kaufmann, 1954; Wohlstetter, 1959; Schelling, 1966; Brodie, 1973). Military superiority was assumed to impart credibility to threats. Second wave theorists grappled with the problem of making threats credible against another nuclear power like the Soviet Union where the cost of implementing a threat could be intolerably high. In such a conflict, Thomas Schelling argued, war is no longer a contest of strength but "a contest of nerve and risk-taking, of pain and endurance." Schelling described a series of tactics, most notably the threat that leaves something to chance, to convey resolve when threats to initiate war were not credible (Schelling, 1966; Clausewitz, 1976).

The putative lessons of Munich also led first and second wave theorists to stress the importance of reputation. States that had honored their commitments and implemented their threats would be taken more seriously by their adversaries. States or leaders with poor reputations would have difficulty in imparting credibility to threats even when they possessed military advantages. Schelling took this argument a step further and argued that commitments were a seamless web; failure to uphold any commitment would encourage communist adversaries to question all of them (Kaufmann, 1954; Wohlstetter, 1959; Schelling, 1966; Brodie, 1973).

Third wave theorists questioned the logic of inferring a state's resolve from its past behavior on the grounds that not all challenges were equally grave (Jervis, 1979, 1989). The first empirical studies of conventional deterrence found that defenders, like many deterrence theorists, worried that adversaries would draw far-reaching inferences about their resolve if they did not stand firm whenever challenged. But these studies also indicated that challengers—the relevant point of reference—generally paid little attention to defenders' past performance when estimating their resolve. More recent studies of deterrence, based on Soviet and Chinese documents and interviews, reveal that Soviet and Chinese leaders never doubted American resolve but often felt threatened by it (Zhang, 1993; Lebow & Stein, 1994; Hopf, 1994; Herring, 1995).

Some third wave theorists argued that the balance of interests was a better predictor of resolve than bargaining reputation. Drawing on work by Glenn Snyder and Thomas Schelling, Robert Jervis urged analysts to distinguish between intrinsic interests (the inherent value in what is at stake) and strategic interests (the degree to which retreat would endanger other interests or the actor's bargaining reputation). In contrast to Schelling, third wave theorists tended to see strategic interests as a more important determinant of perceived resolve. Early empirical research suggested that the relationship between interest and resolve was complex. Richard Betts, for example, found that the balance of interests explained American risk propensity better than it did Soviet restraint. He speculated that the difference might be accounted for by American beliefs about the importance of interests (McConnell, 1979, Maoz, 1983; Betts, 1987; Huth, 1988; George & Simons, 1994; Paul 1994).

Role distinctions are axiomatic to deterrence, and theorists of all three waves maintain that they influence resolve and perceptions of resolve. Deterrers are assumed to have an innate advantage over challengers because demands to change the status quo are more difficult to justify and sustain than actions to preserve it. This is one reason why Schelling thought deterrence easier to achieve than compellence. Others have noted that actors intent on upsetting the status quo must bear the onus of moving first. Challenges to the status quo raise the prospect of further encroachments, and allow defenders to make plausible arguments that the cost of accepting changes in the status quo is greater than the cost to challengers of tolerating it (Kaplan, 1959; Schelling, 1966; Snyder, 1971; Jervis, 1989).

For first and second wave deterrence theorists—and the American national security establishment—the military balance was the most important structural component of deterrence and compellence. Second wave studies of Cold War confrontations, especially of the Cuban missile crisis, maintained that the American military superiority compelled Khrushchev to withdraw the Soviet missiles in Cuba. Some argued this was due to the favorable strategic nuclear balance, and others to American conventional superiority in the Caribbean basin (Wohlstetter & Wohlstetter, 1965; Abel, 1966; Horelick & Rush, 1966; Allison, 1971; Betts, 1987; Bundy, 1988; Garthoff, 1989; George & Simons, 1994). Later studies suggested that the link between the military balance and crisis outcomes was more tenuous (Jervis, 1979, 1989; Lebow, 1982; Betts, 1987; Bundy, 1988; Garthoff, 1989; Lebow and Stein, 1994; Herring, 1995). Still other scholars questioned the importance of the military balance, contending that it should be viewed as one of many factors affecting the success of deterrence and compellence (George & Smoke, 1974; Snyder & Diesing, 1977, Karsten et al., 1984). Empirical cases studies of conventional deterrence failures support this criticism. They find the military balance less important than would-be challengers' estimates of future changes in the balance, and that usable military options are a more important determinant of deterrence success than overall military capability (Lebow, 1981; Jervis et al., 1985; Lebow & Stein, 1987; George & Simons, 1994).

Third wave theorists hypothesized that a state's resistance to encroachments of its interests—and the credibility of its promises to resist—are roughly proportional to the interests it has at stake. Robert Jervis argued that a state's resolve will also be influenced by judgments about how strongly motivated its adversary is to prevail. When both protagonists have core concerns at stake they will be highly motivated to prevail, but even small concessions can significantly affect the balance of motivation. The bargaining advantage will shift in favor of the state making a concession because its remaining interests are likely to be more important and recognized as such by the other side (Jervis, 1989). Jervis also makes the case for role. He maintains that evidence from Cold War crises indicates that defenders practicing deterrence usually had "significant bargaining advantages over challengers trying to compel" (Jervis, 1989). This proposition is hard to test because of the difficulty of distinguishing between the behavioral consequences of roles and interests. Most of the putative advantages of the deterrer derive from its presumed interest in defending the status quo.

Controversies about the relative importance of bargaining reputation, military balance, interests and role conceptions have obscured the more important shared assumptions among deterrence theorists. They all believe that asymmetries of one kind or another are critical determinants of resolve and, by extension, of the outcomes of deterrence and compellence encounters (see Figure 1.6).

For first, second and most third wave theorists, the relationship between resolve and outcome is mediated by threats to go to war in support of one's commitments or demands. These can be direct threats to use force or escalation with its attendant risk of loss of control (Schelling's threat that leaves something to chance) (Lebow, 1985, 1988; Betts, 1987; Quester, 1989; Rhodes, 1989). Credible threats are the mechanism for transforming favorable bargaining asymmetries into bargaining advantages and more favorable outcomes. Only the crudest formulations of deterrence and compellence assume a one-to-one relationship between bargaining advantages and crisis outcomes (Organski & Kugler, 1980; Kugler, 1984).

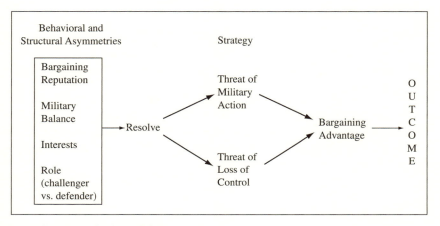

Figure 6.1   Coercive bargaining.

More sophisticated analyses also consider the skill of leaders to be important (Schelling, 1966; Zagare, 1987; George & Simons, 1994).

The political assumptions of deterrence and compellence

The links between asymmetries, resolve, threats and outcomes rest on four political assumptions:

1 Military advantage, more important interests, and the role of defender provide the basis for resolve. A state with military advantages, more important interests at stake, and defending, not challenging, the status quo, can communicate resolve more effectively than its adversary.
2 The credibility of threats is determined by the balance of resolve.
3 Bargaining advantage in crisis is derived from the credibility of threats to use force or risk war through loss of control. The two threats are not mutually exclusive and may be reinforcing.
4 If these threats are applied with finesse, the outcome of a crisis should reflect, although not directly mirror, the structural asymmetries inherent in the context of the bargaining.

The transformation of bargaining asymmetries into resolve, credible threats, and more favorable outcomes also entails behavioral assumptions about how protagonists understand and interpret the meaning of asymmetries, assess risks, and respond to one another's threats. The feasibility of deterrence and compellence as strategies of conflict management ultimately depends on the validity of these assumptions. There has been very little discussion of these assumptions in the literature and virtually no attempt to test them empirically.

The behavioral assumptions of deterrence and compellence

1 Challenger and defender agree about their respective roles.
2 Protagonists will make roughly similar assessments of the military balance and its implications for their respective resolve.
3 Protagonists will have the same understanding of their respective interests.
4 Leaders can to some degree shape adversarial estimates of the risks of war.
5 Leaders can make reasonable estimates of the risks of war inherent in their escalatory initiatives.

Roles

All formulations of deterrence are based on the dichotomous division of protagonists into challenger and defender. These role definitions are critical to the identification of deterrence encounters. They are also important independent variables for second and third wave theorists who describe role as an important determinant of the balance of interests and resolve. These context-free, technical definitions of role bear little relationship to the way actual protagonists conceive of themselves. Challenger and defender take on meaning in reference to the status quo, and this is also determined subjectively and frequently contested by protagonists (Kolodziej, 1987; Jervis, 1989; Lebow & Stein, 1990). Case studies indicate that both protagonists in deterrence and compellence encounters are likely to see themselves as the defender and their adversary as the challenger. If second and third wave theorists are right, these self-perceptions will have important consequences for their estimates of the balance of interests, resolve and strategic behavior (Millett, 1968; Betts, 1987; Lebow & Stein, 1990a, 1990b).

Military balance

The military balance is often portrayed as a structural attribute of the international environment, but case studies indicate just how difficult it can be to estimate accurately (Wohlforth, 1987, 1993; Friedberg, 1988). Divergent estimates of the military balance, or trends in the balance, have been a contributing cause of international tensions and wars. In deterrence and compellence encounters, clashing estimates of the balance can result in different readings of the balance of resolve (Lebow, 1981). Theories of deterrence and compellence further assume that leaders share the same understanding of the importance of the military balance for resolve. Here too, case studies reveal significant differences among leaders and within the same leadership elites. Some policy makers regard military superiority as directly exploitable and expect to impose terms on their adversaries commensurate with their military advantages. Others do not consider military superiority a fungible asset. When adversaries disagree about the military balance or its political meaning, attempts to infer resolve from estimates of the balance are likely to be misleading (Whiting, 1960; Spanier, 1965; Jervis, 1979).

Interests

International Relations specialists increasingly acknowledge the subjective nature of national and domestic political interests. Interests are social constructions rooted in particular values, visions of community and conceptions of politics (Kratochwil, 1982, 1989; Wendt, 1992). Models of bargaining, including those of deterrence and compellence, generally assume that protagonists can identify one another's interests (Snyder & Diesing, 1977; Stein, 1982). Shared understandings of interests are an essential prerequisite of shared estimates of the balance of resolve. Once again, case studies indicate that leaders find it difficult to comprehend adversarial interests and can be insensitive to adversarial efforts to enlighten them (Jervis et al., 1985; Richardson, 1994; Herring, 1995). Because protagonists are generally more sensitive to their interests than those of their adversaries, they frequently assume they have more stake. If leaders believe that interests are an indicator of resolve, both protagonists will see themselves favored by the balance of resolve.

Estimates of adversarial resolve

Models of deterrence and compellence assume that protagonists communicate resolve through threats and military preparations. First and second wave theorists portrayed threats as the most effective means of signaling resolve (Jervis, 1979). Case studies indicate that threats are always evaluated in context. A threat to go to war by a protagonist perceived to be at a military disadvantage may be dismissed as a bluff (Lebow, 1981). So too will a threat seen to be aimed at a domestic audience (Lebow & Stein, 1994). By contrast, a threat directed a third party can raise significant alarm if it is mistakenly seen as aimed at oneself (Khrushchev, 1961). Moreover, threats and military preparations are only one of the factors that shape estimates of resolve. When other considerations (e.g., ideology, the nature of the political system, the personality and past behavior of leaders) shape these assessments, threats may not have much effect, and target leaders may be relatively impervious to attempts to manipulate their assessments.

Estimates of risk

When leaders want to avoid war, threats to go to war or court it through loss of control involve stressful trade-offs. Leaders must weigh the bargaining advantages escalation is expected to confer against the risk of war inherent in their initiatives. This is very difficult to do in international conflicts where estimates of risk are notoriously unreliable (Jervis, 1979).

General deterrence

In the next three sections I use the origins, politics, and resolution of the Cuban missile crisis to illustrate the difficulties of the behavioral assumptions of deterrence and compellence. I draw on Soviet and American documents and interviews Janice Stein and I conducted with Soviet and American officials in the course of writing We All Lost the Cold War (1994). Although my documentation is from our book, my arguments are novel as our book did not address the theory of bargaining. I start my analysis with general deterrence—the attempts by each superpower prior to the missile crisis to restrain the other through an arms buildup, military deployments and threats. I then take up immediate deterrence—the Kennedy administration's efforts to dissuade the Soviet Union from deploying offensive weapons, especially nuclear-armed missiles, in Cuba. Finally, I examine compellenc—the Kennedy administration's use of military preparations and threats to convince Nikita Khrushchev to withdraw the Soviet missiles from Cuba. My analysis indicates that there are good reasons to question political and behavioral assumptions of deterrence and compellence.

The origins of the Cuban missile crisis reveal that general deterrence, as practiced by both superpowers, was provocative rather than preventive. Soviet officials report that the American strategic buildup, missile deployments in Europe and Turkey and assertions of nuclear superiority exacerbated Soviet strategic insecurities. All of these measures had been envisaged by President Kennedy as prudent, defensive precautions against an expected Soviet challenge to Western interests in Berlin. In practice, they convinced Khrushchev that it was imperative to protect the Soviet Union and Cuba from American political and military challenges. Both leaders, seeking to moderate their adversary, brought about the kind of confrontation they were trying to forestall. General deterrence failed because Kennedy and Khrushchev had a poor understanding of each other's intentions, interests, and willingness to accept risks.

The failure of general deterrence in the course of 1961 illustrates the difficulty of using threats to manipulate the cost-benefit calculus of adversaries. If credible threats (of denial or punishment) always increased the costs of challenges—as deterrence and compellence theories assume—leaders who practice these strategies would not need to know anything about the goals, fears, values, and preferences of their adversaries. But Cuba is one of many crises that indicate that threats can make aggressive behavior more attractive by making the costs of compliance appear intolerable. This is most likely to occur when challenges are made to cope with domestic and foreign vulnerabilities.

Lack of information cannot convincingly explain the Kennedy administration's insensitivity to the likely impact of its policies on Khrushchev. Khrushchev was equally insensitive to Kennedy's strategic and political interests, and he was dealing with the most open political system in the world. The principal barrier to understanding on both sides was one-sided, stereotyped understandings of the nature and dynamics of superpower rivalry.

Americans and Soviets each viewed themselves as the defender and their adversary as the challenger. Their role conceptions had enormous implications for their understanding of their adversary's motives and behavior. Each superpower leader and his advisers believed its adversary to be inherently aggressive, its military forces to have offensive missions, and it leaders committed to exploiting any perceived weakness of their adversary. Each side saw itself as the leading exponent of a morally superior social system, defending it against subversion, intimidation and the possibility of direct attack by the other. Each dismissed the other's protestations of good will—"peaceful coexistence" in the jargon of the day—as mendacious propaganda aimed at currying favor among the naive or discontented.

These role conceptions all but excluded consideration of the possibility that the other superpower could feel threatened and be responding in kind to the other's provocations. The superpowers had an obvious common interest in avoiding nuclear destruction, but neither set of leaders believed that its adversary took this responsibility seriously. Before the missile crisis, this seemingly overwhelming imperative was insufficient to break through the cognitive barrier of mistrust that ideological division and the Cold War had erected between East and West.

Immediate deterrence

In the West, the Cuban missile crisis has always been treated as a direct deterrence encounter with the United States (the defender) trying to prevent the Soviet Union (the challenger) from deploying missiles in Cuba. A mirror image prevailed in the Soviet Union where the "Caribbean crisis" was viewed as an extended deterrence encounter with the Soviet Union (the defender) trying to prevent the United States (the challenger) from attacking its client, Cuba.

The competing role conceptions of the superpowers were reinforced by their conflicting definitions of the status quo. The Kennedy administration never doubted that it was upholding the status quo—a Western hemisphere free of foreign military bases. The Joint Chiefs of Staff warned that Soviet missiles in Cuba would represent a dramatic change to the military status quo by making the United States vulnerable to nuclear attack (Kennedy, 1962b). The president and most of his advisers were more concerned with the threat posed by the missiles to the political status quo. In the words of Theodore Sorensen, they "represented a sudden, immediate and more dangerous and secretive change in the balance of power, in clear contradiction of all US and Soviet pledges. It was a move which required a response from the United States, not for reasons of prestige or image but reasons of national security in the broadest sense" (Sorensen, 1969, 187).

Soviet leaders defined the status quo as Fidel Castro's successful revolution in Cuba. Their military buildup in Cuba was defensive because it sought to "prevent the inevitable armed intervention on the Island of Freedom, which was being prepared by aggressive circles in the USA" (Alekseyev, 1988, 27). For Khrushchev, the missile deployment would restore the strategic status quo that Kennedy had upset by his strategic arms buildup and deployment of Jupiter missiles in Turkey. Khrushchev told his ambassador to Cuba that the missiles would "get even" with the Americans and "repay them in kind...so they can feel what it is like to live in the nuclear gun sites" (Alekseyev, 1988, 29).

Different understandings of the context of the missile deployment led to different estimates of the balance of interests (Betts, 1987). Khrushchev and his advisers never doubted that the Soviet Union had more at stake because it was defending itself from American intimidation and Cuba from American attack. "It is undeniable," Sergo Mikoyan insisted many years later, "that the Soviet Union and the entire socialist camp would have lost much more from the overthrow of Castro than the United States could possibly have gained" (Mikoyan, 1989, interview).

Khrushchev also counted on the deployment's legitimacy to influence the balance of resolve. He wrote to President Kennedy during the crisis to point out that

Soviet economic and military aid to Cuba was acceptable under international law, whereas the 1961 American-backed invasion of Cuba was not (Department of State, 1962). The Cuban missiles, Khrushchev insisted, were no different from the American missiles in Turkey. They were a Soviet "tit" for an American "tat," and Khrushchev expected Kennedy to tolerate them just as he had learned to live with the Jupiters (Burlatsky, 1989; Khrushchev, 1989).

American leaders saw the balance of interests entirely m their favor. American foreign policy interests and Kennedy's political interests would be seriously compromised by the surreptitious introduction of Soviet missiles into Cuba. The CIA and administration officials could find no pressing Soviet interest that required a missile deployment. "We knew," McGeorge Bundy says, "that we were not about to invade Cuba and we saw no reason for the Russians to take a clearly risky step because of a fear that we ourselves understood to be baseless" (Bundy 1988, 416). American leaders all but discounted the possibility, in the words of Arthur Schlesinger, Jr, "that Khrushchev would be so stupid as to do something which as much as invited an invasion" (Hawk's Cay, 1987, 21).

The status quo is the anchor point of deterrence theory. From it, the roles of defender and challenger are derived, as are in part the balances of interests and resolve. But the status quo is not an objective attribute of context. It is a political-historical construct whose definition depends entirely on the perspective of observers (Jervis, 1989). Protagonists rarely have the same understanding of the status quo, or of their respective roles and interests at stake. Like the Soviet Union and the United States on the eve of the missile crisis, they often find it extraordinarily difficult to fathom the other's perspective or to communicate theirs successfully. In the absence of shared understandings, deterrence is likely to be misunderstood, and this increases the likelihood that it will fail.

Compellence

Deterrence is a strategy of crisis and war prevention. Crisis management relies more on compellence, and it was a critical element of President Kennedy's strategy in the missile crisis. Compellence exploits superior military capability to threaten punishment if the target does not comply with one's demands.

The military balance

In 1962, the United States possessed overwhelming strategic and conventional superiority, but this did not strengthen deterrence. The lopsided nature of the strategic balance undermined deterrence by making the Soviet Union feel so vulnerable that Khrushchev and the Soviet military were willing to assume the risks of a secret missile deployment in part to offset their inferiority (Garthoff, 1989). The role of the military balance in the resolution of the crisis was also at variance with the expectations of compellence theory. It offers no support for the "strong" formulation of compellence that expects crisis outcomes to mirror the military balance, and only marginal support for the "weaker" formulation that considers the military balance one of several factors that influence the balance of resolve and, by extension, crisis outcomes.

The military balance was never in dispute. The American navy, supported by carrier and land-based aircraft, dominated the Caribbean and could easily have swept the seas of Soviet and Cuban naval vessels, including submarines. Neither protagonist doubted the one-sided nature of the local conventional or strategic nuclear balance; Soviet military analysts credited the United States with a 17 to 1 advantage in deliverable nuclear weapons (Burlatsky, 1989; Zamyatin, 1991). If military advantage translates into bargaining advantage, Kennedy should have imposed his will on Khrushchev. The outcome was initially portrayed as an unalloyed American triumph, and largely for this reason. Henry Kissinger proclaimed that it "could not have ended so quickly and decisively but for the fact that the United States can win a general war if it strikes first and can inflict intolerable damage on the Soviet Union even it if is a victim of a surprise attack." Other authorities emphasized American conventional superiority and the "escalation dominance" it had conferred (Kissinger, 1962; Kahn, 1965; Schelling, 1966; Herken, 1985; Harvard University, 1987).

The "strong" formulation is undercut by the outcome of the crisis. The crisis was not a one-sided American victory, but a compromise that required Kennedy to make a pledge not to invade Cuba and to remove the Jupiter missiles in Turkey. The commitment to remove the Jupiters was offered as a last minute secret concession. Dean Rusk revealed that Kennedy was actively considering a further concession—public acceptance of Khrushchev's demand for a Cuba-Turkey missile swap. The president's closest advisers think it very likely that he would have taken this extra step if it had been necessary to end the crisis (Rusk, 1987a, 1987c; Bundy, 1988; Lebow & Stein, 1994).

The "weak" formulation ignores the many constraints on the use of military force and how they significantly reduced the bargaining advantages that superiority might otherwise have conferred. It also fails to consider the differences of opinion within each superpower's leadership about the political value of military superiority.

The military balance was instrumental in Kennedy's choice of a crisis strategy. The blockade of Cuba exploited American naval and air superiority in the Caribbean for purposes of political suasion. Conventional superiority also made feasible an air strike against the missiles or an invasion of Cuba; the military forces in Cuba would have been no more capable of resisting a full-scale American invasion than the Western garrison in Berlin could have fended off a determined Soviet assault. President Kennedy resisted demands for military action against Cuba because of the risks of escalation it entailed. He was concerned that an air strike or invasion would kill upwards of 1,000 Soviets and provoke retaliation against Berlin or American missile bases in Turkey. Kennedy was deterred from attacking Cuba for exactly the same reason that the United States expected its militarily insignificant forces in Berlin to discourage a Soviet attack. For President Kennedy and Secretary of Defense Robert McNamara the benefits of conventional military superiority were counter-balanced and largely negated by the expected costs of war. American nuclear superiority was unexploitable because the destruction associated with any nuclear war was too horrendous to contemplate (Lebow & Stein, 1994).

Khrushchev was impressed by American conventional superiority in the Caribbean, and was correspondingly anxious to avoid giving Kennedy any pretext to attack Cuba. He refused to consider horizontal escalation, and had Defense Minister Rodion Malinovsky give strict orders to Soviet forces not to fire at American ships and planes unless they attacked Cuba (Burlatsky, 1987). Khrushchev nevertheless hung tough for most of the first week of the crisis in the hope of extracting some concession from Kennedy in return for withdrawing his missiles.

To the extent that the unfavorable military balance contributed to Khrushchev's restraint and ultimate concessions, it was not in the way predicted by deterrence theorists. Khrushchev was convinced that American hardliners would view the crisis as an irresistible opportunity to attack Cuba and overthrow its communist government. His letters, conversations during the crisis and memoirs bespeak this concern (Khrushchev, 1970; Khrushchev, 1990; Lebow & Stein, 1994). He knew that he would be under enormous political pressure to respond with military action of his own; his generals opposed concessions and would demand retaliation. If the Soviet Union attacked the American missiles in Turkey, the United States might strike at the Soviet Union. Khrushchev withdrew his missiles to forestall tit-for-tat escalation.

What mattered in Washington and Moscow was not the military balance, about which there was no real disagreement, but the political meaning of that balance. The hawks put so much emphasis on the military balance because they believed in the political utility of large-scale violence. Kennedy and McNamara took little comfort in the balance because they regarded military action as dangerous and impractical. The hawks focused on relative cost and gain and assumed their adversaries did the same. Because the Soviet Union was outgunned, Soviet leaders would roll over and play dead. If not, the United States would attack and really kill them for real. For Kennedy and Khrushchev, the relevant consideration was absolute cost, and this would be horrendous in even a purely conventional war. Kennedy took no consolation in the near-certainty that there would be many more dead Russians than Americans.

The military balance was not the determining factor of either resolve or the crisis outcome. Kennedy's choice of the blockade over the air strike, Khrushchev's decision to withdraw the missiles, and Kennedy's willingness to withdraw the Jupiters, reflected their political values and estimates of the risks and costs of escalation. Leaders with different values or conceptions of the feasibility of military action would have made different choices.

Manipulation of risk

Kennedy and Khrushchev used military deployments and threats to influence each other's estimate of their resolve. Each leader nevertheless estimated his adversary's resolve more or less independently of the other's attempts at manipulation. Estimates of resolve, moreover, had only an indirect influence on the resolution of the crisis; they explain the timing but not the substance of the concessions both leaders made.

On Saturday morning, October 27, Kennedy expressed willingness to issue a noninvasion pledge in return for the withdrawal of the Soviet missiles in Cuba. He made another important concession to the Soviets on Saturday night, October 27, when he authorized his brother to tell Ambassador Dobrynin that the United States was prepared to remove its Jupiter missiles in Turkey. That evening he considered a further concession, a public missile exchange, but this proved unnecessary (Dobrynin, 1962; Rusk, 1987a, 1987c; Bundy, 1988; Lebow & Stein, 1994).

Kennedy's willingness to make concessions was largely independent of Khrushchev's attempts to convey resolve. Before announcing the blockade, he had confided to his brother that he would have to make a concession to Khrushchev (Schelesinger, 1965).

The timing of Kennedy's offer to withdraw the Jupiters—as distinct from his predisposition to do so—was influenced by his perception of Soviet resolve. Khrushchev had publicly condemned the blockade as piracy, announced that Soviet sea captains had been ordered to use force to protect themselves, and the pace of construction at the missile sites had increased. But all Soviet ships en route to Cuba had stopped dead in the water before the blockade went into effect, and those vessels likely to be carrying military cargoes had changed course and were returning to the Soviet Union. Kennedy reasoned that Khrushchev was unlikely to escalate the confrontation, but equally unlikely to withdraw his missiles without further pressure. A concession might break this deadlock and obviate the need for additional threats or military action (Lebow & Stein, 1994).

Kennedy's consideration of a further concession on Saturday night, October 27, was based on a different calculus—the apparent need to stave off war. That morning, the Ex Comm received one piece of threatening news after another, culminating in the report that an American U-2 had been shot down over Cuba, probably by a Soviet surface-to-air (SAM) missile. The Soviet air defense network in Cuba was apparently operational and Moscow seemed to have no compunction about shooting down unarmed American aircraft (Kennedy, 1962b, 1969; Hilsman, 1967; Kennedy, 1962b). The Ex Comm speculated that the Soviet Union and Cuba were preparing for battle. Robert Kennedy had "the feeling that the noose was tightening on all of us, on Americans, on mankind, and that the bridges to escape were crumbling" (Kennedy, 1969, 97). "We worried," Dean Rusk remembered, 'about the possibility that Khrushchev might respond with a full nuclear strike; that he might be in such a situation that he could not control his own Politburo, whatever his own personal views were, because he had a major problem on his hands in dealing with his Politburo" (Rusk, 1987b, 21-22).

Khrushchev's concessions were influenced by his estimate of risk. But that estimate also took shape largely independently of attempts to shape it. Khrushchev's major concession, his offer to withdraw the missiles from Cuba in return for a noninvasion pledge, was communicated in his Friday letter. That letter was a response to intelligence that an American invasion of Cuba was imminent. Kennedy had not tried to foster the expectation of imminent invasion. When the missile sites were discovered, McNamara had instructed the joint chiefs to accelerate their preparations for military action against Cuba in case it became necessary to remove the missiles by force. Because of his concern about the escalatory consequences of an air strike or invasion, Kennedy chose a naval blockade, but the military continued to prepare for an invasion and expected to be ready to carry it out by Tuesday, October 30 (Rusk, 1987a, c; Rusk, 1990). McNamara says that Kennedy allowed these preparations to continue because he recognized that any order countermanding them would incur the wrath of the Joint Chiefs and Ex Comm hawks (McNamara, 1987).

For many years, Western students of the crisis attributed Khrushchev's "capitulation" to Robert Kennedy's "ultimatum" that his brother would have no choice but to attack Cuba if the Soviet Union did not immediately agree to withdraw its missiles. But we now know that Kennedy made no ultimatum and that Khrushchev had already decided to withdraw the Soviet missiles from Cuba. Dobrynin's cable reporting his conversation with Kennedy influenced only the timing and manner of Khrushchev's concessions. The cable created a great sense of urgency in Moscow and prompted Khrushchev's extraordinary radio message on Sunday expressing willingness to withdraw the missiles. Perhaps the most important consequence of Kennedy's warning was to provide Khrushchev with a strong argument to justify his retreat to the Presidium (Lebow & Stein, 1994). Khrushchev was desperate to resolve the crisis at least a day before the Kennedy-Dobrynin meeting on Saturday night because he was convinced that the United States was about to attack Cuba and perhaps the Soviet Union as well. Khrushchev did not question Kennedy's commitment to peace, but doubted the president's ability to restrain the American military. His concern was as misplaced as Kennedy's suspicion on Saturday that Khrushchev had been captured by Kremlin hardliners (Lebow & Stein, 1994).

The faulty estimates of both leaders can be traced in large part to their stereotyped understanding of each other's political system. Khrushchev and his colleagues used Marxist-Leninist concepts to analyse the workings of the American government. They saw the president and other public officials as agents of monopoly capitalism, and greatly underestimated their autonomy from Wall Street (Griffiths, 1984) The capitalist class was implacably hostile to Castro because of the threat he posed to American hegemony in Latin America; their most influential organs of opinion like Time and the Wall Street Journal repeatedly called for his overthrow. Khrushchev believed that the CIA and the military took their orders from Wall Street, not from the White House (Khrushchev, 1992).

The American understanding of the Soviet political system was equally flawed. American policy-makers recognized that Khrushchev did not exercise anything close to the dictatorial power of Stalin, but still exaggerated his ability to control Soviet foreign policy at every level. Kennedy and his advisers were insensitive to the possibility that any Soviet political or military initiative could be unauthorized. They assumed, incorrectly, that all of the Saturday's troubling events were part of a coherent strategy, implemented on direct orders from Moscow, and signaled the emergence of a harder line (Kennedy, 1962b). Saturday's events had explanations that nobody in the Ex Comm suspected. The report of Soviet diplomats burning their papers was false, the morning message from Khrushchev was not intended to convey a harder line—it was motivated by Walter Lippmann's call for a public missile swap in the Washington Post, read by the Soviet embassy as a trial balloon sent aloft by the White House—and Khrushchev knew nothing about the movements of the Grozny or the downing of Major Anderson's U-2. That attack was in direct violation of his orders. Khrushchev was firmly in control in the Kremlin and at least as anxious as Kennedy to end the confrontation. He sent conciliatory signals, including continued Soviet restraint in the face of the blockade, and hoped that his messages of Friday and Saturday would provide a mutually acceptable basis for resolving the crisis (Lebow & Stein, 1994).

At critical junctures, Kennedy and Khrushchev misjudged each other's resolve. Khrushchev's assessment of the probability of an American attack against Cuba was inversely proportional to the real threat. The risk of an air strike or invasion was greatest in the week before Kennedy announced the quarantine. For much of that week, the air strike was the preferred option of the president and most of the Ex Comm. While the debate raged between advocates of an air strike and a blockade, Khrushchev lived in a world of illusion; he was sublimely confident that American intelligence would not discover the missiles before he revealed their presence to the world, in the middle of November. After Kennedy's quarantine speech, Khrushchev became increasingly fearful that the United States would attack Cuba. To forestall this, he sent a conciliatory message to Kennedy on Friday and on Sunday afternoon broadcast his acceptance of Kennedy's Saturday proposal. Khrushchev did not realize that Kennedy had become increasingly opposed to any military action because of its escalatory potential. One of the ironies of the crisis is that Khrushchev rushed to make an agreement at the very moment that Kennedy contemplated a further concession.

Risk estimation

Compellence assumes that protagonists gain bargaining advantages by demonstrating willingness to risk war. This tactic can also make war more likely. Compellence requires leaders to weigh carefully the trade-offs between the risks of escalation and the bargaining advantages it is expected to confer. Leaders often fail to consider these trade-offs, or make faulty estimates because of lack of information or inappropriate conceptions.

The difficulty of making trade-offs is illustrated by the wide variance in risk estimates that existed within the American and Soviet leadership groups. In the first week, the debate in Washington between air strike and blockade advocates was primarily an argument about the risk of war associated with the air strike. The hawks—Acheson, Dillon, McCone, Nitze, and the Joint Chiefs—insisted that Khrushchev would not dare respond with military action of his own because the military balance was so unfavorable to the Soviet Union. The president and other Ex Comm members were unconvinced; they worried that military action by either superpower against the other would generate enormous political pressures to retaliate regardless of the military balance. The argument flared up again toward the end of the second week of the crisis when the hawks demanded an air strike on the grounds that the blockade had failed. There was a similar controversy in the Soviet Union. The military argued that Kennedy would back down if Khrushchev stood firm. In Havana, Marshal Sergei Biryuzov and General Igor Statsenko gave permission to shoot down the U-2 on the assumption that it would not provoke an invasion of Cuba. Khrushchev and Malinovsky were horrified by the incident because they evaluated the risks of escalation differently.

Hawks and doves in each superpower based their conflicting assessments of risk on the same information. They were divided by their conceptions. The hawks considered only the military balance. They ignored all of the domestic and foreign policy considerations that loomed so large in Khrushchev's thinking. Kennedy and McNamara were more sensitive to the political costs to Khrushchev of diplomatic or military humiliation, and were correspondingly more cautious. They had no inkling of the broader foreign policy and domestic costs that Khrushchev associated with the failure of his initiative because they did not understand his several reasons for deploying the missiles. Kennedy and McNamara were also insufficiently alert to the danger of loss of control. Along with the Joint Chiefs, they exaggerated their ability to plan or execute military operations with precision. They remained unaware of most of the problems that threatened their management of the blockade and nuclear alert. They also failed to consider the difficulties Khrushchev had in controlling Soviet military forces and incorrectly interpreted instances of insubordination (e.g., the Grozny and the U-2 shootdown) as centrally authorized initiatives.

When threats to go to war are difficult to make credible because of the expected costs of war, leaders are forced to rely on Schelling's risk that leaves something to chance. But a risk that leaves everything to chance—or is characterized by a wide band of uncertainty—makes compellence a highly unpredictable strategy.

Changing preferences

The missile crisis was resolved despite all these difficulties by a clever, public-private deal that might even be described as a Pareto-optimal solution. Is this outcome evidence that rational bargaining is feasible in the most opaque and conflictual contexts? Several features of the crisis belie this interpretation. If rational bargaining could overcome these obstacles, the missile crisis would never have occurred. Both leaders wanted to avoid a confrontation over Cuba because they believed it would be destructive to their respective domestic and foreign policy interests. Because of their faulty understandings of each other's preferences, their efforts to forestall such a confrontation unwittingly brought it about. Even a Pareto-optimal solution to the crisis was a much worse outcome for Khrushchev than no crisis at all—it was a principal catalyst of his removal from power a year later (Hyland and Shryock, 1968).

Traditional interpretations attribute the favorable resolution of the crisis to compellence. But compellence was only partly responsible, and then only indirectly, for the mutual concessions that resolved the crisis. Kennedy, the putative compeller, made, or was prepared to make, concessions in every way equivalent to those made by Khrushchev. Both leaders made concessions because they were anxious to forestall violent confrontation and its attendant risk of escalation. Kennedy's imposition of a naval quarantine of Cuba and American military preparations for a possible invasion of Cuba created the context in which the threat of military confrontation became real, but each leader's fear of war was largely independent of the other's attempts to arouse or manipulate those fears.

On the first day of the crisis Kennedy seemed committed to an air strike, and Ex Comm members are convinced that he would have gone ahead with it if he had had to make a decision that day. It took time for Kennedy's anger to subside and for him to think through the likely political and military consequences of an air strike conducted without prior warning. As the week wore on, Kennedy felt cross-pressured. He increasingly wanted to avoid a military showdown in Cuba, but was unwilling to make any concession that would confirm Khrushchev's apparent belief that he could easily be blackmailed. Kennedy worried that concessions would encourage a new and far more serious challenge to American interests in Berlin. It was better to fight a war in the Caribbean where the United States had a distinct military advantage. By the end of the second week, Kennedy's view of the problem had undergone further evolution—he no longer saw any contradiction between his desire to end the crisis through concessions and his goal of moderating Khrushchev.

The secret messages Kennedy had received from Khrushchev and several free-wheeling discussions between Dobrynin and Robert Kennedy had provided insight into Khrushchev's motives for the missile deployment. Kennedy now considered it likely that Khrushchev had miscalculated the real consequences of the deployment and was anxious to find some way out of the crisis. If so, Kennedy reasoned, concessions that let Khrushchev save face were likely to moderate his future foreign policy. Kennedy's revised estimate of the payoffs associated with concessions made him more willing to make those concessions.

From Khrushchev's perspective, the most significant form of reassurance that Kennedy practiced was self-restraint. Khrushchev was surprised that Kennedy did not exploit the missile crisis to overthrow Castro, and had the power to restrain the American military from doing so. Kennedy's forbearance reduced Khrushchev's fear that the president would use his country's nuclear superiority to try to extract political concessions in the future (Adzhubei, 1989). "Kennedy was a clever and flexible man," Khrushchev observed. "America's enormous power could have gone to his head, particularly if you take into account how close Cuba is to the United States and the advantage the United States had in the number of nuclear weapons by comparison to the Soviet Union" (Khrushchev, 1990, 179).

Clarification of interests and reassurance not only created a zone of agreement, but partially restructured the identities of the superpower leaders (Snyder & Diesing, 1977; Stein, 1991). Before the crisis, Kennedy and Khrushchev saw themselves as pure adversaries. Their back channel communications and secret cooperation during the crisis created a shared identity based on a mutual commitment to peace. Paradoxically, the crisis developed trust between the leaders that provided the foundation for their subsequent steps toward détente.

In bargaining situations that share the characteristics of Cuba, the key to structuring a zone of agreement is to bring about a greater shared understanding of context. Cuba was resolved at least in part because each leader had a better understanding of the other's fears and goals and the domestic and foreign constraints under which he operated. This was the result of information exchange and bargaining about the meaning of the encounter.

The crisis might have been resolved by compellence alone; Khrushchev was convinced that an attack against Cuba was imminent, and perhaps against the Soviet Union as well, and probably would have withdrawn the Soviet missiles without any secret concession on the Jupiters. Such a humiliating outcome would almost certainly have led to very tense post-crisis relations, with Khrushchev, or the hardliners who may have replaced him, intent on revenge. The positive consequences of the crisis were not the result of its outcome—it was still a serious defeat for Khrushchev and his country—but rather how that outcome was understood by Khrushchev and Kennedy and their most intimate advisers. That interpretation was a function of the process that led to agreement, and what it taught the two leaders about each other's motives, willingness to cooperate and strong, mutual commitment to avoid war.

Models of bargaining use outcome as their dependent variable. They code dichotomously as settlement or nonsettlement—or as cooperation and defection, in prisoner's dilemma and related games—and settlements are evaluated in terms of their respective payoffs. These models, or games, assume that payoffs remain unchanged throughout the bargaining because the interests that determine them are stable. The missile crisis indicates that interests can change in the course of

Table 6.1   Kennedy's Changing Preferences

	Interests	Preference
Day 1	(Discovery of missile base construction in Cuba)	Air strike
	1. Demonstrate resolve	
	2. Remove missiles from Cuba	
	3. Safeguard political interests	
	4. Avoid violent confrontations	
Day 3	(Decision to quarantine Cuba)	Blockade with air
	1. Remove missiles from Cuba	strike option in
	2. Demonstrate resolve	reserve
	3. Safeguard political interests	
	4. Avoid violent confrontation	
Day 12	(Robert Kennedy's meeting with Dobrynin)	Noninvasion
	1. Avoid violent confrontation	pledge, secret
	2. Remove missiles from Cuba	missile swap, with
	3. Safeguard political interests	other concessions
	4. Demonstrate resolve	in reserve

bargaining, and as a result of bargaining, and that even when they remain stable, preferences can change if actors reframe the problem and as a result make different assessments of the impact of outcomes on their interests (see Table 6.1). Kennedy's and Khrushchev's preferences changed during the crisis because of their changed understandings of each other's motives. The process of bargaining was critical to the outcome. Bargaining models that hold preferences stable ignore one of the most important features of bargaining—attempts by one or both sides to encourage the other to re-evaluate its interests and the payoffs it associates with different outcomes.

Risk assessment and manipulation

Compellence assumes that credible threats of punishment can prompt concessions. Credible threats exploit favorable asymmetries. If both protagonists are equally skilled in bargaining, the outcome of a crisis should reflect the balance of asymmetries between them.

Attempts to predict crisis outcomes, or to assess them ex post facto, require reasonable estimates of the balance of interests, military capability, roles and other relevant asymmetries. The missile crisis is one of many confrontations that indicate that leaders can make extraordinarily subjective estimates of all these asymmetries. This is why protagonists often disagree about the balance of capabilities and interests, the definition of the status quo, and who is the defender. Estimates of these parameters by analysts, which may bear only a passing resemblance to those of one of the protagonists, have no scientific standing.

Compellence theories assume that estimates of resolve are based on the balance of asymmetries. The missile crisis indicates that judgments about resolve sometimes hinge on different considerations. For Kennedy and Khrushchev, it was the putative character of their adversary's political system. Because Kennedy and the Ex Comm conceived of the Soviet Union as a totalitarian state in which all domestic and foreign policy was controlled at the highest levels, they interpreted all of Saturday's disturbing events as part of a coordinated scenario intended to communicate Soviet readiness for a military showdown. They credited Moscow with enormous resolve despite their belief that it was outgunned and had fewer interests at stake. Khrushchev exaggerated American resolve because he was convinced that Wall Street could order an invasion of Cuba that Kennedy was powerless to stop. Both leaders' estimates of the other's resolve and their corresponding willingness to make concessions were different than the theory of compellence would expect.

New information did little to alter estimates of risk and resolve. During the first week of the crisis, the clashing policy preferences of Kennedy and the hawks reflected their different beliefs about the Soviets. The hawks were influenced by the calculus of compellence; because they were confident that Soviet military inferiority would leave Soviet leaders no choice but to grit their teeth and accept military defeat in Cuba. Kennedy and McNamara worried that Khrushchev would be forced to retaliate for political reasons regardless of the military balance. These different expectations reflected different judgments about Soviet leaders. The hawks believed that they were coldly rational and followers of Lenin's adage that Soviet policy should be like a bayonet thrust—pull back if you hit something hard, but keep going if you strike mush. Kennedy thought Khrushchev more like himself—constrained by domestic political pressures and sensitive to his country's national interests and reputation for resolve.

The different policy preferences of American hawks and doves also reflected their different values. Although hawks thought escalation unlikely, some of them did not shrink from the prospect of all-out nuclear war because they believed the United States would emerge the big winner. Six months before the crisis General Curtis LeMay had assured the administration that the Strategic Air Command could wipe out the Soviet Union with the loss of no more than three American cities. LeMay thought this an acceptable price to pay to remove once and for all the threat posed by the Soviet Union (Bundy, 1987).

LeMay was instrumentally rational; his policy preferences reflected his estimates of the probability of nuclear war. Like Kennedy, he knew that in a few years the Soviet Union, even if attacked first, would still be able to destroy the United States with a retaliatory nuclear strike. LeMay reasoned that the United States should seek a showdown while it was still relatively invulnerable to direct attack. Less fanatic hawks also responded to this logic; they wanted to avoid war but thought it imperative to teach the Soviet Union to respect American interests and resolve to reduce the chance of a future war that would be far more devastating to the United States. By the end of the second week, Kennedy wanted to avoid war at almost any cost because of the incalculable human suffering it would inflict He expected, but had no assurances, that the concessions he contemplated would not be exploited by Khrushchev and lead to new challenges. Kennedy was willing to take this risk because of his abhorrence of war.

Another reason Kennedy, LeMay, and more moderate hawks framed the problem differently was their different estimates of the long-term probability of superpower nuclear war. LeMay judged that likelihood high, and was accordingly willing to exploit the missile crisis as a pretext for preventive war. Moderate hawks concurred, and were willing to risk war in 1962 to lower its long-term probability. Before the crisis, Kennedy, like the moderate hawks, also judged the risk as high. During the crisis, he seems to have rebelled at the policy implications of his estimate and to have gradually convinced himself that the crisis might be resolved diplomatically and provide the basis for a more cooperative superpower relationship. Starting from the premise that war had to be avoided at almost all cost, Kennedy in effect brought his estimate of the long-term likelihood of war in line with his immediate policy preferences. His behavior was the reverse of that predicted by rational models of bargaining that assume leaders base their policies on their estimates of relevant contextual factors.

Kennedy's bias had entirely beneficial consequences—it helped to make his vision of superpower relations self-fulfilling. Other American presidents and Soviet leaders behaved similarly. Despite their generally pessimistic expectations about avoiding war in the long term, Presidents Truman and Eisenhower refused to be stampeded into precipitous action by hawkish advisers. They treated each crisis as an obstacle to be overcome in the struggle to preserve the peace. Their restraint, reciprocated after 1962 by Khrushchev and Brezhnev, transformed the East-West conflict into a more stable and peaceful rivalry. Mikhail Gorbachev based his foreign policy on an even rosier assumption—that Presidents Reagan and Bush could be made willing partners in his effort to end the Cold War. Through dogged perseverance, Gorbachev made his expectations self-fulfilling. In these instances the repeated failure of leaders to act "rationally" in the short term promoted the most rational of outcomes in the long term.

The missile crisis indicates that rational bargaining theories are just a shell. They require additional substantive assumptions about actors' beliefs and values and how they reason. Compellence theory contains one such set of auxiliary assumptions. It applied only to the American hawks, and could have led to a nuclear war if they had had their way. An American air strike and invasion of Cuba would have been opposed by 42,000 Soviet troops in Cuba, not the 10,000 estimated by the CIA, and they were equipped with tactical nuclear weapons. Soviet forces were not authorized to use their nuclear weapons without Moscow's permission, but had the capability to launch them and might have done so in response to an American invasion. Theorists of international bargaining need to develop other bargaining "logics" and specify the conditions in which they apply (Garthoff, 1989; Gribkov & Smith, 1994; Lebow & Stein, 1994).

Information and learning

Game theorists have developed impressive techniques to model games of incomplete information. They assume that actors update and revise their estimates of others' preferences and likely outcomes of their own strategies on the basis of new information. Bayesian learning of this kind may prompt changes in bargaining goals or strategies. The missile crisis is frequently treated as such a game of incomplete information (Brams, 1985, 1990; Nalebuff, 1986; Powell, 1987, 1988; Wagner, 1991; Zagare & Kilgour, 1993; Dupont, 1994).

The new evidence about Cuba indicates that the reality of crisis decision making is not captured well by Bayesian models of learning. Soviet and American policy makers were alert to new information and used it to revise key estimates of each other's intentions or likely responses to their initiatives. Their revisions were sometimes in the direction of greater accuracy (e.g., the Kennedy administration's recognition that Khrushchev's Friday message indicated his desire to find a face-saving way out of the crisis, Khrushchev's judgment on Wednesday that Kennedy's management of the blockade revealed that he was not trying to use it as a pretext for war against the Soviet Union). But just as often new information led to inaccurate estimates (e.g., the Soviet belief that Walter Lippmann's Wednesday column was a feeler authorized by the White House, the Ex Comm's conclusion that the events of Saturday morning reflected the emergence of a new, hardline in the Kremlin, the Presidium's fear on Sunday morning that Kennedy's visit to church might be the prelude to a nuclear attack). More tellingly, both sides usually assimilated information to existing schemas. Those schemas determined its importance and meaning. When valid information was filtered though appropriate schemas, revised estimates were more accurate. When revisions were based on false information or inappropriate schemas, they led to estimates further at variance with reality.

In Cuba, motivation was probably a more important catalyst of learning than information. Kennedy was desperately looking for some justification to make concessions in lieu of using force to resolve the crisis. He was therefore predisposed to accept Dobrynin's characterization of the Cuban missile deployment as defensively motivated and a serious miscalculation from which Khrushchev was looking for a face-saving way of extricating himself. Kennedy was also motivated to believe that concessions would moderate, not embolden Khrushchev in the future. Khrushchev knew he had no choice but to remove his missiles, and was correspondingly predisposed to believe that Kennedy would not seek to humiliate him, would honor his noninvasion pledge, and not exploit his country's military superiority to blackmail him in the near future.

Toward better theory

My critique of compellence indicates that parsimonious models of bargaining encounter two kinds of problem—they ignore some essential features of bargaining, and do not capture well those features they attempt to represent.

The narrow conceptualization of capability offers a striking example of the second kind of problem. Many bargaining models identify relative capability as the most important determinant of outcome; theories of deterrence and compellence are even more restrictive and tend to equate capability with military capability. The ability to inflict suffering can confer bargaining advantage, but it represents only one side of the bargaining equation. The ability to absorb suffering also confers bargaining advantage, and can offset an adversary's superior economic or military capability. The North Vietnamese demonstrated this political truth in their war with the United States; they lost every battle but won the war. Theories of bargaining ignore this component of advantage; it is noticeably absent from Thomas Schelling's classic formulation of deterrence and compellence, and helped to make him insensitive to the dangers of American military intervention in Vietnam (Schelling, 1966; Lebow, 1996c).

Bargaining can usefully be compared to the children's game of rock, scissors and paper. Each of the two protagonists makes a fist behind its back and decides whether to be a rock, scissors, or a piece of paper. At the count of three, they thrust out and open their fist and reveal one (rock), two (scissors) or three (paper) fingers. The rock triumphs over the scissors because it can smash them, but is trumped by the paper that wraps the rock. The scissors in turn defeats the paper because of its ability to cut it. The game highlights the relational nature of power. The American rock (nuclear and local conventional superiority) triumphed in Cuba because Khrushchev was desperate to avoid a humiliating military defeat. But American compellence failed against North Vietnam because Hanoi, although at a serious military disadvantage, did not fear war. North Vietnamese paper (willingness to suffer) wrapped the American rock. Theories of deterrence and compellence, and bargaining theories more generally, need to consider capabilities—and counter-capabilitie—beyond usable military force. They must further recognize that capabilities only translate into bargaining leverage when they enable one actor to inflict meaningful loss or confer meaningful gain on another.

Relational bargaining power is probably best conceptualized in terms of asymmetries, or important inequalities, in the situations of the bargainers (Hirschman, 1945; Knorr, 1975; Baldwin, 1980; Wagner, 1988; Lebow, 1996a). Second and third wave deterrence theorists emphasized two possible inequalities interests and role (defender vs. challenger). Other common asymmetries include resources (including military capabilities), need to settle, available alternatives, time pressure and the reputational and precedent setting consequences of concessions. Asymmetries shape expectations of what an agreement ought to look like. Based on its reading of relevant asymmetries each side estimates how much it can demand and what it must give up. Asymmetries also underlie the strategies of rewards and punishment. Cross cutting asymmetries make it possible for one or both sides to make low-cost concessions. Reinforcing asymmetries permit the advantaged side so to make more credible threats of nonsettlement or punishment.

The balance of asymmetries is rarely self-evident. Bargainers often disagree about which asymmetries are relevant and whom they favor. This leads them to different conclusions about the nature of a fair agreement, and can make agreement more difficult to reach. Bargainers are most likely to disagree, as they did in Cuba, about self-referential asymmetries like interests and roles. Almost by definition, adversaries have different understandings of the origins of their conflict, each other's motives and what they both have at stake. Clashing schemas prompt clashing assessments of interests, roles, and the status quo.

Models of bargaining behavior must rely on actors' understandings of the asymmetries. Some bargainers show more sophistication than theorists in this regard. They attempt to enlighten their opposites about their capabilities or other sources of advantage. Bargainers even try, and sometimes succeed, in creating false impressions of advantage. The exchange of information about asymmetries can be a vital part of bargaining. The construction of a shared, or at least closer, understanding of the balance of asymmetries may be necessary to create a zone of agreement. Even when a zone of agreement already exists, such efforts may produce a more favorable agreement for one side by convincing the other to bring its expectations in line with a revised understanding of the balance. As in Cuba, it may reconcile one or both sides to the outcome and facilitate more harmonious post-crisis relations. Deterrence and compellence take a common understanding of context for granted. They assume that credibility is the most problematic component of either strategy. The missile crisis and recent empirical work on other crises indicate that context is often understood differently by protagonists, and that resolve is questioned less often than deterrence theorists surmise (Hopf, 1994; Lebow &Stein, 1994). These cases suggest that interests and motives are more likely to be misunderstood.

Existing approaches to bargaining fail to consider how preferences form and change. Preferences take shape in context, and are influenced by the schemas actors use to frame bargaining encounters. The missile crisis indicates that two considerations in particular are important—assessments actors make of each others' motives, and their estimates of the consequences of the outcome for other bargaining encounters, interests, and relationships. Kennedy's initial preferences for the air strike, and his later decision to impose a blockade, followed from his belief that toleration of the missiles would invite further Soviet challenges. Kennedy's subsequent willingness to make concessions reflected his revised understanding of Khrushchev's motives. Kennedy's preferences changed in response to information and introspection. These catalysts were related; introspection made the president increasingly reluctant to use force and correspondingly receptive to Dobrynin's efforts to clarify Soviet interests and reassure him about Khrushchev's motives and to find some way out of this crisis.

The missile crisis suggests that new information is most likely to encourage learning when bargainers are open to its implications and use appropriate schemas to interpret the information. Real world bargainers are often motivated to maintain an understanding of their adversary or environment conducive to the attainment of their goals—as Khrushchev did in the months prior to Kennedy's announcement of the blockade. He denied, distorted, ignored and discredited warnings from his advisers that a secret missile deployment was likely to provoke a crisis with the United States (Lebow & Stein, 1994). During the crisis, hawks and doves in both superpowers did not change their views, but assimilated new information to their schemas. Disagreement between hawks and doves about the likely consequences of an air strike has not been resolved by the wealth of new information that has since become available: if anything the controversy has become more acute. Sophisticated approaches to bargaining must recognize that information at odds with existing estimates or expectations is only likely to prompt proportionate reassessment if actors are neutral to its implications or motivated to accept them. Reassessment, when it does occur, may not be gradual and incremental, as Bayesian models suggest, but sudden and dramatic.

Most models of bargaining assume transparency. However, information only takes on meaning in context. When different schemas are used to frame and interpret signals they are almost certain to be misunderstood. In the missile crisis, it led to noise being misinterpreted as signals (e.g., Kennedy's Sunday visit to church), signals mistaken for noise (e.g. Khrushchev's complaints at the Vienna summit about the Jupiter deployment) and signals being recognized as signals but misinterpreted (e.g., Khrushchev's Saturday message). Such misunderstandings not only impede learning but can reinforce erroneous understandings of motives and context, as they did in Washington and Moscow at the height of the crisis.

Cognitive errors of this kind can also confound the strategies of rewards and punishment. Both strategies attempt to reconcile an actor to an outcome by making its acceptance more attractive or its rejection too costly. To do either, bargainers must know why others reject their offers or demands; they need to know something about their preferences. Bargainers often need to estimate others' preferences on the basis of incomplete information. If their estimates are off, their threats or rewards may be inappropriate or insufficient. Worse still, they can provoke the very outcomes they are intended to avoid as Kennedy's and Khrushchev's threats did in the period leading up to the Cuban missile deployment. If their estimates are correct, their threats or offer of rewards must be understood by their targets. If bargainers and their targets frame and interpret signals in different contexts, misunderstandings can arise. Thus, Khrushchev's Saturday message, intended as a reward, was interpreted as a threat. Poorly understood preferences or faulty communication can thus confound the strategies of rewards and punishments and undermine the search for accommodation.

Is better theory possible?

The Cuban missile crisis indicates that international bargaining can be a complex process that is not easily modeled. A theory or model that could have predicted that a Soviet missile deployment in Cuba would provoke an intense, largely non-violent bargaining encounter that would end in a compromise settlement would have had to take into account most, if not all, of the beliefs and processes I have identified as important. Such a theory or model would require numerous independent variables and have to specify the interaction effects among these variables. It would also require accurate estimates of superpower preferences, and some method of mapping changes in preferences occasioned by self-reflection and information.

In the face of such complexity, theory needs to be less ambitious in its goals. The best it can aspire to do is to explain outcomes after they have occurred. An appropriate analogy is the study of earthquakes. Geologists can identify fault lines, state with some certainty that quakes are more likely to occur along these lines than elsewhere, but they cannot predict when they will occur, their magnitude, or where their epicenters will be. After an earthquake, when masses of data have been gathered, they can sometimes explain why such events occurred and took the form they did. Even so, these explanations are usually controversial (Lebow, 1996b).

How typical is Cuba of international bargaining? Parsimonious, rational models may be more appropriate to cases without its complexities. Some bargaining encounters may approximate this ideal. Art auctions at Sotheby's are conducted in accord with long-established procedures, involve experienced buyers who know the procedures and employ shared and well-understood signals to communicate bids. Distortion due to uninformed behavior by novices or faulty communication is infrequent. Scholars attracted to parsimonious models of bargaining assume that international bargaining more closely resembles auctions at Sotheby's than it does superpower confrontations over Cuba. This is an empirical question, and one that needs to be answered through a research agenda of comparative case studies.

I suspect that international bargaining is on the whole closer to Cuba than to Sotheby's. Students of Japanese-American relations, for example, report that bargaining over textiles, automobiles and technology encountered many of the same problems, and for this reason cannot readily be modeled. Unlike Cuba, these negotiations were not one-time encounters, but repetitive engagements that spanned decades and involved negotiators with extensive prior contact, good personal relations and access to trusted third parties as back channels and sources of information about one another's preferences. Japanese-American negotiations were also open in the sense that media in both countries chronicled their progress and offered all kinds of commentary and advice. Despite these advantages, negotiators appear to have made different assessments of the relevant asymmetries, misjudged one another's resolve and estimated the other's resolve independently of its efforts to shape those estimates. For all of these reasons American threats sometimes failed. American and Japanese preferences also changed during the course of bargaining (Schoppa Jr., 1997; Destler & Sato, 1982; Bayard & Elliot,

1994). To understand the course and outcome of many important international negotiations it is necessary to go beyond the simple and often unrealistic assumptions of parsimonious, rational theories of bargaining.

Bibliography

Abel, E. (1966). *The missile crisis.* New York: J.B. Lippincott Co.

Adzhubei, A. (1989). Interview, May 15.

Alekseyev, A. (1988). The Caribbean crisis: As it really was. *Ekho Planety, 33* (November), 27.

Allison, G.T. (1971). *Essence of decision: Explaining the Cuban missile crisis.* Boston: Little, Brown.

Art, R. (1980). To what ends military power. *International Security, 4* (Spring), 10.

Baldwin, D. A. (1980). Interdependence and power: A conceptual analysis. *International Organization, 34* (Autumn), 471–506.

Baldwin, D. A. (1985). *Economic statecraft.* Princeton, NJ: Princeton University Press.

Bayard, T. O., & K.A. Elliot (1994). *Reciprocity and retaliation in U.S. trade policy.* Washington, DC: Institute for International Economics.

Berts, R. K. (1987). *Nuclear blackmail and nuclear balance.* Washington, DC: Brookings.

Brams, S. J. (1985). *Superpower games.* New Haven, CT: Yale University Press.

Brams, S. J. (1990). *Negotiation games.* London: Routledge.

Brodie, B. (1946). *The absolute weapon.* New York: Harcourt, Brace.

Brodie, B. (1973). *War and politics.* New York: Macmillan.

Bundy, M. (1987). Interview, October 12.

Bundy, M. (1988). *Danger and survival.* New York: Random House.

Burlatsky, F. (1987). Interview, October 12.

Burlatsky, F. (1989). *Back to the brink: Proceedings of the Moscow conference on the Cuban missile crisis, January 27–28, 1980.* Moscow Conference on the Cuban Missile Crisis, Moscow, University Press of America.

Clausewitz, C. (1976). On war. In M. Howard & P. Paret (eds.), *The people in arms.* Princeton, NJ: Princeton University Press.

Department of State, U.S. (1962). *Bulletin, 49*(19), November 1973, pp. 640–43, and November 12, 1962, pp. 741–43. In D. L. Larson (ed.), *The 'Cuban crisis' of 1962: Selected documents, Chronology and bibliography*, pp. 183–86. Lanham, MD: University Press of America.

Destler, I. M., & H. Sato, (eds.). (1982). *Coping with US-Japanese economic conflicts.* Lexington: DC. Heath.

Dobrynin, A. K (1962). Telegram to Ministry of Defense, October 27, 1962.I In R. N. Lebow & J. G. Stein (eds.), *We all lost the Cold War.* Princeton, NJ: Princeton University Press.

Dupont, C. (1994). Domestic politics and international negotiations: A sequential bargaining model. In P. Allan & C. Schmidt (eds.), *Game theory and international relations: Preferences, information and empirical evidence*, pp. 156–90. Aldershot: Edward Elgar.

Eckstein, H. (1975). Case study theory in political science. In F. I. Greenstein & N. W. Polsby (eds.), *Strategies of inquiry.* Reading: Addison-Wesley.

Friedberg, A. (1988). *The weary titan.* Princeton, NJ: Princeton University Press.

Garthoff, R. L. (1989). *Reflections on the Cuban missile crisis.* Washington, DC: Brookings.

George, A. L., & W. E. Simons (1994). *The limits of coercive diplomacy.* Boulder, CO: Westview.

George, A. L., & R. Smoke (1974). *Deterrence in American foreign policy: Theory and practice.* New York: Columbia University Press.

Gribkov, A. L., & W. Y. Smith (1994). *Operation Anadyr: US and Soviet generals recount the Cuban missile crisis.* Chicago: Edition Q.

Griffiths, F. (1984). The sources of American conduct: Soviet perspectives and their policy implications, *International Security, 9*(2), 3–50.

Harvard University (1987). *Proceedings of the Hawk's Cay conference on the Cuban missile crisis.* Cambridge, MA: Harvard University Center for Science and International Affairs.

Herken, G. (1985) *Counsels of war.* New York: Alfred Knopf.

Herring, E. (1995) *Danger and opportunity: Explaining international crisis outcomes.* Manchester: Manchester University Press.

Hilsman, R. (1967). *To move a nation: The politics of foreign policy in the administration of John F. Kennedy.* Garden City, NY: Doubleday.

Hirschman, A .O. (1945). *National power and the structure of foreign trade.* Berkeley: University of California Press.

Hopf, T. (1994) *Peripheral visions: Deterrence theory and American foreign policy in the third world, 1965–1990.* Ann Arbor: University of Michigan Press,.

Horelick, A. L., & M. Rush (1966). *Strategic power and Soviet foreign policy.* Chicago: University of Chicago Press.

Huth, P. (1988). *Extended deterrence and the prevention of war.* New Haven, CT: Yale University Press.

Hyland, W. , & R. W. Shryock (1968). *The fall of Khrushchev.* New York: Funk & Wagnalls.

Jervis, R. (1979). Deterrence theory revisited, *World Politics, 31* (January), 289–301.

Jervis, R. (1989). *The meaning of the nuclear revolution: Statecraft and the prospect of armageddon.* Ithaca, NY: Cornell University Press.

Jervis, R., R. N. Lebow, & J. G. Stein. (1985). *Psychology and deterrence.* Baltimore: Johns Hopkins University Press.

Kahn, H. (1965). *On escalation.* New York: Praeger.

Kaplan, M. (1959). *The strategy of limited retaliation.* Princeton, NY: Princeton University Press.

Karsten, P., P. D. Howell et al. (1984). *Military threats: A systematic historical analysis of the determinants of success.* Westport, CT: Greenwood.

Kaufmann, W. W. (1954). *The requirements of deterrence.* Princeton, NJ: Princeton Center for International Studies.

Kennedy, J. F. (1962a). Transcript of "off-the-record meeting on Cuba, October 16, 1962, 6:30–7:55 p. m." John F. Kennedy Library.

Kennedy, J. F. (1962b). Transcript of the White House tape of October 27, 1962. John F. Kennedy Library.

Kennedy, R. F. (1969) *Thirteen days: A memoir of the Cuban crisis.* New York: Norton.

Khrushchev, N. S. (1970). *Khrushchev remembers.* Boston: Little, Brown.

Khrushchev, N. S. (1990). *Khrushchev remembers: The Glasnost tapes.* Boston: Little, Brown.

Khrushchev, N .S. (1992). Khrushchev letter to Kennedy, October 30, 1962. *Problems of Communism, Special Edition* (41), 62–73.

Khrushchev, N. S. (1961). For new victories of the world Communist movement. In *Communism — peace and happiness of the peoples*, pp. 9–68. Moscow: Gospolitizdat. 1.

Khrushchev, S. (1989). Interview, May 17..

King, J. E. (1975). The New Strategy. Unpublished.

Kissinger, H. A. (1962). Reflections on Cuba. *Reporter 22* (November), 21–24.

Knorr, K. (1975). *The power of nations.* New York: Basic Books.

Kolodziej, E. (1987). The limits of deterrence theory. *Journal of Social Issues, 43*(4), 130–1.

Kratochwil, F. V. (1982). On the Notion of "Interest" in International Relations. *World Politics, 36* (October): 1–30.

Kratochwil, F. V (1989). *Rules, norms and decisions: On the conditions of practical and legal reasoning in international relations and domestic affairs.* Cambridge: Cambridge University Press.

Kugler, J. (1984). Terror without deterrence. *Journal of Conflict Resolution, 28* (September), 470–506.

Langlois, J.-P. (1989). Modeling deterrence and international crises. *Journal of Conflict Resolution, 33* (November), 67–83.

Langlois, J.-P. (1991). Rational deterrence and crisis stability. *American Journal of Political Science, 35* (November), 801–32.

Lebow, R. N. (1981). *Between peace and war: The nature of international crisis.* Baltimore: Johns Hopkins University Press.

Lebow, R. N. (1982). Misconceptions in American strategic assessment. *Political Science Quarterly, 97* (Summer), 187–206.

Lebow, R. N. (1985). *Nuclear crisis management.* Ithaca, NY: Cornell University Press.

Lebow, R .N. (1988). Clausewitz and crisis stability. *Political Science Quarterly, 103* (Spring), 81–110.

Lebow, R. N. (1996a). *The art of bargaining.* Baltimore: Johns Hopkins University Press.

Lebow, R. N. (1996b). "Kriege und Erdbeben. Kann die theorie der internationalen politik konfliktpräventiv wirken?" *Internationale Politik, 51* (August), 17–20.

Lebow, R. N. (1996c). Thomas Schelling and strategic bargaining. *International Journal, 51* (Summer), 555–76.

Lebow, R. N. (1996d). Play it again Pericles: A non-realist reading of Thucydides. *European Journal of International Relations, 2*(2), 231–58.

Lebow, R. N., & J. G. Stein. (1987). Beyond deterrence. *Journal of Social Issues, 43*(4), 5–72.

Lebow, R. N., & J. G. Stein. (1990a). Deterrence: The elusive dependent variable. *World Politics, 42* (April): 336–69.

Lebow, R. N., & J. G. Stein. (1990b). *When does deterrence succeed and how do we know?* Ottawa: Canadian Institute for International Peace and Security.

Lebow, R. N., & J. G. Stein. (1994). *We all lost the Cold War.* Princeton, NJ: Princeton University Press.

Lijphart, A. (1971). Comparative Politics and the Comparative Method. *American Political Science Review, 65*, 682–93.

McConnell, J. M. (1979). The "rules of the game": A theory on the practice of superpower naval diplomacy. In B. Dismukes & J. M. McConnell (eds.), *Soviet naval diplomacy*, pp. 240–80. New York: Pergamon.

Maoz, Z. (1983). Resolve, capabilities, and the outcomes of international disputes, 1816–1976. *Journal of Conflict Resolution, 27*(2), 195–228.

McNamara, R. (1987). Interview, October 12..

Mikoyan, S. (1989). Interview, May 17.

Millett, A. (1968). *The politics of intervention.* Columbus: Ohio State University Press.

Nalebuff, B. (1986). Brinkmanship and nuclear deterrence: The neutrality of escalation. *Conflict Management and Peace Science, 9,* 19–30.

Organski, A. F. K., & J. Kugler (1980). *The war ledger.* Chicago: University of Chicago Press.

Paul, T. V. (1994). *Asymmetric conflicts: War initiation by weaker powers.* Cambridge: Cambridge University Press.

Powell, R. (1987). Crisis bargaining, escalation, and MAD. *American Political Science Renew, 81* (September): 717–27.

Powell, R. (1988). Nuclear brinkmanship with two-sided incomplete information. *American Political Science Review, 82* (March), 155–78.

Quester, G. (1989). Some thoughts on deterrence failures. In Stern, P.vC., R. Axelrod, R., & Jerris, R. Radner, (eds.), *Perspectives on deterrence*, pp. 52–64. New York: Oxford University Press.

Rapoport, A. (ed.) (1966). *Systematic and strategic conflict.* New York: World Law Fund.

Rhodes, E. (1989). *Rational deterrence and irrational responses: The logic of nuclear coercion.* New York: Columbia University Press.

Richardson, J. L. (1994). *Crisis diplomacy: The great powers since the mid-nineteenth century.* New York: Cambridge University Press.

Rusk, D. (1987a). Interview, September 21.

Rusk, D. (1987b). Interview with James Glight, May 18.

Rusk, D. (1987c). Letter to James G. Blight, February 25.

Rusk, D. (1990). *As I saw it.* New York: W.W. Norton.

Sagan, S. D. (1994). From deterrence to coercion to war: The road to Pearl Harbor. In A. L. George & W. E. Simons (eds.), *The limits of coercive diplomacy*, pp. 84–5. Boulder, CO: Westview.

Schelesinger, A. M. (1965). *A thousand days.* Boston: Houghron Mifflin.

Schelling, T. C. (1960). *The strategy of conflict.* Cambridge, MA: Harvard University Press.

Schelling, T. C. (1966). *Arms and influence.* New Haven, CT: Yale University Press.

Schoppa Jr., L. J (1997) *Bargaining with Japan: What American pressure can and cannot do.* New York: Columbia University Press.

Snyder, G. (1971). "Prisoner's dilemma" and "Chicken" models in international politics. *International Studies Quarterly, 15* (March), 66–103.

Snyder, G., & P. Diesing (1977). *Conflict among nations.* Princeton, NJ: Princeton University Press.

Sorensen, T. C. (1969). *The Kennedy legacy.* New York: Macmillan

Spanier, J. (1965). *The Truman-MacArthur controversy and the Korean war.* New York: Norton.

Stein, A. A. (1982). When misperception matters. *World Politics, 34* (July): 505–26.

Stein, J. G. (1991). Deterrence and reassurance. In P. E. Tetlock, Jo L. Husbands, Robert Jervis, Paul C. Stern and Charles Tilly (eds.). *Behavior, society, and nuclear war,* pp. 8–72. New York: Oxford University Press. 1: 127-43

Viner, J. (1946). *Implications of the atomic bomb for international relations.* American Philosophical Society.

Wagner, H. (1989). Uncertainty, rational learning, and bargaining in the Cuban missile crisis. In P. Ordeshook (ed.), *Models of strategic choice in politics,* pp. 177–205. Ann Arbor: University of Michigan Press.

Wagner, R. H. (1988). Economic interdependence, bargaining power, and political influence. *International Organization, 42* (Summer), 461–83.

Wagner, R. H. (1991). Nuclear deterrence: Counterforce strategies, and the incentive to strike first. *American Political Science Review, 83* (September), 727–49.

Wendt, A. (1992). Anarchy is what states make of it: The social construction of power politics.*International Organization, 46* (Spring), 391–405.

Whiting, A. (1960). *China crosses the Yalu.* Stanford, CA: Stanford University Press.

Wohlforth, W. C. (1987). The perception of power: Russia in the pre-1914 balance. *World Politics, 39* (April), 353–81.

Wohlforth, W. C. (1993). *The elusive balance: Power and perceptions during the Cold War.* Ithaca, NY: Cornell University Press.

Wohlstetter, A. (1959). The delicate balance of power. *Foreign Affairs, 37,* 211–34.

Wohlstetter, A., & R. Wohlstetter. (1965). *Controlling the risks in Cuba.* London: International Institute for Strategic Studies.

Wolfers, A. (1962). *Discord and collaboration.* Baltimore: Johns Hopkins University Press.

Zagare, F. C. (1987). *The dynamics of deterrence.* Chicago: University of Chicago Press.

Zagare, F .C., & M. Kilgour. (1993). Asymmetric deterrence. *International Studies Quarterly, 37* (March), 1–27.

Zamyatin, L. M. (1991). Interview.

Zhang, S. G. (1993). *Deferrence and strategic culture: Chinese-American confrontations 1949–58.* Ithaca, NY: Cornell University Press.

7 Thomas Schelling and strategic bargaining

If Hans Morgenthau expounded the fundamental tenets of realism and described its principal strategies, Thomas Schelling theorized its tactics.[1] He pioneered the study of strategic bargaining, which describes how states can exploit military, economic and other relative advantages to advance their interests through favorable bargaining outcomes. Like his illustrious predecessor, Schelling is the father of a research tradition that is well-represented in international relations and allied fields. His ideas have also had considerable impact in the policy community, where they continue to shape the way in which policymakers seek to influence adversaries. He received a peace medal from the National Academy of Science and in October 2005, was co-recipient of the Nobel Prize in economics.

In my judgment, Schelling's writings are intellectually elegant but morally flawed. They illustrate the intellectual and policy dangers of ignoring politics, culture and morality in search of deductive, rational understandings. All three problems confound his long-standing goal of developing a parsimonious and universal theory of bargaining. Most interestingly, the examples Schelling mobilizes to illustrate his arguments demonstrate the absurdity of his quest. They make clear—although not to him and his disciples—that tactics, signals, noise and reference points only take on meaning in context, and that context is a function of the history, culture and the prior experience of actors with each other. People cannot communicate without a common language, and Schelling errs in assuming that everyone speaks the language of twentieth century: Western microeconomics. The ultimate irony may be the extent to which Schelling's works on bargaining are unwitting prisoners of a particular language and context. The assumptions he makes about the nature and modalities of coercive bargaining reflect a parochial, American view of the world. They lead him to misrepresent the dynamics of the bargaining encounters he uses to justify his approach.

Readers may wonder why I take on Schelling when there is no longer a Berlin Wall, Cold War, or Soviet Union. I offer three justifications. His two prominent books on bargaining established the intellectual framework for much future work on the subject. His work is emblematic of a more general American approach to the world that seeks, when possible, to substitute a combination of technical fixes and military muscle for political insight and diplomatic finesse. Schelling may be "the best and brightest" representative of a tradition that continues to shape American thinking about strategy and coercive bargaining. He is also an important representative of a broader intellectual development: the colonization by microeconomics of international relations and the social sciences more generally. *The Strategy of Conflict and Arms and Influence* represent crucial imperial outposts in this process. They are fair game for those of us who question the value of framing the study of international relations in this manner.

For different reasons, both the theory and practice of international relations are dominated by the search for technical fixes. In the world of theory, this is motivated by the desire for parsimonious theory and reinforced by general ignorance of history, language and diverse cultures. Study of history, foreign languages, and cultures are on the whole discouraged by top-ranked American graduate programs in international relations. Their narrowness reflects arrogance, but also recognition that any acknowledgment of the relevance of this kind of knowledge would significantly reduce the claims of pure theorists of any orientation for status and resources. In the policy world, ignorance and arrogance certainly play their part. Equally important is the long-standing American commitment to win wars with minimal loss of life—American life. Naval and air forces, and the power projection they allow, have always been attractive to American leaders as means of keeping theaters of military operation far away from American shores. The advent of nuclear weapons threatened to end relative American invulnerability, and the prospect of a nuclear-armed Soviet Union was greeted with outrage and shock. It triggered a search for some way of transforming the threat of mutual nuclear annihilation into mutual security through mutual deterrence. Mutual Assured Destruction was successful—indeed, there is evidence that even minimal deterrence would have worked. Every Soviet and American leader during the Cold War was horrified by the prospect of nuclear war of any magnitude (see Lebow & Stein, 1994, chs. 6, 11, 14). There were nevertheless Soviet and American leaders who sought to exploit momentary, or even longer-term, strategic advantages to achieve offensive political goals. Thomas Schelling is a significant figure here too because of his efforts to provide the theoretical foundations for such efforts.

A theory of coercive bargaining

In *The Strategy of Conflict*, published in 1960, Schelling lays out the principles of strategic bargaining. He distinguishes at the outset between theories that treat conflict as a pathology and seek its causes and treatment, and those that accept conflict as a given and address its management. Some of the latter theories frame conflict as a contest and focus on rational and artful behavior designed to "win." Schelling contends that game theory of this kind can help us understand how parties to conflicts really behave and discover strategies that can control or influence the behavior of others. Such a theory of strategy should start from the premise that parties in conflict generally have common as well as opposing interests, and that in international relations especially, "there is mutual dependence as well as opposition." The most obvious example is the shared interest nuclear-capable adversaries have in avoiding all-out war. For this reason, strategic bargaining is not a zero-sum game in which one side's gain represents an equivalent loss for the other. Winning means making gains "relative to one's own value system," and both sides can accomplish this through bargaining, accommodation and the avoidance of mutually damaging behavior (Schelling, 1960, 4–6).

The Strategy of Conflict assumes that most conflicts take the form of bargaining encounters because the ability of either side to achieve its goals hinges on the choices and behavior of its adversary. "The bargaining may be explicit, as one when one offers a concession; or it may be by tacit maneuver, as when one occupies or evacuates strategic territory. It can, as in the ordinary haggling of the market-place, take the *status quo* as its zero point and seek arrangements that yield positive gains to both sides; or invoke threats of damage, including mutual damage, as in a strike, boycott, or price war, or in extortion" (Schelling, 1960, 5)

Schelling describes deterrence as the quintessential strategy of coercive bargaining. It assumes conflict and common interest between antagonists, and employs threats of punishment to obtain favorable outcomes. Deterrence distinguishes between the threat and application of force, and succeeds only when the threats do not have to be carried out. At its core, deterrence is about the use of threats or war, threats of anything else, and either combined with promises, to condition one's own and an adversary's behavior. Schelling is struck by how central the strategy of deterrence is to so many social domains, among them strategy, law and child rearing, and yet how underdeveloped the theory of deterrence remains. Strategists have devised and refined a number of tactics to impart credibility to threats (e.g., military readiness, stretching a "trip wire" across an enemies route of advance, nuclear sharing), but have not developed any commensurate theoretical structure to integrate these insights and provide a broader perspective on the problem of deterrence. Game theory, he contends, offers a tool to build such a theory and to discern underlying principles hidden in a mass of detail and idiosyncratic situations (Schelling, 1960, 6–16).

Game theory, Schelling writes, encourages us to treat strategy as a "cool-headed," rational activity. Strategy in practice may depart to varying degrees from these assumptions, but it allows a systematic treatment of the subject and the development of a benchmark to assess real-world strategic behavior. Rationality is not one-dimensional, but a collection of attributes, and departures from it can take different forms. They include a disorderly or inconsistent value system, faculty calculation, inefficient communication, and unrealistic behavior that represents a compromise among competing values and preferences among those responsible for policy. As every component of rationality has its irrational counterpart, the rationality assumption allows a formalization of irrationality that may be equally useful in studying real world behavior. It encourages formulation of tactics that might appear irrational, among them a careless attitude toward injury and a reputation for loss of self-control, lapses in comprehension. Many of these tactics, he insists, are routinely practiced by untutored and infirm, and a rational theory of strategy may allow us recapture sound, intuitive and useful notions that have been suppressed by our education and institutions (Schelling, 1960, 16–17). Schelling takes this insight a step further and argues that many seeming attributes of rationality "are strategic disabilities in certain situations." Having a reputation for being cautious and contemplative can make it impossible to impart credibility to a threat that would involve significant mutual damage. Modern civilization is disadvantaged in this regard, in contrast to Machiavelli or the ancient Chinese. We have come to identify peace and stability with trust, good faith and mutual respect. When these attributes are lacking, strategies that assume they are present, or can be brought into being, are bound to fail. Agreements will not work in environments were trust and good faith are lacking and there is no legal recourse for breach of contract. In such situations—and Schelling implies that the Cold War is one of them—"We may wish to solicit advice from the underworld, or from ancient despotisms." They exchanged hostages, drank wine from the same glass to reduce the threat of poison, met in public places to discourage massacres, and exchanged spies to allow for the collection and transmittal of accurate information. A rational theory of strategy could assess the utility and efficiency of these time-honored practices and discover modern equivalents that "Athough offensive to our taste, may be desperately needed in the regulation of conflict" (Schelling 1960, 18–20). A follow-on study, *Arms and Influence* (1966) quickly became one of the classics of the international relations literature. Based on the Henry L. Stimson Lectures, that Schelling gave at Yale University in spring of 1965, it extends the analysis of *The Strategy of Conflict* by elaborating principles and tactics specific to the diplomacy of violence. It goes on to apply them to deterrence, nuclear crises and the Cold War more generally. The most striking aspect of the work is Schelling's emphasizes the psychological and contextual bases of power. James Sebenius rightly calls *Arms and Influence* the first work in the spirit of the negotiation-analytic approach to bargaining (Sebenius, 1992, 324, fn. 4).

As a practicing economist, Schelling might have been expected to privilege material capabilities in his analysis. He makes a ritual genuflection in this direction on the opening page when he observes that with enough military force a country may not need to bargain. But his narrative soon makes clear that military capability is decisive in only the most asymmetrical relationships, and only then when the more powerful party has little or nothing to lose from the failure to reach an accommodation. When the power balance is not so lop sided, or when both sides would lose from non-settlement, it is necessary to bargain. Three other influences are important.

First is *context*, which for Schelling describes the stakes, the range of possible outcomes, the salience of those outcomes, and the ability of bargainers to commit to those outcomes. In straight forward commercial bargaining, contextual considerations may not play a decisive role. In bargaining about price, there will be a range of intervals between the opening bids of buyer and seller. If there is no established market price for the commodity, no particular outcome will have special salience. Either side can try to gain an advantage by committing itself to its preferred outcomes. Strategic bargaining between states is frequently characterized by sharp discontinuities in context. There may be a small number of possible outcomes, and the canons of international practice, recognized boundaries, prominent terrain features, or the simplicity of all or nothing distinctions can make one solution more salient than others. Salient solutions are easier to communicate and commit to, especially when the bargaining is tacit.[2]

The second consideration is *skill*. Threats to use force lack credibility if they are costly to carry out. To circumvent this difficulty, clever leaders can feign madness, develop a reputation for heartlessness, or put themselves into a position from which they cannot retreat. Other tactics can be used to discredit adversarial commitments or minimize the cost of backing away from one's own.

Schelling contends that context usually determines tactics. In the 1962 Cuban missile crisis, the American president, John F. Kennedy, benefited from American military superiority in and around the Caribbean. According to Schelling, the naval blockade and the prospect of an air strike or invasion of Cuba confronted the Soviet chairman, Nikita Khrushchev, with an unpalatable choice between defeat or horizontal escalation with its attendant risk of American nuclear retaliation. The missile crisis was a competition in risk-taking won by the United States because Kennedy could exploit discontinuities in the context. Different steps up the escalation ladder did not carry equal increments of risk. Kennedy committed the United States to a rung on the ladder where, in Schelling's judgment, the next step would have meant a quantum leap in risk. Khrushchev demurred because of his fear of war and because of no vital interest at stake.

The third, and arguably most important, determinant of outcome is *willingness to suffer*. Paraphrasing Carl von Clausewitz, Schelling describes war as a contest of wills. Until the mid-twentieth century, force was used to bend or break an adversary's will by defeating its army and holding its population and territory hostage. Air power and nuclear weapons revolutionized warfare by allowing states to treat one another's territory, economic resources, and population as hostages from the outset of any dispute. War is no longer a contest of strength but a contest of nerve and risk-taking, of pain and endurance. For purposes of bargaining, the ability to absorb pain counts just as much as the capability to inflict it.[3]

Schelling does not say so, but it follows from his formulation that the capacity to absorb suffering varies just as much as the capacity to deliver it. Clausewitz recognized this variation. Increases in both capabilities, he argued, made possible the nation in arms and the revolutionary character of the Napoleonic Wars. By convincing peoples that they had a stake in the outcome of the wars, first the French, and then their adversaries, were able to field large armies, extract the resources necessary to arm and maintain them, and elicit the extraordinary level of personal sacrifice necessary to sustain the struggle (Clausewitz, 1976, Book 8, chapter 3B).

The Clausewitz-Schelling emphasis on pain has wider implications for bargaining. The ability to suffer physical, economic, moral or any other loss is an important source of bargaining power and can sometimes negate an adversary's power to punish. Realist approaches to bargaining tend to neglect this dimension of power and focus instead on the power to hurt and how it can be transformed into credible threats. Schelling also ignores the pain absorption side of the power-pain equation—when analyzing compellence in Vietnam, an oversight, I contend, that led to his misplaced optimism that Hanoi could be coerced into doing what Washington wanted.

The power to punish derives only in part from material capabilities. Leaders must also have the will and freedom to use their power. Schelling observes that Genghis Khan was effective because he was not inhibited by the usual mercies. Modern civilization has generated expectations and norms that severely constrain the power to punish. The American bombing campaign in Vietnam, in many people's judgment the very antithesis of civilized behavior, paradoxically demonstrates this truth. The air and ground war aroused enormous opposition at home, in large part because of its barbarity, and public opinion ultimately compelled a halt to the bombing and withdrawal of American forces from Indochina. The bombing exceeded World War II in total tonnage but was also more restricted. The United States refrained from indiscriminate bombing of civilians and made no effort to destroy North Vietnam's elaborate system of dikes. The use of nuclear weapons was not even considered. Restraint was a response to ethical and domestic political imperatives. Similar constraints limited American firepower in Iraq in the Gulf War of 1990–91, and enabled the Republican Guard and Saddam Hussein to escape destruction.

The ability to absorb punishment derives even less from material capabilities, and may even be inversely related to them. One of the reasons why Vietnam was less vulnerable to bombing than Schelling and Pentagon planners supposed was its underdeveloped economy. There were fewer high value targets to destroy or hold hostage. With fewer factories, highways and railroads the economy was more difficult to disrupt, and the population was less dependent on existing distribution networks for its sustenance and material support.[4] According to North Vietnamese Colonel and strategic analyst Quach Hai Luong, "The more you bombed, the more the people wanted to fight you" (McNamara, Blight & Brigham,194). Department of Defense Studies confirm that bombing "strengthened, rather than weakened, the will of the Hanoi government and its people" (Ibid, 341–2, 191). It is apparent in retrospect that the gap between the protagonists in material and military capabilities counted for less than their differential ability to absorb punishment. The United States won every battle but lost the war because its citizens would not pay the moral, economic and human cost of victory. Washington withdrew from Indochina after losing 58,000 American lives, a fraction of Viet Cong and North Vietnamese deaths even at conservative estimates. As Clausewitz understood observed, political and moral cohesion based on common interests is more important than material capabilities.

A comparison between South and North Vietnam is even more revealing. The South Vietnamese armed forces (ARVN) were larger, better equipped and trained than the Viet Cong or the North Vietnamese, and had all the advantages of American air power, communications and logistics. The Republic of South Vietnam crumbled because its forces had no stomach for a fight. The Viet Cong and North Vietnamese sustained horrendous losses whenever they came up against superior American firepower, but maintained their morale and cohesion throughout the long conflict. Unlike ARVN officers and recruits, who regularly melted away under fire, more Viet Cong and North Vietnamese internalized their cause and gave their lives for it. At the most fundamental level, the communist victory demonstrated the power of ideas and commitment.

Taken collectively, the three determinants of outcomes analyzed by Schelling indicate that interests and material capabilities are only part of the bargaining story. They are at best a useful starting point. Bargainers are not automata who transform interests and power into outcomes; as Schelling acknowledges, they play critical, independent roles. Their skill at commitment, in undermining other's commitments, and in backing away from their own commitments can prove decisive. So can context. It determines the range of available outcomes, and can impart special salience and legitimacy to particular outcomes.

The third determinant, the vulnerability of the other side to punishment, constitutes the most formidable challenge to realist models of bargaining. Power confers influence through the instruments of rewards and punishments. But promises and threats translate into influence only when others crave the rewards or fear the punishments. Threats and promises fail when their targets are willing to forego the expected gains or to suffer the anticipated losses. As the Vietnamese so convincingly demonstrated, this kind of resolve is based only superficially on material capabilities. It is a function of subjectively constructed interests and social cohesion—attributes that are ignored by capability-based theories.

Schelling also differs from traditional deterrence theorists in the conditions he identifies as necessary for successful threats. More traditional realist theories focus on the sufficiency and credibility of threats. Schelling gives these considerations weight, but stipulates two other essential conditions. The threatener needs to know what an adversary treasures and what scares him and how to communicate persuasively what behavior will cause the violence to be inflicted or withheld (Schelling, 1966, 3–4).

The fears and vulnerabilities of an adversary are sometimes transparent, and it is a relatively simple matter to design a threat that exploits them. On other occasions, they are not so obvious, or even opaque. Janice Gross Stein and I have documented instances of threats that provoked the behavior they were designed to prevent because of the unexpected ways in which they influenced the cost-calculus of their targets. Khrushchev's May 1962 decision to deploy missiles secretly in Cuba is a case in point. It was triggered by the Kennedy administration's threats against Cuba, its public pronouncements of strategic superiority, and deployment of Jupiter missiles in Turkey. All of these actions, and more specifically the threats associated with them, were intended to moderate Soviet foreign policy. Instead, they made the consequences of restraint appear more costly to Khrushchev (Lebow & Stein, 1994, ch. 2). Contingency can be equally difficult to communicate. The threatened party may refuse to back down for fear that any concession it makes will be interpreted as weakness and encourage further demands. The strategy of threats involves an inherent contradiction that Schelling does not address. The behavior most likely to give credibility to a threat is also the behavior most certain to convey hostility and convince its target that it will be the victim of aggression, now or in the future, unless it stands firm. Khrushchev sent missiles to Cuba to deter an American invasion, but only convinced Kennedy that he would face a more serious challenge in Berlin if he allowed the missiles to remain (Lebow & Stein, 1994, 98–101). Threats can transform a bargaining encounter into a test of wills in which the goal of not giving in becomes at least as important as safeguarding whatever substantive interests are at stake. This may also have been an important consideration in Hanoi's decision to continue its support for the Viet Cong insurgency in 1964–65.

The need to understand the goals and perspective of the other side puts a premium on information and empathy. So does the need—difficult under the best of circumstances—to frighten and reassure an adversary at the same time. The practice of deterrence and compellence, and strategic bargaining more broadly, demands detailed knowledge about the preference structure of targets, the psychology of threats, and sophisticated use of available communications channels. This knowledge is just as critical to threat making as capability and resolve.

If traditional treatments of bargaining overvalue interests and material capabilities, Schelling errs in the opposite direction by overvaluing tactics. Bargaining skill is undeniably important, at times decisive, but it is almost impossible to make credible threats in the absence of the ability to carry them out. Counterthreats to spurn rewards or suffer punishments also require more than tactical brilliance to make them credible. They must be based on a demonstrable ability to do without, and that in turn depends not only on interests, but on the character of the bargainer or society.

Vietnam, Korea, and signals

Schelling encouraged the belief that violence could be used in manageable and predictable ways to coerce recalcitrant adversaries. His ideas were brought to the attention of the Secretary of Defense, Robert McNamara, by John McNaughton, a former Harvard Law School professor whom Schelling had tutored on strategy and arms control. On Schelling's recommendation, McNaughton was offered and accepted the position of deputy on arms control to assistant secretary of defense for international security affairs Paul Nitze. Within a year, McNaughton had become McNamara's general counsel and by 1964 had succeeded Nitze as assistant secretary of defense. McNaughton was a central player in the 1964–65

Vietnam decisions: he prepared a political-military plan for graduated escalation that became the basis for the Rolling Thunder bombing campaign. He consulted Schelling at the time and asked him what kind of air attacks would be most effective as a political signal.[5]

Arms and Influence is dotted with references to the bombing of North Vietnam. Schelling discusses its purpose, targets, timing, duration, and possible results and repeatedly compares the bombing to the compellent threats used against Khrushchev during the Cuban missile crisis. He is guardedly hopeful that it will convince Hanoi to limit its material support for the Viet Cong insurgency in the South (Schelling 1966, 62, 75ff., 83ff., 136, 141ff., 164, 166ff., 171ff., 175, 186–88, 200). At no point in his analysis, does he suggest any reason why the bombing campaign might not succeed. He actually uses it as the prototype for the future compellence of China using low-yield nuclear weapons to destroy military and industrial targets (Kaplan, 1983, 186). Schelling was not alone in considering such scenarios; the Kennedy administration seriously explored the possibility of attacking China's nascent nuclear establishment (Burr & Richelson, 2000–01).

Schelling might have developed a more jaundiced view of the bombing if he had carried the logic of his arguments a step or two further. Compellence, he observed, pits force against will. To succeed, it must inflict (or threaten to inflict) enough pain to bend or break the adversary's will. How much pain depends on what the adversary believes is at stake. Schelling never asked what North Vietnam had at stake or how much suffering would have to be inflicted on it to get its leaders to cry uncle. Even a casual attempt to answer these questions should have raised some doubts about the feasibility of a bombing campaign.

In its long struggle against the French, the communist-led Viet Minh provided striking evidence of its ability to mobilize and elicit sacrifice from the Vietnamese people. Pentagon analysts were not ignorant of this history, but dismissed the French experience as largely irrelevant. The conventional wisdom in Washington was that the France lost because it lacked the will to fight. This would not happen to the United States. The Pentagon argument explicitly recognized that the war between the Viet Minh and France was a contest in suffering won by the Vietnamese. This makes it all the more remarkable that Schelling and those he advised failed to address the pain side of the compellence equation.

Schelling's argument about coercive diplomacy is a subtle analysis of non-verbal communication. It starts from the premise that communication between adversaries is difficult and makes the counter-intuitive argument that non-verbal signals can sometimes convey resolve and intentions more effectively than written or verbal messages. To succeed, nonverbal signals have to exploit salient and mutually understood attributes of context. For Schelling, the bottom line is not how a signal is framed, but how it is understood. What mattered about the bombing was "What the North Vietnamese understood from the action—how they interpreted it, what lesson they drew, what they expected next, and what pattern or logic they could see in it" (Schelling, 1966, 144). Curiously, Schelling neither asks what Hanoi thought about the bombing, nor proposes any criteria relevant to such an inquiry. He assumes that the complex message the bombing was intended to communicate was heard in high fidelity by the North Vietnamese and Chinese.

Schelling gives two reasons for his confidence. First and foremost was the unambiguous relationship between provocation and response. "When North Vietnamese PT boats attacked American ships on the high seas, the United States conducted a modest reprisal against the naval installations and port facilities used by those boats. It was [also] in the North Vietnamese interest to read the message correctly; [otherwise] certain things might have gone wrong with the enterprise, especially in the response to it, that would have been deplorable to both sides" (Schelling, 1966, 144–45).

Schelling assumes that provocation and response, or tit-for-tat, are objectively defined, shared role definitions. But these roles are generally contested, as they were in this instance. American destroyers in transit through the Gulf of Tonkin were attacked by North Vietnamese PT boats on the night of July 30, 1964. At about the same time, South Vietnamese commandos staged raids on North Vietnamese islands in the Gulf. Hanoi described the PT boat attack as a reprisal raid for the shelling of the nearby islands. Destroyers entered the Gulf a second time, on the night of August 3, just as South Vietnamese PT boats carried out raids in the nearby Rhon River estuary. The subsequent bombing of North Vietnamese port facilities was justified as a response to a second round of attacks against the destroyers on the night of August 3. Hanoi vociferously denied any attack, and a subsequent inquiry by the Senate Foreign Relations Committee found no evidence of one. Robert McNamara, Secretary of State at the time, now acknowledges that no attack occurred, and that the attack two days earlier was a response to covert provocations by the United States and South Vietnam. (McNamara, Blight & Brigham, 157, 166-68, 184-86). North Vietnam interpreted the bombing as an unwarranted provocation that signaled Washington's intent to intervene on behalf of its faltering, puppet regime in the South (*Pentagon Papers*, 1971, 3, 259–61; Kahin, 1986, 217–25).

Schelling's confidence that the North Vietnamese understood the American message because it was in their interest to do so is not derived from any theoretical proposition. Quite the reverse. Schelling contends that nonverbal messages need to exploit shared understandings of context. When interests conflict, there are likely to be different understandings of motives, contexts and roles.

Schelling offers the bombing of Vietnam as an example of how carefully crafted signals can penetrate the fog of crisis. In reality, the bombing illustrates just how difficult it is to use military force to convey political messages. It carried a very different message to Hanoi than the one intended by the administration of Lyndon Johnson. North Vietnamese officials testify that it *reinforced* Hanoi's resolve to step up the insurgency in the South to consolidate the Viet Cong's position before major American combat units arrived in the country. According to Le Duan, party secretary and a member of the North Vietnamese Politburo at the time, the big fear among his colleagues was that giving any appearance of giving in to U.S. pressure would invite further demands (Duiker, 1996, 249–50, 261–62; Turley, 1986, 54–59).

Schelling's misplaced confidence in the clarity of the signal conveyed by bombing had political and intellectual roots. Along with the Pentagon officials he advised, he had a world-view that blinded him to the political realities of Southeast Asia and the likelihood that North Vietnamese leaders could honestly see the situation in a different light. His understanding of context was naively apolitical. His two books emphasize topographical features like river lines and political boundaries and military firebreaks that involved the non-use of certain categories of weapons or the territories on or over which they were used. He assumes that all these elements of context are understood in the same way by adversaries; this is what makes them appropriate vehicles for political messages. In practice, every element of context is socially constructed and has a subjective meaning. In applying this understanding to the Korean War, one of Schelling's key examples of a salient, natural landmark was the Yalu River, which separates North Korea from China. The Yalu, he insists, was like the Rubicon. To cross it would have signaled something. It was a natural place to stop; crossing it would have been a new start (Schelling, 1966, 134). This was also the logic of the Truman administration, which assumed that the People's Republic of China would be reassured if United Nations ground and air forces respected this line. As American forces approached the Yalu, Secretary of State Dean Acheson promised China (with no intended irony) that the United States would treat the Yalu just as it did the Rio Grande! Beijing's Rubicon was the 38th Parallel, and the China had warned that it would enter the war if it was crossed by non-Korean forces. The Truman administration dismissed the parallel as an artificial boundary and the Chinese warnings as incredible, and advanced north toward the Yalu. The consequences are well known. The Korean War was transformed into a Chinese-American war as the result of a marked failure in strategic communication (Tsou, 1963, 575–80; Whiting, 1960, 151–62; Lebow, 1981, 2, 10–13).

The different meanings attached by the United States and China to two lines on the map of Korea had little to do with simple geography. The Chinese communists regarded the United States as the foremost imperial power following the same route of conquest as Japan. They expected American forces to stop only temporarily at the Yalu before advancing into Manchuria. China's security required the preservation of North Korea as a buffer, and the 38th Parallel was the first line of defense and litmus paper test of American intentions (Tsou, 1963, 576–80; Whiting, 1960, 169–71). Because of their benign self-image, American officials were insensitive to Beijing's fears. They saw the 38th Parallel as difficult to defend and too close to the South Korean capital. If they were to halt there, North Korean forces would simply regroup and strike south at their convenience, unless the United Nations maintained a permanent military presence in South Korea. For Washington, the only natural stopping places were the narrow neck of the peninsula, favored by General Omar Bradley, or the Yalu River (Lebow, 1981, 179–83, 202–14).

Schelling's discussion of tacit strategic communication makes repeated reference to gestalt psychology (Schelling, 1960, 104, 107, 108n, 164n). However, his argument violates the fundamental premise of gestalt: that perception is not inherent in any stimulus, but a creation of the mind. Gestalt psychologists rejected elemental approaches that sought to understand perception by breaking it down into its constituent parts. They maintained that perception has properties that cannot be predicted from the study of its parts, just as the properties of a chemical cannot be predicted from knowledge of its individual molecules. The meaning, or properties, of perceptions is determined by the cognitive scheme imposed on them. Different cognitive schemas lead to different perceptions (Koffka, 1935; Köhler, 1938). Much of cognitive psychology is based on this insight, and an important strand of research attempts to understand how different frames of reference develop, change, and influence perception (Fiske & Taylor, 1984, 3–4, 141–42).

Schelling builds his argument on simple exercises of tacit communication: two people arrange to meet at the same time, dividing $100, or find one other in New York City for which they have a map. These problems are abstract and easily resolved; people overwhelming opt for the most salient solution. The stimulus appears to dictate the response. The map coordination game is particularly revealing. Subjects and readers regularly choose the bridge over the river in the center of the map as the natural rendez vous (Schelling, 1960, ch. 3). Schelling's map is imaginary. When one moves to a real map, as in Korea, mountains, rivers and borders have historical, political and even personal associations and meanings. People from different countries and political systems are likely to use different frames of reference that generate different gestalts, and encourage different interpretations of the same geographical features or landmarks.

Because salience is a social construction, tacit communication that uses terrain, coordinates, percentages or other concepts is only likely to succeed when sender and recipient have a common frame of reference. When these frames differ, as they so often do between adversaries, effective signaling requires insight into the other side's perspective. Schelling was attracted to tacit communication as a means of escaping this requirement. But there are no shortcuts to effective communication; Vietnam and Korea were the result of illusions to the contrary.

The political use of force

Arms and Influence was intended as a primer for policy makers who might have to manage nuclear crises with the Soviet Union or Communist China. For Schelling, the fundamental paradox of nuclear bargaining is that threats must be credible to deter or compel, but such threats are extraordinarily difficult to make when nuclear war would be national suicide. Schelling sought to circumvent this constraint with the tactic of commitment.

Schelling had observed the value of commitment in international trade negotiations. The side that "burned its bridges" or convinced its bargaining partner that it could not back down because of public opinion or instructions from its government frequently gained a significant advantage. The other side was forced to accept its offer or allow the negotiations to fail. *Arms and Influence* applies this tactic to strategic bargaining, and cites examples, ancient and modern, where it appears to have been used successfully. He was oblivious to the crucial differences between trade and strategic negotiations. In the former, the cost of failure is almost always bearable, and failure is not necessarily irrevocable; negotiations can often be reopened when circumstances are more auspicious. Failure to resolve a superpower nuclear crisis could have led to the most destructive war in history, and the status quo *ante bellum* could not have been restored once nuclear-tipped missiles had been launched. Burning bridges may be a useful tactic in trade negotiations, but would have constituted the height of irresponsibility in a Soviet-American nuclear crisis.

Schelling may not have recognized this common sense truth, but Kennedy and Khrushchev did. Both leaders behaved with remarkable circumspection in the Berlin and Cuban crises. They carefully avoided committing themselves to positions from which they could not retreat. In Cuba, Kennedy rejected the air strike and invasion options in favor of the less confrontational, initially nonviolent naval blockade. Khrushchev responded by recalling or stopping Soviet ships en route to Cuba in order to prevent a confrontation between them and American destroyers on the picket line. When Soviet forces (in violation of their orders) shot down a U-2 surveillance aircraft over Cuba, Kennedy revoked his prior authorization of a retaliatory air strike against a Soviet surface-to-air missile (SAM) site. He made a secret concession to Khrushchev, and contemplated additional concessions if they became necessary to end the crisis (Lebow & Stein, 1994, ch. 6).

Schelling (1966, 99–105) proposes a second tactic for exploiting the risk of war for political gain: the risk that leaves something to chance. He draws an analogy between nuclear crisis and a variant of chess in which the possibility of mutual loss occurs whenever a queen and a knight of opposite colors cross the center line. A referee then rolls a die and both players lose if an ace comes up. If not, the game continues. "In this way," Schelling writes, "uncertainty imparts tactics of intimidation into the game. A player can assume some risk of catastrophe and force an adversary to share it in circumstances where threats to initiate catastrophe would not be credible" (Ibid., 103).

For Schelling (1966, 92–125), nuclear crises were competitions in risk taking. When both adversaries believe that war would be a catastrophe, the side that demonstrates more willingness to court it gains a bargaining advantage. Kennedy "won" the missile crisis because the naval blockade and invasion preparations maneuvered Khrushchev into a position in which he had to choose between capitulation or military defeat. He could have responded to an American invasion of Cuba with horizontal escalation of his own, against Turkey or Berlin, but the risk of nuclear reprisal was too high (Ibid., 95–97). The evidence does not sustain

Schelling's analysis of Cuba. The outcome of the crisis was not an unalloyed American triumph, but a compromise. Beyond his public pledge not to invade Cuba, Kennedy agreed secretly to dismantle and remove American Jupiter missiles from Turkey within six months. If Khrushchev had hung tough for another few days, it is likely that Kennedy would have agreed to his demand for a public missile swap (Lebow & Stein, 1994, 122–30, 523–26). Even more problematic for Schelling's argument is the difficulty Kennedy and Khrushchev had in assessing and controlling risk.

The probability of catastrophe is known within carefully defined limits by both players in Schelling's imaginary game, and they can decide just how much risk they want to accept. In crisis, this is rarely the case. In Cuba, the risk of war associated with any contemplated escalation was entirely unknown; it was a matter of considerable controversy at the time and remains so today. The hawks in the executive committee of the National Security Council (ExComm) were convinced that the risk was extremely low and that the United States could attack Cuba and the missiles without provoking horizontal escalation. The Soviet Union, they argued, would be restrained by American nuclear superiority. The hawks did not know that the Soviet Union had 42,000 combat troops in Cuba, more than four times the number estimated by the Central Intelligence Agency, or that they were armed with tactical nuclear weapons. Kennedy and McNamara, who were also ignorant of these facts, nevertheless worried that any kind of violent, Soviet-American confrontation in Cuba could trigger off reciprocal escalation that would be extremely difficult to stop. Hawks and doves in possession of the same information developed different scenarios of escalation that led to radically different estimates of risk (Lebow & Stein, 1994, 118–20, 291–98).

Schelling's players can shed risk as easily as they assume it by moving their queen or knight back to the other side of the board. In real crises, de-escalation is more difficult. On Friday and Saturday, October 26–27, Khrushchev was desperate to end the crisis and attempted to communicate his willingness to withdraw the missiles from Cuba. His message raised hope in Washington that the crisis could be resolved. In a follow-up message, received on Saturday morning, Khrushchev sought to tie up loose ends, one of which was the American missiles in Turkey. Khrushchev's ambassador in Washington, the newly appointed Anatoliy Dobrynin, misread Walter Lippmann's column in the *Washington Post* which called for the withdrawal of the Turkish missiles, as a trial balloon sent aloft by the White House. Khrushchev's Saturday message and other developments, most notably the destruction of an American U-2 over Cuba, misled Kennedy and his advisors into worrying that Khrushchev, or hard liners who might have replaced him, were intent on provoking a showdown. Khrushchev's clumsy message and insubordinate behavior by the Soviet military undercut his attempt to deescalate (Lebow & Stein, 1994, 131–35, 300–06).

The Cuban crisis is one of many that illustrate how difficult it is for leaders to estimate risks of war or manipulate their adversaries' estimates of those risks.

At the climactic moment of the crisis, Kennedy and Khrushchev misread one another's intentions, exaggerated the risks, and scurried to make the concessions they both thought necessary to forestall war. Fortunately, they erred in the direction of exaggerated risk assessment. In July 1914, leaders of all the great powers underestimated risk and, through a series of reciprocal mobilizations, brought about a war that all of them would have preferred to avoid.

Reason and risk

There are two glaring omissions in *Arms and Influence*. Schelling never considers what happens when compellence fails. Nor does he consider the ethics of compellence. Good policy is predicated upon considering the possibility that one's chosen course of action will fail, devising indicators to provide timely warning of failure, and preparing fall back alternatives to cope with this circumstance. It is equally difficult to formulate effective policy in a moral vacuum.

Schelling cites Clausewitz but ignores one of the central precepts of his timeless study of war. Clausewitz (1976, Book 1) admonishes princes never to take the first step toward war before they have considered the last. The limited use of force to achieve limited goals appears deceptively easy. But war, he warns, has a logic of its own that tends to the extreme through a process of reciprocal escalation. When this happens, leaders lose control over their commitments, often with disastrous consequences.

Harry Truman intervened in Korea with the limited aim of repelling North Korea's invasion of the South. After General Douglas McArthur's striking success at Inchon, Truman could not resist political and military pressures to send American forces across the 38th Parallel to occupy North Korea. The American advance provoked a wider war with China. In 1964 the Johnson administration mobilized political support for its campaign of aerial compellence against Hanoi. When compellence failed, the United States was drawn into a ground war because it had publicly defined a communist takeover in South Vietnam as unacceptable. American intervention provoked increased North Vietnamese participation and prompted President Richard Nixon to extend the air and ground war into Cambodia. Success remained elusive, but Nixon and his Secretary of State, Henry Kissinger, were extremely reluctant to end American involvement because they believed their nation's prestige was on the line.

Schelling's optimism about compellence appears to derive from his faith in the rationality of leaders. He is confident that nuclear powers will on the whole eschew risks of war and step back from the brink when confronted with such risk. Schelling's reaction to the Cuban missile crisis is revealing. He watched Kennedy's quarantine speech on television on October 22, 1962 at the Harvard faculty club and left with a sense of gloating. "He couldn't imagine how Khrushchev could have done such a dumb, blundering act, and we had him on this one, and the only question was how bad a fall we were going to give him" (Welch, 1989,

100–01). In light of all we know today about the crisis and the difficulty leaders on both sides had in controlling it, Schelling's confidence seems misplaced. It was also questionable in 1962. If Khrushchev had blundered so badly in framing his challenge to the United States, why did Schelling expect that he would behave more sensibly once his missile deception was discovered?

According to Schelling, it is reasonable to risk nuclear war if it will reduce the probability of such a conflagration in the long term. In 1987, he described the Cuban missile crisis as the best thing to happen to us since the Second World War. It taught the Soviet Union that the United States would not buckle under pressure. By demonstrating resolve, Kennedy forestalled a more serious crisis in Berlin and compelled Khrushchev and his successors to moderate their foreign policy. The result, Schelling insists, was worth a one in fifty, or even greater risk of nuclear war (Welch, 1989, 100–01).

Schelling's estimate of risk is arbitrary. His commitment to demonstrate resolve assumes that the Cuban missile deployment was triggered by Khrushchev's belief that Kennedy lacked the will to oppose him. Soviet officials have since revealed that Khrushchev sent missiles to Cuba at least in part to deter an invasion that he believed a reckless Kennedy was preparing to launch. He sent them secretly because he was absolutely convinced that Kennedy would use his navy to prevent an open deployment. Khrushchev also embarked upon his dangerous missile gambit because the American strategic buildup, its missile deployment in Turkey, and assertions of strategic superiority made him feel increasingly insecure. Kennedy saw these measures as prudent, defensive precautions against perceived Soviet threats. His actions had the unanticipated consequence of convincing Khrushchev of the need to protect the Soviet Union and Cuba from American military and political challenges (Lebow & Stein, 1994, ch 2).

Influence and arms

The Strategy of Conflict acknowledges that a theory of bargaining "may prove to be a good approximation of reality or a caricature" (Schelling, 1960, 4). His approach more closely approximates the latter; it does not even capture the process or outcome of the cases to which he applies it. There are many reasons for this, and most of the ones I have examined pertain to the internal logic—or occasionally, illogic—of his arguments and the assumption that so-called objective features of context can be manipulated in ways that are mutually comprehensible to antagonists who fear and distrust one another and are likely to speak different political languages. Schelling's formulation of coercive bargaining is also inadequate for what it excludes. Perhaps the most striking omission is the promise of rewards.

Persuasion can take two forms: threats to make rejection of a proposal too costly, and rewards to make it more attractive. Bargainers commonly rely on carrots *and* sticks to shape others' preferences—this is especially true in international crises where the political cost of appearing to back down in the face of superior threats may be greater than the punishment those threats entail. Giving the other side what it wants is the most obvious way to make accommodation attractive, but it may also be the most costly if any concession by one side represents an equivalent loss by the other. To sidestep this problem, bargainers commonly expand the bargaining set by introducing new issues that allow for side payments. Khrushchev justified his Cuban missile deployment as necessary to protect Cuba from American attack. Kennedy did not want to attack Cuba as he thought it would be a costly operation and risk war with the Soviet Union. He readily acceded to Khrushchev's demand for a non-invasion pledge in return for withdrawal of the missiles. Kennedy was equally pleased with the pledge because it provided him with a compelling justification for exercising restraint in face of growing pressure from American hawks to invade Cuba. Because Khrushchev was absolutely convinced that the United States intended to attack Cuba, he regarded the non-invasion pledge as a significant gain (Lebow & Stein, 1994, 132–35).

Sometimes, the cost associated with a concession is not intrinsic but lies in the negative implications the concession would have for relations with third parties. The missile crisis once again provides a dramatic example. Kennedy agreed to issue a public pledge not to invade Cuba in return for withdrawal of the Soviet missiles. He was also willing to dismantle the American Jupiter missile had deployed in Turkey, but he categorically rejected Khrushchev's demand for a public missile swap because of its expected political consequences. Republicans, joined by dissident hawks from his administration, would accuse him of caving in to the Soviets. On October 27, at the height of the crisis, Robert Kennedy explained to Soviet ambassador Anatoliy Dobrynin that his brother was prepared to remove the missiles in Turkey within six months provided Moscow made no attempt to claim it as a concession. Khrushchev, who had been pushing for a public missile swap, insisted on a private letter from Kennedy acknowledging their understanding. Kennedy refused and Khrushchev did not push, because he had come to realize that secrecy was in his interest too. Cuban leader Fidel Castro was furious with him for agreeing to withdraw the missiles and would have been apoplectic if he had thought that Khrushchev had cut a deal beneficial to the Soviet Union at Cuba's expense. To cover up the concession, the Kennedy inner circle invented the story that the president had asked to have the obsolete Jupiter missiles in Turkey removed before the crisis. Unbeknownst to the president, the State Department had dragged its heels, because the Turks were reluctant to give up the missiles. Kennedy was alleged to have exploded when he learned during the crisis that the missiles were still in place. Administration insiders told this tale to unsuspecting newsmen and latter confirmed it in their memoirs (Lebow & Stein, 1994, 142–43). Assessments of costs and gain are significantly influenced by the reading each bargainer has of the other's motives. The question of motive will be paramount when the other side fears that any concession it makes will be exploited rather than reciprocated. A related fear is that a concession will convey an image of weakness and provoke further demands. Both concerns drove Kennedy and Khrushchev at the outset of the missile crisis. Kennedy and his advisors regarded the secret Soviet missile deployment as a gratuitously aggressive provocation. They expected that if they backed away from their commitment to keep offensive weapons out of Cuba Khrushchev would become more brazen and challenge the Western position in Berlin. Khrushchev and his advisors subscribed to a mirror image of their adversary. They worried that if they withdrew the missiles in response to the blockade Kennedy would become more aggressive about exploiting his country's military advantage (Lebow & Stein, 1994, 115–20).

As the crisis progressed, Kennedy and Khrushchev learned more about each other's motives through their exchange of letters, secret meetings between Robert Kennedy and Anatoliy Dobrynin, and the two country's behavior on the blockade line. By clarifying their respective interests and reassuring the other about their intentions, Kennedy and Khrushchev changed each other's estimates of the cost of concession to the point where the costs were no longer seen as unexpectedly high and the concessions appeared to hold out the prospect of substantial rewards. From Khrushchev's perspective, the most significant form of reassurance that Kennedy practiced was self-restraint. Khrushchev was surprised that Kennedy did not exploit the missile crisis to overthrow Castro and humiliate the Soviet Union. Kennedy's forbearance reduced Khrushchev's fear that the president would use his country's nuclear superiority to try to extract political concessions. "Kennedy was a clever and flexible man," Khrushchev remarked afterwards. "America's enormous power could have gone to his head, particularly if you take into account how close Cuba is to the United States and the advantage the United States had in the number of nuclear weapons by comparison to the Soviet Union." Kennedy's unanticipated ability to restrain the American military encouraged Khrushchev to hope that American hardliners would not succeed in sabotaging détente with Kennedy as they had with Eisenhower. Kennedy's behavior altered Khrushchev's estimate of the possibilities for improved Soviet-American relations. From Khrushchev's new perspective, the expected costs of withdrawing the Soviet missiles were greatly reduced and the possible rewards equally enhanced (Lebow & Stein, 1994, 309–19; Adzhubei interview, Moscow, May 15, 1989; Khrushchev, 179).

The crisis also redefined the context of Soviet-American relations for Kennedy. Khrushchev's restraint along the blockade line, his revealing messages, and Robert Kennedy's meetings with Dobrynin convinced him that the Soviet leader had bungled his way into a crisis that he had not wanted and was desperately searching for a face-saving way to retreat. By Saturday night, when Kennedy approved a missile exchange, he was less fearful that Khrushchev would interpret American concessions as a sign of weakness and respond by becoming more aggressive. He thought that there was some chance that the Soviet leader would see concessions as evidence of his commitment to avoiding war and to reciprocating with tension-reducing measures of his own. Kennedy and Khrushchev independently came to the conclusion that concessions might be more effective in achieving their goals than continued confrontation (Lebow & Stein, 1994, 309–19).

It is possible, even likely, that Khrushchev would have withdrawn the missiles in the absence of any concessions. He was desperately anxious to avoid war and convinced that the Americans would use force against the missile sites and Cuba if they were not withdrawn. Clarification of interests and reassurance made it that much easier for Khrushchev to back down. However, their most important consequence was for post-crisis relations. If Khrushchev had been compelled to withdraw the missiles solely by American threats, he and other Soviet leaders would have been much more resentful in the aftermath of the crisis. Mutual clarification of interests and reassurance provided the basis for the superpowers to move away from confrontation and toward détente. By limiting his analysis to threats, Schelling entirely misses the "hidden history" of the missile crisis and the key dynamics that determined its resolution and implications for subsequent superpower relations.

Schelling's single-minded focus on threats is not accidental, but an expression of his Cold War mindset. Like many other Americans of his epoch he regarded the Soviet Union and its communist partners, China and North Korea, as international gangsters intent on exploiting any weakness of their adversaries to expand their influence and territorial domain. Communists spurned the core values of Western civilization and had nothing more than a tactical interest in any accommodation. "Where trust and good faith do not exist and cannot be made to by our acting as though they did, Schelling wrote in the opening chapter of *Strategy of Conflict* (20) "we may wish to solicit advice from the underworld. . . ." It was not only naive, but dangerous, to consider that the men in the Kremlin, or their allies, could be influenced by soft words, promises and concessions.

For much the same reason Schelling assumed that it was extraordinarily difficult to make credible nuclear threats. If Communist leaders had no respect for human life, thought of the West as soft and would risk war under favorable military circumstances, deterrence—even nuclear deterrence—was far from assured. Most of *Arms and Influence* is a response to this problem. Evidence from Soviet archives and interviews with former Soviet officials indicates that deterrence was far more robust than American presidents and arm chair strategists ever imagined. In perhaps the most comprehensive study of this subject, Ted Hopf examined Soviet reactions to 38 cases of American intervention over a twenty-five year period of the Cold War and could not discovered a single Soviet document that drew any negative inferences about American resolve in Europe or northeast Asia. Nor did American credibility suffer from defeats like Vietnam: Soviet commentators concluded that Washington was just as likely to intervene in the future on behalf of its Third World clients—and just as likely to lose. American successes, like Grenada, were largely unnecessary because the Soviets already regarded American commitments as highly credible (Hopf, 1994). They did make them worry more about *their* deterrent and whether it was sufficient to deter

American aggression. In their mutual concern to reinforce deterrence, leaders of both superpowers resorted to the very kind of tactics Schelling advocated. They tried—with a disturbing degree of success—to convinced each other that they just might be irrational enough or sufficiently out of control to use their nuclear weapons. Each superpower consequently became less secure, more threatened, and less confident about its own deterrent. By 1960, the strategy of deterrence had become an important source of conflict in its own right and in the case of Cuban missile crisis, helped to provoke the kind of conflict it was intended to prevent. The most striking omission in Schelling's analysis is ethics. His only reference to morality concerns the French in Algeria, and is intended to highlight the differences between that conflict and Vietnam. The Algerian rebels waged a war of terror against their French and Algerian opponents. The French Army opposed them with force and sought to eliminate their military capability. When this strategy failed, he observes, the French turned to terror, with no more effect. Algeria showed that relying on coercive terror in return may prove not only degrading, but incompatible with the purpose it is intended to serve. Schelling was naively confident that this would not happen in Vietnam because the United States had found a way to coerce the North Vietnamese government without using force against its population (Schelling, 1960, 174). Hans Morgenthau insisted that both the ends and the means of foreign policy had to be consistent with the prevailing moral code—for both ethical and practical reasons. Schelling's brand of realism—and American policy in Indochina—dispensed with all morality on the grounds that it had no place in a dangerous world populated by cutthroat adversaries and frightened allies. In doing so, they did away with what they publicly proclaimed was the key distinguishing feature between the United States and its communist adversaries.

There is much that is undeniably brilliant in Schelling. His implicit critique of rational models of bargaining, and explicit discussion of how weakness and constraints can be exploited to obtain leverage are important contributions to the bargaining literature. Unfortunately, his analysis of strategic bargaining suffers from ideological blindness, cultural insensitivity and amorality. These failings kept Schelling from fully and properly applying his concept of strategic bargaining to Vietnam and Cuba. If he had, he might have recognized the limits and dangers of coercive diplomacy. *Arms and Influence* could have provided powerful arguments against intervention in Vietnam instead of justification for destructive and pointless escalation.

Post-Cold War American foreign policy suggests that little has changed in the theory and practice of coercive bargaining. The former has become immeasurably more sophisticated, but it is still based on the same questionable assumption that politics and culture can be ignored or finessed because the logic and language of bargaining are universal. This is empirically absurd, and almost every study of international crisis shows how signals are missed or misinterpreted, as are "moves," so central to all formulations of bargaining. Formal bargaining theories may do a good job of capturing behavior in highly formalized settings—like auctions at Christie's—where actors have been socialized to a set of procedures that makes communication transparent and effective. But few bargaining counters in international relations have these characteristics. The problem of influence is more difficult still because it depends on knowledge of others' preferences. In the absence of such knowledge, there is no way of knowing if threats or rewards are likely to influence their cost calculus, or if it does, in the intended direction.[6] There are no technical fixes for these problems. They are context dependent, require knowledge about other actors, their cultures and their preferences. The goal of a parsimonious bargaining theory based on realist principles is a conceit. The most such theories can do is to offer a first cut into a problem, that is to help actors structure their situation and to provide a framework they can fill in with relevant local knowledge.

The policy problem runs on a parallel track. Here too, there is no substitute for local knowledge, and for the same reasons. Policy based on grand schemes, whether those of academic realists like John Mearsheimer or the neoconservative ideologues in the Bush administration are premised on the universal applicability of foundational principles, from which policy options are then deduced. In practice, such initiatives will inevitably run afoul because they do not take local conditions into account, or indeed, other considerations, domestic and international, that influence outcomes. Such a misadventure is currently unfolding in Iraq. It is another tragic illustration of the simple realist view of the world (in contrast to the more sophisticated wisdom of classical realism) that greatly overvalues military and economic capability—and especially, their alleged power to coerce, while ignoring the power of resistance based on appeals to principles, honor and self-esteem.

Notes

1 An earlier version of this article "Thomas Schelling and Strategic Bargaining," appeared in *International Studies*, 51 (Summer 1996), pp. 555–76.

2 This theme is more fully developed in *The Strategy of Conflict.*

3 Clausewitz, *On War*, Book 6, chapter 26, "The People in Arms," makes the same point as Schelling. He observes that the national resistance movement in Spain sought to inflict punishment directly on their adversary.

4 Janice Gross Stein made this argument in the Yorkside Cafeteria in 1965 following Schelling's first lecture on "Arms and Influence," and predicted that the bombing campaign would fail to humble Hanoi.

5 Kaplan, *The Wizards of Armageddon*, 332–35, reports that Schelling recommended that the bombing campaign be given three weeks to show results.

6 More extensive arguments and examples are provided in Richard Ned Lebow, The Art of Bargaining (Baltimore: Johns Hopkins University Press, 1996), and "Beyond Parsimony: Rethinking Theories of Coercive Bargaining," *European Journal of International Relations*, 4, No. 1 (1998), pp. 31–66.

Bibliography

Burr, William, & Jeffrey T. Richelson. (2000-01). Whether to "Strangle the baby in the cradle": The United States and the Chinese nuclear program, 1960–64. *International Security, 25*(1), 54–99.

Clausewitz, Carl von. (1976). *On war* (Michael Howard & Peter Paret, Eds. & Trans.). Princeton, NJ: Princeton University Press.

Duiker, William J. (1996). *The communist road to power in Vietnam*. Boulder, CO: Westview.

Fiske, Susan T., & Shelley E. Taylor. (1984). *Social cognition*. Reading, MA: Addison-Wesley.

Hopf, Ted. (1994). *Deterrence theory and American foreign policy in the third world, 1965–1990*. Ann Arbor: University of Michigan Press.

Kahin, George McT. (1986.) *Intervention: How American became involved in Vietnam*. New York: Knopf.

Kaplan, Fred. (1983). *The wizards of armageddon*. New York: Simon and Schuster.

Koffka, Kurt. (1935). *Principles of gestalt psychology* New York: Harcourt, Brace & World.

Köhler, Wolfgang. (1938).*The place of value in a world of facts*. New York: Liveright.

Khrushchev, Nikita, S. (1990). *Khrushchev remembers: The glasnost tapes* (Jerrold Schecter, Trans.). Boston: Little, Brown.

Lebow, Richard Ned. (1981). *Between peace and war: The nature of international crisis*. Baltimore: Johns Hopkins Press.

Lebow, Richard Ned, & Janice Gross Stein. (1994). *We all lost the cold war*. Princeton, NJ: Princeton University Press.

McNamara Robert S., James G. Blight, & Robert K. Brigham. (1999). *Argument without end: In search of answers to the Vietnam tragedy*. New York: Public Affairs.

The Pentagon papers: The Defense Department history of United States decision making in Vietnam. (1971). Senator Gravel edition, vol. 3. Boston: Beacon Press.

Schelling, Thomas. (1960). *The strategy of conflict* Cambridge, MA: Harvard University Press.

Schelling, Thomas. (1966). *Arms and influence*. New Haven, CT: Yale University Press.

Sebenius, James K. (1992). Challenging conventional explanations of international cooperation: Negotiation analysis and the case of epistemic communities. *International Organization, 46*(1), 322–66.

Turley, William S. (1986). *The second Indochina war: A short political and military history, 1954–1975*. Boulder, CO: Westview.

Tsou, Tang. (1963). *America's failure in China, 1941–1950*. Chicago: University of Chicago Press.

Welch, David A. (Ed.). (1989). *Proceedings of the Hawk's Cay Conference on the Cuban Missile Crisis*. Cambridge, MA: Harvard University Center for Science and International Affairs.

Whiting, Allen S. (1960). *China crosses the Yalu: The decision to enter the Korean war*. New York: Macmillan.

Wirtz, James J. (1991). *The Tet offensive: Intelligence failure in war*. Ithaca, NY: Cornell University Press.

8   Robert S. McNamara:
Max Weber's worst nightmare

This is a timely moment to consider the career of Robert Strange McNamara and its lessons for strategic culture, the American approach to war, and the relationship between policy and ethics. The former secretary of defense has garnered considerable international attention as a result of his central role in Errol Morris's 2004 Oscar-winning documentary, *The Fog of War*. His reprise of Vietnam was projected on to silver screens at a time when images of another American military adventure were appearing nightly on our television screens.

By the fall of 2005, when this essay was composed, the Anglo-American invasion of Iraq had come in many ways to resemble its predecessor. Both interventions were based on lies (the nonexistent Gulf of Tonkin attack against American destroyers on August 4, 1964, and Saddam's nonexistent weapons of mass destruction); leaders consistently underestimated the number of troops they thought necessary to accomplish their missions; counter-occupation insurgencies escalated regardless of the number of troops Washington introduced; the secretaries of defense and their generals consistently predicted "light at the end of the tunnel," blamed insurgencies on foreign infiltration and cited increases in attacks against them as "last gasp" efforts by the opposition; public opinion turned against both wars as casualties mounted; and the press ultimately came to describe them, with good reason, as "quagmires." What explains the "recidivism" of American national security policy?

The career of Robert S. McNamara points us toward at least part of the answer. He is horrified today by the destructiveness of modern warfare; willing to reconsider the goals and strategies of the Vietnam-Indochina War, but categorically unwilling to apologize for his actions in helping to bring it about. He is quick to condemn war in general, but silent when it comes to specific conflicts. After leaving office in February 1968, he refused to speak out against the Vietnam War, or to use his influence for the cause of peace. In a more recent public appearance at Berkeley, he danced around the question of whether the Bush administration should be criticized for its invasion of Iraq. He is bitterly resentful of officials who had the courage to oppose the Vietnam War. In Berkeley, he refused to take a question from, or meet privately with, Daniel Ellsberg, whom he considers a traitor.[1]

On the positive side of the ledger, McNamara deserves qualified praise for his efforts to reduce the risk of nuclear annihilation. As secretary of defense in the Kennedy administration, he fought and won three important battles against the military. He compelled chief of the Strategic Air Command (SAC) General Curtis LeMay to reveal the air force's nuclear war plans to him, only to discover that there was only one option, jocularly referred to as "wargasm," by SAC planners. It mandated the instant use of all available bombers to destroy as much of the communist "bloc" as possible, from Eastern Europe to the South China Sea. McNamara insisted on a variety of options to give the president the possibility of fighting a less destructive war. He championed the strategic doctrine known as "Mutual Assured Destruction" (MAD), primarily as a means of restraining the air force, which was pushing for the purchase of 3,900 Minutemen ICBMs. McNamara's brain trust determined that the "knee of the curve," that point at which additional missiles brought increasingly diminishing returns in their ability to destroy Soviet targets of value, was roughly 1,000. He initially settled on the figure of 900—although the number at one point went as high as 1,300—as the lowest number most likely to gain congressional support.[2]

Most importantly, McNamara provided President Kennedy with the arguments and political backing to resist military demands for air strikes in the Cuban missile crisis. He strongly opposed an air strike against the Soviet missile sites in Cuba on the grounds that it would risk war to preserve American invulnerability to nuclear attack for a few years at best, as the Soviets would deploy ICBM's capable of striking the American heartland before the end of the decade. He also opposed an air strike against Soviet surface-to-air missile (SAMs) sites in Cuba in response to the downing of an American U-2 reconnaissance aircraft over the island and the death of its pilot. Word of the loss came on Saturday morning at the tensest moment of the crisis in Washington. Chairman of the Joint Chiefs of Staff, General Maxwell Taylor, demanded immediate retaliation, as promised earlier by the president, who had foreseen the possibility of this situation arising. McNamara incurred the wrath of the Joint Chiefs and other senior officers by speaking out against the air strike on the grounds that it would invite further escalation. His opposition to the air strike helped the president to stand firm and to avoid the kind of escalation that could ineluctably have led to an American invasion of Cuba. We now know that Soviet forces on that island were armed with nuclear weapons, and had orders to use them against invading American forces and the ships that transported them.[3]

MAD was intended to reduce the likelihood of war by maximizing the deterrent value of the nuclear weapons of both superpowers. McNamara understood that the greatest danger of nuclear war arose from the fear of a crippling first strike. This fear could tempt either side to preempt in a serious crisis, especially if their adversary was detected bringing its forces up to a higher state of alert.

MAD was avowedly a city-busting strategy, and McNamara publicly opposed "war-fighting" strategies that would deploy weapons with sufficient accuracy to destroy enemy command and control and missile silos. In private, he encouraged the modernization of America's strategic arsenal, and the subsequent development of war-fighting capabilities by both superpowers led to a prolonged and intensified arms race.[4]

McNamara and Kennedy were responsible for a massive strategic buildup that continued even after satellite intelligence revealed that there was no "missile gap" in favor of the Soviet Union. Soviet sources indicate that the U.S. buildup, coupled with public and private threats from Kennedy and McNamara's subordinates to exploit their first-strike advantage, were a prime incentive for Khrushchev to send missiles to Cuba in the hope of restoring some kind of balance. They also provoked a counter-buildup by the Soviet Union.[5]

McNamara was also duplicitous in his approach to strategy. He committed the United States publicly to MAD, while secretly encouraging and approving efforts to increase the accuracy and capability of American missiles. In 1966, he authorized enlargement of the Minuteman missile's third stage, leading to the creation of the Minuteman III. His goal was to pave the way for the ultimate deployment of multiple independently retargetable entry vehicles (MIRVs), which would allow a Minuteman missile to deliver up to ten warheads against Soviet targets with a high degree of accuracy. McNamara's advisors recognized that MIRVs would permit the "enhancement of a first-strike capability" for U.S. strategic forces, and "the issue of first strike capability was raised and widely discussed" at the time.[6] The deployment of the Mark-12 MIRV reentry system in 1970 intensified Soviet insecurity, led to the subsequent deployment of MIRVs and larger missiles capable of delivering many more warheads, and provided further impetus to the superpower arms race. By the time of the 1975 Helsinki Agreement, the fundamental territorial and political issues in Europe that had triggered the Cold War were resolved. The Cold War nevertheless intensified over the course of the next decade, and in large part because of strategic insecurities. The development and deployment of ever more capable nuclear weapons and their delivery systems, initially a response to mutual fears of war, now became a principal cause of those fears. McNamara and Kennedy bear at least some share of responsibility for this development.

The consummate technocrat

Like a skilled surfer, young McNamara positioned himself perfectly (MBA in 1939 from Harvard Business School) to ride the crest of the wave, and what a ride it was. From service in the Army Air Force, where he used his technical and organizational skills to facilitate the destruction of Japanese cities, to the Ford Motor Company and its presidency, to secretary of defense in the Kennedy administration, where he played a major—some would say dominant—role in bringing about and managing the catastrophic American intervention in Vietnam. Before that wave dashed itself against the rocks, he had the good fortune to cut loose and find another wave—the World Bank—to carry him to the tidal pool of retirement. Even here, occasional surges of undertow—his books on Vietnam, and now *Fog of War*—threaten to take him back out to open water.

For political scientists, the waves are more important than their rider. And these waves were driven by a powerful current of faith that most problems are amenable to technical solutions, and that clear, logical thinking and good data can discover those solutions and make their implementation more effective and efficient. The technocratic approach to problems has led to remarkable progress, especially in the material domain, but it has not come without costs. In Robert McNamara's case, it is responsible for both his accomplishments and his failings, and presents us with a micro case in which to assess the consequences of policy formulated in an ethical vacuum.

Toward the end of the proto-Enlightenment of fifth-century Athens, Sophocles wrote *Oedipus* to warn his fellow citizens of the danger of rationality divorced from principle. In the seventeenth century, Vico[7] warned that "too much reason could lead back to barbarism." Nietzsche picked up on this theme and posited a sharp opposition between the Apollonian art of sculpture and the nonplastic Dionysian art of music.[8] The world of the intellect is Apollonian, and detrimental to the human spirit. Nietzsche insisted that it had dominated Western philosophy and culture since Socrates. Weber gave Nietzsche's dichotomy[9] a modern twist by reframing it as a conflict between charisma and bureaucracy. He associated charisma with human creativity, which found its fullest expression in the man of culture (*Kulturmensch*). Bureaucracy was stifling this creativity by organizing life around dehumanizing routines and empowering the expert but soulless technician (*Fachmensch*). As reason shaped the structure and ends (*Zweckrationalität*) of all kinds of human activities, including religion, art, and the academy, it led to a corresponding disenchantment with nature and the mysteries of life, and with it, a loss of wholeness and decline in communal identification.

Weber argued that the power of bureaucracy was inexorable because

> From a purely technical point of view, a bureaucracy is capable of attaining the highest degree of efficiency, and is in this sense formally the most rational known means of exercising authority over human beings. It is superior to any other form in precision, in stability, in the stringency of its discipline, and in its reliability. It thus makes possible a particularly high degree of calculability of results for the heads of the organization and for those acting in relation to it. It is finally superior both in intensive efficiency and in the scope of its operations and is formally capable of application to all kinds of administrative tasks.[10]

Bureaucracy encourages "Precision, speed, unambiguity, knowledge of the files, continuity, discretion, unity, strict subordination, reduction of friction and of material and personal costs—these are raised to the optimum point in the strictly bureaucratic organization."[11] Karl Mannheim grasped the most disturbing implication of the Nietzsche-Weber vision: runaway rationality—by individuals or organizations—inevitably leads to irrationality.[12] It finds expression in efforts to impose order and routinized responses on a protean, ever-shifting and ultimately uncontrollable world. At the same time, organizational goals are increasingly generated in response to internal imperatives and are correspondingly detached from external reality and ethics. When he penned these words, Mannheim had Nazi Germany in mind, but his argument, and the Weberian foundation on which it rests, apply equally well, but differently, to the United States. Representatives of the Frankfurt School would make a related and even more influential critique of modernity based on their readings of Marx and Freud.[13] I have chosen to build on the Weber–Mannheim critique because its stresses the role of bureaucracy; Weber correctly foresaw too that socialism "would mean a tremendous increase in the importance of professional bureaucrats" independently of its link to capitalism. He also focuses more directly on the ethical horizons of those who make careers in large bureaucracies.[14]

The United States is less bureaucratic than most European countries, but it is the society in which modernity—which found expression, according to Weber, in the standardization, commercialization and quantitative evaluation of all aspects of life—has gone the furthest. The powers that opposed and retarded its progress in Europe—a well-entrenched aristocracy, conservative, state-supported religions and longstanding class divisions—were nonexistent or weaker in the United States. It is no coincidence that the assembly line, Taylorism, modern advertising, push-button warfare, and a belief that heaven resembles upper-middle-class suburbia, replete with SUVs, are all American inventions. For the same reasons, it is also the country in which science, professionalism and ethnic and religious tolerance have achieved their fullest development or expression.

The career of Robert McNamara provides a stunning illustration of the downside of Weberian modernity. While he was merely an enthusiastic functionary in the American bombing campaign of Japan, that campaign deliberately blurred the distinction between military and civilians and sought to kill, maim and make homeless as many of the latter as possible. One of its great achievements was the fire bombing of Tokyo, in part an experiment to test the premise that a large enough fire would be to a great extent self-sustaining by creating currents to draw in oxygen from beyond its perimeter. The deaths of 100,000 civilians—the estimated casualties of the greatest fire bombing raids on March 9–10, 1945—were a welcome byproduct of organizational self-promotion and scientific curiosity run amok.[15]

The Ford Motor Company did not directly kill people, but it was notorious, even in the auto industry, for treating its workers as expendable resources to be manipulated and coerced in pursuit of profit. McNamara joined the company following his discharge from the Air Force in 1946 at a time when the company was anxious to regain its full authority over the shop floor, which it had agreed to share with trade unions to stimulate wartime production. Ford speeded up the production lines and cut back on relief workers in violation of the agreement it had negotiated with the United Auto Workers. These measures, which put worker safety at risk, were designed to compensate for stoppages in the assembly lines caused by administrative failures in coordinating the flow of parts that fed lines at the Lincoln and River Rouge assembly plants. Ford management refused to recognize the union's competence to raise the issue of production standards, hired thugs to beat up and intimidate protesting workers and, not surprisingly, goaded the UAW into a major and relatively successful strike in 1949.[16] Throughout the 1950s, relations between management and workers remained tense as Ford continued to violate agreements it had signed with the union about production standards and pay structure.

McNamara was part of Ford's management team throughout this period; he became a director in 1957 and president in 1960. He introduced the same methods of operations research that had guided target selection and the logistics of the bombing campaign. By rationalizing the procedures of supply and production—and treating the human component as merely another quantitative input in the process—he brought "efficiency" and profit to Ford. As Weber predicted, organizational goals and procedures became the only yardsticks for evaluating decisions and behavior. Reneging on contractual commitments to unions and workers, and intimidating them to the extent that the company's power permitted, were reasonable actions to the executives and technocrats whose understanding of justice was synonymous with organizational goals. Such a labor policy was not only unethical, it was significantly at odds with substantive rationality, as it led to slowdowns, stoppages of the production line, sabotage and strikes.[17] In the 1960s, an increasingly sizeable percentage of the American automobile market was captured by more efficient European and Japanese firms, much of whose advantage derived from better and more productive relations with their workers.

McNamara moved from Ford to the Kennedy administration, where he became one of the principal architects of the Vietnam War. Intervention in Vietnam was motivated by visceral U.S. anti-communism and an exaggerated fear of falling dominos.[18] Its implementation was characterized by the same arrogance of reason and callousness toward human beings that was so evident at Ford. Intervention, like auto production, was narrowly framed by McNamara and his assistants at Defense as a technical problem. They dismissed the French experience as irrelevant, and never doubted that superior U.S. firepower would compel North Vietnam to accept the political independence of the South. They devised all kinds of quantifiable measures—including the infamous body count—to assess progress toward victory. McNamara and the other hawks in the Johnson administration did not recognize that military intervention was doomed from the outset for reasons that McNamara would ultimately come to understand.

At Geneva in 1954, the Eisenhower administration had insisted on the temporary division of Vietnam, and installed a puppet regime in the South headed by a Northern Catholic refugee, Ngo Dinh Diem. With full American support, Diem renounced the unification provision of the Geneva Accords and the 1956 elections that were to bring it about. By the time the Johnson administration began its air war against North Vietnam in 1964, there were 200,000 U.S. military personnel in the country, plus a large aid mission, all with the purpose of propping up the increasingly unpopular Diem regime. Secure in American support, Diem did his best to roll back land reform, extract rents through every kind of corrupt practice, and murder or imprison opponents who ranged across almost the entire political spectrum. There are still pundits who insist that different military tactics would have led to victory, but this is a pipedream.[19] Vietnam was a political struggle, and American military intervention was a response to loss of that struggle and the impending collapse of its local client. It should have been obvious—and was to many observers at the time—that military intervention could not extract roasting chestnuts from the fire but only make that fire brighter.

Unless we consider "anti-communism" an ethical concern, ethics never entered seriously into the deliberations of the Johnson administration about intervention. Nor did the president and his secretary of defense gave much thought to the possible contradiction between the ends they sought and means they embraced to achieve them. Was the goal of an independent South Vietnam—one that is not controlled by communists—worth the blood and treasure this would entail? And just how much bloodshed was there likely to be? What kinds of strategies and tactics might minimize these human and economic costs and maximize the chances of achieving the desired end? Driven by its foreign and domestic political goals, and cocksure in its expectation of success, the administration entered the fray without ever seriously considering the likely human costs and political downside of military intervention—in contrast to its fixation on the putative costs of nonintervention. It just assumed that the means at its disposal would work. But an American-supported coup against Diem in November 1963, and subsequent behind-the-scenes maneuvering, failed to bring to power governments capable of mobilizing much in the way of popular support. On the military front, the massive use of firepower was often quite arbitrary, sometimes obliterating entire villages and their residents. It was apparent to critics, some of them retired military officers, that American tactics were entirely unsuitable to a guerrilla war, and increased the flow of recruits to the Viet Cong. Even if U.S. policy makers considered ethics only in its narrowest, instrumental sense, they ought to have considered the negative consequences of their behavior for their international reputation. Ironically, concern for reputation was a principal motive for intervention, and here too, no serious analysis was undertaken of the assumptions on which the expectation of falling dominos rested. At a deeper level, rationalization and bureaucratization—just as Weber feared—rode roughshod over the Kantian imperative. People were treated as means, not as ends. Japanese civilians in the 1940s, auto workers in the 1950s and Vietnamese civilians and American conscripts in the 1960s were objects to destroy, exploit or expend. In Vietnam it was done in pursuit of unattainable and thus irrational ends.

Vietnam redux

In recent years, McNamara has reexamined the Vietnam War in two books, the most recent of them based on conferences and discussions with North Vietnamese. Four decades after the fact, he "is aghast at the shallowness of our thinking," recognizes that fears of falling dominoes were misplaced, and maintains a military solution to the problem was never possible and constituted "a dangerous illusion" [all italics are McNamara's].[20] He believes that Kennedy should have turned to France for political assistance in seeking a neutral solution; and that, in retrospect, the entire 1961–4 period was "a large missed [political] opportunity" to do this.[21] He concedes that the pretext for war and its congressional authorization—the August 4 attack on American destroyers in the Gulf of Tonkin—never occurred, and that the attack two days earlier was a response to covert provocations by the United States and South Vietnam.[22] He acknowledges that the extensive bombing of the North that followed the Gulf of Tonkin Resolution was the beginning of a "war of destruction" and entirely counterproductive because it provoked an all-out effort by Hanoi to defeat Saigon before the United States could intervene in force.[23] He dismisses hawkish claims that more bombing or troops might have produced a favorable outcome, and quotes, with seeming approval, the observation of North Vietnamese colonel and strategic analyst Quach Hai Luong that additional combat forces would only have hastened the U.S. defeat. These troops would have been spread out around South Vietnam, providing more targets for the North Vietnamese and Viet Cong strategy of sapping support on the home front through a war of attrition.[24] Air attacks did little damage to an almost totally agricultural country. They also sustained North Vietnamese morale. "The more you bombed." Col. Luong reported, "the more the people wanted to fight you."[25] McNamara cites official DOD studies that support Luong's contention that years of bombing had no effect on Hanoi's capability to wage war or send men and materiel south. Instead, it "strengthened, rather than weakened, the will of the Hanoi government and its people".[26] In the South, McNamara admits, bombing and the introduction of ground troops led to "disdain for the South Vietnamese people themselves." They revealed "an insoluble contradiction" between "the overriding U.S. political objective of the war and the actual situation on the ground in South Vietnam."[27]

McNamara deserves credit for distancing himself from the hawks who still think the war was winnable, and for offering cogent reasons why it was not. His approach to Vietnam is still characterized by the same arrogance that was initially responsible for intervention. Every argument he puts forward about why the war was unwinnable was advanced back in the 1960s by anti-war journalists, some scholars, former government officials and retired military officers. McNamara does not acknowledge this unsettling truth, but rather presents his thesis that the war was unwinnable as a novel discovery that could only have been found by dint of his diligent research of the records and soul-searching talks with former Vietnamese enemies.

How did the Indochina tragedy come to pass? McNamara attributes American political and military misjudgments to an unavoidable "failure of empathy" and "lack of communication" between two such radically different cultures.[28] This self-serving is intended to exonerate the Kennedy administration of responsibility for the war. It is also unsupportable. The administration had access to Vietnamese experts in the State Department and the CIA, former French officials and leading authorities in academia (e.g., Frances Fitzgerald, George Kahin), who predicted the likely Vietnamese responses to American military pressure and were not reticent about opposing the war. The problem was not lack of information or understanding, but cognitive closure. It insulated McNamara and other high officials in the Johnson administration from the experts or from treating seriously what they had to say. Not for the last time, an administration would rely on military power over diplomacy, and organizational routines over creatively crafted responses in pursuit of highly questionable and unrealistic goals. Equally self-serving are McNamara's efforts to make the North Vietnamese admit to their own illusions (e.g., that the United States was a colonial power), and to use this admission to argue that a diplomatic settlement was made equally impossible by North Vietnamese misunderstanding and recalcitrance.[29] It was not the North Vietnamese who spurned neutrality at the end of World War II, or who created a political crisis by dividing Vietnam, importing a Northern Catholic émigré to run the South and supporting him for almost a decade despite the rapacious nature of his regime and violent repression of opponents. Nor did Hanoi escalate the war through bombing and military intervention; most of their military moves, as McNamara now recognizes, were in response to American escalations. The blame is not equal, but squarely on the shoulders of the United States, and those members of the Johnson administration who favored the use of force.

Missing from McNamara's books is any discussion of ethics, and whether carpet bombing, search-and-destroy operations, the torture of captives and the extension of the war to Cambodia under Nixon and Kissinger were justified, even if the political assumptions that prompted them had been valid. McNamara never progresses beyond an evaluation of means independently of the ends they were intended to serve. His latter-day hand-wringing and grudging admission—buried toward the end of one of his books—that many American misconceptions reflected what he refers to in the third person as "the natural arrogance of the powerful"[30] is the closest he comes to an apology. Both his books on the war are clever exercises of self-exoneration and, as such, are a further injustice to the 3.8 million Vietnamese and 58,000 Americans who lost their lives in what he now concedes was an unnecessary struggle.

Now 88 years of age, McNamara, is still in top form. In *Fog of War*, his books and at his Berkeley interview, he always has appropriate factoids at hand. One of those nuggets—the estimate that 160 million people died violent deaths in the twentieth century—comes off his lips with some frequency. Much of this carnage is undeniably attributable to psychopathic leaders like Stalin, Hitler, Mao

Zedong, Pol Pot, and Saddam Hussein. But many wars—like Vietnam and Iraq—
were initiated by leaders who were not evil in the sense of deriving pleasure from
the destruction of other people. The psychopaths could not have wreaked such
destruction, and the saner leaders might have exercised more restraint, if they
had not been served by stables of able and encouraging technocrats. McNamara
might properly reflect upon the sobering thought that one of the reasons why the
last century's death toll was so stunningly high is that there are so many officials
like him in high and low places around the world.

Lessons of the past, wars of the present

Victors write history, and Western histories of World War II have given great
play—and properly so—to the war crimes of Nazi Germany and Imperial Japan
and, once the Cold War began, to those of Stalin's Russia. The war crimes of the
Allies have never been recognized as such, and even muted attempts to offer different perspectives on Hiroshima and Nagasaki have met strong and generally
effective protests from veteran associations, military officers and other conservative groups. The controversy and ultimate cancellation in April 1995 of a planned
exhibit of the *Enola Gay*—the B-29 that dropped the atomic bomb over Hiroshima—at the National Air and Space Museum is a case in point. Museum director Martin Harwit was planning to display photographs of Hiroshima victims
and Japanese understandings of the event alongside traditional American interpretations. The Air Force Association and Veterans of Foreign Wars organized a
letter-writing campaign to members of Congress, planted stories, many of them
false or distorted, in the media and brought pressure to bear on the Smithsonian
Institution, the parent organization of the museum to cancel the exhibit and fire
its director. The Museum, dependent on congressional funding, caved in to the
opposition, and Harwit was all but compelled to submit his resignation.[31]

The bombing of German cities, the fire bombings of Hamburg, Dresden and
Tokyo, and the atomic bombing of Hiroshima and Nagasaki are repeatedly justified as "tit-for-tat" revenge for the bombing of London and Pearl Harbor, or as
unpalatable but necessary actions to save allied lives and hasten the end of World
War II.[32] Professional historians and a few journalists aside, there appears to be
little inclination in the United States or Great Britain to acknowledge that World
War II witnessed inhumane behavior by all participants. It is undeniable that Nazi
Germany was unspeakably evil, and the Japanese were aggressive imperialists
who had no concern for the lives or well-being of those they conquered, captured
or simply exploited for economic and sexual ends. For six decades, the evil of
Axis powers has provided a cover for Anglo-American smugness about their roles
in World War II. As in the *Enola Gay* affair, much of the opposition to any challenge of the prevailing narrative comes from government officials and active duty
and retired military officers.

Postwar Germany did not have the same luxury with respect to its past. There
were pressing political and economic reasons for the Federal Republic (FRG) to

acknowledge and distance itself from the crimes of the Nazi period. Even so, Germany's efforts to address the past and accept responsibility for a war of aggression, extermination campaigns against Jew, Gypsies, and gays, the use of slave labor and other evils, were dilatory and painful, and took several generations to confront. In the 1950s, the Adenauer government began paying reparations to Israel and Holocaust survivors, opened relations with Israel, and *Der Alte* traveled to Jerusalem in 1966. Serious rewriting of German history, memorialization of the sites of past crimes, and efforts to educate the German people about their Nazi past really did not get under way until the 1960s. Known as *Vergangenheitsbewältigung* (literally, overcoming the past), such efforts deepened the foundation of democracy in the FRG, and convinced its neighbors that Germans had become responsible Europeans.[33] It enabled Germany to exercise more leadership in Europe and made reunification with East Germany acceptable to other Europeans.[34] There were other catalysts to be sure, but Germany's struggle with its past helped to stimulate and compel many other European countries, especially those in the east, to embark on similar efforts.[35]

American failure to come to grips with its past has had negative consequences for the country. It has allowed the American military and national security establishment to perpetuate practices that are organizationally entrenched but morally questionable, strategically unjustified and politically counterproductive. Two in particular warrant our attention: the utility of all kinds of bombing, and the value; of using force to sustain or overthrow pro- or anti-American regimes. The debate about bombing, which began almost immediately after World War II, has been conducted almost entirely in utilitarian terms.[36] Studies pro and con have evaluated the extent to which strategic bombing achieved its stated goals in World War II, and with some exceptions (e.g., Sherwin, Walzer, Bundy, the Catholic bishops in the 1980s), American analysts do not pay much attention to the ethical issues that surround bombing.[37] The same is true of bombing for purposes of interdiction in Korea and Indochina, and as a form of compellence against North Vietnam.[38] The national security establishment, and branches of the armed forces for whom it is a central mission, continue to assume that bombing of all kinds is effective, and all the more so since the development of increasingly accurate forms of precision guidance. They further assume, as do many Americans, that bombing is an attractive strategy because of its putative ability to save American lives, even though in the past it has destroyed and maimed millions of other human beings, many of them innocent bystanders and children. War, as Clausewitz taught us, is fought for political ends.[39] Military means must be assessed in terms of how they contribute to those goals, and it does not make sense to use unreflexively means that have most often been counterproductive to the goals sought and, since World War II, damaging to U.S. prestige by virtue of the opposition they arouse at home or from important third parties.

The broader issue of near-unilateral intervention is made problematic by American failure in Indochina. The anti-war movement challenged the moral and political basis of the war, and while public opinion turned against intervention, most Americans were clearly uncomfortable with any interpretation that characterized the United States as the aggressor. A kind of collective amnesia about the war set in, and conservative forces began to propagate the view that America lost the war because of the military restraint it exercised. This restraint in turn is usually explained by lack of support at home, undermined by left-leaning intellectuals and the liberal media. This "stab-in-the-back" thesis gained widespread support, just as its predecessor, the infamous *"Dolchstoss"*—which attributed Germany's defeat in World War I to socialist sabotage on the home front—did in the Weimar Republic. The "yellow ribbon" campaign during the Persian Gulf War of January–February 1991, by demonstrating support for our combat troops, helped to overcome the residual trauma caused by Vietnam and effectively strengthened the hands of those who equate dissent with lack of patriotism.

Continuing belief in the efficacy of bombing and military intervention helped to explain the propensity of the Bush administration to invade Iraq in 2003, just as the national failure to address the human consequences of such activities made opposition more difficult. The debate over intervention in the United States turned on the question of whether or not Saddam had weapons of mass destruction, not on the likely consequences of intervention, the morality of the means that were being used and what implications they might have for the proclaimed goal of making Iraq a democratic, pro-American country.

The United States has been so powerful relative to Vietnam that it has been able to write the history of that conflict even though it lost the war. McNamara's conferences and books are part of this project. We have to consider the possibility that a similar effort to impose meaning on the war will take place in the aftermath of the Iraq intervention, regardless of how negative its outcome for the United States. To the extent that these interpretations build on powerful, preexisting World War II and Vietnam narratives that serve psychological and institutional ends, they hinder American efforts to learn from the past and escape from destructive scripts.

Max Weber recognized that politicians continually face ethical dilemmas, and must sometimes use "morally dubious" means to achieve appropriate ends. He knew too that leaders must trust in their own judgments, as there is no way of judging objectively among competing sets of values. He nevertheless expected good leaders to have values, and to follow an "ethic of responsibility," which entailed efforts to evaluate ends and means in terms of those values. Even so, Weber warned, politics could quickly become tragic because "the eventual outcome of political action frequently, indeed regularly, stands in a quite inadequate, even paradoxical relation to its original, intended meaning and purpose." Tragic outcomes are more likely when policy is made by leaders—like McNamara and top officials in the Bush administration—who refuse to confront the ethical implications of their behavior.[40]

Notes

1 Dean E. Murphy, "In Berkeley, Finding Common Ground on Vietnam." *New York Times*, February 6, 2004, p. A14.

2 McGeorge Bundy, *Danger and Survival: Choices About the Bomb in the First Fifty Years* (New York: Random House, 1988), pp. 319–24; Fred Kaplan, *The Wizards of Armageddon* (New York: Simon and Schuster, 1983), pp. 263–86; Desmond Ball, *Politics and Force Levels: The Strategic Missile Program of the Kennedy Administration* (Berkeley: University of California Press, 1980), pp. 72–3, 134–5; Desmond Ball and Jeffrey Richelson (eds.), *Strategic Nuclear Targeting* (Ithaca, NY: Cornell University Press, 1986), pp. 57–83.

3 Bundy, *Danger and Survival*, pp. 391–462; Richard Ned Lebow & Janice Gross Stein, *We All Lost the Cold War* (Princeton, NJ: Princeton University Press, 1994), pp. 97, 110–48.

4 Kaplan, *The Wizards of Armageddon*, pp. 248–57; Ball, *Politics and Force Levels*, pp. 107–64.

5 Ball, *Politics and Force Levels*, pp. 107–64; Lebow & Stein, *We All Lost the Cold War*, pp. 32–41.

6 Daniel Buchonnet, *MIRV: A Brief History of Minuteman and Multiple Reentry Vehicles* (Livermore, CA: Lawrence Livermore Laboratory, 1976), pp. 9–12; Ted Greenwood, *Making of the MIRV: A Study of Defense Decision Making* (Cambridge, MA: Ballinger, 1975), pp. 65–79.

7 Giambattista Vico, *The New Science*, trans. Thomas G. Bergin & Max H. Fisch (Ithaca, NY: Cornell University Press, 1948).

8 Friedrich Nietzsche, "The Birth of Tragedy," in *Basic Writings of Nietzsche*, ed. and trans. Walter Kaufmann (New York: Modern Library, 1962).

9 Max Weber, *The Methodology of the Social Sciences*, ed. Edward Shils & Henry Finch (New York: Free Press, 1949).

10 Max Weber, *Max Weber on Law in Economy and Society*, ed. Max Rheinstein, trans. Edward Shils & Max Rheinstein (New York: Simon and Schuster, 1968), p. 223.

11 Max Weber, *From Max Weber*, ed. and trans H. H. Gerth and C. Wright Mills (New York: Galaxy, 1958).

12 Karl Mannheim, *Man and Society in an Age of Reconstruction: Studies in Modern Social Structure* (New York: Harcourt and Brace, 1940), pp. 39–75.

13 Max Horkheimer and Theodor W. Adorno [1944]. *Dialectic of Enlightenment*, trans. John W. Cumming (New York: Continuum, 1982); Herbert Marcuse, *One Dimensional Man; Studies in the Ideology of Advanced Capitalist Society* (Boston: Beacon Press, 1964).

14 Weber, *Max Weber on Law in Economy and Society*, p. 224.

15 Williamson Murray and Allan R. Millett, *A War to Be Won: Fighting the Second World War* (Cambridge, MA: Harvard University Press, 2000), pp. 503–8.

16 Robert Asher and Ronald Edsforth, *Autowork* (Albany: State University of New York Press, 1995), pp. 127–54.

17 Asher and Edsforth, *Autowork*, pp. 127–54, 209–26.

18 Frederick Logevall, *Choosing War: The Last Chance for Peace and the Escalation of War in Vietnam* (Berkeley: University of California Press, 1999), pp.43–75; Robert S McNamara, James G. Blight, and Robert K. Brigham, *Argument Without End: In*

Search of Answers to the Vietnam Tragedy (New York: Public Affairs, 1999), pp. 99, 148, 155–6.

19 Jeffrey Record, "Vietnam in Retrospect: Could We Have Won?" *Parameters* 26, 1996–7, pp. 51–65.

20 McNamara et al., *Argument Without End*, pp. 99: 148, 187, 191, 318, 368–9.

21 McNamara et al., *Argument Without End*, pp. 149–50.

22 McNamara et al., *Argument Without End*, pp. 157, 166–8, 184–6.

23 McNamara et al., *Argument Without End*, pp. 157–8, 189.

24 McNamara et al., *Argument Without End*, p. 193.

25 McNamara et al., *Argument Without End*, p. 194.

26 McNamara et al., *Argument Without End*, pp. 341–2, 191.

27 McNamara et al., *Argument Without End*, p. 354.

28 McNamara et al., *Argument Without End*, p. 376.

29 McNamara et al., *Argument Without End*, p. 380.

30 McNamara et al., *Argument Without End*, p. 385.

31 Martin Harwit, *An Exhibit Denied: Lobbying the History of Enola Gay* (New York: Springer-Verlag. 1996); Richard H. Kohn, "History at Risk: The Case of the Enola Gay," in Edward T. Linenthal and Tom Engelhardt, *History Wars: The Enola Gay and Other Battles for the American Past* (New York: Henry Holt, 1996).

32 Paul Boyer, "Whose History is it Anyway? Memory, Politics, and Historical Scholarship," in Linenthal and Engelhardt, *History Wars*, pp. 114–24, 130–9.

33 The term *Vergangenheitsbewältigung* was coined in the late 1950s. At the outset, it was ironic in intent, and often placed in quotation marks to indicate scorn for the self-serving nature of so-called soul-searching inquiries into Germany's Nazi past. The term gradually lost its ironic association and took on a broader meaning. It now refers to all efforts, from writing, to television, to museums, to learning appropriate political and moral lessons from the Nazi era, and applying them to the present.

34 Wulf Kansteiner, *In Pursuit of Germany Memory: History, Television, and Politics After Auschwitz* (Athens, OH: University of Ohio Press, 2005).

35 Richard Ned Lebow, Wulf Kansteiner, and Claudio Fogu (eds.) *The Politics of Memory in Postwar Europe* (Durham, NC: Duke University Press, 2006).

36 United States War Department, The United States Strategic Bombing Survey, Summary Report (European War), 30 September 1945, available at http://www.anesi.com/ussbs02.htm#pagei (accessed November 2005); United States War Department, The United States Strategic Bombing Survey, Summary Report (Pacific War), July 1, 1946, available at http://www.anesi.com/ussbs01.htm (accessed November 2005); Robert Pape, *Bombing to Win: Air Power and Coercion in War* (Ithaca, NY: Cornell University Press, 1996); Gian P. Gentile, *How Effective is Strategic Bombing: Lessons Learned from World War II to Kosovo* (New York: New York University Press, 2000).

37 Martin J. Sherwin, *A World Destroyed: The Atomic Bomb and the Grand Alliance* (New York: Knopf, 1975); Michael Waltzer, *Just and Unjust Wars: A Moral Argument with Historical Illustrations* (New York: Basic Books, 1977); Bundy, *Danger and Survival*.

38 Thomas Schelling, *Arms and Influence* (New Haven, CT: Yale University Press, 1966); Pape, *Bombing to Win*.

39 Carl Clausewitz, *On War*, ed. and trans. Michael Howard and Peter Paret (Princeton, NJ: Princeton University Press, 1976), pp. 75, 80–1.
40 Weber, *From Max Weber*, pp. 75, 121–3, 125–6.

References

Richardson, Elliot L. (1992). "Climate Change: Problems of Law-Making," in Andrew Hurrell and Benedict Kingsbury (eds.). *The International Politics of the Environment*, pp. 166–79. Oxford: Oxford University Press.

Schelling, Thomas C. (1960). *The Strategy of Conflict*. Cambridge, MA: Harvard University Press.

Snidal, Duncan C. (1985). "The Limits of Hegemonic Stability Theory," *International Organization* 39(4): 579–614.

Stokke, Olav S. (1992). "Environmental Performance Review: Concept and Design," in Erik Lykke (ed.), *Achieving Environmental Goals. The Concept and Practice of Environmental Performance Review*, pp. 3–24. London: Belhaven Press.

Strang, David, and Patricia M.Y. Chang (1993). "The ILO and the Welfare State," *International Organization* 47(2): 235–262.

Underdal, Arild (1992). "The Concept of Regime 'Effectiveness.'" *Cooperation and Conflict* 27(3): 227–40.

Underdal, Arild (1994). "Progress in the Absence of Substantive Joint Decisions?" in Ted Hanisch (ed.), *Climate Change and the Agenda for Research*. Boulder, CO: Westview Press.

Victor, David G., Kal Raustiala, and Eugene B. Skolnikoff (eds.). (forthcoming) *The Implementation and Effectiveness of International Environmental Commitments*. Cambridge, MA: MIT Press.

Walton, Richard E. and Robert B. McKersie (1965). *A Behavioral Theory of Labor Negotiations*. New York: McGraw-Hill.

Wendt, Alexander. (1992). "Anarchy is What Stakes Make of It: The Social Construction of Power Polities," *International Organization*, 46(2): 391–425.

Wilson, James Q. (1973). *Political Organizations*. New York: Basic Books.

Young, Oran R. (1979). *Compliance and Public Authority*. Baltimore: The Johns Hopkins University Press, for Resources for the Future.

Young, Oran R. (1994). *International Governance*. Ithaca, NJ: Cornell University Press.

Young, Oran R., and Gail Osherenko. (1993). "Testing Theories of Regime Formation," in Volker Rittberger (ed.), *Regime Theory and International Relations*, pp. 223–51. Oxford: Clarendon Press.

Part IV

Cooperation

9 Reason, emotion, and cooperation

Introduction

Cooperation and its absence are hot topics in international relations. The former is at heart of the European project, and so in some ways is the latter. The survival of NATO beyond the Cold War, and the desire of former communist states to join, illustrates the robust nature of certain forms of cooperation. From the perspective of the Bush administration, the failure of NATO to participate in the so-called Coalition of the Willing, or to assume the kind of "out of area" responsibilities perennially sought after by Washington is a stunning example of noncooperation. Not only alliances but also states and the societies on which they rest are held together by various forms of cooperation, the breakdown of which lead to state collapse and civil war.

Cooperation is also on the front burner of international relations theory. In part, this is a response to the issues that dominate the headlines. More fundamentally, it is a response to the realist framing of the international environment as anarchic. In the absence of a hegemon or other means of enforcing order and contracts, cooperation is supposed to occur on a case-by-case basis, and regarded as anomalous if it outlives the interests or other conditions that brought it about. There is a large and growing literature that attempts to explain enduring forms of cooperation under conditions of anarchy. Some approaches, including those rooted in neo-liberalism and constructivism, contend that some regional systems and. to a lesser extent, the international system have been able to escape the most baneful consequences of anarchy. Modelers have tried to show how a degree of order in the form of cooperation can emerge at the system level as the unintended result of purely selfish behavior at the individual level.

The liberal institutionalist, social capital, and "thin" constructivist approaches are considered competing explanations for cooperation. They nevertheless rely on the same explanatory mechanisms imported from micro-economics. They invoke external stimuli in the form of environmental constraints and incentives, or the behavior of other actors. They also share a common unit of analysis: the egoistic, individual actor.

I begin with a critical review of these several explanations for cooperation that highlights their common limitations and how these limitations arise from common assumptions. I then question the utility of their ontology. Drawing on literature from philosophy, sociology, and psychology, I argue that the concept of the autonomous individual is a fiction of the Enlightenment, and that such actors, when they can be found, are generally regarded as sociopaths.

I then turn to the second assumption: that behavior is primarily a response to external incentives. They are undeniably an important catalyst of behavior, but the definition of an incentive and the reasons why it is important depend on the prior identities and interests of actors. Interests follow from identities, and the latter are shaped by the societies in which actors live and the relationships they have formed. Relationships encourage people to frame their interests in collective terms (e.g., as members of partnerships, families, locales, businesses, ethnic groups, classes, religions, nations). My analysis suggests that actors often develop a more general propensity to cooperate with one another, or with members of a community. Such a propensity not only provides a deeper explanation for case-by-case cooperation, but also accounts for why cooperation can occur in situations where it does not appear to be in the immediate interest of one or more of the parties involved.

The several approaches I critique rely heavily on the role of reason. Calculation is undeniably important to all kinds of cooperation, but so is affect. Emotions, I contend, are absolutely fundamental to creating any general propensity to cooperate with a given group of actors. Recognition of the importance of emotions in this connection is widespread among the world's great philosophical and religious traditions. To understand cooperation, we must look at the interaction between reason and emotion and identity and learning.

My argument draws on ancient Greek psychology and philosophy and its modern counterparts and the nineteenth- and twentieth-century literature in political science and international relations, sociology, and experimental economics.

Four accounts of cooperation

Institutions

Neoliberals direct our attention to formally established bodies (e.g., NATO, IMF, GATT) and the ways in which their rules and procedures can shape the expectations of actors. Relying on concepts from economics, they make far-reaching claims for such institutions. They contend that institutions create strong incentives for cooperation by reducing contractual uncertainty. They provide information and mechanisms that enable, and sometimes compel actors to make binding commitments, thus increasing their costs of defection. Over time, the rewards of working through institutions also reduce the benefits of defection (Keohane, 1989; Stein 1990; Shanks et al., 1996; Hajnal, 1999). John Ikenberry's work represents the most sophisticated attempt to apply this argument to the Western alliance, but he is by no means alone in suggesting that the institutions set up by the United States and its partners have set down deep roots and shape their domestic political, economic, and military practices in ways that make the costs of their disruption extraordinarily high and the benefits of competing orders most uncertain (Ikenberry, 2001, 248, 257–73).

Liberal institutionalists may mistake cause for effect. Leaving aside institutions imposed and maintained by coercion, successful institutions build on prior decisions or inclinations by would-be members to regulate and coordinate their behavior. In the absence of this commitment, these institutions are unlikely to provide the advantages attributed to them. Institutions presuppose common interests or the existence of a community with common values and can become the custodians of their norms and procedures (Kratochwil, 1989, 64). Once in place, institutions have the potential to construct more common interests and identities and strengthen the bonds of community. The real question is why and how a prior inclination to cooperate develops.

The different fate of institutions in West and Eastern Europe nicely illustrates the importance of the above observation. The web of institutions established by Moscow was as broad and encompassing as those set up or encouraged by the United States in the postwar period. They did not survive the emergence of a reformist regime in the Soviet Union, and their collapse helped to bring about the collapse of the Soviet Union itself. As long as institutional compliance was enforced by the Soviet Union, member states acquiesced in their outward behavior, just as individual citizens did within states where communist governments were in power. The German Democratic Republic went to Orwellian lengths of impressing almost one-third of its adult citizens into the role of informer in the hope of denying any private spaces and enforcing institutional control in every nook and cranny of life. Efforts at achieving outward compliance were largely successful throughout the Soviet bloc, but did not readily translate into "mind control." Even in the absence of a functioning civil society, East Europeans especially, kept alternative conceptions of history and society alive (Lévesque, 1997; Evangelista, 1999; English, 2000; Lebow, Kansteiner and Fogu, 2006). Opponents of communist regimes also learned how to exploit the outward manifestations of conformity for their own ends (Milosz, 1990, 54–89). In the Soviet Union, almost from the beginning, historians, social scientists, writers and artists of all kinds wrote fiction and non-fiction, or created works of representational or performing art that superficially reproduced, and even appeared to reaffirm, the official discourse and its associated interpretations, while actually subverting them in subtle ways. Readers, viewers and audiences became increasingly adept in their ability to pick up these cues and read, so to speak, between the lines. In the last decade of the Soviet Union, the practice of "double discourse" became increasingly open, with social scientists sometimes able to criticize existing assumptions or policies provided they opened and closed their books and articles with appropriate genuflections to the Marxist canon.

The Soviet and Eastern European cases indicate, pace Aristotle, that there are clear limits to the power of institutions (Poetics, 660). Reactance theory suggests that compliance can be coerced by means of threats and careful surveillance, but once surveillance ceases, compliance will as well (Brehm & Brehm, 1981). The reaction against the order (and the authority behind it) is likely to be in proportion to the degree to which it was imposed, not negotiated. The communist governments in Eastern Europe and the Warsaw Pact accordingly endured only as long as the power propping them up. Nor do institutions fare well in environments where community is weak or lacking, as evidenced by the failure of some Russian stock markets, African governments and the League of Nations (Frye, 2000). Institutions cannot introduce order into societies that most closely resemble the theoretical world of institutional theorists: an anarchical one populated by self-interested actors. Institutions can consolidate and sustain communities, but are, incapable in and of themselves, of creating them.

Social capital

Scholars have looked beyond institutions to societies themselves—at the domestic and international level—in the hope of discovering underlying reasons for order and cooperation. Deploying Marcel Mauss's thesis about exchange in ancient Greece, Robert Putnam argues that "networks of community engagement foster sturdy norms of reciprocity." "Generalized reciprocity" relieves the recipient of having to balance any particular exchange, and creates expectations of further exchanges. Working within the dominant ontology, Putnam reframes cooperation as a narrow collective action problem, and looks to micro-economics for explanations of why autonomous, rational actors cooperate. Not surprisingly, he comes up with the same mechanisms as institutionalists: transparency and the shadow of the future. Economic and political transactions "in dense networks of social interactions" reduce the incentives people might otherwise have for free-riding and malfeasance by helping increase the flow of information and reducing transaction costs (Durkheim, 1984, xxii–xxiii, 38–39; Mauss, 1990; Putnam, 2000, 21–25, 288–89).

Social capital is subject to the same criticism as liberal institutionalism: at best, it describes a secondary process that is a manifestation of an underlying and unexplained propensity to cooperate. In their desire to offer parsimonious and "scientific" explanations for cooperation, both approaches denude the more complex frameworks from which they derive of their deeper explanatory power. Philosophers and anthropologists have a broader conception of institutions than neoliberals. They include a wide range of informal social practices. They are thought to foster cooperation by shaping the discourse of a culture, and thus the way people think, feel and conceive of themselves and their relations to others. Anthropological and sociological conceptions of exchange are also more encompassing. For the ancient Greeks, as understood by Emile Durkheim and Marcel Mauss, participation in a network of ritual exchange and mutual obligation built community by creating affective ties among individuals, providing important shared experiences, and stretching their identities into what Durkheim called *la conscience collective*. Collective identities transformed the meaning of cooperation for members of a community and made cooperation possible. Durkheim was adamant that contracts—by which he also meant institutions—could not create social order. They could only function effectively in societies where order already existed (Durkheim, 1984, 229–30; Connor, 1996, 217–16).

Constructivism

"Thin" constructivist accounts of cooperation also incorporate individual ontologies and consequential choice mechanisms (Green & Shapiro, 1994, 17–19; Keck & Sikkink, 1998; Risse et al., 1999; Checkel, 2001). Alexander Wendt describes the international system as a social creation, with a structure that is more cultural than material. The system nevertheless comprises objective identities; friend, rival, enemy. They are not produced by agents. although their behavior determines the distribution of these identities. Following Bull, Wendt describes three different kinds of anarchy. A Hobbesian or realist world is one in which enemies predominate, and where actors accordingly have unlimited aims, resort to worst-case analysis and pre-emptive behavior and formulate their interests in terms of relative gains. Lockean or liberal anarchy is populated by rivals who accept the right of other actors to exist, allow for neutrality, pursue more limited aims and engage more successfully in balancing and other strategies of conflict management. Kantian or constructivist anarchy, which Wendt speculates, may be in the process of emerging, is dominated by friendly behavior, security communities and the practice of collective security. The degree of cooperation and its causes differ from one kind of anarchy to another; norms may be observed because of coercion, self-interest or their legitimacy (Bull, 1977, 24–7; Wendt, 1999).

While critical of neorealist and neoliberal theories of cooperation, Wendt buys into their ontology. Like Waltz, he assumes the prior existence of materially constituted, uncomplicated and fully autonomous actors whose "only determinable interest, as they enter the arena of interaction, is survival." They have no identity until they interact with other actors at the system level. Wendt fails to distinguish between cooperation and community. The former refers to collaboration on a case-by-case basis, and the latter to a common "we feeling"—to use Karl Deutsch's phrase—that provides an underlying and continuing basis for compromise and cooperation (Deutsch, 1953). Wendt appears to be saying that the international system can promote the emergence of community by transforming identities, but elsewhere in his book he seems to suggest that it merely strengthens cooperation by recasting interests. Wendt differs from Waltz in that he allows for three different kinds of anarchy, each of which corresponds to a different understanding of international relations. While acknowledging such variation, he fails to account for it. The most obvious explanation would be that actors have pre-social identities (whatever that might be), or at least experiences, that generate the expectations and frames of reference they use to interpret the behavior and motives of others. These identities and cognitive predispositions can only come from domestic or international society. Both remain outside his theory (Inayatullab & Blaney, 1997; Pasic, 1997).

"Tit-for-tat"

The most prominent agent-based explanations are of "tit-for-tat" (TFT). In 1981, Robert Axelrod and W. D. Hamilton used a computer tournament to detect strategies that would favor cooperation among individuals engaged in an iterative game of prisoner's dilemma (Axelrod & Hamilton, 1981; Axelrod, 1984). In a first round, 14 more or less sophisticated strategies and one totally random strategy competed against each other for the highest average scores in a tournament of 200 moves. A very simple strategy emerged as the victor: cooperate on the first move and then copy your opponent's last move for all subsequent moves. TFT won again a second, similar competition involving 62 contestants. TFT has three characteristics that account for its impressive performance: it is nice (cooperates on the first move), retaliatory (punishes defection in the prior move with defection), and forgiving (immediate return to cooperation after one cooperative move by an adversary). Like our other explanations for cooperation, TFT starts from the premise that actors are autonomous and egoistic. Its wrinkle, which gained it so much attention, is its seeming proof that cooperation can emerge at the system level from entirely self-interested behaviour at the agent level. It is a high tech spinoff of Hegel's "cunning of reason."

In the computer tournaments won by TFT, "tits" (punishment) and "tats" (defections) were defined unambiguously, as were their consequences (which were assigned numerical values), and both were evaluated independently by the computer that kept score. None of these conditions can be replicated easily in the real world, where "tits" are readily interpreted as "tats," cooperation as defection and either dismissed as noise (Lebow, 1998). The pattern of interaction between two actors, each of whom believes they are punishing the other for prior defection, is likely to diverge radically from a starting point jointly perceived as mutual cooperation, or of defection and punishment. The Cuban missile crisis was the result of precisely such an escalating spiral of mutually reinforcing defections, with each superpower convinced that its "tat" was a "tit" in response to the other's "tat" (Lebow & Stein, 1994b).

In subsequent tournaments, Axelrod studied the consequences of faulty attribution by introducing a certain degree of randomization in the form of outcomes not chosen by players. Occasionally, when players chose to cooperate or defect, it would appear to their opponent that they had done the reverse. Both players would be informed afterwards if their choice had not been implemented correctly, but they would never be told if opponents' choices were intended or not. Nor did they know how long the game would last. Axelrod explored two ways of coping with this problem: making the response to defection somewhat less than the provocation (generosity), and encouraging the player who had defected by accident that an opponent's defection in response did not call for another defection on his/her part (contrition). Subsequent iterations of these strategies revealed that both of them could cope effectively with noise, but that too much forgiveness invites exploitation (Nowak & Sigmund, 1993; Kraines & Kraines, 1995; Wu &

Axelrod, 1995; Axelrod & Dion, 1998). All of these experiments with noise only further problematized attributions of intent.

In the original and subsequent tournaments, the outcomes of cooperation and defection were still perfectly perceived by all players, the payoffs of all possible combinations of cooperation and defection were known, and all games consisted of reciprocal moves, a structure understood by all players. In the real world, outcomes and their payoffs can only be estimated imperfectly; actors on the same side often make radically divergent estimates of both. Different presidential advisors routinely did this throughout the Cold War when they considered the putative costs and benefits of cooperation in or defection from various arms control regimes. In politics, perception is everything, and it may have at least as much to do with how the other side presents its choices as the choices themselves.

TFT may be the most extreme example of a theory of cooperation based entirely on external stimuli. As we have seen, it requires actors to replicate the previous move of their adversaries. If they cooperate, you cooperate, and if they defect, you defect. The strategy tells us nothing about the original choice of any actor, and it is easy to see that the nature of the world that emerges is critically dependent on the distribution of opening moves. They presumably reflect a prior disposition toward cooperation or defection. Like its competitors, TFT assumes a good part of the cooperation it attempts to explain. In this connection, it is interesting to observe that when Axelrod ran TFT with real American and Soviet defense analysts as players, they subsequently explained their initial and subsequent choices—mostly defection—in terms of their prior expectations about each other's motives (Axelrod, 1997, 30).

Leaving the abstract, transparent domain of games for the often opaque world of international relations, it is difficult to find an interstate rivalry that moved from acute conflict to cooperation by means of TFT. The Cold War ended because Mikhail Gorbachev refused to play TFT. He made a series of conciliatory moves, undeterred by Reagan's repeated unwillingness to reciprocate. Repeated efforts at conciliation in the face of no response or defection convinced many Europeans and Americans of Gorbachev's sincerity, and generated allied and domestic pressure on the Reagan administration to extend the olive branch. Ironically, the first major move the administration made toward cooperation—their "zero option" arms control proposa—was never intended to be taken seriously by the Soviets. Its purpose was to put the onus of the expected failure of arms control on Moscow and make the administration look better in the eyes of its critics. Gorbachev's positive response compelled the administration to follow through on its own offer, and led to an important arms control agreement (Chernayev, 1996; Evangelista, 2004).

At best, TFT describes tactics that may facilitate cooperation in the long run when the outcomes of individual encounters are not critical. It tells us nothing about the reasons why leaders seek cooperation. To understand why Sadat and Gorbachev were moved to extend the olive branch, and willing to assume great risks in the process, we need to examine their internal as well as external incentives—that is, their domestic goals and political needs—and the ways in which both kinds of incentives were refracted through important processes of learning (Gorbachev, 1995; Brown, 1996: Herrmann & Lebow, 2004).

A world of autonomous, egoistic individuals—even the fiction of such a world—when used as a starting point of analysis, fosters the belief that cooperation and commitments should serve purely selfish ends. Working from such an assumption, which rules out social and emotional attachments and commitments and the communities they sustain, it is easy to see why social scientists working in the rational choice tradition must resort to the most extreme forms of intellectual prestidigitation to explain how anything beyond the most short-lived and instrumental kind of collaboration ever occurs. Having coaxed the rabbit of individualism out of their analytical hat, social scientists are now unsuccessfully casting about for tricks to put it back inside.

Are actors individuals?

The realist, liberal, and social capital approaches are generally considered distinct and competitive. All three approaches share a common ontology and logic. Their starting point is the liberal assumption of the autonomous, egoistic actor who, in the words of C. B. MacPherson, is "the proprietor of his person and capacities." Society is conceived of as "a lot of free individuals related to each other as proprietors of their own capacities and of what they have acquired by their exercise" (Macpherson, 1962, 3; Komter, 1996). Proponents of these approaches explain cooperation (or the lack of it, in the case of neorealism) with reference to the incentives (or lack of them) offered by the environment. This ontology, imported into the discipline from economics, has now metastasized through the social sciences and is found at the core of all theories of rational choice. The self-contained individual as the unit of analysis is a socially conditioned choice, and one that imposes serious conceptual limitations on scholarship. It also raises troubling ethical issues.

There is nothing natural about people acting primarily on the basis of individual self-interest. Individual interest is historically conditioned, took millennia to emerge, and has been regarded as unnatural by most people for most of its existence. In traditional societies, people were—and still are—more tightly integrated into communities, and more likely to define their identities in communal terms (Fitzgerald, 1993, 190; Lapid, 1997, 3–20; Yack, 1997). They do not lack a concept of self, but that concept is relationally defined; it is likely to be the sum of socially assigned roles (Durkheim, 1984, 219–222: Finley, 1954, 134). *Persona* is the Latin word for mask and describes the outer face that one presents to the community (Hobbes, 1968, xvi, 112; Andrew, 1986, 98–103; Onuf, 2001). The face defines the self in others' eyes and in one's own mind's eye. This understanding resonates in the modern understanding of identity as a set of meanings "that an actor attributes to itself while taking the perspectives of others" (McCall & Simmons, 1978, 61–100). At the collective level, identities are often defined, and perhaps, even constructed, with reference to "others" and what our understanding of them says about ourselves (Bull, 1977, 33–34, 44; Cederman, 2001).

In ancient Greece, there was no conception of individual self-interest, and none of "self-interestedness" prior to the late fifth century. Unfortunate individuals such as slaves and outcasts, who did not belong to a community, were thought of as liminal people and objects of pity and fear. Durkheim observed that the replacement of the collectivity by the individual as the object of ritual attention is one of the hallmarks of transitions from traditional to modern societies. Indeed, from Rousseau on. Enlightenment and Romantic ideologies emphasized the uniqueness and autonomy of the inner self (Parsons, 1937, 378–90; Berman, 1971; Lukes, 1973; Collins, 1985, 46–82; Norton, 1995). Modernity created a vocabulary that recognizes tensions between inner selves and social roles but encourages us to cultivate and express our "inner selves" and original ways of being (Althusser, 1971, 127–88; Shotter, 1989, 133–51; Butler, 1997; Eakin, 1999; Gergen, 1999). As products of this ideology, we tend to take for granted that our desires, feelings and choices are spontaneous and self-generated, but there is good reason to believe that they are in large part socially constituted. This was certainly the perspective of Thucydides, Plato and Thomas Hobbes (Hobbes, 1968, xiii, 86–87). More recently, Erving Goffman, in the tradition of Durkheim, sought to document the extent to which everyday life is structured by an astonishing variety of rituals that construct and reinforce identities and render the very notion of an autonomous inner self highly problematic (Goffman, 1959, 1962, 1963; Ruggie, 1983, 195–232). Additional empirical support for the social construction of identity comes from psychological research that finds that people have a great sense of their own uniqueness, but then when asked to describe what makes them unique, come up with generally shared or widely valued attributes like honesty, dedication to family, artistic or athletic talent (Bruner, 1994, 41–54; Gergen, 1994, 78–104).

We also think of ourselves as unique because of our idiosyncratic pasts and the ways in which they make us who we are. There may be some biological basis for this claim: Gerald Edelman proposes a theory of neural nets that describes how the nervous system evolves in response to life experiences and becomes a physical representation of the uniqueness of every individual (Edelman, 1992). But memories are not hard-wired. As Vico (1948) suspected, many of our most important memories turn out to be social constructions. Modern psychological work on collective memory begins with Maurice Halbwachs, who argued that "social organization gives a persistent framework into which all detailed recall must fit, and it very powerfully influences both the manner and matter of recall" (Bartlett, 1932; Vygotsky, 1978; Halbwachs, 1980, 296). Decades of research reveals that autobiographical memory is largely unreliable, even the so-called flashbulb memories that involve recall of shocking events along with considerable details of one's personal circumstances at the time the news was received (Brown & Kulik, 1977; Brewer, 1986, 34–49; Rubin, 1986; Holland & Quinn, 1987; Fivush, 1988, 277–82; Polkinghorne, 1988; Bohannon & Symons, 1992, 65–91; Winograd & Neisser, 1992; Collins et al., 1993; Neisser, 1993; Barclay, 1994, 55–77; Neisser, 1994; Pennebaker et al., 1997). Accumulating evidence suggests that to some degree, we remake our memories over time in response to our psychological needs and group identifications (Erikson, 1950; Portelli, 1991).

The psychological literature emphasizes the temporal nature of identity. This consensus is reflected in Donald Polkinghorne's observation that "Self... is not a static thing or a substance, but a configuration of personal events into an historical unity which includes not only what one has been but also anticipation of what one will be." Experiments reveal multiple "remembered selves," whose evocation depends on appropriate priming or the social milieu in which the person is situated at the time (Neisser, 1981, 1993; Spence, 1982; White, 1989; Polkinghorne, 1991; Fivush, 1988). Memory studies suggest that the concept of the authentic self is deeply problematic. We appear to evolve over time, and the best we can do is call up imperfect and selective representations of what we once were—or would like to think we were (Eakin, 1990, x).

Identities and interests at the state level depend on international society. Leopold von Ranke, a nineteenth-century precursor of Kenneth Waltz, defined a great power in terms of its capabilities (Von Laue, 1950, 203). However, since the modern state system emerged, many more authorities have considered great power status something akin to the Greek conception of *hēgemonia* in that it can only be conferred by other powers (Lebow, 2003, 122, 126, 276–89). Membership in the international system, and even more, great power status, carries responsibilities (Hinsley, 1963, 4–5, 133–37, 142–44, 160–61, 180–82, 191–93; Butterfield, 1966, 132–18; Bull, 1977, 203). Grotius, Pufendorf, Vattel, Wolff, and more recently, the English School and some constructivists, elaborated these responsibilities and the rules to which member states must adhere (Manning, 1962; Bull, 1977; Butterfield & Wight, 1977; Wight, 1977, Donelan, 1978; Watson, 1992; Buzan, 1993; Onuf, 1998; Brown, 2001). In the words of Hedley Bull, member states conceive of themselves as "bound by a common set of rules in their relations with one another, and share in the working of common institutions" (Bull, 1977, 16). International society theorists insist that these rules and norms are for the most part obeyed because they enable states to pursue their interests in a more efficient and less violent way.[1] Oran Young observes that new states have little choice but to participate in these practices and institutional arrangements. According to Bull, rules and norms makes anarchy more of a Lockean than a Hobbesian world because they enable trade, civilized social relations and some degree of security in the absence of a sovereign (Bull, 1977, 46–51; Clark, 1989, 2; Buzan 1993).

Building on John Searle's distinction between "brute" and "social" facts, Kratochwil contends that international society must, of necessity, precede the state system because it creates the constitutive frameworks in terms of which actors relate. These rules—particularly those surrounding sovereignty—determine who qualifies as an actor (Searle, 1969, 1995; Kratochwil, 1989, 25–28; Ruggie, 1998, 22–25, 32–36, chapter 2). Identities come through naming and participation in society. States, like people, are socialized into membership and its attendant responsibilities. Germany and Japan went through such a process in the aftermath of World War II, and some other former dictatorships are in varying stages of transformation (Klotz, 1995; Solingen, 1995, 1998; Berger, 1996, 317–156; Checkel, 1997a, b; Gurowitz, 1999; Cortell & Davis 2000). The Soviet Union also underwent an evolution of this kind. At the outset, Bolsheviks conceived of the Soviet Union as a temporary political unit and world revolutionary force antagonistic to the existing state system. Stalin accepted the state system as a temporary, if necessary, evil. His successors came to embrace their membership in it and sought external recognition as a superpower. By the time of Gorbachev, membership in international society had helped to undermine traditional communist identities, making possible an end to the Cold War (Herman, 1996; Checkel, 1997a; Lévesque, 1997; English, 2000; Herrmann & Lebow, 2004).

Hedley Bull conceived of international society as "thin" in comparison to domestic societies. For the English School as a whole, it was not a half-way house between anarchy and world government, but a Pareto-optimal solution to the problem of balancing cultural diversity against the need for order (Bull 1977; Dunne, 1998, 11). The postwar transformations of Germany, Japan, and the Soviet Union, and more recently, of South Africa and the countries of Eastern Europe, suggest that international society, especially Western regional society, is "thicker" than Bull and his colleagues imagined.

There are also striking parallels between individual and collective actors in the realm of memory. I have previously noted the connection between memory and identity, and how individual memories are at least in part socially constructed. Individuals rewrite their pasts, not always consciously, in response to cues from peer groups and the wider society. Psychologists speculate that one important incentive for doing so is the expected rewards of group membership and solidarity (Robinson, 1976; Brewer, 1986; Baddeley, 1992; Edwards and Potter, 1992; Hyman, 1992; Neisser, 1992, 1994). There is growing evidence that collective memory is also socially constructed. The events that people recall as well as the emotions and meanings attributed to them are significantly affected by commemorations and discourses propagated by authorities and other institutions and groups (Herf, 1997; Olick & Robbins, 1998; Molasky, 1999; Novick, 1999; Peitsch, 1999; Yoneyama, 1999; Deak, 2000; Lebow, Kansteiner and Fogu, 2006) A recent cross-national study of the politics of memory in postwar Europe, found that postwar memories of World War II and the Holocaust evolved considerably over the course of five decades, and were shaped by a complex interplay between top-down and bottom-up forces, both of which were significantly influenced by international, cross-national and trans-national discourses and interventions. External influences were most important in Germany, seeking to regain its standing in Western and international society, and more recently, in those Eastern European countries admitted to, or seeking admission to the European Union (EU) and NATO. Some of the Eastern European states are in the process, often self-consciously, of bringing their memories and the identities they help to construct into line with those sanctioned and promoted by the EU and NATO (Lebow, Kansteiner and Fogu, 2006).

Modern society's emphasis on individualism and free choice creates an entrenched predisposition to exaggerate the uniqueness of the inner self. Uniqueness can only exist as distinction, so identity is relational by definition. The Greek word for fame (*kleos*) derives from the verb to hear (*kluein*). It indicates recognition, as Homer recognized, that fame requires heroic deeds, bards to sing about those deeds, and people willing to listen and be impressed by them. Modern people need each other just as much to acknowledge, praise, or vilify achievements. Kant captured this tension nicely when he observed that each person seeks "to achieve a rank among his fellows, whom he cannot stand, but also cannot stand to leave alone" (Kant, 1992, 8, 20–21). Some decades back, David Riesman, Reuel Denney, and Nathan Glazer distinguished between "inner" and "other" direction. Inner-directed people acted in response to their own set of values and goals. Other-directed people had goals and values shaped by others and behaved in the ways intended to gain their approval (Riesman et al., 1950). However, this distinction is exaggerated because even inner-directed people need to define themselves in opposition or in contrast to the identities and roles being foisted on them by society. Inner selves and individual identities cannot exist apart from society because membership and participation in society—or its rejection—is essential to the constitution of the self.

Sociopaths aside, the rest of us are embedded in a web of relationships—a social habitus, to use Mauss's language—that begins with families and personal relationships and extend out to business or professional ones and some mix of social, sporting, civic, or religious groups and generally go beyond this to ethnic, regional, and national identifications. We enter into these relationships because we recognize that many of the good things in life require, or are at least enhanced by, sharing and acting in concert with other people. Relationships and the affective ties and loyalties they generate give our lives meaning and direction. They not only constitute the cement of community, they teach us who we are. We have multiple identities—something well-documented by psychologists—and many of them collective in the sense that we equate our well-being with that of others (Tajfel, 1981; Durkheim, 1984, xl–xli, 170–172: Tajfel & Turner, 1986; Brewer, 1991, 1996; Kaufman, 2001). As Norbert Elias puts it, the "I" is embedded in the "we." Scholars must start from the structure of relations between individuals in order to understand the identity of any of them (Burkitt, 1991; Elias, 1991, 61–62). The most compelling proof that the world is not composed of egoistic actors is the behavior of people who actually separate themselves from all social ties. For Greek playwrights, the individual freed from the bonds of family and community was something to be feared and pitied. Ajax, Antigone, Deianeira, and Electra were destructive to themselves, their families and their societies. We observe the same phenomenon at the international level. From Nazi Germany to North Korea, states that reject world society and seek to become truly autonomous actors have became self-destructive pariahs.

The concept of individual identity emerged only gradually from collective conceptions of identity based on roles (Elias, 1978, 1982). According to Amartya Sen, self-interest was not used as the first principle of an economic model until the late nineteenth century.[2] Other economists insist that this did not happen until the publication in 1942 of Joseph Schumpeter's influential theory of political and economic behavior (Schumpeter, 1963; Mansbridge, 1990). Readers might object that some of the greatest modern philosophers, including Hobbes, conceived of the state of nature as composed of fully autonomous, egoistic and rational individuals who negotiated social contracts to escape from violence and disorder. But this represents a misreading of Hobbes. For Enlightenment philosophers, contracts were convenient fictions that allowed them to reconcile self-interest with authority and provide a logical foundation for order. None of them, with the possible exception of Locke, conceived of human beings as autonomous and rational, or believed that contracts could be negotiated in a state of nature. Hobbes was adamant that contracts required trust, the very condition that was lacking in the state of nature. Order could only be imposed by a Leviathan (Hobbes, 1968, xvii, 117; Jencks, 1979, 63–86; Kratochwil, 1989, 113–17). He was equally certain that any analogy between the state of nature and international politics was inappropriate. States do not have the same incentives to leave the state of nature. While even the strongest man needs to sleep, states can keep a constant watch by having people work in shifts (Kratochwil, 1989, 3–4, 113–16).

For liberal philosophers, autonomous rational agents and the contracts they negotiated, performed the same role that such agents do for contemporary theories of rational choice—with one big difference. Grotius, Hobbes, and Locke used contracts as thought experiments to help them construct deductive foundations for political orders. They never intended or expected that their systems, or the assumptions on which they were based, would be taken literally as recipes for community, or used to explain or predict political behavior. Modern social science, and rational choice in particular, is an expression, product, and even vehicle of modernity. It crystallizes modernity's constitutive pathology of trying to turn abstract discourse into concrete reality. Its proponents believe that their assumptions, if not fully descriptive of reality, provide a close enough fit for them to model complex human behavior. Modern realism may be the most extreme example of this conceit, but it is only one example of a class of approaches that dominate international relations and social science more generally.

Internal vs. external motivation

The dominant ontology has another core assumption: actors respond primarily to external stimuli. Realist, liberal, and institutionalist approaches all focus on the constraints and opportunities created by the environment. They reward certain kinds of behavior and punish others, and shape actors indirectly through a process of natural selection, or directly by influencing their cost calculus. The latter may be accomplished by creating a "shadow of the future," lowering information costs or establishing a pattern of interactions that makes coordination more efficient for everyone. Cooperation may emerge as the unintentional outcome of cumulative self-interested behavior (Olson, 1965; Stigler & Becker, 1977; Gammon, 1992). "Tit-for-tat," considered by many one of the most robust theories of cooperation, is a prominent representative of this approach; it assumes that actors will cooperate or defect in response to the previous choices of others with whom they interact (Axelrod, 1984). As we have seen, this premise is also central for Alexander Wendt, for whom behavior is shaped by external incentives and constraints. His "alter" and "ego" construct their system on the basis of mutual interactions, and once that system is established, it creates strong incentives for both the founders and other actors to conform (Wendt, 1999, 326–336). Theories of this kind sometimes allow for differences in the character of actors: Bueno de Mesquita, for example, introduces a distinction between risk prone and risk averse actors—but these actor-level characteristics are second-order refinements for theories that rely on environmental cues as their principal mechanisms (Bueno de Mesquita, 1981, 34–35).

By contrast, theories of foreign policy at the state level are based on differences among actors. They build typologies of strong and weak states and societies, modernizing and traditional elites or democracies vs. other forms of government. Classical realists operate at this level of analysis; Morgenthau's theory is founded on a three-fold typology of foreign policy goals. The democratic peace is the most recent effort to explain cooperation—or at least the absence of war—in terms of state level characteristics. The burgeoning literature on the democratic peace developed largely in response to the empirical finding that democracies do not fight one another, and much of the discussion is about the robustness and significance of this finding. The democratic peace remains under-theorized, and there is no agreement about the mechanisms responsible for it. Building on Kant, Michael Doyle contends that democracies have liberal cultures that eschew war and violence, putting a premium on peaceful conflict resolution. They value what Kant calls "the spirit of commerce," which structures cooperation and community through trade. Other scholars suggest that elections make leaders answerable to public opinion, that transparent democratic processes make war preparations difficult to hide for both these reasons, democratic states expect other democratic states to act peacefully (Russet, 1993; Owen, 1994; Ray, 1994, 1995; Williams, 2001). Most of these explanations, by reinforcing economic and political costs, also take the form of external constraints on leaders. Only the Kantian variant stresses the internal causes of peace: common practices that construct common discourse and identities that have subtle but powerful influences on expectations and behavior (Honing, 1993; Williams, 2001). As currently formulated, democratic peace theory, like its institutionalist counterpart, may mistake symptoms for causes.[3]

Many philosophers, ancient and modern, have sought the explanation for cooperation within the minds of actors.[4] Grotius, Pufendorf, Hobbes, and Smith recognized that people need each other to achieve their individual goals, and that recognition of this need impels them toward society and the social life (Grotius, 1925, 11; Pufendorf, 1934, ii, 154–78; Smith, 1976, I 10, II ii–iii, 85). Feelings were central for the liberal philosophers. Hobbes considered "fellow-feeling" and the sympathy for others it engendered to be natural proclivities of human beings (Hobbes, 1968, 126). Adam Smith thought that moral ideas derived from feelings of empathy. Our ability to experience the pain and pleasure of others, and our desire to have them experience ours, keeps us from being entirely selfish. Feelings are responsible for ethics because they provide the incentive to understand and evaluate our behavior as others see and experience it (Smith, 1976). While not insensitive to the role of emotions, Kant emphasized the central role of reason in producing knowledge and self-enforcing ethics. Social antagonism provides an incentive for us to develop our rational faculties. We use these faculties to advance our own selfish ends, primarily by means of calculation and communication with others.[5] When our reason fully develops, it grasps the fundamental law of humanity: the absolute equality and dignity of all human beings. Reason now becomes the vehicle for helping us overcome our competitive propensity and to cooperate with other human beings on the basis of equality to achieve common goals. For Kant, like the liberal philosophers, cooperation is not so much a response to external stimuli as it is an expression of the internal moral development of human beings (*Groundwork of Metaphysics*, 4, 428–29, 435; *Conjectural Beginning of Human History*, 8, 114; *Metaphysics of Morals*, 6, 314, 27.463, in Lectures on Ethics; Schneewind, *The Invention of Autonomy*, 521). This was held true of states as well as individuals, and the basis for a "perpetual peace" founded on a civitas gentium (Doyle, 1983a, b, 205–35, 323–53; 1986; Onuf, 1998, 230–32).

German idealist philosophers and many representatives of the Anglo-American liberal tradition looked back to Aristotle's conception of human beings as political animals who could only find fulfillment in the life of the polis. According to Aristotle, the polis was created and maintained by affection and friendship (*philia*), because these bonds encourage us to define our happiness in terms of the well-being of our family, friends and fellow citizens. *Philoi* (friends) constitute expanding circles of affective networks that cumulatively add up to the civic project (*koinonia*) (Aristotle, Politics, 1253a2–3). Citizenship is the active sharing of power among equals in contrast to the hierarchical relations of the traditional family (*oikos*) (Plato, *Republic*, 419a–421a; Aristotle, *Nicomachean Ethics*, Books 9–10, 1155a23, b29–b31; *Politics*, 1280b29–1280b40). Plato considered friendship the foundation of community because it created an atmosphere of trust in which meaningful dialogue and justice became possible. Plato's dialogues allow Socrates to demonstrate in practice that it is the surest route for reaching common conclusions in a cooperative way. For Plato and Aristotle, philosophy encouraged the kind of introspection that had the potential of turning the soul toward justice.[6] Hannah Arendt argued that the absence of *philia*, and a resulting inability to see the world through the eyes of other people, is what made Adolf Eichmann into "one of the greatest criminals" of the twentieth century (Arendt, 1964, 287–88; Euben, 1996, 327–59).

Kant thought that guest friendship (*xenia*) was probably the one universal standard of honorable conduct (Kant, 1991). Many of the world's great moral-philosophical traditions share more fundamental understandings of human beings, among them the belief that affection and reciprocity are the basis for cooperation and community. The Mishnah says that "The reward for a good deed is another good deed; and the penalty for a transgression is another transgression" (Pikey Avot, 4.2). Kong Fuzi (our Master Kong), known as Confucius in the West, insisted that rulers treat people as they would like to be treated, and that such behavior was sustained by filial devotion, humaneness and ritual. These sentiments and practices give rise to loyalty and reciprocity (Schwartz, 1985, 56–134; Bloom, 1999a, 41–44; 1999b, 49).

Experimental economists have found empirical support for the universality of reciprocity as a principle. One of their more robust findings is the extent to which people are willing to forego material gain to punish others who would deny their equality (Sigmund, 1995; Binmore, 1998; Falk et al., 1999; Nowak et al., 2000; Henrich, 2001). The standard format for this research is a game in which two players must decide how to share $100 or an equivalent sum of money. A coin toss determines the roles of proposer and responder. The proposer makes a single offer to share the money on any basis he or she wants, and the responder can accept or reject the offer. The two players are kept apart and both are informed beforehand that no further communication will be allowed beyond the initial offer and response. If the proposer's offer is accepted, the $100 is distributed in accordance with the terms of that offer. If it is rejected, neither side receives any money. In almost all cultures, two-thirds of the proposer's offer the responder 40–50% of the total: only 4 out of 100 offer less than 20%. More than half of all responders reject offers of less than 20%. They prefer to forego any gain to prevent proposers from making what, in their judgment, is an unfair gain. A review of the literature concludes that the experiments "all point to one conclusion: we do not adopt a purely self-centered viewpoint but take account of our co-player's outlook. We are not interested solely in our own payoff but compare ourselves with the other part and demand fair play" (Sigmund et al., 2002, 82–87). Experimental economists and game theorists have struggled to come up with explanations for behavior seemingly so at odds with the logic of homo economicus. Some acknowledge a widespread concern for fairness and reciprocity, but others suggest that participants fail to understand the game, and incorrectly expect a second round. Still others hypothesize that the game reveals an evolutionary atavism: for millions of years people lived in small groups whose functioning depended on trust and openness.

"Our emotions are thus not finely tuned to interactions occurring under strict anonymity" (Sigmund et al., 2002, 85). Sophisticated social scientists can look the truth in the face and not see it—when it violates their cherished assumptions.

Greek and modern philosophers, the Jewish and Confucian traditions, classical realism, and at least some social scientists, point us toward a similar understanding of the origins of cooperation and civil order (Melucci, 1989; Dawes et al., 1990; Calhoun, 1991; Morris & Mueller, 1992; Sen, 1992). Cooperation is possible when people recognize its benefits. This recognition is not brought about by external constraints and opportunities, but by introspection and experience. They bring some of us—individuals, communities, and states—to deeper understandings of our interests and the recognition that we cannot become ourselves outside of close relations with other people. At every level of interaction, from personal relationships to business and politics, we become willing to forego certain short-term gains to sustain these relationships and the principles of justice on which they rest. Viewed in this light, the emergence of the European community, the end of the Cold War and the survival of NATO represent triumphs of higher-order learning (Lebow, 1994). By contrast, the foreign policies of the Bush administrations, like the corporate policies of Enron, Arthur Anderson, and WorldCom, are a retrogression to a more primitive, self-centered, and inevitably counterproductive way of thinking about oneself and the world.

Interests, order, and ethics

For the Greeks and many modern philosophers, cooperation and the civic project (*koinonia*) is ultimately an expression of our innate sociability. Man is a political animal, as Aristotle so aptly put it, and we are driven by our instincts to associate with others to realize our own needs and potential (Aristotle, *Poetics*, 1253a30). Relationships and the commitments they entail are not simply instrumental means to selfish ends, but important ends in their own right. We become who we are through close association with others. In the words of Charles Taylor, dialogue allows us to "become full human agents, capable of understanding ourselves, and hence of defining our identity" (Taylor, 1991, 33). If identity depends upon community, interests depend on identity. One of the reasons that Hobbes invoked the state of nature was to show that deprived of an identity, we all become more or less identical, and our only interests are the fundamental requisites of survival—food, clothing, shelter, and sex. Identity confers interests because it gives us social purpose and allows for differentiation.

Cooperation is no more anomalous than conflict. Both kinds of behavior are expressions of our fundamental nature and needs. Cooperation enables and sustains the relationships and communities that give us identities and interests, and conflict arises when the identities and interests of individuals or groups are at odds or clash with those of other individuals and groups. Cooperation and conflict are often framed as polar opposites, but at a deeper level, as the Greeks understood, they are closely related and even symbiotic.

Greek poets, playwrights, and philosophers framed the problem of choice differently than do modern social scientists. Their principal concern was with human goals, and they distinguished between two kinds of human impulses: appetite (to *epithumétikon*) and spirit (to *thumoeides*). The former pertained to bodily needs, like food, shelter, and sex, and all their more sophisticated expressions. The latter was manifested in the competitive quest for recognition, understood as the basis of self-esteem. Plato and Aristotle (1984) maintained that reason generates desires of its own and was a third source of motivation. Their understanding of reason was much richer than the modern conception of reason as merely instrumental. Through the application of reason people could apprehend the ends of life and restrain and train the appetite and spirit to collaborate with it to promote happiness (eudaimonia) and well-being (Plato, *Republic*, 441c1–441c2, 441e4, 442c5–442c6, 580d7–580d8, 8505d11–8505e1; Aristotle, *Nicomachean Ethics*, 1.7.1098a4, 1.13.1102b13–1.13.1102b31, 7.4.1147b25–7.4.1147b28, b31–b35, 1148a8–1148a9, 1247b18–1247b19). In healthy individuals, the appetite and spirit accept the rule of reason and coexist in psychological balance. Plato's Socrates acknowledges that few people fully attain this state of mastery, but insists that the closer they come, the happier they are (Plato, *Republic*, 441d12–442b4, c6–c8, 443c9–444a3, 472b7–472d2, 588c7–588d5).

In theory, all one's appetites could be satisfied in a purely selfish and autonomous way. More sophisticated, and presumably, pleasurable indulgence of appetites whether it be shelter, nourishment, or sex—require sharing and the willing participation of others. The spirit, by its very nature, can only be developed and satisfied in a social context. External honor and standing is a relational concept. It is a scarce commodity because if it were available for everyone, no one could possess it. Worlds in which they matter—and this encompasses most societies—are highly competitive. Paradoxically, they also require high degree of consensus and cooperation. Honor or standing is only meaningful when recognized and praised by others. Indeed, they are most often conferred by others, as was *hēgemonia* in ancient Greece and great power status today. In the absence of a society with important shared values, and institutions, or at least, procedures for recognizing accomplishments and establishing standing, external honor cannot exist. Internal honor is also a product of socialization, although it only requires individual validation. It has often functioned historically to restrain power, uphold important social values, and by doing so, has contributed significantly to the maintenance of the social and political order.

Greeks thought people were motivated by fear, interest, and honor. Interest and honor were expressions of the appetite and spirit, respectively (Thucydides, *The History of the Peloponnesian War*, 1.75.3). Fear becomes an increasingly dominant motive when either the appetite or spirit breaks free of the constraints and threatens the well-being, self-esteem—or the survival—of other actors. Fear transforms liberal or constructivist worlds into realist ones because its behavioral consequences tend to make the expectations that aroused it self-fulfilling. Thucydides provides a blow-by-blow account of how this happened in Athens, Corcyra, and in Hellas more generally, in the run up to and during the course of the Peloponnesian War. His Melian Dialogue is among the earliest and certainly the most famous description of foreign policy in a harsh, realist environment. Thucydides does not intend it to seen as the norm, but rather as pathology (Lebow, 2003, 124–125, 145–148).

In liberal and constructivist worlds, there are two levels of cooperation: an underlying and diffuse expectation of cooperation, and case-by-case cooperation. The latter is greatly facilitated and sustained by the former. Conflict may be acute, but is nevertheless contained within well-defined limits. In pre-Peloponnesian War Greece, war among *poleis* was a common occurrence, just as it was in Europe for most of the eighteenth century, but its ends and means—and its casualties—were limited. In fully realist worlds, conflict, not cooperation, is the default, and any cooperation that occurs is the result of case-by-case assessments of self-interest. Like the game of Diplomacy—which models such a world—defection is frequent when actors perceived it to serve their interests.

Toward the top of the international relations research agenda must be the question of the nature of world(s) in which we live? Realists, liberals, and constructivists make broad claims about the utility of their respective paradigms for studying international relations. All three paradigms are relevant because there is more to the international system than is captured by a single paradigm. It is mixed in a double sense. The system is a composite of a number of regional systems with widely varying characteristics. The North Atlantic area, Australasia, and many parts of the Pacific rim are characterized by a high degree of cooperation. The North Atlantic is sometimes described as the core region of an expanding "pluralist security community," in the language of Karl Deutsch (1957). The Middle East and South Asia, by contrast, are primarily realist in their inter-state interactions. Other regions, like Southeast Asia, Latin America, and Africa, fall somewhere in between. Like sophisticated colors that appear uniform to the eye but are in fact blends of primary colors and other pigments, each region is characterized by some mix of realism, liberalism, and constructivism, and one, moreover, that is constantly in flux. Understanding the particular mix in any region, its stability and, if unstable, its likely trajectory or course are fundamental to the study of its politics. Such an effort leads us to address a more general set of questions about how these different worlds arise, evolve, interact and transform themselves.

Of particular interest are the paths that lead to and away from starkly realist worlds. Neorealists have always maintained that states cannot escape from realist worlds anymore than firms can escape from the market. They are something akin to Stephen Hawking's conception of black holes: singularities from which—in violation of the laws of quantum mechanics—no information can escape. Hawking has recently questioned his own longstanding interpretation, conceding that information may escape after all. The ability of Greece at the end of the Peloponnesian Wars and Europe at the end of the religious wars, and again, after World

War II, to reconstitute sophisticated and restrained orders in the aftermath of destructive spirals into political black holes, indicates that movement away from realist worlds is possible. We need to know more about how and why this process occurs.

One part of the explanation involves the independent role of reason. For Plato, reason had desires of its own: its purpose was to discover the ends of life and educate the spirit and appetite so they would want to collaborate harmoniously to achieve these ends. For Hume, the quintessential Enlightenment philosopher, this relationship was reversed. Reason became "slave to the passions," and its only role was to find efficient means of turning goals into achievements—what Max Weber would later call "instrumental reason." Social science, in contrast to ancient philosophy, is overwhelmingly focused on means. Not ends. It treats ends as either exogenous (as it does preferences) or something that reason readily infers from the environment (e.g., the putative concern for relative gain in an anarchical international system). Unlike classical realism, modern realism, and much of social science misses or ignores the ways in which reason can promote new understandings, reshape ends and constrain or rechannel appetites and the spirit. As I have argued in the body of the chapter, it may be this latter kind of learning that brings about cooperation at the individual and international levels and is thus a proper—indeed, essential—subject of social science.

As we have seen, the world's great philosophical and religious traditions emphasize the role of emotions, not just of reason, in bringing about the fundamental disposition to cooperate. Affection builds empathy, which allows us to perceive ourselves through the eyes of others. Empathy in turn encourages us to see others as our ontological equals and to recognize the self-actualizing benefits of close relationships with others. From Socrates to Gadamer, philosophers have also argued that dialogue has the potential to make us recognize the parochial and limited nature of our understandings of justice. Affection and reason together make us seek cooperation, not only as a means of achieving specific ends, but of becoming ourselves. They bring many of us—individuals and social collectivities—to the recognition that self-restraint, that is, self-imposed limitations on our appetites and spirit, are essential to sustain the kinds of environments in which meaningful cooperation becomes possible.

Social science as a whole has given short shrift to the role of emotions. It is undeniably central to psychology, but for some decades that field attempted to subsume emotion to cognition, and it is only in recent years, that emotions have been a more important subject of study in its own right. Important exceptions include: Clore (1992, 2002), Damasio (1996), Gray (1987), and McDermott (2004). In political science, emotions have always been recognized as important, but a few studies aside (Marcus et al., 2000), our discipline has primarily stressed their negative influence on behavior.[7] The time is long overdue for both disciplines to acknowledge and study the positive contribution of emotions, harnessed to reason, to order and cooperation.

Notes

1 Kratochwil (1989) argues that they reduce the complexity of choice-situations and are guidance devices that bring conceptual order to the environment. They facilitate goals, shared meanings, justify behavior, and enable communication in the broadest sense. At a deeper level, they influence choices by helping to structure processes of categorization, deliberation and interpretation.

2 Sen (1978, 317–344) attributes this innovation to Edgeworth (1881).

3 Thompson (1996) argues that "zones of peace" may be a necessary antecedent for democratic states to emerge. Such zones also depend on the construction of some degree of common identity.

4 The most important exceptions may be Hume and Hegel. Hume (1964, 105), explains society entirely in terms of the selfish motives of actors. For Hegel, (1942, 199, 209E), the family is a unit of feeling, held together by affection. But cooperation in what he calls 'civil society' is brought about by the "cunning of reason," which, like Smith's "invisible hand," is an external mechanism. Schneewind (1998, 4) reminds us that the emphasis on internal motivation is part of the general assault, during the seventeenth and eighteenth centuries, on traditional conceptions of morality based on obedience. Enlightenment moral philosophers conceived of morality as self-governance, and this in turn provided the justification for people to assume control of the lives in a wide range of domains. Reid, Bentham, and Kant are all important figures in this transition. Taylor (1989, 83) makes a similar argument.

5 In Kant's terminology, human experience results from intuitions (*Anschauungen*) and concepts (*Begriffe*). Objects are given to us through sensibility (*Sinnlichkeit*), which produces intuitions. Objects are also thought about, leading to understanding (Verstand), and through understanding to concepts. Critique of Pure Reason (1881) Axi–xii, A19–20/B33–34, 738–9, B766–7; What Does it Mean to Orient Oneself in Thinking?, (1786), 8, 144–146, in Religion and Rational Theology; Critique of the Power of(Judgment, 5, 293–298: Ideal Toward a Universal History, 18, 20–21 (Wood, 1970).

6 *Dialektikē* derives from dialegesthai (to engage in conversation). Plato, Republic, 509d–511d, 531d–534e.

7 An important exception is Marcus,G,. W. Neuman, and M. Mackuen, Affective Intelligence and Political Judgment (University of Chicago Press, 2000).

References

Althusser, L. (1971). Ideology and ideological state apparatuses (Notes toward an investigation). In B. Brewster (trans.), *Lenin and philosophy and other essays,* New York: Monthly Review Press. 127–88.

Andrew, J. (1986). *Worlds apart: The market and the theater in Anglo-American thought, 1550–1750*, Cambridge: Cambridge University Press.

Arendt, H. (1964). *Eichmann in Jerusalem: A report on the banality of evil*, New York: Viking.

Aristotle (1984). *The complete works of Aristotle: The revised Oxford translation*, Barnes, J. (Ed.). 2 vols., Princeton, NJ: Princeton University Press.

Axelrod, R. (1984). *Evolution of cooperation*. New York: Basic Books.

Axelrod, R. (1997). *The complexity of cooperation: Agent-based models of competition and collaboration,* Princeton, NJ: Princeton University Press.

Axelrod, R., & Dion, D. (1998). The further evolution of cooperation. *Science, 242,* 1385–1390.

Axelrod, R., & Hamilton, W. D. (1981). The evolution of cooperation. *Science, 211(4489),* 1390–1396.

Bartlett, C. (1932). *Remembering: A study in experimental and social psychology. New York: MacMillan.*

Baddeley, A. (1992). Is memory all talk? *The Psychologist, 5,* 447–448.

Barclay, C. R. (1994). Composing protoselves through improvisation. In U. Neisser & R. Fivush (eds.), *The remembering self: Construction and accuracy in the self narrative,* (pp. 55–77).Cambridge: Cambridge University Press.

Berger, T. U. (1996). *Norms, identity, and national security in Germany and Japan.* In P. J. Katzenstein (ed.), The culture of national security: Norms and identity in world politics, (pp. 317–56). New York: Columbia University Press.

Berman, M. (1971). *The politics of individualism: Radical individualism and the emergence of modern society.* London: Allen & Unwin.

Binmore, K. G. (1998). *Game theory and the social contract: Just playing.* Cambridge: MIT Press.

Bloom, I. (1999a). Confucius and the Analects. In W. T. de Bary & I. Bloom (eds.), *Sources of Chinese tradition, volume I: From earliest times to 1600.* New York: Columbia University Press.

Bloom, I. (1999b). Selections from the Analects.I In W. T. de Bary & I. Bloom (eds.*), Sources of Chinese tradition, volume I: From earliest times to 1600.* New York: Columbia University Press.

Bohannon, J. N., & Symons, V. L. (1992). Flashbulb memories: Confidence, consistency, and quantify.I In E. Winograd & U. Neisser (eds.), *Affect and accuracy in recall.,* New York: Cambridge University Press. 65-91.

Brehm, S. S., & Brehm, J. W. (1981). *Psychological reactance: A theory of freedom and control.* New York: Academic Press.

Brewer, M. (1991). The social self: On being the same and different at the same time. *Personality and Social Psychology Bulletin, 17,* 475–82.

Brewer, M., & Miller, N. (2001). *Intergroup relations.* Pacific Grove, CA: Brooks-Cole.

Brewer, W. F. (1986). What is autobiographical memory. In D. C. Rubin (ed.) *Autobiographical Memory* (pp.. 34–49)., Cambridge: Cambridge University Press.

Brown, A. (1996). *The Gorbachev factor.* Oxford: Oxford University Press.

Brown, C. (2001). World society and the English school. An international society perspective on world society. *European Journal of International Relations, 7,* 423–442.

Brown, R., & Kulik, J. (1977). Flashbulb memories. *Cognition, 5,* 73–99.

Bruner, J. (1994). The "remembered self." In U. Neisser & R. Fivush (eds.), *The remembering self: Construction and accuracy in the self sarrative.* (pp. 41–54). Cambridge: Cambridge University Press..

Bueno de Mesquita, B. (1981). *The war trap.* New Haven, CT: Yale University Press.

Bull, H. (1977). *Anarchical society.* London: Macmillan.

Burkitt, I. (1991). *Social selves: Theories of the social formation of personality.,* London: Sage.

Butler, J. (1997). *Excitable speech: The polities of the performative.* New York: Routledge.

Butterfield, H. (1966). The balance of power.I In H. Butterfield & M. Wight (eds.), *Diplomatic investigations: Essays in the theory of international oolitics*. Cambridge, MA: Harvard University Press.

Butterfield, H., & Wight, M. (eds.) (1977). *Diplomatic investigations; Martin Wight, systems of states* (pp. 132–148. Leicester: Leicester University Press.

Buzan, B. (1993). From international system to international society: Structural realism and regime theory meet the English school. *International Organization, 47.* 327–352.

Calhoun, C. (1991). The problem of identity in collective action. In J. Huber (ed.) *Macro-micro linkage in sociology* (pp. 51–76). Beverly Hills, CA: Sage.

Cederman, L. (2001). *Constructing Europe's identity: The external dimension*. London: Lynne Rienner.

Checkel, J. T. (1997a). *Ideas and international political change: Soviet/Russian behavior and the end of the cold war*. New Haven, CT: Yale University Press.

Checkel, J. T. (1997b). Norms, institutions and national identity in contemporary Europe. *International Organization, 51,* 31–63.

Checkel, J. T. (2001). Why comply? Social learning and European identity change. *International Organization, 55,* 553–588.

Chernayev, A. (1996). *My six years with Gorbachev* (R. D. English & E. Tucker, trans. and ed.). College Park: University of Pennsylvania Press.

Clark, I. (1989). *The hierarchy of states: Reform and resistance in the international order.* Cambridge: Cambridge University Press.

Clore, G. (1992). Cognitive phenomenology: Feelings and the construction of judgment. In L. Matin & A. Tesser (eds.), The construction of social judgment (pp. 133–63). Hillsdale, NJ: Erlbaum.

Clore, G., Wyer, R. S., Dienes, B., Gasper, K., Gohn, C. L., & Isbell, L., et al., (2002). Affective feelings as feedback: Some cognitive consequences. In L. Martin & G. Clore (eds.), *Theories of mood and cognition*. Mahway, NJ: Erlbaum.

Collins, A. E., Gathercole, S. E., Conway, M. A., & Morris, P. E. M. (eds.). (1993). *Theories of memory*. Hillsdale, NJ: Lawrence Erlaum.

Collins, S. (1985). Categories, concepts or predicaments? Remarks on Mauss' use of philosophical terminology. In M. Carrithers, S. Collins, & S. Lukes (eds.), *The category of the person: Anthropology, philosophy, history*. Cambridge: Cambridge University Press.

Connor, R. (1996). Civil society, Dionysiac festival, and the Athenian democracy. In J. Ober & C. Hedrick (eds.), *Dēmokratia: A conversation on democracies, ancient and modern*. Princeton, NJ: Princeton University Press.

Cortell, A. P., & Davis Jr., J. W. (2000). Understanding the domestic impact of international norms: A research agenda. *International Studies Review, 2,* 65–90.

Damasio, A. (1996). *Descartes' error: Emotion, reason, and the human brain*. New York: Putnam.

Dawes, R., Van der Kragt, A. J. C., & Orbell, J. (1990). Cooperation for the benefit of us—not me, or my conscience. In J. J. Mansbridge (ed.), *Beyond self-interest* (pp. 97–110). Chicago: University of Chicago Press.

Deak, I., Gross, J. T., & Judt, T. et al. (eds.) (2000) *The politics of retribution in Europe: World war II and its aftermath*, Princeton, NJ: Princeton University Press.

Deutsch, K. W. (1953). *Nationalism and social communication*. Cambridge: MIT Press.

Deutsch, K.W. et al. (1957). *Political community and the North Atlantic area*. Princeton, NJ: Princeton University Press.

Donelan, M. (ed.). (1978). *The reason of state*. London: Allen & Unwin.

Doyle, M. W. (1983a). Kant, liberal legacies, and foreign affairs: Part 1. *Philosophy and Public Affairs, 12*, 205–235.

Doyle, M. W. (1983b). Kant, liberal legacies, and foreign affairs: Part 2. *Philosophy and Public Affairs, 12*, 323–353.

Doyle, M. W. (1986). Liberalism and world politics. *American Political Science Review, 80*, 1151–1169.

Dunne, T. (1998). *Inventing international society: A history of the English school*. New York: St. Martin's Press.

Durkheim, E. (1984). W. D. Halls (trans.), *The division of labor in society*. New York: Macmillan.

Eakin, J. P. (1990). *Making selves: How our lives become stories*. Ithaca, NY: Cornell University Press.

Eakin, J. P. (1999). *How our lives become stories: Making selves*, Ithaca, NY: Cornell University Press.

Edelman, G. M. (1992). *Bright air, Brilliant fire: On the matter of the mind*. New York: Basic Books.

Edgeworth, F. Y. (1881). *Mathematical psychics: An essay on the application of mathematics to the Moral sciences*. London: C. K. Paul.

Edwards, D., & Potter, J. (1992). The chancellor's memory: Rhetoric and truth in discursive remembering. *Applied Cognitive Psychology, 6*, 187–215.

Elias, N. (1978). *The history of manners: The civilizing process I*. Oxford: Basil Blackwell.

Elias, N. (1982). *State formation and civilization: The civilizing process II*. Oxford: Basil Blackwell.

Elias, N. (1991). M. Schröter (ed.), & E. Jephcott (trans.), *The society of individuals*. Oxford: Basil Blackwell. 61-82.

English, R. D. (2000). *Russia and the idea of the West: Gorbachev, intellectuals and the end of the cold war.*New York: Columbia University Press.

Erikson, E. H. (1950). *Childhood and society*. New York: Norton.

Euben, J. P. (1996). Reading democracy: "Socratic" dialogues and the political education of democratic citizens.In J. Ober & C. Hedrick (eds.), *Dēmokratia: A conversation on democracies, ancient and modern* (pp. 327–59). Princeton, NJ: Princeton University Press.

Evangelista, M. (1999). *Unarmed forces: The transnational movement to end the cold war*, Ithaca, NY: Cornell University Press.

Evangelista, M. (2004). Turning points in arms control. In R. K. Herrmann & R. N. Lebow (eds.), *Ending the cold war* (pp. 83–106). New York: Palgrave.

Falk, A., Fehr, E., & Fischbacher, U. (1999). *On the nature of fair behavior*. Institute for Empirical Research in Economics, University of Zurich, Working Paper No. 17, August.

Finley, M. . (1954). *The world of Odysseus*. New York: Viking Press.

Fitzgerald, T. K. (1993*). Metaphors of identity*. Albany: State University of New York Press.

Fivush, R. (1988). The function of event memory. In U. Neisser & E. Winograd (eds.), *Remembering reconsidered: Ecological and traditional approaches to the study of memory*. Cambridge: Cambridge University Press.

Frye, T. (2000). *Brokers and bureaucrats: Building market institutions in Russia.* Ann Arbor: University of Michigan Press.

Gammon, W. (1992). The social psychology of collective action. In A. D. Morris & C. McClure Mueller (eds.), *Frontiers in social movement theory.* New Haven, CT: Yale University Press.

Gergen, K. J. (1994). Mind, text, and society: Self-memory in social context. In U. Neisser & R. Fivush (eds.), *The remembering self: Construction and accuracy in the self narrative.* Cambridge: Cambridge University Press.

Gergen, K. J. (1999). *An invitation to social construction.* London: Sage.

Goffman, E. (1959). *Presentation of self in everyday life.* New York: Doubleday.

Goffman, E. (1962). *Behavior in public places: Notes on the social organization of gatherings.* New York: Free Press.

Goffman, E. (1963). *Stigma: Notes on the management of spoiled identity.* New York: Simon & Schuster.

Gorbachev, M. (1995). *Memoirs.* New York: Doubleday.

Gray, J. (1987). *The psychology of fear and stress.* Cambridge: Cambridge University Press.

Green, D. P., & Shapiro, I. (1994). *Pathologies of rational choice theory: A critique of applications in political science.* New Haven, CT: Yale University Press.

Grotius, H. (1925). *De jure belly ac paces Libras tress.* F. W. Kelsey (trans.), Oxford: Oxford University Press.

Gurowitz, A. (1999). Mobilizing international morms: Domestic actors, immigrants and the Japanese state. *World Politics, 51,* 413–445.

Halbwachs, M. (1980). F. J. Ditter Jr. & V.Y. Ditter (trans.). *The collective memory.* New York: Harper & Row.

Hajnal, P.I . (1999). *The G7/G8 System: Evolution, role and documentation.* Brookfield, VT: Ashgate.

Hegel, G. W. F. (1942). T. M. Knox (trans.) *Philosophy of right.* Oxford: Oxford University Press.

Henrich, J., Boyd, R., Bowles, S., Camerer, C., Fehr, E., & Gintis, H. (2001). In search of homo economicus: Behavioral experiments in 15 small-scale societies. *American Economic Review, 91,* 73–78.

Herf, J. (1997). *Divided memory: The Nazi past and the two Germanies.* Cambridge: Harvard University Press.

Herrmann, R. K., & Lebow, R. N. (eds.). (2004). *Ending the cold war.* New York: Palgrave.

Herman, R. G. (1996). Identity, norms, and international security: The Soviet foreign policy revolution and the end of the cold war. In P.J. Katzenstein (ed.), *The culture of national security: Norms and identity in world politics* (pp. 271–316). New York: Columbia University Press.

Hinsley, F. H. (1963). *Power and the pursuit of peace.* Cambridge: Cambridge University Press.

Hobbes, T. (1968). C..B. Macpherson (ed.). *Leviathan.* Harmondsworth: Penguin.

Holland, D., & Quinn, N. (eds.). (1987). *Cultural models in language and thought.* Cambridge: Cambridge University Press.

Honing, B. (1993). *Political theory and the displacement of politics.* Ithaca, NY: Cornell University Press.

Hume, D. (1964). T. H. Green & T. H. Gorse (eds.), *The philosophical works, vol. II.* Aileen: Sciatica.

Hyman. Jr, I. E. (1992). Multiple approaches to remembering. *The Psychologist, 5,* 450–451.

Ikenberry, G. J. (2001. *After victory: Institutions, strategic restraint and the rebuilding of order After Major wars.* Princeton, NJ: Princeton University Press.

Inayatullab, N., & Blaney, D. L. (1997). Knowing encounters: Beyond parochialism in international relations theory. In Y. Lapid & F. Kratochwil (eds.), *The return of culture and identity in IR theory.* Boulder, CO: Lynne Rienner.

Jencks, C. (1979). The social basis of unselfishness. In H. J. Gans, N. Glazer, J. Gusfield, & C. Jencks (eds.), On the making of Americans: Essays in honor of David Riesman (pp. 63–86). Philadelphia: University of Pennsylvania Press.

Kant, I. (1991). Perpetual peace. In H. Reiss (ed.) & H. B. Nisbet (trans.), Kant's political writings (pp. 105–18). Cambridge: Cambridge University Press.

Kant, I. (1992). *Ideas toward a universal history, in Cambridge edition of the writings of Immanuel Kant.* Cambridge: Cambridge University Press.

Kaufman, S. (2001). *Modern hatreds: The symbolic politics of ethnic war.* Ithaca, NY: Cornell University Press.

Keck, M., & Sikkink, K. (1998). *Activists beyond borders: Advocacy networks in international politics.* Ithaca, NY: Cornell University Press.

Keohane, R. O. (1989). *International institutions and state power: Essays in international relations theory.* Boulder, CO: Westview.

Klotz, A. (1995). *Norms in international regimes: The struggle against apartheid.* Ithaca, NY: Cornell University Press.

Komter, A. E. (1996). *The gift: An interdisciplinary perspective.* Amsterdam: Amsterdam University Press.

Kraines, D., & Kraines, V. (1995). Evolution of learning among Pavlov strategies in a competitive environment with noise. *Journal of Conflict Resolution, 39,* 439–466.

Kratochwil, F.V. (1989). *Rules, norms, and decisions: On the conditions of practical and legal reasoning in International relations and domestic affairs.* New York: Cambridge University Press.

Lapid, Y. (1997). Culture's ship: Returns and departures in international relations theory. In Y. Lapid & F. Kratochwil (eds.), *The return of culture and identity in IR theory* (pp. 3–20). Boulder, CO: Lynne Rienner.

Lebow, R. N. (1994). The long peace, the end of the cold war, and the failure of realism. *International Organization, 48* (Spring), 249–277.

Lebow, R. N., & Stein, J. G. (1994). *We all lost the cold war.* Princeton, NJ: Princeton University Press.

Lebow, R. N. (1998). Beyond parsimony: Rethinking theories of coercive bargaining. *European Journal of International Relations, 4*(1), 31–66.

Lebow, R. N. (2003). *Tragic vision of politics: Ethics, interests, and orders.* Cambridge: Cambridge University Press.

Lebow, R. N., Kansteiner, W. and Fogu. C. (2006). *The politics of memory in postwar Europe.* Durham, NC: Duke University Press.

Lévesque, J. (1997). *The enigma of 1989: The USSR and the liberation of Eastern Europe,* Keith Martin (trans.). Berkeley: University of California Press.

Lukes, S. (1973). *Emile Durkheim: His life and work. A historical and critical study.* Palo Alto, CA: Stanford University Press.

Macpherson, C. B. (1962). *The political theory of possessive individualism: Hobbes to Locke.* Oxford: Oxford University Press.

McCall, G., & Simmons, J. (1978). *Identities and interactions*. New York: Free Press.

McDermott, R. (2004). The feeling of rationality: The meaning of neuroscientific advances for political science. *Perspectives in Politics, 2*, 691–706.

Manning, C. A. W. (1962). *The nature of international society*. London: London School of Economics.

Mansbridge, J. J. (1990). The rise and fall of self-interest in the explanation of political life. In J. J. Mansbridge (ed.), *Beyond Self-interest* (pp. 3–24). Chicago: University of Chicago Press.

Marcus, G., Neuman, W. R., & Mackuen, M. (2000). *Affective intelligence and political judgment*. Chicago: University of Chicago Press.

Mauss, M. (1990). W. D. Halls (trans.), *The gift: The form and reason for exchange in archaic societies*. New York: Norton.

Melucci, A. (1989). *Nomads of the present*. London: Hutchinson.

Milosz, C. (1990). *The captive mind*. New York: Vintage.

Molasky, M. (1999). *The American occupation of Japan and Okinawa: Literature and memory*. London: Routledge.

Morris, A., & Mueller, C. (eds.). (1992). *Frontiers in social movement theory*. New Haven, CT: Yale University Press.

Neisser, U. (1981). John Dean's memory: A case study. *Cognition, 9*, 1–22.

Neisser, U. (1992). The psychology of memory and the socio-linguistics of remembering. *The Psychologist, 5*, 451–452.

Neisser, U. (ed.). (1993). *The perceived self: Ecological and interpersonal sources of self-knowledge*. Cambridge: Cambridge University Press.

Neisser, U. (1994). Self-narratives: True and false. In U. Neisser & R. Fivush (eds.), *The remembering Self: construction and accuracy in the self narrative* (pp. 1–18). Cambridge: Cambridge University Press.

Norton, R. E. (1995). *The beautiful soul: Aesthetic morality in the eighteenth century*. Ithaca, NY: Cornell University Press.

Novick, P. (1999). *The holocaust in American life*. New York: Houghton-Mifflin.

Nowak, M. A., & Sigmund, K. (1993). A strategy of win-shift, lose-stay that outperforms tit-for-tat in the prisoner's dilemma game. *Nature, 364*, 56–58.

Nowak, M. A., Page, K. M., & Sigmund, K. (2000). Fairness versus Reason in the Ultimatum Game. *Science, 289*, 980–994.

Olick, J., & Robbins, J. (1998). Social memory studies: From "collective memory" to the historical sociology of mnemonic practices. *American Review of Sociology, 24*, 105–140.

Olson, M. (1965). *The logic of collective action*. Cambridge: Harvard University Press.

Onuf, N. G. (1998). *The republican legacy*. New York: Cambridge University Press.

Onuf, N. G. (2001). *The rise of the liberal world: Conceptual developments from Thomas Hobbes to Henry Wheaton*. Paper presented at Center of International Studies; University of Southern California, October 17.

Owen, J. (1994). How liberalism produces the democratic peace. *International Security, 19*, 87–125.

Parsons, T. (1937). *The structure of social action*. New York: McGraw-Hill.

Pasic, S. C. (1997). Culturing international relations theory: A call for extension. In Y. Lapid & F. Kratochwil (eds.), The return of culture and identity in IR theory (pp. 85–104). Boulder, CO: Lynne Rienner.

322   *Cooperation*

Peitsch, H. et al. (eds.) (1999). *European memories of the second world war.* New York: Berghahn.

Pennebaker, J. W., Paez, D., & Rimé, B. (1997). *Collective memory of political events: Social psychological perspectives.* Mahwah, NJ: Erlbaum.

Plato (1996). *Republic,* I. A. Richards (ed. and trans.). Cambridge: Cambridge University Press.

Polkinghorne, D. E. (1988). *Narrative knowing and the human sciences.* Albany: State University of New York Press.

Polkinghorne, D. E. (1991). Narrative and self-concept. *Journal of Narrative and Life History, 1,* 135–153.

Portelli, A. (ed.). (1991). Uchronic dreams: Working-class memory and possible worlds. In *The death of Luigi Trastulli and other stories: Form and meaning in oral history* (pp. 99–116). Albany: State University of New York Press.

Pufendorf, S. (1934). *De jute nature et gentium libri octo* (C. H. Oldfather, & W. A. Oldfather,Trans.).Oxford Oxford University Press.

Putnam, R. D. (2000). *Bowling alone: The collapse and revival of American community.* New York: Simon & Schuster.

Ray, J. L. (1994). How liberalism produces the democratic peace. *International Society, 20,* 87–125.

Ray, J. L. (1995). *Democracy and international conflict: An evaluation of the democratic peace proposition.* Columbia: University of South Carolina Press.

Riesman, D., Denney, R., & Glazer, N. (1950). *The lonely crowd: A study of the changing American character.* New Haven, CT: Yale University Press.

Risse, T., Ropp, S. C., & Sikkink, K. (eds.). (1999). *The power of human rights: International norms and domestic change.* Cambridge: Cambridge University Press.

Robinson, J. A. (1976). Sampling autobiography. *Cognitive Psychology, 8,* 588–595.

Rubin, D. C. (ed.). (1986). *Autobiographical memory.* Cambridge: Cambridge University Press.

Ruggie, J. G. (1983). International regimes, transactions, and change: Embedded liberalism in the postwar economic order. In S. D. Krasner (ed.), *International regimes* (pp. 195–232). Ithaca, NY: Cornell University Press.

Russet, B. (1993). *Grasping the democratic peace: Principles for a post-cold war world.* Princeton, NJ: Princeton University Press.

Schneewind, J. B. (1998). *The invention of autonomy: A history of modern moral philosophy.* New York: Cambridge University Press.

Schumpeter, J. (1963). *Capitalism, socialism and democracy.* New York: Harper & Row.

Schwartz, B.I. (1985). *The world of thought in ancient China.* Cambridge: Harvard University Press.

Searle, J. (1969). *Speech acts: An essay in the philosophy of language.* Cambridge: Cambridge University Press.

Searle, J. (1995). *The construction of social reality.* New York: Free Press.

Sen, A. K. (1978). Rational fools: A critique of the behavioral foundations of economic theory. In H. Harris (ed.), *Scientific models and men.* Oxford: Oxford University Press.

Sen, A. K. (1992). Goals, commitments and identity. *Journal of Law, Economics, and Organization, 20,* 341–355.

Shanks, C., Jacobson, H .K., & Kaplan, J. H. (1996). Inertia and change in the constellation of international governmental organizations, 1981–1991. *International Organization, 50,* 593–628.

Shotter, J. (1989). Social accountability and the social construction of "you." In J. Shotter & K. J. Gergen (eds.), *Texts of identity*. London: Sage.

Sigmund, K., (1995). *Games of life: Explorations in ecology, evolution and behavior*. Harmondsworth: Penguin.

Sigmund, K., Fehr, E., & Nowak, M. A. (2002). The economics of fair play. *Scientific American, 286*, 82–87.

Smith, A. (1976). D. Raphael and A. L. Macfie (eds.), *The theory of moral sentiments*. Oxford: Oxford University Press.

Solingen, E. (1995). The political economy of nuclear restraint. *International Security, 19*, 126–169.

Solingen, E. (1998). *Regional orders at century's dawn: Global and domestic influences on grand strategy*. Princeton, NJ: Princeton University Press.

Spence, D. P. (1982). *Narrative truth and historical truth: Meaning and interpretation in psychoanalysis*. New York: Norton.

Stein, A. A. (1990). *Why nations cooperate: Circumstance and choice in international relations*. Ithaca, NY: Cornell University Press.

Stigler, G., & Becker, G. (1977). De Sustibus non est Disputandum. *American Economic Review, 67*(2), 76–90.

Tajfel, H. (1981). *Human groups and social categories*. Cambridge: Cambridge University Press.

Tajfel, H., & Turner, J. (1986). The social identity theory of intergroup behavior. In S. Worchel & W. Austin (eds.), *Psychology of intergroup relations* (pp. 7–24). Chicago: Nelson-Hall. .

Taylor, C. (1989). *Sources of the self: The making of modern identity*. Cambridge, MA: Harvard University Press.

Taylor, C. (1991). *The malaise of modernity*. Toronto: Anansi Press.

Thompson, W. R. (1996). Democracy and peace: Putting the cart before the horse? *International Organization, 50*, 141–174.

Laue, T. H. von (1950). *Leopold von Ranke: The formative years*. Princeton, NJ: Princeton University Press.

Vico, G. (1948). G. Bergin and M .H. Fisch (trans.) *The new science*. Ithaca, NY: Cornell University Press.

Vygotsky, L. S. (1978). M. Cole (ed.), *Mind in society: The development of higher psychological processes*. Cambridge, MA: Harvard University Press.

Watson, A. (1992). *The evolution of international society*. London: Routledge.

Wendt, A. L. (1999). *Social theory of international politics*. Cambridge: Cambridge University Press.

Wight, M. (1977). *Systems of states*. Leicester: Leicester University Press.

Williams, M. (2001). The discipline of the democratic peace: Kant, liberalism and the social constructivism of security communities. *European Journal of International Relations, 7*, 525–554.

White, R. T. (1989). Recall of autobiographical events. *Applied Cognitive Psychology, 18*, 127–135.

Winograd, E., & Neisser, U. (eds.). (1992). *Affect and accuracy in recall*. New York: Cambridge University Press.

Wood, A. W. (1970). *Kant's moral religion*. Ithaca, NY: Cornell University Press.

Wu, J., & Axelrod, R. (1995). Coping with noise: How to cope with noise in the iterated prisoner's dilemma. *Journal of Conflict Resolution, 39*, 183–189.

Yack, B. (1997). *The fetishism of modernities: Epochal self-consciousness in contemporary social and political thought.* Notre Dame, IN: University of Notre Dame Press.

Yoneyama, L. (1999). *Historical traces: Time, space, and the dialectics of memory.* Berkeley: University of California Press.

10 Building international cooperation

The reconciliation of former enemies like France and Germany, Egypt and Israel, China and the United States, and the Soviet Union and the United States encourages cautious optimism about the ability of leaders and peoples to extricate themselves from deadly quarrels. This optimism must be tempered by recognition that reconciliations are not always complete or irreversible. Egypt and Israel signed a peace treaty that has endured almost 20 years, but their relations remain cool and social contacts between their peoples are limited. The Soviet Union's reconciliation with the West was brought about by a reformist regime and opposed by nationalists and traditional communists who might one day gain power in Russia. Sino-American relations, well on their way toward normalization in the early 1980s, have become more conflictual as a result of Tienamien Square, trade disputes, and differences over Taiwan.

These caveats are intended to qualify, not to deny, the fundamental nature of the transformation that has occurred in these several relationships. In the past, ideological conflict, territorial disputes, and contested spheres of influence led to arms races, hostile alliances and wars, or the expectation of war. Today, the threat of war is remote, and perhaps nonexistent in the case of France and Germany, and the leaders of all these former enemies are committed to resolving by diplomatic means whatever problems arise between them.

International relations scholars offer varied assessments of this phenomenon. One school of thought questions how lasting such reconciliations are likely to prove, and predicts that international relations will be as violent in the future as it was in the past. Other scholars are more optimistic about these relationships and about international relations in general, and have offered a variety of justifications for their optimism. The burgeoning literature on accommodation distinguishes between conflicts that ended in the aftermath of a military victory that enabled one protagonist or its allies to remake the institutions of the other (e.g., France-Germany, Japan-United States), and those where political accommodation was reached without victory by regimes that had previously been committed to confrontation (e.g., Egypt-Israel, Soviet Union-United States). Research on the former has emphasized the positive role of democratic governments, transnational institutions, and norms. Research on the latter has given more importance to international and unit level structural constraints and the allegedly beneficial consequences of general deterrence.

This chapter addresses only accommodations that have been brought about by political compromise. I begin by examining the claims that can be explained by structural factors, in particular, by changes in the distribution of capabilities or general deterrence success. I find these claims unconvincing. Structural factors are undeniably important but only part of the story. Political considerations, independent of structure, appear to have played the decisive role in accommodation. I develop my argument with reference to the East-West and Israeli-Arab conflicts. They are recent and dramatic examples of accommodation, and they are also cases in which the most far-reaching claims have been made for structural explanations.

Declining capabilities

Until recently, there was very little political science literature devoted to the problem of change. Power transition theory, an important exception, sought to explain hegemonic war in terms of the rising capabilities of challengers and the declining capabilities of hegemons.[1] Since the end of the Cold War, change has attracted the attention of theorists, and realists have tried to explain the volte face in Soviet foreign policy under Mikhail Gorbachev in terms of that country's declining capabilities. They contend that the withdrawal from Afghanistan, the liberation of Eastern Europe, and the acceptance of one-sided arms treaties were all part of a rational attempt to manage decline.[2] This explanation is fundamentally flawed.

Decline is not determining

As power transition theories predict, decline sometimes leads to war. In this century alone, Germany, Austria-Hungary and Japan went to war to stem their on-going or expected decline. Great Britain, and the Soviet Union, realists acknowledge, attempted to manage their declines through diplomacy and disengagement.[3] If decline provokes war and accommodation, we need intervening variables to account for these divergent outcomes.

This problem is compounded by the fact that war and accommodation are only two of the possible responses to decline. Leaders can also practice denial, try to shift the burdens of empire on to allies, or implement reforms intended to reverse decline. The Russian, Austrian, Ottoman and British empires all engaged in extensive denial. Britain, for much of the first half of the twentieth century, and the United States, from the 1960s to the end of the Cold War, sought to convince their allies to shoulder a greater defense burden. Leonid Brezhnev and Mikhail Gorbachev sought to revitalize the Soviet economy and stem decline through programs of reform.

Structural theories of war and accommodation are at the very least underspecified. They need to identify all the possible responses to decline and the conditions associated with them. They also need to recognize that there is enormous variation within any of these categories of response. Brezhnev and Gorbachev both responded to decline with reforms, but they were very different in their domestic and foreign substance.

Action at a distance

Since the time of Aristotle, physics has assumed that one body can only influence another if it has some form of contact with it. This can be direct, as in the collision of two billiard balls, or indirect, as in the case of electro-magnetism, whose force is transmitted from one body to another by subatomic particles.

The action at a distance problem is endemic to structural theories in the social sciences. Some structural theories try to finesse it by employing a passive construct of structure modeled on Darwin's concept of natural selection. For Darwin, structure consists of a set of constraints set by the physical environment that reward or punish certain kinds of attributes or behavior. Individuals who display these attributes or behavior are more likely to survive to the age of reproduction. Over time, therefore, individuals with these traits (or particular species) will become more numerous. Kenneth Waltz uses structure in this Darwinian sense in his theory of international relations.[4]

The actors in Darwin's struggle for survival are oblivious to the constraints of structure. Their physical or behavioral changes are the result of random mutations, a small minority of which confer competitive advantages in their environment. Structural theories in the social sciences run into trouble when they posit structures that have a direct effect on behavior. To avoid action at a distance they require a mechanism through which structure is mediated. The mechanism is people who modify their behavior in light of their understanding of structure. Most balance of power theories, for example, predict shifts in alliance patterns in response to shifts in the relative capabilities (and motives) of actors. For the balance of power to work as specified, leaders must be sensitive to these underlying changes and free to act in response to them.

Structural theories of this latter kind invariably assume that actors make timely and accurate assessments of their environments. If so, they need not be considered. Behavior can be inferred directly from structure. Actors, like electrons, are merely a conveyer belt. Realist theories that attribute the Soviet Union's accommodation with the West to its declining capabilities thus assume that Gorbachev understood the nature and implications of that decline and acted to cut his country's losses.[5]

From the perspective of East-West relations, Gorbachev's most significant act was his willingness to allow Eastern Europe to break free of communism and Soviet control. Realist analyses treat Gorbachev's retreat from Eastern Europe as an attempt to strike the best deal possible with the West, or simply to shed an expensive and unmanageable sphere of influence.[6]

Officials close to Gorbachev, however, deny that he was pursuing a policy of retrenchment. His public repudiation of the use of force to maintain existing governments in Eastern Europe was intended to undermine Warsaw Pact hard-line leaders, all of whom bitterly condemned glasnost and perestroika, and to encourage their replacement by Gorbachev-like reformers. Reform-oriented communist leaders in Eastern Europe were expected to strengthen Gorbachev's position in the Politburo and to make Soviet-bloc relations more equitable and manageable.[7]

Gorbachev's policies backfired. His call for change triggered off popular revolutions that swept away communist governments and left him no choice but to accept this fait accompli and the once unthinkable absorption of East Germany by its Western nemesis. Gorbachev had failed to grasp the extent of popular and elite antagonism to communism in Poland, Hungary, Czechoslovakia, and East Germany.

Gorbachev's domestic assessments were equally inaccurate. The Soviet Union's precipitous economic decline followed his reforms and was at least in part caused by them. Gorbachev unwittingly undermined communism in the Soviet Union, was blind to the growing threat of a conservative coup against him, and to the extent to which his domestic and foreign policies encouraged the centrifugal forces of nationalism that would lead to the breakup of the Soviet Union. Given Gorbachev's unquestioned commitment to socialism, it seems extremely unlikely that he would have behaved as he did, at home or abroad, if he and his advisers had understood the likely consequences of their policies. Domestic democratic reforms and the hands-off policy toward Eastern Europe were the result of—and probably could not have occurred without—strikingly *unrealistic* expectations about those consequences.

Structural explanations for Mikhail Gorbachev's foreign policy are guilty of *post hoc ergo propter hoc* analysis. Knowing Gorbachev's policies and their outcomes, they posit structures and assessments that must have led to these policies and outcomes. Those outcomes, however, were unwanted and unexpected, and the policies in question were carried out for other reasons. To explain Gorbachev's policies—and those of Sadat, Rabin, and Arafat—it is necessary to consider their goals, understand the foreign and domestic constraints and opportunities confronting them, and their assessments of the likely consequences of the various courses of action they saw open to them.

General deterrence

The second structural explanation for accommodation is successful general deterrence. General deterrence is a long-term strategy intended to discourage a military challenge. The defender strives to maintain a favorable military balance, or at least enough military capability to convince a challenger that a resort to force will be too risky or costly.[8]

Deterrence is not entirely unrelated to the distribution of capabilities. General deterrence success depends on adequate military capabilities, and in some conflicts may require a favorable balance of military power. Successful deterrence, however, also requires willingness to use those capabilities, and that willingness must be credibly communicated to a would-be challenger. Deterrence thus has an important psychological-political component that is related to physical capabilities but by no means synonymous with them. The deterrence and distribution of capabilities explanations overlap the most in number three below, where military competition becomes the focus and yardstick of a broader competition in capabilities.

Some scholars, and many more journalists and politicians, have credited general deterrence with winding down the Cold War and Arab-Israeli conflicts. Three kinds of claims have been made:

1 *General deterrence success.* The military capability and resolve of a defender deter a challenger from using force. The challenger tried and fails to reverse the military balance and weaken the defender's resolve by building up its military capability, concluding alliances with other dissatisfied states, and threatening the defender's allies. After some years, the challenger reluctantly concludes that deterrence is robust and that it is a waste of resources to continue the conflict. Gorbachev's efforts to end the Cold War have been described as the result of such a learning process.[9]

2 *Repeated defeat.* The same learning process leads to accommodation, but as a result of successive military defeats. The leaders of Egypt, Jordan, and Syria embraced diplomacy only after five unsuccessful and costly wars (1948, 1956, 1967, 1969–70, 1973) convinced them that Israel could not be destroyed or defeated. To achieve key foreign policy goals, they had to work with Israel.[10]

3 *Lost competition.* In this variant, general deterrence not only restrains the challenger, but convinces it that military competition with the defender is impractical. The challenger hastens to make an accommodation before the military balance turns decisively against it with all the negative political consequences that this would entail. This is the logic of those who argue that the Carter-Reagan arms buildup and Strategic Defense Initiative compelled the Soviet Union to end the Cold War on terms favorable to the West.[11]

General deterrence may contribute to the resolution of certain kinds of conflicts, but the claims made for it to date in East-West and Arab-Israeli relations remain unsubstantiated. They also encounter serious conceptual and empirical problems.[12]

Defining deterrence success

Repeated Arab defeats may well have been a catalyst for rethinking the relationship with Israel. There are no conceptual grounds, however, for describing this process as a general deterrence success. Deterrence succeeds when the military capability and resolve of a defender convince a challenger to refrain from using force. The five Arab-Israeli interstate wars were the result of general and immediate deterrence failures. Whatever Arab learning occurred was the result of Israel's ability to defend itself, inflict costly defeats on its adversaries and occupy their territory. Military defeat should not be confused with deterrence. Doing so violates the almost-universal definition of deterrence in the literature, transforming the strategy into a heads-I-win, tails-you-lose proposition.

Determining deterrence success

Deterrence failures are readily identifiable. They result in highly visible crises or wars. Deterrence successes are more elusive. Immediate deterrence is triggered by the belief that general deterrence is failing and that a military challenge is likely or probable. This expectation may be wrong but it is almost always a response to some kind of threatening adversarial behavior. These threats may be absent in general deterrence encounters. If general deterrence succeeds over time, a challenger may never consider military action or make explicit threats. The more successful general deterrence, is the fewer traces it leaves.

Assessments of general deterrence are also less reliable that those of immediate deterrence because they depend on counterfactual argument. Immediate deterrence success can in theory be documented; researchers need only ascertain that a challenger intended to use force but decided against it because of the defender's display of capability and resolve. When there are no immediate preparations to use force, and possibly no considerations of such preparations, there is no behavioral evidence to indicate the success of general deterrence. Claims for success rest on the unprovable assertion that resorts to force would have been made in the absence of deterrence.

The counterfactual basis of claims of general deterrence success also make it extraordinary difficult to distinguish between a success and a case that lies outside the scope of the theory. In immediate deterrence, this is an empirical not a theoretical problem. If the investigator is able to establish that an adversary neither considered nor planned a military challenge, the case is not an immediate deterrence encounter; the practice of deterrence—assuming it occurred—was unnecessary to forestall a use of force. In identifying cases of general deterrence, this test will not work. We would expect no active consideration of initiating hostilities in both a general deterrence success and a relationship where deterrence was unnecessary. To distinguish between these situations the investigator needs to ascertain why force was not considered—and leaders themselves may not know the answer to this question.

General deterrence also differs from immediate deterrence in its temporal dimension. General deterrence must be assessed over the course of an adversarial relationship. How well and how long does it have to work to be considered successful? We have no theoretical criteria for making such judgments. This gives considerable latitude to investigators and encourages arbitrary assessments.[13]

In the Middle East, it is easy to make the counterfactual argument that Israel would have been destroyed as a state and its Jewish inhabitants killed or expelled if they had lacked the means and will to defend themselves. Arab states went to war in 1948 with the publicly proclaimed objective of destroying Israel and remained committed to it for many years afterwards. The counterfactual argument is compelling because of the repeated failure of general and immediate deterrence and the evidence this provided of Arab intentions.

General deterrence in the Cold War confronts all of these problems: the absence of war makes it difficult to assess the role of deterrence in keeping the peace. Lack of evidence about Soviet intentions and calculations has not prevented many scholars and journalists from hailing the success of deterrence in restraining the Soviet Union. They take as axiomatic that the Kremlin sought military conquests and was only kept in check by Western military capabilities and resolve. This is a political not a scientific argument.

The evidence that has emerged since the end of the Cold War does not lend much support to deterrence claims. The Soviet military prepared to invade Western Europe just as the Strategic Air Command prepared to annihilate the Soviet bloc with nuclear weapons. There is not a scintilla of evidence, however, that leaders on either side ever considered carrying out these plans or sought a decisive military advantage for the purpose of carrying out a first strike. Rather it suggests that Soviet and American leaders alike were terrified by the prospects of nuclear war.[14]

General deterrence cannot be discounted. The Soviet Union never possessed nuclear and conventional military superiority and we do not know how its leaders would have behaved in that circumstance. It is also impossible to substantiate or rule out other explanations for absence of war. John Mueller has made the case for self-deterrence, and argues that memories of recent conventional warfare and its costs encouraged caution in Moscow and Washington.[15] In *We All Lost the Cold War*, Janice Gross Stein and I offered a political explanation for the long peace: we argue that neither superpower was ever so unhappy or threatened by the status quo that it was prepared to risk, let alone start, nuclear war to challenge or overturn it.[16]

More evidence from the Soviet archives may permit more effective discrimination among these competing explanations. Judging from what has happened in other historical controversies, for example, the origins of the First World War, I suspect that more evidence will only fuel controversy.

On the basis of the evidence at hand, I offer several observations about the role of general deterrence in facilitating conflict resolution in general and in the cases under discussion.

Deterrence is insufficient

For purposes of general deterrence, the Cold War and Middle East must be regarded as fundamentally different kinds of conflict. If neither superpower ever wanted or intended to initiate hostilities against the other, general deterrence was irrelevant, redundant, or provocative. In conflicts like the Middle East, where at least one of the protagonists would go to war if it thought it could win or otherwise gain from hostilities, general deterrence was relevant and may sometimes have succeeded in preventing war.

Even in the second kind of conflict, deterrence is at best a necessary but insufficient condition for accommodation. The fact that a challenger recognizes it cannot win a war does not mean its leaders are prepared to end that conflict and extend the olive branch to their adversary. Frustration does not necessarily lead to enlightenment; there is ample evidence that it often does the reverse. Leaders can continue the struggle by other means (e.g., economic boycotts, terrorism, subversion) or wait for more favorable circumstances, as Egypt and Syria did between 1949 and 1967 and 1967 and 1973.

Soviet-American relations provide the most dramatic evidence against the proposition that accommodation follows upon the recognition that an adversary cannot be overcome by military means. Leaders of both superpowers recognized the impossibility of a meaningful military victory from the outset of the Cold War. That conflict nevertheless endured for almost a half-century. Investigators need to look elsewhere to explain its demise.

Role conceptions

General deterrence distinguishes between a challenger, who is prepared to resort to force to alter the status quo, and a defender, who practices deterrence to discourage the use of force and defend the status quo. Conflict arises because of the challenger's goals and willingness to use force to advance them. As long as the defender remains committed to the status quo, it follows that relations between the protagonists can only improve when the challenger accepts the status quo or agrees to try to change it by peaceful means.

The role conceptions of general deterrence are politically naive. The responsibility for international conflict is rarely one-sided, nor is its origin necessarily the result of a challenge to the status quo. In both the Middle East and East-West conflicts, *all* the parties involved saw themselves as defenders and their adversaries as challengers. They often envisaged the policies that their adversaries judged to be provocative as justifiable efforts to defend or restore the status quo. These attributions cannot have been entirely self-serving because scholarly opinion is also deeply divided about the causes of these conflicts, the relative responsibility of the protagonists, and the nature of the roles they played over the years.

Even conflicts that begin as deliberate challenges to an unambiguous status quo are likely over time to evolve into something more complex. A defender may respond to a challenge by mobilizing its citizenry and allies, redirecting and expanding its military capability, forging alliances with its adversaries and trying to exploit its challenger's vulnerabilities. These actions can trigger conflict spiral that sustains confrontation long after its initial causes have disappeared. The Cold War may be a case in point. It began as a struggle for influence in Central Europe and endured three decades after de facto accommodation had been reached about the political-territorial status quo in Central Europe and almost two decades after the superpowers and their allies had formally recognized that status quo in the Final Act of the Helsinki Accords.

Resolution of most international conflict requires reorientation in thinking and policy by *both* sides. This can be very difficult to accomplish. Important political and economic groups within the protagonists may have developed vested interests in conflict and make it difficult for conciliatory leaders to gain power or implement their foreign policy agenda. Leaders who express interest in accommodation may not be taken seriously by their adversary. They also risk being rebuffed by public opinion, important allies or exploited by their adversary. The East-West and Middle East conflicts provide ample illustrations of all of these problems and indicate that a leader's commitment to reduce conflict is only the first and by no means sufficient step toward accommodation. Attempts to explain the transformation of the East-West and Middle East conflicts—or any enduring international rivalry—need to explain shifts in goals of both sides and the emergence of the domestic and foreign conditions that encourage or facilitate accommodation.

Two pathways to accommodation

I hypothesize that leaders will consider conciliatory foreign policies when: (1) they expect improved relations with adversaries to confer important domestic and international benefits, or prevent important domestic and international losses; (2) have reason to believe that their adversaries will respond positively to their conciliatory overtures; (3) consider it feasible to mobilize enough domestic support to sustain and implement a policy of accommodation.

The first condition is the most important because it addresses the incentives for accommodation. The second and third conditions pertain to feasibility. Leaders who expect to profit or stave off loss through accommodation are not likely to attempt such a policy unless they judge it to have a reasonable chance of success. Success will depend on the response of the adversary; both sides must cooperate to wind down or resolve a conflict. Leaders must also have the authority or support to carry out and sustain a policy that almost certainly represents a sharp break from accepted practice. The three conditions tell us nothing of substance about the conditions in which leaders see accommodation as conducive to the attainment of their broader political objectives. Case studies of accommodation are helpful in this connection and suggest two distinct "pathways" to accommodation.

In the first pathway, *the principal catalyst for accommodation is the commitment by leaders of one of the protagonists to domestic reforms and restructuring.* I have described this pathway elsewhere and documented the links between domestic reform and conciliatory foreign policies in the Anglo-French, Egyptian-Israeli and East-West conflicts.[17] Here I provide a brief overview of the argument in the latter two cases.

In the early 1970s Egypt's economy was in a shambles. President Anwar el-Sadat concluded that socialism from above had failed and that Egypt had to liberalize its economy. Sadat was also convinced that such a domestic transformation required some resolution to the Arab-Israeli conflict. When the 1973 war failed to achieve this end by military means, Sadat searched actively for a diplomatic solution which would create the stable climate necessary to attract foreign investment and aid from the West.[18]

Sadat expected that a peace agreement with Israel brokered by the United States would create the conditions for the successful liberalization of the Egyptian economy. The United States would provide extensive economic aid and technical assistance to jump start the Egyptian economy. In a more secure and stable environment, foreign investment from the capitalist countries would flow into Egypt, accelerating economic growth. Only if the Egyptian economy grew could Egypt begin to address the fundamental infrastructural and social problems that it faced. Peace with Israel was important not only because of the direct benefits that it would bring—the return of the Sinai oil fields and an end to humiliation—but because of the opportunity it provided to open Egypt to the West and particularly to the United States.[19]

Mikhail S. Gorbachev's efforts to transform East-West relations were also motivated in large part by his commitment to domestic restructuring. Perestroika required an accommodation with the West; this would permit resources to be shifted from military to civilian investment and production, and attract credits, investment, and technology from the West. According to Foreign Minister Shevardnadze, the chief objective of Soviet foreign policy became "to create the maximum favorable external conditions needed in order to conduct internal reform."[20]

For Gorbachev and his closest advisers there was another important link between foreign and domestic policy. In the view of *perestroichiks*, the conflict with the West had been kept alive and exploited by the communist party to justify its monopoly on power and suppression of dissent.[21] "New thinking" in foreign policy would break the hold of the party old guard and the influence of the military-industrial complex with which it was allied.[22]

For committed democrats like Shevardnadze, perestroika and glasnost also had an ideological component. For the Soviet Union to join the Western family of nations, it had to become a democratic society with a demonstrable respect for the individual and collective rights of its citizens and allies. Granting independence to the countries of Eastern Europe was the international analog to emptying the Gulags, ending censorship in the media, and choosing members of the Supreme Soviet through free elections. Perestroika, Shevardnadze explained, "was understood to be universally applicable and could not be guided by a double standard.

If you start democratizing your own country, you no longer have the right to thwart that same process in other countries."[23]

The second mediating condition of a conciliatory response is the understanding leaders have of the consequences of confrontation. Leaders are more likely to pursue conciliatory foreign policies when they believe confrontation has failed. In all three cases, leaders recognized that confrontation had failed, had been extraordinarily costly, and was unlikely to succeed in the future.

Sadat's peace initiative took place in the aftermath of military failure, a costly war in which Egypt was frustrated in its battlefield goals. Egyptian officials recognized that military conditions in 1973 had been optimal—Egyptian and Syrian armies were armed with the latest weapons, mounted a joint attack, and achieved surprise—yet the war ended with Egyptian armies on the verge of a catastrophic military defeat. It was clear to Sadat and his generals that, even under the best possible conditions, Egypt could not hope to defeat Israel. Sadat thus began to search for a diplomatic solution that would return the Suez Canal to Egypt. He sought to involve the United States as a mediator, broker, and guarantor of a peace settlement.

Mikhail Gorbachev's search for accommodation was also a reaction to the failure and costs of confrontation. Under Leonid Brezhnev, the Soviet Union had steadily built up its conventional and nuclear arsenals in a bid for military superiority. Brezhnev and many of his colleagues, and the Soviet military establishment, were convinced that a shift in the correlation of forces in favor of the socialist camp would compel the West to treat the Soviet Union as an equal superpower. Nixon and Kissinger's interest in détente, which came at a time when the Soviet Union was drawing abreast of the United States in strategic nuclear capability, confirmed their view of the political value of military forces.[24]

Soviet leaders reasoned that additional forces would further improve their position vis à vis the West and continued their buildup into the 1980s. Their policy had the opposite effect. Moscow's seeming pursuit of strategic superiority coupled with its more assertive policy in the Third World handed American militants a powerful weapon to use against détente. The Carter administration was forced to begin its own strategic buildup and then to withdraw the proposed SALT II Treaty from the Senate. The apparent upsurge in Soviet aggressiveness and Carter's seeming inability to confront it, contributed to Reagan's electoral landslide and support for his more extensive military buildup and anti-Soviet foreign policy.

Soviet foreign policy analysts in the institutes were sensitive to the ways in which Brezhnev's crude military and foreign policy had provoked a pernicious American reaction. Their critiques of Soviet policy circulated widely among the Soviet elite. These analyses were especially critical of the increasingly costly intervention in Afghanistan. They also took Brezhnev and the military to task for their deployment of SS-20s in Eastern Europe and the western military districts of the Soviet Union. They maintained that the commitment of NATO to deploy Pershing II ballistic missiles and ground launched cruise missiles (GLCMs), which Moscow found so threatening, was a predictable response to Moscow's provocative and unnecessary deployment of highly accurate short- and intermediate range nuclear systems.[25]

The overarching theme of these analyses was that the Brezhnev buildup had provoked the same kind of pernicious overreaction in the United States that the Kennedy-McNamara buildup of the 1960s had in the Soviet Union. Soviet attempts to intimidate China with a massive buildup along its border were said to have had the same effect. A different and more cooperative approach to security was necessary.

Soviet failures in Afghanistan and in managing relations with the United States and Western Europe prompted a fundamental reassessment of foreign policy on the part of intellectuals and politicians not associated with these policies. Gorbachev and Shevardnadze maintain that their foreign policy views were formed in reaction to Brezhnev's failures and were significantly shaped by the analyses of Soviet critics in the foreign ministry and institutes. Both men had long conversations with analysts and foreign ministry critics of Brezhnev's policies before they decided to withdraw from Afghanistan. Such individuals were also instrumental in Gorbachev's and the Politburo's decision to accept on-site inspection, which helped to break the logjam in arms control.[26]

The Gorbachev revolution in foreign policy is reminiscent of the French experience in a second important way. The humiliation of Fashoda was the catalyst for a major shift of power within France that facilitated the emergence of a new foreign policy line. Soviet officials agree that economic stagnation and the running sore of Afghanistan paved the way to power for a reform-oriented leader. Once in the Kremlin, Gorbachev exploited Afghanistan and the deployment by NATO of Pershing us and GLCMs in Western Europe to discredit the militants and gain the political freedom to pursue a more conciliatory policy toward the West.[27]

The third condition facilitating accommodation is the expectation of reciprocity. *Leaders will be more likely to initiate conciliatory policies when they believe that their adversary is more likely to reply in kind than to exploit their overtures for its unilateral advantage.* In many, if not most, adversarial relationships, leaders fear that any interest they express in accommodation, or any concessions they make, will communicate weakness to their adversary and prompt a more aggressive policy rather than concessions in kind. Given the serious foreign and domestic costs of failed efforts at accommodation, leaders are only likely to pursue conciliatory policies when they expect such policies to be reciprocated.

Anwar el-Sadat had reason to suppose that Israel might respond positively to an offer of a peace treaty. He made extensive private inquiries about Prime Minister Menachem Begin. He asked Nicolae Ceauçescu of Rumania, who had met Begin several times, whether the prime minister was sincere in his interest in peace and if he could fulfill any commitment that he made. Reassured by the Romanian leader, Sadat sent his Deputy Premier, Hassan Tuhami, to meet secretly in Morocco with Israeli Foreign Minister Moshe Dayan to explore the outlines of an agreement. Dayan assured Tuhami that Israel would consider returning the Sinai to Egypt in exchange for a full peace. Only when his expectations of reciprocity were confirmed did Sadat undertake his public and dramatic visit to Jerusalem.

For the Soviet Union, the importance of the expectation of reciprocity is best illustrated by the different policies of Nikita Khrushchev and Mikhail Gorbachev, the two Soviet leaders most interested in accommodation with the West. Gorbachev was able to pursue—and to persevere with—his search for accommodation because of the positive evolution of superpower relations since the height of the Cold War in the early 1960s.

Gorbachev was much less fearful than Khrushchev that the United States and its allies would exploit any Soviet concession. Khrushchev's intense fear of the West had severely constrained his search for accommodation. He was unprepared to gamble, as Gorbachev did, that conciliatory words and deeds would generate sufficient public pressure on Western governments to reciprocate. Khrushchev did make some unilateral concessions; he reduced the size of the armed forces and proclaimed a short-lived moratorium on nuclear testing. When his actions were not reciprocated, he felt the need to demonstrate firmness to buttress his position at home and abroad. His inflammatory rhetoric strengthened the hand of militants in the West who all along opposed accommodation with the Soviet Union.[28]

Gorbachev succeeded in transforming East-West relations and ending the Cold War because the West became his willing partner. Unlike Khrushchev, whose quest for a German peace treaty frightened France and West Germany, Gorbachev's attempt to end the division of Europe met a receptive audience, especially in Germany and Western Europe. Disenchantment with the Cold War, opposition to the deployment of new weapons systems, and a widespread desire to end the division of Europe, created a ground-swell of support for exploring the possibilities of accommodation with the Soviet Union. Western public opinion, given voice by well-organized peace movements, was a critical factor in encouraging Gorbachev and his colleagues in their attempts at conciliation.

Gorbachev was intent on liberalizing the domestic political process at home and improving relations with the West. Within a month of assuming office, he made his first unilateral concession—a temporary freeze on the deployment of Soviet intermediate range missiles in Europe. This was followed by a unilateral moratorium on nuclear tests and acceptance of the Western "double zero" proposal for reducing intermediate-range nuclear forces (INF) in Europe. In subsequent speeches and proposals, he tried to demonstrate his support for sweeping arms control and a fundamental restructuring of superpower relations. President Ronald Reagan continued to speak of the Soviet Union as an "evil empire" and remained committed to his quest for a near-perfect ballistic missile defense.

To break this impasse, Gorbachev pursued a two-pronged strategy. In successive summits he tried and finally convinced Reagan of his genuine interest in ending the arms race and restructuring East-West relations on a collaborative basis. When Reagan changed his opinion of Gorbachev, he also modified his view of the Soviet Union and quickly became the leading dove of his administration. Gorbachev worked hard to convince Western publics that his policies represented a radical departure from past Soviet policies. The Soviet withdrawal from Afghanistan, freeing of political prisoners, and liberalization of the Soviet political system, evoked widespread sympathy and support in the West and generated strong public pressure on NATO governments to respond in kind to Gorbachev's initiatives.

Gorbachev's political persistence succeeded in breaching Reagan's wall of mistrust. At their Reykjavik summit in October 1986, the two leaders talked seriously about eliminating all of their ballistic missiles within 10 years and making deep cuts in their nuclear arsenals. No agreement was reached because Reagan was unwilling to accept any restraints on his Strategic Defense Initiative. The Reykjavik summit, as Gorbachev had hoped, nevertheless began a process of mutual reciprocation, reassurance, and accommodation between the superpowers. That process continued after an initially hesitant George Bush became Gorbachev's full-fledged partner in ending the vestiges of 40 years of Cold War.

A second, different pathway to accommodation is through vulnerabilities that leaders believe can only be addressed through collaboration with their adversaries. This was probably the fundamental cause of the ongoing rapprochement in the Middle East between Israel and the Palestinians and Israel and Jordan.

Prime Minister Yitzhak Rabin, an experienced military officer, was convinced by Iraqi SCUD attacks during the Gulf War that Israel faced an increasing threat of biological and chemical attacks from its determined enemies. The civilian population would be increasingly at risk as there was no adequate defense against such weapons. Although Israel could retaliate, it could not adequately deter in Rabin's judgment. It was accordingly in Israel's interest to reach an accommodation with the Palestinians and Syria.

The other driving factor was Rabin's preoccupation with the United States. The U.S.-Israeli relationship had always been a preoccupation for Rabin. The Bush administration had put tremendous pressure on Israel over loan guarantees, tying them to a freezing of settlements on the West Bank. The two issues—the threat of unconventional attacks, and the need to repair the rift in U.S.-Israeli relations—combined to stimulate interest in accommodation.

The pressures on Yasir Arafat were greater. The PLO was at its lowest point in its history. Following the Gulf War, Arafat and the PLO had lost the financial support of the Gulf countries and Arafat was unable to pay the salaries of his large staff in the West Bank and Gaza. In both territories, the Intifada had been captured by indigenous Palestinian leaders who operated with growing autonomy. Hamas, vocally antagonistic to the PLO, was growing stronger. Arafat was also pushed toward accommodation by the disappearance of the Soviet Union and the loss of its support.

The two pathways have several features in common that in turn have important implications for the study of accommodation.

Domestic politics

Sadat and Gorbachev were intensely focused on their domestic agendas, and adopted foreign policies they thought would advance those agendas. Domestic considerations were also critical for Rabin and Arafat. For at least three of the four leaders the link between domestic and foreign policy was the reverse of that posited by most theories of foreign policy. By ignoring domestic politics, existing theories fail to capture some of the most important motives for foreign policy change.

Biased assessment

Risk assessments can be significantly influenced by what is at stake. Studies of immediate deterrence failures document numerous instances of leaders who committed themselves to aggressive challenges of adversarial commitments to cope with pressing strategic and domestic problems.[29] Because they believed that these problems could only be overcome through successful challenges they convinced themselves, sometimes in the face of strong disconfirming evidence, that their challenges would succeed. Gorbachev's behavior indicates that a commitment to accommodation can encourage the same kind of motivated bias in information processing. In the absence of any real evidence and against the advice of prominent advisers, he convinced himself that he could change Ronald Reagan's view of arms control and of the Soviet Union and achieve the kind of breakthrough essential for a wider political accommodation. Gorbachev's success suggests the corollary that expectations of reciprocity can sometimes be made self-fulfilling, just like expectations of conflict.

Gorbachev's other miscalculations had less satisfactory results from his perspective. His public call for reform in Eastern Europe set in motion a chain of events that led to the overthrow of seven communist governments, demise of the Warsaw Pact and the reunification of Germany under Western auspices. Gorbachev's domestic economic and political reforms accelerated the decline of the Soviet economy and were the proximate causes of communism's collapse and the breakup of the Soviet Union.

Sadat also made serious miscalculations. Above all, he miscalculated the short-term consequences of accommodation with Israel. He expected the process to move quickly, so that Arab opposition to it would not have a chance to coalesce and organize. He further expected the Gulf states to support, at least tacitly, any accommodation that was backed by the United States. Finally, he expected that accommodation would result in a flood of foreign investment in Egypt. All these calculations were wrong and put Sadat into a difficult political position. His political isolation at home and abroad and the failure of the peace process to address or assist the Palestinians were contributing causes to his assassination.

These miscalculations had many causes, but perhaps the most fundamental one was the contradictory nature of the goals these leaders sought. Gorbachev wanted to make the Soviet Union a freer, more productive country with more equitable relations with its Warsaw Pact allies and the West. He also wanted to preserve the core of political communism and its command economy. He deluded himself into believing that these objectives were not only compatible, but reinforcing, when in reality the former could only be achieved at the expense of the latter.[30] Sadat was also involved in a fundamental contradiction between his desire for rapid economic growth and his commitment to autocratic and corrupt government. He also deluded himself into believing that he could have peace with Israel and continue to receive much needed financial aid from the Gulf states.

Our cases give rise to a disturbing speculation. Would Sadat and Gorbachev have pursued their respective accommodations if they had had a better understanding of their consequences? Did accommodation depend on gross wishful thinking by the leaders responsible for initiating it? If so, what theoretical implications does this have for scholars attempting to explain and predict such accommodations—and, more importantly, for leaders contemplating them? Would they—and their countries—have been better off eschewing accommodation? This is, of course, the contention of embittered Russian communists and uncompromising Arab nationalists.

Structural explanations assume that leaders are more or less interchangeable; rational leaders who confront the same combination of constraints and opportunities will respond in similar ways. Our cases indicate enormous variation. Brezhnev and Gorbachev both recognized the need to reinvigorate the Soviet economy, but implemented strikingly different reform programs and related foreign policies, just as Rabin and Shamir adopted different policies to safeguard Israel's security. These differences cannot be attributed to changing circumstances. Opponents of Sadat, Gorbachev, Rabin, and Arafat would not have pursued accommodation, and they were not powerless because of their opposition to accommodation; the choice of leader in all cases was determined by other issues and considerations.

Approaches that focus on the decisive and independent role of leaders confront a difficult challenge. They ultimately need to explain why different leaders adopt different policies. We have taken a step in this direction by identifying some of the political visions, pressures and learning experiences that appear to promote accommodation. Our propositions need to be tested in other cases and in other periods of the East-West and Middle East conflicts. Were these conditions present in other cases and at other times, and were they associated with attempts at accommodation? Other cases also need to be examined to identify other possible pathways to accommodation. If our findings prove valid, they will have some explanatory and predictive value. They take us only part way to our goal, however. They tell us nothing about the reasons why leaders develop the particular visions, goals and lessons that prompt them to seek accommodation.

The challenge posed by this question is most evident in the case of Sadat. He was almost unique among the Egyptian political elite in his belief that accommodation with Israel was advisable and feasible. His commitment to economic restructuring was controversial but more widely shared.

The beliefs and goals of leaders are also difficult to explain when they are more widely shared. An important segment of the Soviet elite also favored economic reform, liberalization of the political system, withdrawal from Afghanistan and improved relations with the West. Gorbachev was a relative latecomer to foreign policy and appears to have adopted many of his foreign policy goals from his most liberal advisers. Why did Gorbachev assimilate these views and not those of the more conservative officials with whom he worked? A number of explanations have been proposed (e.g., generational learning, domestic politics, coalition building), and they all encounter problems.[31]

Caveats

My propositions represent a tentative step toward a more comprehensive theoretical explanation of accommodation. They need to be tested and incorporated into a broader theory that more fully specifies the domestic and other conditions that prompt policy makers to extend the olive branch to their adversaries.

The first step in testing my propositions would be to search my three cases for other times in which any of the three conditions was present. Evidence that other attempts at conciliation were made under similar conditions would strengthen their claim to validity. The finding that my three conditions were present on one or more occasions and no attempt at conciliation was made would indicate that they are insufficient. It would trigger a search for additional conditions and evidence also present in the three attempts at conciliation investigated in this chapter. The finding that additional attempts at conciliation were made under different conditions would point to the existence of different pathways to accommodation.

My propositions also need to be tested in other cases. To do this I need to construct an appropriate data set. Ideally, it should include the universe of twentieth-century cases of attempted conciliation. This would allow the testing of propositions about the conditions under which conciliation is attempted and the conditions under which it succeeds. Once again, the next step would be to see if the conditions associated with conciliation were present on occasions when conciliation was not attempted.

This chapter examined only one pathway to accommodation. In all three cases, leaders sought to resolve long-standing international conflicts because they regarded it as essential or extremely beneficial to the success of their domestic reforms. I fully expect that a search of other cases would reveal additional incentives and pathways to accommodation. One alternative incentive is mutual fear of a third party. It played a role in Anglo-French relations in the years between 1905 and 1914, and was probably central to the Sino-American rapprochement of the 1970s. Economic incentives may have been critical in the partial accommodations between the two Germanys during the era of *Ostpolitik* and the two Chinas today.

There is also the important question of how leaders respond to conciliatory initiatives. Successful accommodation requires reciprocity. My first pathway describes how a leader adopts a more conciliatory foreign policy to facilitate domestic restructuring. The other side must respond positively, reassure the initiator of its own interest in accommodation, and both sides must work together to resolve outstanding differences between them and institutionalize their new relationship.

Prior to 1986 there were four unsuccessful attempts to transform Soviet-American relations: by the post-Stalin troika in 1953–55, Nikita Khrushchev in 1959–60, Leonid Brezhnev and Richard Nixon from 1969 to 1973, and Jimmy Carter from 1976 to 1979. The Khrushchev and Carter experiences show the dangers of unsuccessful attempts at accommodation. Both leaders came under blistering criticism from hardliners at home and sought to protect themselves by intensifying confrontation with their adversary.[32]

Reciprocity is essential but by no means inevitable, as Soviet-American relations illustrate. We need to study successful and unsuccessful attempts at accommodation and develop propositions that explain divergent responses. The explanations for reciprocity may prove quite different from those of initiation. This is not a problem in the second pathway that delineates how similar kinds of incentives move both sides simultaneously toward accommodation.

What is accommodation?

Research on accommodation has focused almost entirely on independent variables; researchers have advanced a series of competing propositions to explain accommodation in general and the East-West and Arab-Israeli accommodations in particular. We also need to focus attention on the dependent variable. Just what do we mean by accommodation? Is it a sharp decline in the probability of war (Israel-Egypt)? Must relations improve to the point where war becomes almost unthinkable (United Kingdom-France, United States-United Kingdom, France-Germany)? Or is it something in between (Russia-United States)?

A decline in the probability of war leads to, or reflects, an improved relationship. Reconciliation, however, requires more than removal of the threat of war. If the Anglo-French and Franco-German experiences can be taken as guides, it requires resolution of important outstanding issues, the building of close economic and social ties and a fundamental compatibility in political institutions and values.

There are different degrees of accommodation, and researchers need to specify the kind of accommodation they mean. Toward this end it would be helpful to identify the stages relationships can pass through from outright hostility to full reconciliation. This would allow for more appropriate case comparisons. If, as we suspect, conflicts move (or fail to move) from one stage to another for different reasons, it would also break down the dependent variable into more analytically meaningful categories.[33]

For scholars interested in peace, the probability of war will initially remain the critical dependent variable. Peace, however, ultimately depends on the quality of the broader relationship. Conflicts in which the probability of war has been sharply reduced but otherwise remain frozen (Israel-Egypt, Greece-Turkey) can readily heat up in response to regime changes or other threatening developments. This can also happen in relationships where accommodation has gone further. There is growing concern at the moment about the future of Chinese-Taiwan relations, and this is in spite of growing levels of investment and social intercourse.[34]

Broader relationships are important in a second sense. Accommodation is not a stochastic process; it is more likely to occur under some circumstances than others. The pathways we have described require domestic or strategic incentives, the expectation of reciprocity and the ability to mobilize adequate domestic support behind the peace process, and any agreement and whatever implementation it requires. These conditions are more likely to develop after a conflict has been ongoing for some time. They may also reflect accumulated frustration and costs on both sides.

The East-West conflict provides the best illustration of this proposition. Most analyses of the end of that conflict understandably focus on the policies of Mikhail Gorbachev. Major improvements in East-West relations, however, took place long before Gorbachev came to power in 1985. By 1985, that conflict was characterized by a fundamental stability. Twenty-three years had elapsed since the last war-threatening crisis. The superpowers took each other's commitment to avoid war for granted and had signed a series of arms control and rules-of-the-road agreements to regulate their strategic competition and interaction. These accords weathered the shocks of the Soviet invasion of Afghanistan and Reagan's commitment to Star Wars. Gorbachev's initiatives were built on this preexisting foundation.[35]

Gorbachev's policies initiated the final phase of a reconciliation that had been proceeding fitfully since the death of Stalin. Gorbachev would never have contemplated, or have been allowed to carry out, his domestic reforms, asymmetrical arms control agreements, and encouragement of reform in Eastern Europe, if the majority of the Central Committee had expected a hostile West to respond aggressively to a visibly weaker Soviet Union. The willingness of Gorbachev and his key associates to make unilateral concessions without apparent fear of their foreign policy consequences indicates that for them the Cold War had already receded into the past. They were discarding its atavistic institutional remnants to facilitate cooperation with their former adversaries and reap its expected benefits.

All three of our accommodations illustrate the important role of ideas. The fundamental, underlying cause of the resolution of the East-West conflict was a dramatic shift in the Soviet conception of security. The rejection of confrontation in favor of "common security" paved the way for the series of unilateral gestures that broke the logjam of East-West conflict. This conceptual revolution was preceded by an earlier and equally important conceptual breakthrough: the recognition by superpower leaders that they both feared nuclear war and were committed to its prevention. This recognition was responsible for the stability that characterized East-West relations from the mid-1960s. Both changes in conception were largely independent of capabilities. Analysts need to look elsewhere, to learning and how elite conceptions are shaped through personal and national political experiences, and reading and personal contacts with one another, advisers, intellectuals and diplomats, scientists and journalists who can function as conveyer belts of ideas and information between adversaries.[36]

Arab-Israeli accommodation also involved learning, but of a different kind. Arab leaders recognized that they could not win a war. Once that recognition set in, the advantages of accommodation should have been obvious: territory regained, occupation ended, an improved relationship with the United States, and greater economic opportunities in the region and through the vehicle of American aid. Although defeat drove home these lessons to Sadat, it did not to most of his contemporaries. More recently, Palestinians and Israelis alike are deeply divided on the issue of peace. Proponents and opponents alike draw diametrically opposed policy lessons from the shared historical experiences.

Our analysis indicates that structural explanations of accommodation are inadequate. At best, declining capabilities and deterrence success represent necessary but insufficient conditions for accommodation. The visions of leaders, the concrete goals, and their understanding of the constraints and opportunities they confront provide a more compelling explanation of accommodation. These considerations cannot be accounted for with reference to any of the so-called structures prominent in the foreign policy and international relations literature. This is not to say that political visions—for example, the increasing preference of elites for democratic governments and market economies—are not themselves a reflection of underlying conditions. Ultimately, the explanation for accommodation must be sought in an understanding of the complex interplay of structure and politics.

Notes

1 For example, George Modelski, "The Long Cycle of Global Politics and the Nation-State," *Comparative Studies of Society and History* 20 (April 1978): 214–35; Charles F. Doran and Wes Parsons, "War and the Cycle of Relative Power," *The American Political Science Review* 74 (December 1960): 947–65; William R. Thompson, ed., *Contending Approaches to World System Analysis* (Beverly Hills, CA: Sage, 1983); A. F. K. Organski and Jacek Kugler, *The War Ledger* (Chicago: University of Chicago Press, 1980); Raimo Väyrynen, "Economic Cycles, Power Transitions, Political Management and Wars Between Major Powers," *International Studies Quarterly* 27 (December 1983): 389–418; Robert Gilpin, *War and Change in World Politics* (New York: Cambridge University Press, 1981). This literature is reviewed by Jack S. Levy, "Declining Power and the Preventive Motivation for War," *World Politics* 40 (October 1987): 82–107.

2 See, for example, Daniel Deudney and G. John Ikenberry, "The International Sources of Soviet Change," *International Security* 16 (Winter 1991/92): 74–118, and

"Soviet Reform and the End of the Cold War: Explaining Large-Scale Historical Change," *Review of International Studies* 17 (Summer 1991): 225–50; Kenneth A. Oye, "Explaining the End of the Cold War: Morphological and Behavioral Adaptations to the Nuclear Peace," in *International Relations Theory and the End of the Cold War*, ed. Richard Ned Lebow and Thomas Risse-Kappen (New York: Columbia University Press, 1994), 57–84; William C. Wohlforth, "Realism and the End of the Cold War," *International Security* 19 (Winter 1994/95): 91–129.

3 Gilpin, War and Change, 192–97; Wohlforth, "Realism and the End of the Cold War," and Aaron L. Friedberg, *The Weary Titan: Britain and the Experience of Relative Decline, 1895–1905* (Princeton, NJ: Princeton University Press, 1988).

4 Kenneth N. Waltz, *Theory of International Politics* (Reading, MA: Addison-Wesley, 1979). See Richard Ned Lebow, "The Long Peace, The End of the Cold War, and the Failure of Realism," in Lebow and Risse-Kappen, *International Relations Theory and the End of the Cold War*, 46–49, for a critique of Waltz's use of Darwin.

5 Hans Morgenthau, *Politics Among Nations: The Struggle for Power and Peace* (New York: Knopf, 1948), Part 3, recognized this problem, and acknowledged that leaders do not always grasp the imperatives of structure and that their policies are influenced by nonmaterial factors like ideology. Morgenthau's theory was not determinist, and he invoked nonmaterial considerations to explain behavior at variance with his theory. Wohlforth, "Realism and the End of the Cold War," 97–98, also acknowledges that "decision makers' assessments of power are what matters." At the outset of his article, he uses the word perception in its psychological sense, and appears to acknowledge the inherently subjective nature of assessment. Later on, however, when discussing Soviet policy, perception represents objective and rational understanding of capabilities. What Wohlforth appears to concede in his theory section he takes back in its empirical application.

6 John Mearsheimer, "Back to the Future: Instability in Europe After the Cold War," *International Security* 15 (Summer 1990): 5–56; Kenneth N. Waltz, "The Emerging Structure of International Politics," *International Security* 18 (Fall 1993): 44–79; Valerie Bunce, "Soviet Decline as a Regional Hegemon: the Gorbachev Regime and Eastern Europe," *Eastern European Politics and Societies* 3 (Spring 1989): 235–67; "The Soviet Union Under Gorbachev: Ending Stalinism and Ending the Cold War," *International Journal* 46 (Spring 1991): 220–41; Oye, "Explaining the End of the Cold War"; Wohlforth, "Realism and the End of the Cold War."

7 For evidence, see Stephen F. Cohen and Katrina vanden Heuvel, *Voices of Glasnost: Interviews with Gorbachev's Reformers* (New York: Norton, 1989), passim; Jack F. Matlack, Jr., *Autopsy of an Empire: The American Ambassador's Account of the Collapse of the Soviet Union* (New York: Random House, 1995), 68–154; Archie Brown, *The Gorbachev Factor* (New York: Oxford University Press, 1996), chap. 7.

8 Patrick Morgan, *Deterrence, A Conceptual Analysis* (Beverly Hills, CA: Sage, 1977), is generally credited with this distinction.

9 Daniel Deudney and G. John Ikenberry, "The International Sources of Soviet Domestic Change," *International Security* 13 (Winter 1991/92): 74–118; Oye, "Explaining the End of the Cold War." Learning and adaptation to unsuccessful competition are also important components of the explanations for the shift in Soviet policy in the arguments of Michael W. Doyle, "Liberalism and the End of the Cold War," and Jack Snyder, "Myths, Modernization, and the Post-Gorbachev World," in Lebow and

Risse-Kappen, *International Relations Theory and the End of the Cold War*, 85–108, 109–26.

10 Elli Lieberman, "The Rational Deterrence Theory Debate and the Role of Deterrence in Enduring Rivalries." Unpublished paper.

11 Wohlforth, "Realism and the End of the Cold War"; John Mearsheimer, "Back to the Future"; Waltz, "The Emerging Structure of International Politics"; Bunce, "Soviet Decline as a Regional Hegemon."

12 For a discussion of the methodological problems of studying general deterrence, see Richard Ned Lebow and Janice Gross Stein, *When Does Deterrence Succeed and How Do We Know?* (Ottawa: Canadian Institute for International Peace and Security, 1990); Gary Goertz, "Enduring Rivalries and the Study of Deterrence," paper prepared for the Conference on Great Power Rivalries, held on April 27–29 at the Center for the Study of International Relations at the University of Indiana.

13 In his analysis of Israeli-Syrian relations, Yair Evron, *War and Intervention in Lebanon* (Baltimore: Johns Hopkins University Press, 1987), maintains that general deterrence succeeded between 1975 and 1985 because the two countries fought only one major war. Evron counts any year without a war as a success, making deterrence 90% successful during the decade. He also begins his ten-year period in 1975, conveniently excluding the Israeli-Syrian conflicts of 1973 and 1974. Robert Jervis, "Rational Deterrence: Theory and Practice," *World Politics* 41 (January 1989): 183–207, also notes the arbitrary use of temporal indicators of success.

14 On Khrushchev and Brezhnev, see Richard Ned Lebow and Janice Gross Stein, *We All Lost the Cold War* (Princeton, NJ: Princeton University Press), 1994 esp. chap. 14.

15 John Mueller, *Retreat From Doomsday: The Obsolescence of Major War* (New York: Basic Books, 1989).

16 Lebow and Stein, *We All Lost the Cold War*.

17 Richard Ned Lebow, "The Search for Accommodation: Gorbachev in Comparative Perspective," in Lebow and Risse-Kappen, *International Relations Theory and the End of the Cold War*, 167–86.

18 See Janice Gross Stein, "The Political Economy of Strategic Agreement: The Linked Costs of Failure at Camp David," in *Domestic Politics and International Negotiation: An Integrative Perspective*, ed. Peter Evans, Harold Jacobson, and Robert Putnam (Berkeley: University of California Press, 1993), 77–103.

19 Ibid.

20 Eduard Shevardnadze, *The Future Belongs to Freedom*, trans. Catherine A. Fitzpatrick (New York: Free Press, 1991), xi.

21 Author's interviews with Fedor Burlatsky, Cambridge, October 12, 1987; Vadim Zagladin, Moscow, May 18, 1989; Oleg Grinevsky, Vienna, and New York, October 11, and November 10, 1991; Georgiy Arbatov, Ithaca, New York, November 15, 1991; Anatoliy Dobrynin, Moscow, December 17, 1991.

22 For a good discussion of "new thinking" in foreign policy, see David Holloway, "Gorbachev's New Thinking," *Foreign Affairs* 68 (Winter 1988/89): 66–81.

23 Shevardnadze, *The Future Belongs to Freedom*, xii.

24 Lebow and Stein, *We All Lost the Cold War,* chap. 8.

25 Author's interviews with Oleg Grinevsky, Vienna, October 11, 1991, New York, November 10, 1991, Stockholm, April 25, 1992; Leonid Zamyatin, Moscow, Decem-

ber 16, 1991; and Anatoliy Dobrynin, Moscow, December 17, 1991. See also, Sarah E. Mendelsohn, "Explaining Change in Foreign Policy: The Soviet Withdrawal from Afghanistan," Columbia University dissertation, 1993, and the forthcoming Cornell University dissertation of Robert Herman, "Soviet New Thinking: Ideas, Interests and the Redefinition of Security."

26 Ibid., and Shevardnadze, *The Future Belongs to Freedom*, passim.
27 Ibid.; Interviews with Oleg Grinevsky, Vadim Zagladin,, and Anatoliy Dobrynin.
28 Lebow and Stein, *We All Lost the Cold War*, chap. 3, on Khrushchev's strategy.
29 Richard Ned Lebow, *Between Peace and War: The Nature of International Crisis* (Baltimore: forms Hopkins University Press, 1981); "Deterrence Failure Revisited: A Reply to the Critics," *International Security* 12 (Summer 1987): 197–213; Janice Gross Stein, "Calculation, Miscalculation, and Conventional Deterrence I: The View from Cairo," and "Calculation, Miscalculation, and Conventional Deterrence II: The View from Jerusalem," in Robert Jervis, Richard Ned Lebow, and Janice Gross Stein, *Psychology and Deterrence* (Baltimore: Johns Hopkins University Press, 1985), 34–59, 60–88; Lebow and Stein, *We All Lost the Cold War*, Richard Ned Lebow and Janice Gross Stein, "Deterrence: The Elusive Dependent Variable," *World Politics* 42 (April 1990): 336–69, on how not to study immediate deterrence.
30 Lebow and Stein, *We All Lost the Cold War*, chap. 3, argue that there was a similar contradiction in Khrushchev's goals and that it was a fundamental cause of many of his most important foreign and domestic policy miscalculations.
31 See, for example, Thomas Risse-Kappen, "Ideas Do Not Float Freely: Transnational Coalitions, Domestic Structures, and the End of the Cold War," in Lebow and Risse-Kappen, 187–222, Sarah E. Mendelsohn, "Internal Battles and External Wars: Politics, Learning and the Soviet Withdrawal from Afghanistan," *World Politics* 45 (April 1993): 327–60; George Breslauer, "Explaining Soviet Policy Change: The Interaction of Politics and Learning," in *Soviet Policy in Africa: From the Old to the New Thinking*, ed. George Breslauer (Berkeley, CA: Berkeley-Stanford Program in Soviet Studies, 1992); Jeff Checkel, "Ideas, Institutions, and the Gorbachev Foreign Policy Revolution," *World Politics* 45 (January 1993): 271–300; Coit D. Blacker, *Hostage to Revolution: Gorbachev and Soviet Security Policy, 1985–1991* (New York: Council on Foreign Relations, 1993). For a critical review of some of these explanations see Janice Gross Stein, "Political Learning by Doing: Gorbachev as Uncommitted Thinker and Motivated Learner," in Lebow and Risse-Kappen, *International Relations Theory and the End of the Cold War*, 223–58.
32 Lebow and Stein, *We All Lost the Cold War*, chap. 3; Raymond L. Garthoff, *Détente and Confrontation: American-Soviet Relations from Nixon to Reagan* (Washington, D.C.: Brookings, 1985), 563–1009.
33 Some useful work has been done in this connection by scholars studying enduring rivalries. See, for example, Palmira Brummett, "The Ottoman Empire, Venice, and the Question of Enduring Rivalries"; Gary Goertz, "Enduring Rivalries and the Study of Deterrence"; Edward Ingram, "Enduring Rivalries: Britain and Russia"; Jack S. Levy and Salvatore Ali, "Economic Competition, Domestic Politics, and Systemic Change: The Rise and Decline of the Anglo-Dutch Rivalry, 1609–88"; Paul W. Schroeder, "The Enduring Rivalry between France and the Habsburg Monarchy, 1715–1918"; William R. Thompson, "The Evolution of a Great Power Rivalry: The Anglo-American Case"; John A. Vasquez, "Are There Patterns in Interstate

Rivalries?" All these papers were prepared for a Conference on Great Power Rivalries, held on April 27–29, 1996 at the Center for the Study of International Relations at the University of Indiana.

34 *New York Times*, August 21, 1995, A1.

35 This point is also made by Richard K. Herrmann, "Conclusion: The End of the Cold War—What Have We Learned?" in Lebow and Risse-Kappen, *International Relations and the End of the Cold War*, 259-84.

36 Sec, for example, Risse-Kappen, "Ideas Do Not Float Freely"; Rey Koslowski and Friedrich V. Kratochwil, "Understanding Change in International Politics: The Soviet Empire's Demise and the International System," in Lebow and Risse-Kappen, *International Relations and the End of the Cold War*, 127–66; John Mueller, "The Impact of Ideas on Grand Strategy," in *The Domestic Bases of Grand Strategy*, ed. Richard Rosecrance and Arthur A. Stein (Ithaca, NY: Cornell University Press, 1993), 48–62; Mary Kaldor, "Who Killed the Cold War?" and Metta Spencer, "Political Scientists," *Bulletin of the Atomic Scientists* 51 (July/August 1995), 57–61 and 62–68.

Part V

Ancient Greeks and modern international relations

11 Thucydides the constructivist

Movements establish genealogies to legitimize themselves. To make Christianity more attractive to Jews, the New Testament traces Jesus's lineage to King David. Realists claim Thucydides as their forebear. In recent years, a number of international relations scholars have offered more subtle readings of his history that suggest realism is only one facet of his work.[1] I make a more radical assertion: Thucydides is a founding father of constructivism. The underlying purpose of his history was to explore the relationship between *nomos* (convention, custom, law) and *phusis* (nature) and its implications for the development and preservation of civilization.[2] His work shows not only how language and convention establish identities and enable power to be translated into influence but also how the exercise of power can undermine language and convention. Thucydides' understanding of these relationships was insightful and points to the possibility, indeed the necessity, of a symbiotic and productive partnership between two currently antagonistic research traditions.

Realists and their critics

Since the time of Thomas Hobbes, Thucydides has been celebrated as a realist, as someone who stripped away all moral pretenses to expose the calculations of power and advantage that of necessity motivate successful political actors (Bury, 1975; de Ste. Croix, 1972; Kagan, 1969; Meiggs, 1972). Neorealists assert that his history vindicates their emphasis on the system level and contains implicit propositions about power transition and the onset of hegemonic war as well as the inability of norms and conventions to keep the peace under conditions of international anarchy (Gilpin, 1986; Waltz ,1979). Other realists, most notably Michael Doyle (1997), offer more nuanced readings that attempt to understand Thucydides in the context in which he wrote. A growing number of scholars challenge the claims of neorealists, and some question whether Thucydides is adequately characterized as a realist.

Detailed analysis of Thucydides' history in the mid-nineteenth century called into question its consistency and unity. This research gave rise to the *Thucydidesfrage*, a controversy about how many distinct parts there are to the history, the order in which they were written, and what this reveals about the evolution of the author's thinking over approximately two decades of research and writing. Thucydides was considered a coldly detached and dispassionate rationalist, a scientist in the tradition of Hippocrates, in search of an "objective" and timeless understanding of politics and war. Because ordered thought and presentation are absolutely essential to such an enterprise, scholars assumed that Thucydides would have "cleaned up" his manuscript to remove all the inconsistencies if he had lived long enough.

The postwar attack on positivism in social sciences and history encouraged a rethinking of Thucydides. Wallace (1964), Bowersock (1965), and Stahl (1966) made the case for a passionate and politically engaged writer who can be considered a critic of the scientific approach to history. Connor's *Thucydides* (1984) represents a dramatic break with the past in that it attempts to restore a "unitarian" reading of the history. To Connor, Thucydides is a masterful postmodernist who carefully structures his text to evoke an intended set of responses. He uses omissions, repetitions, and inconsistencies in the form of arguments and judgments that are "modified, restated, subverted, or totally controverted" (p. 18) to tell a more complex story and convey a more profound understanding of the human condition. Ultimately, Connor (pp. 15–8) argues, "the work leads the reader—ancient or modern—far beyond the views and values it seems initially to utilize and affirm."

Thucydides' careful attention to language is the starting point of another seminal study, *When Words Lose Their Meaning*, by James Boyd White (1984). According to White, people act in the world by using the language of the world. To understand their behavior and the social context that enables it, we need to track the ways in which words acquire, hold, or lose meanings and how new meanings arise and spread. White contends that Thucydides recognized this truth, and his conception of meaning transcends the lexical to encompass understandings of self, manners, conduct, and sentiment. Changes in meaning involve reciprocal interactions between behavior and language, which are tracked by Thucydides in his speeches, debates, and dialogues. As the Peloponnesian War progresses, the terms of discourse that function at the outset in intelligible ways shift and change, and the language and community (*homonoia*) constituted by it deteriorate into incoherence.

When the Athenians can no longer use the traditional language of justification for their foreign policy, they struggle to find an alternate language, and they finally resort to assertions of pure self-interest backed by military clout. Such a language is not rooted in ideas, is unstable, and deprives its speakers of their culture and identities. By using it, the Athenians destroy the distinctions among friend, colony, ally, neutral, and enemy and make the world their enemy through a policy of limitless expansion. In effect, they abandon the culture through which self-interest can intelligently be defined, expressed, and bounded. By the time of the Sicilian debate, the Athenians can no longer speak and act coherently, and this failure is the underlying reason for their empire's decline. For Thucydides and for White, the history of the Athenian empire not only indicates the tension between justice and self-interest but also reveals that they validate and give meaning to each other.

Garst (1989) relies on White's arguments to accuse neorealists of having a narrow definition of power and of unfairly projecting it onto Thucydides. Thucydides shows that Athenian imperialism was successful when power was exercised in accord with well-defined social conventions governing Greek speech and behavior. These conventions are ignored as the war progresses. The Melian Dialogue and the Sicilian debate reveal how the Athenians destroyed the rhetorical culture through which their interests as an imperial power were intelligently formulated and expressed. Their foreign policy became a policy of coercion and limitless expansion. For Garst, this process illustrates the power of agency and reveals that foreign policy is rarely, if ever, a mechanical response to a balance of power.

For Crane (1998), Thucydides' history is a realist classic because it reveals how the strong dominate the weak and interests trump justice. But Thucydides considered such behavior a fundamental departure from traditional Greek practice, in which foreign policy was an extension of aristocratic family connections and enmeshed leaders and their *poleis* in a web of mutual obligations. The Corinthian plea to the Athenian assembly not to ally with Corcyra, based on Corinth's prior restraint during the Samian rebellion, reflects this approach and uses the time-honored language and arguments of reciprocity. The Athenians reject the appeal because they formulate their interests and foreign policy on the basis of immediate interests. They act as if alliances are market transactions: short-term exchanges unaffected by past dealings. Thucydides considered this approach to politics destructive of the relationships that are the true source of security and prosperity. Pericles, who speaks for Thucydides (2.60.2–4) on this question in his funeral oration, insists that the individual is nothing without the state, but at the time of the Sicilian debate Alcibiades asserts that the state counts for nothing if it does not support him as an individual (6.92.2–5). The single-minded focus on self-interest was the underlying cause of discord at home and reckless expansionism abroad. Crane believes that Thucydides' goal was to reconstitute the "ancient simplicity" (*euethēs*) of the aristocracy in a new, rationalized form.

Rahe (1996) also acknowledges two sides to Thucydides: the hard-headed analyst of power politics and the critic of realism. Thucydides' portrayal of post-Periclean Athens shows how lust (*erōs*) for power ultimately made prudent calculation of advantage and calibration of means and ends impossible. The Melian Dialogue and the debate over the Sicilian expedition indicate that Athenians had lost all sense of measure and proportion; they had become impervious to reasoned argument and therefore to the risks inherent in their initiatives. Thucydides wants readers to recognize that without moral boundaries human beings develop unlimited ambitions. The sober construction of self-interest requires restraint, which in turn requires acceptance and internalization of the claims of justice and human decency.

Forde (1989; 1992) and Orwin (1994) approach Thucydides from a more Straussian perspective. Forde criticizes neorealists for ignoring justice, a concern that was central to such early postwar realists as Hans Morgenthau and John Herz. He contends that Thucydides, like Plato, recognized the possibility of reconciling justice and interest through the citizen's love for and identification with his polis—the principal theme of Pericles' funeral oration. In post-Periclean Athens,

citizens put their self-interest first, and this led to acute discord, domestic instability, and defeat. For Orwin, Thucydides paints an "unflinching" portrait of the
harshness and even brutality of the time but with the goal of showing how human
beings, through their "humanity," can transcend both the security dilemma and
crippling domestic discord. To do this they must take justice seriously.

Ober (1989, 1998) blends the traditions of classical and international relations
scholarship. He invokes Austin's (1975) conception of performative speech acts
and Searle's (1995) distinction between brute and social facts to analyze Athenian
politics (Ober, 1998). He argues that Searle's all-important distinction between
social and brute facts becomes blurred in the context of the awesome power
wielded by the Athenian assembly. Debates and decisions became "social facts"
because successful orators imposed their own speech-dependent meanings on
brute facts. As brute facts and social meanings diverged, the latter became the
basis of policy, and this led to disaster. In this conflict between words (*logoi*) and
deeds (*erga*), Ober contends that Thucydides' sides with the latter. The history
attempts to reconstruct erga through the application of scientific principles of
data collection and evaluation (*technē*) to the past, and by doing so it points the
way to a similar process in everyday politics.

My analysis builds on these works but differs from them in important respects.
I take issue with some of their interpretations or reach the same conclusion by
different routes. My main difference with my political science and classical colleagues concerns the purpose of the history; I contend it is about the rise and
fall of civilization and what might be done to salvage it.[3] My analysis builds on
Connor's insight that the structure of Thucydides' text provides clues for reconciling some of his seeming inconsistencies. Toward this end, I identify four layers
to the history: (1) the nature and relationships among power, interest, and justice;
(2) Athens as a tragedy; (3) the relationship between nomos (convention, custom and law) and phusis (nature); and (4) the relationship between erga and logoi
and its implications for civilization. Each layer addresses a different question,
and the successive answers can be read back to provide a deeper understanding
of the questions posed by previous layers. For Connor, omissions, repetitions,
inconsistencies, and subverted sentiments and arguments are intended to move
readers to deeper understandings. I see them playing this role within levels, and
I argue that Thucydides offers the structure of his narrative, choice of language,
and implicit references to other fifth-century texts—Herodotus' *History*, the Hippocratic corpus, and the tragedies of Aeschylus, Sophocles, and Euripides—as
"signs" (*sēmata*) to move us from one level of the text to the next.

There are sound historical and textual reasons for reading Thucydides this way.
Fifth-century sophists considered themselves teachers and intended their works
or oral presentations as courses of study. They opened with the statement of a
problem and simple responses to it and went on to develop increasingly complex and sophisticated arguments that often undercut their initial argument. At
the deepest levels, their arguments were left implicit to encourage students to

draw the intended conclusions for themselves. Sophists dominated Athenian philosophy during the second half of the fifth century and had considerable political influence. Pericles himself was their principal patron. Sophists were subversive of the old aristocratic order in the deepest sense, for they maintained that *arete* (excellence, especially the kind that made a man a respected leader) could be acquired through study, not just through heredity and lifelong association with men of good breeding. Thucydides rejected some Sophist teachings—he was undoubtedly troubled by the social consequences of Sophist ridicule of objective standards of justice. But he was greatly attracted to their style of argument, which he adopted for his own and quite different purposes.

In his treatment of the origins of the Peloponnesian War, Thucydides provides a striking example of his use of the sophistic method. At the onset (1.23.5–6) he attributes the war to "the growth of the power of Athens, and the alarm which this inspired in Sparta, made war inevitable." He goes on to describe Athens and Sparta making their respective cases before the court of public opinion. By his use of the word prophasis, which was widely used before the law courts as a rationalization for suits, Thucydides signals to more sophisticated readers that charge and countercharge are little more than propaganda that obscures the real causes of the war (Rawlings, 1981). The subsequent narrative and paired speeches of Book I describe the deeper causes: Sparta's fear for its way of life, which is threatened by the political, economic, and cultural transformation of Greece spearheaded by Athens; the ability of third parties to manipulate Sparta for their own parochial interests; and the miscalculation of leaders throughout Greece at critical junctures of the crisis (Lebow, 1991, 1996).

Thucydides requires a dedicated and thoughtful audience. Readers must be willing to recognize multiple levels of analysis as well as the questions and arguments specific to these levels, and they must ponder the implications of any apparent contradictions. The history cannot be read in a linear manner; one must move back and forth between sections of the text to grasp the contrasts and ironies embedded in structure and language and the ways in which different contexts and orders of presentation encode insights and interpretations. Not all inconsistencies can be resolved in this way, and those that remain are intended to draw attention to tensions inherent in the situation and the possibility of a deeper truth that helps reconcile them. Heraclitus taught that the world is a battleground between opposing forces and that philosophers must look beneath the surface to find the deeper unity that unites them. Thucydides, as did Plato, thought and wrote in this binary tradition.

Power, interest, and justice

Almost all the works I have discussed address questions of interest and justice in the history. There is a near consensus that Thucydides' depiction of the so-called realism of the Athenians does not reflect his own views. Justice must be considered because it provides the language for any reasonable formulation of interest. Otherwise, interests are equated with power and result in policies of aggrandizement. White (1984), Garst (1989), Forde (1992), Orwin (1994), Rahe (1996), and Crane (1998) develop this thesis from the "inside out" perspective of Athenians attempting to manage, protect, and expand their empire. Thucydides is also interested in the "outside in" perspective: how allies, enemies, and neutrals respond to Athens and its policies. His work documents not only the process by which Athens succumbed to a foreign policy of limitless expansion but also the reasons such a policy was bound to fail.

As noted elsewhere (Richard Ned Lebow and Robert Kelly,"Thucydides and Hegemony: Athens and the United States," *Review of International Studies* 27 (October 2001), pp. 1–17.

> Thucydides distinguished between *hēgemonia* and *archē*, both of which are most frequently translated as hegemony. For fifth- and fourth-century Greeks, hēgemonia was associated with *timē*—the gift of honor (Meiggs, 1972; Perlman, 1991]). *Timē* was bestowed informally by free consent of the Greek community as reward for achievements, and retained by consent, not by force. Sparta and Athens were so honored because of their contributions during the Persian Wars. Athens also earned *timē* because her intellectual and artistic accomplishments made her the "school of Hellas." *Archē* connoted something akin to our notion of political control, and initially applied to authority within a city state and only later to rule or influence over city states.

The semantic field of *archē* was gradually extended to encompass tyranny.

By 416, when the assembly voted to occupy Melos and subdue Sicily, Thucydides makes it clear that the Athenian empire was an *archē* based primarily on military might. The structure and language of the Melian Dialogue mark a radical break with past practice. The Melians deny the Athenian envoys access to the people, granting only a private audience with the magistrates and the few (*oligioi*). The exchange consists of brachylogies: short, blunt, alternating verbal thrusts, suggestive of a military encounter. The Athenians dispense with all pretense. They acknowledge they cannot justify their invasion on the basis of provocations or their right to rule. They deny the relevance of justice, which only comes into play between equals. "The strong do what they can, and the weak suffer what they must," and the Melians should put their survival first and submit (Thucydides, 5.89). The Melians warn that the Athenian empire will not last forever, and if the Athenians violate the established norms of justice and decency their fall "would be a signal for the heaviest vengeance and an example for the world to mediate upon" (5.90). The Athenians insist they are only concerned with the present and the preservation of their empire. The Melians suggest it is in their mutual interest for Melos to remain neutral and a friend of Athens. The Athenians explain that neutrality would be interpreted as a sign of weakness by other island states "smarting under the yoke" (5.99) and would serve as a stimulus to rebellion. "The fact that you are islanders and weaker than others renders it all the more important that you should not succeed in baffling the masters of the sea" (5.91–9). Contemporary Greeks would have been shocked by the failure of Athens to offer any justification (*prophasis*) for its invasion of Melos and by its repudiation of the Melian offer of neutrality on the grounds that "your [Melian] hostility cannot so hurt us as your friendship" (5.95). Fifteen years into the war the Athenians repudiate, indeed invert, core Greek values.

The rhetorical style of the envoys reinforces the impression conveyed by their words. Dionysius of Halicarnassus (1975, 31) considered their language "appropriate to oriental monarchs addressing Greeks, but unfit to be spoken by Athenians to Greeks whom they liberated from the Medes." Thucydides seems to have modeled his dialogue on a passage in Herodotus (7.8), in which the Persian king Xerxes discusses with his council of advisors the wisdom of attacking Greece (Connor, 1906; Cornford, 1984). The language is similar, and the arguments run parallel; Xerxes alludes to the law of the stronger and the self-interest of empires. Herodotus (8.140, 144) also describes an offer of peace and friendship that Xerxes made to Athens and Sparta on the eve of his invasion. The Athenians spurn his olive branch and accept the danger of confronting a seemingly invincible force in the name of Greek freedom and cultural identity, just as the Melians reject an Athenian offer of alliance because of the value they put on their freedom. These parallels would not have been lost on contemporaries. For Thucydides, as for many Greeks, the Athenians of 416 have become the Persians of 480, the symbol of rank depotism in the Greek world.

The Melians offer a long view on the fate of empires. The Athenians focus on the immediate future, and in their pursuit of short-term gain alienate allies and dry up whatever reservoir of good will their early heroic behavior had created. By the time of the Melian Dialogue, they have antagonized even neutrals and close allies, which makes their fear of the security dilemma self-fulfilling. Thucydides tells us through the voice of the Melians that raw force can impose its will at any given moment, but few empires have the military and economic capability to repress their subjects indefinitely. Allies who see themselves as exploited will sever the bonds when the opportunity arises. Oppression also leaves memories that inhibit future attempts at empire building. In 378, when Athens tried to form the Second Athenian Confederacy, most of Greece resisted. *Hēgemonia* is an essential precondition of sustainable empire.

Realists define the national interest in terms of power. Many regard international law and associated norms as impediments to state interests unless they provide a rhetorical cover for policies whose real purpose it is to maximize power and influence. Thucydides opposed such a narrow view of state interests. Pericles was praiseworthy because he made foreign policy responsive to his vision of long-term Athenian interests, and he used his personal standing and rhetorical skills to win popular support for these policies. The demagogues who followed him were at best successful tacticians. They advocated foreign policies they expected to be popular with the masses and were more interested in their own fortunes than those of their polis. Pericles understood that the overriding interest of Athens was preservation of the empire, and this required both naval power and legitimacy. To maintain the latter, Athens had to act in accord with the principles and values that had earned *hegemonia*, and it had to offer positive political and economic benefits to allies. Because post-Periclean Athens consistently chose power over principle, it alienated allies and third parties, lost *hegemonia*, and weakened its power base. The Melian Dialogue and the Sicilian expedition are pathological departures from rational self-interest.

Athens as tragedy

Fifth-century tragedies dramatized the lives of individuals to convey insights into human beings and their societies as well as critically examine or reaffirm fundamental values of the community. Cornford (1907) and Euben (1990), among others, have discussed Thucydides' relationship to tragedy and the structural similarities between his history and the tragedies. Alker (1988; 1996) contends that the history might be read as the tragedy of the empire's rise and fall and the Melian Dialogue as a "morality play" about might and right. Bedford and Workman (2001) suggest that Thucydides adopted the tragic form to develop his critique of Athenian foreign policy. I believe he wanted readers to experience his history as a tragedy and to move from emotional involvement with the story to contemplation of its general lessons, just as they might with a theatrical production.

In his only statement about his intent, Thucydides (1.22) offers his history as "an aid for the interpretation of the future, which in the course of human things must resemble it if it does not reflect it." The cyclical pattern he has in mind is not just about the growth and decline of empires but, more generally, how success spawns excessive ambition, overconfidence, and self-destructive behavior.

The Greek literary tradition was largely an oral one, and Herodotus, author of the first long historical narrative, was paid to read sections of it aloud (Luce, 1997). His words are chosen with their sounds in mind, and his style, *lexis eiromenē* (literally, speech strung together), is related to epic poetry. He introduces an idea or action, defines it by approaching it from different perspectives, and expands its meaning through the apposition of words, phrases, and clauses. Opinion is divided about Thucydides, who wrote at a time when the oral tradition was declining (Havelock, 1963; Lain Entralgo, 1970). Thucydides can be appreciated if read aloud, but it would be difficult to grasp deeper layers of meaning. His text is written in a complex and idiosyncratic style that requires careful analysis to discover and work through its purpose. Thucydides makes extensive use of parallels in setting, structure, and language with other passages in his work and those of other writers. He intended his history to be read and studied.

The embedding of oral forms in a literary text is common to Herodotus, Thucydides, and Plato. In *The Iliad*, from which so much of this tradition derives, paired and group speeches are as important as narrative and mark critical moments of decision and turning points. The speeches are also vehicles for moving thematically toward greater depth, compassion, and ethical sophistication. In Thucydides, the speeches highlight critical junctures, sometimes suggest their contingency, but always examine opposing courses of action and the justifications provided for them. They also track the progression—really the descent—of Greece from relatively secure societies bound together by convention, obligation, and interests to a condition of disorder and even anarchy, a transformation to which I shall return.

Another commonality in the Greek literary tradition is the use of heroes to provide continuity and structure to the text. Modern writers on the origins, course, and consequences of wars frequently acknowledge the prominent role of key actors, but they almost always provide some kind of general, sociological framework to understand and assess the decisions and behavior of these people (Herwig, 1997; Murray & Millet, 2000; Weinberg, 1994). Herodotus and Thucydides do the reverse; they rely on the words, actions, and fate of heroes to move the narrative along and give it meaning. Herodotus uses the story of Croesus to set up the central saga of Xerxes. Solon warns Croesus to recognize his limits and restrain his ambitions, and Xerxes receives similar advice from Artabanus. Both men nevertheless embark upon ambitious military ventures that end in catastrophe. Early in Book One, Thucydides (1.9–11) uses the story of Agamemnon and the Trojan War—in which an alliance held together by naval power confronts a major land power—to provide an overview of what will follow. Elsewhere in the history, the stories of individuals and cities prefigure the fate of more important personages and major powers, especially Athens.

There is a more fundamental difference in the way ancient Greek and modern historians approach heroes. Most contemporary works dwell on the particular mix of background, personal qualities, and experience that make people distinct as individuals. They do this even when these figures are intended to be emblematic of a class, movement, or set of shared life experiences. Herodotus and Thucydides hardly ever take note of idiosyncratic attributes; like the authors of epic poetry and drama, they are interested in using individuals to create archetypes. They stress the qualities, especially strengths and weaknesses, their heroes share with other heroes. The typicality, not the uniqueness, of actors and situations is a central convention of fifth-century poetry, tragedy, and prose. Even Pericles, whom Thucydides offers as the model of a modern man of politics, is a stereotype. He is the sum of qualities that make him an ideal leader in a transitional democracy and a benchmark for his successors. All subsequent leaders possess different combinations of some of his qualities but never all of them—to the detriment of Athens. Nicias displays honesty and dedication but lacks the skill and stature to dissuade the assembly from undertaking the Sicilian expedition. Alcibiades has intelligence and rhetorical skill but uses them to advance his career at the expense of his city.

Greek tragedies consist of archetypical characters who confront archetypical situations. The tragic hero, like his Homeric predecessor, is a self-centered, narcissistic figure who revels in his own importance and comes to believe that he is not bound by the laws and conventions of man. These manifestations of ego and their consequences are often explored through a standard plot line: Success carries with it the seeds of failure. Success intoxicates heroes; it encourages them to form inflated opinions of themselves and their abilities and to trust in hope rather than reason. It makes them susceptible to all kinds of adventures in which reason would dictate caution and restraint. The Greeks used the word *atē* to describe the aporia this kind of seduction induces and associated it with *hamartia* (missing the mark). *Hamartia* leads the hero to catastrophe by provoking *nemesis* (wrath) of the gods.

Herodotus frames his treatment of Croesus and Xerxes in terms of this progression (Beye, 1987). Intoxicated by his riches, Croesus misinterprets the oracle who tells him that a great empire will be destroyed if he invades Persia. He is defeated and only saved from being burned at the stake by the mercy of his adversary. Xerxes is an ambitious but cautious leader who accumulates enormous power. His exaltation and pride nevertheless grow in proportion to his success, and *atē* makes him vulnerable to *hamartia*. At first, he resists Mardonius's suggestion to exploit the revolt of the Ionians to invade Greece and add Europe to his empire. Subsequent dreams change his mind and lead him to a fatal error of judgment. His sense of omnipotence leads him to attempt to punish the Hellespont for washing away his bridge across it in a storm. Nemesis at Salamis is inevitable, and from the perspective of Herodotus and Greek tragedy, the destruction of the Persian fleet and, later, army represents less a triumph of the Greeks than a failure of Xerxes.

Thucydides begins where Herodotus leaves off and shifts the locus of the narrative from Persia to Greece. The Athenians, the principal agents of Xerxes' nemesis, repeat the cycle of success, overconfidence, miscalculation, and catastrophe. Indeed, the Athenian victory over Xerxes at Salamis, which marks the emergence of Athens as a military power, sets the cycle in motion. Athens achieves a string of victories until ambition and overconfidence lead to military and political disasters: the complete annihilation in 454 of the expedition to Egypt, the revolt of Erythrae and Miletus in 452, and the defeat at Coronea in central Greece in 446 (Thucydides 1.104, 109–10). These setbacks temporarily compel Athenians to recognize the limits of their power. In 449 they make peace with Persia, and in 446 they agree to the Thirty Years' Peace with Sparta. Under Pericles, Athens devotes its energies to consolidating the sprawling empire. But like Xerxes, Pericles is unable to exercise restraint in the longer term. Convinced of his ability to control events at home and abroad, he persuades an initially reluctant assembly to seize the opportunity of alliance with Corcyra in the erroneous expectation that the worst possible outcome will be a short war in which Sparta will discover the futility of opposing Athens. This initial *hamartia* leads to war, plague, the death of Pericles, a prolonged war, and abandonment of Pericles' defensive strategy. A second hamartia, the Sicilian expedition, urged on the assembly by Alcibiades, leads to nemesis.

Cleon, intended to represent a figure intermediate between Pericles and Alcibiades, shows none of Pericles' caution or thoughtfulness. He is as unscrupulous as Alcibiades—Thucydides calls him "the most violent man at Athens"—but not as clever in his pursuit of power (Thucydides 3.36). He launches a stinging verbal attack on Nicias, accusing him and his troops of cowardice in facing the Spartans in Pylos. Nicias offers to stand aside and let Cleon assume command of his forces. Cleon discounts this as mere rhetorical posturing, but Nicias then resigns his command. Cleon tries desperately to back down, but the assembly, remembering his earlier bravura, will not let him do so (4.24–9). Cleon is forced to sail for Pylos, where he and Demosthenes succeed, much to Cleon's surprise and relief, in overwhelming the Spartans in short order (4.29–42). In the aftermath of his victory, Sparta sued for peace to secure the return of its hostages, and the Archidamian phase of the Peloponnesian War comes to an end.

Not content with the peace, Alcibiades convinces the assembly to renew the war and embark upon a policy of imperial expansion. Thucydides regards the decisions to ally with Corcyra and conquer Sicily as the most fateful decisions of the assembly; each is a *hamartia*, and together they lead to nemesis. In discussing these decisions, he suggests the real motives of the assembly and hints at the contradictions these entail as well as the unexpected and tragic consequences that will follow (1.44; 4.65). The decision to ally with Corcyra requires a second debate in which the assembly reverses itself. This also happens in the punishment of Mytilene and the Sicilian expedition (1.44; 3.36; 6.8). But the most important similarity, which sets the Corcyra and Sicilian decisions apart from other events in the history, is that Thucydides provides "archeologies" that establish the background for the momentous events that will follow (Thucydides 1.2–13, 6.2–6; see Connor, 1984; Rawlings, 1981). He not only heightens the connection through his use of this analytical parallel but also suggests that we read the Sicilian debate as a new beginning, a history within the history that describes decisions and events that deserve equal billing with those that led to the war.

Nicias does his best to dissuade the assembly, which is utterly ignorant of the size and population of Sicily, from sailing against an island so large, distant, and powerful. As does Artabanus in his plea to Xerxes, Nicias urges (6.9–14) the Athenians to keep what they have and not risk "what is actually yours for advantages which are dubious in themselves, and which you may or may not attain." Alcibiades, cast in the role of Mardonius, makes light of the risks of the expedition and greatly exaggerates its possible rewards to the assembly. He does not attempt to rebut the arguments of Nicias but makes a calculated, emotional appeal to a receptive audience. Nicias comes forward a second time (6.20–3) and, recognizing that direct arguments against the expedition will not carry the day, tries to dissuade the assembly by insisting on a much larger force and more extensive provisions than originally planned. To his surprise, the more he demands from the assembly, the more eager it becomes to support the expedition, convinced that a force of such magnitude will be invincible (6.24–6).

There are striking similarities in plot and language between Thucydides' account of the Athenian assembly and Herodotus' depiction of Xerxes at Abydus (Connor, 1984; Rahe, 1996). Thucydides describes the Sicilian expedition as more extravagant than any Greek campaign that proceeded it by virtue of its *lamprotēs* (splendor) and *tolma* (audacity). These are words used by Herodotus and other Greeks to describe Xerxes' court and military plans. Readers of Thucydides would have found his work old-fashioned. He could assume that they were familiar with the works of Aeschylus, Sophocles, Euripides, and Herodotus and that most would recognize his personification of Athens as a tragic hero and the mordant comparison he intended between Athens and Persia. This format and analogy would encourage readers to consider the story of Athens as the basis for generalizations about Greece and the human condition.

Nomos versus Phusis

Greek city-states were isolated from one another and the wider world by mountain ranges or large bodies of water. In the fifth century, economic growth, immigration, and improvements in shipbuilding enabled the Greeks to expand their travel and trade and learn more about the customs of other peoples. In the process, they began to question their long-standing belief that their social practices were gods-given and moved toward a position of cultural relativism. In Athens there was an intense, century-long debate about the relative importance of human nature (*phusis*) and convention (*nomos*) (Finley, 1942/1967; Kerford, 1981). Pindar, who declared that custom is the master of us all, and Herodotus, who offered a detailed and nonjudgmental account of the diversity of human practices, anchored one pole of this debate. Sophocles resisted their agnosticism and relativism. Plato, in his *Protagoras* and the *Republic*, would offer the most sophisticated defense of the underlying importance of innate qualities.

Realists and some classicists assert that for Thucydides phusis trumps nomos (Crane, 1998; de Ste. Croix, 1972; Romilly, 1990). They cite references in speeches to universal laws that govern human behavior and behavior that appears to lend substance to these claims. One example is the justification for empire the Athenian envoys offer to the Spartan assembly on the eve of the war. They are doing nothing more than acting in accord with "the common practice of mankind" (*hē anthrōpeia phusis*) that "the weaker should be subject to the stronger" (Thucydides, 1.76). The Athenians give the same justification to the Melians. If neorealists and their classical allies are right, then human drives for dominance (*archē*), ambition (*philotimia*), and self-aggrandizement (*pleonexia*) will sooner or later undermine and defeat any effort to construct an international order based on norms, conventions, law, and underlying common interests. Is this inference warranted?

Heraclitus maintains that nature (*phusis*) tends to conceal itself, and its seemingly contradictory manifestations have an underlying unity (*harmonia*) that can be discovered through reflection. Thucydides bases his inquiry on this assumption and searches for some means of getting beneath the established social order and day-to-day behavior to discover what truths lie underneath. Plato attempts something similar and for much the same reason. Thucydides models his inquiry on medical research (Cochrane, 1929). Hippocrates and his followers chart the course of diseases in the human body, noting the symptoms that appear at the onset and how these build to a critical moment or crisis stage that leads to death or recovery. Thucydides applies this method to the social diseases of revolution and war; he describes their manifestations and charts their course through the body politic to the point of social strife and the disintegration of civil society. As physicians sought to learn something about the nature of the human body from studying the progression of illness, so Thucydides hoped to learn about the human mind.

Thucydides (2.47–54) makes the link between physical and social diseases explicit in his analysis of the Athenian plague of 430–28. He begins by noting the common view that the disease arrived in Athens via Africa but refuses to speculate about its causes. Following Hippocratic tradition, "I shall simply set down its nature, and explain the symptoms by which perhaps it may be recognized by the student, if it should ever break out again" (2.48.3). He describes in clinical detail the onset of the disease, subsequent symptoms, variation in the course of the illness, the suffering and fatality it causes, and the disfigurement of survivors.

The plague left the city crowded with dead and dying. Bodies accumulated and decayed in houses, half-dead creatures roamed the streets in search of water, and sacred places were full of the corpses of those who came there seeking relief. As rich and poor died off in large numbers, the social fabric began to unravel. "Men, not knowing what was to become of them, became utterly careless of everything, whether sacred or profane" (2.52.3). Family responsibilities were ignored in violation of the most fundamental ethical principle of Greek society: the obligation to help one's own *philoi*. People were increasingly afraid to visit one another, and many sufferers died from neglect. Sacred rituals were ignored, burial rites were dispensed with, and corpses were disposed of in any which way. Some residents resorted to "the most shameless modes of burial, throwing the bodies of their family or friends on the already burning pyres of others" (2.52.3). "Lawless extravagance" became increasingly common, and men "cooly ventured on what they had formerly done in a corner" (2.53.1). Those who suddenly inherited wealth "resolved to spend quickly and enjoy themselves, regarded their lives and riches as alike things of the day" (2.53.2). Fear of the gods and human laws all but disappeared, as "each felt that a far severer sentence had been already passed upon them all and hung over their heads, and before this felt it was only reasonable to enjoy life a little" (2.53.4).

The other stasis that Thucydides records in detail is political: the revolution, civil violence, and moral disintegration of Corcyra in the 420s (3.70–81). As in the account of the plague, he begins with a detailed, precise, almost day-by-day description of what transpired. This sets the stage for a more impressionistic account, followed by generalizations based on that account, and he ends with a depiction of the gravest atrocities. Violent conflict between democratic and oligarchic factions, intervention by the foreign allies of both, and internal revolution culminate in seven days of "butchery" in which Corcyreans, consumed by hatreds arising from private and political causes, kill as many of their enemies as they can lay their hands upon. As in Athens, every convention is violated: "Sons were killed by their fathers, and suppliants dragged from the altar or slain upon it, while some were even walled up in the temple of Dionysus and died there" (3.81.4–5).

Just as the plague ushers in an era of lawlessness and boldness (*tolma*) that significantly affects domestic politics and foreign policy, so the Corcyrean revolution, for much the same reason, is the precursor of similar developments in other cities. After Corcyra, Thucydides (3.82) tells us, "the whole Hellenic world" is convulsed as democratic factions seek to assume or maintain power with the help of Athens, and oligarchs do the same with the support of Sparta. "The sufferings which revolution entailed upon the cities were many and terrible, such as have occurred and always will occur, as long as the nature of mankind remains the same, though in a severer or milder form, and varying in their symptoms, according to the variety of the particular cases" (3.82.1).

These extreme situations bring out the worst in human beings, and the passage just quoted can be read as support for the universality and immutability of human nature. But Thucydides (3.82.2) modifies his generalization in the next sentence: "In peace and prosperity states and individuals have better sentiments because they do not find themselves suddenly confronted with imperious necessities; but war takes away the easy supply of daily wants, and so proves a rough master that brings most men's characters to a level with their fortunes." The arrow of causation is reversed; stasis does not so much reveal the hidden character of people as it shapes that character. People who have little to live for behave differently from people who have much to lose. The qualifier "most" is important because it indicates that not everyone responds the same way to social stimuli, not even in the most extreme situations. In his description of the plague, Thucydides (2.51) uses parallel constructions to describe how some people, fearful of succumbing to the disease, isolated themselves at great costs to friends and family; others placed honor above survival, and "honor made them unsparing of themselves." Some survivors participated in the greatest excesses, whereas others were unstinting in administering to the ill and dying. The same bifurcated response can be observed at the other end of the spectrum, in secure and prosperous societies: The majority of people adhere to social and religious conventions, and a minority is unconstrained and destructive in behavior.

Thucydides has a less deterministic understanding of human nature. By removing the constraints and obligations arising from convention, stasis permits the fullest expression of the worst human impulses, but in some people it brings out the best. The plague and Corcyrean revolution, and the wide range of other "tests" to which human beings are subjected in the course of the Peloponnesian War, indicate that human nature encompasses a range of needs, desires, and impulses, some of them contradictory (Kokaz, 2001). People appear driven by their needs for self-preservation, pleasure, recognition, and power but also by needs for love, honor, and esteem. The Melian Dialogue offers a nice counterpoint to the Corcyrean revolution in this respect. Opposition to Athens is futile, but the Melians choose to resist because they value freedom more than self-preservation.

The Hippocratic physicians taught that phusis varied according to the environment. Some believed that traits acquired through social practice (*nomos*) could, over time, modify nature (*phusis*). Thucydides believes that behavior is the result of a complex interaction between the two. If human nature could not be harnessed for constructive ends, civilization would never have developed. This conclusion refocuses our attention on the meta-theme of Thucydides' narrative: the rise and fall of Greek civil society and the circumstances in which positive and negative facets of human nature come to the fore.

Logoi and Erga

Ober (1998) maintains that Thucydides privileges *erga* over *logoi*. From Thucydides' perspective, both deeds and words are social constructions, but he gives pride of place to *logoi*. Social facts and social conventions create the intersubjective understandings on which all action depends. Social facts often misrepresent brute facts, but Thucydides considers this discrepancy a double-edged sword. It can prove destructive, as it did in the Sicilian debate, for the reasons Ober describes. But it is potentially beneficial, if not essential, to the maintenance of community. Democratic ideology in Athens exaggerated the equality among classes and downplayed political, economic, and social inequalities. It reconciled the *dēmos* to the existing social order and muted the class tensions that led to violent conflict and civil wars in many other polities. The Athenian democratic ideology rested on myths: on social facts at variance with reality and on a history that bore only a passing relationship to so-called empirical facts, as the Archeology in Book One convincingly demonstrates.

It is no coincidence that observations about words (Thucydides, 3.82) follow directly on a discussion of how the Corcyrean revolution affected the rest of Hellas. "Revolution ran its course from city to city, and the places which it arrived at last, from having heard what had been done before, carried to a still greater excess the refinement of their inventions, as manifested in the cunning of their enterprises and the atrocity of their reprisals" (3.82.3). Language is the vector by which the disease of revolution spreads, but it is also a contributing cause of constant movement (*kinēsis*) and destruction (Saxonhouse, 1996). Not just in Corcyra but throughout much of Greece, "words had to change their ordinary meanings and to take those which were now given them." Thucydides (3.82) gives a string of examples, and all indicate the extent to which meanings and the values they expressed were subverted:

> Reckless audacity came to be considered the courage of a loyal supporter; prudent hesitation, specious cowardice; moderation was held to be a cloak for unmanliness; ability to see all sides of a question, incapacity to act on any. Frantic violence became the attribute of manliness; cautious plotting a justifiable means of self-defense. The advocate of extreme measures was always trustworthy; his opponent a man to be suspected. To succeed in a plot was to have a shrewd head, and to divine a plot still shrewder; but to try to provide against having to do either was to break up your party and to be afraid of your adversaries.

Words are the ultimate convention, and they also succumbed to stasis. Altered meanings not only changed the way people thought about one another, their society, and their obligations to it but also encouraged barbarism and violence by undermining longstanding conventions and the constraints they enforced. Thucydides (3.82.8) attributes this process to "the lust for power arising from greed and ambition; and from these passions proceeded the violence of parties once engaged in contention." Politicians used "fair phrases to arrive at guilty ends" and degraded and abased the language.

Thucydides follows the introductory remarks in Book One with the so-called Archeology (1.2–21), in which he describes the rise of Hellenic culture. In contrast to other fifth-century accounts of the rise of civilization, less emphasis is placed on agriculture and the development of material technology and more stress is given to the power of tyrants to cobble together small settlements into increasingly larger kingdoms and alliances. He portrays archaic Greece as being in constant movement as a result of frequent migrations due to population growth, depletion of local agricultural resources, and the depredations of pirates and invaders. Civilization, defined as a state of peace and rest (*hēsuchia*), only became possible when communities combined to undertake common action, including the suppression of piracy. Common action required common understanding; language was the vehicle of this understanding and the very foundation of political stability and civilization. Civilization is also due to a reinforcing cycle of *logoi* and *erga*. The Archeology sets the stage for the history of decline that follows.

Greeks distinguished men from animals by their ability to speak and their preference for cooked meat. The word *omos* (raw) is used three times by Thucydides (3.94, 3.36, 3.82.1): to describe an Aetolian tribe so uncivilized that "they speak a language that is exceedingly difficult to understand, and eat their flesh raw"; in the Mytilenian debate, to characterize what many Athenians think about the previous day's decision to execute all the Mytilenians; and to describe the stasis that convulsed the Greek world beginning with the revolution in Corcyra. Rahe (1996) suggests that the word is used on the last two occasions to indicate that the war, plague, and revolutions reversed the process described in the Archeology. The measure of rest (*hēsuchia*) and peace civilization brought about was disrupted by the movement (kinesis) of war, which undermined conventions (*nomoi*), including those of language, and encouraged the kind of brazen daring (*tolma*) that provoked "raw" and savage deeds. The Greeks became increasingly irrational and inarticulate (*alogistos*) and, like animals, no longer capable of employing the logos (rational facilities and language) necessary for communal deliberation.

Is the rise and fall of civilization inevitable? Greek myth and saga portray a largely unalterable world, but one that is only tenuously connected to the time in which the audience dwells. The great playwrights carried on this tradition, and the tragic sense of life depends on the inevitability of nemesis and the immutability of things (Beye, 1987). Like the plots of so much myth and epic, tragedy also relies on the intervention of the gods and the power of situations to generate pressures and psychological states that move the action along and leave limited choice to the individual. In *Agamemnon* (176–83), Aeschylus explains that "Zeus shows man the way to think, setting understanding securely in the midst of suffering. In the heart there drips instead of sleep a labor of sorrowing memory; and there comes to us all unwilling prudent measured thought; the grace of gods who sit on holy thrones somehow comes with force and violence." Orestes confronts a dilemma not of his own making and from which there is no exit. The chorus, whose lines I quote, reminds us that the most he can do is preserve his dignity and learn from his suffering. Herodotus imported this tradition into prose. His Xerxes has no control over his fate; the power of Persia and the insolence of the Greeks compel him to attempt their conquest. When he has second thoughts, the gods intervene through Mardonius to push him to invade Greece, just as the Argives are compelled to make war against Troy by Athena, who speeds down from Olympus to convince Odysseus to prevent their departure (Homer, 2.135–210).

For Herodotus, the stories of Croesus and Xerxes are concrete manifestations of a timeless cycle of *hubris-atē-hamartia-nemesis* that can be expected to repeat itself so long as humans walk the earth. The same attitude of resignation and acceptance has been attributed to Thucydides. Some of his actors do articulate this perspective. The Athenian envoys at Sparta portray themselves as prisoners of history and seem to understand that they are playing roles in a grand, historical drama, although not yet framed as a tragedy (1.75). Pericles warns his countrymen that one day they, too, will be forced to yield "in obedience with the general law of decay" (2.64).

Thucydides is not as pessimistic as many realist readings suggest. Why would he invest decades in the research and writing of the history and offer it as a "possession for all time" if he thought human beings and their societies were the prisoners of circumstance and fate? He must have believed that people possess at least some ability to control their destiny. The appropriate analogy is to psychotherapy. Freudian therapy assumes that people will repeatedly enact counterproductive scripts until they confront and come to terms with the experiences that motivate this behavior. This can only be achieved through regression; people must allow themselves to relive painful experiences they have repressed and come to understand how these shape their present behavior. Sophists relied on a somewhat similar process. Their works were offered as courses of study that engage the emotions and mind. By experiencing the elation, disappointment, anguish, and other emotions a story provoked, and by applying reason to work through its broader meaning and implications, readers could gain enlightenment. Hippocratic physicians put great store in the curative power of words. Euripides' Phaedra and Andromache describe words as sources of power and psychological compensation. The plays of Aeschylus are based on the maxim of *pathei mathos*, of learning and transcending one's situation through the pain associated with understanding that situation. There is ample Greek precedent for Thucydides' project.

Like analysts, neither sophists nor tragic playwrights tell people what lessons to learn; all believe that genuine understanding can only be internalized and influence behavior if it arises from a process of cathartic self-discovery. Thucydides' history encourages Athenians and other Greeks to relive traumatic political experiences in the most vivid way and to work through their meaning and implications for their lives and societies. I believe he harbored the hope that such a course of "therapy" could help free people of the burdens of the past and produce the kind of wisdom that enables societies to transcend their scripts.

Transcending old scripts requires an alternative vocabulary. Crane (1998) argues that Thucydides wanted to reconstruct the aristocratic ideology, the "ancient simplicity" to which he was born and raised. He was undeniably attracted to the "ancient simplicity." Evidence for this lies in the location of his discussion of it in the text (3.83), which follows his description of stasis at Corcyra. The intended inference is that religion, honor, and aristocratic values promote a tranquil and secure social and political order, and their decline removes restraints to unprincipled self-aggrandizement.

The passage is unabashedly nostalgic but also brutally realistic. The ancient simplicity had not merely declined; it had been "laughed down and disappeared" (Thucydides, 3.83). Here and elsewhere Thucydides recognizes the gulf between the old and the new, and he knows the life-style associated with the ancient simplicity has passed and cannot readily be restored. Greece, and especially Athens, has been transformed by what can only be called a process of modernization. Population growth, coinage, trade, the division of labor, major military undertakings, and empire have given rise to new classes, new ideas and values, and new social and political practices to cope with a more complicated and competitive world. The Athenian empire has become so powerful that it no longer needs to rely on the standard pattern of client-patron relations, based on obligation and the mutual exchange of favors and services. Success has made the traditional system of political relationships and the values on which it rested look old-fashioned and unnecessary, even a hindrance. The fate of Sparta also testifies to this change. Its influence in Greece derived largely from the symbolic capital it had accumulated in the form of reliability in the eyes of others, especially allies. Spartans had gone to war to preserve this capital and in the vain hope that defeat of Athens would stave off the changes that threatened their traditional way of life. Sparta emerged as the victor in the war, but it was no longer the same polis. Spartans had to become more like their adversary to defeat it, which is perhaps the most compelling evidence that the old ways were doomed.

Thucydides recognizes the impracticality of trying to turn the clock back; the aristocratic order and its values had become anachronistic, and the effort to reimpose oligarchic rule at the end of the Peloponnesian War failed miserably. He has a subtler project in mind: Adapt older values and language to present circumstances to create a more workable synthesis that can accommodate progress but mitigate its excesses. Ober (1998) contends that Thucydides looked to Periclean Athens for his model. It functioned well because of the balance of power between the masses and the smaller elite of rich, influential, and powerful men (*hoi dunatoi*). The need of each group to take the other into account and the presence of leaders such as Pericles, who mediated and muted these class-based tensions, led to policies that often reflected the interest of the community (*hoi Athēnaioi*), not merely the democratic or aristocratic faction.

In Book One, Thucydides portrays Pericles as someone who personifies the ancient simplicity but has mastered the new arts of oratory and statecraft. His success in governing Athens under the most trying circumstances may have convinced Thucydides that such an amalgam was desirable and possible. But his praise of Pericles is another one of his judgments that is in part subverted later in the text. In Book Four, Thucydides offers Hermocrates of Syracuse as another role model (Connor, 1984; Monoson & Loriaux, 1998). He is intended to be a counterpoint to Pericles and a more accurate guide to how foreign policy restraint can be sold to the public and a more peaceful international order maintained.

In his appeal to Sicilians for unity against Athens, Hermocrates inverts key realist tenets of foreign policy that are associated with Pericles (Thucydides 4.59–64). Connor (1984) observes that the "law of the stronger" becomes an injunction for the weaker to unite, and Hermocrates (4.62) goes on to exploit the widespread fear of Athens to justify forethought and restraint but urges common defensive action. On the eve of war Pericles sought to inspire confidence in his fellow citizens, but Hermocrates wants to intensify their fears. Athens and its enemies attributed Athenian success to ingenuity, speed of execution, and confidence in the ability to face challenges (Thucydides 1.68–71, 2.35–46). Hermocrates finds strength in the restraint and caution that come from recognition of the limits of knowledge and power and contemplation of the future with an eye toward its unpredictability. Pericles urged his countrymen to spurn Sparta's peace overtures, but Hermocrates favors accommodation and settlement. Successors of Pericles, especially Cleon and Alcibiades, encouraged the Athenians to contemplate the rewards from imperial expansion. Hermocrates implicitly urges his audience to consider the advantages they already possess and the loss that war may entail. Hermocrates—and Thucydides—had an intuitive grasp of prospect theory (Levy, 1992, 1996; Tversky & Kahneman, 1992), which is based on the robust psychological finding that people are generally more concerned with preventing loss than they are with making gains.

Sophists pioneered the rhetorical strategy of "anti-logic." Zeno silenced his opponents by showing how their arguments also implied their negations and were thus contradictory (Kerford, 1981). Thucydides makes extensive use of antilogic. He examines every so-called law of politics, appears to validate it, but ultimately subverts it by showing the unintended and contradictory consequences that flow from its rigorous application. This is most obvious with the principles espoused by demagogues like Cleon, but it is also true of more honorable politicians like Pericles. Thucydides did not spoon feed conclusions; he wanted readers to draw them by reflecting on his narrative, speeches, and dialogues. Hermocrates' speech is the most overt attempt to point readers in the right direction. Through emotions and intellect—feeling the pain of the rise and fall of Athens and grasping the reasons this occurred—readers could experience the history as a course of "logotherapy." Its larger purpose was to make them wary not only of the sweet and beguiling words of demagogues but also, as Monoson and Loriaux (1998) suggest, of any politician who advocates policies at odds with conventions that maintain domestic and international order. This caution is the first and essential step toward the restructure of language and the reconstitution of conventions that can permit economic and intellectual progress while maintaining political order.

Thucydides the constuctivist

Fifth-century Greece experienced the first *Methodenstreit*. "Positivists" insisted on the unity of the physical and social worlds as well as the existence of an ordered reality that can be discovered through the process of inquiry. They were opposed by "constructivists," who regarded the social world as distinct and human relations as an expression of culturally determined and ever evolving conventions.[4] Early Greek thinkers accepted the divine nature of the world and considered human customs part of an overall, unified scheme of nature. The goal of the Ionian protophysicists was to discover the original principle, the *archē*, that determined all the other regularities, social and physical, of the universe. Reality was out there, waiting to be described in terms of impersonal forces and the agency that also expressed those forces. In the fifth century, sophists directed their inquiry away from nature to human beings. According to Jaeger (1939–45, 1.306), "the concept of *phusis* was transferred from the whole universe to a single part of it—to mankind; and there it took on a special meaning. Man is subject to certain rules prescribed by *his own* nature."

This shift coincided with exposure to alien cultures and the discovery of practices that differed remarkably from those of the Greeks. People in these cultures also found different meanings in the same events. Philosophical inquiry and experience of cultural diversity combined to encourage a subjectivist epistemology in which nomos was contrasted with *phusis* and considered by many a more important determinant of human behavior. The deeds themselves (*auta ta erga*) and concept of the "real world" became problematic, as did the assumption that either could be understood through observation. Democritus (1956, fragments 9 and 11), proclaimed that things were "sweet by convention, bitter by convention, hot by convention, cold by convention," and he went on to reason that all observation was illegitimate. Such skepticism encouraged the belief that truth was relative (Lloyd, 1978).

Given sophistic epistemology, it is not surprising that it spawned a cognate to postmodernism. Protagoras, who is the best known representative, regarded all claims to knowledge as nothing more than rhetorical strategies for self-aggrandizement. Justice was a concept invoked by the powerful to justify their authority and advance their parochial interests. Philosophical nihilism reached its fullest expression in Critias, who defined justice in terms of power and found justification for this in human practice—the very argument the Athenian envoys made at Melos. Critias is good grist for the mill of any contemporary critic of postmodernism. A politician and one of the thirty tyrants who briefly ruled Athens after its defeat in 404, he was infamous for his corruption and brutality (Guthrie, 1969; Strauss, 1986). Plato represented a reaction to the sophists; he was horrified by their reduction of law to custom and by the equation of justice with tyranny. He parodied sophists in his dialogues (see especially *Protagoras*) and argued against their efforts to explain physical and social reality purely in terms of its phenomenal aspects. He sought to restore objectivity and the status of universal laws by discovering an underlying, ultimate reality that would provide a foundation for a universal nation of justice and social order (Guthrie, 1969; Kerford, 1981).

Like contemporary constructivists, Thucydides was fascinated by convention (nomos) and the role it played in regulating human behavior. The history makes clear that he regarded conventions not only as constraints but also as frames of reference that people use to understand the world and define their interests. It may be going too far to claim that Thucydides initiated the "linguistic turn" in ancient philosophy, but he certainly shared the constructivist emphasis on the importance of language, which he thought enabled the shared meanings and conventions that make civilization possible. His history explores the relationship between words and deeds and documents the double-feedback loop between them. Shared meanings of words are the basis for conventions and civic cooperation. When words lose their meaning, or their meaning is subverted, the conventions that depend on them lose their force, communication becomes difficult, and civilization declines. Thucydides exploited the growth and evolution of the Greek language for purposes of expression and precision, and he probably coined more neologisms that any other fifth-century author. One goal of the history is the considered restoration of traditional meanings of words to help resurrect the conventions they sustained.[5] In this sense, he anticipates Plato.

The core of constructivism is hard to define because there is so much variation among authors. In a thoughtful analysis of this literature, Hopf (2002) suggests that constructivism has two components. The first is appreciation of social structure, whether understood sociologically, as in the thin institutionalist accounts of Finnemore and Sikkink (1998) and others, or linguistically, as attempted by Kratochwil and Ruggie (1986), Kratochwil (1989), Onuf (1989), and Ruggie (1998). The second component is the acceptance of the mutual constitution of agents and structures (Kratochwil 1989; Kratochwil and Ruggie 1986; Onuf 1989). Constructivism, in its thicker linguistic version, is interested in the logic of intelligibility, that is, what makes some actions more imaginable and thus more probable than others. The thin version gives more weight to the role norms play in advancing interests than to the creation of norms by identities.

Thucydides is undeniably a constructivist and may have been the original practitioner of the thicker linguistic version. His history examines how language shapes the identities and conventions in terms of which interests are defined. He drives this point home in the most graphic way by showing that it is impossible to formulate interests at all when conventions break down and the meaning of language becomes subverted. Traditional Greek social intercourse, domestic and "international," was embedded in a web of interlocking relationships and obligations and governed by an elaborate set of conventions. Dealings with foreigners were an extension of domestic relations. There was no specific word for international relations—the closest is *xenia*, which generally is translated as "guest friendship."

War was not infrequent but was limited in means and ends. With rare exceptions, the independence and social system of other city-states were respected; wars were waged to establish precedence and settle border disputes. Combat was highly stylized and was designed to minimize casualties and allow individuals to gain honor through the display of heroism. Truces were obligatory to permit both sides to gather their dead and the victor to erect a trophy (Adcock, 1957). With the introduction of the hoplite phalanx and later developments against massive Persian armies, the character of war changed somewhat, but most conventions were still observed. They did not break down until late in the Peloponnesian War, when even the quasi-sacred truces that enabled proper disposal and honoring of the dead often were no longer observed.

To the extent that realist readings of Thucydides address the breakdown of conventions, these changes are attributed to the effects of war, which is "a rough master" (3.82.2). This explanation is not convincing, because the Persian wars were equally harsh, yet most conventions held. Modern analogies spring to mind. The American Civil War was brutal by any standard, but both sides generally observed the conventions of war. Confederate mistreatment of African American prisoners of war was the principal exception, but even this reflected a convention. Troops on both sides behaved in ways that baffle us today. At Bloody Angle at Gettysburg, New Yorkers refused to follow orders to fire on the remnant of retreating Alabamians and instead threw their caps into the air and cheered them for their bravery. In World War I, German and Allied armies behaved on the whole quite honorably toward each other and civilians, in sharp contrast to World War II, especially on the Eastern front, which approximated Thucydides' depiction of barbarism. The differences were not due to the harshness or duration of war but to the character of the political systems. When language was subverted and conventions ignored or destroyed, as in Nazi Germany, the rational construction of interest was impossible, war aims were limitless, and the rules of warfare were disregarded.

Thucydides takes the constructivist argument another step and implies that civil society is also what actors make of it. Following Hobbes, most realists maintain that the distinguishing feature of domestic society is the presence of a Leviathan that overcomes anarchy and allows order to be maintained. For Thucydides, the character of domestic politics runs the gamut from highly ordered, consensual, and peaceful societies to those wracked by anarchy and bloodshed. It is not a Leviathan that is critical but the degree to which citizens construct their identities as members of a community (*homonoia*, literally, being of one mind) or as atomistic individuals. When the former view prevails, as it did in Periclean Athens and in Greece more generally before the Peloponnesian War, conventions restrain the behavior of actors, whether individuals or city-states. When the latter dominates, as in Corcyra and almost in Athens after 412, civil society disintegrates, and even a Leviathan cannot keep the peace. The domestic environment in these situations comes to resemble the war-torn international environment, and for the same reasons.

Conclusion

The history drives home the truth that a strong sense of community is equally essential to domestic and international order. Some rational choice formulations—again following Hobbes—acknowledge this reality and recognize that it is necessary to preserve the rules of the game if actors collectively are to maximize their interests. They highlight the paradox that a focus on short-term interests—by individuals, factions, or states—can undermine the order or environment on which the rational pursuit of interest depends. Thucydides would regard the tragedy of the commons as an unavoidable outcome in a culture in which the individual increasingly is the unit to whom advertisers and politicians appeal and in terms of whom social scientists conduct research. He would not find it surprising that a significant percentage of the citizens of such a society cannot see any reason for or imagine any benefit that might accrue from paying taxes.

The importance of community, and of identities defined at least partly in terms of it, was not lost on traditional realists. Morgenthau, (1951/1982, 61) cited Edward Gibbon's observation that the balance of power functioned well in the eighteenth century because Europe was "one great republic" with common standards of "politeness and cultivation" and a common "system of arts, and laws, and manners." As a consequence, the "mutual influence of fear and shame imposed moderation on the actions of states and their leaders" and instilled in all of them "some common sense of honor and justice" (p. 60). However much they desired to increase their power at the expense of their neighbors, they limited their ambitions because they recognized the right of others to exist and the fundamental legitimacy of the international political order. Morgenthau regards the breakdown of this sense of community as the underlying cause of both world wars and the threat to humanity posed by the Cold War. The same objection can be raised about liberal, institutionalist approaches that stress the role of institutions in creating and maintaining order. Those institutions may flourish and function as they do—when they do—because of an underlying sense of community.

Thucydides' history suggests that interest and justice are inextricably connected and mutually constitutive. On the surface they appear to be in conflict, and almost every debate in his history in one form or another pits considerations of interest against those of justice. But Thucydides, like Democritus, is interested in the underlying and often hidden nature of things. At that level, the history shows that interests cannot be intelligently considered, formulated, or pursued outside a *homonoia* and the identities it constructs and sustains. The creation and maintenance of *homonoia* depends on enduring individual commitments to justice and respect for other human beings (or political units). In the most fundamental sense, justice enables interests.

Materialist interpretations of Thucydides, which overwhelmingly are realist, offer a superficial and one-sided portrayal. Constructivist readings must avoid this error. Thucydides is both a realist and a constructivist. Stasis and *homonoia* represent two faces of human beings; both are inherent in their phusis. Materialism and constructivism are equally germane to the study of international relations. They need to build on Thucydides' research program, that is, discover the conditions that underlie stasis and homonoia and what caused transitions between them. For this reason alone, the history is "a possession for all time."

Notes

1 All English references to Thucydides in this article refer to *The Landmark Thucydides: A Comprehensive Guide to the Peloponnesian War*, ed. Robert B. Strassler (New York: Free Press, 1996).

2 *Nomos* first pertained to customs and conventions before some of them were written down in the form of laws and, later, to statutory law. Hesiod makes the first known usage, and Plato later wrote a treatise, *Nomoi*, in which he suggests that long-standing customs have higher authority than laws. *Nomos* can refer to all the habits of conforming to an institutional and social environment. *Phusis* is used by Homer to designate things that are born and grow and can be derived from the verb *phuein*, and later it became associated with nature more generally.

3 We must distinguish between Greek civilization and civilizations more generally. Thucydides certainly had in mind the restoration of civil society and international

order in Athens and Greece. Did he look beyond Greece geographically or historically? Fifth-century Greeks were aware of other contemporary (e.g., Egypt, Persia)
and past (Mycenaean and Homeric) civilizations. Thucydides had a clear sense of the
rise and fall of civilizations and describes his history "as a possession for all time,"
so it is reasonable to infer that he looked to a future readership beyond the confines
of Greece.

4 I do not want to exaggerate the parallels between ancient and modern philosophies
of social inquiry; there were important differences in ideas and the relative timing
of social and scientific advances. In the modern era, advances in mathematics have
contributed to modern science and, ultimately, the social sciences. In Greece, the age
of mathematical discovery came after these philosophical debates were under way.
Athenian interest in mathematics began a generation after Thucydides; Euclid wrote
his *Elements* at the end of the fourth century, and Archimedes made his contributions
almost a century later.

5 Well before Thucydides, Greek philosophy debated the importance and meaning of
language. There was some recognition that it mediated human understanding of reality and thus constituted a barrier to any perfect grasp of that reality. An attempted
solution was to assert that names are not arbitrary labels but imitations of their
objects. Others (e.g., Hermogenes) insisted that words are arbitrary in origin and do
not represent any reality. Socrates tried to split the difference by arguing that things
have a fixed nature that words attempt to reproduce, but the imitation is imperfect,
and this is why languages vary so much. Moreover, all attempts at imitation become
corrupted over time.

Considerable effort went into recapturing the meaning of words and names in the late
fifth century, and Thucydides must be situated in that tradition. I see no evidence that he
believed in the original meaning of words, but certainly he wanted to restore earlier meanings, supportive of homonoia, that had been subverted. Plato, in *Phaedrus*, 260b, makes a
similar argument when he discusses a skilled rhetorician who convinces someone to use
the name "horse" to describe a donkey and thus transfers the qualities of one to the other.
He is clearly tilting at rhetoricians and politicians who advocate evil as good.

References

Adcock, F. E. (1957). *The Greek and Macedonian art of war.* Berkeley: University of
    California Press.
Aeschylus (1938). Agamemnon. In *The complete Greek drama*, vol. 1, Whitney J. Oates &
    Eugene O'Neill, Jr. (eds.). New York: Random House. Pp. 167–225.
Alker, Hayward R. (1988). The dialectical logic of Thucydides' melian dialogue. *Ameri-
    can Political Science Review*, 82 (September), 806–20.
Alker, Hayward R. (1996). *Rediscoveries and reformulations: Humanistic methods for
    international studies.* Cambridge: Cambridge University Press.
Austin, J. L. (1975). *How to do things with words*, 2d. ed., J. O. Urmson & Marina Sbisà
    (eds.). Cambridge: Harvard University Press.
Bedford, David, & Thom Workman. (2001). The tragic reading of the Thucydidean trag-
    edy. *Review of International Studies*, 27 (January), 51–67.
Beye, Charles Rowan. (1987). *Ancient Greek literature and society*, 2d rev. ed. Ithaca, NY:
    Cornell University Press.

Bowersock, Glen P. (1965). The personality of Thucydides. *Antioch Review*, 35(1), 135–45.

Bury, J. B., & Russell Meiggs. (1975). *A history of Greece to the death of Alexander the Great*, 4th rev. ed. New York: St. Martin's.

Cochrane, Charles. (1929). *Thucydides and the science of history*. Oxford: Oxford University Press.

Connor, W. Robert. (1984). *Thucydides*. Princeton, NJ: Princeton University Press.

Cornford, F. M. (1907). *Thucydides mythistoricus*. London: Arnold.

Crane, Gregory. (1998). *Thucydides and the ancient simplicity: The limits of political realism*. Berkeley and Los Angeles: University of California Press.

Democritus. (1956). In *Die Fragmente der Vorsakratiker*, Hermann Diels & Walther Kranz (eds.). Berlin: Weidmannsche Verlagsbuchhandlung, 56–7.

De Ste. Croix, G. E. M. (1972). *The origins of the Peloponnesian war*. London: Duckworth.

Dionysus of Halicarnassus. (1975). *On Thucydides*, W. Kendrick Pritchett (trans.). Berkeley: University of California Press.

Doyle, Michael W. (1997). *Ways of war and peace*. New York: Norton.

Ellis, J. R. (1991). The structure and argument of Thucydides' archeology. *Classical Antiquity*, 10(2), 344–75.

Euben, J. Peter. (1990). *The tragedy of political theory: The road not taken*. Princeton, NJ: Princeton University Press.

Finley, John H., Jr. (1967). *Thucydides*. Ann Arbor: University of Michigan Press. (Original work published 1942)

Finnemore, Martha, & Kathryn Sikkink. (1998). International norm dynamics and political change. *International Organization*, 52 (Autumn), 887–918.

Forde, Steven. (1989). *The ambition to rule. Alcibiades and the politics of imperialism in Thucydides*. Ithaca, NY: Cornell University Press.

Forde, Steven. (1992). Varieties of realism: Thucydides and Machiavelli. *Journal of Politics*, 54 (May), 372–93.

Garst, Daniel. (1989). Thucydides and neorealism. *International Studies Quarterly*, 33(1), 469–97.

Gilpin, Robert. (1986). The richness of the tradition of political realism. In Robert O. Keohane (ed.), *Neorealism and its critics* (pp. 301–21) . New York: Columbia University Press.

Guthrie, W. K. C. (1969). *A history of Greek philosophy*, 5 vols. Cambridge: Cambridge University Press.

Havelock, Eric A. (1963). *Preface to Plato*. Cambridge, MA: Harvard University Press.

Herodotus. (1958). *The histories of Herodotus of Halicarnassus*, Harry Carter (trans.). New York: Heritage Press.

Herwig, Holger H. (1997). *The first world war: Germany and Austria-Hungary, 1914–1918*. London: Arnold.

Homer. (1951). *The Iliad of Homer,* Richmond Lattimore (trans.). Chicago: University of Chicago Press.

Hopf, Ted. (2002.). *Social Construction of International Politics: Identities and Foreign Policies, Moscow, 1955–1999*. Ithaca, NY: Cornell University Press.

Jaeger, Werner. (1939–45). *Paideia: The Ideals of Greek Culture*, 3 vols. Gilbert Highet (trans.). Oxford: Blackwell.

Kagan, Donald. (1969). *The outbreak of the Peloponnesian war.* Ithaca, NY: Cornell University Press.

Kerford, G. B. (1981). *The Sophistic movement.* Cambridge: Cambridge University Press.

Kokaz, Nancy. (2001). Moderating power: A Thucydidean perspective. *Review of International Studies,* 27 (January), 27–49.

Kratochwil, Friedrich V. (1989). *Rules, norms, and decisions: On the conditions of political and legal reasoning in international relations and domestic affairs.* Cambridge: Cambridge University Press.

Kratochwil, Friedrich V., & John Gerard Ruggie. (1986). International organization: A state of the art on an art of the state. *International Organization,* 49 (Autumn), 753–75.

Lain Entralgo, Pedro. (1970). *The therapy of the word in classical antiquity.* E. J. Rather & John M. Sharp (ed. And trans.). New Haven, CT: Yale University Press.

Lebow, Richard Ned. (1991). Thucydides, power transition theory, and the causes of war. In Richard Ned Lebow & Barry S. Strauss (eds.), *Hegemonic rivalry: From Thucydides to the nuclear age.* Boulder, CO: Westview. 125-68.

Lebow, Richard Ned. (1996). Play it again Pericles: Agents, structures and the peloponnesian war. *European Journal of International Relations,* 2 (June), 231–58.

Lebow, Richard Ned, & Robert Kelly. (2001.). Thucydides and hegemony: Athens and the United States. *Review of International Studies,* 27 (October). 1-17

Levy, Jack S. (1992). An introduction to prospect theory. *Political Psychology,* 13 (June), 171–86.

Levy, Jack S. (1996). Loss aversion, framing and bargaining: The implications of prospect theory for international conflict. *International Political Science Review,* 17 (2), 179–95.

Lloyd, Geoffrey E. R. (1978). *Magic, reason and experience: Studies in the origins and development of Greek science.* Cambridge: Cambridge University Press.

Luce, T. J. (1997). *The Greek historians.* London: Routledge.

Meiggs, Russell. (1972). *The Athenian empire.* Oxford: Oxford University Press.

Monoson, S. Sara, & Michael Loriaux. (1998). The illusion of power and the disruption of moral norms: Thucydides' critique of Periclean policy. *American Political Science Review,* 92 (June), 285–98.

Morgenthau, Hans J. (1982). *In defense of the national interest: A critical examination of American foreign policy.* Lanham, MD: University Press of America. (Original work published 1951)

Murray, Williamson, & Allan R. Millet. (2000). *A war to be won: Fighting the second world war.* Cambridge, MA: Harvard University Press.

Ober, Josiah. (1989). *Mass and elite in democratic Athens: Rhetoric, ideology, and the power of the people.* Princeton, NJ: Princeton University Press.

Ober, Josiah. (1998). *Political dissent in democratic Athens: Intellectual critics of popular rule.* Princeton, NJ: Princeton University Press.

Onuf, Nicholas Greenwood. (1989). *World of our making: Rules and rule in social theory and international relations.* Columbia: University of South Carolina Press.

Orwin, Clifford. (1994). *The humanity of Thucydides.* Princeton, NJ: Princeton University Press.

Perlman, Shalom. (1991). Hegemony and Arche in Greece: Fourth-century views. In Richard Ned Lebow & Barry Strauss (eds.), *Hegemonic Rivalry: From Thucydides to the Nuclear Age* (pp. 269–86). Boulder, CO: Westview.

Rahe, Paul A. (1996). Thucydides critique of realpolitik. In Benjamin Frankel (ed.), *Roots of realism* (pp. 105–41). Portland, OR: Frank Cass.

Rawlings, Hunter R., III. (1981). *The structure of Thucydides*. Princeton, NJ: Princeton University Press.

Romilly, Jacqueline de. (1990). *La construction de la vérité chez Thucydide*. Paris: Julliard.

Saxonhouse, Arlene W. (1996). *Athenian democracy: Modern myth-makers and ancient theorists*. South Bend, IN: University of Notre Dame Press.

Searle, John R. (1995). *The construction of social reality*. New York: Free Press.

Stahl, Hans-Peter. (1966). *Thucydides: Die Stellung des menschen im geschichlichen Prozess*. Munich: C. H. Beck.

Strauss, Barry S. (1986). *Athens after the peloponnesian war*. Ithaca, NY: Cornell University Press.

Thucydides. (1996). *The landmark Thucydides: A comprehensive guide to the peloponnesian war,* Robert B. (ed.). Strassler. New York: Free Press.

Tversky, Amos, & Daniel Kahneman. (1992). Advances in prospect theory: Cumulative representation of uncertainty. *Journal of Risk and Uncertainty,* 5 (2), 297–323.

Wallace, W. P. (1964). "Thucydides." *Phoenix,* 18 (4): 251–61.

Waltz, Kenneth. (1979). *The theory of international politics*. Reading, MA: Addison-Wesley.

Weinberg, Gerhard L. (1994). *A world at war: A Global history of world war II*. Cambridge, MA: Harvard University Press.

White, James Boyd. (1984). *When words lose their meaning: Constitutions and reconstitutions of language, character and community*. Chicago: University of Chicago Press.

12 Power, persuasion, and justice

The ancient Greeks' conceptions of power are embedded in the writings[1] of fifth- and fourth- century playwrights, historians, and philosophers. They enrich our understanding of power in several important ways. They highlight the links between power and the purposes for which it is employed, as well as the means used toward these ends. They provide a conceptual framework for distinguishing enlightened from narrow self-interest, identify strategies of influence associated with each, and their implications for the survival of communities.

In the field of international relations, power has been used interchangeably as a property and a relational concept.[2] This elision reflects a wider failure to distinguish material capabilities from power, and power from influence. Classical realists—unlike many later theorists—understood that material capabilities are only one component of power, and that influence is a psychological relationship. Hans Morgenthau insisted that influence is always relative, situation specific and highly dependent on the skill of actors.[3] Stefano Guzzini observes that this political truth creates an irresolvable dilemma for realist theory. If power cannot be defined and measured independently from specific interactions, it cannot provide the foundation for deductive realist theories.[4]

Liberal conceptions also stress material capabilities, but privilege economic over military power. Some liberal understandings go beyond material capabilities to include culture, ideology and the nature of a state's political-economic order; what Joseph Nye, Jr. calls "soft power." Liberals also tend to conflate power and influence. Many assume that economic power—hard or soft—automatically confers influence.[5] Nye takes it for granted that the American way of life is so attractive, even mesmerizing, and the global public goods it supposedly provides so beneficial, that others are predisposed to follow Washington's lead. Like many liberals, he treats interests and identities as objective, uncontroversial, and given.[6]

Recent constructivist writings differentiate power from influence, and highlight the importance of process, Habermasian accounts stress the ways in which argument can be determining, and describe a kind of influence that can be fully independent of material capabilities. They make surprisingly narrow claims. Thomas Risse considers argument likely to be decisive only among actors who share a common "lifeworld," and in situations where they are uncertain about their interests, or where existing norms do not apply or clash.[7] Risse and other advocates of communicative rationality fail to distinguish between good and persuasive arguments—and they are by no means the same. Nor do they tell us what makes for either kind of argument or how we determine when an argument is persuasive without reasoning backwards from an outcome. Thicker constructive approaches build on the ancient Greek understanding of rhetoric as the language of politics, and consider the most persuasive arguments those that sustain or enable identities. According to Christian Reus-Smit, "all political power is deeply embedded in webs of social exchange and mutual constitution—the sort that escapes from the short-term vagaries of coercion and bribery to assume a structural, taken-for-granted form—ultimately rests on legitimacy."[8]

Like thick constructivist accounts, the Greeks focus our attention on the underlying causes of persuasion, not on individual instances.[9] They offer us conceptual categories for distinguishing between different kinds of argument, and a politically enlightened definition of what constitutes a good argument. The Greeks appreciated the power of emotional appeals, especially when they held out the prospect of sustaining identities. More importantly, they understood the transformative potential of emotion; how it could combine with reason to create shared identities, and with it, a general propensity to cooperate with or be persuaded by certain actors.

Persuasion and power

Given the complex nature of my argument, it is useful to begin with a short discussion of the relationship between power and persuasion (a principal form of influence), followed by an overview of the principal points I intend to make. First, however, I want to address a stock objection that is invariably raised when Greek ideas or practices are imported into a modern setting. Because they arose in such a different context, they are sometimes described as alien, even irrelevant, to industrial, mass societies. It would certainly be unrealistic to expect that some Greek practices would work the same way for us as it did in fifth century Athens. While human practices vary enormously across time and cultures, human nature does not. Certain human needs appear to be universal, as do pathologies associated with human desires, information processing, and decision making. Hubris, one of the self-destructive behavioral patterns described by Greek tragedy, is a widespread phenomenon. In our age, as in antiquity, powerful actors tend to become complacent about risk and put their trust in hope rather than reason and overvalue their ability to control their environment, other people, and the course of events.[10] Greek concepts, applied with finesse and suitable caveats, can shed important light on contemporary politics.

For the Greeks and moderns alike, power and persuasion are closely linked in theory and practice. The strategic interaction literature encourages us to consider influence as derivative of power, if mediated by agency. Of course, in practice, power can be used to achieve some ends (e.g., genocide) that have little or nothing to do with persuasion. However, as Clausewitz so aptly observed, military force usually has the broader goal of persuasion; self-defense, for example, is intended to convince an aggressor that it should break off its attack because it will not succeed or prove too costly.[11] Persuasion can involve the threat, as opposed to the application; deterrence and compellence only succeed when force does not have to be used. Persuasion can rest on rewards, as do strategies of reassurance. Defense, deterrence and many forms of reassurance ultimately depend on material capabilities. Persuasion can be based on other kinds of power, including moral, rhetorical and influence over important third parties. The degree to which persuasion is an expression of power really depends on how expansive a definition of power we adopt.

We need to distinguish the goal of persuasion from persuasion as a means. As noted above, efforts at persuasion (the goal) rely on the persuasive skills of actors (the means) to offer suitable rewards, make appropriate and credible threats, or marshal telling arguments. Aeschylus, Sophocles, Thucydides, and Plato recognize the double meaning of persuasion, and like their modern counterparts, devote at least as much attention to persuasion as a means as they do to it as an end. Unlike many contemporary authorities, their primary concern is not with tactics (e.g., the best means of demonstrating credibility) but with ethics. They distinguish persuasion brought about by deceit (*dolos*), false logic, coercion, and other forms of chicanery from persuasion (*peithō*) achieved by holding out the prospect of building or strengthening friendships, common identities, and mutually valued norms and practices. They associate persuasion of the former kind (dolos) with those sophists who taught rhetoric and demagogues who sought to win the support of the assembly by false or misleading, arguments for selfish ends. *Peithō*, by contrast, uses dialogue to help actors define who they are, and this includes the initiating party, not just the actor(s) it seeks to influence. *Peithō* constructs common identities and interests through joint understandings, commitments: and deeds. It begins with recognition of the ontological equality of all the parties to a dialogue, and advances beyond that to build friendships and mutual respect. *Peithō* blurs the distinction between means and ends because it has positive value in its own right, independently of any specific end it is intended to serve.

Some of the Greek authors I examine—Sophocles in particular—treat *peithō* and *dolos* as diametrically opposed strategies. This reflects the tendency of Greek tragedy to pit characters with extreme and unyielding commitments to particular beliefs or practices against each other in order to illustrate their beneficial and baneful consequences. I do the same, while recognizing, as did the Greeks, that pure representations of any strategy of influence are stereotypes. *Peithō* and *dolos* like other binaries I describe, have something of the character of ideal types. Actual strategies or political relationships approach them only to certain degree, and in practice, can be mixed.

Sophocles, Thucydides, and Plato consider *peithō* a more effective strategy than *dolos* because it has the potential to foster cooperation that transcends discrete issues, builds and strengthens community and reshapes interests in ways that facilitate future cooperation. For much the same reason, *peithō* has a restricted domain; it cannot persuade honest people to act contrary to their values or identities. *Dolos* can sometimes hoodwink actors into behaving this way. In contrast to *peithō*, it treats people as means not ends—a Kantian distinction implicit in Sophocles and Plato.[12] *Dolos* is almost always costlier in a material sense because it depends on threats and rewards. States whose power is primarily capability-based, and whose influence is largely exercised through *dolos*—the Greeks referred to such a political unit as an *archē*—often felt driven lo pursue foreign policies intended to augment their capabilities. Like Athens, they may try to expand beyond the limits of their capabilities. *Peithō*, by contrast, encourages self-restraint.

Dolos is most often a strategy of the powerful, as they have the resources to employ it most effectively. For the playwrights it is also associated with the domination of *archē*. Along with violence, it is quintessential expression of this kind of rule. It can also be used by the weak to subvert the authority of the powerful. In Euripides' *Hecuba*, the Trojan queen Hecuba tricks her enemy Polymestor in order to tie him up. His Medea is at a double disadvantage because she is a barbarian as well as a woman, but triumphs over Jason by means of chicanery.

There is another key distinction between Greek and many modern understandings of power that derives from fundamental differences in their psychology. Since the Enlightenment, Western philosophers and social scientists have generally attributed all human desires to the appetite, and emphasized the instrumental role of reason in helping people satisfy their appetites. The Greeks had a richer understanding of motives. They posited three kinds of desire: appetite, spirit, and reason. Appetite encompassed all physical desires, including security and wealth. The concept of spirit embodies the insight that all human beings value and seek self-esteem, a desire that can come into conflict with appetite. For Plato and Aristotle, self-esteem is acquired by emulating and excelling at qualities and activities admired by one's society, and thereby winning the respect of others. The spirit is angered by impediments to self-assertion in private or public life, and driven to seek revenge for all slights of honor.

Self-esteem and appetite not infrequently come into conflict in politics, which, almost by definition, makes some actors dominant over others. Subordinates may be moved to accept domination by their appetite (because it will make them more secure, wealthier or more powerful vis a vis third parties) and to oppose it by their spirit (which insists on resistance in the name of self-esteem). Classical realists from Thucydides to Morgenthau understood this tension, and the corollary that power must be masked to be effective. Subordinate actors need to be allowed, or at least encouraged, to believe that they are expressing their free will, not being coerced, are being treated as ends in themselves, not merely as means, and are respected as ontological equals, even in situations characterized by marked power imbalance.

The different demands of appetite and spirit have important implications for strategies of influence. Capability-based theories of influence like realism assume that influence is proportional to power, measured in terms of material capabilities. Generally speaking, the weaker the state, the less likely it is to oppose the wishes of a powerful interlocutor. Cases where weaker powers (or factions) go to war against strong ones (e.g., Athens vs. Persia, Melos vs. Athens), or strenuously resist them (e.g., North Vietnam vs. the United States, Chechnya vs. Russia) are anomalous from a realist perspective. The Greek understanding of the psyche suggests that capability-based influence always has the potential to provoke internal conflict and external resistance because of how it degrades the spirit—and all the more so when no effort is made to give it any aura of legitimacy through consultation, institutionalization, soft words, and self-restraint. *Peithō* is least likely to generate resistance, especially when initiated by an actor whose right to lead—which the Greeks associated with *hēgemonia*—is widely accepted. It helps to explain why lesser powers often fail to form alliances to balance against a power that is dominant or on its way to becoming so. The general acceptance of Chinese regional hegemony by most of the countries of the Pacific rim offers a good contemporary example.[13]

The balance of material capabilities is not irrelevant for the Greeks and classical realists. It influences acceptance or rejection of subordinate status, but not for the reasons commonly assumed. Small powers may offer less resistance because it is not as severe a blow to their self-esteem to give way to an actor many times more powerful. Resistance is most likely to be pronounced in honor-based societies—regardless of their relative power—where self-esteem takes precedence over appetite. This may be one reason why the initial Iraqi euphoria at the overthrow of Saddam Hussein quickly turned into opposition to the United States as an occupier. This transition was facilitated by American occupation policy, which aimed—but never really succeeded—in addressing Iraqi appetites (by providing security, food, electricity, etc.); to the exclusion, and often the detriment, of satisfying Iraqi needs for self-esteem.

My analysis points to an interesting and complex relationship between power and ethics. While recognizing that might often makes for right, it reveals that right can also make might. Of equal importance, it provides a discourse that encourages the formulation of longer-term, enlightened self-interests predicated on recognition that membership and high standing in a community is usually the most efficient way to achieve and maintain influence. Such commitments also serve as a powerful source of self-restraint. For all of these reasons, ethical behavior is conducive—perhaps even essential—to national security.

Thucydides and Athens

Thucydides' account of the Peloponnesian War encodes a profound analysis of the nature of power and influence. Central to it is the distinction he makes between *hēgemonia* and *archē*. For fifth and fourth century Greeks, *hēgemonia* was a form of legitimate authority associated with *timē* (honor and office), which in this sense also meant the "office" to which one was accordingly entitled. Sparta and Athens earned *timē* by virtue of their contributions and sacrifices to Greece during the Persian Wars. *Timē* was also conferred on Athens in recognition of her literary, artistic and intellectual, political and commercial accomplishments that had made her, in the words of Pericles, the "school of Hellas."[14] *Archē* meant "control," and initially applied to authority within a city state, and later to rule or influence of some city states over others.

The years between the Battle of Salamis (480 B.C.E.) and the outbreak of the Peloponnesian War (431) witnessed the gradual transformation of the Delian League into the Athenian empire. Athens removed the treasury from Delos, imposed its silver coinage and weights and measures on most of its allies, and made the Great Panathena an empire festival. It intervened in the domestic affairs of allies to support democratic factions and, when necessary, used force to extract tribute from restive allies. By 430, Pericles acknowledged that the Athenian empire had many attributes of a tyranny, but could proclaim, with some justification, that it also retained important features of *hēgemonia*.[15] There were few revolts in the early stages of the Peloponnesian War. They became more frequent after Sparta's successes in Chalcidice, and there was a rash of defections after Athens' defeat in Sicily.[16]

After Pericles' death from the plague in 429, Athens' military strategy changed, and with it, relations with allies. Pericles had urged his countrymen "to wait quietly, to pay attention to their fleet, to attempt no new conquests, and to expose the city to no hazards during the war."[17] Cleon and Alcibiades spurned his sober advice in favor of an offensive strategy aimed at imperial expansion. As Pericles had foreseen, this offensive strategy aroused consternation throughout Greece and appeared to lend substance to Sparta's claim that it was the "liberator of Hellas." The new strategy required more resources and compelled Athens to demand more tribute from its allies, which provoked resentment and occasionally, armed resistance. Rebellion elicited a harsh response, and several cities were starved into submission. Siege operations required considerable resources, making it necessary to extract more tribute, triggering a downward spiral in Athenian-allied relations that continued for the duration of the war.[18] By 416, the year the assembly voted to occupy Melos and subdue Sicily the Athenian empire had increasingly become an *archē* based on military might. The structure and language of the Melian Dialogue reveal how much the political culture of Athens had changed. It consists of *brachylogies*: short, blunt, alternating verbal thrusts, suggestive of the lunge and parry of a duel. The Athenian generals, Cleomedes and Tisias, dispense with all pretense. They acknowledge that their invasion cannot be justified on the basis of their right to rule or as a response to provocations. They deny the relevance of justice, which they assert only comes into play between equals. "The strong do what they can and the weak suffer what they must," and the Melians should put their survival first and submit.[19] The Melians warn the Athenians that their empire will not last forever, and if they violate the established norms of justice and decency their fall "would be a signal for the heaviest vengeance and an example for the world to meditate upon." The Athenians insist that they live in the present and must do what is necessary to preserve their empire. The Melians assert that that empire is best served by a neutral and friendly Melos. The Athenians explain that their empire is held together by power (*dunamis*, power in action) and the fear (*phobos*) it inspires. Other island states would interpret Melian neutrality as a sign of Athenian weakness and it would therefore serve as a stimulus for rebellion. "The fact that you are islanders and weaker than others renders it all the more important that you should not succeed in baffling the masters of the sea."[20] Contemporary Greeks would have been shocked by Athens' rejection of the Melian offer of neutrality on the grounds that "your hostility cannot so hurt us as your friendship (*philia*),"[21] Friendship was widely recognized as the cement that held the polis together. Fifteen years into the war the Athenians had inverted a core Greek value.

Pericles understood that the overriding foreign policy interest of Athens was preservation of its empire, and that this required naval power *and* legitimacy. To maintain *hēgemonia*, Athens had to act in accord with the principles and values that it espoused, and offer positive political and economic benefits to allies. Post-Periclean leaders consistently chose power over principle, and by doing so, alienated allies and third parties, lost *hēgemonia* and weakened Athens' power base Viewed in this light, the Melian Dialogue and the Sicilian expedition are not only radical departures from rational self-interest but the almost inevitable result of the shift in the basis of Athenian authority and influence from *hēgemonia* to *archē*.

Thucydides' account of the Peloponnesian War is rich in irony. Athens, the tyrant, jettisoned the traditional bonds and obligations of reciprocity in expectation of greater freedom and rewards only to become trapped by a new set of more onerous obligations. The post-Periclean empire had to maintain its *archē* by constantly demonstrating its power and will to use it. Toward this end, it had to keep expanding, a requirement beyond the capabilities of any state. The Melian operation was part of the run up to the invasion of Sicily motivated in part by this goal—where the same Athenians who slaughtered most of the Melians and sold the remainder into slavery would meet a similar fate at the hands of the Syracuse.

Archē

The Greeks generally used two words to signify power: *kratos* and *dunamis*. For Homer, *kratos* is the physical power to overcome or subdue an adversary from such action. Although fifth-century Greeks did not always make a clear distinction between these words, they tended to understand *kratos* as the basis for *dunamis*. It is something akin to our notion of material capability. *Dunamis*, by contrast, is power exerted in action, like the concept of force in physics.

Archē—rule over others—is founded on *kratos* (material capabilities) and, of necessity, sustains itself through *dunamis* (displays of power). Superior material capability provides the basis for conquest or coercion. Influence is subsequently maintained through rewards and threats. Such a policy makes serious demands on resources, and encourages an *archē* to increase its resource base. Athens did this through territorial and commercial expansion, but even more through the extraction of tribute, which permitted a major augmentation of its fleet.

Archē is always hierarchical. Control will not admit equality, and an authoritarian political structure is best suited to the downward flow of central authority and horizontal flow of resources from periphery to center. Once established, the maintenance of hierarchy becomes an important second order goal, for which those in authority are often prepared to use all resources at their disposal. Athenians explicitly acknowledged that Melian independence, by challenging that hierarchy, would encourage more powerful allies to assert themselves, which could lead to the unraveling of their empire. The Soviet Union, another classic *archē*, periodically intervened in Eastern Europe for the same reason.

There are three underlying causes for the failure of *archē*: a decline in material capability, overextension and inadequate resolve. The first, a loss of *kratos*, was an underlying cause of the slow decline and shrinkage of all great colonial empires in the nineteenth and twentieth centuries. Power transition theorists have identified a range of responses of great powers—most of whom were also empires—to relative loss in capabilities (e.g., preventive war, retrenchment), but have been unable to explain why they chose the strategies they did.[22] The distinction, or more accurately, the continuum characterized by *archē* on one end and *hēgemonia* on the other, offers some analytical purchase. The closer a system resembles an *archē*, at home or abroad, the more likely it is to resort to repression, look for opportunities to assert authority, and consider preventive war. In modern times, the Ottoman, Russian, and Austro-Hungarian empires adopted these strategies—all three in the case of Austria-Hungary—in response to their relative declines in *kratos*. There was fear in Constantinople, St. Petersburg and Vienna, as there would be in Moscow a half-century later, that any perception of weakness or lack of resolve would invite serious challenges by domestic or foreign opponents. Britain, by contrast, was a constitutional democracy and faced the prospect of a serious colonial rebellion only in Ireland—a territory it had governed as an *archē*. It had more leeway to consider other strategies, most notably retrenchment, which it began to put into effect in the Far East early in the twentieth century. Further evidence for this proposition is that shifts from repression to retrenchment often follow democratic transitions within a metropole (e.g., Spain, Portugal, and Gorbachev's Soviet Union).

Successful *archē* also requires self-restraint. There are diminishing returns to territorial expansion and resource extraction. At some point, further predation encourages active resistance and makes maintenance of *archē* even more dependent on displays of resolve, suppression of adversaries and the maintenance of hierarchy. All these responses require greater resources, which in turn encourages more expansion and resource extraction. For political, organizational and psychological reasons, self-restraint is extraordinarily difficult for an *archē*.

Hierarchy without constitutional limits or other restraints—the political basis for *archē*—makes it easier to ignore the interests and desires of domestic opinion and client states, isolates those in authority from those whom they oppress, and narrows the focus of the former on efforts to maintain or enhance their authority. Over time, it can produce a ruling class—like Athenian citizens, slave owners in the American antebellum South, the former Soviet *nomenklatura* or the present day Chinese Communist Party—whose socialization, life experiences and expectations make the inequality on which all *archē* is based seem natural, and for whom rapacity and suppression of dissent has become the norm.

Thucydides offers the political equivalent of what would become Newton's third law of motion: an *archē* is likely to expand until checked by an opposite and equal force.[23] Imperial overextension—*dunamis* beyond that reasonably sustained by *kratos*—constitutes a serious drain on capabilities, especially when it involves an *archē* in a war the regime can neither win nor settle for a compromise peace for fear of being perceived as weak at home and abroad. In this circumstance, leaders become increasingly desperate and may assume even greater risks because they can more easily envisage the disastrous consequences to themselves of not doing so. Athens threw all caution to the winds and invaded Sicily, not only in the expectation of material rewards, but in the hope that a major triumph in *Magna Grecia* would compel Sparta to sue for peace. In our age, Austria-Hungary invaded Serbia to cope with nationalist discontent at home, Japan attacked the United States hopeful that a limited victory in the Pacific would undermine resistance in China, and Germany invaded Russia when it could not bring Britain to, its knees. All of these adventures ended in disaster.

Archē is based primarily on material capabilities, and will last only as long as those capabilities sustain the requisite level of rewards, threats and punishments. Resolve enters the picture as subordinates and third parties periodically assess an *archē*'s will to use its capabilities to sustain itself and its hierarchical structure. Resolve can be strengthened by superior capability, but there is no direct relationship between capabilities and resolve. A decline in capabilities can make it appear all the more important to demonstrate resolve, as it did for Russia and Austria-Hungary in 1914, both of whom, like Athens, feared that any perceived failure of will would be the catalyst for greater internal opposition and foreign policy challenges.

Will can erode independently of capabilities. France in the 1930s is a textbook case of how internal division can make external resolve all but impossible. The Soviet Union under Gorbachev experienced a crisis of will, but for a different reason. A meaningful percentage of the Soviet elite—including the general secretary and his closest advisors—had lost faith in Soviet-style communism, and embraced values inimical to maintaining the unchallenged authority of the communist party at home and of Soviet authority in Afghanistan and Eastern Europe. Gorbachev's public encouragement of reform in Eastern Europe and refusal to use the Red Army to maintain pro-Soviet regimes, led to revolution in Romania and tumultuous but less violent upheavals elsewhere in the region. These developments, which began with Gorbachev's domestic reforms, were part of a chain of events that led to the collapse of the Soviet Union. The Soviet case indicates that hierarchy, at home and abroad, can serve as a useful mechanism for asserting authority and extracting resources, but its maintenance ultimately becomes a litmus test—for rulers and ruled alike—of the capability and resolve of an *archē*.[24]

The Gorbachev experience has suggested to some that an *archē* must remain firm at all costs; that repression, à la Tienamen Square, is a more efficacious response to opposition than concession and reform. This may be true in the short-term, but it is almost surely Counterproductive in the longer-term. Crude forms of extraction, accompanied by repression, are far less efficient than pluralist, collaborative and democratically organized efforts. Stalin's forced collectivization and five year plans were credited with saving the Soviet Union from Germany, but it seems likely that continuation of Lenin's New Economic Policy would almost certainly have resulted in more growth.[25] East Germany, Cuba, and, above all, North Korea, offer dramatic illustrations of the limitations of hierarchical, state-run economies.

Archē seems to have been more successful in pre-modern times when it did not run so counter to popular expectations or general political practice. In the course of the last century, liberal democracy and material well-being increasingly became, if not the norm, the aspiration of growing numbers of peoples. Repressive regimes were most secure in countries whose populations—as in Stalin's Soviet Union and present day North Korea—could effectively be isolated from other societies and governments and information about their practices and achievements. These regimes illustrate two paths to failure. In North Korea, over five decades of the closest approximation to a "totalitarian" regime have brought the country to the brink of economic breakdown and widespread starvation. The scope of the latter is only limited by foreign aid, and, while nobody can predict how the end will come, the days of communism in North Korea are surely numbered—and so too may be its survival as a state.

The Soviet Union weathered the Stalin-imposed famine of the 1930s (here too foreign aid was helpful), barely survived the war, and struggled unsuccessfully for the next half-century to improve its economy beyond the value added by growth in its labor force. And yet, communism was not brought down by its inability to perform economically, although this was a source of disenchantment for intellectuals acquainted with the higher living standard of the West. So too was knowledge of non-Marxist ideas and political life elsewhere by high party officials and *apparatchiki*. Loss of faith in the political system encouraged the naïve hope that democratic reforms could restore idealism, reinvigorate the command economy, revitalize the system, and make it more like Western European social democracies.[26] Instead, *glasnost* and *perestroika* led to the rapid unraveling of the economy and political system by unleashing an array of long pent up contradictory demands and subversive activities with which the system could not cope. China has sought to avoid this outcome, and finesse the dilemmas of *archē* by encouraging economic development through the partial introduction of capitalism while maintaining the iron grip of the communist party on the reins of political power.

The verdict on the Chinese experiment is not yet in, but there are good reasons to think that economic growth will only heighten dissatisfaction with the communist party and lead to some kind of showdown if it does not allow a peaceful devolution of power. If so, China, even more than the Soviet Union, will become a victim of a process of unintended consequences of the kind nicely described by classical Marxist theory. Feudalism gave rise to capitalism, and capitalism was expected to give rise to socialism as much by virtue of its successes as its failures. High feudalism generated wealth that secular princes and those of the church spent on various forms of conspicuous consumption. This encouraged the growth of artisan and commercial classes, the rebirth of urban centers, and ultimately, the rise of the bourgeoisie who overthrew feudalism. Mature capitalism was supposed to impoverish a large working class while giving it, through necessary job training and military service, the organizational and military capabilities to rebel against their oppressors. China's, extraordinary economic development has given rise to an ever growing class of successful entrepreneurs, scientists, intellectuals and artists who constitute a growing source of opposition to the Party. This class has become large enough, and some sufficiently outspoken, to make the regime both insecure but increasingly dependent on them for economic growth. The problem is exacerbated by increasing unrest in the countryside, where the corruption and high-handedness of party officials prompts an average of 150 protests a day.[27] Such a situation is by its very nature highly unstable.[28]

Persuasion

As I noted in the introduction, the ancient Greeks distinguished persuasion based on deceit (*dolos*), false logic, and other forms of verbal chicanery, from persuasion (*peithō*) based on honest dialogue. *Peithō*; is characterized by frankness and openness and it accomplishes its goal by promising to create or sustain individual and collective identities through common acts of performance. As a form of influence, it is limited to behavior others understand as supportive of their identities and interests. It is nevertheless more efficient than *archē* because it does not consume material capabilities in displays of resolve, threats or bribes.

The contrast between the two strategies is explored in Aeschylus' *Oresteia*. In *Agamemnon*, the first play of the trilogy, Clytemnestra employs *dolos* to trick her husband, just back from the Trojan War, into walking on a red robe that she has laid out before him. She wraps him up in the robe to disable him so she can kill him with a dagger. In the next play, Libation Bearers, Orestes resorts to dolos to gain entrance to the palace and murder Clytemnestra and her consort, Aegisthus. In the final play, the *Eumendides*, Athena praises *peithō* and the beneficial ends it serves and employs it to end the Furies' pursuit of Orestes, terminate the, blood feuds that have all but destroyed the house of Atreus and replace tribal with public law.[29] Dolos is clearly linked to violence and injustice. Even when used to achieve justice in the form of revenge it entails new acts of injustice that perpetuate the spiral of deceit and violence. The only escape from the vicious cycles is through *peithō* and the institutional regulation of conflict, which have the potential of transforming the actors and their relationships. This transformation is symbolized by the new identity accepted by the Furies—the *Eumenides*, or well-wishers—who, at the end of the play; are escorted to their new home in a chamber beneath the city of Athens.

Although the trilogy is ostensibly about the house of Atreus and the regulation of family and civic conflict, it is also about international relations. Many of the major characters are central figures in the Trojan War. Helen is married to Menelaus, and her seduction and abduction by Paris triggers the Trojan War. Menelaus' honor can only be redeemed by the recapture of Helen and destruction of the city that has taken her in. Agamemnon, his brother and king of Argos, leads the Greek expedition against Troy. The *Oresteia* open with his return to Argos after a 10 year absence. In the interim, his wife Clytemnestra has taken Aegisthus, son of Thyestes, for a consort. Among her motives for murdering her husband is his earlier sacrifice at Aulis of their daughter Iphigenia in response to the prophecy that it was necessary to secure favorable winds for the departure of the Greek fleet to Troy.

The curse of the Atridae and the Trojan War are also closely connected in their origins: both are triggered by serious violations of guest friendship (*xenia*), one of the most important norms in heroic age Greece. In Aeschylus' version, the troubles of the Atridae clan begin with Thyestes' seduction of his brother Atreus' wife. This violation of the household is followed by another more terrifying one. Atreus pretends to forgive Thyestes and allows him to return home where he is invited to attend a feast. In the interim, Atreus has murdered two of Thyestes three children and put them in a stew which he then serves to Thyestes. This gives Aegisthus, the surviving son, a motive for seducing Clytemnestra and assisting her in the murder of Agamemnon, the son of Atreus. The curse of the Atridae and the Trojan War unfold as a series of escalating acts of revenge. If the curse of the Atridae can be resolved through *peithō* and the institutional regulation, this might be possible for the internecine conflicts among the community of Greeks, as they arise from the same causes and are governed by the same dynamics.

Peithō is also central to Sophocles' *Philoctetes,* produced in 409, five years before Athens' defeat in the Peloponnesian War. Greek tragedy was deeply affected by two decades of war, the plague, the breakdown of Athenian civic culture and the reemergence of intense factional conflict. Sophocles and Euripides are less convinced than Aeschylus, writing more than a generation earlier, that reason and dialogue can successfully overcome, or at least, mute conflict. Their plays suggest that civic conflicts are multiple, cross-cutting and endemic, and correspondingly more difficult to resolve. They nevertheless search for some way of restoring a civilizing discourse in the intensely partisan and conflictual environment of late fifth century Athens.

Like many tragedies, the *Philoctetes* is set during the Trojan War. Philoctetes' father had been given Heracles' bow because he had lit that hero's funeral pyre. Philoctetes inherited the bow, and trained himself to become a master archer. En route to Troy, he was bitten in the leg by a snake and left with a foul-smelling, suppurating wound. The resulting stench, and Philoctetes' repeated cries of pain, led the Geeks to abandon him on the island of Lemnos while he slept. After years of inconclusive warfare, the Greeks receive a prophecy that Troy will only be conquered when Philoctetes and his bow appear on the battlefield. They dispatch Odysseus and Achilles' son Neoptolemus to retrieve archer and bow, and the play opens with their arrival on the island.

Odysseus lives up to his reputation as a trickster; he resorts to soft words (*logoi malthakoi*) to persuade Neoptolemus to go along with his scheme to pretend friendship with Philoctetes in order to steal the bow. He does this by creating a seemingly irreconcilable conflict between two important components of his identity: the honorable man who would rather fail than resort to dishonesty and deceit, and the Greek committed to the defeat of Troy. Odysseus presents his argument at the very last moment, giving Neoptolemus no time for reflection.

Philoctetes is an honorable, friendly, and generous person, with whom Neoptolemus quickly establishes a genuine friendship. When Philoctetes grows weak from his wound, he gives his bow to Neoptolemus for safekeeping, and when he awakes from his feverish sleep, is delighted to discover that Neoptolemus has kept his word and not abandoned him. In the interim, the chorus had pleaded unsuccessfully with Neoptolemus to sneak off with the bow. Neoptolemus then half-heartedly tries to persuade Philoctetes to accompany him to Troy on the spurious grounds that he will find a cure there for his wound. Philoctetes sees through this deceit, and demands his bow back. Neoptolemus initially refuses, telling himself that justice, self-interest, and above all, necessity, demand that he obey his orders to bring the bow back to Troy. Philoctetes is disgusted, and Neoptolemus' resolve weakens. Odysseus returns and threatens to force Philoctetes to board their ship, or to leave him on the island without his bow. Odysseus appears to have won, as he and Neoptolemus depart with the bow. However, Neoptolemus, who has finally resolved his ethical dilemma, returns to give back the bow because he recognizes that what is just (*dikaios*) is preferable to that which is merely clever (*sophos*). Odysseus threatens to draw his sword, first against Neoptolemus, and then against Philoctetes. Neoptolemus refuses to be intimidated, as does Philoctetes, who draws his bow and aims an arrow at Odysseus. Neoptolemus seizes his arm and tells him that violence would not reflect honor on either of them. Philotetes then agrees to proceed voluntarily with Neoptolemus and Odysseus to Troy.

Odysseus fails to grasp the essential truth that our principal wealth is not material, but social and cultural. It consists of the relationships of trust we build with neighbors and friends through honest dialogue, and the communities which this sustains. Odysseus is willing to use any means to accomplish his ends because he lacks any definition of self beyond the ends he can accomplish. He is incapable of interrogating those ends or the means by which they might be obtained. His attempts to exercise power through deceit and threats fail, leaving him something of an outcast.[30] Odysseus comes close to imposing his will on both his protagonists, and fails only because Neoptolemus and Philoctetes have established a friendship based on mutual trust and respect. His emotional attachment puts Neoptolemus back in touch with his true self and the values that make him who he is, and give him the resolve and the courage to return to Philoctetes with his bow, apologies for having obtained it dishonorably and face down an enraged Odysseus. The emotional bond Neoptolemus and Philoctetes establish also leads Philoctetes to imagine an encounter between himself and Heracles, who tells him that it is his fate to go to Troy with Neoptolemus and there win glory. He agrees to proceed because he too has been restored as a full person through his relationship with Neoptolemus.

Gorgias (circa 430 B.C.E), described language (*logos*) as a "great potentate, who with the tiniest and least visible body achieves the most divine works." When employed in tandem with persuasion (*Peithō*) it "shapes the soul as it wishes."[31] Thucydides exalts the power of language and its ability to create and sustain community, but recognizes how easily it can destroy that community when employed by clever people seeking selfish ends. I have argued elsewhere that one of the key themes of his text is the relationship between words (*logoi*) and deeds (*ergā*).[32] Speech shapes action, but action transforms speech. It prompts new words and meanings, and can subvert existing words by giving them meanings diametrically opposed to their original ones. The positive feedback loop between *logoi* and *erga*—the theme of Thucydides' "Archeology"—created the *nomoi* (conventions, customs, rules, norms, and laws) that made Greek civilization possible. His subsequent account of the Peloponnesian War shows how the meaning of words were twisted and transformed to encourage and justify deeds that defied *nomos*, and how this process was responsible for the most destructive forms of civil strife (*stasis*) that consumed Hellas.[33] For Thucydides, *dolos* was an important cause of war. It is pronounced in the opening speeches of the text: the appeals of Corcyraeans and Corinthians to the Athenian assembly to persuade and dissuade it from entering into a defensive alliance with Corcyra.[34]

Words are the ultimate convention, and they too succumb to *stasis* in the sense that civilized conversation is replaced by a fragmented discourse in which people disagree about the meaning of words and the concepts they support, and struggle to impose their meanings on others is as Odysseus did with Philoctetes. Altered meanings changed the way people thought about each other, their society and obligations to it, and encouraged barbarism and violence by undermining long-standing conventions and the constraints they enforced. Thucydides attributes this process to "the lust for power arising from greed and ambition; and from these passions proceeded the violence of parties once engaged in contention." Leaders of democratic and aristocratic factions

> sought prizes for themselves in those public interests which they pretended to cherish, and, recoiling from no means in their struggles for ascendancy,

engaged in the direct excesses; not stopping at what justice or the good of the state demanded, but making the part caprice of the moment their only standard, and invoking with equal readiness the condemnation of an unjust verdict or the authority of the strong arm to glut the animosities of the hour.[35]

Thucydides gives us few examples of *peithō*. Arguably, the most significant is Pericles' funeral oration, which turns a solemn recognition of the sacrifices of the fallen into an uplifting commemoration of Athens and its values, and how they are maintained by the love, sacrifice, and the self-restraint of its citizens. Pericles speaks in a forthright manner, acknowledging that the Athenian empire has come in some ways to resemble a tyranny. It nevertheless retains its *hēgemonia* and achieves excellence (*aretē*) by demonstrating generosity (*charis*) to its allies.[36] "In generosity," he tells the assembly, "we are equally singular, acquiring our friends by conferring not by receiving favours."[37] *Charis* encouraged loyally, self-restraint and generosity based on the principle of reciprocity. With *philia* (friendship), it was the foundation of interpersonal, civic and inter-polis relations.

To this point in the argument, I have stressed the beneficial consequences of *peithō* and the negative consequences of *dolos*. Are there circumstances in which dolos may be necessary or beneficial, and *peithō* damaging? The ending of *Philoctetes* leaves us with the thought that *peithō* and *dolos* may be usefully combined. Heracles tells Achilles that he cannot capture Troy without the assistance of Philoctetes, but working together like twin lions hunting, they shall overcome Ilium. Philoctetes will use Heracles' bow to kill Paris, Troy's leading warrior, and Odysseus, as myth as has it, would devise the scheme of the "Trojan horse" to gain the Greeks entry into the City.

Thucydides' Mytilenian debate is sometimes cited as a less ambiguous example of *dolos*. In this episode, Diodotus convinces the Athenian assembly not to execute all Mytilenian adult males, but only a limited number of aristocrats who can be held responsible for the rebellion. He openly acknowledges that it is no longer possible to defend a policy in the name of justice; Athenians will only act on the basis of self-interest. He carries the day by using his considerable rhetorical skill to mask an appeal based on justice in the language of self-interest.[38] Modern examples abound. Franklin Roosevelt has been almost uniformly praised by historians for the rhetorically dishonest, but strategically effective, when he committed American naval forces to engage German submarines in the Atlantic before America entered the war. Modeling himself on Roosevelt, Lyndon Johnson campaigned as the peace candidate and promptly exploited an alleged attack on American naval vessels in the Gulf of Tonkin to intervene militarily in Vietnam. As that war ended in disaster, historians condemn Johnson's deception. George W. Bush and his advisors made multiple false claims to gain public and congressional approval for an invasion of Iraq. It is too early to offer a definitive judgment, but it seems highly likely that history will judge Bush's *dolos* at least as critically as it has Johnson's.

Leaders routinely believe that they know better than public opinion what is good for their countries, and feel justified to use *dolos* to achieve their policy goals. Even when their policies are in the national interest, they risk exacerbating the political problem by making the public less responsive to honest, and inevitably more complicated, arguments in the future. Thucydides uses the sequence of Pericles' funeral oration, the Mytilenian and Sicilian debates to track this decline. More often than not, *dolos* is simply a political convenience; leaders use it because it is the only way, or at least the easiest way, of gaining popular support.

Plato's opposition to *dolos* was unyielding for these reasons. He understood that rhetoric was at the heart of politics, and sought to develop dialogue as an alternative to speeches that so easily slipped into reliance on *dolos*. Quite apart from dialogue's ability to produce consensual outcomes through reason, the free exchange of ideas among friends and the give-and-take of discussion had the potential to strengthen the bonds of friendship and respect that were the foundation of community. Plato portrays Socrates' life as a dialogue with his polis, and his acceptance of its death sentence as his final commitment to maintain the coherence and principle of that dialogue. Plato structures his dialogues to suggest that Socrates' positions do not represent any kind of final truth. His interlocutors often make arguments that Socrates cannot fully refute, or chooses not to, which encourages readers to develop a holistic contemplation of dialogue that recognizes that unresolved tensions can lead to deeper understandings and form the basis for collaborative behavior.[39]

The Socratic emphasis on dialogue has been revived in the twentieth century, and is central to the thought and writings of figures as diverse as Mikhail Bakhtin, Hans-Georg Gadamer, and Jürgen Habermas. Bakhtin suggests that even solitary reflection derives from dialogues with others against whom or with whom we struggle to establish ourselves and our ideas.[40] Habermas's "critique of ideology" led him to propose a coercion-free discourse in which participants justify their claims before an extended audience and assume the existence of an "ideal speech situation," in which participants are willing to be convinced by the best arguments.[41]

Greek understandings of *peithō* have much in common with, but are not entirely the same as, Habermas' conception of communicative rationality. Habermas puts great emphasis on reasoned argument among equals, and its ability to persuade—an outcome so essential to democracy. *Peithō* values reason, but less for its ability to convince than its ability to communicate openness and honesty. These values help to build the trust and friendship on which the underlying propensity to cooperate and be persuaded ultimately depend.

Gadamer's conception of dialogue is closer to the Greeks. For Gadamer, dialogue "is the art of having a conversation, and that includes the art of having a conversation with oneself and fervently seeking an understanding of oneself."[42] It is not so much a method, as a philosophical enterprise that puts people in touch with themselves and others and reveals to them the prior determinations, anticipations, and imprints that reside in their concepts. Experiencing the other through dialogue can lead to *exstasis*, or the experience of being outside of oneself. By this means, dialogue helps people who start with different understandings to reach a binding philosophical or political consensus. Critical hermeneutics in its broadest sense is an attempt to transgress culture and power structures through a radical break with subjective self-understanding.[43]

This framing of persuasion has important implications for the theory and practice of power and influence. In contrast to *archē*, which is created and sustained by violence, threats, and *dolos*, *hēgemonia* is created and sustained by *peithō* and rewards. It is only possible within a community whose members share core values, and is limited to activities that are understood to support common interests and identities. *Peithō* can also help to bring such a community into being. While it is the strategy of influence associated with *hēgemonia*, it is largely independent of material capabilities. However, it can help to sustain those capabilities because it does not require the constant exercise of *dunamis*.

As we observed, *hēgemonia* is an honorific status conferred by others in recognition of the benefits an actor has provided for the community as a whole. It is a reputation for excellence and honor. Material capabilities come into the picture in so far as they provide the raw materials that facilitate the attainment of excellence and honor. Athens was greatly inferior to Persia in its material capabilities, but its willingness to take on that empire at the risk of annihilation made it all the more praiseworthy and honorable. As Pericles recognized (to a point), but his successors did not, self-restraint and generosity were the most effective way to enhance Athenian reputation and influence.

Peithō can function independently of *hēgemonia*. Actors at any level of social interaction who earn the respect of their interlocutors by making claims supported by arguments that appeal to their interlocutors' feelings, opinions, and interests— and offer them the possibility of reaffirming their identities—are likely to have some influence. A recent example is the success of a diverse coalition of NGOS who coordinated their efforts to persuade a majority of the world's states to negotiate and ratify the International Criminal Court.[44] Osama Bin Laden wields influence for much the same reason, albeit within a very different community.

Motives

The Enlightenment rejected Aristotelian *telos* and largely reduced reason to a mere instrumentality, to "the slave of the passions," in the words of David Hume.[45] Our cognitive abilities help us satisfy our appetites by identifying appropriate outlets for them. Freud's model of the mind is a classic post-Enlightenment formulation: the ego, which embodies reason, mediates between the impulses of the libido and the external environment. Strategic choice, the dominant paradigm in contemporary social science, is based on a similar understanding of reason; it assumes that actors rank order their preferences and act in ways best calculated to achieve them.

The modern focus on reason as instrumentality encouraged a shift away from consideration of the ends we seek, or should seek, to the means of satisfying our appetites. The behavioral sciences reflect this shift in their emphasis on strategic interaction. Social scientists acknowledge the critical importance of preferences, but have made no sustained effort to understand what they are, how they form or when and why they change. Their ontology is unsuited to the task. The best they can do is derive preferences from deductive theories—as neorealists do when they stipulate that relative power is the principal end that states seek in an anarchic international environment—or try to infer them on the basis of behavior. By making human, institutional or a state preferences unidimensional, theorists greatly oversimplify human motivation, and their theories offer a poor fit with reality. To acknowledge multiple motives requires additional theories to stipulate which motives predominate under what conditions. Such theories would have to be rooted in sophisticated understandings of human psychology and culture.

Unlike our theories, life is wonderfully complex. People and collectivities are moved by a diverse array of motives—which they understand only imperfectly. Their preference hierarchies shift in response to ever-changing internal and external stimuli. Realists greatly oversimplify reality by assuming that states seek power, just as economists do when they assume that people seek wealth. Political scientists and economists alike have devoted surprisingly little thought to the nature and scope conditions of this most fundamental of their propositions. Some actors do seek power or wealth as ends in themselves. For others, perhaps most, power or wealth are instrumentalities; they are means of achieving security, comfort, reputation, honor, a good life, or some other end or combination of goals.

Assume for the sake of the argument that states have a preference for power when making political choices.[46] To have a workable theory of politics, we would need to know the kinds of choices that actors frame as political (as opposed to economic, social, or religious, etc.). We also need to know why they seek power, because only then can we begin to estimate how they will assess trade-offs between power and other values (e.g., wealth, reputation, rectitude), and what they will risk in the pursuit of power. There is no way to analyze means without seriously considering ends.[47]

This truth was well-known to the ancient Greeks who framed the problem of choice differently than modern social scientists. Their principal concern was human goals, and from an early date they thought people were motivated by fear, interest and honor. Interest and honor were expressions of the appetite and spirit respectively, categories to which we will return momentarily. Fear becomes a motive, and possibly, the dominant one, when either the appetite or spirit breaks free of restraints normally imposed by reason and threatens the well-being, self esteem, and perhaps, survival, of other actors.

In Book One, Thucydides invokes all three motives to explain the actions of Athens and Sparta that led to war. In their speech to the Spartan assembly, the Corinthians describe the Athenians as driven by *polypragmosunē*: literally, "trespass," but widely used in the late fifth century by critics of modernity to signify a kind of metaphysical restlessness, intellectual discontent and meddlesomeness that found expression in *pleonexia* (envy, ambition, search of glory, monetary greed, lust for power and conquest).[48] Athens cannot resist the prospect of gain held out by the Corcyraean proposal of alliance. Thucydides is equally critical of Sparta. King Archidamus offers the Spartan assembly an accurate account of Athenian power and urges his compatriots to reflect carefully before embarking on a war that they are likely to pass on to their sons. His argument carries less weight than the emotional plea of the ephor Sthenelaïdas, who insists that the Athenians have wronged long-standing allies and deserve to be punished. In Athens, Pericles appeals to the Athenian appetite for wealth and power, while in Sparta, Sthenelaïdas speaks to his countrymen's spirit and yearning for honor. In showing the disastrous consequences of the unrestrained pursuit of either desire, Thucydides reaffirms the importance of the traditional Greek value of the middle way (*meden agan*), something that could only be attained in practice when reason constrains both appetite and spirit.[49]

Plato articulated a similar understanding of motivation, but embedded it in an explicit theory of human psychology. In his *Republic*, Socrates identifies three distinct components of the psyche: appetite, spirit and reason. Appetite (*to epithumētikon*) includes all primitive biological urges—hunger, thirst, sex, and aversion to pain—and their more sophisticated expressions. Socrates uses the example of thirst, which he describes as a desire for a drink qua drink, to argue that appetites are a distinct set of desires and not means to other ends. He divides appetites, as he does all desires, into those that are necessary and unnecessary. The former are appetites we are unable to deny and whose satisfaction benefits us. The latter are those we could avoid with proper training and discipline. Appetite includes the unnecessary desire for wealth, which is unique to human beings and, he insists, has become increasingly dominant. He acknowledges that we require some degree of coordination, even reflection, to satisfy our appetites, but no broader conception of the meaning of life.[50]

Plato's Socrates infers that there are desires beyond the appetites because someone can be thirsty but abstain from drink to satisfy other desires. The principal alternative source of desire is the spirit (*to thumoeides*), a word derived from *thumos*, the alleged internal organ that roused Homeric heroes to action. Socrates attributes all kinds of vigorous and competitive behavior to *thumos*. It makes us admire and emulate the skills, character and positions of people considered praiseworthy by society. By equaling or surpassing their accomplishments, we gain the respect of others and buttress our own self-esteem. The spirit is honor-loving (*philotimon*) and victory-loving (*philonikon*). It responds with anger to any impediment to self-assertion in private or civic life. It desires to avenge all slights of honor or standing to ourselves and our friends. It demands immediate action, which can result in ill-considered behavior, but can be advantageous in circumstances where rapid responses are necessary.[51]

The spirit requires conceptions of esteem, shame, and justice. They are acquired through socialization, and tend to be common to a family, peer group and perhaps, the wider society. Plato has Socrates distinguish spirit from appetite and reason. His defining example is Leontius, who experiences pleasure from looking at corpses, but is angry at himself for indulging his shameful appetite. The spirit can come into conflict with reason. When Odysseus returns home in disguise, he is enraged to discover that some of Penelope's maids have become willing bedmates of her suitors. He suppresses his anger because it would reveal his identity and interfere with his plans to address the more serious threat posed by the numerous and well-armed suitors.[52] Examples abound in international relations, and, I submit, include the choice faced by the Bush administration in the aftermath of the events of September 11, 2001. Strategic reason would have dictated a measured response, designed to capture those responsible through police action and diplomatic pressure and reduce the likelihood of further terrorism against the United States and Americans abroad. The invasion of Afghanistan, motivated in large part by the perceived need to defend American honor—widely shared by the American people—failed to accomplish either goal. The Bush administration did not respond like Odysseus.

Reason (*to logistikon*), the third part of the psyche, has the capability to distinguish good from bad, in contrast to appetite and spirit which can only engage in instrumental reasoning. Socrates avers that reason has desires of its own, the most important being discovery of the purposes of life and the means of fulfilling them. It possesses a corresponding drive to rule (*archein*)—the root from which archē is derived. Reason wants to discipline and train the appetite and the spirit to do what will promote happiness (*eudaimonia*) and well-being.[53]

Greek understandings of human motivation shed additional light on the respective costs and benefits of *archē* and *hēgemonia*. I have stressed the ways in which the resource extraction characteristic of *archē* arouses opposition on the part of subordinate individuals and peoples. We tend to associate such opposition with the appetite, but the Greeks would expect the spirit to inspire at least as much resentment and opposition. The spirit is angered by slights to honor, and in many societies there are few things more dishonorable than visible subordination. The spirit is a universal attribute of human beings, but its relative importance varies from culture to culture. In so-called shame cultures, honor takes precedence over appetite—even at the risk, or near-certainty, of death. Herodotus explains Athenian resistance to Persia in terms of honor, as Thucydides does with Melos. Those states like Thebes that 'Medized, that is, made their peace with advancing Persian armies, were ever after thought to have behaved dishonorably.

The importance of honor in shame cultures offers an interesting perspective on Iraqi resistance to Anglo-American occupation. The Bush administration expected its forces to be hailed as liberators, and initially they were welcomed by many Iraqis. The Americans had no plans for a rapid transfer power to an independent Iraqi or international authority. They assumed light control over the reins of civilian authority, headed by an American puppet exile with little to no local support. American forces increasingly came to be seen as an army of occupation. Violent resistance triggered equally violent reprisals and set in motion an escalatory spiral—of the kind Aeschylus wrote about—which further cast the Americans in the role of occupiers. Insensitive to the needs of the spirit, American authorities belatedly attempted to win over the Iraqi people by satisfying their appetites—e.g., restoring electricity, providing gasoline and diesel fuel, rebuilding schools and hospitals, and doing their best to provide security. These programs—which the Bush administration repeatedly cited as evidence of its goodwill and commitment—did nothing to placate the spirit, and were run in a manner that further highlighted Iraqi subordination. The same was true of dilatory American efforts to create an independent Iraqi governing authority and repeated public insistence that Washington would continue to have the last word on all important matters. Interviews with Iraqis from all walks of life indicated fury at their perceived insubordination. One respondent angrily admitted that Saddam may have killed thousands of Iraqi civilians, and the Americans only hundreds. The American occupation was still intolerable, as he put it, because at least "Saddam was one of ours."[54]

The spirit can strengthen *hēgemonia* if it is managed in way to confer honor on those who are subordinate. The Athenian Empire grew out of the Delian League, an alliance to liberate those Greek communities still under the Persian yoke. Member states willingly accepted Athenian leadership because it was considered essential to their common goal, one from which all would gain honor (*timē*). Even in the early days of empire, many Greeks apparently felt a sense of pride in being part of such a powerful and glorious enterprise. Pericles almost certainly encouraged this sentiment by using a sizeable portion of the allied tribute to construct the Parthenon, the Athena Parthenos and Propylaea, all of which bespoke the wealth and grandeur of Athens and its empire.

Pericles understood that power must be masked to be effective. In his funeral oration, he describes Athens as a democracy (*dēmokratia*), but Thucydides tells us that the constitutional reforms of 462–61 created a mixed form of government (*xunkrasis*). Behind the outward form of democracy lay the de facto rule of one man (*ergōi de hupo tou prōtou andros archē*)—Pericles.[55] The democratic ideology, with which he publicly associated himself, moderated class tensions and reconciled the *dēmos* to the economic and political advantages of the elite in a Gramscian manner. When the gap between ideology and practice was both exposed and made intolerable by the behavior of post-Periclean demagogues, class conflict became more acute, and politics more vicious, leading to the violent overthrow of democracy by the Tyranny of the Thirty in 404 and its equally violent restoration a year later.

The founding fathers of the post-World War II order—some of whom, like George C. Marshall, regularly cited Thucydides in their writings and speeches—recognized this political truth. They created economic, political, military and juridical institutions that, at least in part, tended to restrain powerful actors and reward weaker ones, providing the latter with strong incentives to retain close relations with the dominant power. American hegemony during the Cold War was based on the sophisticated recognition that the most stable orders are those "in which the returns to power are relatively low and the returns to institutions are relatively high."[56] Influence depended as much on self-restraint as it did on power.

Power and ethics

In modern discourses, ethics and behavior are generally considered distinct subjects of inquiry because they are understood to derive from different principles. Many modern realists consider these principles antagonistic; not all the time to be sure, but frequently enough to warrant the establishment of a clear hierarchy with interest-based considerations at the apex. For the Greek tragedians—and I number Thucydides among them—there was no dramatic separation between ethics and interest. Their writings show how individuals or states that sever identity-defining relationships enter a liminal world where reason, freed from affection, leads them to behave in self-destructive ways. The chorus in Antigone proclaims in the first stasimon: "When he obeys the laws and honors justice, the city stands proud. ...But when man swerves from side to side, and when the laws are broken, and set at naught, he is like a person without a city, beyond human boundary, a horror, a pollution to be avoided."[57]

Behavior at odds with the accepted morality of the age undermines the standing, influence and even the hegemony of great powers. The Anglo-American invasion of Iraq is the latest example of this age-old phenomenon. The national security elite of the United States still considers its country "the indispensable nation" to whom others look for leadership. Public opinion polls of its closest allies—countries like Canada, Japan and the countries of Western Europe—indicate that the United States has lost any *hēgemonia* it may once have had, and is overwhelmingly perceived as an *archē*, and one that many people believe is the greatest threat to the peace of the world.[58] In the run up to the invasion of Iraq, it surely behaved as an *archē*; the Bush administration's duplicitous claims about weapons of mass destruction and false claims that the purpose of an invasion was to remove these weapons and introduce democracy to Iraq were a quintessential exercise in deceit (*dolos*). Its subsequent occupation began with efforts to protect only those assets of strategic or economic value to the Bush regime (e.g., the oil ministry and refineries), and was followed by the installation of an American proconsul, unwillingness to share authority with any international organization, and the denial of contracts for the rebuilding of Iraqi infrastructure to companies from countries that had not supported the war. Such behavior is typical of an *archē* who can no longer persuade but must coerce and bribe; and, Blair's Britain aside, this is the basis of the so-called coalition of the willing.

At least as far back as Homer, Greeks believed that people only assumed identities—that is, became people—through membership and participation in a community. The practices and rituals of community gave individuals their values, created bonds with other people and, at the deepest level, gave meaning and purpose to peoples' lives. Community also performed an essential cognitive function. To take on an identity, people not only had to distinguish themselves from others, but "identify" with them. Without membership in a community, they could do neither, for they lacked an appropriate reference point to help determine what made them different from and similar to others. This was Oedipus' problem; because of his unknown provenance, he did not know who he was or where he was heading. His attempt to create and sustain a separate identity through reason and aggression was doomed to failure

For the Greeks, this pathology extended beyond individuals to cities. There is reason to believe that Sophocles intended Oedipus as a parable for Periclean Athens. Like Oedipus, Athens' intellectual prowess became impulsiveness, its decisiveness thoughtlessness, and its sense of mastery, intolerance to opposition. Oedipus' fall presages that of Athens, and for much the same reasons. The United States would do well to consider the extent to which the unilateral foreign policies that it has pursued since the end of the Cold War are taking it down the same path as Oedipus and Athens. Its unilateral foreign policies, often accompanied by "in your face" rhetoric, have opened a gulf between itself and the community of democratic nations that has previously allowed it to translate its power into influence in efficient ways. Once outside this community, and shorn of the identity it sustained, Washington must increasingly use threats and bribes to get its way, and like Athens and Oedipus, the goals it seeks are likely to become increasingly short-sighted and irrational. If this comes to pass, it will be another tragic proof of arguably the most fundamental truth of politics: that friendship and persuasion create and sustain community, and community in turn enables and sustains the identities that allow rational formulation of interests. In the last resort, justice and power are mutually constitutive.

Notes

1 Robert A. Dahl, "Power," in *International Encyclopedia of the Social Sciences*, ed. David L. Sills (New York: Free Press, 1968), 12, 405–15; Steven Lukes, *Power: A Radical View* (New York: Macmillan, 1974), and its recent revision (London: Palgrave, 2004); Stefano Guzzini, "Structural Power: The Limits of Neorealist Power Analysis," *International Organization* 47, no. 3 (1993): 443–78, and "The Enduring Dilemmas of Realism in International Relations," *European Journal of International Relations* 10, no. 4 (2004): 533–568.

2 Hans J. Morgenthau, *Politics Among Nations: The Struggle for Power and Peace* (New York: Knopf, 1948), 14ff., 270–74, and *In Defense of the National Interest: A Critical Examination of American Foreign Policy* (Lanham, MD: University Press of America, 1982), 48, 52–54.

3 Guzzini, "Enduring Dilemmas of Realism".
4 Dahl, "Power."
5 Joseph S. Nye, Jr., *Soft Power: The Means to Success in World Politics* (Washington, DC: Public Affairs Press, 2004), and "The Decline of America's Soft Power," *Foreign Affairs* 83 (May/June 2004): 16–21. For a critique of Nye see Christian Reus-Smith, *American Power and World Order* (London: Polity, 2004), 64–65.
6 Thomas Risse, "'Let's Argue!'": Communicative Action in World Politics," *International Organization* 54, no. 4 (2000): 1–40; Neta C. Crawford, *Argument and Change in World Politics: Ethics, Decolonization, and Humanitarian Intervention* (Cambridge: Cambridge University Press, 2002).
7 Reus-Smith, *American Power.*
8 Martha Finnemore and Stephen J. Toope make this argument in the context of compliance with international law. See Finnemore and Troope, "Alternatives to 'Legalization': Richer Views of Law and Polities," *International Organization* 55, no. 3 (2001): 743–58.
9 For an elaboration of this theme see Richard Ned Lebow, *The Tragic Vision of Politics: Ethics, Interests and Orders* (Cambridge: Cambridge University Press, 2003).
10 Carl von Clausewitz, *On War,* ed. and trans. Michael Howard and Peter Paret (Princeton, NJ: Princeton University Press, 1976), bk. 1.
11 *Gorgias*, Plato's Socrates maintains that rhetoric, as practiced by sophists, treats others as means to an end, but dialogue treats them as ends in themselves and appeals to what is best for them. See also the *Republic*, 509d-511d, 531d-534c.
12 David C. Kang, "Getting Asia Wrong: the Need for New Analytic Frameworks," *International Security* 27, no. 4 (2003): 57–85.
13 Thucydides, 2.4
14 Ibid., 2.63.
15 On the Samian revolt see Russell Meiggs, *The Athenian Empire* (Oxford: Oxford University Press, 1972), 188–92.
16 Thucydides, 2.65.7.
17 Meiggs, *Athenian Empire*, 205–54.
18 Thucydides, 5.89.
19 Ibid., 5.91–99.
20 Ibid., 5.95.
21 A. F. K. Organski, *World Politics*, 2nd ed. (New York: Knopf, 1967), 202–03; A. F. K. Organski and Jacek Kugler, *The War Ledger* (Chicago: University of Chicago Press, 1980); and Robert Gilpin, *War and Change in World Politics* (New York Cambridge University Press, 1981), 200–01.
22 James Boyd White, *When Words Lose Their Meaning: Constitutions and Reconstitutions of Language, Character, and Community* (Chicago: University of Chicago Press, 1984); and Lebow, *Tragic Vision of Politics*, chs. 2, 3 and 7.
23 Raymond L. Garthoff, *The Great Transition: American Soviet Relations and the End of the Cold War* (Washington, DC: Brookings, 1994); Archie Brown, *The Gorbachev Factor* (Oxford: Oxford University Press, 1996); Jacques Lévesque, *The Enigma of 1989: The USSR and the Liberation of Eastern Europe,* trans. Keith Martin (Berkeley: University of California Press, 1997); Robert D. English, *Russia and the idea of the West: Gorbachev, Intellectuals, and the End of the Cold War* (New York Columbia University Press, 2000).

24 Alexander Erlich, *The Soviet Industrialization Debate 1924–1928* (Cambridge, MA: Harvard University Press, 1967); Alec Nove, "Was Stalin Really Necessary?", *Problems of Communism* 25, no. 4 (1976): 49–62, and *An Economic History of the Soviet Union*. rev. ed. (Harmondsworth: Penguin, 1982).

25 Lévesque, Enigma of 1989.

26 Joseph Kahn, "For the Chinese Masses, an Increasingly Short Fuse," *International Herald Tribune*, December 31, 2004, 1–2.

27 Maurice Meisner, *Mao's China and After: A History of The People's Republic*, 3rd ed. (New York: Free Press, 1999); and Bruce Dickson, "Who does the Party Represent?" From "Three Revolutionary Classes" to "Three Represents," in *Stale and Society in 21st-century China*, eds. Peter Hays Gries and Stanley Rosen (New York. Routledge 2004), 141–158.

28 Aeschylus, *Eumenides*, lines 958–74. Aeschylus' *Prometheus* also explores different kinds of persuasion and shows how they can fail.

29 Bernard Knox, *The Heroic Temper: studies in Sophoclean Tragedy* (New York Cambridge University Press, 1982), ch. 5; James Boyd White, *Heracles' Bow: Essays on the Rhetoric and Poetics of the Law* (Madison: University of Wisconsin Press, 1985), 3–27; and Alasdair MacIntyre, *After Virtue,* rev. 2nd ed. (Norte Dame: Norte Dame University Press, 1984), 134.

30 Gorgias, frg. 82, BII, pp. 8, 13–14 in Hermann Diels and Walther Kranz, *Die Fragmente der Vorsokratiker*, 7th ed. (Berlin: Weidmannsche Verlagsbuchhandlung, 1956).

31 Lebow, *Tragic Vision of Politics*, ch. 4

32 Lebow, "Thucydides the Constructivist," *American Political Science Review* 95, no. 3 (2001): 547–60, and *Tragic Vision of Politics*, ch.4..

33 Lebow, *Tragic Vision of Politics*, 154–59.

34 Thucydides, 3.82.

35 Ibid., 2.34.5.

36 Thucydides, 2.40.4.

37 Ibid., 3.36–49. See Clifford Orwin, *The Humanity of Thucydides* (Princeton, NJ: Princeton University Press, 1994), 161.

38 John M. Cooper, "Socrates and Plato in Plato's Gorgias," in M. Cooper, *Reason and Emotion: Essays on Ancient Moral Psychology and Ethical Theory* (Princeton, NJ: Princeton University Press, 1999), 28–75.

39 Mikhail Bakhtin, *Problems of Dostoevsky's Poetics* (Minneapolis: University of Minnesota Press, 1984); Michael Holquist and Katerina Clark, *Mikhail Bakhtin* (Cambridge, MA: Harvard University Press, 1984); and James Wertsch, *Voices of the Mind* (Cambridge: Harvard University Press, 1991).

40 Jürgen Habermas, *The Theory of Communicative Action*, 2 vols., trans Thomas McCarthy (Boston: Beacon Press, 1984–87), 2 and *Moral Consciousness and Communicative Action*, trans. Christian Lenhardt and Shierry Weber Nicholsen (Cambridge, MA: M. I. T. Press, 1990).

41 Hans-Georg Gadamer, "Reflections on My Philosophical Journey," in *The Philosophy of Hans-George Gadamer*, ed. Lewis Edwin Hahn (Chicago: Open Court, 1997), 3–63, 33; and Johannes Fabian, "Ethnographic Objectivity Revisited: From Rigor to Vigor," in *Rethinking Objectivity*, ed. Allan Megill (Durham, NC: Duke University Press, 1994), 81–108.

42   Hans-George Gadamer, *Truth and Method*, 2nd ed., trans. Joel Weinsheimer and Donald G. Marshall (New York: Crossroad, 1989), "Plato and the Poets," in *Dialogue and Dialectic*, trans. P. Christopher Smith (New Haven, CT: Yale University Press, 1980), 39–72, and "Reflections on My Philosophical Journey," in *The Philosophy of Hans-George Gadamer*, ed. Lewis Edwin Hahn (Chicago: Open Court 1997), 17, 27.

43   Fanny Benedetti and John L. Washburn, "Drafting the International Criminal Court Treaty: Two Years to Rome and an Afterword on the Rome Diplomatic Conference," *Global Governance* 5, no. 1 (1999); Marlies Glasius, "How Activists Shaped the Court," Crimes of War Project Magazine (2003). Available at http://www.crimesof-war.org/icc_magazine/icc-glasius.html#top; accessed February 28, 2005..

44   David Hume, *A Treatise of Human Nature*, eds., David Fate Norton and Mary Norton (Oxford: Oxford University Press, 2000), 2.3.3.4, and *An Inquiry Concerning the Principles of Morals,* ed. Tom L. Beauchamp (New York: Oxford University Press, 1998), Appendix I, 163.

45   Morgenthau, *Politics Among Nations*, 3rd ed. (New York: Alfred A. Knopf, 1960). 5.

46   Harold Lasswell is one of the few social scientists who addressed this problem He posited a plurality of motives, each of which could serve as an end in itself or a means toward achieving other ends. See Lasswell, *Politics: Who Gets What, When, How* (Cleveland: Meridian Books, 1958), Postscript, 202–03.

47   Thucydides uses polypragmosyne only once in his text, to characterize Athenians as 'hyperactive' (6.87.3), but it is widely used by other authors to describe Athens. See Victor Ehrenberg, "Polypragmosyne: A Study in Greek Politics," *Journal of Hellenic Studies* 67 (1947): 46–67; John H. Finley, "Euripides and Thucydides," *Harvard Studies in Classical Philology* 49 (1938): 23–68; and June W. Allison "Thucydides and Polypragmosyne," *American Journal of Ancient History* 4 (1979) 10–22.

48   Ibid., 1.80–85, 86–88, for the two speeches. The war developed as Archidamus predicted, and Sparta was forced to sue for peace after a sizeable number of its hoplites were taken prisoner on the island of Sphacteria in 426 Athens subsequently broke the truce and was defeated in 404, but Sparta's victory left it weak and unable to maintain its primacy in Greece.

49   Plato, *Republic,* 439b3-5, c2-3, 553c4-7, 558d11-e3, 559a3-6 and 580d11-58la7.

50   Plato's conceptions of the *thumos* are developed in Books V, VIII and IX of the *Republic*.

51   Homer, *Iliad*, Book 20, 1–37; and Plato, *Republic*, 439el-440b.

52   Plato, *Republic*, 441c1-2, 441e4, 442c5-6, 580d7-8, 8505d11-el.

53   Interviews conducted and quote provided by Prof. Shawn Rosenberg.

54   Thucydides, 2.37.1 and 2.65.9–10.

55   G. John Ikenberry, *After Victory: Institutions, Strategic Restraint, and the Rebuilding of Order After Major Wars* (Princeton, NJ: Princeton University Press, 2001), esp. 248, 257–73.

56   Sophocles, *Antigone*, 267–69.

57   Lebow, *Tragic Vision*, 314–15.

58   Bernard Knox, *Oedipus at Thebes* (New York: Norton, 1970), 99; and J. Peter Euben, *The Tragedy of Political Theory: The Road Not Taken* (Princeton, NJ: Princeton University Press, 1990), 40–41.

13 Tragedy, politics, and political science

It is a great pleasure to participate in a thoughtful symposium on an important topic. My reading of Frost, Mayall, and Rengger indicates a broad area of agreement concerning the likelihood that complicated policies, domestic or foreign, are likely to have unintended, largely negative consequences. These authors believe that such problems are more likely in a world characterized by competing ethical perspectives. Frost is more optimistic than either Mayall or Rengger that a transformation of the international system is nevertheless possible. Drawing on Oakeshott's rejoinder and correspondence with Morgenthau, Rengger questions the utility of tragedy to transcend the arts and make a useful contribution to the practice and study of international relations. My own position is closest to Frost's, and the reasons for this will be apparent in the course of "unpacking" this debate.

Let us begin with the broad areas of agreement. Frost tells us that many highly regarded students of international relations (e.g., Morgenthau, Niebuhr, Butterfield, and most of the English School) consider tragedy central to international relations. They associate the potential for tragedy with ethical, religious and cultural diversity. Efforts to impose one's own code on other actors in these circumstances will almost certainly encounter resistance because it threatens their identities as well as their interests.[1] As all political behavior is "a struggle for power over men," and "degrades man by using him as a means to achieve fundamentally corrupt ends," the potential for tragedy is omnipresent.[2] For Morgenthau, tragedy has another broader cause: the "sin of pride," which blinds us to the realities of international affairs.[3]

Building on Aristotle's reading of Greek tragedies, Frost offers a more precise and useful definition of tragedy. It describes "a special relationship between an act undertaken for ethical reasons and its negative or painful consequences." Tragic accounts are narratives that illustrate a chain of events linking an ethical decision to an unintended negative consequence by means of an agon, or contest between actors. Their denouement comes when surviving actors recognize what has happened and are overwhelmed by grief. In their efforts to protect what is important to them, the contestants end up destroying it. This reversal, called a peripeteia by Aristotle, is the irony that deepens the sense of tragedy. Tragedy arises, Frost and Aristotle agree, because the world is full of actors not only with clashing ethical perspectives, but with strong, unyielding commitments to them.[4]

Morgenthau's evocation of "the sin of pride" directs our attention to an important component of tragedy for the Greeks: the idea of hubris.[5] For tragedians, and Greeks more generally, hubris is a category error. People commit hubris when they confuse themselves with the gods in their belief that they can transcend human limitations. The tragic playwrights understand hubris as the result of otherwise commendable character traits and commitments. Thucydides associates it with cleverness, self-confidence, forethought, decisiveness, initiative and risk taking, the very qualities that lead to political success. For Pericles, and the citizens of Athens, success stimulates the appetite for further successes while blinding them to the attendant risks. Hubris is manifest as overconfidence in one's own judgment and ability to control events. It encourages leaders and followers to mistake temporary ascendancy for a permanent state of affairs.

Hubris leads us back to Frost's description of tragedy through the mechanisms responsible for policy failure. The kind of bad judgment and irrational risk taking that hubris encourages angers other actors because it most often finds expression in efforts to control and impose one's values on them. Such conflicts presuppose the prior existence of the clashing ethical perspectives that lie at the core of Frost's understanding of tragedy. Invoking an understanding of hubris that harks back to the *Iliad*, Aristotle defines it as "the serious assault on the honor of another, which is likely to cause shame, and lead to anger and attempts at revenge."[6]

Hubris leads us beyond Frost's characterization of tragedy by focusing our attention on the role of agency, and, more specifically, on the kinds of actors most likely to succumb to hubris. For Homer and the tragedians, they are invariably the powerful: kings and warriors like Agamemnon, Ajax, and Creon, who lose their self-control and respect for the nomos that legitimizes their power and fame. Oedipus is an interesting variant on this theme. He remains respectful of the laws of humankind, but loses sight of the limits of human knowledge and power. He gains a kingdom and a queen by winning two contests: the first with his father Laius at the crossroads, and then with the Sphinx outside Thebes. He loses his wife and throne by "winning" another contest, this time with himself. Against the advice of his wife and chief advisor, he uses his authority and formidable intellect to prove to himself that he can discover the cause of the Theban plague. Oedipus reflects the Greek understanding of the human dilemma. Tragedy is inescapable, and efforts to circumvent it by power and intellect risk making it more likely.

Mayall and Rengger pick up on this aspect of tragedy. Mayall agrees with Frost that awareness of tragedy is "a necessary antidote" to the hubris of progressive thought and its unwillingness to accept responsibility for initiatives carried out in its name that fail to produce their intended outcomes. Mayall acknowledges that progress has been made in some regions toward banishing war and enhancing human rights, but denies that it constitutes "uncontested evolution toward a global human rights culture."[7] He questions the existence of a global civil society and the appeal of a universal standard on which it is based. International environments are not always hospitable to progressive projects, he warns. And agreement about core values and strategies—so essential to cooperation—is even difficult among actors who share common "lifeworlds."[8] More fundamentally, he doubts the ability of human beings to transcend the tragic dimension of politics. "Even if one pattern of behavior with tragic consequences can be avoided, another is always likely to loom up from beyond the horizon."[9] Rengger concurs, observing that such a pessimistic outlook is common to realists, who view the political world as one of "recurrence and repetition." They consider the tension between moral self-understanding and the imperatives of political life as unavoidable and insurmountable.[10] Greek tragedians, Thucydides included, were undeniably realists in this sense. They believed that the cycle of hubris, *atē*, *hamartia*, and *nemesis* would repeat itself as long as humans stride the earth.

It is useful to distinguish two levels of coping with tragedy. First, and least visionary, is an attempt to finesse some tragedies by knowledge of their existence and general causes. Sensitivity to ethical dilemmas, knowledge of one's own and others' identities, self-restraint in the pursuit of goals, efforts to gain support for them by persuasion instead of coercion, and tentative rather than all-out commitments to goals may have the potential to reduce vulnerability to tragedy. There is also the more ambitious goal of altogether transcending the tragic condition. Enlightenment philosophers, liberals, and socialists have all shared this vision, which rests on the ability of reason to construct an order that will harmonize human interests and allow general fulfillment of human needs.

Morgenthau fits comfortably into the first category, and Rengger believes that Frost, Mayall and I do too. Rengger represents my position accurately, quoting lines from *Tragic Vision of Politics* to the effect that immersion in tragedy can encourage conceptions of self and order that act as antidotes to hubris.[11] Hubris, of course, is only one cause of tragedy, and the possibility remains of tragedies arising from clashing ethical imperatives.

Frost is primarily interested in tragedy as a normative theory that allows us to frame and understand ethical dilemmas and their consequences more clearly. With respect to policy, he draws largely pessimistic conclusions. Well-intentioned people acting ethically can produce negative outcomes. If such outcomes are possible in interactions among people in the same family, church, or state, "the chances of progress will be even slighter when we encounter people with ethical systems sharply opposed to ours."[12] He follows with a strong argument against the beneficial consequences of awareness and learning. Central to the dynamics and dramatic power of tragedy is the assumption that full knowledge of the consequences of their actions would not have dissuaded actors from making the same agonizing choices. Their choices are constrained because they flow from their identities; they act as they must, making the ensuing conflicts unavoidable. Their choices are generally responsible ones. Aeschylus, Sophocles, Euripides, and Shakespeare's characters carefully consider the likely consequences of their behavior and are blindsided by possibilities they did not, or could not, have predicted. Tragedy cannot be prevented by knowledge of past tragedies or more careful decision-making.[13]

Frost is a great believer in the benefits of global civil society, but recognizes that it poses ethical dilemmas with possibly tragic outcomes. As citizens of states and global society, we routinely confront "lose-lose" dilemmas that force us to choose between the individual rights of global citizens and the seeming interests of our national units. Tragedy nevertheless has a transformative potential because of its ability to bring these dilemmas to our attention, intensify our dissatisfaction with the conditions responsible for them, prompt us to search for most just arrangements and commit us to their realization in practice. The interaction of reason and emotions in this way was an underlying cause of the transformation of the Republic of South Africa and postwar Western Europe.[14]

Mayall agrees that the peaceful overthrow of apartheid in the Republic of South Africa and the institutionalization of peaceful inter-state relations in Europe are impressive achievements, but denies that they are evidence of an "uncontested evolution toward a global human rights culture."[15] In his view, current efforts by Western powers to promote democracy are as much rhetorical as real, and provoke opposition by would-be losers to the extent they are taken seriously. They are also unrealistic—as Kant recognized—in the absence of a universal, cosmopolitan culture, and one, moreover, that recognizes group as well as individual rights. Such a culture would require serious constraints on sovereignty, which are simply not in the offing. The more feasible alternative is an imperial democracy imposed by the United States, which, like other empires, demands the rights and privileges it denies subject people. Rather than promoting a global civil society, such an informal empire is more likely to collapse "under the combined force of cynical hypocrisy abroad and savage attack from the unassimilated at home."[16]

Rengger is just as pessimistic. Realist thinking, he reminds us, derives its intellectual and moral power from its recognition that political necessity almost always trumps ethical considerations. Nothing has changed in this respect since the end of the Cold War. Conflict and war "seem to be everywhere ascendant," aspirations for a new world order have been exposed as "facile and deluded," and Hobbes' famous twins—Force and Fraud—"seem once more to be in the driving seat of international affairs."[17] Rengger also doubts that knowledge about tragedy can make the world less tragic. He cites Morgenthau in support. In *Scientific Man versus Power Politics*, where Morgenthau discussed his understanding of tragedy, he argued that human beings are flawed and can never overcome their imperfections.[18] If Morgenthau is right, Rengger insists, "then even the relatively modest hopes entertained by Mayall or Lebow might well turn out to be mistaken."[19]

Rengger's reading of *Scientific Man versus Power Politics* is unimpeachable, but this work does not represent Morgenthau's final position on human fallibility. Morgenthau wrote the book in the immediate aftermath of the worst and most widespread instance of human barbarism. His marginal life in Germany, academic humiliation in Geneva, loss of position and possessions in Madrid, anxious wanderings in Europe in search of a visa to a safe haven, struggles to survive economically in New York and Kansas City, and loss of his grandparents in the

Holocaust darkened his mood and sapped his faith in human reason. Morgenthau was nevertheless too intellectually curious, reflective, and open-minded to allow his *Weltanschauung* to ossify. His intellectual growth did not stop with his early postwar books, but continued throughout his career. By the 1970s, he became convinced that the Cold War had been resolved de facto by mutual acceptance of the postwar political and territorial status quo in Europe. He regarded with interest and approval Western European efforts to build a more peaceful continent on the twin foundations of parliamentary democracy and supranational institutions. Both transformations, he explicitly recognized, were based on learning and reason.[20]

Even more than Frost and Mayall, Rengger doubts the normative value of tragedy. He draws on the fascinating exchange between Hans Morgenthau and Michael Oakeshott following the publication of Scientific Man versus Power Politics. Oakeshott was favorably impressed by Morgenthau's book, but not by his invocation of tragedy. He insisted that tragedy was art, not life.[21] Morgenthau stuck to his guns and wrote back that tragedy was "a quality of existence, not a creation of art."[22] The two men came out of different intellectual traditions. For Morgenthau, steeped in German literature and philosophy, tragedy was a natural discourse, and a language he found useful to frame his opposition to the liberal and idealistic assumption that reason and goodwill could construct institutions that would promote more or less harmonious social relations at every level of interaction. Oakeshott thought and wrote in a highly idiosyncratic framework. Both discourses serve their purposes admirably, and there may be some intellectual payoff to having parallel ways of authoring critiques. A relevant analogy is to the damaging consequences of hyper-individualism. Sophocles and Thucydides have much to say about this subject, and use the tropes and forms of Greek tragedy to examine the causes and destructive effects of such behavior at the family, state and inter-polis levels. Tocqueville, drawing on the writings of Montesquieu and Condorcet, has made a similar argument by using the concept of "self-interest well understood."[23] Once again, we benefit from multiple discourses, which are more reinforcing than cross-cutting, and enrich our understanding of a phenomenon by framing it differently.

None of our authors argues that knowledge of tragedy has much practical value. Such a claim is, however, implicit in Thucydides, just as it is explicit in the later Morgenthau. Why would Thucydides have invested decades in researching and writing his history and offer it as a "possession for all time" if he thought human beings and their societies were prisoners of circumstance and fate? He must have believed that people possess at least some ability to control their destinies. Psychotherapy assumes that people will repeatedly enact counterproductive scripts until they confront and come to terms with the experiences that motivate this behavior. This can only be achieved through regression; people must allow themselves to relive painful experiences they have repressed and come to understand how they shape their present behavior. Sophists relied on a somewhat similar process. Their works were offered as courses of study that engage the emotions and mind. By experiencing the elation, disappointment, anguish, and other emotions a story provoked, and by applying reason to work through its broader meaning and implications, readers could gain enlightenment. Neither sophists nor analysts tell readers or analysands what lessons to learn; both believe that lessons can only be learned and come to influence behavior when they are the result of a process of cathartic self-discovery. Thucydides' account of the Peloponnesian War encourages Athenians and other Greeks to relive traumatic political experiences in the most vivid way and to work through their meaning and implications for their lives and societies. I believe he harbored the hope that such a course of "therapy" could help free people of the burdens of the past and produce the kind of wisdom that could enable some societies to transcend their scripts.[24]

Frost believes that civil society in the West is the product of this kind of learning. He is hopeful that a global civil society will emerge that will promote human rights and peaceful inter-state relations. Mayall insists that an effective global civil society requires preconditions which are not present in today's world. He may be right, but cultural diversity and lack of democracy in China, many Muslim countries, and much of Africa do not preclude the possibility of making some progress toward global civil society. Movement toward democracy in many Pacific rim countries over the course of the last two decades is convincing evidence of precisely this kind of progress. It is also possible that more favorable conditions will emerge in other regions of the world—and in the United States—at some future time.

Rengger bases his pessimism on the twin pillars of tragedy and history. Tragedy and social progress are not necessarily mutually exclusive. If the frequency and scope of tragedy can be reduced through learning, progress is possible even if universal harmony and accurate prediction of the consequences of human behavior are not. History teaches Rengger that fear-based worlds have always been the default condition of international relations. But the future need not resemble the past. Until the second half of the twentieth century, death by infectious disease was unavoidable—unless one died of some other cause. Enormous progress has been made in reducing the effects of pathogens, and we may be on the cusp of major breakthroughs with respect to mortality itself. If young doctors and scientists did not have faith in the possibility of progress, none of these advances would have been made. Politics is different from science and medicine in the sense that faith in progress can have negative consequences when it is based on incorrect assumptions and leads to naïve and unsuccessful policies. This is, after all, one of the principal insights of tragedy. Policies tempered by the lessons of tragedy and history, and implemented by skillful leaders, do hold out the prospect of progress. The so-called lessons of history can be a real impediment to progress if they are uniformly pessimistic. Realism has the unfortunate potential to make our expectations of a fear-based world self-fulfilling—just as naïve notions of escaping from them can make them even more fearful.

Is a belief in progress compatible with tragedy? Mayall and Rengger would have us believe not. For classical Greeks, *sophrosunē* (the restraint imposed on desires by reason) was the antidote to hubris. Given the limited ability of ancients to control their environment, *sophrosunē* took the form of accommodation to the vagaries of life and acceptance of its hard realities. The Greek emphasis on *sophrosunē* and the Enlightenment belief in the ability of human beings to harness and tame their environment represent two extreme responses—both based on the exercise of reason. If thoughtful Greeks could observe our world, and rethink their understanding of the human condition in light of modern conditions and possibilities, they might conclude that the golden mean—the *medan agan*, so central to their approach to life—describes a position somewhere between ancient acceptance and modern activism. If so, it would find expression in cautious hopes for progress, tempered by awareness of the dangers of forgetting the inherent limitations of human beings.

Notes

1 Mervyn Frost, "Tragedy, Ethics and International Relations," *International Relations*, 17(4), 2003, pp. 477–95.
2 Hans Morgenthau, *Scientific Man versus Power Politics* (Chicago: University of Chicago Press, 1947), p. 167.
3 Hans Morgenthau, *Politics Among Nations* (New York: Alfred Knopf, 1948), note 4, p.11; and, "The Political Science of E. H. Carr," *World Politics* I, October 1948, pp. 127–34.
4 Frost, "Tragedy, Ethics and International Relations," pp. 480–84: Aristotle, *Poetics*, 11.1452 a 32 and 24.1460 a 27–31.
5 Morgenthau errs in reading into tragedy Judeo-Christian understandings of sin, a concept that was alien to classical Greek culture.
6 Aristotle, *Rhetoric,* 1378 b 28–9.
7 James Mayall, "Tragedy, Progress and the International Order: A Response to Frost," *International Relations*, 17(4), 2003, p. 498.
8 Alfred Schutz, *Structures of the Life World*, vol. 2 (Evanston, IL: Northwestern University Press, 1989).
9 Mayall, "Tragedy, Progress and the International Order," p. 499.
10 Nicholas Rengger, "Tragedy or Scepticism? Defending the Anti-Pelagian Mind in World Politics," *International Relations*, 19 (Spring 2005), pp. 321–28.
11 Rengger, "Tragedy or Scepticism?": Richard Ned Lebow, *The Tragic Vision of Politics: Ethics, Interests, and Orders* (Cambridge: Cambridge University Press, 2003), p. 364.
12 Frost, "Tragedy, Ethics and International Relations," p. 484.
13 Frost, "Tragedy, Ethics and International Relations," pp. 485–6.
14 Frost, "Tragedy, Ethics and International Relations," pp. 493–4.
15 Mayall, "Tragedy, Progress and the International Order," p. 498.
16 Mayall, "Tragedy, Progress and the International Order," p. 502.
17 Rengger, "Tragedy or Scepticism?"
18 Morgenthau, *Scientific Man vs. Power Politics.*

19 Morgenthau, *Scientific Man vs. Power Politics.*
20 Lebow, *The Tragic Vision of Politics,* chapter 5.
21 Rengger, "Tragedy or Scepticism?," p. 326, quoting Oakeshott.
22 Hans J. Morgenthau, letter to Michael Oakeshott, May 22, 1948, Morgenthau Papers, B44, quoted in Rengger, "Tragedy or Scepticism?," p.326.
23 Alexis de Tocqueville, *Democracy in America*, trans. and ed. Harvey C. Mansfield and Delba Winthrop (Chicago: University of Chicago Press, 2000), II, pt. 2, chapter 8, p. 501.
24 Lebow, *Tragic Vision of Politics*, chapters 4 and 7 for elaboration of this argument.

Part VI

Conclusions

14 The future of international relations theory

Richard Ned Lebow

My editor has asked me to address three themes in the final chapter of this volume: the future of international relations, international relations theory, and my research agenda. I can only speak with assurance about the last; it is the only one over which I have any control. Even here, research plans get sidetracked or transformed, and new projects emerge in response to developments in the world, intriguing ideas from colleagues and publications to which one feels compelled to respond. My introduction presents my career as a logical progression, but students of autobiography tell us that these narratives impose an order in retrospect that was not apparent at the time, and perhaps never existed.

George Bernard Shaw dismissed all autobiographies—his own included—as a tissue of lies.[1] Psychological research indicates that our most vivid memories—so called flashbulb memories of where we were, what we said, and what we did when we first learned of dramatic events like Pearl Harbor, the Kennedy assassination, or 9/11—are more often than not socially constructed.[2] Evidence abounds that we remake our memories over time in response to psychological needs and group pressures.[3] Psychologists speak of multiple "remembered selves," with the evocation of any one of them dependent on a person's social setting at the time.[4] Memory studies indicate that the concept of the authentic self is deeply problematic. We evolve over time, in response to internal and external stimuli. The best we can do is call up imperfect and selective representations of what we once were—or would like to think we were.[5]

Undeniably, if unwittingly, my account of my intellectual development reflects these several processes. It strikes me as accurate, but then I may be the least reliable witness. Accounts of the future are rooted in the past, not the real past—whatever that is—but our socially constructed, psychologically motivated, and ideologically filtered recall of the past and its putative lessons. We use past and present to organize our thoughts and expectations about the future. They generate the categories we use to make sense of the world, identify challenges and issues that require attention and select strategies to cope with them.

The present and future are every bit as slippery as the past. As my work on deterrence indicates, we routinely use the present to confirm tautologically the lessons of the past. Cognitive and motivated biases make us insensitive to information that is contrary to our expectations or threatens important goals. Although we recognize the future is indeterminate, we try to understand it in terms of linear projections of the past. Despite ample evidence indicating the open nature of the social world, we routinely consider only closely related events and causes when predicting future trends. At the turn of the twentieth century, the *New York Times* lamented the growth of horse drawn traffic in Manhattan because of the health and other hazards it created. An official study examined the growth or horse traffic over the last 50 years and assumed that the demand for horses would continue to grow at the same rate. They came to the disturbing conclusion that by 1950, the populated parts of Manhattan would be covered by up to six feet of manure. They failed to consider the possibility that other means of transportation, particularly the automobile, would supplant the horse.

In the Introduction, I used the example of the social-political revolution of the 1960s to illustrate the pitfalls of linear projections in open systems. The lesson has not been learned well by scholars or policymakers. On the eve of the first George W. Bush administration, I participated in a forecasting project with participants from CIA, State, Treasury, Defense, and the NSC. The goal was to identify the likely changes in the European political, economic, and military environment and the kinds of opportunities and challenges they might present to the new administration over the course of the next four years. Participating officials and analysts were subdivided into smaller working groups, each addressing their acknowledged area of the expertise. We were instructed to devise and evaluate alternative scenarios of issues of current concern, which included Europe's economy, military procurement policies, relations with the United States and Russia, and illegal immigration. When the working groups reported their conclusion to the plenary session, each one not surprisingly offered three scenarios: a more or less straight-line projection of present trends, an augmented, and a diminished linear projection. They offered an opinion as to which was most likely, and the leaders of the exercise combined them in a package of scenarios to present to the new administration. What was billed as an attempt to think "out of the box" compelled intelligent and well-informed participants to stay within the box. They could not consider problems or issues not currently on the agenda—terrorism, for example—that might become paramount in the very near future. Given the way the exercise was structured, there was no way of ruling out scenarios that were mutually exclusive (e.g., a decline in the European economy but an increase in European defense spending). Most importantly, there was no way to explore the ways in which any of the posited outcomes might interact synergistically to produce entirely novel and unexpected results.

We cannot make accurate predictions in many key areas of life, but neither can we throw our hands up in the face of uncertainty, contingency, and unpredictability. In a complex society, individuals, organizations, and states require a high degree confidence in the short-term future and a reasonable degree of confidence in the longer-term future to make plans and commit themselves to decisions, investments and policies. Consider the real estate market. In the absence of some assurance about future interest rates, banks could not offer mortgages—or offer them at rates anyone could afford—houses could not be bought or sold, people could not move to accept jobs—even they could be offered—and the economy would go into a precipitous decline.

Human beings cope with the dilemma of uncertainty by doing their best to control the future to make their expectations self-fulfilling. To continue with our example of interest rates, the Federal Reserve Bank was established to regulate them, and has been careful to raise and lower interest rates by small increments, usually quarter-points, well spaced over time. Our efforts at control extend to nature itself, which modern societies have sought to tame with varying degrees of success. In pre-technological societies, this deep-seated human need for mastery of the environment finds expression in efforts to ward off tragedies and bring about desired outcomes by propitiating the gods. Prayer is alive and well in our society—and becoming more prevalent according to some surveys—despite the absence of any evidence for its efficacy. This phenomenon suggests that we need to believe in our ability to control, or at least influence, the future, and all the more so in recognizably uncertain and dangerous times.

Our second strategy for coping with uncertainty is denial. We convince ourselves that the future will more or less resemble the past or deviate from it in predictable and manageable ways. We remain unreasonably confident in this belief despite the dramatic discontinuities of even the recent past—consider the end of the Cold War, the breakup of the Soviet Union, the events of 9/11, and the sharp downturn in the economy produced by synergistic interaction of the bursting of dot.com bubble, 9/11, and corporate corruption. The so-called behavioral revolution in social science is part and parcel of this project. Its bedrock assumption is that the social environment is sufficiently ordered to be described by universal, or at least widely applicable, laws. These supposed regularities allow for some degree of prediction. Faith in this project has hardly diminished despite the inability of several generations of behavioral "scientists" to discover such laws or make any but the most banal predictions with any degree of success. Political scientists, sociologists, and economists were largely blind-sided by all the major changes that occurred in recent years (i.e., the end of the Cold War, rise of the religious right, and the recession in the late 1990s and early 2000s). Key theories from these disciplines—especially those from international relations—have also been wrong on a series of lesser predictions. We generally refuse to take seriously, and sometimes even punish, people who challenge our most comforting illusions. It is hardly surprising that those in control of major university departments and governmental funding agencies have done their best over the decades to marginalize academic critics of the behavioral revolution.

There is a certain irony to our quest for order. As Herodotus observed in ancient Egypt, the absolutely certainty of yearly Nile floods encouraged and sustained a large, wealthy society that became increasingly moribund, mired in tradition and immune to innovation. By contrast, the hardscrabble agriculture of Greece and its vulnerability to the elements put a premium on individual initiative and experimentation. It led to a more open and less-stratified society that was less populous and stable but more brilliant in its accomplishments.[6] Modern history is rich in similar comparisons. The quest for order and predictability was carried to extremes in the Soviet Union, the communist regimes of Eastern Europe and North Korea—and with disastrous consequences; North Korea is the only one of these regimes still extant, and its future is far from promising. Even governments and institutions that value difference and tolerate a high degree of dissent struggle with its implications and consequences. They are highly bureaucratized, and unpredictability and disorder are inimical to those who run and staff these organizations. Serving on a college admissions and finance committee taught me that it is theoretically possible to search for and even reward rebels and free-thinkers of all kinds, but only with great effort.

The preceding discussion suggests the presence of two related and seemingly irresolvable tensions. The first is between our need for order and predictability on the one hand and the longer-term benefits of novel and unexpected challenges on the other. The second is between our need for order and predictability and our reluctance to recognize the extent to which it is unobtainable. Both tensions have profound implications for international relations and its study. In the first instance, they promote unwarranted expectations of continuity and resistance to challenges, even though change they may be beneficial. Hans Morgenthau, who was unusual in this respect, believed that the purpose of social science, and of international relations theory in particular, was to identify novel problems, propose possible solutions and bring them to the attention of the public and policymakers. "All good theory," he insisted, "is practical theory, which intervenes in a concrete political situation with the purpose of change through action."[7] In reality, postwar international relations theory has more often sought to buttress the illusions of policymakers and public alike that the future is likely to resemble the present and is best addressed with the intellectual resources we already have at hand.

Explaining change

Much ink has been spilled on how realism, or at least some of its most prominent exponents, have contributed to this mindset by insisting on the fundamental continuity of international relations and the inability of states and regions to escape the consequences of anarchy through cooperative ventures. Holding the structure of bipolarity constant blinded many scholars to the ways in which the character of superpower relations had evolved over the course of the decades. So did the general propensity in international relations theory to seal off events and processes in the international realm—a so-called system with alleged properties of its own – from developments within the actors who constituted the system. To some degree this was also true in the policy world. When I served as a scholar-in-residence in the CIA during the Carter administration, enormous human and technical assets were deployed to study the Soviet economy, military capabilities, and strategies for using those capabilities—all prime concerns of realist analyses of foreign policy. There was nobody whose full-time assignment was to monitor Soviet nationality problems.

Most theories of international relations have a fundamental problem with change because of their reliance on so-called "structures" as independent variables. Realism and liberalism posit structures at the system or unit level (e.g., anarchy, democracy) and deduce from them implications for system stability and patterns of selection or adaptation. These theories need to assume a certain stability in the character and duration of the structures that do their primary analytical work. Neorealism acknowledges hierarchy as an alternative to anarchy, but describes transitions between the two ordering principles as rare, the Roman Empire being the last example of hierarchy. Realists of all stripes expect somewhat more frequent variation in the polarity of anarchic systems, and more change still in the balance of power within multipolar systems. Realists have little incentive to think about movement away from anarchy because it would put them and their theories out of business.

Changes in polarity and the balance of power are not threatening to realists because they provide the variation necessary for their theories. However, this only works if these changes have the same implications independently of the context in which they occur. Realists accordingly treat all bi- and multipolar systems as fully comparable, and power transition theories do the same for transitions, assuming that rising and declining hegemons, from ancient Greece to the present, resort to the same strategies in similar circumstances. Separating international relations from the context in which it occurs, precludes the possibility of anticipating or explaining change because the causes and indicators are change embedded in that context. Neither the United States—generally described as the hegemon—nor the Soviet Union—aka the challenger—behaved according to the predictions of any power transition theory. The United States never seriously contemplated war against the Soviet Union while it was a hegemon, and the Soviet Union never contemplated war against the United States while it was a rising challenger, co-hegemon or declining challenger. Students of the Cold War have invoked nuclear weapons, memories of World War II, the democratic political culture of the United States and learning by Soviet leaders to explain mutual war avoidance and the peaceful end of the Cold War.[8] Regardless of which explanation, or combination of them, accounts for the absence of war, they all derive from the context in which the Soviet-American rivalry took place, and, with the possible exception of nuclear weapons, lie outside any realist theory.

Liberalism encounters the same problem when it invokes state structure as an explanatory variable, as the democratic peace research program does. Even the most casual reading of Tocqueville, or of Arthur Schlesinger, Jr.'s classic study of the Jacksonian era, indicates that democracy was not the same thing in the early nineteenth century as it is in the early twenty-first century.[9] Nor is there any consensus about what democracy is today, and which states qualify as democracies. Some students of comparative politics contend that the problem of definition has become increasingly acute because so many authoritarian regimes hold elections and allow carefully constrained opposition parties to give the appearance of democracy.[10] Democracy is nevertheless treated as an historical constant and relatively unproblematic category in many studies intended to test the so-called democratic peace. To the extent that theories require stable structures, they make it correspondingly difficult to address change. Attempts to conceptualize change solely from the perspective of structure verge on the oxymoronic. As Marxism to its credit recognizes, structures themselves are never constant, but develop and evolve over time.

Any order we examine is in a state of flux. Our understanding of it, as Henri Bergson put it so nicely, is a "snapshot" that freezes the moment and gives it an artificial appearance of stability.[11] Equilibrium is simply not a useful concept in studying political order, even in the short term. It assumes a state or states of equilibrium to which the system returns. Even small perturbations and the accommodations to which they lead can shift these equilibria. One accommodation often leads to new pressures, or confronts them as circumstances change, generating pressure for new accommodations. As the system evolves, its equilibria shift in small increments and over time diverge significantly from their starting points. We should not think of the stability of orders with reference to any kind of steady state, but rather in terms of multiple, successive, and short-lived accommodations. This reality renders deeply problematic the concept of stability. Some of the most "stable" political systems—measured in terms of their longevity—are those that have evolved dramatically over the course of time, so much so in some cases that comparisons between these systems at T and T + 5 suggest that we are looking at two very different systems. Georgian England compared to late Victorian Britain, or Victorian Britain compared to Tony Blair's Britain are cases in point. The institutions governing the country were more or less unchanged, but their membership, procedures, and the roles they played in society were greatly transformed.

Shifts in the nature of accommodations along any fault line can be dampened or amplified as they work their way through the society. Order is an open system. None of its key components can be studied in isolation from the rest of the social world, because important sources of instability and change for the components in question can emanate from any of them. Physical scientists study non-linear processes by modeling them. They often start with linear processes that are reasonably well-understood, to which they add additional variables, and arbitrarily vary their value, or rate of change, in the hope of discovering the outer boundaries of linearity, and beyond them, possible patterns or domains of order that may develop in non-linear domains. Turbulence is the paradigmatic example. At a certain point, flow becomes unpredictable. Within this turbulence, areas of stability may form, where flow can be described by linear models or equations. The Great Red Spot of Jupiter is a temporary island of relative stability in a storm raging throughout the atmosphere of Jupiter. It may be that seemingly durable political orders are best understood as temporary islands of relative stability—they are still in a state of flux, just less so—in a sea of non-linear political turbulence. By identifying such islands, the ways in which they evolve, maintain their apparent stability, and where they come up against the edge of chaos, we can learn a lot about the processes that build, maintain, and destroy orders.

The problem of political order is more complex because of the decisive role of agency. Our reflections about the past, expectations about the future and the causal links we construct between past and future, do much to shape the present. These constructions are highly subjective and allow much free play to the human imagination. They may, in the words of Rousseau, "recall a past which no longer exists, or anticipate a future that will often never come to pass."[12] For all these reasons, a theory of international relations must be more a theory of process than of structure. It might be constructed around a typology of ideal types of political orders, each associated with distinctive kinds of goals and behavior. Real orders would at best approximate these ideal types, and almost certainly contain characteristics of multiple orders. These mixed worlds would also be lumpy, in that they would reveal considerable regional variation. As with great attractors in chaos theory, we might search for the most stable kinds of orders as well as the routes by which systems move toward or away from relatively stable states. To do this, we also require a theory of disorder, that is of the kinds of changes, and their causes, that move systems away from relatively ordered to less ordered states. I am currently working on such a theory. The first volume, tentatively entitled *Recognition, Honor and Standing: A Paradigm of Politics and International Relations*, will be published by Cambridge University Press.

Levels of analysis

Kenneth Waltz uses the term "reductionist" in a pejorative way to describe theories of international relations that reach down to lower levels of analysis to explain patterns of behavior at the system level. However, theories at the system level fail for two reasons: unit structure and the norms governing their interactions introduce enormous variation in their behavior. Nor can theories at the system level account for change when its causes reside at other levels of analysis. A realistic theory must take state structure, domestic politics, other sub-state processes and individuals into account. One way to do this, as yet unexplored, is a theory of process that bridges levels by describing the dynamics that translate changes at one level of analysis into changes at others. To the extent that these dynamics are universal, or at least common to a variety of orders, such a theory would not be limited to particular types of changes or the historical epochs in which they occur. The quintessential model for such theory of process is evolution, whose validity extends across the entire span of life on earth, if not to the cosmos beyond.

Even if the dynamics of order are the same, or similar across orders, there would still be differences across levels of social aggregation. The most important divide is between groups and societies on the one hand and nations on the other. They differ with respect to the overlap between legal and social norms, the extent to which behavior conforms to norms of both kinds, and the nature of the mechanisms that can be used to encourage or enforce conformity. In developing his concept of organic solidarity, Emile Durkheim observes, and subsequent research tends to confirm, that legal and social norms are more congruent, and informal mechanisms of social control more effective, in smaller and less developed societies (e.g., villages and towns) where the division of labor is relatively simple.[13] Moral disapproval of deviance is also more outspoken in these settings, where it is a powerful force for behavioral conformity. So too is tolerance of deviation when it is understood as closing ranks against outside interference.[14] On the whole, however, tolerance of deviance varies directly with the division of labor; it is most pronounced in larger and more complex social systems. Order is more difficult to achieve and sustain at higher levels of social aggregation.

According to Durkheim's formulation, what distinguishes international and regional from domestic systems is not the absence of a Leviathan, but the robustness of the social order. If so, the difference between domestic systems on the one hand and regional and international systems on the other is one of degree, not of kind. This does not make regional and international orders any easier to sustain. They are likely to have competing, rather than reinforcing, norms, and more glaring contradictions between norms and behavior. In these orders, moral outrage is generally a strategy of the weak, and is frequently associated with agents who are not even recognized as legitimate actors. Some striking instances aside—among them, the boycott of South Africa to end *Apartheid*, the Montreal Protocol and subsequent agreements to ban chlorofluorocarbons (CFCs) and restore the ozone layer—moral suasion only occasionally serves as a source of social control or catalyst for change. As informal mechanisms of control are more important than formal ones in domestic societies, their relative absence—and not the absence of central authority, as realists insist—may be *the* defining characteristic of the regional and international society and their respective political systems.[15] The lack of normative consensus, paucity of face-to-face social interactions and the greater difficulty of mutual surveillance, all but preclude effective social control at the regional and international levels. That we observe any degree of order at these levels is truly remarkable, and makes it a particularly interesting puzzle.

Regional and international orders are set apart by another phenomenon: the human tendency to generate social cohesion by creating distinctions between "us" and "others." This binary—which may be endemic to all human societies— was first conceptualized in the century in response to the an emerging pattern in Western Europe of promoting domestic cohesion and development by means of foreign conflict. Immanuel Kant theorized that the "unsocial sociability" of people draws them together into societies, but leads them to act in ways that break them up. He considers this antagonism innate to our species, and an underlying cause of the development of the state. Warfare drove people apart, but their need to defend themselves against others compelled them to band together and submit to the rule of law. Each political unit has unrestricted freedom in the same way individuals did before the creation of societies, and hence is in a constant state of war. The price of order at home is conflict among societies. The "us" is maintained at the expense of "others."[16]

Hegel builds on this formulation, and brings to it his understanding that modern states differed from their predecessors in that their cohesion does not rest so much on preexisting cultural, religious, or linguistic identities as it does on the allegiance of their citizens to central authorities who provide for the common defense. Citizens develop a collective identity through the external conflicts of their state and the sacrifices it demands of them. "States," he writes in the *German Constitution*, "stand to one another in a relation of might," a relationship that "has been universally revealed and made to prevail." In contrast to Kant, who considers this situation tragic, Hegel rhapsodizes about the life of states as active and creative agents who play a critical role in the unfolding development of the spirit and humankind. Conflict among states helps each to become aware of itself by encouraging self-knowledge among citizens. It can serve an ethical end by uniting subjectivity and objectivity and resolving the tension between particularity and universality.[17]

International relations as a zone of conflict and war was further legitimized by the gradual development of international law and its conceptualization of international relations as intercourse among sovereign states. The concept of sovereignty created the legal basis for the state and the nearly unrestricted right of its leaders to act as they wish within its borders. It also justified the pursuit of national interests by force beyond those borders so long as it was in accord with the laws of war. Sovereignty is a concept with diverse and even murky origins, that was first popularized in the sixteenth century. Nineteenth and twentieth century jurists and historians, many of them Germans influenced by Kant and Hegel (e.g., Heeren, Clausewitz, Ranke, Treitschke) developed a narrative about sovereignty that legitimized the accumulation of power of central governments and portrayed the state as the sole focus of a people's economic, political and social life. Without empirical justification, they described the 1648 Treaty of Westphalia as ushering in a novel, sovereignty-based international political order. The ideology of sovereignty neatly divided actors from one another, and made the binary of "us" and "others" appear a natural, if not progressive, development, as it did conflict and warfare among states.[18] This binary was reflected at the regional level in the concept of the European "system," which initially excluded Russia and the Ottoman Empire as political and cultural "others." There was no concept of the "international" until the late eighteenth century, and its development reflected and facilitated the transformation of the European system into an international one in the course of the next century. Here too, sharp distinctions were initially made between the European "us" and Asian and African "others," most of them societies that were not yet organized along the lines of the European state. The antagonism that Kant describes reasserted itself at the regional and international levels.

Twentieth century international relations theory took shape against the background of the Westphalia myth, which became foundational for realists. Their writings make interstate war appear the norm, and enduring cooperation an anomaly that requires an extraordinary explanation. They pluck lapidary quotes out of context from Thucydides, Machiavelli, and Hobbes to lend authority to their claims that the international arena is distinct from the domestic one and that anarchy and warfare are its norm. Watered-down versions of the realist world view dominate foreign policy communities on a nearly world-wide basis. Sovereignty and untrammeled pursuit of the national interest have revealed themselves to be mutually constitutive. They are also, in part, self-fulfilling, as foreign policies based on narrow constructions of self-interest, made possible by the legal edifice of sovereignty, appear to confirm realist depictions of international relations and the fundamental differences they assert exist within states and between them. Writing in the mid-1960s, before the emergence of constructivism, Martin Wight lamented that the realist project precluded any serious theorizing about international society. The "theory of the good life," he lamented, is only applicable to orderly societies, and realists framed the international arena as a "precontractual state of nature," where no real theory is possible.[19] Within this framework, the most theorists could do was to describe patterns of interaction among units.

If the challenge of studying order at the international level is intriguing, the prospect of doing so is a little less daunting than it used to be. There has been mounting criticism of "us" and "other" dichotomies, and of the false, or at least exaggerated, binary constructed by historians, jurists and realists between domestic and international politics.[20] Important differences between politics at these levels nevertheless remain, and between both of them and individual behavior. One of the key insights of the Enlightenment, since elaborated by social science, is the extent to which systems produce outcomes that cannot be predicted or explained by knowledge about the actors that constitute the system. It is nevertheless impossible, as the neorealist enterprise unwittingly demonstrates, to build good theories solely on the basis of system-level characteristics and processes.

A wise scholar might be tempted to stop here. There are, however, reasons to forge ahead. The most powerful one is normative. Justice is best served by an ordered world, but one that must be pliable enough to allow, if not encourage, the freedom, choice and overall development of individual actors. No existing order can be considered just, but many domestic orders—social and political—come closer to meeting the conditions in which justice might become possible than do regional orders or the international system. Failed states (e.g., Somalia, Afghanistan, Haiti) and the international system as a whole are undeniably the most unjust and least stable political orders, and the most in need of our attention, practical as well as theoretical. Understanding both levels of "order" in comparison to other levels, can provide insights that cannot be gained by studying them in isolation. Given the connection between theory and practice, it is important to create an alternative narrative that lends additional support to those scholars and practitioners who are attempting to move beyond narrow concepts of sovereignty and understandings of regional and international relations that assume that war is an unavoidable fact of life. For intellectual, ethical, and practical reasons alike, we need to pursue our investigations even if our answers are partial, tentative and certain to be superseded.

The goal of theory

Variants of positivism, arguably the dominant approach to theory in the social sciences, model themselves on a traditional, some would say, outmoded, conception of the physical sciences. They seek universal laws with predictive capability, and regard explanation and prediction as logically equivalent.[21] Over a century ago, Max Weber noted that neither this goal nor its enabling conditions are possible in the social world where behavior is rooted in ever evolving cultural contexts and influenced by human reflections on the meaning and causes of prior outcomes. For these reasons, a theory that convincingly explains a phenomenon that has occurred in the past, can fail to predict its reoccurrence even when the constellation of seemingly relevant variables and background conditions are the same.[22] Social laws, when they can be found, have a short shelf-life because the moment people came to understand such regularities they take them into account in their deliberations and strategies. The so-called January effect on the New York Stock Exchange is a good illustration. A large fraction of the annual gains in this market used to occur in January, but no longer did so the moment the phenomenon was discovered and publicized.[23]

There are two reasonable approaches to social theory. The first aims at "local knowledge" in the form of propositions that more or less hold true in circumscribed domains. For millennia power found expression, and in part, fed on territorial expansion by conquest. Egypt, Assyria, China, Persia, Macedon, Rome, Ottomans, Moguls, Spain, France, Britain, and Russia founded empires with their armies or navies. The size and duration of the ancient empires was governed by demographic crises, succession struggles, tax constraints, and the permeability of frontiers. Modern empires had to confront nationalism and problems of legitimacy at home and among subject peoples. Despite the recent resurrection of the term to describe American hegemony, empire has become an anachronism. Military conquest is not only frowned on by the international community, but increasingly difficult to translate into political authority—as the Anglo-American coalition discovered in Iraq. Power itself has undergone considerable evolution; its basis has gradually shifted from military to economic and technological, and now includes an important cultural component. The costs and benefits of different strategies for wielding influence have arguably changed even more dramatically.

Local theoretical knowledge is also problematic because it requires awareness of the boundaries within which it is valid. The conception of causality on which deductive-nomological models are based requires empirical invariance under specified boundary conditions. Bounded invariance is only possible in closed, linear systems. Open systems can be influenced by external stimuli, and their structure and causal mechanisms can evolve as a result. Rules that describe the functioning of an open system at time T do not necessarily do so at T + 1. The boundary conditions may have changed, rendering the statement irrelevant, another axiomatic condition may have been added, or the outcome may be subject to multiple conjunctural causation. There is no way to know *a priori* from the causal statement itself if any of these conditions pertain. Nor will complete knowledge about the system at time T—if that were possible—allow us to project its future development. Empirical invariance does not exist in open systems, and seeming probabilistic invariances may be causally unrelated. As physicists are the first to admit, prediction in open systems, especially non-linear ones, is difficult, if not impossible.

All social systems, and many physical and biological systems, are open. This includes economics, which claims to be the most scientific of the social sciences. One of its seemingly robust regularities that approached the status of a law was that lower unemployment leads to higher inflation. Joseph Stiglitz acknowledges that this law had to be "repealed" in the early 1990s because high technology generated new, higher-paying jobs that replaced manufacturing jobs that had moved offshore. Greater productivity led to higher profits, which, combined with low interest rates and greater consumption, the latter stimulated by psychological as much as economic factors, produced robust growth and with it, higher employment.[24] In international relations, the last three transformations of the international system—those associated with World War I, World War II, and the end of the Cold War—were the result of non-linear confluences that changed not only the polarity, but the "rules" of the system.[25]

In cognitive psychology, election studies, and certain branches of economics, researchers have been able to construct propositions useful for theoretical and practical ends. Such knowledge is at best probabilistic. It is also precarious, because the conditions on which it depends can change without warning. No matter how rigorously formulated, local knowledge can never contain full information about its limits or the conditions in which they will be transgressed. This becomes apparent only in retrospect, and sometimes at considerable cost. The Asian economic crisis of the early 1990s is a prime example. Rapid growth allowed some Asian countries to attract hundreds of billions of dollars of short-term international loans in the early 1990s. When short-term money managers began to lose faith in the Thai and South Korean economies, the IMF pressured their governments to maintain exchange rates by raising interest rates to restore investor confidence. Such a strategy had often worked in the past, yet the more Asian governments tried to defend their currencies, the more panic they incited. Money managers hastened to withdraw their funds before local currencies collapsed. Urged by the IMF and Washington, the Russian, South African, and Brazilian economies subsequently pursued the same policy with similar, disastrous results. In the aftermath, the IMF and many prominent economists came to recognize that greater sophistication on the part of investors and the greater mobility of capital had changed the rules of the game. They needed different strategies to cope with the problem of investor confidence.

The second kind of theory does not get around this problem, and starts from acceptance of its existence. It recognizes that social outcomes are shaped by context—including cultural understandings and practices—chance events, timing, process, and forces outside of theories applicable to the domain in question. It seeks to identify the underlying dynamics of social interactions or patterns of behavior associated with them. It eschews prediction in favor of explanation on the assumption that the former is the more reasonable goal. It nevertheless aspires to offer policy makers a useful framework for organizing their thoughts and making a "first cut" at whatever problem or decision they confront.

The theory of evolution is the outstanding example of such a theory in the natural world. It understands evolution as the result of biological change and natural selection. The former is a function of random genetic mutation and mating. The latter depends on the nature and variety of ecological "niches" and the competition for them. Niches, in turn, are shaped by such factors as continental drift, the varying output of the sun, changes in the earth's orbit, and local conditions that are hard to specify. Biologists recognize that all the primary causes of evolution are outside the theory of evolution and are either random, or interact in complex, non-linear ways, that make prediction impossible. Certain kinds of outcomes can be "ruled out" in a probabilistic sense, but almost never absolutely. Historical and theoretical work has resulted in a robust theory that permits scientific reconstruction of the past in the context of a logic that explains why things turned out the way they did. Darwinian theory, widely regarded as one of the seminal scientific advances of the modern era, challenges the belief, all too common in political science, that prediction is the principal, or even only, goal and test of a scientific theory.

The theory of evolution is intended to account for both the diversity of life and the common convergence of forms. In contrast to most theories of international relations, structure is its dependent rather than independent variable. It is a theory of change that says nothing about context; it acknowledges that everything that produces or sustains change is outside the theory. It overcomes this seeming paradox by being a theory of process that describes the dynamics that help to account for the outcomes we observe.

Greek tragedy is arguably the first "proto" theory of process in the political realm. One of its principal plot lines concerns the causes and effects of hubris.

The tragic hero, like his Homeric predecessor, is a self-centered, narcissistic figure who revels in his own importance and comes to believe that he is not bound by the laws and conventions of man. These manifestations of ego and their consequences are explored through a standard plot line: success intoxicates heroes and leads them to inflated opinions of themselves and their ability to control man and nature alike. They trust in hope (*elpis*), and become susceptible to adventures where reason would dictate caution and restraint. The Greeks used the word *atē* to describe the aporia this kind of seduction induces, and that *hamartia* (miscalculation) it encourages. *Hamartia* ultimately results in catastrophe by provoking the wrath of the gods (*nemesis*). The *Persians* of Aeschylus, produced in the spring of 472, at the height of Themistocles' power, is an early example of this genre, and seemingly intended as a cautionary tale about the consequences of hubris. Herodotus and Thucydides apply the pattern to Persia and Athens respectfully to explain their imperial overstretch and the *nemesis* to which it led at Salamis and Sicily.[26] This tragic plot line arguably also explains the underlying reasons and dynamics of the Bush administration's disastrous invasion of Iraq.

Among the moderns, Carl von Clausewitz is perhaps the first modern thinker to develop a social theory based on explicit recognition of the unbridgeable gap between general laws and specific cases. Like the Greeks, he seeks to describe a universal dynamic, in this case associated with the phenomenon of war, that could order an activity made remarkably diverse by different human practices, levels of organization and technology and the purposes for which it was waged.[27] He describes international relations as a constant struggle for dominance in which political units expand their power until opposed by equal and opposite political-military forces. They wage war to achieve goals unattainable by political means. The amount of force used should be a function of the goal: just enough to bend or break the will of an adversary. This is extraordinarily difficult in practice because once emotions are engaged, as they are whenever violence is used, it becomes difficult to keep war from spiraling out of control. A process of reciprocal escalation (*Wechselwirkung*) works to propels war to its maximum potential. The opposite tendency of friction acts to constrain it. Context makes every case unique, and negates the possibility of waging war by formula or of determining in advance the strength of these opposing tendencies. Reason, skill, and luck determine how successful leaders are judging how much force to use, how to apply and contain it, and whether or not it succeeds in achieving its intended ends.[28]

Hans Morgenthau approaches international relations with a similar understanding.[29] Following Weber, he maintains that all politics at all levels of aggregation are about domination; actors seek to compel others to do their will. Attempts to wield power meet resistance from those who interests or self-esteem are threatened. It provokes balancing in the form of alliances and counter efforts to augment one's own power to enable more effective resistance. Politics everywhere consists of continuous efforts to gain, assert and resist power, legitimize or delegitimize it in the minds of those over whom it is exercised, or compel them to do your will by other means. International relations is different only in so far as the struggle for power is less embedded in a set of restraining norms than is usually the case within political units. In practice, however, there is wide variation in the goals political units seek and the means they use to achieve them.

Clausewitz and Morgenthau believe that the purpose of theory is to order the world and provide a framework useful for negotiating contemporary challenges. Clausewitz finds the dialectic a useful rhetorical means of encapsulating this understanding. Thesis represents war in theory, antithesis everything in practice that defied the application of theory, and synthesis, the blending of theoretical and practical wisdom to formulate and attain feasible real world goals. Morgenthau never found such an elegant solution to the problem of distinguishing between theory and practice, although he certainly conceives of the balance of power in both ways. It is a universal mechanism and strategy that transcends culture and epoch, but its operation depends on a variety of contextual factors, among them the quality of leadership. Like Clausewitz, he understands the social world as "a chaos of contingencies," but "not devoid of a measure of rationality." Theory could order the world and structure the choices of leaders, but the choices others made, and the outcomes of any interaction would always be uncertain because of the inherent complexity of the social world. The best a theory could do was "to state the likely consequences of choosing one alternative as over against another and the conditions under which one alternative is more likely to be chosen or more successful than another."[30]

Clausewitz and Morgenthau envisaged their theories as merely a first step toward understanding a complex reality. Theories had to be supplemented by insights derived from experience and intuition. These insights might provide finer grained understanding and guidance. Their heroes are the soldiers and statesmen who were guided less by theory than by genius. There is admittedly something mystical in their conceptions of leadership, and Clausewitz considered his greatest intellectual failure his inability to develop a theory of genius. Experience is a more ordinary phenomenon and undoubtedly important in all kinds of human endeavors. We must nevertheless not overvalue its ability to bridge the gap between theory and practice. Bail and parole, release from mental institutions, admissions to college and professional schools, and extending of credit all rely on predictions of who is likely to succeed. For many of these decisions, actuarial data is available. Although some of this data is of dubious value, numerous studies show it is still better for purposes of prediction than the *ad hominen* judgments of "expert" professionals.[31] In international relations we have no base rates and must depend on the less reliable combination of theory and experience. We must remain wary of claim that "local knowledge" can bridge the gap.

Forward reasoning

The logic of my argument suggests that point prediction in international relations is impossible. A more useful approach may be the development of scenarios, or narratives with plot lines that map a set of causes and trends in future time.[32] This forward-reasoning strategy is based on a notion of contingent causal mechanisms, in opposition to the standard, neopositivist focus on efficient causes. It should not be confused with efforts by some to develop social scientific concepts directly analogous to evolutionary mechanisms (such as variation or selection) in biology to explain, for example, transformations in the international system or institutions, or conditions for optimum performance in the international political economy.

Scenarios are not predictions or forecasts, where probabilities are assigned to outcomes; rather, they start from the assumption that the future is unpredictable, and tell alternative stories of how the future may unfold. Scenarios are generally constructed by distinguishing what we believe is relatively certain from what we think is uncertain. The most important "certainties" are generally common to all scenarios that address the same problem or trend, while the most important perceived uncertainties differentiate one scenario from another.

This approach differs significantly from a forecasting tournament or competition, where advocates of different theoretical perspectives generate differential perspectives on a single outcome in the hope of subsequently identifying the "best" or most accurate performer. Rather, by constructing scenarios, or plausible stories of paths to the future, we can identify different driving forces (in lieu of independent variables, since it implies a force pushing in a certain direction rather than what is known on one side of an "equals" sign) and then attempt to combine these forces in logical chains that generate a range of outcomes, rather than single futures.

Scenarios make contingent claims rather than point predictions. They reinsert a sensible notion of contingency into theoretical arguments that would otherwise tend toward determinism. Scholars in international relations tend to privilege arguments that reach back into the past and parse out one or two causal variables that are then posited to be the major driving forces of past and future outcomes. The field also favors variables that are structural or otherwise parametric, thus downplaying the role of both agency and accident. Forward reasoning undercuts structural determinism by raising the possibility and plausibility of multiple futures.

Scenarios are impressionistic pictures that build on different combinations of causal variables that may also take on different values in different scenarios. Thus it is possible to construct scenarios without pre-existing firm proof of theoretical claims that meet strict positivist standards. The foundation for scenarios is made up of provisional assumptions and causal claims. These become the subject of revision and updating more than testing. A set of scenarios often contains competing or at least contrasting assumptions. It is less important where people start, than it is where they are through frequent revisions, and how they got there.

A good scenario is an internally consistent hypothesis about how the future might unfold; it is a chain of logic that connects "drivers" to outcomes. Consider as an example one plausible scenario at the level of a "global future" where power continues to shift away from the state and toward international institutions, transnational actors, and local communities. The state loses its monopoly on the provision of security and basic characteristics of the Westphalian system as we have known it are fundamentally altered. In this setting, key decisions about security, economics and culture will be made by nonstate actors. Security may become a commodity that can be bought like other commodities in the global marketplace. A detailed scenario about this transformation would specify the range of changes that are expected to occur and how they are connected to one another. It would identify what kinds of evidence might support the scenario as these or other processes unfold over the next decade, and what kind of evidence would count against the scenario or indicate a branching off point. Moreover, evidence that counts *against* one scenario, might count *for* another. Evaluations of evidence as events unfolded would then determine which scenario appeared to be playing out, or whether the same scenario had started to evolve in unanticipated directions. The same drivers could be at play in multiple scenarios, but how changes in technology, human agency, and transnational networks interact is less certain and these interactions can lead outcomes along very different trajectories.

This method is simply a form of process tracing, or increasing the number of observable implications of an argument, in future rather than past time. Eventually, as in the heuristics of evolutionary biology, future history becomes data. But instead of thinking of data as something that can falsify any particular hypothesis, we need to think of it as something capable distinguishing or selecting the story that was from stories that might have been. Such storylines are not linear, but as contingent in a way our scenario methodology tries to capture.

A central choice in developing scenarios is whether to begin with drivers—the "causal forces" or the plot line in the story—or the outcomes or resolution of the stories. There are several reasons to start with drivers. From the perspective of traditional social science, it is cleaner in principle to reason from cause to effect when possible. Pragmatically, scenario thinkers are more likely to generate results that contain surprises or challenging combinations of events when they begin from beliefs or ideas about fundamental causes, rather than from preconceived notions of the most likely outcome states. People who work on particular problems and have done so for a long time typically carry around in their heads a set of plausible outcomes, or "official futures," that they believe are likely and relevant to their concerns. One of the purposes of constructing scenarios is to encourage scholars and experts to think outside of these confines about plausible, different futures.

In summary, scenario thinking is disciplined by beginning with the identification of the several factors (causes), which scholars believe are most important to the future of a political relationship. They can then distinguish between what is most certain and what is most uncertain. Uncertainty in this context can mean that scholars are uncertain about the 'value' of the variable, or about the causal impact of the variable, or both. The three or four most important, uncertain causes can then be identified, as well as a narrative explication of the key uncertainties at play and the nature of their possible interactions. These critical uncertainties become the basis of different plot lines. By assigning different "values" to these variables, and combining them in different ways, scholars can reason to a set of plausible end-states. These end-states should be plausible within existing conceptual frameworks, but, when possible, challenging to "official futures." Scholars can then develop the narrative pathways that could generate the outcomes by moving from a highly abstract framework toward increasingly precise—and compelling—causal stories that specify assumptions, major drivers, limiting conditions, and implications. As part of these narratives, scholars must specify the trends that weave through their stories, and can be monitored as time passes.

Rather than prediction, laying out such a scenario and its alternatives encourages students of international affairs to consider a range of drivers, to identify the critical uncertainties, to develop different plot lines by varying these uncertainties, and to develop indicators of different paths to monitor trends as they unfold. Just as counterfactual analysis is a useful tool for evaluating the strength of competing explanations and recognizing the contingency of outcomes that actually occurred, forward reasoning opens our analyses to the possibilities of alternative futures, but forces discipline in tracing likely paths created by important drivers in combination with significant uncertainties.

Perhaps the most important contribution forward reasoning can make to international relations is to confront us repeatedly with surprises. Whatever theories or suppositions guide scenario generation, our expectations will be frequently, if not regularly, confounded given the power of agency and the open nature of all social systems. Discrepant outcomes can always be explained away or somehow made consistent with existing theories of international relations—as with realism and the end of the Cold War—by various conceptual sleights of hand. Forward reasoning actively seeks to rebut its own expectations, and considers discrepant information as valuable as confirming information. Such an approach, if it does nothing else, encourages openness and humility, both of which are currently in very short supply in our discipline.

Perhaps the most important contribution forward reasoning can make to international relations is to confront us repeatedly with surprises. Whatever theories or suppositions guide scenario generation, our expectations will be frequently, if not regularly, confounded given the power of agency and the open nature of all social systems. Discrepant outcomes can always be explained away or somehow made consistent with existing theories of international relations—as with realism and the end of the Cold War—by various conceptual sleights of hand. Forward reasoning actively seeks to rebut its own expectations, and considers discrepant information as valuable as confirming information. Such an approach, if it does nothing else, encourages openness and humility, both of which are currently in very short supply in our discipline.

Notes

1 George Bernard Shaw, *An Autobiography, 1856–1898* (New York: Weybright and Talley, 1969), pp. 1–4.

2 R. Brown and J. Kulik, "Flashbulb Memories," *Cognition* 5 (1977), pp. 73–99; J. N. Bohannon and V. L. Symons, "Flashbulb Memories: Confidence, Consistency, and Quantify," in *Affect and Accuracy in Recall,* eds. E. Winograd and U. Neisser, pp. 65–91 (New York: Cambridge University Press, 1992); Ulric Neisser, "John Dean's Memory: A Case Study," *Cognition,* 9 (1981), pp. 1–22; D. P. Spence, *Narrative Truth and Historical Truth: Meaning and Interpretation in Psychoanalysis* (New York: Norton, 1982); R. T. White, "Recall of Autobiographical Events," *Applied Cognitive Psychology,* 18 (1989), pp. 127–35; D. E. Polkinghorne, "Narrative and Self-Concept," *Journal of Narrative and Life History,* 1 (1991), pp. 135–53.

3 Donald E. Polkinghorne, *Narrative Knowing and the Human Sciences* (Albany: State University of New York Press, 1988). See also Craig R. Barclay, "Composing Protoselves Through Improvisation," in *The Remembering Self: Construction and Accuracy in the Self Narrative,* eds. Ulric Neisser and Robyn Fivush, pp. 55–77 (Cambridge: Cambridge University Press, 1994); W. F. Brewer, "What is Autobiographical Memory," in *Autobiographical Memory,* ed. D. C. Rubin, pp. 34–49 (Cambridge: Cambridge University Press, 1986); Robyn Fivush, "The Function of Event Memory," in, *Remembering Reconsidered: Ecological and Traditional Approaches to the Study of Memory,* eds. Ulrich Neisser and E. Winograd, pp. 277–82; (Cambridge: Cambridge University Press, 1988), Dorothy Holland and Naomi Quinn, eds., *Cultural Models in Language and Thought* (Cambridge: Cambridge University Press, 1987); R. D'Andrade, "Some Propositions About the Relation Between Culture and Human Cognition," in *Cultural Psychology: Essays in Comparative Human Development,* eds. James W. Stigler, Richard. A. Shweder, and Gilbert H. Herdt, pp. 65–129 (Cambridge: Cambridge University Press, 1990); D. C. Rubin, ed., *Autobiographical Memory* (Cambridge: Cambridge University Press, 1986); A. E. Collins, S. E. Gathercole, M. A. Conway, and P. E. M. Morris, eds., *Theories of Memory* (Hillsdale, NJ: Erlbaum, 1993); E. Winograd and U. Neisser, eds., *Affect and Accuracy in Recall* (New York: Cambridge University Press, 1992); Ulric Neisser, ed., *The Perceived Self: Ecological and Interpersonal Sources of Self-Knowledge* (Cambridge: Cambridge University Press, 1993); Ulric Neisser and Robyn Fivush, *The Remembering Self: Construction and Accuracy in the Self Narrative* (Cambridge: Cambridge University Press, 1994); James W, Pennebaker, Dario Paez and Bernard Rimé, *Collective Memory of Political Events: Social Psychological Perspectives* (Mahwah, NJ: Erlbaum, 1997). For broader studies, that relate changes in memory to life histories and political events, see Erik H. Erikson, *Childhood and Society* (New York: Norton, 1950); Alessandro Portelli, "Uchronic Dreams: Working-Class Memory and Possible Worlds," in *The Death of Luigi Trastulli and Other Stories: Form and Meaning in Oral History* (Albany: State University of New York Press, 1991).

4 Ulric Neisser, "John Dean's Memory: A Case Study," *Cognition,* 9 (1981), pp. 1–22; D. P. Spence, *Narrative Truth and Historical Truth: Meaning and Interpretation in Psychoanalysis* (New York: Norton, 982); R. T. White, "Recall of Autobiographical

Events," *Applied Cognitive Psychology*, 18 (1989), pp. 127–35; D. E. Polkinghorne, "Narrative and Self-Concept," *Journal of Narrative and Life History*, 1 (1991), pp. 135–53.

5 Paul John Eakin, *Making Selves: How Our Lives Become Stories* (Ithaca, NY: Cornell University Press, 1990).

6 Herodotus, *The History,* trans. David Grene (Chicago: University of Chicago Press, 1987), 2.10–11, in the Nile and 2.123-81 on Egyptian customs.

7 Morgenthau, *Scientific Man vs. Power Politics* (Chicago: University of Chicago Press, 1946), pp. 72–73, 119-22.

8 Richard K. Herrmann and Richard Ned Lebow, "What Was the Cold War? When and Why Did it End?," in *Ending the Cold War,* eds. Richard K. Herrmann and Richard Ned Lebow, pp. 1–30 (New York: Palgrave-Macmillan, 2003)

9 Tocqueville, Alexis de, *Democracy in America*, trans. and ed., Harvey C. Mansfield and Delba Winthrop (Chicago: University of Chicago Press, 2000); Arthur Schlesinger, Jr., *The Age of Jackson* (Boston: Little, Brown, 1945).

10 Larry Diamond, "Thinking About Hybrid Regimes," *Journal of Democracy* 13, no. 2 (April 2002), pp. 21–35.

11 Henri Bergson, *Creative Evolution*, trans. Arthur Mitchell (New York: Modern Library, 1944), p. 232.

12 Jean-Jacques Rousseau, *Les Rêveries du promeneur solitaire* (Paris: Bordas, 1985), p. 5.

13 Emile Durkheim, *The Division of Labor in Society*, trans. W.D. Halls (New York: Macmillan, 1984), pp. 400–401.

14 Brian Lavery, "Scandal? For an Irish Paris, It's Just a Priest With a Child," *New York Times*, January 22, 2005, p. A6, describes local support for a 73-year-old Roman Catholic priest who fathered the child of a local school teacher and unwillingness to talk about it to representatives of outside media. The local bishop was also been supportive and did not remove the priest from his pastoral duties.

15 International society and system are distinct but overlapping, and given the complexity of contemporary political, economic and social relations, it is probably impossible to distinguish the two categorically.

16 Immanuel Kant, "Idea for a Universal History with a Cosmopolitan Purpose," in *Kant: Political Writings*, ed. Hans Reiss, pp. 44–47 (Cambridge: Cambridge University Press, 1991); *Perpetual Peace*, in *Kant: Political Writings*, pp. 93–130. Quote on p. 112.

17 Hegel, *The German Constitution*, pp. 15–20; *Elements of the Philosophy of the Right* and "The Philosophical History of the World," for the development of his thought on the state.

18 Kant, "Idea for a Universal History with a Cosmopolitan Purpose," pp. 41–53; *Perpetual Peace*.

19 Wight, Martin, "Why There is No International Theory," in, eds., *Diplomatic Investigations: Essays in the Theory of International Politics,* eds. Martin Wight and Herbert Butterfield, pp. 17–35 (Cambridge, MA: Harvard University Press, 1968).

20 For example, R. B. J. Walker, *Inside/Outside: International Relations as Political Theory* (Cambridge: Cambridge University Press, 1993); Giorgio Agamben, *Homo Sacer: Sovereign Power and Bare Life* (Stanford, CA: Stanford University Press, 1998).

21 Gary King, Robert Keohane, and Sidney Verba, *Designing Social Inquiry* (Princeton, NJ: Princeton University Press, 1994), is an influential example.

22 Max Weber, "'Objectivity" in Social Science and Social Policy," *Max Weber, The Methodology of the Social Sciences*, eds. Edward A. Shils and Henry A. Finch, ch. 2 (Glencoe, Il: Free Press, 1949 [1904]).

23 Richard Thayer, "Anomalies: The January Effect," *The Journal of Economic Perspectives*, 1 no. 1 (Summer 1987), pp. 197–201.

24 Joseph E. Stiglitz, *The Roaring Nineties* (New York: Penguin, 2003), pp. 88–89.

25 Richard Ned Lebow, "Contingency, Catalysts and International System Change," *Political Science Quarterly* 115 (Winter 2000–01), pp. 591–616.

26 Richard Ned Lebow, *The Tragic Vision of Politics: Ethics, Interests and Orders* (Cambridge: Cambridge University Press, 2003), ch. 4 for an analysis and comparison.

27 Carl von Clausewitz, *On War*, trans. Michael Howard and Peter Paret (Princeton, NJ: Princeton University Press, 1976); Lebow, *Tragic Vision of Politics*, ch. 5.

28 Clausewitz, *On War*, Book One.

29 Lebow, *Tragic Vision of Politics*, ch. 5, for Morgenthau's approach to theory.

30 Hans J. Morgenthau, "The Purpose of Political Science," in *A Design for Political Science: Scope, Objectives and Methods*, ed. James C. Charlesworth , p. 77 (Philadelphia: American Academy of Political and Social Science, 1966).

31 Robyn Dawes, *House of Cards: Psychology and Psychotherapy Built on Myth* (New York: The Free Press, 1994), ch. 3.

32 This section of the conclusion is drawn from Steven Bernstein, Richard Ned Lebow, Janice Gross Stein, and Steven Weber, "Social Science as Case-Based Diagnostics," in Richard Ned Lebow and Mark Irving Lichbach, *Theory and Evidence in Comparative Politics and International Relations* (New York: Palgrave-Macmillan, 2007).

Name index

Subject index